›››› *Canadian Marketing in Action*

# Canadian Marketing in Action

**KEITH J. TUCKWELL**
*St. Lawrence College*

Prentice-Hall Canada Inc.
Scarborough   Ontario

》》》》 **TO PAST MEMORIES,
PRESENT TIMES AND FUTURE PROSPECTS**

Canadian Cataloguing in Publication Data

Tuckwell, Keith J. (Keith John), 1950–
   Canadian marketing in action

Includes bibliographical references.
ISBN 0–13–117375–8
1. Marketing.   2. Marketing – Canada.   I. Title.

HF5415.T83   1991      658.8      C90–094759–4

Prentice-Hall, Inc., Englewood Cliffs, New Jersey
Prentice-Hall International, Inc., London
Prentice-Hall of Australia, Pty., Ltd., Sydney
Prentice-Hall of India Pvt., Ltd., New Delhi
Prentice -Hall of Japan, Inc., Tokyo
Prentice-Hall of Southeast Asia (Pte.) Ltd., Singapore
Editora Prentice-Hall do Brasil Ltda., Rio de Janeiro
Prentice-Hall Hispanoamericana, S.A., Mexico

ISBN 0–13–117375–8

Production Editor: Jamie Bush
Project Editor: David Jolliffe
Production Coordinator: Florence Rousseau
Interior Design and Page Layout: Robert Garbutt Productions
Cover Design: Gail Ferreira-Ng-A-Kien
Cover Image: © Guido Rossi/The Image Bank Canada
Typesetting: Colborne, Cox & Burns

    2   3   4   5   AGC   95   94   93   92   91

Printed and bound in the U.S.A. by Arcata Graphics Inc.

# »»» **Contents**

# PART FOUR >>> PRODUCT

## PART FIVE >>> PRICE

# PART SIX >>> PLACE

## 12   *Distribution Planning and Physical Distribution*    341

# *Preface*

The essence of marketing is to develop, produce and market a product that meets the needs of a target market. A textbook is no different from any other product. This textbook originated because the education market in Canada wanted a good, wholly Canadian resource for teaching marketing.

Certainly the market for this textbook is competitive: several longstanding and successful books are readily available to teachers and students. What, then, makes *Canadian Marketing in Action* unique and worthy of your consideration? Among the unique features of the book are the following:

## 1. Practical, Student-Oriented Approach

The book balances a thorough account of the principles and theories of marketing with a clear picture of the actions required to implement the principles successfully.

## 2. Canadian Perspective

The text is written from a Canadian viewpoint. No American co-authors influence the direction this book takes or the emphasis it places on topics.

## 3. Content Coverage

All traditional marketing theory is included: environments, segmentation and target marketing, buying behaviour, consumer and business marketing, and the 4Ps. In addition, emerging areas of importance such as direct marketing, event marketing, services and nonprofit marketing and global marketing are given an in-depth treatment.

## 4. Action Vignettes

An exciting feature of the text are its "Marketing in Action" vignettes. All are Canadian, and all illustrate companies with which your students are familiar. These vignettes help marketing come alive for the students, communicating the dynamism and risk of the marketing profession.

### 5. Canadian Cases

The textbook contains 22 cases of varying length written specifically for introductory marketing students. The cases are ideal for in-class discussion or take-home assignments.

### 6. Pedagogy

The design of the text helps students learn the chapter material, while communicating the excitement and pace of marketing itself. Photos, tables, charts and graphs illustrate text material; vignettes capture the essence of real world marketing and sample advertisements augment the Canadian perspective. A full glossary appears at the end of the text, and all key terms appear in bold face in text copy and in colour in the margins of the chapters.

### 7. Supplements

No marketing text is complete without a full supplementary package for the instructor and student. The following materials are available for *Canadian Marketing in Action*:

#### Instructors Manual
Prepared by the author, the manual includes chapter summaries, answers to chapter questions, additional illustrations of key concepts, and guidelines for answering case questions.

#### Overhead Transparency Masters
Culled from the textbook, or specifically designed to complement chapter content, these masters may be copied onto acetates for use in class.

#### Colour Transparencies
Providing additional information, these 140 transparencies include material not found in the text that can be easily integrated into lectures.

#### Videos
Each video illustrates a marketing concept by depicting real companies addressing real problems. Video topics include L.L. Bean, Shopping in the U.S.S.R., and the concern with oat bran. The videos are free upon adoption. Please contact your local Prentice-Hall representative for fuller information.

#### Test Bank
More than 1200 questions have been prepared to help test your students on the material they have studied. The test bank is available in hard copy and in disk format.

#### "The Mart" by N. Maddox and D.A. Schellinck (Dalhousie University)
Similar to computerized cases, this supplement gives students a taste of the real decisions marketing managers make, and of the risks and effects of each decision. Organized around the 4Ps, this item can be bought separately or shrink-wrapped with the text.

# Organization of the Textbook

The book is divided into eight sections of study:

## Part 1 · Marketing Today

The initial section presents an overview of contemporary marketing, its processes and practices, and examines the controllable and uncontrollable environments that influence marketing.

## Part 2 · Marketing Planning

This part examines the marketing planning process and how marketing contributes to the achievement of company objectives. The concepts of market segmentation and positioning are presented in detail along with a discussion of the role and process of marketing research.

## Part 3 · Buying Behaviour

The focus of this section is the behaviour and decision-making of consumers and customers from business and industry. The procedures for purchase decisions followed by both the consumer and business markets are examined in depth.

## Part 4 · Product

The middle part of the text examines the marketing mix. How products are developed, marketed and managed is investigated.

## Part 5 · Price

The role of price in the marketing mix is shown in this section. The discussion deals with pricing strategies, the role of pricing in achieving corporate objectives, and methods for determining prices. How the price function is managed in business organizations is also probed.

## Part 6 · Place

This section centres on the roles of distribution planning, physical distribution, wholesaling, and retailing. How each area is considered in the marketing mix is carefully examined.

## Part 7 · Promotion

The promotion section explores various elements of the strategic promotion mix, including advertising, public relations, sales promotion, personal selling, event marketing and sponsorships.

## Part 8 • Emerging Areas of Marketing

Marketing is a constantly evolving discipline. With this in mind, Part 8 presents some of the key areas of contemporary marketing practice. The nature and role of direct marketing, the unique considerations of services and nonprofit marketing, and the emerging importance of global marketing are all investigated.

The format of each chapter is consistent. Each chapter starts with a list of learning objectives directly related to the key concepts presented in the chapter. Key terms appear in bold print and are highlighted in the margin. "Marketing in Action" vignettes are included to illustrate various concepts in an applied manner. Chapter summaries appear at the end of the chapter along with a key term summary list and review and discussion questions.

The Appendices contain a detailed marketing plan provided by the Ontario Ministry of Tourism and Recreation, and a marketing mathematics section expands on the content presented in the pricing chapters. Finally, a glossary of key terms and definitions appears at the end of the textbook.

〉〉〉〉

## Acknowledgements

Many organizations and individuals have contributed to the development of this textbook. I would like to sincerely thank the following organizations for their special cooperation and contribution.

Air Canada Cargo
Apple Canada Inc.
A&W Food Services of Canada Limited
A.C. Nielsen Company of Canada Limited
Beatrice Foods Inc.
BMW Canada Inc.
Campbell's Soup Company Limited
Canada Trust
Canadian Direct Marketing Association
Canadian National Railways
Canon Canada Inc.
Clarkson Gordon/Woods Gordon
Discount Car and Truck Rentals
Dofasco Inc.
Domtar Inc.
Ford Motor Company of Canada Limited
Holiday Inns of Canada Limited
Inco Limited
Jaguar Canada Inc.
Journey's End Corporation
Labatt Breweries Limited
3M Canada Inc.
Mennen Canada Inc.
Mita Copystar Canada Limited

NCR Canada Ltd/Ltee
Nabisco Brands Limited
Nissan Automobile Company (Canada) Limited
Ontario Ministry of Tourism and Recreation
Petro-Canada Inc.
Postal Promotions Limited
Pratt & Whitney Canada Inc.
Procter & Gamble Inc.
Silcorp Limited
The Bradford Exchange Limited
Toshiba Canada Limited
Volkswagen Canada Inc, Porsche Division

For undertaking the tedious task of reviewing the textbook at various stages of development, I am indebted to many colleagues. The input provided by each of you was appreciated. I would like to sincerely thank

Ian Aldworth      *Seneca College*
Ross Crain      *Seneca College*
Dwight Dyson      *Centennial College*
Susan Eck      *Seneca College*
Neville Ferrari      *Humber College*
Wendy Kennedy      *Algonquin College*
Hal Link      *St. Clair College*
David Nowell      *Sheridan College*
Morie Shacker      *British Columbia Institute of Technology*
Robert Stamp      *George Brown College*
Tom Thorne      *Loyalist College*
Colin Young      *Ryerson Polytechnical Institute*

For contributing cases to the textbook I would like to thank two of my St. Lawrence College colleagues, Ron Kelly and Gerry McCready.

From Prentice-Hall Canada Inc., I would like to pass on an exceptional thank you to the Project Editor, David Jolliffe. Your comments, suggestions and guidance along the way were appreciated. Your grasp of the content and your understanding of the book's direction produced a sound working relationship. It was a pleasure to work with you!

I would also like to thank the Managing Editor, College Division, Yolanda de Rooy for seeing the wisdom in pursuing such a project, and for providing me with the opportunity to write Canada's first truly Canadian marketing textbook.

Thanks also to Jamie Bush, Production Editor, for shepherding the book through production and to Maria Amuchastegui for her diligent photo research.

Finally, I must thank the members of the Tuckwell family for their patience and understanding throughout the process. To Esther, Marnie, Graham and Gordie . . . thank you!

Keith J. Tuckwell
1991

# PART ONE

# *Marketing Today*

# CHAPTER 1

# Contemporary Marketing

*LEARNING OBJECTIVES*

After studying this chapter, you will be able to

1. Define marketing and describe its role and importance in contemporary organizations.

2. Define utility and describe the five types of utility.

3. Trace how marketing has evolved over time to become the focal point of business activity.

4. Explain the variety of activities that embrace contemporary marketing practice.

5. Outline the stages in the marketing process.

6. Identify the relationships between marketing and other functional departments of an organization.

7. Describe the key issues confronting the practice of marketing in Canada.

## 〉〉〉 *The Importance of Marketing*

Marketing, in the 1990s, is an exciting and dynamic field. It is an activity that influences us daily, both consciously and unconsciously. To begin understanding the role of marketing, examine any recent purchase you have made. Ask yourself one question: "What influenced me to buy this product?" Some answers might be:

1. The price was reasonable.
2. The quality was better than that of the other options available.
3. It was available when I needed it.
4. The advertisements attracted me to the product.
5. It was on sale in a store that I visit frequently.

All of these matters — price, quality, availability, advertising and promotion — are determined by marketers.

Let's look at a purchase decision from the viewpoint of the business that markets it. What did the business do to get you to make the purchase? Take the example of a Sony colour television. To get the customer to buy the product, Sony has it placed in convenient locations, such as department stores, its own Sony stores or specialty stores that sell audio, video and television equipment. Sony prices the colour television competitively or at a price justified by the quality it represents, and it makes the set available at a time when the customer wants it. Sony also creates an awareness of and interest in the television by presenting its benefits in advertising. All of these endeavours are part of marketing. Marketing, it may be said, gets a customer to buy by presenting and delivering a package of satisfactions. Its goal is to create these satisfactions.

Marketing has become Canada's hottest business topic. In today's extremely competitive global marketplace, where customers are faced with virtually unlimited choices among products, the quality of an organization's marketing activity will determine whether it succeeds or fails. In many business organizations of the past, the marketing function was misunderstood; it was put under the control of a marketing department that operated independently of other parts of the business organization. Today the emphasis has shifted so much that the entire culture of the organization is apt to be marketing oriented.

## The New Corporate Culture

corporate culture
marketing culture

**Corporate culture** refers to the values, norms and practices shared by all employees of an organization. The **marketing culture** is the philosophy or attitude of an organization regarding how it should deal with customers. Today, given the quality of products and service options available to customers in virtually every purchase decision, organizations, in order to survive, have had to foster a marketing culture that gives the customer the first and final say. Business organizations today exist, above all, to serve their customers, and all employees contribute to this effort. Successful businesses, such as IBM, McDonald's, and others, think "customer" all the time. Marketing is the driving force in their business operations. These types of companies encourage all employees — senior executives, salespeople, production workers, accountants, clerks, and secretaries — to think of the customer as king. As a result, all the activities and services they offer are designed to satisfy that customer. In effect, all employees are now part of a marketing team and share in a common goal of being in the customer satisfaction business.

According to management authority Peter Drucker,

Marketing requires separate work and a distinct group of activities. But, it is, first, a central dimension of the entire business. It is the whole business as seen from the point of view of its final result, that is from the customer's point of view[1]

# >>>> *Marketing Defined*

What is marketing? The American Marketing Association, an international association of academics and marketing practitioners, defines marketing as "the process of planning and executing the conception, pricing, promotion and distribution of ideas, goods and services to create exchanges that satisfy individual and organizational objectives."[2]

In today's competitive marketing arena, however, there are some concerns over this definition. It does not truly recognize the activities of non-profit organizations that engage in a variety of marketing activities, and it oversimplifies the role of business objectives. These objectives usually include targets for profit, market share, and sales volume. At times they may conflict with each other. For example, a firm in a very competitive growth market may have the objective of increasing its market share, but the marketing costs of achieving this objective may actually reduce profits or even create losses temporarily.

*marketing*

For these reasons, we will define **marketing** as the process of anticipating, stimulating, developing, managing and satisfying customer needs through exchanges between the organization and the customer. This definition recognizes that different marketing organizations can have different objectives. For example, the driving forces behind product-oriented businesses, service-oriented businesses and non-profit businesses are quite distinct. The objectives may differ, but each type of business organization carefully plans its marketing strategy.

In this definition, the needs referred to are those of final consumers, business customers, wholesalers and retailers, non-profit organizations, governments, and other institutional customers. Exchange involves the transfer of something of value in return for something else. In the exchange process, a transaction occurs as soon as people agree to trade with each other. There is a transfer, from seller to buyer, of ownership or of the right to use the product or service. For instance, an exchange occurs when a consumer presents cash or a credit card to pay for a pair of Nike running shoes at a Foot Locker store. It must be pointed out that an exchange does not necessarily entail a transfer of ownership. The rental of a videotape at a local video shop is an exchange, but in this case the customer does not acquire ownership of the tape, only the temporary right to use it.

## Marketing Provides Satisfactions

*utility*

All Canadian businesses and service organizations perform two basic functions. First, they use market research and consumer analysis to identify customer needs, and, second, they develop, produce, and market a product or service that meets those needs. These business organizations create what is known as utility. **Utility** is defined as the want-satisfying power of a product or service. There are five types of utility.

form utility

1. **Form utility** is created by production of a good or service. Using an idea or concept developed from marketing research, the production department combines raw materials and component parts to form a finished product. For example, raw materials such as steel, rubber, plastics and fibreglass are combined with components such as glass windows, pre-assembled engines, batteries, and so on to form an automobile. The vehicle is designed to meet the needs and wants of the potential market, as identified by marketing research. Once an automobile is designed and produced, the responsibility for market acceptance shifts to those responsible for marketing planning. The marketing activity focuses on time, place, information, and ownership utility.

place utility

2. **Place utility** concerns having the product readily available at a location convenient for the customer. If a retailer announces a big sale of colour televisions, there had better be inventory on hand to accommodate those customers who will immediately take advantage of the savings offered. People expect goods to be conveniently available.

time utility

3. **Time utility** creates satisfaction by having the product or service available when it is needed by customers. In the growth and expansion of drive-through facilities and in the extended operating hours of fast food restaurants can be seen examples of businesses providing time utility. Extended banking hours and the availability of instant teller machines are other examples.

information utility

4. **Information utility** concerns the availability of knowledge about a product or service. Market planners develop a message, a list of features and benefits, and present them in such a way that the product will be attractive to potential customers. To this end, advertising is commonly placed in various media — television, radio, newspapers, and magazines. Promotional incentives such as coupons and contests also send out messages about a product for the customer to evaluate.

ownership utility

5. **Ownership utility** refers to an exchange process at the point of purchase. Possession and ownership of a product or service transfers from the seller to the buyer. Therefore, ownership utility occurs when the buyer pays for the product or service. The acceptance of trade-ins, lay-away plans and instant credit approval programs are ways of making ownership easy.

## ⟩⟩⟩⟩ *The Evolution of Marketing*

The practice of marketing has evolved over time. Business organizations have moved through several eras, each with a different emphasis, first on production, then on sales, and eventually on marketing.

### The Production Era

production era

In the **production era** firms paid little attention to what customers needed. Instead, they concentrated on what they were capable of producing. They worked on the assumption that customers would purchase the product so long as they could afford it. Businesses realized profits by making and distributing a limited variety of products as efficiently as possible. Henry Ford's classic statement, "They can have any colour of car as long as it's black," illustrates the philosophy behind the production era.

## The Selling Era

selling era

As manufacturers added new product lines and as more and more competition entered the market, customers had a greater selection of products. Consequently, the emphasis shifted from production to selling. In the **selling era** the belief was that the more the company sells, the more profit the company makes. But companies that paid little attention to costs found that such was not always the case. At the same time customers became increasingly demanding of quality, performance, dependability, and so on in the products manufacturers were selling.

The advent of the selling era was the earliest attempt to match potential customers with a product or service. In the automobile industry competing firms built a variety of models and then searched for a consumer market to buy them. Their efforts focused on advertising to get customers into the dealer showrooms.

## The Marketing Era

marketing era

In the **marketing era** all planning revolves around the customer. The resources of the firm are directed at determining and satisfying customer needs. Essentially the task of the organization is to determine the needs and wants of a target market and deliver a set of satisfactions in such a way that it is perceived to be of better value than a competitive product. The goal of determining and satisfying customer needs is

marketing concept

referred to as the **marketing concept**.

Companies such as IBM, Coca-Cola, General Motors, The Royal Bank of Canada, Canon Canada Inc., and all of their major competitors practice the marketing concept. Refer to the Marketing in Action vignette "Kellogg's Stays Close to Home" for an illustration of how the marketing concept works.

Firms applying the marketing concept realize a profit by staying one step ahead of competitors in the delivery of desired satisfactions to customers. In doing so, they also concentrate on operating their production, sales, and distribution systems efficiently. There is a closer working relationship among the various departments of a business since each must contribute to achieve common company goals. Organizations adopting the marketing concept make what they can market instead of marketing what they can make. When Lee Iacocca, then President of the Ford Motor Company, launched the Ford Mustang in 1964 he set the stage for the marketing concept in the automobile industry. Remarking on the failure of the Edsel in the 1950s he stated that

> whereas the Edsel had been a car in search of a market it never found, here was a market in search of a car. The normal practice in Detroit was to build a car and then try to identify the buyers. We were in a position to move in the opposite direction and tailor a new product for a hungry new market.[3]

## >>>> *MARKETING IN ACTION*

### *KELLOGG'S STAYS CLOSE TO HOME*

In the late 1970s and 1980s, the cereal market wasn't going anywhere, and key players in the market, including General Mills and Quaker Oats, diversified into livelier markets. General Mills entered the retailing business through Eddie Bauer stores, and Quaker Oats entered the restaurant business through Magic Pan Restaurants. Kellogg's, however, did not diversify.

Hindsight, being perfect, confirms that Kellogg's strategy of sticking to the business it knew best, that is, cereals, was a prudent one. Three factors combined to make Kellogg's successful: marketing savvy, product innovation, and advertising power.

Kellogg's remained committed to the cereal business because it recognized what its rivals didn't: that there was a generation of young adults who were becoming obsessed with getting rid of high-fat, cholesterol-laden breakfasts, and who wanted to consume, instead, high quantities of fiber. This recognition sparked new interest in the adult segment of the dry packaged cereal market in the United States and Canada.

What did Kellogg's do? To appeal to those concerned about health and fitness, Kellogg's launched Müslix, an upscale granola product of European heritage; Nutrific, a mixture of barley, bran, almonds and raisins; and Pro-Grain, a honey-coated multi-grained cereal. At the same time, Kellogg's did not forget its existing, core brands. Frosted Flakes, Rice Krispies, Special K, and Corn Flakes all held their market share during this time. In 1989, the company successfully launched Common Sense Oat Bran and Whole Wheat cereal in Canada. This new product cashed in on the country-wide interest in dietary fibre. Oat bran enjoys status as a trendy health food as a result of research reports showing that

*Müslix, a high-fibre cereal introduced by Kellogg's, was aimed at the health-conscious consumer*

a diet high in soluble fibre, such as that found in oat bran, may help to reduce cholesterol levels.

What was the overall effect on Kellogg's business? From 1982 to 1987, Kellogg's total market share in the cereal business increased from 38 percent to 43 percent. In contrast, General Mills launched several new products for the children's presweetened cereal market, but did not gain a share point.

Kellogg's new product introductions were accompanied by extensive advertising support and appropriate strategies. Catering to the health craze, Nutrific came with a small booklet which included height and weight charts, cholesterol count charts, a nutrition guide, and a checklist of exercises. Advertising shifted from lifestyles and concentrated primarily on the product benefits appropriate for a healthy lifestyle. All of these marketing activities resulted in significant growth for Kellogg's cereal products in a market that was not growing at the time.

Adapted from Rebecca Fannin, "Crunching the competition", *Marketing & Media Decisions*, March 1988, p.70.

The degree to which a business or non-profit organization has adopted the marketing concept is reflected in all of its operations. From the moment they make a telephone enquiry, customers form personal impressions about the supplier's consumer orientation. Was the telephone answered promptly? Was the person who received the call friendly and courteous? Did the organization convey the impression that it wanted to serve the potential customer's needs? Modern marketing-oriented organizations ensure that staff are trained in both product knowledge and customer service skills.

## The Societal Marketing Concept

**societal marketing concept**

Many researchers and market planners believe that contemporary marketing activity has gone beyond the marketing concept. Kotler, McDougall, and Armstrong's explanation of the **societal marketing concept** states that

> the organization's task is to determine the needs, wants, and interests of target markets and to deliver the desired satisfactions more efficiently and effectively than competitors, in a way that preserves or enhances the consumer's and society's well being.[4]

The three major components of the societal marketing concept are satisfying consumer needs, delivering satisfactions better than competitors and being conscious of conducting business activities in the best interests of society (see figure 1.1).

Satisfying customers needs better than the competition is the first key to successful marketing practice. However, in certain product categories, some organizations have lost sight of this concept and have placed an unreasonable emphasis on their competitors instead of on the consumer. The advertising wars that erupted in the mid- and late 1980s in the soft drink and fast food restaurant markets illustrate this point. The campaign launched by Pepsi-Cola, called the "Pepsi Challenge", created much controversy in the marketplace. Burger King's campaign, which compared flame-broiled burgers to McDonald's fried hamburgers, created similar controversy. Companies and brands such as these become obsessed with the competitive situation, and place the competitor front and center in their marketing strategies, perhaps at the expense of consumers they should be attempting to satisfy.

The societal marketing concept focuses on the well-being of consumers and society. Consumer and environmental groups will often attack companies and industries that market products of questionable value or products that are harmful. For example, the tobacco industry in Canada is constantly under attack from the Non-Smokers Rights Association, which argues that the marketing and advertising

**FIGURE 1.1**  Elements of the Societal Marketing Concept

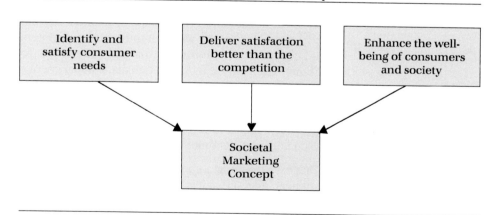

FIGURE 1.2    Evolution of Marketing

| Phase | Characteristics |
|---|---|
| Production Era | • Sell what you can produce.<br>• Limited or no choice for customer.<br>• Profit based on production efficiency. |
| Selling Era | • Products matched to consumer needs (quality, variety, etc.).<br>• Choices more readily available.<br>• Profits based on expanded sales. |
| Marketing Era | • All activity revolves around the consumers and their satisfaction.<br>• Extremely competitive, since the consumer has a wide choice of products and services.<br>• Profits based on efficient production and marketing. |
| Societal Marketing Concept | • Fulfill society's expectations (e.g., for a safe environment).<br>• Being good corporate citizens.<br>• Profits based on efficient production and marketing in an extremely competitive market and on satisfying informed consumer groups. |

of a product directly linked to health deterioration is morally wrong. Companies that adhere to societal marketing concepts take such social considerations and consumer reactions into account in their marketing planning.

Refer to figure 1.2 for a summary of the evolution of marketing.

## The Importance of a Consumer Orientation

The best way of demonstrating the importance of a consumer orientation is to examine the behaviour of the unhappy customer. Business people know that dissatisfied customers pass the word on to friends and relatives. For a business organization, such negative information has a high cost. A recent study conducted by Consumer and Corporate Affairs Canada, a department of the federal government, found that:

1. Ninety-six percent of unhappy customers never complain, but 90 percent of those who are dissatisfied will not buy the product again.
2. Each unhappy customer will tell his or her story to at least nine other people.[5]

The cost of getting a consumer to make an initial purchase is very high. Some researchers suggest that it is five times more costly to get a new customer to buy than to keep an old one. Therefore, in accordance with the marketing concept, it is in the firm's financial best interests to keep current customers satisfied. The products provided by a firm must live up to the expectations created by its own marketing efforts; otherwise, much will be lost.

## 〉〉〉〉 *Marketing Today*

Marketing in practice embraces a host of activities designed to attract, satisfy, and retain customers. Included in these activities are market analysis and marketing research, consumer analysis, product, price, distribution and promotion planning, and a consideration of social responsibilities. The following illustrates the fundamental concepts and provides examples of these activities. Refer to figure 1.3 for a summary of marketing activities.

**FIGURE 1.3**   Marketing Activities

| Activity | Responsibilities |
| --- | --- |
| Market Analysis and Research | Evaluation of economic and competitive influences which affect the firm's marketing strategies and activities. |
| Consumer Analysis | Evaluation of consumer needs, behaviour and the purchase process as well as the identification of defined target markets. |
| Product Planning | Design and development of goods and services, packaging, brand names and accessories that meet the needs of the marketplace. Decisions on product modification and deletions (withdrawal) are also part of product planning. |
| Price Planning | The establishment of fair and profitable pricing strategies that include list prices, discounts, and purchase and credit terms. |
| Distribution Planning | Organizing transactions between manufacturers (suppliers) and wholesalers and retailers. The focus is on warehousing, inventory management, transportation, and wholesaling and retailing. |
| Promotion Planning | Combining the promotion elements of advertising, sales promotion, personal selling and public relations to generate consumer interest in a product, service or idea. |
| Social Responsibility | Marketing safe products in an ethical manner. Being socially responsible and acting as a good corporate citizen for the well-being of society. |
| Marketing Management | The planning, implementation, evaluation, and controlling of marketing activity. The firm analyzes all available information and makes the appropriate decisions as to the goods and services offered for sale. |

## Market Analysis and Research

Market analysis is the first step in the organization's decision-making process. Using a variety of the information sources and marketing research techniques that are readily available, the organization collects appropriate information to determine if a market is worth pursuing. The factors included in market analysis are market demand, sales volume potential, production capabilities, and the availability of the resources necessary to produce and market the product or service. Through market research, Journey's End identified that of the three price categories in the motel market, the lowest priced, or budget, segment was the emerging and growth segment. Today it is a leader in this market segment.

## Consumer Analysis

Consumer analysis deals mainly with monitoring behaviour changes within Canadian society. Business organizations use marketing research procedures to evaluate changes in consumers' tastes and preferences, attitudes and lifestyles, so that marketing strategies can be adjusted accordingly. For example, consumer analysis identified a new emphasis on health and fitness; this led to the introduction of many new food and beverage products such as low calorie margarine, light soft drinks, beer and alcohol products, and the emergence of fresh food restaurants like Cultures. Similarly, the emergence of two-income households where both the husband and wife were employed full-time outside the home created a whole new market for convenience products and tremendous growth in the fast food restaurant business. See the Marketing in Action feature "Demand You Say?" for an example of how social change affects marketing activity.

### >>>> MARKETING IN ACTION

*DEMAND, YOU SAY?*

From 1981 to 1986 the frozen breakfast market in North America doubled in size. The market for 1992 is estimated to be worth $992 million in retail volume.

A research study conducted by Packaged Facts Inc. of New York concluded that three factors contributed to such tremendous growth. The trends that sharp marketers capitalized on were: a steady increase in the use of microwave ovens; the popularity of fast food breakfasts (McDonald's, Harvey's and others), which created a demand for similar store-bought breakfasts; and the efforts of nutritionists in convincing North Americans of the importance of eating a good breakfast.

McCain Foods Limited

*McCain Foods, with headquarters in Florenceville, N.B., competes for a share of the frozen-breakfast market*

Adapted from "Breakfast boom owed to microwave", *Canadian Grocer*, August 1987, p.10.

# Product Planning

Using information gained from market and consumer analysis, organizations develop new products or modify existing products and services to meet the changing needs of the marketplace. In the automobile industry, firms like General Motors, Ford and Chrysler offer complete product lines to meet these needs; that is, they offer products to satisfy all price segments of the car market. Products like the Cadillac are tailored to meet the needs of those seeking a high income and status, while a medium-priced Chevrolet station wagon would appeal to a suburban household with several children. The Mercury Tracer offers economical transportation to buyers who are concerned about price, and then there are cars such as the Corvette or Pontiac Firebird Trans Am, which appeal to young, trendy, sporty customers.

# Price Planning

Marketing organizations are very conscious about the importance of price in today's marketplace. Pricing involves developing a strategy that provides reasonable profit for the firm while making the product or service attractive to the customer. Factors which play a role in price activity include the prices of competing products and how much it costs to make the product. Then, profit has to be added into the price. Generally, consumers will be attracted to products that offer good value for the price. As an example, a base price of $8 995 for a two-door Honda Civic Hatchback offers consumers economical transportation value, when compared to higher priced and more luxurious types of cars.

# Distribution Planning

Distribution is concerned, first of all, with transactions between manufacturers, middlemen, and retailers who ultimately sell the product to the consumer. Food processors such as McCains, Weston's and Kraft General Foods all market their product lines through a variety of chain stores and independent distributors. To illustrate these transactions, let's consider the example of Maxwell House coffee. This product is produced by Kraft General Foods in a manufacturing facility in LaSalle, Quebec. From there it travels by truck transport to the A&P Distribution Centre or some similar customer in Toronto, where it is stored until an A&P retail outlet places an order for it. From the distribution center it is sent to the retail outlet by truck, along with other goods ordered. The second major aspect of distribution is determining efficient means of transportation. Depending on such factors as cost, distance, and time, a business organization may use water, air, rail, truck or even a pipeline to deliver goods.

# Promotion Planning

Promotion involves the development and implementation of media advertising campaigns, consumer and trade promotion activities, personal selling programs, public relations, and publicity. This is the most visible area of marketing, and these activities play a major role in creating an image for the product or service. For consumer products such as Crest toothpaste or Pepsi-Cola, virtually all forms of promotion activity are used. These and similar products must be sold through distributors — wholesalers and retailers — on the basis of promotion activity that includes temporary price discounts and allowances. To generate consumer interest in the product and to increase purchase levels in retail stores, intensive, multi-media campaigns are mounted and often combined with periodic couponing or some other consumer promotion activity.

## Social Responsibility

All business organizations are obligated to offer for sale safe, ethical, and useful goods and services. They must not deceive customers and must treat all customers fairly. The firm must be concerned with society's well-being. Companies that market products that are of questionable quality or that are harmful will come under attack from governments, consumers, and environmental groups.

## Marketing Management

In addition to planning marketing activity, an organization must manage that activity effectively and efficiently. Depending on the nature of the organization, marketing activity is managed on a geographic basis, on the basis of customer accounts (type of customer), by product line, or by category of product. The Moore Corporation, a large Canadian business forms company, is an example of a firm that manages marketing according to the type of industry served. They develop specific strategies for different industries: strategies for the telecommunications industry are quite different from those for the health care industry. Companies such as Procter & Gamble and John Labatt Limited use a product management system whereby each brand or group of similar brands is assigned to a manager, who is responsible for planning the marketing activity for the product. In this system, the same product could require different marketing strategies according to how consumers' needs and lifestyles vary in different Canadian locations. For example, the strategies used to advertise Labatt's Blue in urban Ontario may be quite different from the advertising strategies used in the Maritimes.

# ⟩⟩⟩⟩ *The Marketing Process*

The marketing process involves several distinct stages (see figure 1.4). Initially, the task of the marketing organization is to determine the needs of consumers, specifically, to identify a group of consumers who have similar needs. Determining need is the responsibility of marketing. Once consumer needs are known, marketing can develop a product concept that will satisfy those needs. New product concepts must then be thoroughly tested through marketing research so that market acceptability can be determined. As part of the research, the production department often designs

**FIGURE 1.4** The Marketing Process

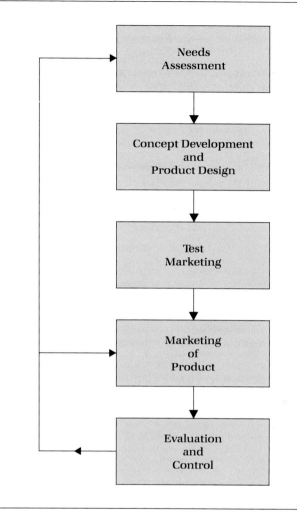

a prototype and has it assessed by potential users. Input from these users often results in design modifications to the product.

When the organization is confident that the product or service will satisfy customer needs, a marketing plan is developed. The initial phase of planning involves a thorough market analysis and consumer analysis. The initial implementation stage may involve a test market. Test marketing involves placing a product for sale in one or more geographic markets and observing its performance under conditions similar to the ones proposed in the marketing plan. Once the test product and marketing plan have been evaluated, a regional or national "rollout" of the product or service follows.

To complete the marketing cycle, research is usually conducted periodically so that the organization is certain that the product continues to meet the changing needs (tastes, preferences, habits and lifestyles) of the volatile marketplace. Only through a constant monitoring process can a firm stay in touch with its customers and their changing needs.

# The Role of Marketing in an Organization

Earlier in the chapter, it was stated that the corporate culture of contemporary business in Canada has acquired a marketing focus. However, marketing is but one function in an organization, and its role and importance within the operational framework can vary from one organization to another. Its function must be integrated into the total operations. Let's examine some of the roles and relationships of the major operational areas of a typical business (see figure 1.5).

## *Marketing*

The objective of marketing is to identify, attract, and retain a loyal group of customers for all products and services offered by the organization. The marketing department develops strategies and operational plans, using a unique combination of the product, price, distribution and promotional factors. While marketing generates revenues for the firm, the marketing department must interact with other departments to plan and implement strategies.

## *Research and Development*

The objective of the research and development department is innovation. Business organizations invest considerable sums of money in development programs in hopes of discovering the breakthrough product that will move the company forward.

**FIGURE 1.5    The Functional Areas of Business**

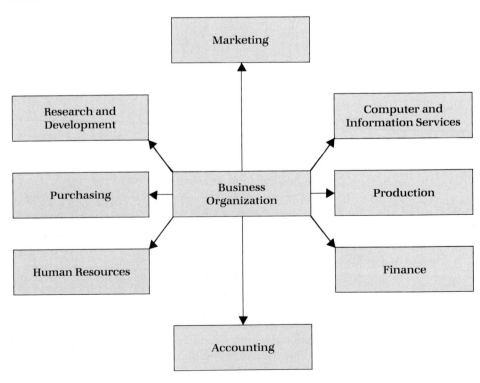

Research and Development also seeks to improve quality and reduce costs in order to contribute to the financial well-being of the company. Marketing is responsible for testing new developments generated by Research and Development.

### Production

The objective of the production or manufacturing operation is to produce all company products efficiently. Its areas of concern include production capability, plant capacity, quality control, inventory management and cost reduction. Production manufactures the goods ordered by the customers and, as a result, plays a key role in keeping customers satisfied.

### Finance

The finance department acts as a monitoring agent. Its concern is with the short-term and long-term financial position of the organization. As such, the department ensures that other operational areas, including marketing, stay within budget guidelines, that the firm focuses on profitable items, and that the costs of borrowing and debt management are kept as low as possible. Finance oversees the financial resources of the organization and in this capacity relies heavily on the sales forecasts provided by marketing.

### Accounting

The accounting department provides other operational areas with transaction details. It monitors costs and continuously provides up-to-date cost reports, which the marketing department uses to develop pricing strategies.

### Purchasing

The role and responsibility of Purchasing is to secure reliable and uninterrupted sources of raw materials, parts, supplies and packaging materials. Its primary concern is to be efficient. To do so it attempts to place the largest possible orders in order to get the lowest possible prices, while trying to maintain low inventories so that costs in this area are kept to a minimum. The quality of the materials thus purchased has a direct influence on the quality of the product that is produced and marketed by the company.

### Human Resources

The human resources department is responsible for the recruitment, selection, development and motivation of employees. Managers ensure that adequate numbers of qualified staff are available in other functional areas in the short-term and long-term.

## The Scope of Marketing Activity

Marketing activity in Canada embraces government, all forms of business, non-profit organizations, and the manufacturing industry. Supporting these marketing-based organizations are service specialists that include advertising agencies, marketing research specialists, direct marketing groups, media communications, transportation and distribution firms.

The scope of the marketing activity is such that it includes many areas, among them target marketing, positioning strategies, product development, packaging, brand names and trademarks, marketing research, advertising, sales promotion, personal selling, wholesaling, retailing, and physical distribution.

Marketing plays a role in the daily lives of Canadians. Either consciously or subconsciously people are bombarded with messages each day, messages that influence attitudes, beliefs and lifestyles. Some critics believe that marketing adds unnecessary costs to products; that marketing promotes a materialistic society; that marketing pushes on the public products that are not really needed; and that marketing wastes valuable natural resources. On the positive side, marketing can be said to contribute to the quality of Canadian life. The innovations in packaging in the drug industry, such as child-proof or tamper-proof bottles, or the development of new products and services, such as wheelchair porchlifts and recycling ventures, to meet changing needs show that marketing is a positive force. Marketing affects Canadians in many ways. The changing demographic structure in Canada (e.g., two income families and the need for expanded day care facilities) has given new meaning to the word *convenience*. The result has been numerous marketing innovations — microwave ovens, automatic banking machines, convenience food products and the growth of fast food restaurants. Furthermore, many business organizations make significant financial contributions to support arts, entertainment, athletic and other non-profit endeavours in Canada. The quality of life is strongly reinforced by today's modern marketing organizations.

## ⟩⟩⟩⟩ *Current Issues in Marketing*

Contemporary marketing practice in Canada faces three major issues or challenges. First, marketing activity must be conducted in a manner that is socially responsible. Second, marketing activity must be ethical, and third, marketing must consider directly the interests of the consumers being served. Let's briefly examine each issue.

### Social Responsibility

social responsibility

**Social responsibility** can be defined as the possession of a corporate conscience that anticipates and responds to social problems. The thrust of social responsibility is such that firms must be concerned with more than making a profit. That there was an endless supply of natural resources such as water, air and energy used to be taken for granted. In the 1970s and 80s this feeling changed. Environmental groups, governments, and consumers mounted intense media pressure against firms that did not show a social conscience. Because of an increasing acceptance of the social marketing concept, firms started to act more responsibly with respect to the consumers they serve and to society in general. At times firms are still caught in a delicate situation. Sometimes product and packaging innovations offer tremendous cost-saving opportunities for the firm, but are harmful to society. Such products include non-returnable soft drink bottles, which create waste; exploding glass bottles, which plague the soft drink business and cause danger for an unsuspecting public; and foam and plastic packaging materials, which destroy the earth's ozone layer.

In the 1980s, ecological issues came to the forefront. Ecological matters that marketing organizations must be aware of today include pollution, recycling, and the preservation of scarce natural resources. Pollutants judged to be dangerous must be eliminated from the environment and safe substitutes found. For example, consider the fluorocarbons used in spray-can products in the 1970s (hair sprays, deodorants, etc.). The propellants from these types of products drifted into the atmosphere and could, potentially, have destroyed the ozone layer that protects the earth fom the sun's ultra-violet rays. In reaction to a potentially dangerous situation and pressure from concerned groups, the industry developed alternatives such as a pump spray can and new aerosol propellants.

Recycling refers to the reprocessing of used materials for reuse. Canadian businesses generate billions of tonnes of waste annually: plastics, glass bottles, paper and metal containers and so on. Wherever possible, recycling should be considered by companies, since it can contribute to the maintenance or slower depreciation of many of Canada's natural resources. Recyclable cans in the beer industry and returnable soft drink bottles represent contributions to such maintenance. For an example of what some firms are doing about recycling see the Marketing in Action feature "New Venture in Recycling."

## 〉〉〉〉 *MARKETING IN ACTION*

### *NEW VENTURE IN RECYCLING*

Protecting the environment is a high priority for business and industry today. Although pollutants still exist, there is a spirit of cooperation among governments, concerned environmental groups, and business and industry, and a common interest in taking action. Profit plays a major role in this new attitude; for companies, it doesn't pay anymore to be a polluter. Companies that violate pollution standards can face stiff fines; senior executives can be jailed for continued negligence; and high clean-up costs can be levied against companies that are in violation of regulation or legislation. Clearly the environment is an important issue to Canadians, and it is because of this growing public concern that firms are taking action.

Citing a fundamental shift in society, Domtar Inc. of Canada and U.S.-based Dow Chemical Corporation considered forming a joint venture company to capitalize on the recycling of plastic bottles. The venture project was to involve the retrieval of polyethylene terephthalate (PET) and high density polyethylene (HDPE) plastics from the trash of both countries. The biggest users of

*Companies such as Domtar are responding to the growing public concern about the environment*

plastics are the milk, soft drink, and household products industries. Both Dow and Domtar believed that the waste management issue would create a fundamental shift in society and that recycling would become normal practice. Although this particular venture proved not to be financially viable, these firms showed a willingness to preserve the environment and make better use of resources.

Adapted from "Domtar, Dow cash in on recycling", *Toronto Star*, September 27, 1988, p.F11.

## Ethical Behaviour

Ethical behaviour in business organizations cannot be taken for granted. The Competition Act in Canada broadly governs most of the marketing activity as does other more specific legislation. Despite the legislation, business firms have been caught conducting their marketing activity in less than ethical ways. Examples of unethical

**FIGURE 1.6    A Socially Responsible Advertising Message**

practices include bait and switch advertising (enticing a consumer to a store for a certain product and then trading them up to a more expensive one) and double ticketing (causing confusion by having two price tags on an item).

The banning of tobacco advertising in Canada (Bill C-51) is a very controversial issue. On one side is the Non-Smokers Rights Association pushing hard for the ban because of the documented health hazards of smoking; on the other side is the tobacco industry, arguing that it is within its rights to advertise since tobacco products are legally sold in Canada.

The advertising of alcohol products such as beer, wine and liquor are also carefully scrutinized by the Canadian public. Considerable objections have been raised regarding the use of "lifestyle advertising" to promote the sale of these products. Critics argue that too much of the "good life" is presented without mention of harmful side effects and potential long-term health problems. To their credit, the industry and individual companies allocate some marketing funds to developing advertising messages that stress moderation and the need for socially responsible behaviour. An example of this form of advertising appears in figure 1.6.

## Consumerism

**consumerism**

Consumerism is the term that refers to a direct relationship between a marketing organization and the consumers it serves. **Consumerism** is defined as "a social force within the environment designed to aid and protect the consumer by exerting legal, moral and economic pressure on business."[6] Consumerism came to the forefront in the 1960s. In the United States, two major events were responsible for the true start of a consumerism era. The first was President John F. Kennedy's announcement of a Consumer Bill of Rights. Kennedy stated that consumers had four basic rights:

1. The right to choose freely.
2. The right to be informed.
3. The right to be heard.
4. The right to be safe.

These rights have formed the foundation of government legislation and consumer protection laws in both Canada and the United States. The second major event that fuelled consumer protection activity was the publication in 1965 of Ralph Nader's book, *Unsafe at Any Speed*, an attack on the automobile industry and, in particular, on the ill-fated Chevrolet Corvair.

In Canada, consumerism was recognized with the formation of the federal government's Consumer and Corporate Affairs Ministry in 1967. Provincial ministries entered the scene in later years. Consumer and Corporate Affairs Canada is responsible for administering consumer protection legislation in Canada through various acts, primarily the Competition Act. The principle role of the consumer ministry is to promote the fair and efficient operation of the Canadian marketplace through the following means:

1. Establishing and administering rules and guidelines for business conduct.

2. Making sure information is accurate so that consumers can make informed decisions.

3. Maintaining and encouraging competition among businesses.

4. Establishing, administering and enforcing standards for trade in commodities and services.

5. Providing protection from product related hazards.

6. Encouraging the disclosure and diffusion of technological innovation.[7]

Refer to the Marketing in Action vignette "Rules, You Say?" for an illustration of the role of a consumer affairs ministry.

## ⟩⟩⟩⟩ *MARKETING IN ACTION*

### *RULES, YOU SAY?*

The Canadian auto repair industry has frequently been under attack by consumer groups. Complaints have centred on the high cost of repairs, the poor itemization of the work completed, and the general untrustworthiness of the shop doing the work. In response, the Ontario government finally produced legislation aimed at protecting consumers from abuses in this industry. The Ministry of Consumer Affairs now requires all Ontario repair outlets (dealerships, used car firms, auto body shops, brake and muffler shops, and windshield replacement shops) to

1. Provide warranties on new and reconditioned parts and labour.

2. Provide written estimates and advise customers if there is a fee for the service involved in itemizing costs, hours, parts to be used, and total costs.

3. Post labour rates.

4. Itemize shop supplies that are charged to customers.

5. Offer to return removed parts.

To protect insurance companies, the new law makes it an offence to charge insurance firms more than consumers. Repair shops who do not abide by the law face fines of up to $2 000 and/or

*Ontario auto-repair outlets must abide by strict new rules*

a jail term of up to one year. Corporations can face fines up to $25 000.

Adapted from Janice Turner, "Strict new rules for car repairs", *Toronto Star*, October 2, 1988, p.F5.

The Consumers Association of Canada (CAC) also represents consumers. This association is primarily funded by the federal government, but also raises money to support its cause through the sale of the *Canadian Consumer* publication. The mandate of the CAC is to represent the consumer interest whether it be with governments, organizations, or other self-interest groups. As a result of the government legislation that protects consumers and of the role that consumerism plays in today's marketplace, business organizations must be attuned to the needs of the customers they serve. Their marketing behaviour must be such that all customers are treated fairly and all practices must be in accordance with existing regulation and legislation.

## 〉〉〉〉 S U M M A R Y

In today's competitive marketplace it is the quality of an organization's marketing activity that determines the success, even the survival, of that organization. Given this situation, businesses are adopting a marketing-oriented corporate culture whereby all employees of an organization, in every activity they perform, must consider the satisfaction of customer needs as the main priority.

Marketing in practice embraces many activities that culminate in an overall plan. These activities include market analysis and marketing research, consumer analysis, determining product and price, and devising distribution and promotion strategies. In addition, marketers must consider the well-being of society in their planning process.

Marketing creates utility, which is defined as the want-satisfying power of a product or service. There are five types of utility: form, place, time, information and ownership. The text defines marketing as the process of anticipating, stimulating, developing, managing, and satisfying customer needs as they are identified through exchanges between an organization and its customers. This definition indicates that marketing has many objectives — for example, contributing to profit, increasing market share, and establishing a reputation for a product, service, or company. Marketing is an activity that is integrated into the firm's total operation. It interacts with other areas such as research and development, production, accounting and finance, and purchasing.

The marketing activity has evolved over time. Early Canadian business development saw much of the organization's profit-making activity centered on creating production efficiency. Gradually, business philosophy shifted to an emphasis on selling, and for the first time business organizations started to look at the needs of consumers and to offer a greater selection pf products. Businesses believed that the key to increasing profits was to increase sales regardless of the costs involved. Thus, in the past 25 years, the marketing concept, which focuses directly on satisfying consumer needs, has taken precedence. In addition, businesses today are sensitive to the needs and well-being of society in general. They must, while conducting their activities, consider ethics, social responsibility, and the strong need to keep consumers satisfied. The result has been increased customer service and a more caring business environment.

## 〉〉〉〉 KEY TERMS

| | | |
|---|---|---|
| corporate culture | promotion | selling era |
| marketing culture | utility | marketing era |
| marketing | form utility | marketing concept |
| market analysis | place utility | societal marketing concept |
| consumer analysis | time utility | social responsibility |
| product | information utility | ethical marketing |
| price | ownership utility | consumerism |
| distribution | production era | |

## 〉〉〉〉 REVIEW AND DISCUSSION QUESTIONS

**1.** Briefly explain the role of the various activities associated with marketing.

**2.** Briefly describe the concept of utility and explain the five different types of utility.

**3.** How does the definition of marketing in this text differ from that of the American Marketing Association?

**4.** How important is marketing to a contemporary business organization? To a non-profit organization?

**5.** McDonald's is the established leader in the fast food restaurant business. What factors have contributed to its success?

**6.** What is the difference between the marketing concept and the societal marketing concept?

**7.** Select a prominent retail operation in your own hometown (chain or independent retailer), and analyze how they have or have not made use of the marketing concept.

**8.** Identify and describe the activities of any large Canadian corporation whose marketing activities you judge to be socially responsible.

**9.** Briefly explain what you feel are the negative and the positive aspects of the marketing activity.

## 〉〉〉〉 REFERENCES

1.  PETER DRUCKER, *Management Tasks, Responsibilities and Practices* (New York: Harper & Row, 1973), p.63.

2.  American Marketing Association, "AMA Board Approves New Definition", *Marketing News*, March 1, 1985. p.1.

3.  LEE IACOCCA and WILLIAM NOVAK, *Iacocca: An Autobiography* (Toronto: Bantam Books, 1984), pp.64-65.

4.  PHILIP KOTLER and GORDON McDOUGALL, *Marketing Essentials* (Toronto: Prentice-Hall Canada Inc., 1985), p.13.

5. WILLIAM BAND, "Customer Service: The Real Competitive Edge", *Sales & Marketing Management in Canada*, November 1987, p.56.

6. DAVID CRAVENS and GERALD HILLS, "Consumerism: A Perspective for Business", *Business Horizons*, 1970, p.21.

7. Consumer and Corporate Affairs Canada, *Annual Report*, March 31, 1988, p.3.

# CHAPTER 2 〉〉〉〉

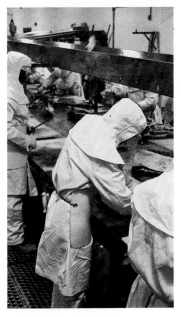

# Marketing Environments

---

**LEARNING OBJECTIVES**

After studying this chapter you will be able to

1. Describe the role and nature of the controllable variables in the marketing decision-making process.

2. Explain the concept of the marketing mix.

3. Illustrate the role that environmental factors have on the consumer marketplace and marketing mix strategies.

---

The environment in which marketing operates is constantly changing. Problems, opportunities, successes, and failures are largely dependent upon an organization's ability to adapt to changing conditions. Those businesses that anticipate change and its impact on their operation will be able to develop new strategies for success. To foresee and adjust to changes, a company must look at two kinds of phenomena: controllable variables and uncontrollable variables. Variables such as product and price are controllable since decisions in these areas are made within the organization. Variables such as the economy, the competition, and technology are external to the firm, and therefore, uncontrollable. The uncontrollable variables definitely have an impact on the type of decisions made regarding the controllable variables.

## ⟩⟩⟩⟩ *The Controllable Marketing Variables*

marketing mix

The controllable variables are referred to as the marketing mix. The **marketing mix** is defined as a combination of the marketing elements that are used to satisfy the needs of a target market and achieve organizational objectives. The elements are

**FIGURE 2.1    The Marketing Mix**

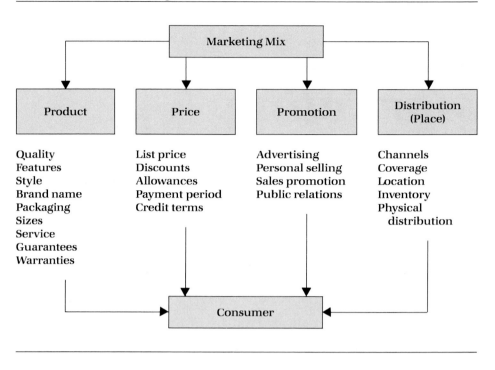

referred to as the "4 Ps": product, price, place or distribution, and promotion. In planning marketing strategies for a company, product, or service, decisions are made for each element of the marketing mix. Refer to figure 2.1 for an illustration of these decisions. Let's examine the four key decision areas of the marketing mix.

## Product Strategy

product strategy

The most critical decision for a firm is determining what products or services to market. **Product strategy** involves making decisions on variables such as product quality, product features, brand name and packaging, customer service, guarantees and warranties. The variable elements of product strategy can be further subdivided on the basis of tangibility (characteristics perceptible by touch) and intangibility (characteristics not perceptible by touch). Products like the IBM PS/2 microcomputer are well known for product quality, performance, and dependability. The product has an extensive list of features and a customer service program backed by a company with an excellent reputation. IBM's product combines the characteristics of tangibility and intangibility. The physical characteristics of IBM's product can be clearly seen and demonstrated for customers at the point of purchase. This is tangibility. A feature such as service is intangible and will only be recognized by the customer should problems occur with the equipment after purchase. In contrast, a brand of beer like Labatt's Blue is by and large not that distinguishable from competing products on the basis of tangible characteristics like taste and appearance or on the basis of price and distribution, which are controlled by government regulation. As a result, product strategy for Blue will touch on subtle differences in taste (tangibility) but rely heavily on intangible factors such as heritage to distinguish itself from competitive brands. It is common for a beer advertisement to mention the beer's brewing history or its established reputation.

**differential advantage**

**product differentiation**

Product strategy attempts to establish a **differential advantage** for a product, which then becomes the focal point of the marketing activity for that product. This process is referred to as **product differentiation**, which is defined as a strategy that focuses on the unique attributes of a product in order to distinguish one brand from all others. For example, the differential advantage of Maytag appliances is service (i.e., the lack of service required for Maytag products), as demonstrated by the idle repairman in their advertising. Maxwell House prides itself on the taste of its coffee, boasting that it is good until the last drop, while Zenith emphasizes its television's superior quality, claiming that the quality goes in before the name goes on.

## Price Strategy

**price strategy**

**Price strategy** involves the development of a pricing structure which is fair and equitable for the consumer while being profitable for the organization. Since most products are marketed in a competitive market, organizations are free to establish prices according to what the market will bear. A host of factors are considered when a price strategy is established, including the cost of the product, the location of the customer, the desired profit level and the degree of competition. Generally, the less distinguishable a product is from its competitors (a condition referred to as *low differential advantage*), the less flexibility there is with price. It should be pointed out that price is subject to regulation in certain markets and service sectors, and planned increases in price must be approved by governments or government agencies. For example, prices are controlled in the cases of hydroelectric power, telephone rates, cable television, beer, wine, and alcohol.

In addition to setting a price, organizations also establish price policies. Price policies cover trade allowances, discount programs, and credit terms. A business can provide these additional incentives, and customers can evaluate them while making their purchase decision.

## Promotion Strategy

**promotion strategy**

**Promotion strategy** involves another group of mix elements; it is a company's blending of advertising, sales promotion, personal selling, and public relations activity, which enables the company to present to a target market a consistent and persuasive message about a product or service.

Advertising is a persuasive form of marketing communications, designed to stimulate a positive response (usually a purchase) from a defined target market. In advertising, decisions are made on the content, style and tone of the message (i.e., what to say and how to say it). For some products a humorous appeal may be used, while in other cases celebrities may be used to endorse the product. The use of emotional appeals is another common technique in advertising. Which media to use is another strategic decision to be made. Should the organization attempt to reach the masses through network television advertising, or should a selective audience be reached by a specialized targeted magazine?

Sales promotion is divided into two areas: consumer promotion and trade promotion. Consumer promotions center on the use of coupons, cash refunds, contests, and other incentives that are designed to encourage consumers to make immediate purchases. Trade promotions include rebates, trade allowances, and performance allowances, and are designed to encourage distributors to carry and resell a product.

Personal selling involves face-to-face communications or other direct forms of communication (e.g.,telemarketing) between marketing organizations and potential buyers.

The linking of the various promotional efforts is vital for the success of the organization. For example, advertising and sales promotion will create awareness and interest for a product or service. Personal selling will create the desire and action to obtain the product; it is the activity that closes deals (achieves purchase).

Public relations deal with a firm's relationships and communications with its various publics. These include not only customers but other groups such as shareholders, employees, governments, suppliers and distributors. Public relations embraces activities such as public affairs, issues management, government relations, community relations, industry relations, media relations, and publicity. Generally, public relations is intended to complement the other promotion and marketing strategies that an organization implements.

## Place or Distribution Strategy

**distribution strategy**
**marketing channel**

**Distribution strategy** refers to the selection and management of marketing channels and the physical distribution of products. A **marketing channel** is a series of firms or individuals that participate in the flow of goods and services from producer to final users or consumers. An IBM microcomputer may be sold directly to a school or business by a company sales representative or it may be sold to a computer store like Computerland or Compucentre, which in turn sells it to the final user. A product like dog food will move from a manufacturer like Quaker Oats to a wholesaler like National Grocers to a retailer like IGA, which in turn sells to the consumer. Each situation represents a different kind of channel.

Distribution decisions must establish which type of channel to use, the degree of market coverage desired (i.e., how intense will coverage be), the location and availability of product, inventory (the amount of product stored at manufacturing or warehousing facilities), and transportation modes (air, rail, water, transport, and pipeline). Developing effective and efficient distribution systems requires that an organization work closely, and develop a harmonious relationship, with distributors (wholesalers and retailers) who resell a product in the channel. In addition to figure 2.1, refer to the Marketing in Action vignette "Recipe for Success: Mix Gasoline with Milk," which shows the integration of a variety of distribution elements. This joint venture concept between convenience stores and oil companies shows how basic marketing strategies of two different businesses have combined to satisfy consumers' needs and add to organizational profits.

## >>>> *MARKETING IN ACTION*

### *RECIPE FOR SUCCESS: MIX GASOLINE WITH MILK*

Did you know that one out of every five gallons of gasoline sold in the U.S. was sold through convenience store outlets. Similar trends are emerging in Canada. Oil companies and convenience store chains are rapidly moving into each other's turf at an alarming rate, and the traditional gas station is disappearing just as fast.

Shell Canada was the first oil company in Canada to add a convenience store to one of its gas stations in 1974, but it wasn't until 1984 that rapid expansion occurred. In western Canada, Shell launched its own convenience store chain, Circle K, to tie in with its gas stations. A total of 70 outlets are now in operation.

Convenience store chains are also entering the gasoline business through joint ventures. Southland Canada Inc. operates 7-Eleven Stores, 220 of which sell gas. Others to enter the field include Mac's and La Maisonnée stores (Silcorp Limited of Canada) and Neighbours (Petro-Canada).

Why the invasion of each other's turf? For the convenience store retailer, gasoline profit margins are not the bait. The pumps are traffic builders which translate into customers. An executive of 7-Eleven claims that 35 percent of people who buy gasoline also pick up something in the convenience store. In many cases the customer must enter the store to pay for the gas. Also, the location of the corner gas station is ideal for convenience stores.

*Mac's is one of a number of convenience store chains entering the gasoline business through joint ventures*

Fcr oil companies with low profit margins in gasoline sales it is hard to justify sitting on prime corners selling only gasoline. Profit margins are the main reasons gas stations are selling milk, snack foods, and other basic necessities. Gross margins on variety store items are around 35 percent compared to 7 percent for gasoline.

As these firms progress further into the 1990s, more expansion and conversion of gas stations is anticipated. Joint ventures between oil companies and convenience store chains will be quite commonplace.

Adapted from Kenneth Kidd, "Gasoline, milk, oil, muffins: an appetising business mix", *Toronto Star*, August 7, 1988, p.F1.

## Public Image: The 5th P

For any business organization, large or small, a good company reputation is an important asset. Nevertheless, business organizations, particularly large ones, often ignore their corporate image as they become engrossed in the marketing and image of individual brands, product lines, or services. As discussed in chapter 1, businesses today are more in tune with consumer needs and societal concerns than ever before (they follow the societal marketing concept), and as a result, a fifth P is gaining recognition: the firm's **public image.**[1] A reputation is important enough that a firm should pay special attention to it.

**public image**

A good example of a firm neglecting its company image is Nestlé. Nestlé attracted consumer complaints about the marketing practices it employed to promote its

**FIGURE 2.2**   The Public Image Mix

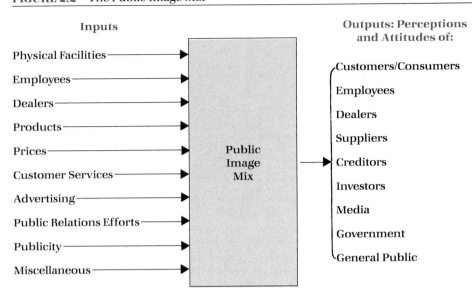

*Source*:  William Band, Coopers & Lybrand. Reproduced with permission.

infant formula in Third World countries. Rather than taking action, the company ignored complaints, then attempted a counterattack on its critics through aggressive public relations. The result was a full-fledged consumer boycott of Nestlé products. The company finally relented but suffered from massive amounts of negative publicity.[2] There are several inputs which, if used and managed properly, will contribute to a positive public image. Refer to figure 2.2 for a summary of these public image inputs.

## >>>> *The Uncontrollable Marketing Variables*

In developing marketing strategies, an organization must consider the external variables that exist in the marketplace. It is the unpredictability of these variables that makes marketing a dynamic field. For example, if interest rates rise, spending by consumers has a tendency to drop, which affects all kinds of industries: housing, automobiles, major appliances for the home, recreation and leisure activities, among others. A rippling effect occurs that extends to suppliers to these industries. When market planners develop marketing strategies, they must constantly monitor and evaluate the effect of the following uncontrollable variables:

1. The competition.
2. The economy.
3. Consumer characteristics.
4. Laws and regulations.
5. Technology.

See figure 2.3 for a visual illustration of the uncontrollable marketing variables.

FIGURE 2.3    Uncontrollable Marketing Environment

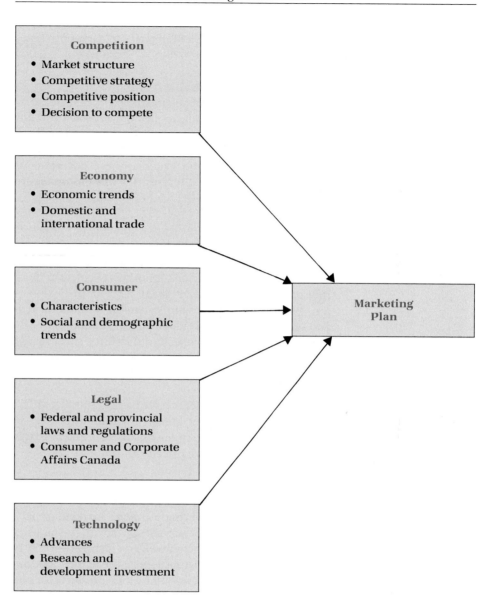

## The Competition

The activity of competitors is probably the most thoroughly analyzed aspect of marketing practice, as competitors are constantly striving to find new and better ways of appealing to similar target markets. The competitive environment that an organization operates in must be defined and analyzed, and the strategies of direct and indirect competitors must be monitored and evaluated.

### *Market Structures*

In Canada, a business operates within one of four different types of market structure, each of which has a different impact on marketing strategy.

#### *Monopoly*

monopoly

In a **monopoly**, one firm serves the entire market and, therefore, theoretically controls all marketing mix elements: product, price, place, and promotion. In Canada, however, where monopolies are regulated by government, their control is limited. Examples of monopolistic but regulated markets include telephone service, cable television within geographic areas, electricity, and water. Since consumers do not have a choice in matters such as these, governments at all levels must regulate price and service availability, ensuring that customers are treated fairly.

#### *Oligopoly*

oligopoly

In an **oligopoly** a few large firms dominate the market. The marketing activity, in an oligopolistic market, focuses on variables other than price. The beer industry in Canada is a good example. The industry is controlled by two large breweries: Labatt and Molson. It is very difficult for others to enter the market and be successful unless they are satisfied with a very small piece of the action. Amstel Breweries of Hamilton, Ontario, is a good example. Amstel is noted for regional beers such as Grizzly and Steeler. Keith's India Pale Ale in the Maritimes and Big Rock beers in Alberta are other examples. What makes it difficult for small firms to compete is the fact that large breweries are extending their reach in Canada by adding popular U.S. brands to their product lists. Brands such as Miller, Budweiser, and Coors are now national in scope in Canada.

Generally, firms compete on the basis of product differentiation and promotion in an oligopoly. In the beer industry, subtle differences in taste may not be all that important, but the image of the brand as created by marketing could be a vital factor in the consumer's purchase decision.

#### *Monopolistic Competition*

monopolistic competition

In a market characterized by **monopolistic competition** there are many firms, large or small, each offering a unique marketing mix based on price and other variables. The product or service uses any of the mix elements to differentiate itself from competitors. Products are clearly distinguished by brand names. In effect, each competitor is striving to monopolize the market, but due to the presence of strong competition, there are always substitute products for consumers.

The automobile industry in Canada is an example of a market which is straddling oligopoly and monopolistic competition. The influx of foreign car makers and the business they have captured has made this market more competitive than ever. Domestic automakers such as General Motors, Ford, and Chrysler control the largest piece of the market. They compete with each other for a greater share of the market by offering a variety of cars in all price segments (e.g., economy cars, mid-priced compacts, and high-priced luxury cars). All cars are identified by brand names such as Buick Regal, Oldsmobile Cutlass, Ford Probe, Ford Tempo, Pontiac Sunbird, Plymouth LeBaron, Dodge Caravan, and so on. The domestic automakers must also be concerned about competition from Japanese and European manufacturers. Initially, cars from these countries concentrated on the small car segment, but now they market a variety of products and cover all price segments of the market.

The structure of most markets in Canada lies between monopoly and pure competition. Most Canadian industries are highly concentrated and best described as oligopolies or as monopolistically competitive.[3]

### Pure Competition

pure competition

In a market where **pure competition** exists, there are many small firms marketing similar products; therefore, the differential advantage is not that clear to consumers. Since firms are smaller, they have less control of the marketing variables, particularly in the area of price and distribution. For example, channel members (wholesalers and retailers), faced with a wide choice of products but limited space to store them, will be very selective about what they carry and as a result have a significant influence on the availability of a manufacturer's product to the consumer market. Food distribution is a good example: several large retailers such as Safeway, A&P, Loblaws, Sobey's, and Provigo have a tendency to dominate the regional markets they operate in. If their buyers decide not to carry a certain product, it will not be available in any of their retail outlets. They only have so much shelf space and, therefore, are interested in lines that will turn over quickly. Less popular lines with lower turnover are always in jeopardy.

New firms can easily enter a purely competitive market, so existing firms, in order to remain competitive, must ensure that there is an adequate supply of products available at a low price and with widespread distribution. Frequently, it is price (low price) which maintains a competitive advantage for any one product.

### Competitive Strategies

Once an organization has identified the characteristics of the market it operates in, its attention shifts to the strategies of competitors. Competitors from direct and indirect sources must be monitored. Types of competitive information that are routinely monitored and evaluated include the following:

1. *Market Share*   How much of the total business does each competitor have? What are the share trends on a national and regional basis?

2. *Market Segment Trends*   An assessment is made of where competitors are strong and weak. Such analysis may be done on a geographic basis (e.g., strong in Ontario, weak in Quebec), or on the basis of product or market category (e.g., a firm may be noted for its strength in the premium-priced segment but weak in low-priced segments).

3. *Marketing Activity Assessment*   An analysis is also conducted of 4P activities which have played an influencing role in a competitor's market share performance. In which marketing variables lie their strengths? Weaknesses?

4. *Innovation*   In addition to assessing existing products, a company investigates whether the competition introduced any new product or packaging innovations, and what effect the innovation had on the market. For example, what influence did it have on market share or consumer purchase decisions?

direct competition

**Direct competition** is competition from alternate or substitute products and services that satisfy the needs of a common target market. For example, in the toothpaste market, Crest competes directly with Colgate, Aqua Fresh, Close Up and others. In the coffee market, Maxwell House competes with Nabob, Nescafé, Taster's Choice, other national brands, and many private-label store brands. Firms must also consider **indirect competition**. For example, a fitness club must think not only of other clubs around town, but also of indirect competition from other ways in which consumers may spend their leisure and recreation hours, and their dollars. Consumers may, for example, consider spending their leisure hours in attending a sporting event, going to the theatre, or enrolling in a continuing education course at a local high school, college, or university. Therefore, the owner of the fitness club must develop strategies for competing with the array of recreation alternatives available to consumers.

*indirect competition*

### The Competitive Position

*market share*

A firm's market share reflects its competitive position in the marketplace. **Market share** is the sales volume of one competing company or product expressed as a percentage of total market sales volume. Competing products are classified in many ways. Kotler describes and classifies competitors as follows:[4]

*market leader*

1. **A market leader** is the largest firm in the industry and is a leader in strategic actions (e.g., new product innovation, pricing and price increases, and aggressive promotion activity). Examples of leaders include IBM computers, Goodyear tires, and Canadian Tire in automotive and general merchandise retailing; as regards the beer industry, Labatt's Blue is the largest selling brand of beer in Canada.

*market challenger*

2. **A market challenger** is a firm or firms (product or products) that is attempting to gain market leadership through aggressive marketing efforts. Perhaps the best example is the battle between Pepsi-Cola (the challenger) and Coca-Cola (the leader). While the claims and counter-claims of these two giants are often confusing to consumers, Coca-Cola still retains leadership in the soft drink business. Pepsi-Cola, however, uses more aggressive marketing strategies. The Pepsi Challenge advertising campaign, which showed Coke drinkers preferring the taste of Pepsi in blind taste tests, is a good example. Read the Marketing in Action account ''Battle Grounds Drawn in Toy World'' for an illustration of the impact of competition. This vignette shows how a market challenger attempts to do battle with a true market leader.

*market follower*

3. **A market follower** is generally satisfied with its market share position. Often, it has entered the market late and has not incurred the research and development costs that innovators do. As a result, it follows the leaders on product, price, distribution and other marketing actions.

*market nichers*

4. **Market nichers** practice niche marketing. Niche marketing is now a popular term in marketing jargon. It refers to the concentration of resources in one or more distinguishable market segments. An appropriate analogy for market nichers is that of the big fish in a small pond, as opposed to a little fish in a big pond. In order to market niche, an organization differentiates itself on the basis of market specialization, geographic specialization, product features, special expertise in service, or other areas of strength. Examples of market nichers are Maytag Appliances (dependable and repair-free), Canada Dry (a brand known for its variety of drink mixers as

## 〉〉〉〉 *MARKETING IN ACTION*

### *BATTLE GROUNDS DRAWN IN TOY WORLD*

What is the most popular toy doll in North America? Barbie is in her thirty-first season, and her manufacturer, Mattel Toys, claims that 98 percent of girls between three and ten years of age own a Barbie doll. That's a successful product.

Many others have tried to compete with Barbie, but were unsuccessful. One such manufacturer, Hasbro Inc., introduced Jem to the market (sort of a "Barbie gone wild" doll) with much fanfare, but it was withdrawn from the market within two years. Hasbro sold seven million dolls over this period and viewed the project as unsuccessful.

The moral to this case is quite simple. Don't go head-to-head with a number one item unless your product is "clearly delineated, clearly differentiated". Barbie's position in the doll market is almost impregnable, since she has the most accessories and play environments, as well as an enviable wardrobe.

Undaunted by past failure, Hasbro attacked again with the introduction of Maxie. Maxie is positioned as a younger, less sophisticated doll than Barbie, available at a lower price. Maxie's launch was quite different from Jem's. First, Maxie's image is simpler, so that young girls can identify with her, and her supporting props represent activities that are less glamorous that those of Jem.

What are the chances for success this time around? Well, Hasbro invested one million dollars

*Barbie® doll through the years: (left to right) 1989 Super-star Barbie, 1977 Barbie, 1968 Barbie, and the original Barbie of 1959*

developing Maxie and the company states that 10 percent of the $400 million doll market would be satisfactory. But the odds of success were low, and in 1990 Hasbro had stopped manufacturing the doll. On average, 6 000 new toys are introduced each year and roughly 75 percent fail — most within the first year. Fierce competition makes the toy market a tough market to crack.

Adapted from Barbara Carton, "Maxie takes on Barbie in doll land", *Toronto Star*, July 31, 1988, p.F4.

---

opposed to being a mainstream soft drink beverage), and Cross Pens (premium-priced quality pens are their only product line). Speedy Muffler's concentration on the muffler and brake repair segment of the automotive repair market is another example of niche marketing. The subject of niche marketing is discussed in more detail in the market segmentation section of chapter 4.

### *The Decision to Compete*

Given that all businesses monitor and evaluate competitive activity closely, some critical decisions have to be made regarding the manner and degree in which a firm will compete in any given market. Making the decision to enter a market requires that three questions be answered[5]. Let's examine each question briefly.

### *Should the Firm Compete?*

To answer this question, businesses take into account a number of considerations. First, an organization will review the overall direction it is taking as a company to see if competing in a particular market will fit the objectives and philosophy expressed in its mission statement. It will also want to know if participation in that market could be profitable. If it could be profitable, will the company have the resources (time, dollars and expertise) to sustain the venture? John Labatt Limited sold its Catelli Foods Division in 1988, a $200 million operation, because it did not feel equipped to compete with major packaged-goods companies in the wake of free trade between Canada and the United States. According to George Taylor, president of Labatt's Food Division, "For Catelli to take full advantage of the growth opportunities in the 1990s, a major commitment by Labatt to the North American retail packaged food business would be required. Labatt's strategy was to concentrate on its core businesses, that being beer and institutional foods."[6]

### *How Many Market Segments Should the Firm Compete in?*

The resources of any organization affect the decision on what markets to compete in. Large multi-product companies operate in numerous market segments and are capable of providing brands with competitive levels of marketing support. Companies with products in the market leader and market challenger classifications fit into this situation (e.g., Procter & Gamble, Nabisco Brands, McCain's Foods, and other major packaged goods companies). Conversely, many smaller companies with limited resources will niche or concentrate their efforts in selected markets and do their best to stay competitive there. Specialized retail operations such as Kettle Creek Canvas Company, Chatham Run, and Mark's Work Wearhouse are examples of organizations that concentrate in specific market segments.

### *How Should the Firm Compete?*

Once market segments have been identified, the next major issue is the development of the best marketing strategy for satisfying that market. An organization considers the uncontrollable marketing variables, determines the role and importance of the marketing mix elements (4 Ps), and implements an appropriate action plan to satisfy their target market needs.

## The Economy

The economy has significant impact on the marketing activity of an organization. Canada's economic situation is measured by variables such as the gross national product (GNP), inflation, unemployment, real income, and interest rates. These indicators determine how conservative or how aggressive an organization's marketing efforts will be. Let's examine these economic issues briefly by defining each term:

1. *Gross National Product*  The GNP is the total value of goods and services produced in a country on an annual basis.

2. *Inflation*  Inflation refers to a rising price level for goods and services that results in reduced purchasing power.

3. *Unemployment*   The unemployed are people actively looking for work who do not have jobs.

4. *Real Income*   This is income adjusted for inflation over time.

The relationships among these economic variables are dynamic. For example, if, during a given period, widespread cost increases drive prices up beyond, say, the means of moderate income groups, the purchasing of goods and services will decrease. When prices rise at a higher rate than incomes, there is less money available for discretionary purchases by consumers. The consumer will concentrate on necessities instead. Thus inflation, by slowing down the economy, contributes to unemployment. It also shrinks real income (e.g., a $30 000 income in 1992 is worth less than a $30 000 income in 1991 or previous years). In the early 1980s the interest rates and mortgage rates skyrocketed to the 18–20 percent range temporarily, and as a result the purchase of homes dropped dramatically. This drop in demand affected all industries that supply the home building industry. Consequently, unemployment in these industries rose considerably. In such times, industry marketing strategies tend to be conservative.

The converse is also true. If inflation rates are reasonable from year to year, interest rates are lower and unemployment decreases, resulting in a healthier economy. In this situation consumers are more apt to spend; therefore, marketing activity becomes more aggressive. These conditions prevailed in Canada in the mid- and late 1980s.

The state of the economy also affects the value of the Canadian dollar. Changes in the value of the Canadian dollar have a special impact on the marketing activities of international marketing organizations that export to the United States and other world markets. When, for instance, the Canadian dollar is worth less than the U.S. dollar, Canadian-produced goods become more attractive to and marketable among American buyers, since the prices of our goods in their market are lower than those of their own goods. Conversely, if the Canadian dollar is higher in value than the U.S. dollar, our goods become less attractive because the prices of Canadian goods are higher than U.S. ones in their market. In this case, exports to the U.S. would probably decline.

### Free Trade: Canada and the United States

Free trade came into effect as of January 1, 1989. Under the agreement between the two countries, tariffs are to be lowered gradually and phased out over a ten-year period. This agreement is largely based on the Auto Pact, which was put into place in 1965. The Auto Pact was a bilateral agreement that led to the integration of North American production and marketing of automobile products into one large market. Safeguards were built into the Auto Pact to ensure that production of cars in Canada did not drop below a certain proportion of cars sold in Canada.[7]

**dumping**

The major incentive for Canada to pursue free trade was the protectionist attitude that was growing in the United States at the time. Fearful of a growing trade deficit, the U.S. was ready to interfere with the flow of imports into their country. The U.S. was concerned over products entering their country that were subsidized by the exporting country, and products that were dumped into their country. **Dumping** is the practice of selling products at significantly lower prices in foreign markets than

FIGURE 2.4    Some Benefits and Costs of Free Trade

**Benefits**

1.  Once it gains access to the large United States market, Canada will benefit from cost reductions because of economies of scale in production.

    *Example:*    A Canadian plant will produce a product or select group of products for the entire North American market, instead of for Canada only.

2.  There will be gains in efficiency due to increased competitiveness within the Canadian economy as Canada becomes more open to import competition.

    *Example:*    Oligopolistic industries that dominate Canada can hold prices at high levels. New competition from U.S. products will lower prices for Canadian consumers. Firms will look at ways to become more efficient in their operations rather than rely on price increases to protect profit margins.

**Costs**

1.  Substantial adjustment costs will be incurred, and this will affect certain regions, the economic sectors, and the labour force.

    *Example:*    Certain industries such as wine, food processing and textiles will be directly affected. Plant shutdowns and layoffs will occur.

2.  Non-economic matters such as political, social and cultural values are at risk.

    *Example:*    The loss of a Canadian identity is objectionable to many, as is the abolishing or watering down of social programs such as universal medical plans, unemployment insurance, and pension plans.

---

in a country's domestic market. Canada's domestic automakers accused Hyundai Motor Company of South Korea of dumping Ponys, small, low-priced cars it made in the mid-eighties, in Canada. This car was very successful initially, mainly due to its significant price advantage. Over time the price advantage gradually disappeared and sales of the Pony slowed down. Eventually, the Pony was discontinued, and many of their original buyers returned to North American automobiles for their next purchase.

The free trade agreement calls for a free trade area, where the movement of goods and services is to be free, but each country is able to impose its own restrictions on the movement of labour and capital within the area as well as its own tariffs and trade policies on the rest of the world. Refer to figure 2.4 for a summary of the benefits and costs of free trade and to the Marketing in Action feature "Free Trade: Canada and the United States" for further details on this issue.

### *The Impact of Free Trade on Marketing Practice*

People employed in marketing may be vulnerable to job loss as a result of free trade with the United States, since marketing activity and planning could become centralized in the U.S. headquarters of multinational companies. Is there a need to duplicate marketing organizations in two countries to serve one market? Marketing activity in Canada is usually planned on an east-west basis giving due consideration to language, social, and cultural differences. With free trade, a north-south orientation will

## 〉〉〉〉 *MARKETING IN ACTION*

### *FREE TRADE: CANADA AND THE UNITED STATES*

Windsor-Essex County Development Commission

*The Free Trade Agreement allows goods and services to flow with increasing ease across such borders as the Detroit River between Windsor, Ontario, and Detroit, Michigan*

The free trade agreement between Canada and the United States will result in a shakeout in the North American market, with companies and industries on both sides of the border gaining benefits or suffering consequences. To assess the gains and losses is virtually impossible, particularly when the economies will intermingle more. Economists generally agree, however, that when tariffs are removed, the costs of producing goods will be the single most important factor determining whether firms locate in Canada or in the U.S.

There are some good examples of free trade benefiting Canada. General Motors has invested close to $1 billion in its Oshawa, Ontario plant (Oshawa Autoplex), making it one of the most technologically advanced assembly plants in North America. Car models built in this facility will serve the entire North American market. Jobs and production are not at risk there. The Goodyear Tire and Rubber Company of Akron, Ohio, announced that a $150 million state-of-the-art tire plant would be built in Napanee, Ontario, resulting in approximately one thousand jobs for that region.

On the negative side, Canada's food processing industry is expected to be in jeopardy. In 1987-88, RJR Nabisco sold off its coffee, candy, and pet food lines in Canada in order to concentrate on fewer product lines. Manufacturing facilities were reduced from 29 to 17 and its work force from 6 800 to 4 000. In 1987, Montreal-based Dominion Textiles had 8 000 or 73 percent of its employees in Canada, 2 400 in the U.S., and 600 in Europe. By the end of 1988, the Canadian work force dropped to 6 800, about half of the total. Michael Dufour, a Domtex executive, explained that "the advent of free trade will only fuel our strategy of expanding outside of Canada". Domtex was closing Canadian plants and acquiring U.S. facilities because of the lower production costs there (labour rates in this industry are estimated to be 20 percent higher in Canada).

Procter & Gamble is integrating Canadian plants into their overall North American supply base. An aging plant in Hamilton, Ontario, which produced a variety of product lines, is now only producing toilet soaps for the total market. Another of their Canadian plants produces only selected detergent products for sale in Canada and export to the U.S.

Considering the arguments for and against free trade, it is clear that the effects will be difficult to measure. What is more important, perhaps, is the question of whether a consolidated North American market will help U.S. and Canadian companies compete against Asian and European industry. What do you think?

Adapted from "Getting ready for the great North American shakeout", *Business week*, April 4, 1988. p.43., and Konrad Vabuski, "Where will investment go under free trade?", *Toronto Star*, August 14, 1988, p.F1.

occur, and the marketing power base will shift to the south. Canada will operate with efficient plants that produce selected goods for the entire market, and in this way will create an efficient distribution system to serve the Canadian (northern) market.[8] Where marketing strategies are concerned, Quebec may suffer as a result of this new arrangement: the truly unique needs of that province will be less important to a U.S.-based marketing organization once that province represents only 2 percent of the North American market. To an organization managed by Canadians, on the other hand, Quebec represents a possible 28 percent of its consumption, so there is a strong case for original marketing and advertising strategies.

## Consumer Characteristics

The nature and characteristics of consumers are other unpredictable variables that influence marketing strategies. Market planners must analyze demographic and social trends and develop appropriate strategies to address the changes that occur. These trends refer to changes in age, income, occupation, education, location of residency, and lifestyle, among many other variables. Data from the 1986 census suggest that the age distribution of the Canadian population is continuing to change. While the growth rate in total population has declined over the past twenty years, certain categories are growing much faster than average. Changes in the age distribution of the population are due to variations in the birth rates in recent years; the baby boom of the fifties was followed by a "baby bust" in the late sixties and seventies. Generally, the Canadian population is maturing. This phenomenon will have an impact on school systems, the labour force, family formation, health care, and the demand for products and services. The important social and demographic (or sociodemographic) trends influencing marketing activity in Canada are as follows:[9]

1. Population growth is low, with a 0.6 percent rate projected for the next few years (1988-1998).
2. The population is aging, and by 1999 half of the population will be over 35 years, at which time seniors will play an increasingly dominant role.
3. There will be higher income growth among wealthier Canadians (e.g., 20 percent of affluent families account for 40 percent of education and recreation expenditures in Canada).
4. There will be more highly paid women occupying managerial and professional positions.
5. The baby boom segment (those born in the 1950s) is a growing percentage of the total population.
6. Baby boomers are creating their own "mini-child boom."
7. Market segments composed of ethnic groups other than the British will continue to grow (e.g., 50 percent of Ontario's population is now non-British).
8. Marriage delays have created and will continue to create a growing singles market segment.

Figure 2.5 provides a visual illustration of population trends by age. Note the growth in the 25–44 year segment and the 55 + year segment.

All of these factors are interrelated in terms of the effect they have already had on Canadian marketing activity. Refer to figure 2.6 for information regarding cause-and-effect relationships between consumer change and marketing practice.

FIGURE 2.5    Population Trends By Age Classification

|  | Population | | |
|---|---|---|---|
|  | 1976 | 1981 | 1986 |
| 19 yr. and under | 35.8% | 31.9% | 29.0% |
| 20–34 | 25.0 | 27.0 | 26.8 |
| 35–54 | 22.1 | 22.5 | 24.5 |
| 25–54 | 37.8 | 39.9 | 42.4 |
| 55 + | 17.1 | 18.6 | 19.7 |
| Population (in thousands) | 22 993 | 24 343 | 25 309 |

*Source*:  Adapted from Statistics Canada, *Canada Year Book 1988*, Ottawa: Supply and Services Canada, 1987, Cat. No 11-402E/1987, p. 2–18. Adapted with the permission of the Minister of Supply and Services Canada, 1990.

FIGURE 2.6    Influence of Sociodemographic Trends on Marketing Activity

| Sociodemographic Trend | Effect on Marketing Activity |
|---|---|
| Growth in new ethnic markets in urban areas | Marketing strategies and plans targeted at specific ethnic groups (see the Sun Life Marketing in Action vignette in chapter 7) |
| Growth in baby boom segment (families with double incomes, or no children) | Influx of renewed activity for upscale goods and services such as fitness clubs, travel, restaurants and expensive toys |
| Growth in numbers of wealthy Canadians | Increased marketing of banking and financial services and fund raising by charitable and private organizations |
| Women working outside the home | Increased demand for day-care services, convenience foods, and fast food restaurants |
| "Greying" society (number of people 55 + years increasing) | Increased emphasis on leisure and recreation, travel, and financial services. Greater demand for health care services |

# Laws and Regulations

Yes, Canada is a free enterprise society, but in any society of this nature the consumer can be subjected to unscrupulous business practices — practices which serve only the needs of the business using them. Consequently, numerous laws and regulations (some voluntary and some involuntary) have been put into place to protect consumer rights and ensure that organizations conduct business in a competitive manner. As indicated in chapter 1, ignorance of the law is not a legitimate defence for a business; companies must act according to the law or face the perils of the judicial system.

The focal point of the legal environment for marketing and other business practice in Canada is **Consumer and Corporate Affairs Canada**, a ministry of the federal government. Consumer and Corporate Affairs Canada was created in 1967 with the principal mandate of bringing together a number of related laws that would help consumers and businesses function in Canada. The mandate of this department was updated in 1987–88 with the adoption of a new **Competition Act** which replaced the original Consumer and Corporate Affairs Act.[10] The purpose of the Competition Act is three-fold:

1. To maintain and encourage competition in Canada.
2. To ensure that small and medium size businesses have an equitable opportunity to participate in the Canadian economy.
3. To provide consumers with product choice and competitive prices.

There are three bureaus within Consumer and Corporate Affairs Canada that influence business and marketing activity: the Bureau of Competition Policy, the Bureau of Consumer Affairs, and the Bureau of Corporate Affairs.

**Consumer and Corporate Affairs Canada**

**Competition Act**

### Bureau of Competition Policy

This bureau enforces rules that govern and promote the efficiency of a competitive Canadian marketplace. Its chief instrument for carrying out these functions is the Competition Act. Among the trade practices that the Bureau of Competition routinely reviews are mergers and acquisitions. The bureau seeks to ensure that monopoly situations are not created, that competition is not affected negatively, that no price fixing or other pricing infractions occur, and that advertising does not misrepresent a product or mislead the consumer.

### Bureau of Consumer Affairs

This bureau promotes a safe, orderly, and fair marketplace for consumers and businesses. In consultation with other government agencies and organizations that represent business groups, it establishes and enforces regulations and programs that protect the interests of consumers. The bureau also ensures that dangerous products are identified and that certain products that cause injury are removed from the market. In this respect, Bill C-70, An Act to amend the Hazardous Products Act in 1988, created the Workplace Hazardous Materials Information System (WHMIS), a program aimed directly at protecting workers through the identification and monitoring of hazardous materials. The legislation under the jurisdiction of Consumer Affairs Canada includes the Canadian Packaging and Labelling Act, the National Trademark and Labelling Act, and the Weights and Measures Act.

### Bureau of Corporate Affairs

This bureau provides a regulatory framework for the business community in Canada. Its intent is to ensure orderly conduct among businesses across the country, to encourage economic development, and to promote creativity, innovation, and the exploitation of technology. Legislation administered by Corporate Affairs includes the Bankruptcy Act, the Canada Corporations Act, the Patent Act, and the Copyright Act.

# Technology

Technology will probably be the greatest single force shaping the Canadian marketplace in the next decade and beyond. The technological environment consists of the discoveries, inventions, and innovations that provide marketing with opportunities. New products, new packaging, cost-reduced formulae for existing products, and the use of substitute materials are all the result of technological advancement, as are automation and the use of robotics in the manufacturing process.

As technology accelerates, the length of time a product remains on the market will become shorter. Constant developments in the small computer industry mean that even very recent innovations become obsolete. Consequently, buyers of the equipment are in a constant state of confusion when trying to decide what and when to purchase.

Research and development is a major investment for many industries in Canada. Consult the Marketing in Action account "Northern Telecom and Canada's Largest Private R&D Company" for an illustration of the role and importance of research

## ⟩⟩⟩⟩ *MARKETING IN ACTION*

### *NORTHERN TELECOM AND CANADA'S LARGEST PRIVATE R&D COMPANY*

Northern Telecom is committed to the development and production of the highest quality telecommunications systems, making research and development a key priority. The company consistently invests between 12 and 13 percent of revenues annually in research and development. It owns 70 percent of Bell-Northern Research Ltd. (BNR) of Ottawa, the country's largest private-sector research establishment, with Bell Canada owning the remaining 30 percent. BNR operates R&D facilities in six locations in Canada as well as locations in the United States and the United Kingdom.

Northern Telecom traces its origin back to 1882, when the Bell Telephone Company of Canada established a manufacturing facility to produce telephones. It has become the world's leading supplier of fully digital telecommunications switching equipment. The corporation now conducts business in more than 70 countries and operates 40 manufacturing plants in Australia, Canada, France, Malaysia, The People's Republic of China, the Republic of Ireland, and the United States. Research and development is conducted at 21 of these facilities.

The corporation manufactures a complete line of telecommunications equipment for telephone companies, private corporations, educational institutions, government agencies, hospitals, offices, and residences. Its products include

*BNR technologist Conrad Lafrance monitors a computer-controlled voice simulator, shown moving in an arc above Northern Telecom's new Meridean Norstar M7310 telephone*

switching and transmission systems, fiber optics and communications cable, subscriber switching systems, telephones and other terminals, outside plant equipment, and other products for public and private telecommunications networks as well as a wide range of software that delivers advanced features and applications to the company's diverse customer base.

It is R&D, such as that conducted by BNR, that helps Northern Telecom to be an important player in the international telecommunications market. Investment in research and development is crucial to maintaining a presence in a global market that is expected to grow by $300 billion U.S. annually through the year 2000.

Adapted from Gayle MacDonald, "R&D: the lifeblood of nortel's global high-tech empire", *Financial Post*, October 3, 1988, p.26 and information from Northern Telecom.

and development. In Canada, the telecommunications industry accounts for 20 percent of R&D spending, and as a result of this investment it has established itself as a major exporter and global competitor.[11] Other industries in Canada where R&D investment is high include computer hardware and software, aerospace and biotechnology. See figure 2.7 for an illustration of how technology plays a role in the advertising strategy at Dofasco.

**FIGURE 2.7**   Technology and Advertising Strategy

**FIGURE 2.8** Inputs for Satisfying Customers

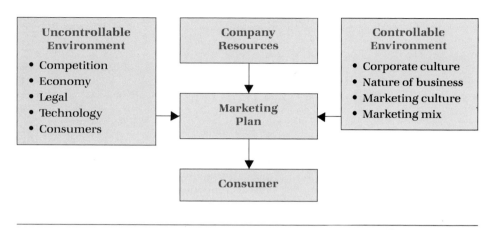

Biotechnology derives from the science of living organisms. It has created, among other things, hardier grains, beefier cattle, faster growing trees, and test-tube babies. Biotechnology is also finding ways to reduce the amounts of garbage discarded each year, turning the waste into useful by-products.[12] Genetic manipulation or genetic engineering will grow in the future. The technology needed to eliminate, through breeding, the undesirable characteristics of plants and animals already exists. Perhaps someday this technology will be used to create humans who are healthier, smarter, and stronger! The problem with such technology is that the pace of the advancements are so rapid that society does not have time to understand their consequences.

To conclude this chapter, refer to figure 2.8. This chart provides a visual summary of the various elements that an organization must consider in its quest to satisfy consumers.

## 〉〉〉〉 S U M M A R Y

The environment that marketing operates in is dynamic, and organizations must therefore constantly anticipate and react to change. How an organization handles change is a key factor in determining its degree of success or failure in the marketplace.

From a management viewpoint, there are certain elements which marketing can control. These elements or controllable variables are referred to as the marketing mix. The marketing mix consists of strategic decisions for four variables (the 4Ps): product, price, place (or distribution), and promotion. A 5th P, public image, is receiving greater attention in contemporary marketing practice. In marketing planning, the decisions made regarding these variables combine to form a marketing strategy for a product, service, or company.

Decisions about the marketing mix are influenced by certain uncontrollable variables. These variables, though beyond the control of the organization, have a significant influence on the direction of its marketing activity. In studying the uncontrollable variables, an organization analyzes the competition, the economy, the laws and regulations, the consumers, and the changes in technology.

## ⟩⟩⟩⟩ KEY TERMS AND CONCEPTS

marketing mix
product strategy
differential advantage
product differentiation
price strategy
promotion strategy
distribution strategy
marketing channel

public image
monopoly
oligopoly
pure competition
direct competition
indirect competition
market share

market challenger
market follower
market nichers
dumping
Consumer and Corporate Affairs
   Canada
Competition Act

## ⟩⟩⟩⟩ REVIEW AND DISCUSSION QUESTIONS

**1.** Since marketing organizations can choose their target markets, why are consumers considered part of the uncontrollable environment?

**2.** What is the differential advantage for the following organizations or products? **(a)** McDonald's **(b)** Canadian Tire **(c)** Pampers **(d)** Journey's End Motels **(e)** Zellers **(f)** Pepsi-Cola

**3.** Identify an organization that you would characterize as a market challenger. Briefly describe the nature of its marketing activity.

**4.** Identify and briefly explain the elements of the marketing mix.

**5.** Explain what niche marketing is and briefly describe two examples of the concept in practice.

**6.** What is the purpose of the Competition Act?

**7.** Briefly explain how the characteristics of consumers affect marketing activity.

**8.** How important is technology and what impact will it have on marketing organizations in the future?

**9.** "There is too much regulation and control of marketing activity in Canada." Discuss this statement.

**10.** "Consumer protection laws are in conflict with the free enterprise system." Discuss this statement.

## ⟩⟩⟩⟩ REFERENCES

1. WILLIAM A. BAND, "Build Your Company Image to Increase Sales", *Sales & Marketing Management in Canada*, December 1987, p.10.

2. *Ibid.*, p.12.

3. ALEXANDER MACMILLAN and BOHUMIR PAZDERKA, *Microeconomics*, 3rd Canadian Edition (Scarborough, Ontario: Prentice-Hall Canada Inc., 1989), p.182.

4. PHILIP KOTLER, *Marketing Management: Analysis,* *Planning and Control*, 5th edition (Englewood Cliffs, New Jersey: Prentice-Hall, 1984), Chapter 12.

5. BECKMAN, BOONE and KURTZ, *Foundations of Marketing*, 4th Canadian Edition (Toronto: HBJ Holt Canada Inc., 1987), p.24.

6. OLIVER BERTIN, "Free Trade Blamed for Decision to Sell Catelli", *The Globe and Mail*, December 6, 1988, p.B7.

7. ALEXANDER MACMILLAN and BOHIMUR PAZDERKA, *Microeconomics*, 3rd Canadian Edition (Toronto: Prentice-Hall Canada Inc., 1989), p.341.

8. ELLIOTT ETTENBERG, "Portrait of a Marriage", *Marketing*, September 15, 1988, pp. 17-18.

9. JO MARNEY, "Ad Researchers Trade Secrets", *Marketing*, December 5, 1989, p.16.

10. Consumer and Corporate Affairs Canada, *Annual Report*, March 31, 1987, p.3.

11. CLARKSON GORDON/WOODS GORDON, *Tomorrow's Customers*, 21st Edition, 1988, p.13.

12. BRUCE GATES, "Biotech Revolution", *Financial Post*, December 5, 1988, p.33.

# ›››› PART TWO

# *Marketing Planning*

# CHAPTER 3

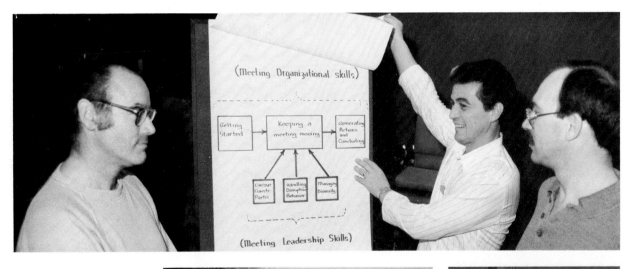

# Strategic Marketing Planning

Before developing a marketing plan — a document that outlines the direction and activities of an organization, product, or service — a marketer must consider the plan for the rest of the organization. Marketing strategies are directly influenced by the overall business plan or corporate plan. A corporate plan provides direction to all operational areas of a business, from marketing and production to human resources and information systems. To understand marketing planning, therefore, it is imperative that we know the planning process of an organization, and appreciate the interaction of plans at different levels of the organization. This chapter presents business planning at two distinct levels, that of corporate planning and that of marketing planning, and describes the components of each type.

# ⟩⟩⟩⟩ *The Business Planning Process*

Strategic business planning involves three variables: objectives, strategies, and execution or tactics. Let's first define these planning variables:

objectives

1. **Objectives** are statements that outline what is to be accomplished in the corporate plan or marketing plan. For instance, how much profit or market share is to be achieved over a one-year period.

strategies

2. **Strategies** are statements that outline how the objectives will be achieved. Strategies usually identify the resources necessary to achieve objectives, such as funds, time, people, and type of activity.

execution
(tactics)

3. **Execution**, or **tactics**, refers to the plans of action that outline in specific detail how the strategies are to be implemented. Tactical plans usually outline the specific activity, cost, timing, and personnel involved in implementation.

A diagram of the business planning process as it applies to marketing is provided in figure 3.1.

## Planning Versus Strategic Planning

planning

**Planning** is the process of anticipating the future business environment and determining the courses of action a firm will take in that environment. For example, a firm will look at trends in the areas of demography, the economy, changing technology, politics, and culture, and then develop a plan that will provide for growth in such changing times. **Strategic planning** is the process of determining objectives (stating goals to achieve), and identifying strategies (on how to achieve the goals) and tactics (specific action plans) that will contribute to the achievement of objectives within the framework of the business environment.

strategic planning

Strategic planning is a comprehensive process done at most levels of an organization. A **corporate plan** originates at the top of the organization and is largely based on input from senior executives such as the president and vice-presidents. Such plans are usually not elaborate documents, since their purpose is to identify corporate objectives that are to be achieved over a specified period. The corporate plan acts as a guideline for planning in the various operational areas of the company. In

corporate plan

FIGURE 3.1   Business Planning Process—Marketing Orientation

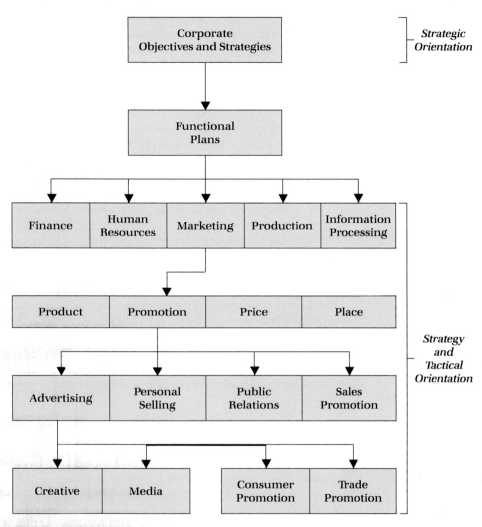

Each level of planning provides guidance for the next level.

the case of the marketing department, the vice-president of Marketing and the Marketing staff refer to these corporate objectives as they conduct their individual product, division or market planning. Marketing plans also contain objectives, but tend to be more strategic in nature and to outline the activities that will be implemented to achieve objectives.

Business planning throughout the organization begins and ends at the corporate or senior management level, or at the level of the corporate plan. Senior management formulates the overall strategic direction for the organization and establishes the financial objectives the company should aspire to achieve (sales, profits, return on investment). Then, in accordance with the objectives and directions passed down from the senior management level, the marketing department develops plans, objectives, strategies, and tactics for individual products, divisions, or target markets, depending on the nature of the organization's marketing management system.

Marketing plans consider such matters as the marketing mix (product, price, place, and promotion), target market characteristics, and control mechanisms. When the marketing plans are devised they can be very specific in nature. As we can see in figure 3.1, specific objectives, strategies, and tactics are developed for each of the 4Ps. Promotion can then be further subdivided into advertising, personal selling, sales promotion and public relations, with individual plans written for each of these divisions. Advertising could itself be divided between creative plans and media plans, and so on. As this planning process indicates, each plan is related to another. The phrase "a chain is only as strong as its weakest link" is an appropriate description of these relationships. Strategic planning attempts to coordinate all activity in such a manner that elements from various areas work together harmoniously. For example, in the case of marketing and advertising, all activity must present a consistent message regarding the company or its products in order to create a favourable impression in the minds of consumers. One weak link in the chain can create conflict or confuse the target market. For example, the selling price could be made too high in relation to the customer's perception of quality. Inconsistent activity spread over numerous company products could seriously disrupt attempts to achieve marketing and corporate objectives.

Strategic business planning is an applied problem-solving and decision-making effort through which managers act to ensure the future success of their organization, products and services. It forces management to think about the future, set clear objectives and find a way of coordinating company efforts.

## Management's Role in the Planning Process

Typically, the vice-presidents of all of the operational areas of a business form the top management or executive branch of the organization. Marketing personnel reporting to the vice-president of Marketing include marketing managers, sales managers, product managers, and distribution managers. The number and the type of these managers depend on the manner in which marketing responsibility is divided within the firm. These positions are usually classified as mid-management. Lower level managers may be present in the organization as well and include sales supervisors, assistant brand managers, warehouse supervisors, and traffic and distribution coordinators.

The role and involvement of these managers in the planning process depend on their location in the organization hierarchy. The roles of each of the three basic levels of management are as follows.

### Top Management

Senior executives of an organization devise long-range strategic plans (three to five years and beyond) concerning the overall health, well-being, and future of the organization. Strategic plans as developed by senior executives outline the overall objectives of the organization and identify the strategies and resources required to implement them. These executives are not involved with operational plans directly, though they are responsible for key decisions that involve the financial resources of the firm.

## Mid-Management

Mid-management includes the operational managers from the various functional areas of an organization (marketing, human resources, production and so on). Their responsibility encompasses a mixture of strategic and tactical planning. The nature of the planning at this level is based on the direction and guidance provided by top management; that is, the plans mid-management generates in operational areas are designed to help fulfill overall company objectives. Operational plans tend to be short-range (usually one year) and are more specific in nature. In the case of marketing plans, the objectives, strategies, and tactics are formulated in clearly worded statements.

## Lower Level Management

Typically, the planners at lower levels of management include supervisory personnel. These people are primarily involved in day-to-day operations. Their main role is to create and implement short-range plans that will help achieve the operational objectives developed by mid-management. As a group, lower level managers are mainly concerned with tactics, that is, with implementation as opposed to strategic planning.

It should be noted that when planning occurs in an organization there is a discussion among the various levels of management. For example, a sales plan may involve a national sales manager, regional sales managers (from geographic areas) and sales supervisors at various stages of the planning cycle. Drafting a marketing plan may require the participation of an assistant brand manager, product manager, marketing manager, and vice-president of Marketing, depending on the stage of the planning cycle. Refer to figures 3.2 and 3.3 for a visual illustration of management's role in

**FIGURE 3.2**  Role of Management in Planning

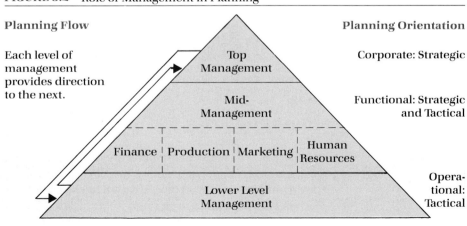

FIGURE 3.3    Planning Orientation of Different Management Levels

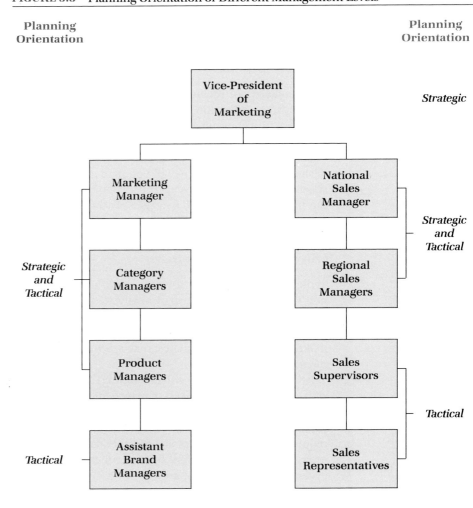

planning. Note that the nature of planning shifts from a strategic orientation at the top of the organization to a tactical orientation at the bottom.

## ⟩⟩⟩⟩ *Corporate Planning*

In figure 3.1, business planning is divided into two distinct categories: corporate planning and functional planning, which includes marketing planning. Let's clearly distinguish between each type of planning. First of all, corporate planning. It usually includes three variables. It begins with the production of a mission statement for the organization; it then involves devising corporate objectives and strategies for which the mission statement is used as a guide.

# Mission Statement

mission statement

A **mission statement** is a statement of the organization's purpose. It reflects the operating philosophy of the organization and indicates the direction the organization is to take. Such statements are concerned with the opportunities the company seeks to pursue in the marketplace. They are marketing-oriented and only work if the company's products and services are designed and marketed to fit the demands of the customers. Stemming from the marketing concept, mission statements not only recognize customer needs, but also consider the competition, and, particularly, the need to produce quality products that will have a long life cycle. The statement below is the mission statement for Dominion Textiles Inc.

> The mission of Dominion Textiles Inc. is to serve worldwide markets profitably with quality textile and textile related products while seeking opportunities to apply corporate resources to areas other than textiles. The fundamental goal of the corporation is to attain and sustain leadership positions in selected market segments, concentrating on quality of product and customer service.[1]

Since corporate plans provide direction to all functional areas of the company, they need to be long-term, broad in scope, and to consider the overall well-being of the organization.

# Corporate Objectives

corporate objectives

**Corporate objectives** may state what market share is desired of a particular market segment, what sales and level of profitability are sought for a product or for the company, and how much return on investment is to be achieved. Objectives may also include statements on where the company might diversify, what businesses to acquire, or other goals. Good objective statements are written in quantifiable terms so that they can be measured for attainment. To illustrate, the corporate objectives of Dominion Textiles follow:

> *Sales:* To increase sales volume significantly, targeted to reach $2 billion within three years (from $1.8 billion in 1988).
>
> *Return on Investment:* To achieve a return on common shareholders equity of 18 percent within the next three years.[2]

Similar statements can be developed for other objectives. These objectives, decided upon by senior management, provide the framework for the development of more detailed plans in the operational areas of the organization.

# Corporate Strategies

corporate strategies

After the **corporate objectives** are confirmed, the organization identifies strategies, which basically outline how the objectives are to be achieved. The factors considered when strategies are being developed are marketing strength, the degree of competition within markets the company operates in, financial resources (e.g., the availability of investment capital or the company's ability to borrow required funds), research and development capabilities, and commitment (i.e., the priority the company has placed on a particular goal). Here are the strategy statements of Dominion Textiles Inc.:

1. To focus on business segments which enable the corporation to maintain and enhance their leadership position.

2. To pursue the principle of decentralization by placing decision-making authority at the lowest appropriate levels.

3. To identify acquisitions and other opportunities in primary businesses in order to grow not only in textiles but also to effect diversification into new products and markets.

4. To expand programs to link business opportunities around the globe.[3]

As in the case of objectives, corporate strategy can follow numerous directions. To illustrate the concept of strategy development, let's assume a company establishes growth as a primary objective. What alternatives for growth are available to the company? This company could achieve growth through any one of, or combinations of, the following avenues.

### Becoming More Aggressive in Current Markets

Pepsi-Cola's use of the Pepsi Challenge (comparative taste tests with Coca-Cola) as a marketing platform is a good example of aggressive marketing activity. Aggressive activity by one firm could force another to compete as aggressively, with no real change occurring in the market share position. However, constant pressure and market share gains by Pepsi-Cola did result in Coca-Cola's changing the formula for Coke.

### Entering New Markets with Existing Products

McDonald's restaurants began with suburban locations (where most people live). Having established a base market, McDonald's began to move into downtown locations (where people work) and highway restaurants on major autoroutes. Competitors such as Burger King and Wendy's have pursued similar strategies in order to remain competitive. In this example, new markets are based on location. Swiss Chalet's expansion into smaller urban markets (less than 100 000 population) is another example of developing markets. Previously, Swiss Chalet concentrated on locations in large cities.

### Developing New Products for Current Markets

This strategy stems from shifting consumer attitudes and preferences for product categories. To meet changing tastes and desires, breweries, for example, have introduced light beers (Blue Light, Molson Light, Foster's Light, Moosehead Light, etc.) and dry beers (Molson Special Dry and Labatt's Dry). These segments offered opportunities for growth in a total market that was stagnating. In many product categories — food, alcohol, tobacco, and soft drinks, for example — the segments for "light" products are growing faster than other segments. There, growth is partly attributed to consumers' concern for improving their physical well-being. These products are marketed in accordance with prevailing consumer attitudes. In the hotel industry,

Holiday Inns of Canada has made a similar pitch to the health-conscious consumer by including elaborate fitness centers in their major hotels across the country in an attempt to attract more business.

### *Gaining Control of the Channel of Distribution*

The Dylex Corporation's ownership of a variety of retail clothing chains (Tip Top, Fairweather's, Big Steel, Thrifty's, and many others) and F.W. Woolworth's ownership of sports and leisure wear stores (Foot Locker, Lady Foot Locker, Champs, Northern Reflections, and Canary Island) both represent attempts to gain an increasing control of a market. The strategy in each case is to use a mix of retail store types to appeal to a broad cross-section of demographic groups (i.e., to groups that differ widely in terms of age, income, sex, etc.). The store image and the quality and price of the product lines vary from one of their chains to another, and appeal to different segments of the population. The sum of all store operations adds up to a wide control of the retail clothing market in Canada.

### *Acquiring Other Companies*

acquisition

Strategies based on **acquisition** have become increasingly prominent since the 1980s. In the advertising business, mergers are occurring on a global scale. In Canada, several of the large agencies have merged to form even larger operations. Coca-Cola purchased Dr. Pepper; Pepsi-Cola purchased The Seven Up Corporation; and Chrysler acquired American Motors. In every case, the company pursued the acquisition in order to gain a stronger foothold in the market it competes in. Robert Campeau's takeover of several large American department store chains (in 1988 the Campeau Corporation purchased, for about $10 billion, Allied Stores Corp., Federated Department Stores Inc., and their subsidiary companies) is another example of acquisition. This was Campeau's attempt to gain control of one of the largest retailing empires in the United States.

### *Diversifying into New Markets*

diversification

The decision to diversify into new markets often brings risk, since current management often lacks experience in the market under consideration. Nonetheless, the pursuit of growth involves such diversification strategies. **Diversification** refers to a firm's movement into a totally new area — a new industry, a new market, or a new product category. John Labatt Limited is a company strongly associated with the Canadian brewing industry, but as a company it has diversified over the years, and is now comprised of three major groups. Labatt Brewing is the brewing group; Chateau-Gai Wines is the packaged foods group; and Ault Foods and Ogilvie Flour Mills form the agricultural products group. Canadian National (CN) is another example of a company that has diversified. From a strong base in railway transportation, it has diversified into trucking, hotels, the CN Tower, telecommunications, and real estate development.

See the Marketing in Action vignette ''Diversification at Imasco'' for a good example of how a Canadian firm uses acquisition and diversification strategies to its advantage.

## ⟩⟩⟩ *MARKETING IN ACTION*

### *DIVERSIFICATION AT IMASCO*

What's Imasco? Imasco is an acronym for Imperial and Associated Companies, created to diversify Imperial Tobacco into new lines of business. And diversify it did. Today, Imasco is a leading North American consumer products and services company.

In Canada, Imasco owns Imperial Tobacco, Canada Trust, Shoppers Drug Mart/Pharmaprix, and The UCS Group (United Cigar Stores). Imperial Tobacco commands 58 percent of the Canadian tobacco market, and its leading brands, Player's and du Maurier, are first and second in national market share. Shoppers Drug Mart operates 633 outlets nationally and is by far Canada's largest drug store group. The UCS Group operates Canada's largest chain of retail gift, tobacco, and convenience stores, with 531 retail outlets across the country.

Imasco's most significant acquisition was of the Genstar Corporation in 1986. Its main reason for acquiring Genstar was that it wanted to gain control of Canada Trust, Canada's largest trust company. Canada Trust was attractive because it is a strongly managed market leader in a consumer industry experiencing above average growth, namely financial services. The cost of the acquisition was $2.6 billion. To finance the deal Imasco sold off all of Genstar's assets except Canada Trust.

Imasco also has a large presence in the United States, with over 3300 Hardee's Restaurants (corporate and franchised) in 40 states competing in the fast food industry. In April 1990 Hardee's completed the purchase of the 600-unit Roy Rogers chain, which will be converted to the Hardee's trademark. The acquisition consolidates Hardee's position as the third largest fast food hamburger chain in America.

All of Imasco's operating companies are leaders in industries that serve the individual consumer directly.

Imasco is an acquisition-oriented company.

*In Canada, Imasco owns Imperial Tobacco, Canada Trust, Shoppers Drug Mart/Pharmaprix, and the UCS Group (United Cigar Stores)*

According to Purdy Crawford, the chairman, president and chief executive oficer, success is based on a few basic criteria which all major acquisitions must meet:

1. The targeted acquisition must be well-positioned in the consumer goods or service sector.

Imasco Limited

While Imasco's corporate structure is decentralized, its management group has a strong sense of unity. An important common thread is the corporate business plan, which sets out Imasco's overall mission and identifies a set of convictions, objectives and strategies that are common to every one of its operating companies. Some of the most important elements are:

1. Operational excellence and an emphasis on increasing the productivity of assets.
2. The delivery of goods and services that are of the highest quality and integrity.
3. Recognition of the importance of responding to the changing needs of customers in a more timely and effective way than competitors (which includes a heavy emphasis on research and development, marketing, and merchandising activities).
4. The careful application and enhancement of corporate and brand trademarks, which it considers among its most valuable assets.

Imasco has diversified and conducts business only in the sectors it knows. Its management style also reflects an understanding of the Corporation's strengths and weaknesses. The message for any firm is to understand your capabilities, set a direction and do the essentials like marketing better than anyone else.

Adapted from Purdy Crawford, "Achieving growth through diversification — Imasco's strategy for success", *Business Quarterly*, Summer 1987, p.91 + .

2. It must have a very capable management group in place.
3. It must have above average growth potential and be capable of making a meaningful and immediate profit contribution.
4. It must be based in North America, preferably Canada.

In analyzing its past acquisitions, Imasco feels that these criteria have been met. Each company has grown substantially since being acquired.

# Portfolio Management

portfolio analysis

One way for an organization to proceed with strategic planning is through portfolio analysis. **Portfolio analysis** is used for companies that are divided into strategic units according to the business categories or market segments in which they operate. It is a process of reviewing these units. For example, a company could be divided according to the industries they serve (consumer goods division, industrial goods division, institutional goods division), or by key product categories (soaps and detergents, toiletries and personal care products, paper products and food products). Some portfolios are strong; some are weak. The task of strategic planners is to assess the strengths and weaknesses of each portfolio and recommend additions and deletions where necessary. Decisions of this nature are usually based on the respective profit contributions of the various portfolios.

strategic business
unit (SBU)

The first step in this task is to identify the portfolios which comprise the company. These are referred to as strategic business units (SBUs). A **strategic business unit (SBU)** is a unit of the company that has a separate mission and objective, and that can be planned independently of other company businesses. An SBU can be a division of the company, as in the Labatt's example cited earlier; a complete product line, perhaps under one brand name; or a single brand operating in its own market segment. Figure 3.4 illustrates strategic business units in several large diversified companies.

Companies provide their SBUs with varying levels of marketing support. The growth potential of each unit determines the level of marketing support (time, dollars and activity) it receives; the units are not equal. For example, units with little growth potential or slow growth rates will not be supported to the same extent as a unit whose growth potential is significant. In fact, funds will be channelled away from slow growth units into high growth units. The basic criteria for this type of decision-making is stated in two questions.

## How attractive or profitable is the SBU market?

For example, the fax machine market (facsimile machines that attach to telephones and send copies of documents to distant locations in seconds) is booming. Entrance into such a market may look profitable, but there are so many firms competing with each other that a significant investment would be required, even for a small return. In a fragmented market, where many brands compete for the same purchase, such a strategy would be questionable. In such cases, when the profits anticipated are not realized, many manufacturers voluntarily withdraw from the market.

## How strong is the firm's SBU in the market?

Does the SBU dominate, challenge, or follow the market? How much of the company's resources will be needed to alter its current market position? Answers to these types of questions, which are found through detailed analysis of the market and competition, will guide the firm as it decides what strategy is best. What market share the SBU has often determines whether a company will stay in that market and how much of the company's resources will be allocated to it.

**FIGURE 3.4**   Strategic Business Units of Diversified Companies

**General Foods (SBUs based on division and product lines)**

| | |
|---|---|
| Coffee Division | Maxwell House, Chase & Sanborn, Sanka, Brim, Heritage, Postum, Mellow Roast, International Blends, Baker's Baking Products |
| Consumer Foods Division | Kool Aid, Tang, Quench, Crystal Light, Awake, Country Time, Post Cereal (Grape Nuts, Alpha Bits, Honey Comb, Sugar Crisp, Fruit 'n Fibre and others), Jell-O, Dream Whip. Minute Rice, Stove Top Stuffing, Shake 'n Bake and Certo |
| Hostess Division | Complete range of potato, corn, tortilla, meat and nut snack foods under Hostess brand name |

**General Mills (SBUs based on nature of business)**

| | |
|---|---|
| Bluewater Seafood Division | Frozen Seafood Products |
| Consumer Foods Division | Lancia, Bravo, Big "G" Cereals, Betty Crocker, Nature Valley |
| Restaurants | Red Lobster |
| Retailing | Eddie Bauer |

**Molson Companies (SBUs based on industry)**

| | |
|---|---|
| Brewing | Canadian, Export, Coors, and others |
| Chemicals | Diversey Corporation |
| Retail Merchandising | Beaver Lumber, Lighting Unlimited, Crown Stores |
| Venture Capital | Grayrock Shared Ventures Limited (partnership with North American Life Assurance) |
| | Ohlmeyer Communications (Hockey Night in Canada) |

# Boston Consulting Group Model

The Boston Consulting Group (BCG) devised a strategic planning matrix that was popularized in the early 1970s. The matrix combines two variables, market share and market growth, in order to place strategic business units (divisions, products, or brands) into four basic categories. The strategies for each category and the resources allocated to each are as varied as the businesses that a company may operate in. The problems and opportunities facing the four categories are quite different (see figure 3.5). The four categories in this matrix are stars, cash cows, question marks or problem children, and dogs.

**stars**

1. **Stars** are SBU's that have a high market share in a high growth market. Their position in the market is usually the result of a significant marketing investment, and profits are generally quite good, although they can be threatened by the high degree of competition. Stars are usually high profile divisions, or popular brands (often referred to as glamour brands) within a company.

**cash cows**

2. **Cash cows** are SBU's that have a high market share in a low growth market. Such a position is the sign of a well-established and successful product in a mature market. The task of marketing is to maintain a cash cow's position while spending as little as possible on marketing support. This type of product generates cash flow for investment in other developing products, such as stars and question marks, or for the development of new products.

**question marks/
problem children**

3. **Question marks**, or **problem children**, are products that have a low market share in a high growth market. Management spends a significant amount of time and money on these products in an attempt to improve their position. The potential is there, but the results aren't. Over time, some difficult decisions have to be made regarding question marks. Should management continue its support in an effort to build the question mark's market share, or should it withdraw its support and reinvest its funds in less difficult situations?

**dogs**

4. **Dogs** are characterized by low market share in low growth markets. Facing rather bleak prospects, a product in this category will not receive marketing support and will be phased out when it cannot sustain itself financially.

**FIGURE 3.5**   Boston Consulting Group Matrix

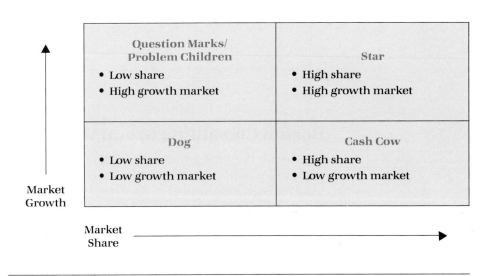

As can be seen by the BCG matrix descriptions, certain categories exist or are maintained to support others. Specifically, any cash flow or profits generated by cash cows are directed at stars or question marks. Otherwise, the company can invest in new product development. Strategically, this concept is sound, for an organization is forced to look at its strengths and weaknesses so that a scarce resource (money) can be invested in growth products. In this regard, SBUs have a life cycle, and, consequently, no division or product line within an organization can expect unlimited, perpetual marketing support. In a typical life cycle, the SBU might start as a question mark. While dissatisfied with the SBU's present position, the firm continues to invest in marketing it because of its potential for growth. Due to good strategic decisions, the SBU may then move to the star category; the product has become successful and perhaps a market leader. The market then matures as new innovations occur. As a result, the SBU becomes a cash cow; support is cut or reduced, and available resources are channelled into new attractive areas. Finally, due to lack of support and a market that is dying because the products have become obsolete, the SBU slips into the dog category.

## The New Breed of Strategic Planning

In contemporary business practice, more forward or visionary thinking is occurring than previously. Executives are spending much more time determining the long-term direction the firm should be taking. They are looking at the future and planning how to get there. The process of strategic planning, particularly in large organizations, is becoming more informal at the corporate management level, where qualitative judgements are combined with quantitative analysis. At lower levels of management, traditional and formal planning still prevails, as in the case of, for example, the design and implementation of annual marketing plans.

Today, organizations tend to concentrate their efforts on winners instead of on developing corrective action programs to improve the situation of losers. For example, very large corporations that play the takeover game, lusting after the acquisition of profitable new ventures, lose sight of the customers they serve and neglect the satisfaction of their needs. Success, in these companies, is due not to their managers' efforts or to their savvy in developing a business. Instead, they gain success by buying out profitable ventures that were developed and nurtured by others. Examples include Campeau's takeover of the U.S. retailing giants Allied Stores and Federated Department Stores, and the takeover of RJR Nabisco by Kohlberg Kravis Roberts & Company, a private merchant banking firm.

Rather than building better products, some corporations have become obsessed with the takeover game, with wheeling and dealing, with power plays and leveraged financing. More detailed information on this new breed of strategic planning can be found in the Marketing in Action feature "Corporate Empire: Taking Over RJR Nabisco."

## ⟩⟩⟩ *MARKETING IN ACTION*

### *CORPORATE EMPIRE: TAKING OVER RJR NABISCO*

The 1980s will be known as the decade in which acquisitions and mergers came to the forefront of North American business activity. It was a period when the large became larger and the word "mega" took on new meaning. It was a strategic switch from the past: companies involved in what appeared to be merger-mania were not focused on producing better products. To improve the financial well-being of shareholders, companies focused on buying out competitors or other profitable companies in order to gain dominance in the marketplace. Ross Johnson, a Canadian sometimes described as one of America's toughest marketing men, has been a player in this takeover game.

One of the biggest stories of the 1980s was the battle for control of RJR Nabisco that occurred between Kholberg Kravis Roberts & Company (KKR), a merchant banking company and ultimate winner in the sweepstakes, and a group headed by Ross Johnson, who was then the president and chief executive officer of RJR Nabisco. As the bidding was escalated between the two parties (KKR ultimately paid $24 billion U.S.), it was clear that Ross Johnson would be a winner financially, whether he got control or not. He stood to gain simply by selling out to KKR, but the gains would have been much greater had his own takeover bid been successful.

Both offers for control of RJR Nabisco involved what is known as a leveraged buyout. A leveraged buyout is described as follows:

> a publicly owned company is purchased from its shareholders using a 10 percent equity and a lot of debt. Equity is raised from the buyers' own funds and financial institutions. The funds are invested in the target firm often in concert with its managers who are encouraged to stay on and improve the company. They will then sell their shares back to the stock market, usually in a year or two when stocks rise in value. The return on investment in such cases can run as high as 50 percent, quite an attractive opportunity. In 1988, leveraged buyouts in the United States had an estimated value of $90 billion.

Who is Ross Johnson? Ross Johnson was the chief executive officer of the nineteenth largest company in the United States, RJR Nabisco (revenues of $16 billion a year). He rose rapidly to the top of the corporate ladder, and in the process utilized a different style of strategic planning. The pinnacle of his activities was his privatization takeover attempt of his own company. Referred to as a corporate raider from the inside, he used a strategy that appeared to put personal gain ahead of corporate gain.

Where did Ross Johnson come from? After graduating from the University of Manitoba with a commerce degree, he started in an accounting job at Canadian General Electric. A few years later he was in marketing at CGE, operating the lamp division in Toronto. Studying at night he received his MBA from the University of Toronto. He switched to retailing when he joined the T. Eaton Company, rising to the position of merchandising manager within a few years. His strategy was to move to get ahead. At CGE, the bureaucratic structure was frustrating; at Eaton's, the family dynasty was a stumbling block, so he switched again to GSW, which was then a small appliance manufacturer. By 1971, he was with Standard Brands as president and chief executive officer. Standard Brands product line included Chase & Sanborn coffee, Planter's Nuts, Lowney's chocolates, Royal dessert products, and many others. In 1973, he was recruited to New York to head up the International Division of Standard Brands, and a few years later, at the age of 44, became the president and chief executive officer of the entire Standard Brands Company.

The strategies he used to gain dominance emerged in 1981, when he merged Standard Brands with arch-rival Nabisco. In the merger, he became the number two man in the corporate hierarchy, a situation that only lasted three years. Within three years of becoming president of Nabisco Brands, Johnson and the Nabisco board of directors would repeat history by surrendering Nabisco to RJ Reynolds Industries to form RJR

Canapress Photo Service

*Ross Johnson, formerly the president of RJR Nabisco*

Nabisco. At that time RJR Industries was controlled by Tylee Wilson who was firmly entrenched as the chief executive officer. Johnson asked the new board to make a choice between himself and Wilson, and again he won, becoming chief executive officer of the merged company. In two cases, then, Johnson merged a smaller company into a larger one, and became the head man both times.

What was Johnson's management style? To say the least, Johnson's style was very different from what you read about in textbooks like this one. He appears to be somewhat of a maverick (a successful maverick). In terms of taking action he states that "when you have most of the facts you go. You can't wait to be absolutely sure you're right. By then you're probably wrong again." His strategy, then, was to go for it — to make snap decisions rather than watch opportunities pass by. Businesses normally make money by building useful products at a reasonable price, one that would be fair to consumers and profitable for companies. In the 1980s this concept was put to the test as companies became obsessed with financial power plays, corporate wheeling and dealing, and creative accounting. Johnson is an example of this new breed of planner. Not loyal to established company brands, he had been known to sell off brands that, while profitable, were not leaders. His actions were often quick, and surprising to executives who worked for him. According to James Westcott, a Toronto-

based management consultant, Johnson viewed a plan as something you depart from, rather than something that guides you.

Despite having done things that appeared questionable, at the time, Johnson was very successful. Many critics say that he turned chaos into an effective management tool, for unpredictability in his actions has been quite commonplace. For example, he completely reorganized Reynolds Tobacco when he took over — staff were cut at head office, and then many were hired back in another division of the company; he bought a wine company one day, only to sell off a liquor company a few days later; and then he moved the 112-year-old tobacco company, steeped in tradition, from Winston-Salem, N.C., to Atlanta, Ga. As Johnson himself has said: "I kept everybody confused. It's like being a magician. You let them know what's in your left hand so you can be working all the time with your right hand." Executives who worked for Johnson became accustomed to changing jobs. Such chaos would normally create unrest, but for Johnson it generally resulted in a capable, loyal, and motivated executive staff. According to John Greeniaus, president of Nabisco USA, and a Johnson follower from Standard Brands in Canada: "Some people would find this environment unsettling, but they're people who want to spend their lives in jobs where nothing happens."

Johnson's strategies of selling off businesses were profitable for the corporations he was in charge of. Over the years, he sold off brands such as Canada Dry, Chase & Sanborn, and Del Monte frozen foods and these were only small dealings within corporate mergers and acquisitions. The strategies employed here involved selling off businesses in order to gain funds to pay down the company's debt, give it more marketing clout, or make strategic acquisitions that would ensure marketing dominance.

Adapted from Larry Black, "Cowboy capitalist", *Report on Business Magazine*, January 1989, pp.32-41.

# ⟩⟩⟩⟩ *Marketing Planning*

The marketing department operates within the parameters established by the senior management or executive branch of the organization. The objectives, strategies, and action plans developed by marketing are designed and implemented to contribute to the achievement of overall company objectives. Where planning is concerned, the major areas of marketing responsibility include:

1. The identification and selection of target markets.

2. Establishing marketing objectives, strategies, and tactics.

3. Managing the marketing function internally based on the organization structure.

4. The evaluation and control of marketing activities implemented.

marketing planning

**Marketing planning** is the analysis, planning, implementation, evaluation, and control of carefully formulated and coordinated initiatives, done with a view to satisfying target market needs while achieving organizational objectives. Marketing planning involves the analysis of relevant background information and historical trend data and the development of marketing objectives and strategies for all products and services within the company. The decisions on product, price, promotion, and distribution are outlined, in integrated form, in the marketing plan of each product. Other elements of marketing planning include target market identification, budgeting, and control mechanisms. In contrast to strategic corporate plans, marketing plans are short-term in nature (one year), specific in scope (they deal with one product and outline precise actions), and combine the elements of strategy and tactics (they are action oriented). They are also subject to change on short notice as a

**FIGURE 3.6**    Some Differences Between Corporate and Marketing Planning

| Element | Corporate Plan | Marketing Plan |
|---------|---------------|----------------|
| Orientation | Strategic | Strategic and tactical |
| Frequency | Three to Five Years and beyond | One year |
|  | Minor updating annually | Updated annually |
| Scope | Corporate | Specific |
|  | Decisions on overall direction, objectives, strategies and resources | May be: Divisional, Product line, Brand, Area |
| Flexibility | Inflexible due to long range direction | Very flexible |
|  | Alterations based on formal reviews | Modification based on economic, competitive activity |

FIGURE 3.7    Marketing Planning Process

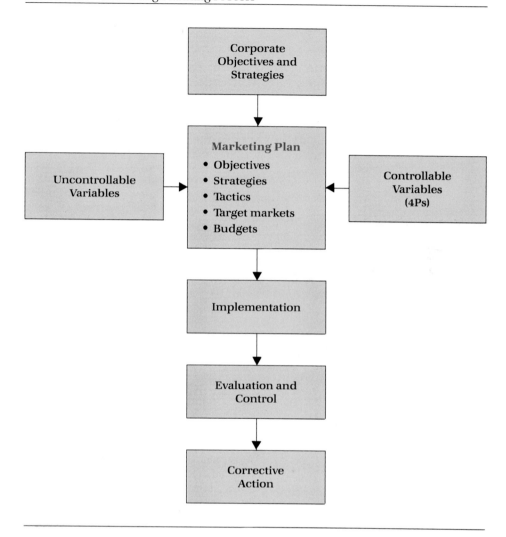

result of economic shifts or competitive activity. Figure 3.6 contains a brief summary of corporate plans compared to marketing plans and figure 3.7 summarizes the stages of marketing planning. The following is a description of the various elements of marketing planning.

## Market Analysis

As a preliminary to marketing planning, a variety of information is compiled and analyzed. Information that is typically reviewed at this stage of planning includes:

1. *Market Size and Growth*   A review is made of trends in the marketplace over a period. Is the market growing, remaining stable, or declining?

2. *Regional Market Importance*   Market trends and sales volume trends are analyzed by region to determine areas of strength or weakness and areas to concentrate on in the future.

3. *Market Segment Analysis*   The sales volume for a total market and for segments within a market are reviewed. For example, the coffee market is analyzed in terms of regular ground coffee, instant coffee, decaffeinated coffee and flavoured coffee.

4. *Seasonal Analysis*   An examination of seasonal or cyclical trends during the course of a year is conducted. For example, special events such as Christmas, Mother's Day, Halloween, and others often have an impact on sales volume.

5. *Consumer Data*   Current users of a product are profiled according to such factors as age, income, gender, lifestyle, and location.

6. *Loyalty*   A review is made of the degree of loyalty customers exhibit towards a product or brand. Are customers loyal or do they switch brands often?

7. *Other Trends*   Factors such as trends in pack size (regular size, single size, family size, etc.), colours or scents of product sold (for products like nail polish and other cosmetics), flavour analysis (ice cream or other types of food), or other relevant areas are important in the planning process.

8. *Media*   Trends in competitive spending on media advertising will influence advertising and budgeting.

Generally, this type of analysis focuses on market, competitor, and brand information, and sets the stage for new directions in strategic marketing planning, modifications to current strategy, or the maintenance of current strategy.

## Marketing Objectives

marketing objectives

**Marketing objectives** are statements identifying "what" a product or service will accomplish over a one-year period. Typically, marketing objectives concentrate on sales volume, market share, and profit (net profit or return on investment), all of which are quantitative in nature and measurable at the end of the period. Objectives that are qualitative in nature could include new product introductions, new additions to current product lines, product improvements, and packaging innovations.

To illustrate the concept of marketing objectives, consider the following sample statements:

*Sales Volume:* To achieve a unit volume of 200 000 units by the end of the year, an increase of 10 percent over the current year.

*Market Share:* To achieve a market share of 30 percent in twelve months, an increase of four share points over the current position.

*Profit:* To generate an after budget profit of $600 000 in the next twelve months.

*Product:* To launch a new package design in the fourth quarter of this year.

# Marketing Strategies

marketing strategies

These are essentially the "master plans" for achieving marketing objectives. **Marketing strategies** identify target markets and satisfy those target markets with a combination of marketing mix elements (the 4Ps) within budget constraints. This definition identifies three important variables in the development of marketing strategy.

target market

1. *Target Market*   When developing a marketing plan, the planner identifies those target markets that represent the greatest profit potential for the firm. A **target market** is a group of customers perceived as having certain characteristics in common: similar needs, habits, and lifestyles. Is there one primary user group, or are there several user segments who have a need for the product or service? In answering these questions, the planner defines the target market in terms of demographic (age, income, gender, education and occupation), psychographic (lifestyle), and geographic (location) characteristics.

2. *Marketing Mix*   At this stage of the planning process, the role and importance of each element in the marketing mix and those activities that comprise each element of the mix are identified. The task is to develop a plan of attack so that all 4P elements combine to achieve marketing objectives.

3. *Budget*   The corporate plan has already identified a total marketing budget for the company, giving consideration to the overall profit concerns for the forthcoming year. The allocation of the budget must be spread across all company products and be based on the firm's analysis of current priorities or profit potential. Managers responsible for product planning must develop and justify a budget that allows enough funds for the implementing of strategies identified in their marketing plan, and for the achievement of the financial objectives identified for the product. The final stage of the budgeting process is the allocation of funds among the activity areas in the plan (advertising, sales promotion, personal selling, etc.).

4. *Marketing Execution*   Often referred to as marketing tactics, this type of planning focuses on specific program details that stem directly from the strategy section of the plan. In general terms, a tactical plan outlines what activity will be implemented, how much it will cost, what the timing will be, and who will be responsible for implementation. Detailed tactical plans for all components of the plan — advertising, sales promotion and marketing research — are included here.

## *Common Types of Marketing Strategies*

Marketing strategies are classified according to the combinations of products and markets that a firm competes in. Multi-product organizations employ many different strategies simultaneously. Generally, product-oriented marketing strategies are classified as market penetration, market development, product development, diversification, and harvest (see figure 3.8).

### FIGURE 3.8   Common Marketing Strategies

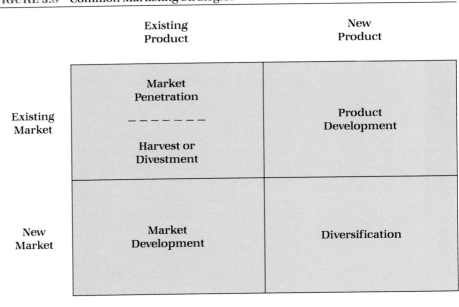

## Market Penetration

market
penetration

Strategies centered on **market penetration** are aimed at improving the market position of existing products in existing markets. Essentially, the strategies are meant to increase the number of sales made to present users. In this respect, the 4Ps are modified so that a better formula for getting customers to buy is developed. For example, a price reduction could be considered, or a new commercial message could be used, or any combination of 4P activity. Companies will constantly review their marketing mix strategies throughout the life of a product.

## Market Development

market
development

A company pursuing a strategy based on **market development** attempts to market existing products to new target markets. Such strategies attempt to attract consumers with different demographics or lifestyles. To illustrate, a hotel chain such as the Westin or Sheraton may receive most of their business from business travellers during the week. To spur weekend business, these hotels assemble and market family package plans (weekend holidays) at very reasonable prices. Other businesses may grow by taking a successful regional product and rolling it out into other regions or into the national market. For example, Schooner Beer was originally brewed by Oland Breweries, a subsidiary of Labatt's, for the Maritimes market. It is now marketed in Ontario as well. The Marketing in Action vignette "A&W's Revival Plan" illustrates how a company combined marketing development and diversification strategies to improve its position in the marketplace.

## Product Development

product
development

In the case of a strategy involving **product development**, new products are offered to current target markets, or modified existing products are marketed to current users. Such initiatives may include the introduction of new sizes, flavours,

## 〉〉〉〉 *MARKETING IN ACTION*

### *A & W's REVIVAL PLAN*

You probably don't remember when, but A & W was once a leading restaurant in the hamburger segment of the fast food business. Its first Canadian restaurant, the popular drive-in, opened in Winnipeg in 1956. For over twenty years the drive-in served as a meeting place for Canadian teens who ordered hamburgers from pony-tailed waitresses.

In the mid-seventies, A & W fell on hard times. Consumers' tastes and habits were changing and A & W customers deserted the drive-in, preferring instead the walk-in sit-down style of McDonald's. By 1976, A & W found itself in fourth place, behind MacDonald's, Burger King, and Harvey's, and profits were declining rapidly.

The parent company, Unilever Canada Limited encouraged senior A & W executives to take action. What then contributed to A & W's revival? First, why the rapid decline? Company executives admit that they did not forecast the decline in drive-in popularity. Their growth plans were based on the opening of new outlets each year. In 1976 there were 298 A & W outlets across Canada, eighty-five of which were corporately owned. The remainder were independent franchises.

In planning for the future, A & W experienced a painful retrenchment, but new strategies that came out of it paved the way to success. New plans focused on product and place. Here's what A & W did:

1. In terms of product, the basic menu of the sixties was retained. A & W felt that the adult skew (e.g. growth of baby boomer segment) of the marketplace still wanted their hamburgers to have distinctive quality and flavour.

2. As for changes in location and style, the restaurants were shifted from drive-in style and located in shopping malls, in order to capitalize on the constant flow of pedestrian traffic (e.g. storefront operations in food courts) in malls.

3. Profitable drive-in locations were converted to combination drive-through and sit-down res-

A & W Food Services of Canada Ltd.

*For over twenty years, the drive-in served as a meeting place for teens, who ordered hamburgers from pony-tailed waitresses. As part of its revival plan, A & W began to situate its restaurants in shopping malls, capitalizing on the constant flow of pedestrian traffic*

taurants that would compete more directly with other chains.

4. To diversify further, A & W entered the soft drink industry through a distribution agreement with Coca-Cola. As of 1987, A & W surpassed Hire's (Crush Canada Inc.) to become the top selling root beer in Canada.

In its most recent move, A & W has purchased the franchise rights in western Canada for Cultures, a popular fresh food restaurant now located in eastern Canada. Cultures is successfully positioned to take advantage of the health and fitness segment of the Canadian population.

As a result of all of these new strategies, A & W is now in a heated battle for second place with Burger King, Harvey's, and Wendy's.

Adapted from David Baines, "A & W's recipe blends old with new", *Financial Times of Canada*, August 1987, pp. 11, 17.

colours, and improvements to the taste (if it is a food product). Expansion of a product line by line extensions is also common. This involves the use of the same brand name on new products or related products (a family of products). For example, Hostess is synonymous with potato chips, corn chips, tortillas, meat snacks, and nut snacks. In all cases, the product appeals to the target market of the original product — potato chips. The target market now has more product variety to choose from.

### Diversification

**diversification**

**Diversification** refers to the introduction of a new product to a completely new market. In effect, the company is entering unfamiliar territory when it uses this strategy. Such a strategy requires substantial resources for research and development, initially high marketing expenses, and a strong commitment to building market share. To illustrate, a consumer packaged goods company in the food business could diversify by entering the institutional food service market and selling its products to hotels, restaurants, and other institutions. The same company may decide to enter the restaurant business, as General Mills did with Burger King and Red Lobster Restaurants, a move that was definitely a new venture for the company at the time.

### Harvest

**harvest**

With a **harvest** strategy, also called a divestment strategy, the organization elects to divorce itself from a product or, as sometimes happens, from an entire division of the company through sale or liquidation. As discussed in the previous chapter on free trade, John Labatt decided to sell its Catelli Foods division for competitive reasons. It is more common for a company to withdraw a product from the market very late in the product's life. For example, it may be classified as a dog and be unable to support itself financially. Rather than allowing the product to become a financial drain, the company makes the decision to withdraw it. When you think of sewing machines, the name Singer probably comes to mind first. Interesting is the fact that Singer no longer makes sewing machines. Singer got out of the sewing machine business to concentrate on new high technology opportunities.

## Marketing Control

**marketing control**

Since clearly defined and measurable objectives have been established by the organization, and by the marketing department for its products and services, it is important that results be evaluated against the plan and against past performance. This evaluation indicates whether current strategies need to be modified or whether new strategies should be considered. **Marketing control** is the process of measuring and evaluating the results of marketing strategies and plans, and taking corrective action to ensure that marketing objectives are attained.[4] According to this definition, marketing control involves three basic elements:

1. Establishing standards of marketing performance expressed in the form of marketing objectives.
2. Periodically measuring actual performance (of the company, division or product) and comparing it to standards.
3. Taking corrective action (e.g., developing new strategies) in those areas where performance does not meet standards.

**FIGURE 3.9**   Marketing Control Process

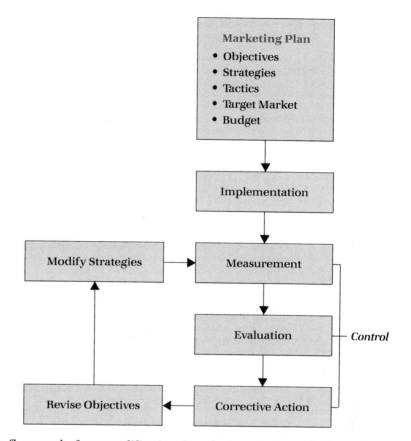

The flow results from modifications based on quarterly marketing and financial reviews in a one year plan/implementation cycle.

Refer to figure 3.9 for a diagram of the control process. The nature of an organization's control process can vary. The degree of control and frequency of evaluation is left to the discretion of management. For evaluating the effectiveness of marketing strategies, there are three primary measures or indicators. These are marketing activity plan reviews, financial reviews, and strategic control reviews.

## Marketing Activity Reviews

A marketing plan's effectiveness, that is, whether or not the strategies achieve the desired results, can be measured by several key indicators. Since marketing objectives tend to focus on sales volume and market share, sales and market share tend to be the principal measures of success, but other measurements can also be made. To make these evaluations, organizations often implement marketing activity reviews on a quarterly basis, though the frequency of the reviews can depend on the size of the organization. Large organizations tend to follow rigid planning cycles which have the review process built in. The more frequent the reviews, the more opportunity there is to make strategic adjustments during the course of a year.

Sales analysis involves two distinct measures: actual versus plan, and actual versus sales of a year ago. This type of analysis can be done for products, product lines, divisions, customers, territories, and regions. Usually the sales managers and marketing managers or product managers review sales performance together and mutually agree on revised figures and strategies for the balance of the year. Understanding why sales are up or down is the responsibility of both marketing managers and sales managers. Collectively, any revised figures to which the managers agree have an impact on the financial well-being of the company and affect the activities of other operational areas of the company.

Market share analysis includes competitors in the evaluation process. Did a product's market share increase, remain stable, or decrease compared to a year ago, or what have the share trends been from period to period? What is the competitor doing? Are they gaining or losing market share? The evaluation of these standards will certainly help determine the need for strategy adjustments. In the case of this type of analysis, managers attempt to link their marketing activities to share performance, in an effort to determine which activities are effective and which are ineffective.

## Financial Reviews

As part of the organization's marketing control process, periodic profit reviews are conducted. Key variables in a profit review are up-to-date sales forecasts, costs, and marketing budgets. If, in reevaluating these variables, the organization does not feel that profit objectives will be achieved for the period, the marketing department may be asked to trim its marketing budgets. Such reductions could be implemented in several ways: by product, by division, or by region. Certain activities could be reduced or eliminated if necessary. For example, all advertising could be cut in order to save all other activities. At this stage, there would be much negotiation between mid-management and top management, for mid-managers would want to protect their own areas. Priorities are established through such negotiation, and funds are withdrawn from those activities that will feel the effects the least. Generally speaking, the entire review process is an interactive one involving various levels of management. If there is candid discussion by all participants, the primary benefit of such a review is the new strategies that emerge from it.

## Strategic Control

**strategic control**

**Strategic control** is more long-term in nature. Since conditions in the marketplace (economy, technology, competition, and governments) change rapidly, marketing strategies become outdated. Strategic reviews tend to be more common in multi-product, multi-division companies. These reviews are intensive in nature and are conducted every three to five years. The frequency of strategic reviews testifies to the recognition that it takes time to implement and evaluate fairly the effectiveness of marketing activity. Within this framework, marketers reassess marketing strategies for all products annually, during preparation of the marketing plan. Marketing plans are usually developed on a product-by-product basis, or by division, or by some other strategic business unit.

**FIGURE 3.10** Contents of a Marketing Audit (Sample Model)

A company collects and analyzes the following information in the marketing planning process:

**Environmental Factors**
- Competition
- Economy
- Culture
- Politics
- Technology

**Market**
- Size and growth rate
- Degree of competition

**Target Market**
- Customer profile
- Purchase frequency
- Characteristics that influence purchase

**Company**
- Philosophy and mission
- Skills and expertise
- Financial resources
- Objectives and strategies

**Marketing Strategy**
- Objectives
- Strategies (including financial resources)

**Marketing Information**
- Marketing information system
- Formal planning system

**Marketing Control**
- Cost analysis
- Productivity analysis
- Profit analysis

**Marketing Function (Division, Product Line, or Product)**
- Strategies for product, price, place, promotion

**Competition**
- Who and how many?
- Strengths and weaknesses

**marketing audit**

The primary instrument for evaluating strategic direction and overall effectiveness of marketing activity is a marketing audit. A **marketing audit** is a systematic, critical, and unbiased review and appraisal of the marketing department's basic objectives and policies and of the organization, methods, procedures, and people employed to implement the policies.[5] A marketing audit covers all marketing areas. It is usually conducted by external consultants—marketing experts removed from the internal operations and political environment of the organization. The task of the auditor is to evaluate the plans and the quality of the marketing effort. Are the resources (time, personnel, and money) adequate? While such an external audit may seem unnecessary, internal managers are often too close to their area of responsibility to evaluate its work properly. They may implement strategies that have worked well in the past but may not be suitable for the future. The audit may prevent such inappropriate strategies from being implemented. An example of a marketing audit is included in figure 3.10.

# 〉〉〉〉 *Planning Dichotomy: Long-Term Versus Short-Term*

A dichotomy exists in strategic marketing planning. Ideally, marketing planners would like to adopt a long-term perspective, that is, develop a plan, secure necessary resources, and see it completely implemented so that a healthy profit results. However, even though success requires long-term commitment, marketing executives must constantly try to balance the long-term against the short-term.

Unfortunately, the quarterly financial reviews discussed in the previous section take their toll on long-term plans. A financial review often results in the cutting of budgets and a retreat to short-term profit protection, even if these things occur at the expense of long-term objectives. Budget cutting may conflict with long-term expectations when it comes to measurable variables such as market share, since preserving market share, particularly in the face of competition, largely depends on a firm's ability to maintain a certain marketing budget. Constantly sacrificing long-term goals for short-term gain will affect the ability of an organization to compete. Companies that follow this procedure are practising tactical maneuvers instead of plotting strategic initiatives. Firms should get away from relying so heavily on short-term sales and profit objectives as the only means of measuring success or failure.

In *Thriving on Chaos*, Tom Peters suggested that firms measure the wrong elements; they focus on immediate costs and profits instead of on variables such as the quality of products and service, company flexibility, and employee innovation, factors which guarantee long-term revenue and company gain. Peters identifies three critical factors in gaining long-term competitive advantage:[6]

1. *Customer Responsiveness*   Achieving responsiveness involves the creation of a differential advantage through, for example, superior quality and better service. Firms measure responsiveness by consulting customer complaint records, by responding to customer requests, and by doing research to determine perceived quality of the product.

2. *Fast Paced Innovation*   This is the ability to respond quickly and continuously to a changing marketplace. Success and failure are measured in terms of the number of successful new products introduced to the market. Determining the difference between sales of new and old products would be another way of measuring success. How many new product introductions have failed? What is the firm's success rate for new product introductions?

3. *Flexibility*   This refers to the firm's ability and willingness to change: to change, for example, people, processes, and programs when necessary. This can be measured in terms of the firm's ability to react. Does internal bureaucracy inhibit or encourage change?

## ⟩⟩⟩⟩ *Contingency Planning*

**contingency plan**

In contemporary marketing, an organization must be flexible in order to take advantage of new developments in the marketplace. Throughout the planning cycle, a firm is presented with new threats and opportunities that can make a plan obsolete rather quickly. Consequently, the wise marketing manager builds a contingency plan into a master plan. A contingency is the possibility of something happening that poses a threat to the organization. A **contingency plan** involves the identification of alternate courses of action that can be used to modify an original plan if and when new circumstances arise.

A contingency plan is generally based on "what if" or "worst case" situations. If these situations develop, the organization is ready to implement alternate strategies. Some events that would require alternate action would be 1) the competition increasing its level of media advertising, 2) the competition reducing price to build market share, 3) a new competitive product entering the market, 4) Canada Post going on strike and so jeopardizing a direct mail campaign, or 5) union workers in one's plant going on strike and so limiting access to product. Such situations add a dimension to strategic marketing planning and force the manager to plan for the unexpected at all times.

## 〉〉〉〉 S U M M A R Y

The quality of marketing planning in an organization is influenced by the business planning process itself. In terms of marketing, two different but related plans are important: the corporate plan and the marketing plan. Each plan is based on the development of corporate objectives, strategies, and tactics. A corporate plan provides direction to a marketing plan; a marketing plan provides direction to the various components of marketing such as advertising and sales promotion.

Business planning is a problem-solving and decision-making effort that forces management to look at the future and to set clear objectives and strategies. All levels of management play a role in planning. Planning by top management has a strategic orientation; mid-management a strategic and tactical orientation; and lower management a tactical orientation.

Business planning is divided into two broad areas: corporate planning, and operational planning for the functional department of a business, of which marketing planning is a part. Other departments such as Production, Human Resources, and Finance prepare their own plans as well. Corporate planning starts with the development of a mission statement, followed by corporate objectives and strategies. Some of the more common corporate strategies include: penetration through increased marketing activity, entering and developing new markets, new product development programs, investment in the channels of distribution, acquisition, and diversification.

Strategy is often developed with reference to portfolio analysis. For such an analysis, the firm is divided into strategic business units (profit centres), which may be divisions of a company, product lines, or individual brands. Strategic planning and analysis assesses the strengths and weaknesses of each strategic business unit (SBU). Analysis using the Boston Consulting Group matrix takes into account the dynamics between market growth and market share. The matrix divides products into four categories: stars, cash cows, question marks or problem children, and dogs. The strategy for each is quite different.

Strategic marketing planning involves reviewing and analyzing relevant background information, establishing appropriate marketing objectives and strategies, identifying target markets, accessing budget support and control procedures. The more commonly used marketing strategies include: market penetration, market development, product development, diversification, and harvesting. Once strategies are implemented, they are subject to evaluation. The evaluation and control process attempts to draw relationships between strategic activity and results. The organization determines which activities are effective or ineffective and then alters its strategy as needed. Due to uncertainty in the marketplace, wise marketing planners build contingency plans into the overall marketing plan. Such plans force planners to consider in detail the environments which influence marketing activity.

## ⟩⟩⟩ KEY TERMS

| | | |
|---|---|---|
| objectives | diversification | target market |
| strategies | portfolio analysis | market penetration |
| execution (tactics) | strategic business unit (SBU) | market development |
| planning | stars | product development |
| strategic planning | cash cows | diversification |
| corporate plan | question marks/problem children | harvest |
| mission statement | dogs | marketing control |
| corporate objectives | marketing planning | strategic control |
| corporate strategies | marketing objectives | marketing audit |
| acquisition | marketing strategies | contingency plan |

## ⟩⟩⟩ REVIEW AND DISCUSSION QUESTIONS

**1.** In planning, what is the basic difference between objectives, strategies, and tactics?

**2.** What is the relationship between a corporate plan and a marketing plan?

**3.** In this chapter, marketing strategies are described as the "master plans" for achieving marketing objectives. What does this mean?

**4.** Briefly explain the difference between the terms within each of the following pairs: **(a)** objectives and strategies **(b)** acquisition and diversification **(c)** market penetration and market development **(d)** stars and cash cows **(e)** marketing control and marketing audit

**5.** Briefly explain the role of the various levels of management in the planning process.

**6.** Explain the significance of the "strategic business unit" concept in marketing planning.

**7.** Briefly describe the strategies for each of the four categories of the BCG matrix.

**8.** Marketing evaluation and control procedures tend to be quantitative in nature. Is this the best approach for measuring the effectiveness of marketing strategies? Can you suggest any alternatives?

**9.** "Corporate strategies focus too much on profits and too little on satisfying customers." Discuss the issues surrounding this statement.

**10.** "Large corporations which acquire other large corporations do more harm than good in a competitive marketplace." Is this statement fact or fiction? Defend your position and provide appropriate examples to substantiate your views.

## 〉〉〉 REFERENCES

1. Dominion Textiles Inc., *1988 Annual Report*, p.2.
2. *Ibid.*
3. *Ibid.*
4. PHILIP KOTLER, GORDON McDOUGALL and GARY ARMSTRONG, *Marketing*, Canadian Edition (Toronto: Prentice-Hall Canada Inc., 1988), p.64.

5. E. JEROME McCARTHY, STANLEY J. SHAPIRO and WILLIAM D. PERRAULT, *Basic Marketing* (Homewood, Illinois: Irwin, 1986), p.742.
6. WILLIAM BAND, "Use the Right Measures to Track Marketing Performance", *Sales & Marketing Management in Canada*, February 1988, p.33.

# C H A P T E R  4  〉〉〉〉

# Market
# Segmentation

**LEARNING OBJECTIVES**

After studying this chapter you will be able to

1. Define a market and distinguish among consumer goods markets, industrial goods markets, and business goods markets.

2. Describe the process used and the information needed to identify and select target markets.

3. Define market segmentation and explain the influence of this concept on marketing activity.

4. Describe the various types of segmentation strategies commonly used in contemporary marketing practice.

5. Explain the concept of positioning and its role in contemporary marketing practice.

## >>>> What is a Market?

market

Before discussing market segmentation, let's define what a market is. A **market** is a group of people who have a similar need for a product or service, the resources to purchase the product or service, and the willingness and ability to buy it. As this definition indicates, a market, or potential market, possesses four basic characteristics:

1. People with common needs.
2. People with financial resources to buy (purchasing power).
3. People who are willing to buy.
4. People with the ability to buy (authority to buy).

## Types of Markets

Traditionally, markets have been placed in two broad categories: consumer goods and industrial goods. Since some marketing to business and industry that was considered part of industrial goods marketing is now referred to as business-to-business marketing, a third classification must be identified. This new classification eliminates the connotations of manufacturing associated with "industrial" marketing. This text will divide or segment the total market into three broad categories: consumer goods, industrial goods, and business goods.

consumer goods

1. **Consumer goods** are products and services which are ultimately purchased for personal use. Any commonly purchased item serves as an example: a type of coffee or soft drink, toothpaste, a chocolate bar or other snack food item, or a registered retirement savings plan purchased at a local bank or through an insurance company.

industrial goods

2. **Industrial goods** are products such as raw materials, supplies, and other firms' finished products, purchased to be used directly or indirectly in the manufacture of other goods for resale. A company like General Foods Inc., which manufacturers and markets Maxwell House coffee, purchases coffee beans for processing, and glass jars, paper labels, and plastic lids for packaging in order to form their finished product — a jar of instant coffee. These ingredients and materials are all industrial goods.

business goods

3. **Business goods** are products, purchased by business, government, institutions, and industries, that facilitate the operations of an organization. Such goods might include a wide array of business equipment such as photocopiers, telephone systems, and related equipment; facsimile machines for message transmission; company automobiles for the sales force; word processing and computer equipment.

# ⟩⟩⟩⟩ *Identifying and Selecting Target Markets*

## Mass Marketing

A business organization has two basic options once it has determined the best target marketing strategies to use. The firm can adopt a strategy of mass marketing or use market segmentation to its advantage.

mass marketing

When it is **mass marketing**, a business organization uses one basic marketing strategy to appeal to a broad range of consumers, not addressing any distinct characteristics among the consumers. In effect, the nature of the product or service is such that it enjoys widespread acceptance. In contemporary practice, this type of marketing is the exception rather than the rule, but certain products and services are suited to this approach.

When the production concept was followed, mass marketing was appropriate because consumers were offered a limited choice. Products came in one form for everybody; they did not cater to different tastes and desires. Marketing made a general appeal. In today's environment, where great competition exists, firms are striving to differentiate their products in order to make them more attractive to potential users. Using marketing research information to advantage, the firm identifies different segments in need of specialized products and services. Consequently, mass marketing is used less.

To illustrate mass marketing, let's examine the muffler business in Canada. The two main competitors are Speedy Muffler King and Midas Muffler. Both firms offer a similar product line, which includes replacement mufflers, shock absorbers, and brake systems. At one time or another, all car owners will be in need of their products. As a result, each firm must create a high level of awareness among all car consumers so that it will be remembered when its products are needed. Factors such as age, income, lifestyle, and location, which are typically used to identify targets, are not important in the purchase of a replacement muffler. When the consumer needs a muffler, he or she will seek the best option available based on his or her knowledge of what is available.

Supermarket marketing is another example of mass marketing. In the Canadian west, Safeway dominates the market. Their strategy is to attract the widest possible range of consumers to their store locations. In Ontario, A&P and Loblaws are market leaders; as is Provigo in Quebec, and Sobey's in the Maritimes. In all cases, market strength is held by a few chains addressing a common need among consumers: the need for food. The characteristics of the consumers who shop at these chain stores are irrelevant. The goal of these stores is to expand their existing customer base and take market share from their competitors.

A problem commonly associated with mass marketing is that sales are emphasized at the expense of profits. It is true that an expanded consumer base will add to sales, but the organization must consider the costs associated with gaining the sales. In Ontario, Dominion Stores once dominated the food retailing business. But at length they faced stiff competition from A&P, Loblaws and Food City. When price wars broke out and certain competitors undertook extensive store remodelling plans, Dominion's marketing strategies stayed relatively stable, except that it participated in the price war. Dominion suffered as a result of this strategy: going for sales regardless of the costs was a contributing factor in the demise of this chain (most stores were ultimately sold to A&P). Today, A&P is the largest food retailer in Ontario.

An advantage of mass marketing is that the organization can create a consistent and well known image for itself. In the example of Speedy Muffler King, the company has used many different advertising approaches over the years, but the message remains the same: at Speedy the customer gets prompt, courteous, and reliable service, and a guarantee of product quality.

## Market Segmentation

**market segmentation**

**Market segmentation** is the division of a large market (mass market) into smaller homogeneous markets (segments or targets) based on common needs and/or similar lifestyles. Segmentation strategies are based on the premise that it is preferable to tailor marketing strategies to distinct user groups, where the degree of competition may be less. If segmentation strategy is employed, the organization does not mass produce or mass market. Instead, the firm specializes by concentrating on large portions of a particular segment of the population. In this regard, organizations will pursue segments where opportunities are the greatest (e.g., where competition is less or where their product can be clearly distinguished from the competition that does exist).

To maximize profits, the firm commonly has to operate in many different segments. A segmentation strategy enables a firm to control marketing costs, allowing it to make profits. Regional marketers, using a regional brand, can therefore compete, within their own region, with national marketers using a national brand, even though they could never compete nationally due to costs. On the downside, segmenters must be alert to shifting consumer trends and taste patterns, since a dramatic shift in any particular segment could put a segment marketer out of business. Hence, the need exists to operate in many segments.

Another advantage of segmentation is that the organization can generate a distinct "niche" for itself, or for a product line or brand that it markets. Niche marketing is discussed in detail later in this chapter.

# ⟩⟩⟩⟩ *Target Markets to Pursue*

Segmentation is the identification of target markets worth pursuing, with the company's assessment based on the profit potential these markets offer. A multi-product firm competing in diverse markets develops distinct marketing strategies for each of the target markets it perceives to have the greatest profit potential. To identify and select the target markets worth pursuing, the organization will use marketing research to learn the demographic, geographic, psychographic, and behaviour-response characteristics of the segments. Identifying segments on such bases allows the marketer to see what target markets exist and to devise strategies for reaching them. Let's examine each one of these segmentation variables.

## Demographic Segmentation

demographic
segmentation

**Demographic segmentation** is defined as the division of a large market into smaller segments based on combinations of age, sex, income, occupation, education, marital status, household formation, and ethnic background. In Canada, two major demographic trends will influence the direction of marketing activity in the future: the aging population and the evolving ethnic mix. These factors along with other demographic variables will be discussed in this section. For further information on the aging population and ethnic mix refer to chapter 7.

### Age and Sex

Traditionally, the group encompassing people of 18 to 34 years of age has been given the most attention by marketers, since this group has, in the past, comprised the largest segment of the population. This strategy will change, however, since the Canadian population is aging. It is estimated that between 1986 and 1996 there will be a 7 percent decline in the number of Canadians under the age of 35.[1] Baby boomers (those people born in the late forties and fifties) will be entering middle age (people in the 36–49-year age range), and this older group will become a major buying influence. According to projections, in 1996, there will be 1.6 million more people in the 35–49 year age range, an increase of 32.4 percent from 1986.

In addition, the "grey revolution" will be increasingly apparent. This term applies to the 50 years-plus market. By 1996, almost 7.6 million Canadians representing 28 percent of the population will be over the age of 50, compared to 22 percent in 1986.[2] Refer to figure 4.1 for a breakdown of the Canadian population by age distribution. In comparison to past generations, the over-50 age group is expected to be not only larger but also quite different in the next decade. The current emphasis on health and physical fitness suggests that this group will not be old either physically or in their outlook. It is expected that more marketing strategies will isolate and pursue these older age groups (35 to 49, 50 to 64, and 65-plus). New products will have marketing strategies that appeal to these age groups and existing products will need changed strategies if they are to survive.

To illustrate the impact of older age groups on marketing activity, consider the growth of "light" products in the 1980s. Marketers developed many light products and low calorie products, in addition to their regular products, to take advantage of the aging population and its concern for health. For example, there are light ketchups, margarines, dairy products such as sour creams and cream cheeses, salad dressings, frozen dinners, and many more. Light products appealed to consumers who were over the age of thirty years (late baby boomers). In the beer market, light products were introduced using established brand names to gain quicker acceptance in the marketplace (Blue Light, Bud Light, Coors Light, Export Light, and Oland's Lite). In the beer market, the light segment accounted for 13 percent of total volume in 1988, a segment worthy of pursuit by the major breweries.[3]

In their young years, baby boomers were influenced by lifestyle marketing appeals, but, as they age, the fun-and-games, youth-oriented approach of the 1970s and 1980s will become decreasingly effective. Effective marketing strategies aimed at boomers are expected to become factual, to stress quality, and to appeal to the buyer's good judgement. Since this group will be thinking about retirement planning, the financial services industry will receive a boost. As an example, the London Life "Freedom 55" advertising campaign stressed the benefits of life insurance for people over the age of 55 years. This was a unique approach in an industry strongly associated with the negative. The campaign illustrated living patterns that everyone, not just high income earners, can enjoy through careful retirement planning.[4]

**grey market**

In the **grey market**, marketers must be conscious of the outlook of seniors (65 plus years). Many current seniors are active, interested people in pursuit of new interests. With mortgages paid off and few obligations, many seniors have income from a variety of pensions and investments. Seniors have growing spending power, are living longer, and therefore represent attractive opportunities, particularly among organizations that deal in housing, health care, entertainment, and recreation. In 1986, this segment included 2.7 million Canadians, and by 2001, this figure will swell to four million, a huge potential market.[5]

**FIGURE 4.1**   Population by Age Distribution Percentage, 1976–1986

|  | 1976 | 1981 | 1986 |
|---|---|---|---|
| 0–9 yr. | 15.7% | 14.6% | 14.3% |
| 10–19 | 20.1 | 17.4 | 14.7 |
| 20–34 | 25.1 | 26.9 | 26.8 |
| 35–49 | 16.7 | 17.4 | 19.5 |
| 50–64 | 13.6 | 13.9 | 14.1 |
| 65 + | 8.8 | 9.7 | 10.6 |
| Total | 100.0 | 100.0 | 100.0 |
| Total Population (in thousands) | 22 993 | 24 343 | 25 354 |

*Source*:  Adapted from Statistics Canada, *Canada Year Book 1988*, Ottawa: Supply and Services Canada, 1987, Cat. No 11-402E/1987, p. 2–18. Adapted with the permission of the Minister of Supply and Services Canada, 1990.

Sex has always been a primary means of distinguishing product categories: personal care products, magazines, athletic equipment, and fashion are all categorized according to the sex of the buyer. Due to the increasing presence of women in the workforce outside the home (a significant change from earlier generations), and the changing roles of men and women in Canadian households, the marketing orientation will become increasingly "unisex," as both sexes will buy and use similar products.

Between 1980 and 1987, the percentage of the employed work force consisting of women over the age of sixteen went from 46.7 percent to 51.3 percent. At the same time, the corresponding figure for men went from 74.3 percent to 70.9 percent.[6] Refer to figure 4.2 for a summary of employment figures by age and sex. A significant trend is also occurring in the 25 to 34 year category of women. As of 1986, two out of every three Canadian women in this age group were working outside the home, an increase of 20 percent in ten years.[7]

These trends affect marketing strategy. Organizations that have traditionally marketed to the housewife are forced to change their approach. Retailers and home service organizations (electricians, plumbers and delivery services, etc.) have to adjust to the two-person working family and operate outside of the traditional working hours, as do many professionals such as doctors and dentists. The 1980s saw the opening of storefront dental clinics (e.g., Tridont Health Care Inc.), which were open during business and non-business hours. The banking industry pursued new opportunities by offering extended hours, Saturday openings, and by installing automated teller machines to serve customers when banks are closed.

The automobile industry has recognized the distinct benefits of sex segmentation, particularly since more women entered the workforce. A Consumer Council survey conducted by the magazine *Chatelaine* in 1985 indicated that women can influence a car purchase as much as 80 percent of the time.[8] What influences a man to buy a car is quite different from what influences a woman. Strategies directed at men focus on styling and road handling, while strategies directed at women emphasize quality, safety, reliability, and fuel economy. General Motors targets marketing funds directly

**FIGURE 4.2    Percentage of Men and Women Employed, by Age, 1980 and 1987**

|  | Canada | |
|---|---|---|
|  | 1980 | 1987 |
| **Men** | | |
| 16–24 yr. | 66.0 | 64.3 |
| 25–44 | 90.6 | 87.4 |
| 45 + | 61.9 | 55.0 |
| Total | 74.3 | 70.9 |
| **Women** | | |
| 16–24 yr. | 58.0 | 60.7 |
| 25–44 | 57.9 | 67.2 |
| 45 + | 29.2 | 30.2 |
| Total | 46.7 | 51.3 |

*Source*: Statistics Canada, *Canadian Social Trends*, Autumn 1988, p. 15. Reproduced with the permission of the Minister of Supply and Services Canada, 1990.

at women. In 1987, it spent $39.7 million in media advertising, with 8 percent of it channeled towards women.[9] General Motors products popular with women include the sporty Fiero and Sunbird models, and the Oldsmobile Cutlass Calais.

In the expensive sports car category, Mazda RX models and Toyota Celica have successfully positioned themselves to appeal to women with career aspirations. BMW traditionally targeted its advertising to the upscale male market, but recently it introduced to the Canadian market a model specifically for women, the 325i Cabriolet. The car was priced in the $40,000 range, and positioned as a less expensive alternative to the Mercedes Benz SL roadster, so as to appeal to upscale, career-minded women.[10]

### Income, Occupation, and Education

Generally, these three variables have a close relationship with each other. Higher incomes are usually associated with certain professions such as medicine, law, and dentistry, which, in turn, are usually associated with backgrounds of higher education. People in these occupations earn incomes above that of the average Canadian.

In Canada, there are some regional disparities in household incomes, with many regions suffering from higher-than-average rates of unemployment due to the depressed state of Canada's resource industries. Knowledge of household income is critical to marketers because it highlights areas of market potential, that is, areas where buying potential is significant, whether it be a region, an area of a city, or a residential neighbourhood.

Wealthy Canadians now form a larger segment of the population than in previous decades, due mainly to the number of dual-income families. These households are defined as having an income in excess of $50 000 annually. This more affluent group represents a notable marketing opportunity, since the top 20 percent of affluent families account for

1. Forty-seven percent of education expenditures
2. Forty-four percent of savings and financial securities expenditures
3. Forty-two percent of spending on recreation
4. Forty-two percent of gifts and charitable donations[11]

What effect does affluence have on marketing strategy? With the emergence of a mature, affluent target market, which already places an emphasis on fitness and recreation and on the home as an entertainment centre, marketers anticipate a continuing high demand for leisure products, home entertainment units, high quality fashion, and travel. Recognizing the affluence of this market, marketers will appeal to it on the basis of status and achievement, encouraging its members to acquire products that are in line with their income and occupation.

### Marital Status and Household Formation

Statistics relating to marriage and divorce between 1980 and 1985 indicate a decline in the number of marriages each year and a high but relatively stable divorce rate. The divorce rate remains significantly higher than it was in the 1960s and 1970s. This trend is partly due to changes in divorce laws, which have made the process of getting divorced much less complicated, and to the fact that young married couples are deciding on divorce much earlier than was the case with previous generations. These developments have created new types of household formations, such as single parent families.

As of 1986, four out of five Canadian families lived in the traditional family comprised of husband, wife, and children. A growth in the number and size of traditional families has slowed due to delays in marriage, to the increasing number of single-parent families (in which the parent is widowed or divorced), and to the aging population now moving past the prime family-forming years. In 1961, there were 3.9 members in the average household, today there is only 3.1.[12]

Another significant trend is the growth in the "singles" segment. A tendency to postpone marriage, together with a high divorce rate, has increased the number of single-person households, which now account for 20 percent of all Canadian households.[13]

Canadian household formations have also changed due to the growing number of people living together without being married. Between 1981 and 1986, common-law unions increased sharply, while the number of married couples rose by only a small amount. The percentage of people living in union, either in a commom-law partnership or in a legal marriage, decreased only slightly between 1981 and 1986.[14] In effect, growth in common-law unions compensated for marriage declines and had a stabilizing effect on household formations, an important factor affecting marketing strategy.

Marketing strategists must consider these trends, along with the age and sex trends mentioned earlier. These developments indicate that there will be a continuing demand for a variety of types of housing (new housing, resale housing, condominiums, and apartments). The housing demand in turn creates demand for furnishings, appliances, decoration and entertainment products for the homes, and a range of products and services related to household upkeep (see figure 4.3). The Marketing in Action vignette entitled "Today's Indulged Children" provides some interesting insight into how changing demographic trends have influenced the children's market and marketing activity.

**FIGURE 4.3**   Necessities of the Modern Household

|  | **Percentage of Homes That Own** |
|---|---|
| Televisions | 99% |
| Telephones | 98 |
| Cassette and Tape Recorders | 70 |
| Cable Television | 69 |
| Microwave Ovens | 54 |
| VCRs | 52 |
| Cable Converters | 41 |
| Home Computers | 13 |
| Pay Television | 11 |
| Compact Disc Players | 8 |
| Camcorders | 3 |

Canadian households are becoming more and more "new tech." Items such as microwave ovens and VCRs, which were luxuries a few years ago, are now commonplace.

*Source*: Adapted from information included in *The Royal Bank Reporter*, Fall 1989.

## ››› *MARKETING IN ACTION*

### *TODAY'S INDULGED CHILDREN*

Numerous demographic trends in Canada have created and will continue to create profitable opportunities for businesses that direct their activities at the children's market. Some of these demographic trends are having a profound effect on the way children are raised. These trends include the following:

1. Children of the baby boom generation (adults born in the late 1940s and 1950s) are having their own children, thus creating a mini-boom.

2. There are more mothers who work outside the home and more dual-income families, which have higher levels of disposable income, than ever before. Canadians over the age of 45 are the most prosperous group; they are often young grandparents with money to spend.

3. Due to the divorce rate, there is a greater incidence of split or lone-parent families than in previous decades.

4. Family sizes are much smaller as fewer children are in the household. As a result, there are higher disposable incomes that can be spent on the children. Smaller households are the result of people delaying marriage and the greater number of two-earner families.

The mini-boom of the 1980s created a huge new demand for trendy and expensive clothing, accessories, and toys for babies and children. Businesses catering to the under-twelve age group are burgeoning, with designer clothes boutiques, bookstores, video outlets, and toy shops springing up everywhere. The children's market in Canada has been estimated to be worth $3.5 billion.

What are the children like today who are being indulged with the latest in clothing, toys, and entertainment? They are demanding and very status-conscious. Those in the nine- to twelve-year age group are aware of the status associated with certain brand names. Such status consciousness stems from the parent's attitudes and those of their peers who purchase the "right" type of products. They will purchase the $400 baby stroller when a less expensive model would

*Laura Ashley "Mother and Child" bath products for children are designed to be safe for sensitive skin. Also, their containers are unbreakable and easy to squeeze, and have specially designed spouts that prevent spilling.*

perform the same function. The children want the labels their parents wear. They demand Esprit, Benetton, Beaver Canoe, and other such labels on their clothing. The little ones get the best of toys such as Fisher-Price, and they wear OshKosh clothing and Weebok sneakers.

It could be said that these children are the victims of parents who feel guilty about not spending more time with them. To make up for this shortcoming, they compensate with a "spare no expense" attitude. Given these circumstances, marketing organizations have taken action. In Square One, a huge regional mall in the booming community of Mississauga, Ontario, one section of the mall is known as Kids Place. Here, there are twelve stores selling nothing but toys, shoes, clothing, and accessories. Other retailing developments include:

1. Laura Ashley Shops — They carry a line of

bath products for babies called "Mother and Child".

2. Dalmy's — It has opened a group of children's retail clothing outlets.

3. Roots — It now sells miniature sweatshirts.

4. Bata Industries Limited — This well-known company has opened a chain of shoe and clothing stores called Bubblegummers.

5. Coles Book Stores — This book retailer has opened a chain of stores specializing in children's needs called Active Minds.

6. Creative Kids — A relatively new company which uses direct selling techniques (specifi-

cally home parties similar to those used by Tupperware), it is now a five-million-dollar-a-year business.

All of these examples show how a marketing organization uses demographic trends to develop appropriate strategies that are in keeping with the changing needs of the marketplace. The key to success is evolving with the market rather than standing pat and relying on existing businesses.

Adapted from Jennifer Hunter, "Baby it's yours", *Report on Business Magazine*, January 1989, pp.44-47.

## Ethnic Mix

The Canadian birthrate is declining on an annual basis (refer to figure 4.4), and as a result it is expected that immigrants will account for most of whatever growth occurs in the 1990s. Canada's ethnic diversity will present new opportunities. In some regions and large cities, ethnic communities in concentrated locations are accessible market niches for marketing organizations to pursue.

In Ontario, almost half of the population is now of non-British origin, quite a change from the past. In cities like Toronto and Vancouver, Chinese and continental European groups have developed their own neighbourhoods, resulting in a multicultural mosaic in these cities. For example, Italians represent 5 percent of Ontario's population and 10 percent of Toronto's. People of German origin represent 17 percent of Saskatchewan's population and 10 percent of Alberta's. In total, almost one-third of Canada's population has neither English nor French as its mother

**FIGURE 4.4   Canada's Population Growth, 1961–1986**

|  | Population (in thousands) | Increase during Intercensal Period | Average Annual Growth Rate |
|---|---|---|---|
| 1961 | 18 239 | 13.4% | 2.5% |
| 1966 | 20 015 | 9.7 | 1.9 |
| 1971 | 21 568 | 7.8 | 1.5 |
| 1976 | 22 993 | 6.6 | 1.3 |
| 1981 | 24 343 | 5.9 | 1.1 |
| 1986 | 25 354 | 4.2 | 0.8 |

*Source*:  Adapted from Statistics Canada, *Canada Year Book 1988*, Ottawa: Supply and Services Canada, 1987, Cat. No 11-402E/1987, p. 2–14. Adapted with the permission of the Minister of Supply and Services Canada, 1990.

tongue, and this group is growing faster than the rest of the population.[15] In the 1990s, the successful targeting and meeting of the needs of various ethnic groups promises to be profitable for firms venturing into these sub-markets.

## Geographic Segmentation

**geographic segmentation**

**Geographic segmentation** refers to the division of a large geographic market into smaller geographic or regional units. The Canadian market can be divided into five distinct areas: the Maritimes, Quebec, Ontario, the Prairies, and British Columbia. Geographic considerations used in conjunction with demographics provide the marketer with a clear description of the target market, and from this description marketing strategies can be developed. Gone are the days when a national brand applied the success of an Ontario-based strategy to all other parts of Canada. The most obvious difference is in Quebec, where the language and cultural characteristics necessitate the use of original marketing strategies. When all segmentation variables are combined, it becomes clear that the activities that influence the French-speaking business executive are quite different from those influencing the Prairie farmer, or the west coast fisherman. Consequently, marketing organizations must assess opportunities on a regional basis. The significance of the various provinces and marketing regions is outlined in figure 4.5.

**FIGURE 4.5**   Population Trends by Province and Region

| Province and Region | 1981 Actual (in thousands) | 1986 Actual (in thousands) | 1986 Percentage of Total | 1986 Region's Percentage of Total | 1992 Projection (in thousands) |
|---|---|---|---|---|---|
| Newfoundland | 568 | 568 | 2.2% | | 575 |
| Prince Edward Island | 123 | 127 | 0.5 | | 134 |
| Nova Scotia | 847 | 873 | 3.4 | | 911 |
| New Brunswick | 696 | 710 | 2.8 | | 732 |
| Maritimes | 2 234 | 2 278 | 8.9 | 8.9% | 2 352 |
| Quebec | 6 438 | 6 540 | 25.8 | 25.8 | 6 707 |
| Ontario | 8 625 | 9 114 | 36.0 | 36.0 | 9 881 |
| Manitoba | 1 026 | 1 071 | 4.2 | | 1 127 |
| Saskatchewan | 968 | 1 010 | 4.0 | | 1 005 |
| Alberta | 2 238 | 2 375 | 9.4 | | 2 553 |
| Prairies | 4 232 | 4 456 | 17.6 | 17.6 | 4 685 |
| British Columbia | 2 744 | 2 889 | 11.4 | 11.4 | 3 122 |
| Yukon/Northwest Terr. | 69 | 76 | 0.3 | 0.3 | 90 |
| Canada | 24 343 | 25 354 | 100.0 | 100.0 | 26 836 |

*Source*:  Adapted from "Financial Post Survey of Markets," *Financial Post Projections*, 1988, and from Statistics Canada, *Canada Year Book 1988*, Ottawa: Supply and Services Canada, 1987, Cat. No. 11-402E/1987, p. 2–14. Adapted with the permission of the Minister of Supply and Services Canada, 1990.

Geographic regions are sub-divided into urban and rural areas. Within urban metropolitan areas, the market can be divided further based on location: urban downtown, suburban, and regional municipalities that surround large cities. It is estimated that 75 percent of Canada's population lives in areas classified as urban and that three cities (Toronto, Montreal and Vancouver) account for 30.5 percent of the population.[16] Refer to figure 4.6 for a review of Canada's twenty largest cities.

Considering the distribution of Canada's regional and urban population, it is not surprising that successful marketing strategies have an urban orientation. These strategies may also differ according to location within the urban area. The attitudes, opinions, and lifestyles of a downtown urban dweller may be quite different from those of the suburban dweller. For example, in many inner city neighbourhoods today, there is a comparatively high incidence of young, upscale households (the different types of households discussed earlier). In contrast, the suburban household tends to be more traditional in nature. Suburban dwellers are likely to be married, have children, own a large family automobile, have a second car, live in new homes, commute downtown to work, and so on. Both of these groups may require the same products; however, the strategies used to reach these groups can be very

**FIGURE 4.6**  Canada's Top Twenty Markets by Population

| Market (Metropolitan Area) | 1981 Actual (in thousands) | 1986 Actual (in thousands) | 1986 Percentage | 1986 Accumulated Percentage | 1992 Projection (in thousands) |
|---|---|---|---|---|---|
| 1. Toronto | 3 130 | 3 427 | 13.5% | 13.5% | 3 924 |
| 2. Montreal | 2 862 | 2 921 | 11.5 | 25.0 | 3 014 |
| 3. Vancouver | 1 268 | 1 381 | 5.5 | 30.5 | 1 561 |
| 4. Ottawa-Hull | 744 | 819 | 3.2 | 33.7 | 936 |
| 5. Edmonton | 741 | 785 | 3.1 | 36.8 | 845 |
| 6. Calgary | 626 | 671 | 2.7 | 39.5 | 732 |
| 7. Winnipeg | 592 | 625 | 2.5 | 42.0 | 668 |
| 8. Quebec | 584 | 603 | 2.4 | 44.4 | 632 |
| 9. Hamilton | 542 | 557 | 2.2 | 46.6 | 578 |
| 10. London | 327 | 342 | 1.4 | 48.0 | 362 |
| 11. St. Catharines-Niagara | 343 | 343 | 1.4 | 49.4 | 344 |
| 12. Kitchener | 288 | 311 | 1.2 | 50.6 | 343 |
| 13. Halifax | 278 | 296 | 1.2 | 51.8 | 322 |
| 14. Victoria | 241 | 256 | 1.0 | 52.8 | 276 |
| 15. Windsor | 251 | 252 | 1.0 | 53.8 | 258 |
| 16. Saskatoon | 175 | 201 | 0.8 | 54.6 | 213 |
| 17. Oshawa | 186 | 203 | 0.8 | 55.4 | 228 |
| 18. Regina | 171 | 186 | 0.7 | 56.1 | 184 |
| 19. Sudbury | 156 | 149 | 0.6 | 57.2 | 141 |
| 20. Saint John | 121 | 121 | 0.5 | 56.7 | 123 |

*Source*: "Canadian Markets 1987/88," *Financial Post Projections*, and Statistics Canada, *Canada Year Book 1988*, Ottawa: Supply and Services Canada, 1987, Cat. No. 11-402E/1987, p. 2–17. Adapted with the permission of the Minister of Supply and Services Canada, 1990.

different. Similar comparisons can be made between the urban dweller and the rural dweller. The differences in need, attitude, and outlook on life create constant challenges for marketing organizations.

**geodemographics**

The combination of geographic and demographic segmentation has spawned the use of the term **geodemographics**. This term is concerned with the marketing strategy of isolating dwelling areas (e.g., areas within a city) according to geography and demographics, a strategy based on the assumption that people seek out residential neighbourhoods in which to cluster with their lifestyle peers. The description of younger, higher income households clustering in redeveloped downtown areas and dual income, traditional families concentrating in suburbia are applications of the geodemographic concept. Applying the same principle on a regional basis, practitioners refer to regional marketing strategies as micro-marketing. **Micro-marketing** involves the development of marketing strategies on a regional basis, for which it is necessary to give consideration to the unique needs and geodemographics of different regions.

**micro-marketing**

Many Canadian marketing organizations are moving away from "broadstroke" national marketing strategies toward the use of strategies based on regional considerations and opportunities. Refer to the Marketing in Action vignette on page 100, "Sears' New Stores", for an illustration of marketing strategies based on geodemographics.

## Psychographic Segmentation

**psychographic segmentation**

The use of geodemographics has been the traditional way to segment Canadian markets, but in today's competitive marketplace, marketing organizations have added a more sophisticated variable referred to as psychographics. **Psychographic segmentation** is market segmentation based on the differing lifestyles — activities, interests, and opinions — of consumers. Psychographic segmentation is multidimensional: it considers a variety of the factors that affect a person's purchase decision. Such information is advantageous to marketers because it tells them not only who buys, but why they buy.

Psychographics examines lifestyles as reflected in observed activities, values, attitudes, interests, and beliefs. Such examination helps marketers understand why two people who are demographically identical behave in very different ways and purchase different types of products and services. When organizations target psychographically, they present products that are in line with the lifestyle of the target market, so that the personality of the product matches the personality of the target.

The advent of psychographics and psychographic research has occurred because the values of the baby boom generation have continually changed. This generation included the "hippie" of the sixties, the "me generation" of the seventies, and the "yuppies" of the eighties. New needs have emerged for the individual as attitudes, opinions, and beliefs have shifted with the changing lifestyles. To understand and address the changing needs, marketers had to research and profile them.

Psychographic research was pioneered by Stanford Research Institute in California (now SRI International) in 1976. At that time, it profiled nine American lifestyles: survivors, sustainers, belongers, achievers, emulators, I-am-Me's, experientials, the

## ⟩⟩⟩ *MARKETING IN ACTION*

### *SEARS' NEW STORES*

In contemporary marketing there is a movement towards geodemographic marketing. Geodemographic segmentation clusters potential customers into neighbourhood lifestyle categories. These clusters are assigned demographic features as well as socioeconomic or lifestyle characteristics.

Sears is a good example. It has used geodemographic segmentation as a portfolio management tool for years. Sears geocodes its credit-card customer base to determine its best customers and to identify what growth segments to target. This information helps Sears to determine what merchandise is best suited to the needs of a particular geodemographic area.

Sears recently opened two new stores in Chicago on this basis. One store is located downtown, in Chicago's Old Town district, an area that has a heavy concentration of apartment dwellers and singles. The store offers services such as hardware, home improvements, ready-to-assemble furniture, and concession services such as a bakery, café, floral shop, and optical department. The other store is located in the suburban south side of Chicago, an area consisting of single-family households with children. The store offers more clothing than the other store, as well as a Kids & More department and a collection of shops for moms and kids, with a design based on extensive research with mothers and children. Both stores offer a variety of national brands along with the Sears lines of merchandise. The movement to differentiating urban stores from suburban stores is expected to continue in the Sears chain of stores in both the U.S. and Canada.

In Canada, Sears has adopted a different strategy. In an effort to grow, Sears opened six department stores in 1988 in smaller cities such as Truro, N.S., and Timmins, Ontario, markets that competitors like Eaton's and The Bay weren't interested in. Referred to as mini-stores, they are about half the size of the conventional Sears department store and stock a limited variety of

*Sears' new location in St. Thomas, Ontario*

goods, mainly family fashions, appliances, and household items. Operating costs are lower due to cheap rents and to the fact that fewer employees are needed in each store. In the stores already open, sales per square foot are twice that of the traditional, larger store, according to G.J. Reddington, president and chief executive of Sears in Canada.

The movement to regional marketing, the emergence of the mini-store concept, and Sears' already strong position in the sale of appliances and home goods have helped keep Sears ahead of its department-store rivals. At the same time, both Eaton's and The Bay continue to focus on the sale of clothing, a slumping market in general. These strategies will serve to further differentiate the competitors and give Sears a competitive advantage in the marketplace.

Adapted from Lynn Coleman, "Marketers advised to go regional," *Marketing News*, May 8, 1989, pp.1,8., and Barrie McKenna, "Mini-stores ring up big returns for Sears," *Financial Post*, May 8, 1989, p.8.

societally conscious, and the integrateds.[17] In Canada, numerous psychographic research studies have been conducted, resulting in a variety of descriptive classifications. Goldfarb Consultants of Toronto has classified Canadians into six psychographic cells, in two broad segments; traditionalists and non-traditionalists.[18]

## Canadian Psychographic Classifications

### Traditionalists

Among the traditionalists, *day-to-day watchers* (25 percent of the population) represent the status quo who watch the world pass by. They dislike society's unremittingly fast pace. For them, family satisfaction takes priority over the satisfaction of the individual. They are motivated by security and loyalty factors, and familiar products appeal to them. In terms of marketing, they are influenced by the dominance of brand name, by authority figures as presenters of products, and by quality. They respond to promotions (which encourage them to obtain what they cannot usually afford) and watch a great deal of television.

*Old-fashioned puritans* (18 percent) represent a group who prefer simpler times. The family is important to them, but the ethics of individualism dominate. They are firm believers in government, law, and social order. They shop for value at established stores. They are motivated by value and a combination of reasonable price and quality. Therefore, they respond to messages stressing good value. They purchase large sizes (to save money), and they will respond to coupons if they perceive that value can be had from them.

*Responsible survivors* (12 percent) represent the frugal segment of the population. They are somewhat insecure about spending, and shop for the lowest price. Income is not a factor; they have money, but do not enjoy spending it. This group is motivated by price, likes generic (private label and no-name) products, and shops at low end retailers such as Bi-Way and Kresge's, which offer low prices for low quality merchandise. Marketing activity should emphasize price to attract responsible survivors, and since television is an important aspect of their lifestyle, it is an effective way to reach them.

### Non-Traditionalists

*Joiner activists* (16 percent) are idealists looking for self-improvement. They reject the status quo, are liberal-minded, and have a tendency to make carefully considered decisions. This group is motivated by information (they evaluate their options before making a purchase decision). Marketing activity should use techniques that appeal to rationality and stress quality, service, and dependability. Because they are information-oriented, a variety of print and broadcast media can be used to reach them.

*Bold achievers* (15 percent) are aggressive, confident individuals who set high goals for themselves. They aspire to be at the top, to lead, to obtain power and responsibility. They are innovators and as such are willing to try new products.

Achievers can be motivated on an emotional level by status-, prestige-, and success-based appeals. They will purchase products that reflect their success. They tend to respond to premium (high) prices, expensive packaging, and exclusivity. They do not want products that others can have easily. Refer to figure 4.7 for an illustration.

**FIGURE 4.7**    An Advertisement Aimed at an Achiever, or Status-conscious Individual

THE NEW BMW 5-SERIES

Many successful individuals become so caught up in their professional lives that they lose sight of the other side of the equation.

After all, achievement deserves some reward. And such rewards often have the added benefit of expanding one's horizons, leading to a more balanced life.

For some of these individuals, the new BMW 535i and 525i may represent a most appropriate reward. Because while these luxury sports sedans move confidently through professional and social situations, they would be equally at home on a racing circuit.

The 5 Series automobiles are, in fact, a unique fusion of the practical and the bold. A fusion that denies neither the mind nor the heart. The cars satisfy at every level.

And to drive one of these cars, to drive it well in good country, for the downright good fun of it, may lead one to a more earthbound perception of reality, a healthy remove from one's normal round.

And that has value in itself, does it not?

THE ULTIMATE DRIVING EXPERIENCE

*Self-indulgents* (14 percent) are a group that resents authority. They are "me-first" types, heavily into self-gratification. They have impulsive tendencies, even in major purchases, because they seek instant gratification. Products that differentiate them from their peers have strong appeal. Price is not a factor; gratification is very much a factor. Marketing messages should highlight the gratification factor as a source of motivation.

### Illustrations of Psychographics in Use

To illustrate the application of psychographics, let's examine the classic case history of Merrill, Lynch, Pierce, Fenner & Smith Inc. In 1971, the firm introduced an advertising campaign featuring a thundering herd of bulls and the slogan "Bullish on America". The advertisements were to appeal to affluent, investment-oriented individuals. The campaign did not work until a new advertising agency entered the picture and revamped the campaign in 1979. The new agency, Young & Rubicam, developed ads featuring a single bull and the slogan "A Breed Apart". This strategy was successful. According to Ken Solmon, vice-president and director of Research Services at Y & R in Toronto,

> they didn't create the bull. But because it was running in the herd, it was a belonger advertisement, when they wanted to talk to achievers, who see themselves as individuals. The guy is not a cow running in the herd; he's a leader who runs ahead of the pack.[19]

Psychographic information shows how an individual's interest in a product depends on his or her lifestyle. Diversified auto-makers such as General Motors, Ford, or Chrysler design and market a range of cars in order to satisfy the lifestyle requirements of the Canadian lifestyle groups. Trendy sports cars with European styling appeal to bold achievers, while a family station-wagon, full-sized sedan, or mini-van appeals to the old-fashioned puritan. Other products for which psychographic segmentation has been used to advantage include soft drinks, beer, alcohol, tobacco, sports equipment and leisure sportswear, and fashion. Clothing stores such as Holt Renfrew and other upscale boutiques appeal to bold achievers and self-indulgents. The middle-of-the-road groups, like joiner activists and old-fashioned puritans, are likely to shop for clothing at established department stores (Simpsons, Eaton's, and The Bay), and national chains such as Fairweather, Tip Top and Suzy Shier. In contrast, responsible survivors are likely to purchase clothing in discount department stores (K-Mart, Woolco and Towers), and low end retail chains.

Marketing organizations should be cautious about how they use psychographic information. It is very unlikely that all people are the same in any lifestyle classification. However, the collection and knowledge of such information will enhance geodemographic information and provide insight into how to plan effective marketing strategies.

As a result of demographic, geographic and psychographic information, certain products will enjoy success in Canada in the 1990s. Profitable opportunities will exist for convenience products, upscale baby products, quality products, technology-based products used in the home, and customized products (see figure 4.8).

FIGURE 4.8   Products of the Future

| Product | Rationale |
|---|---|
| Upscale Baby Products | The baby boomers have had or are now having their own children. The more affluent of these parents can spend more on their children. Look for "posture-perfect" baby strollers, designer baby clothes, and technologically sophisticated toys. |
| "Make it Snappy" Products | The increased number of two income families means that fewer people have the time available for household chores. Tomorrow's successful products and services will reduce the time it takes to do some of these or avoid them altogether. Expect more: microwave ovens and cookware for them, built-in vacuum systems, stain resistant carpets and fabrics, snow removal, house cleaning, and gardening services, home delivery of groceries, walk in health care and dentists, mega-stores and convenience everything. Service providers will increasingly have to offer their skills when the customer wishes to buy, rather than when the vendor wants to sell. This could lead to night work for many professionals and extended hours for many retailers, perhaps even seven day shopping. |
| Quality above All Else | Canadians seem to love technologically nifty products. One trend is a shift from repeat buys of lower cost, functionally adequate items to higher cost, quality merchandise. Look for increased demand for upscale kitchen and laundry appliances, including European makes and designs; extended warranties on many consumer durables to support quality claims; look for well-built, fully equipped but smaller homes; look for the growth of luxury and exotic foods at-home and away-from-home. |
| More "Fad" and "Technology as Toy" Products | The demand for variety and novelty could result in more short life products. Expect: more introductions and subsequent discontinuations of perfumes, shampoos, cosmetics, toys, beers, candies, breakfast cereals and consumer electronics. Fads are by nature difficult to predict, but many are likely to be technologies in search of a customer, such as glow-in-the-dark chemical wands. Some old fads continue to return to a new audience — look at skateboards. Home video games are being re-introduced. Everything electronic will continue to appeal to the love for novelty. Within 10 years expect family rooms to have entertainment centres covering a wall with components such as a TV in "surround-sound" stereo, |

**FIGURE 4.8**   (continued)

| | |
|---|---|
| | with high definition, flat and square screen TV integrated with VCR's, audio equipment, digital audio tape recorders, home computers and information retrieval and dissemination systems. Before the end of the century, 3-D hologram movies could be part of the system. |
| Customized Products | Increasing fragmentation of consumer markets into smaller and smaller niches will likely lead marketers to the ultimate niche market — customized products and services. We will have come full circle from the days of the early pioneer craftsmen. For the first time since the industrial revolution, production economics of scale need not be determinants of cost. Robotic technology can make production for the custom market close to that for the mass market. Expect more: custom clothing, perfumes, shoes and programmable consumer electronics. |
| Re-emergence of Style | Convertible automobiles are making a comeback. New homes have Scarlett O'Hara staircases sweeping to the second floor. Clothing, cosmetics and hairstyles are more dramatic than a few years ago. Watch for new products that recognize style as a basis for differentiation: new design fridges, stoves and automobiles. |

*Source*:  Clarkson Gordon/Woods Gordon, *Tomorrow's Customers*, 21st Edition, 1987, p. 10. Reprinted with permission

## Behaviour Response Segmentation

**behaviour response segmentation**

**Behaviour response segmentation** is used in conjunction with other segmentation variables. It involves dividing buyers into groups according to the occasions they might have for using a product; to the benefits they require of a product; to the frequency with which they use it and to the degree of their brand loyalty.

### Occasion For Use

In the case of the occasion-for-use segmentation strategy, marketers, in order to increase the consumption of a product, show how the product can be used for various occasions. For example, advertisers show products such as milk, eggs, and orange juice being consumed at times other than their traditional mealtimes. Other products are associated with special occasions and are promoted heavily at these times. Flowers and chocolates, for example, are associated with Valentine's Day, Mother's Day, Easter, and Christmas.

### Benefits Sought

Benefit segmentation is based on the premise that different consumers try to gratify different needs when they purchase a product. For example, a car buyer may place great emphasis on either style or road-handling ability; a shampoo buyer may want conditioning or dandruff control. If the target market is rational in nature, benefits will focus on quality, price, efficiency, and dependability. If the target is influenced by emotion, different forms of presentation (sex, fear, love, status, etc.) can be used. To see the difference, consider a product such as blue jeans. An inexpensive, private-label brand purchased at a junior department store will perform the same function as a high-priced, designer label brand purchased at a high-end fashion retailer. The reason people buy one brand of jean instead of another derives from a combination of demographic (age, income, education, and occupation) and psychographic variables (activities, interests and opinions).

### Usage Rate

Frequency of use is an important segmentation variable. Marketers will conduct research to distinguish the characteristics of a heavy user from those of a medium or light user. Very often, an 80/20 rule applies, in that 80 percent of a product's sales volume comes from 20 percent of the users (heavy users). To attract more heavy users, the heavy user demographic and psychographic profile can be used to present the product. The benefits of the product are communicated in a manner that will attract those potential users. A firm may also decide to pursue medium and light users. Many more of these users would have to be attracted to the product in order to generate a level of consumption equivalent to that offered by a heavy user. Appealing to a variety of users with different backgrounds, attitudes, and lifestyles can be costly and complicate the development of marketing strategies.

### Loyalty Response

The degree of brand loyalty has an influence on segmentation strategy. As with usage rate segmentation, the marketing organization should conduct research to determine the characteristics of brand-loyal users. Strategies would then be developed to attract users with similar profiles and behaviour tendencies. From a marketing viewpoint, consideration must be given to users with varying degrees of loyalty. For example defensive activities (for defending or retaining market share) are directed at maintaining the loyalty of medium and heavy users. Distributing coupons on the package for use on the next purchase is an example of defensive activity. Offensive tactics (ones that go on the offense or attack), such as trial coupons delivered by the media, are also employed to attract new users and users of competitive brands. Because brand-switching does occur, marketers must be conscious of customers at both ends of the loyalty spectrum.

Consumers can be divided into three categories, where loyalty is concerned:[20]

1. *Brand-Loyal* These consumers gravitate consistently to the same brand or pool of brands (alternatives that are perceived to be equal in terms of quality, value, price, availability, and so on). For example, Reebok and Nike running shoes may be perceived as equal, as are candy bars such as Kit Kat, Coffee Crisp, and Crispy Crunch. A competitive product that offers superior benefits can sway the purchase decision of these consumers. For example, the image of Duracell batteries

lasting longer helps maintain loyalty; this brand is seen as being more dependable than Energizer or Eveready.

2. *Inertia Driven*    Although such consumers are brand-loyal, their loyalty is based on habit rather than reason. They don't know why they buy the same brand all the time; they simply do it. This group is hard to switch to a new product, and any attempt by marketers to create a switch requires price and promotion incentives.

3. *Brand Promiscuous*    These consumers are irrepressibly mobile. They are always switching and are up for grabs with each purchase. They, too, are influenced by price and promotion incentives, but they always look for the best deal available at the time of purchase.

# ⟩⟩⟩⟩ *Common Marketing Strategies*

Assuming that the marketing organization has identified and selected the target markets it wishes to pursue, the next decision to be made concerns the degree of coverage and activity in the various segments. This section will focus on specific segmentation strategies: market differentiation, niche marketing or market concentration, and market integration.

## Market Differentiation

market
differentiation

**Market differentiation** involves targeting several market segments with several different products and marketing plans (different marketing strategies for each product and segment). Market differentiation is often referred to as multiple segmentation, since the organization appeals to two or more distinct segments.

To understand the use of market differentiation, consider the following examples. Procter & Gamble is a large, diversified consumer-packaged-goods company that operates in many segments: household cleaning products, consumer food products, and institutional food and cleaning products, to name a few. In the consumer-cleaning-products market they dominate the laundry detergent segment with brand names such as Tide, Bold, Cheer, Gain, Era, and Ivory Snow. They market many brands in powdered and liquid forms to satisfy the different needs of the targets they pursue. A company such as Kraft General Foods Inc. dominates the coffee market in many segments (e.g., regular ground coffee, instant coffee, decaffeinated coffee, and flavoured coffee) with brands like Maxwell House, Sanka, Yuban, and Mellow Roast. They face stiff competition from Nestlé, which markets brands such as Nescafé, Taster's Choice, and Encore. Most, if not all, consumer-packaged-goods companies practice market differentiation: they are multi-product companies operating in a variety of market segments.

In the automobile market, market differentiation is also common. The three North American automakers all offer a range of products in a variety of price segments (economy to mid-price to luxury models). For example, the Ford Motor Company offers the Escort and Tracer models in the economy segment; the Taurus and Sable in the mid-price segment; and the Lincoln Continental and Lincoln Mark VII in the luxury segment. In the business equipment market, companies such as IBM, Apple Computer, and Canon pursue opportunities based on type of market. All companies gear their strategies to the needs of different segments. Strategies are tailored to the business-and-industry segment, the institutional segment, and the personal-home-use segment. Refer to figure 4.9 for an illustration of how Canon differentiates its copiers from those of competitors.

The main advantages of market differentiation are that sales are maximized by a participation in numerous segments and that profits should increase, assuming that the company has adequately differentiated its product from competitive offerings. On the risk side, the costs of differentiation can be high, since the company offers a group of product variations, operates in new distribution channels, and promotes a multitude of brands. Since financial resources for marketing are usually scarce, a

**FIGURE 4.9**  Differentiation Strategy

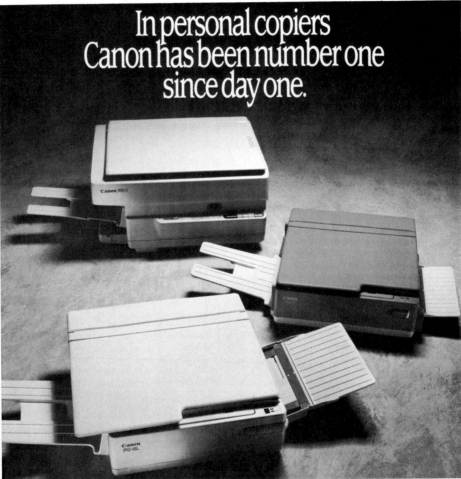

*Canon's strategy is to stress product variety for meeting diverse copying needs.*

company is generally careful and evaluates potential revenues against the costs of obtaining them, in order to ensure that adequate profits are achieved.

## Niche Marketing

niche marketing

**Niche marketing**, or market concentration, is defined as targeting a product line to one particular segment and committing all marketing resources to the satisfaction of that segment. To set the stage for a discussion of niche marketing strategies, consider the motorcycle market. Many of the large companies in the market are Japanese-based, including Honda, Suzuki, and Yamaha. All firms offer a complete line of motorcycles in a variety of price segments; they use market differentiation. In contrast, a company such as U.S.-based Harley Davidson Inc. specializes in the super-heavyweight segment (engines of 850 cubic centimetres and larger). Harley Davidson is a niche marketer, for they clearly distinguish their product by size, looks, and appearance. Unlike its Japanese competitors, which promote the high-tech look, Harley looks "tough or mean" and has the image of being made the U.S. way. As a measure of Harley Davidson's success, the company controlled 54 percent of the super-heavyweight segment in the United States in 1988. In Canada, their share is 30 percent based on sales of a ninety-dealer network nation-wide.[21]

Niche marketing is a good strategy for small companies which have limited resources, and small divisions of large companies. The segments pursued are quite small, so the key to success lies in finding opportunities that do not require large economies of scale in production and distribution. Attractive niches have the following characteristics:

1. The niche is sufficiently large and has enough purchasing power to be profitable.
2. It is of negligible interest to major competitors, so that there is little threat from these firms.
3. The firm has the required skills and resources to serve the segment effectively.
4. The firm can defend itself from an attacking competitor.

In the case of Harley Davidson, these characteristics apply. The super-heavyweight segment only represents about 5 percent of the total motorcycle market, but Harley's domination of that segment keeps competitors at bay, and provides adequate profits and marketing resources to sustain their presence. Japanese competitors are more concerned with the less serious riders so their appeal is to the mainstream motorcycle market.

Another good example of niche marketing occured in 1988, when Carling O'Keefe revived the Black Label brand. Black Label was a popular brand back in the 1950s and 1960s, but by the 1980s it had virtually disappeared from the market. Carling appealed to an upscale market using the theme "The Legend is Black". In describing the targeting strategy, Bruce McCallum, the vice-president and creative director of Palmer Bonner BCP, O'Keefe's advertising agency, stated that

> we're recognizing that our beer drinker is individualistic. This is not a large percentage of the population but its large enough to go after. It's not an age group, but a psychographic segment, a melange of people who don't want to be identified with the mainstream.[22]

To further separate Black Label from mainstream beer brands, Carling employed an innovative advertising strategy that used black and white print advertisements and fifteen-second-long black and white television commercials. For these commercials, the image was reversed so that figures appeared like photographic negatives.

To successfully implement a niche marketing strategy, an organization should consider four basic steps.[23]

### Identifying the Niche

When identifying market niches, an organization evaluates market opportunities in order to determine ways of differentiating product offerings or of finding target groups that are dissatisfied with current product or service offerings. As an example, Reed Products Inc., a New England-based company developed first aid kits for specific injuries — wounds, burns, poisonings, and eye trauma. Traditional first aid kits go for the mass market. In developing this niche Reed recognized that seventy million Americans incur serious home injuries each year and that most people do not have the right supplies available for treatment.

Other good examples of niche marketers include BMW and Jaguar in the automobile market, cars that appeal strictly to an upscale, status-conscious market segment (refer to figure 4.7). In the pizza business, Domino's Pizza avoids head-on competition from large chains such as Pizza Hut and Mother's Pizza by concentrating on home delivery only. In more general terms, some of the options available for niche marketing strategies are as follows:

1. *Customer Size Specialization*   This strategy involves tailoring efforts to small customers only, who are often neglected by larger marketing organizations.

2. *Job Specialization*   A marketer following this strategy would produce and market custom-designed products (produced according to customer specifications).

3. *Customer Specialization*   This entails producing and selling a product to only one or a few firms (e.g., private label products for supermarkets or department stores which use the store's brand names).

4. *Quality and Price Specialization*   Operating only in certain price segments (low price or high price) is the nature of this strategy. Hewlett Packard only markets expensive and sophisticated calculators.

5. *Service Specialization*   If competitive products are similar, an organization could provide additional services to distinguish itself. Banks, for example, promote services that make money available to clients during non-traditional business hours. Retail stores offer credit terms and layaway plans to encourage purchase.

### Exploiting the Niche

Once the niche is identified, the organization must decide whether to enter it. Factors considered in this decision include the threat of competition (will the idea be easy to duplicate?) and how long the new opportunity will last (will consumer preferences and tastes change quickly or will technology outdate the idea?).

Firms using a niche strategy must be able to mobilize rapidly. Otherwise, opportunities will be missed. They must be able to enter into and withdraw from a market quickly, if necessary. For example, there was tremendous demand for smoke-detectors in the late seventies and early eighties. Many firms entered the market late (too late) and suffered financially. It was the type of product where repeat purchase was not a factor.

## Expanding the Niche

Once a firm has entered a segment it must decide on ways to broaden the customer base. A company like Frito Lay continues to expand their snack food business from the original potato chip base. Today they offer a complete range of snacks, in a variety of sizes and flavours, that appeal to similar target markets. Toys 'R Us, the unique toy retailer, expanded the toy market by promoting the sale of toys year round through a new distribution system. They capitalized on changing demographics (e.g. the mini- baby boom and the higher level of disposable income among dual income parents) discussed earlier in this chapter.

## Defending the Niche

Profitable market niches do not go unnoticed by competitors. Being first into a niche does create advantage, but if competition enters, the opportunities begin to level off. Usually, a firm will defend a segment as long as the product is contributing profits; otherwise it moves to more attractive situations. Defensive strategies are developed by making shifts in the marketing mix. The firm can improve or modify the product, lower its price, seek out new channels of distribution, or experiment with new forms of advertising. As an example, Japanese car-makers, which at one time marketed only small, economy models, have gradually moved their product line upward to compete effectively with domestic manufacturers in the North American market. For a summary of the key elements of niche marketing strategies refer to figure 4.10.

**FIGURE 4.10**   Niche Marketing Strategies

| Step | Strategy |
|---|---|
| 1. Identify the Niche | Market research reveals<br>• New ways to differentiate products<br>• Dissatisfied or untapped segments<br>Concentrate on company strength and careful use of resources |
| 2. Exploit the Niche | Tactical selection of segment to enter<br>• Avoid ease of competitive entry<br>• Offer added value to differentiate<br>• Be mobile in entering or withdrawing |
| 3. Expand the Niche | Protect current position while expanding the niche<br>• Efficient use of marketing mix<br>• Expand customer base<br>• Meet changing needs<br>• New channels of distribution |
| 4. Defend the Niche | Defensive orientation in marketing mix<br>• Improve product<br>• Lower price<br>• New channels<br>Pursue new opportunities at right time |

# Market Integration

market integration

**Market integration** is an expansion from a single segment into other similar segments. Market integration is followed for several reasons:

1. The needs of consumers change; as consumers mature, their needs, attitudes, and outlooks alter.

2. New competition enters a particular segment, posing a threat to firms already there; in other words, the segment becomes more fragmented.

3. Products and markets reach the maturity stage of the product life cycle and are threatened by new technology, which brings new, innovative products.

The following developments apply to McDonald's and Burger King, the arch-rivals in the fast-food restaurant business, and show market integration at work:

1. Burger chain opens and appeals directly to children and teens.

2. Target market is expanded to include young adults, since the original target market is getting older.

3. A family restaurant concept is adopted so that the restaurant is presented as an informal place to enjoy a family meal.

4. The menu is expanded to include items that will have broader market appeal; fish, chicken, and ribs are added over a period of time.

5. The hours of operation are expanded to appeal to different users, as a result of changing demographics; late night ''drive-throughs'' are opened and breakfast menus cater to early morning travellers.

6. The restaurants appeal to a seniors segment on the basis of meal economy and social opportunity.

7. A general appeal is made to all age groups through product variety and extended hours of operation, as well as through additional services such as birthday parties and play areas. Marketing strategies for individual segments complement each other.

This example illustrates how changes in marketing occur over time. Marketing organizations realize that standing still results in competitive disadvantage and, ultimately, the demise of the product or company. In effect, market integration is a strategy that lies between market differentiation and mass marketing. It is based on the premise that one way to expand volume and market share is to appeal to users of similar products in other market segments. Such an objective usually involves using a marketing strategy that is different from the original strategy, in order to appeal to the new market targets.

The Marketing in Action vignette entitled ''What is the Blue Zone?'' illustrates many concepts discussed in this chapter, including market segmentation (particularly market integration), and the use of demographic and psychographic information and lifestyle positioning (discussed in the next section of this chapter). For a summary of commonly used marketing strategies refer to figure 4.11.

**FIGURE 4.11** Market Segmentation Continuum

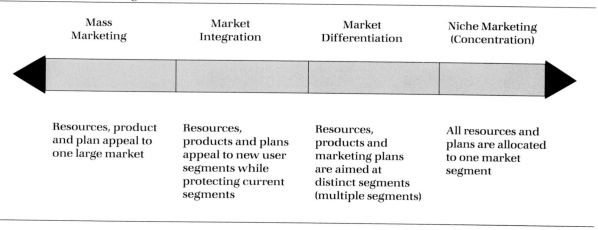

| Mass Marketing | Market Integration | Market Differentiation | Niche Marketing (Concentration) |
|---|---|---|---|
| Resources, product and plan appeal to one large market | Resources, products and plans appeal to new user segments while protecting current segments | Resources, products and marketing plans are aimed at distinct segments (multiple segments) | All resources and plans are allocated to one market segment |

## >>>> MARKETING IN ACTION

### WHAT IS THE BLUE ZONE?

In a market worth more than $2 billion, the Big Two beer-makers are locked in constant market warfare. Their goal is to expand market share in a market showing few signs of real growth. One of the most interesting maneuvers in the beer market in recent years has been the strategy used to market Labatt's Blue, Canada's market leader.

#### Canada's Top 5 Beer Brands

| | | |
|---|---|---|
| 1. | Labatt's Blue | 18% |
| 2. | Molson Canadian | 12 |
| 3. | Coors/Coors Light | 8 |
| 4. | Molson Export | 7 |
| 5. | Miller/Miller Light | 5 |

*Source:* "Financial Post estimates", *Financial Post*, August 1, 1988, p.11.

Blue represents enormous business opportunities for Labatt's. The brand has an image of quality and tradition; it is an established leader in terms of consumers' awareness and acceptance; it appeals to a wide range of beer consumers, and it enjoys a high level of marketing support and commitment from company management.

The question, then, is why Labatt's would launch a very contemporary campaign called the "Blue Zone" to run concurrently with the "Call for the Blue" mainstream campaign. Let's examine the situation in more detail. As an established brand, Blue had strong appeal with older age groups (thirties and forties) yet weaker appeal with the young adult segment (19–24 years old). Also, Blue was facing stiff competition from brands like Canadian, Export, and Coors (Molson brands), whose images were being changed as a result of advertising strategies directed at the young adult target market.

One way for a company to build overall market share for a brand is to protect current business while pursuing new targets. At risk in this situation is some of the existing business, since it is usually given less attention, but the company hopes that the new business will compensate, and net gains will occur. This was the game plan for Labatt's Blue.

Marketing research indicated that the young adult segment (19–24 years old) perceived Blue to be becoming older and less exciting than other more targeted brand alternatives. It was the type of beer that their dads would drink. Capturing the interest of the young adult beer consumer, so

Labatt Brewing Company Ltd.

*Example of a "Blue Zone" advertisement used in the Labatt's campaign*

Given these trends and the competitive situation, the management responsible for Blue developed a marketing strategy to "re-energize" the brand. The result was the "Blue Zone", a curiosity campaign aimed at the young adult segment. Advertising copy encouraged consumers to enter the Blue Zone "someplace close . . . sometime soon". But what was the Blue Zone? According to Blue brand manager David Kincaid, it's a state of mind that will remain undefined. Research indicated that people had different interpretations for the Blue Zone. Some thought it was the ultimate party while others thought it was a quiet evening with someone special. Regardless, it was the difference in interpretation that provided the impetus for the campaign.

The Blue Zone strategy built upon Blue's existing strengths (consumers' perception of the beer's quality, dependability and tradition) as it complemented the mainstream "Call for the Blue" campaign, while presenting a fresh new approach that appealed to the young adult segment. The Blue Zone, and the mystery that surrounds it, demonstrates that Labatt's understands the needs and attitudes of the young adult beer consumer. Marketing activities were tailored to the needs and priorities shared by the target market: to have fun, to cut loose periodically, to be adventurous and take safe risks, and to live for the moment.

The use of a dual marketing strategy for Blue is unique and innovative, but the ultimate success of it rests with the consumer. Some critics see the dual message as confusing, and possibly it will alienate some current users. Others view it as a new approach offering tremendous advantage. Successful, multi-faceted positioning strategies for existing products can save a company the considerable sums of money that would be needed to research, develop and launch a new product for each one of the target segments. Perhaps the innovative approach by Labatt's Blue will be the wave of the future. Initial results are proving promising.

*Source:* Personal interview with Mr. David Kincaid, Brand Manager, Labatt's Breweries Limited, December 2, 1988.

that the brand could evolve with the target market as its members matured, became important to the marketers of Blue. If efforts were not directed at attracting these new consumers while they were in a trial stage (experimenting with a variety of brand alternatives), long-term market share erosion could occur. The following facts demonstrate the importance of the young adult segment to the beer market:

1. Young male adults account for almost one-third of the total male consumption of beer.

2. Per capita consumption among young male adults is 14.5 bottles per week compared to 10 per week for the average male; that is, the young adult male consumes almost 50 percent more than the average beer consumer.

3. This age group (19–24 years old) is a trend setter that influences brand trial and acceptance.

# ⟩⟩⟩⟩ *Market Positioning Concepts*

positioning

**Positioning** can be defined as the creation of appropriate marketing appeals, which make a product, service, or company desirable in the minds of customers. Positioning is frequent in today's marketing activity because of the increasing level of competition. It involves designing and marketing a product to a target market in such a way that it will be distinguished from the competition. The manner by which a product is distinguished will have an effect on buyer's perceptions of the product and on the position it occupies in the buyer's mind. Therefore, positioning is a means of segmenting a market in two different ways:

1. Designing and marketing a product to meet the needs of a target market.
2. Creating the appropriate appeals to make the product stand out in the minds of the target market (through marketing mix activity).

Positioning is concerned with matching the product to the needs of the target market. The matching process involves an assessment of competitive marketing activity to determine opportunities worth pursuing. In figure 4.12 a market is analyzed on the basis of the value offered consumers — the relationship between price

**FIGURE 4.12**   Market Positioning Grid

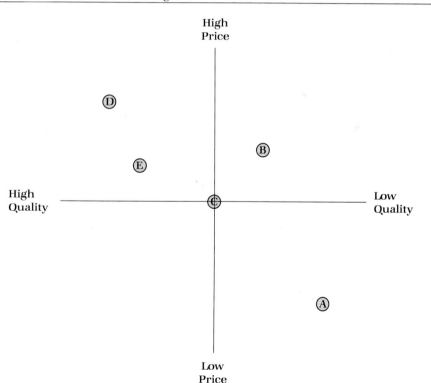

Knowing that price and quality are important factors to consumers, Brand E perceives an opportunity to market a high quality product at a more reasonable price than its competition.

and quality. The assumption in the figure is that price and quality are important factors in the purchase decision and that four competing brands exist on the market:

1. Brand A — low price, low quality
2. Brand B — high price for quality offered
3. Brand C — medium price and quality
4. Brand D — high price, high quality

A fifth competitor (Brand E) is considering entering the market. Among a variety of options available, Brand E could either locate on the grid to compete directly with an existing competitor, or locate to appeal to a different segment. As shown in figure 4.12, Brand E is positioned to appeal to a segment demanding higher quality at a reasonable price. In this case the firm would sacrifice its profit margin on each unit sold, since it is more costly to manufacture and market a product for this market segment. However, if marketing mix activity is effective in communicating the value offered, higher unit volume is generated and compensates for lower profit margins. Such are the decisions of business.

# Types of Positioning

## Head-On Positioning

In head-on positioning, one brand is presented as equal to or better than another brand. This strategy is usually initiated by the number two brand in the market. The strategy is to show people who declare they regularly use one brand actually choosing another product. The best example of this strategy was the Pepsi Challenge used in the 1980s. In Pepsi-Cola advertising, Coke drinkers were shown indicating a preference for the taste of Pepsi in blind-folded taste tests of both products. Burger King also experimented with this strategy when it stressed the consumer's preferring the flame-broiled burgers available at its outlets over the fried burgers available at McDonald's.

Head-on positioning requires financial commitment, since the brand leader is likely to react with increased marketing spending. A direct counterattack by the brand leader is unlikely, as it prefers to let its number one position and product benefits work for it. In effect such a company uses brand dominance positioning.

## Brand Dominance Positioning

Brands that are market leaders can utilize their market share position to help position themselves in the minds of consumers. Marketing communications are designed to clearly state that the product is successful, a market leader, and highly acceptable to a majority of users. The Coca-Cola advertising campaigns, centering on themes such as "Coke is It" and "It's the Real Thing", are examples of brand dominance communications.

## Product Differentiation

**product differentiation**

**Product differentiation** is a strategy that focuses on the unique attributes or benefits of a product — those features that distinguish one brand from its competitors. The Seven-Up "Un-Cola" advertising campaign is a classic illustration of product differentiation. In this campaign, Seven-Up was presented as a clear, crisp, refreshing alternative to the dominant cola brands. Seven-Up was attacking the perceived weakness in cola products — the presence of caffeine. A brand of toothpaste might be differentiated on the basis of its ability to prevent cavities, freshen breath, whiten teeth, or perhaps perform several or all of these functions. A company might claim for its brand of detergent equal performance with higher-priced brands while focusing on price as its differential advantage. Figure 4.9 shows how Canon copiers are differentiated from competitive offerings.

### Technical Innovation Positioning

Technical innovation is more important for a company as a whole than for individual products. Companies seeking to instill an image of continued technical leadership will use this strategy to position themselves as representing the leading edge of technology. Such a position, if firmly established in the minds of customers, will benefit new products when they are introduced to the market. Dofasco Inc. is an example of a company using this strategy (refer to figure 4.13 on page 118).

### Lifestyle Positioning

In crowded markets where product attributes are perceived as similar by the target market, firms must look for alternate ways of positioning their products. The addition of psychographic information has allowed marketers to develop marketing communications based on the lifestyle of the target market. Essentially, the product is positioned to "fit in" or match the lifestyle of the user. The Jaguar advertisement that appears in figure 4.14 on page 119 is a good illustration of lifestyle advertising. The ad visually demonstrates how Jaguar is a natural part of the contemporary lifestyle of an upscale, urban couple. The copy in the advertisement provides a more rational presentation, focusing on the quality and tradition that the target market has come to expect from Jaguar.

Generally, lifestyle positioning uses emotional appeals such as love, fear, sex, and humour. An example of lifestyle positioning is the Chanel No. 5 commercial that shows a sunbathing woman at one end of a swimming pool and an imaginary man at the other end who lunges into the pool and then steps out toward the woman. Their slogan, "Share the Fantasy", is meant to pique the imaginations of potential customers.

## Repositioning

**repositioning**

In a competitive marketplace, marketing organizations must be ready to alter their positioning strategies. It is unrealistic to assume that the positioning strategy that is adopted initially will be appropriate throughout the life cycle of a product. Therefore, products will be repositioned based on the prevailing environment in the marketplace. **Repositioning** is defined as changing the place that a product occupies in the consumer's mind in relation to competitive products. The need to reposition occurs for two primary reasons. First, the marketing activity of a direct competitor may change, and, second, the changing preferences of the target market will cause a product to adapt.

**FIGURE 4.13**   Meeting Customer Needs through Technological Leadership

**FIGURE 4.14**   Positioning to the Lifestyles of Bold Achievers

## The Jaguar V12 XJ-S Convertible
## An elegant new perspective.

With its finely crafted soft top retracted, it is a beautiful, open-air, two-passenger, masterpiece of automotive excitement and artistry. Activate the electronic roof control, and it is instantly, smoothly transformed into a magnificent sports coupe. It is the elegant new Jaguar XJ-S Convertible, and it is an automobile whose appeal extends far beyond its manifest physical beauty.

Above all else, the Jaguar Convertible is an uncompromising performance machine. Beneath its gracefully sloping hood, it is endowed with Jaguar's advanced 5.3 litre, 12-cylinder May head engine. Modified for racing, this V12 engine powered the TWR Jaguar Racing Team to victory in the world's two most demanding races: the grueling 24 Hours of Le Mans, and the equally arduous 24 Hours of Daytona.

Settle in behind the wheel. Turn the key and this intrepid power plant springs to life with a seductive purr that only hints at its vast reserve of controlled power. On the road, the suspicion can be quickly confirmed.

Jaguar engineered, road and race-proven handling systems offer precise control under the most adverse driving conditions. Four-wheel independent suspension, with anti-dive geometry, minimizes dive on acceleration and braking. A sophisticated anti-lock braking system (ABS) greatly reduces skid potential, even when opposing wheels are positioned on different road surfaces. In every aspect of its performance, it reacts with the controlled power and refined grace of a feline thoroughbred in full stride.

Within the driver and passenger compartment, gracious comfort reigns supreme. Uncluttered elegance is enhanced by the supple richness of matched leather, and the elegant warmth of hand-polished burl walnut veneers. Virtually every creature-comfort amenity is, as you would expect, standard. At around $85,000, it is, without question, a worthy investment for an automobile destined to become a timeless classic.

For more information, contact your nearest Jaguar dealer. Or, if you choose, send your business card to Jaguar Canada Inc., Indell Lane, Bramalea, Ontario, L6T 4H3.

**JAGUAR**
A BLENDING OF ART AND MACHINE

### *Reacting to Competitive Activity*

This situation is best explained by an example. When, in April, 1985, Coca-Cola stunned the competing soft drink manufacturers, its own bottlers, and its consumers by altering its formula for making the cola, Coca-Cola was trying to reposition its flagship brand as a slightly sweeter, less filling soft drink. The company decided to do so in the United States (Canada followed shortly thereafter) when it realized that its share of supermarket sales was slightly behind that of Pepsi-Cola. The new formula was extensively tested among consumers, and was preferred over the original Coca-Cola and Pepsi-Cola. However, by July of 1985, the company announced the return of the original product as Coca-Cola Classic. The episode shows a company, in reaction to the competition, attempting to reposition its product, but in this case failing. As mentioned earlier, the company underestimated consumers' emotional attachment to the original product. The market dictated that the company alter its strategy again.

### *Reacting to Changing Consumer Preference*

Analyzing consumer trends leads to repositioning strategies. The demographic trends discussed earlier in the chapter are the major influences on strategy change. To illustrate, the trend towards eating more meals out of the home is a boon for restaurants such as McDonald's, Burger King, and Wendy's. However, as consumers become bored with the hamburger and other established food items offered at these restaurants, they seek out other alternatives such as chicken and pizza. To protect business, restaurants like McDonald's are constantly under pressure to test new products and expand menus to remain competitive (refer back to the discussion on market integration). Changes in positioning, then, come out of demographic and psychographic shifts in the market that companies must analyze continuously.

## ⟩⟩⟩⟩ S U M M A R Y

This chapter discussed the key concepts associated with marketing strategy and market segmentation. A market was defined as a group of people having a similar need for a product or service, the resources required to purchase the product or service, and the willingness to buy it.

In terms of market segmentation, organizations must identify their target markets as precisely as possible. They do so by making good use of information provided by demographics (age, sex, income, education, occupation, and so on), geographics (regional location and location within a region), and psychographics (activities, interests and opinions). The organization will constantly monitor trends in these areas so that they can adapt their marketing strategies accordingly.

Behaviour response segmentation is another variable which can be used to develop more effective marketing strategies. This type of segmentation deals with the occasions consumers have for using a product, the benefits sought by consumers from a product, the frequency with which they use it, and the degree of their loyalty to a particular brand. Once the organization has identified and selected the target markets to pursue, it must decide on what degree of coverage and activity there should be in each segment. They can choose between mass marketing and the various types of market segmentation strategies, which include product differentiation, niche marketing, and market integration. Any combination of strategies could be used, and such combinations are common in larger organizations that operate in many different types of markets.

Positioning involves designing a product or service to meet the needs of a target market, and then creating the appropriate marketing appeals so that the product stands out in the minds of consumers. Some common positioning strategies include head-on comparisons with competitors, product differentiation, technical innovation, brand dominance, and lifestyle approaches. As a product matures, factors such as competitive activity and changing consumer preferences force re-evaluation of positioning strategies.

## >>>> KEY TERMS

market
consumer goods
industrial goods
business goods
mass marketing
market segmentation
demographic segmentation

grey market
geographic segmentation
geodemographics
micro-marketing
psychographic segmentation
behaviour response segmentation

market differentiation
niche marketing
market integration
positioning
product differentiation
repositioning

## >>>> REVIEW AND DISCUSSION QUESTIONS

**1.** Identify the four characteristics that must be present for a market to exist.

**2.** Is mass marketing an appropriate strategy in today's competitive marketplace?

**3.** What is the difference between demographic segmentation, geographic segmentation, and psychographic segmentation?

**4.** Explain why it is important for marketing organizations to monitor demographic trends in Canada.

**5.** Is it appropriate in today's marketing environment to use a common national marketing strategy ? Discuss.

**6.** Briefly explain the difference between market differentiation and market integration.

**7.** Cite some examples of niche marketers in your local community. What are the risks associated with being a niche marketer?

**8.** Explain the relevance of positioning and repositioning in marketing practice.

**9.** "To succeed in the future, products and services must be repositioned to appeal to older target markets". Comment on the implications of this statement.

**10.** Can one product be successfully positioned to be attractive to several different target markets? Discuss and provide examples to verify your position.

**11.** "The value of lifestyle marketing communications is questionable, as little is actually stated about the product". Evaluate the validity of this statement, using examples of your own choice.

## ›››› R E F E R E N C E S

1. CLARKSON GORDON/WOODS GORDON, *Tomorrow's Customers in Canada*, 20th Edition, 1985, p.2.

2. *Ibid.*

3. "The Summer Beer Battle", *Financial Post*, August 1, 1988, p.11.

4. Information provided by London Life Insurance Company, London, Ontario.

5. GAYLE MACDONALD, "Older Market Gives Developers a New Niche", *Financial Post*, August 29, 1988, p. 47.

6. Statistics Canada, *Canadian Social Trends*, Autumn Issue, 1988, p.15.

7. CLARKSON GORDON/WOODS GORDON, Tomorrow's Customers, 21st Edition, 1987, p.8.

8. MARGARET BREAM, "It's Sugar and Spice and Four on the Floor", *Marketing*, May 9, 1988, pp. 39-40.

9. *Ibid.*

10. "BMW Changes Its Approach to Female Market", *Marketing*, September 8, 1986, p.8.

11. CLARKSON GORDON/WOODS GORDON, Tomorrow's Customers in Canada, 21st Edition, p.5.

12. Statistics Canada, *Canada Year Book 1988* (Ottawa: Supply and Services Canada, 1987, Cat. No. 11-402E/ 1987), p.2-7.

13. *Ibid.*

14. Statistics Canada, "Common Law Unions", *Canadian Social Trends*, Autumn 1988.

15. CLARKSON GORDON/WOODS GORDON, *Tomorrow's Customers*, 21st Edition, p.7.

16. Statistics Canada, *Canada Year Book 1988*, p.2-3.

17. IAN PEARSON, "Social Studies", *Canadian Business*, December 1985, pp. 69-70.

18. ELLIOTT ETTENBERG, "Psychographics: The art of finding out why, not just who", *Sales & Marketing Management in Canada*.

19. PEARSON, "Social Studies", p.70.

20. MARION CHANKOWSKY, "Segmentation strategy will get you around the promotion clutter", *Marketing*, October 3, 1988, pp.22-24.

21. COLIN LANGUEDOC, "The thunder of a big Harley has mystique", *Financial Post*, August 15, 1988, p.18.

22. JIM McELGUNN, "Black Label acquires certain cachet", *Marketing*, June 27, 1988, p.12.

23. ALLAN J. MAGRATH, "Niche marketing: Finding a Safe, Warm Cave", *Sales & Marketing Management in Canada*, May 1987, p.40.

# C H A P T E R 5 ›››››

# Marketing Research

Since a considerable amount of money is invested in the design, development, and marketing of goods and services, a marketing organization is very concerned about protecting its investment. In addition, its desire to remain competitive and be knowledgeable about changing consumers' needs makes it necessary to collect appropriate information, before and after critical decisions are made. Past experience and intuitive judgement are not sufficient to carry an organization through the 1990s. Carefully planned marketing research is the tool that provides organizations with the insight necessary to take advantage of new opportunities. This chapter will discuss the marketing research process and the impact it has on marketing planning and business decision-making.

## ⟩⟩⟩ *Marketing Research: Role and Scope*

Research provides an organization with information. It does not guarantee that proper decisions and actions by the firm will result from the research information. The old saying that "some information is better than no information" puts the role of marketing research into perspective. A vital marketing tool, it is used to help reduce or eliminate the uncertainty associated with making business decisions. Simply put, reliable research data reduces the risk for the manager who is responsible for making a key decision.

**marketing research**

The American Marketing Association defines **marketing research** as[1]

> the function which links the consumer, customer, and public to the marketer through information — information used to define marketing opportunities and problems; generate, refine, and evaluate marketing actions; monitor marketing performance and improve understanding of marketing as a process.
>
> Marketing research specifies the information required to address these issues; designs the method for collecting information; manages and implements the information collection process; analyzes the results; and communicates the findings and their implications.

This chapter will discuss the key components of this definition.

### The Scope of Marketing Research

Marketing research focuses on markets and the marketing mix (product, price, promotion, and place). Refer to the Marketing in Action vignette "Wendy's Big Classic" for an illustration of how Wendy's used marketing research in designing a new product. Regardless of the nature of the research study, the information obtained will assist managers in their decision-making. Figure 5.1 provides a list showing the scope of marketing research activity.

## ⟩⟩⟩ *MARKETING IN ACTION*

### *WENDY'S BIG CLASSIC*

In preparation for the launch of a new hamburger in 1986, Wendy's (U.S.) invested $1 million in taste tests. The goal was to develop the right product mix to satisfy American palates. What research was conducted? Taste tests were conducted with 5 200 people in six different cities. The company tested:

1. Nine different buns (hard and soft, square and round, seeds and seedless, warm and cold).

*Wendy's "Big Classic"*

Wendy's Restaurants of Canada Inc.

FIGURE 5.1    Some Typical Applications of Marketing Research

### Markets

- Forecasting demand for goods and services
- Identifying target markets
- Identifying new product needs
- Trend information and analysis (e.g., economic trends influencing marketing activity)

### Products

- Testing new product concepts; products
- Comparative product tests
- Package design evaluation
- Product changes (e.g., new varieties, formula changes)

### Prices

- Alternate pricing strategies
- Price/value analysis
- Effect of price increases on users

### Promotions

- Sales territory analysis
- Advertising effectiveness (motivation and intent to purchase)
- Media selection evaluations
- Testing message alternatives
- Evaluating sales promotion alternatives

### Place

- Site and location analysis
- Evaluation of transportation alternatives
- Test markets
- Inventory analysis

---

2. Forty different sauces.
3. Three types of lettuce (chopped, shredded and leaf).
4. Four different containers in ten different colours.
5. Five hundred names, including the Hunk, the Chief, the XL, the Hot 'n Juicy, and the Max.

The final product that emerged was a square beef patty, topped with leaf lettuce, two tomato slices, raw onion rings, dill pickles, ketchup, and mayonnaise on a corn-dusted, hearth-baked kaiser bun. The burger is packaged in an almond-coloured styrofoam box with a dome sculpture resembling the bun's top. Oh yes, the name was the "Big Classic"! Are you hungry?

Adapted from "Hamburger the winner in $1 million taste test", *Toronto Star*, September 21, 1986, p.B2.

# Acquiring Information

Essentially, there are three broad categories of research: basic research, applied research, and fact gathering.

**basic research**

1. **Basic Research** is often referred to as true research. It is research undertaken to simply develop new knowledge and discover new information. The discovery of a cold nuclear fusion process resulted from basic research, since the process was investigated without consideration of any specific application.

**applied research**

2. **Applied Research** refers to the undertaking of research to resolve a specific problem. In effect, this type of research has a sense of direction and list of objectives it must achieve. Marketing organizations practice applied research. For example, firms conduct research to find out what factors are contributing to declines in market share or in sales volume.

---

## ❯❯❯❯ *MARKETING IN ACTION*

### *A FEW WORDS ABOUT JAPANESE RESEARCH*

When Sony researched the market for a lightweight, portable cassette player, results showed that consumers wouldn't buy a tape player that didn't record. Company chairman Akio Morita introduced the Walkman anyway, and the rest is history. Today it's one of Sony's most successful products.

The Japanese question why North American companies do so much consumer research, when so much information is readily available by simply visiting and consulting with retailers, free information at that. While the Japanese do some research, they have a tendency to trust their instincts when making big decisions. In this regard, they rely on two types of data: soft data, which are based on visits to retailers, and hard data, which consist of company shipment reports and inventory levels. This data is the true reflection of the prevailing consumer behaviour.

When the Japanese do conduct consumer research they interview people who have bought the product, or a product like the one under review. When Toyota wanted to learn what North American car buyers preferred about small cars, they talked to Volkswagen owners about their likes and dislikes. Volkswagen of Germany was the leading foreign seller of small cars in North America at the time.

*One of Sony's most successful products. Sony is a registered trademark of Sony Corporation Tokyo, Japan*

Photo courtesy of Sony of Canada Ltd.

In contrast to North American companies, the Japanese do not scrutinize an undifferentiated mass public to learn about general attitudes and values. The Japanese focus on real situations as they are occurring, and they react quickly to meet market expectations. In the markets for cars, audio equipment, cameras, video equipment, and many others, they have been quite successful using this approach.

Adapted from K. Johannson and Ikijuro Nonaka, "Market research the Japanese way," *Harvard Business Review*, May–June 1987, pp.16-18.

fact gathering

3. **Fact Gathering** concerns the compilation of already discovered data, originally published for reasons that have nothing to do with the specific problem under investigation by a particular researcher. For example, a market planner will consult reference materials on the impact of price increases on sales volume. Such information is considered when a price increase is being contemplated.

Marketing executives combine these approaches in the acquisition of information. Rare are the days now when executives make million-dollar decisions based simply on subjective analysis, or on their feelings, intuitions, and hunches. Such decisions lack substantiation and are criticized by other executives if they lead to failure. Yet sometimes the unscientific approach is still followed. For an alternate viewpoint on this topic, consult the Marketing in Action vignette "A Few Words about Japanese Research".

Prudent marketing decision-makers combine their intuition and the judgement they have derived from experience with all other information sources available. They will use the scientific method, which implies that the data generated is reliable, to confirm or reject their own beliefs. The key elements of the scientific method are that

1. Awareness of a problem is reached through exploratory investigations.
2. Proper information sources and methodologies of collecting information are delineated.
3. Alternate solutions are thoroughly evaluated.
4. Data is properly analyzed and interpreted.
5. Specific actions taken are based on research findings.

# ⟩⟩⟩⟩ *Types of Marketing Research*

## Exploratory Research

exploratory
research

**Exploratory research** serves to clarify the nature of a problem. It is meant to pinpoint or describe the problem through informal investigations, so that the right type and methods of primary research can be undertaken to resolve it.

## Descriptive Research

descriptive
research

**Descriptive research** is undertaken for the purpose of identifying the characteristics of consumer groups, that is, to identify the demographic, psychographic, and geographic characteristics of a target market.

## Performance Evaluation

performance
evaluation

**Performance evaluation** acts as a control mechanism, for it determines the effectiveness of marketing strategy or marketing mix activity. For example, a company may decide to test its television commercials to determine their impact on the target market. Depending on the results, the company could discontinue, modify, or continue the use of these messages.

### Causal Research

**causal research**

**Causal research** is conducted to determine cause-and-effect relationships. For example, if price is reduced to a certain level, what will be the corresponding effect on sales? The company could change any of its marketing mix variables in a test situation and leave other variables constant. Theoretically, different mix options could be tested in different markets to determine which mix would be most effective for use on a larger scale, either regionally or nationally.

## ⟩⟩⟩ *The Marketing Research Process: Problem Awareness*

The research process is a systematic one with many steps: problem awareness, exploratory research, secondary data collection, primary research, data transfer and processing, data analysis and interpretation, and recommendations (see figure 5.2). In the problem awareness stage an attempt is made to specify the nature of the difficulty. Many practitioners of marketing research state that the proper identification of a problem is the first step in finding its solution. Therefore, it is essential that a problem be precisely defined. After all, a business organization does not want to waste valuable time and money collecting information that will not lead to action. Defining a **problem** involves developing a clearly-worded statement that provides direction regarding the topic to be investigated.

## ⟩⟩⟩ *Exploratory Research*

Exploratory research is research that helps define the precise nature of a problem through the use of informal analysis. This informal analysis is often referred to as the

**funnelling**

funnelling process. **Funnelling** is the process of narrowing a subject into manageable variables so that specifically directed research can be conducted. Funnelling is

**situation analysis**

accomplished by means of a thorough **situation analysis**. For such analysis, the researcher collects information from knowledgeable people inside and outside the organization and from secondary sources. Many variables are analyzed as potential problem areas, and through the funnelling process areas that appear to be unrelated are eliminated.

To illustrate exploratory research and the funnelling process, let us assume that market share for a product is declining. Finding the cause of the decline would be to identify the problem. Identifying the true nature of the problem is the task of exploratory research. In order to find the problem, the researcher investigates a number of matters: advertising strategies, pricing strategies, product quality, availability and distribution, and any other marketing mix element. As this analysis

**FIGURE 5.2**   Marketing Research Process

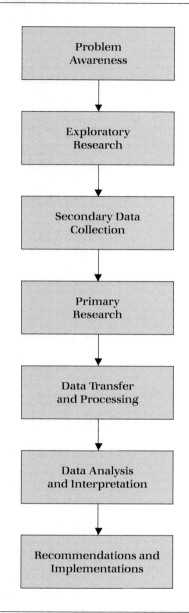

unfolds, it should become apparent which elements are contributing to the market share decline.

This process is needed because, when research is initiated, a problem of a general nature is usually presented. But if primary research is needed, that is, if the problem is not resolved through secondary research, it can only be conducted if problems are specific in nature or narrow in scope. The exploratory process narrows the scope of the problem until a resolvable problem is arrived at, or until purposeful primary research can be conducted. The results of exploratory research can be used to ensure

**FIGURE 5.3    Exploratory Research**

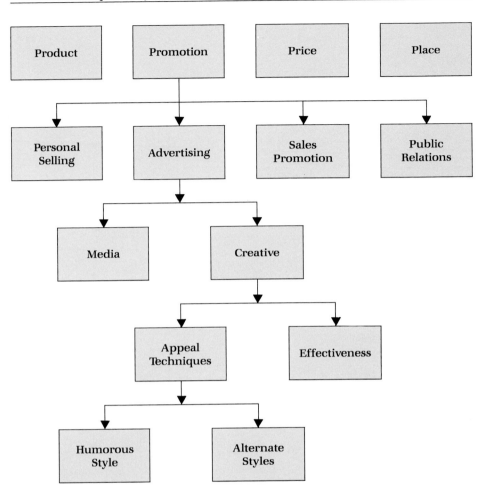

The purpose of exploratory research is to narrow the scope of investigation until a specific problem is identified. In this case, the problem concerns styles of advertising. Research would, therefore, be undertaken on such styles.

that the general description of the problem contains no false assumptions. Refer to figure 5.3 for a diagram of the exploratory research process. When considering this diagram, assume that the sales of a product are declining. Finding out why there is a decline would be to determine the problem. According to the diagram, the company could follow several routes in order to pinpoint the problem. The isolation of a "creative" problem in this illustration (a problem dealing with the advertising message) assumes that other areas have been evaluated, at least informally, and rejected as the source of the problem.

Sometimes the problem is both pinpointed and resolved through discussions held with people knowledgeable in the area of concern or through the collection and consideration of secondary data. Given the declining sales situation, numerous people could be consulted. Reliable sources would include product managers (who are probably responsible for the entire investigation), sales managers, distribution managers, wholesalers and retailers, advertising agency personnel, and whomever else may be relevant.

## 〉〉〉〉 *Secondary Data Collection*

secondary data

**Secondary data** is data which has been compiled and published for purposes unrelated to the specific problem under investigation. It is available from both internal and external sources (see figure 5.4) and is used by marketing organizations to identify those demographic, economic, and social trends that affect marketing strategy. It also is used to profile consumer and business market segments.

**FIGURE 5.4** Secondary Data Sources

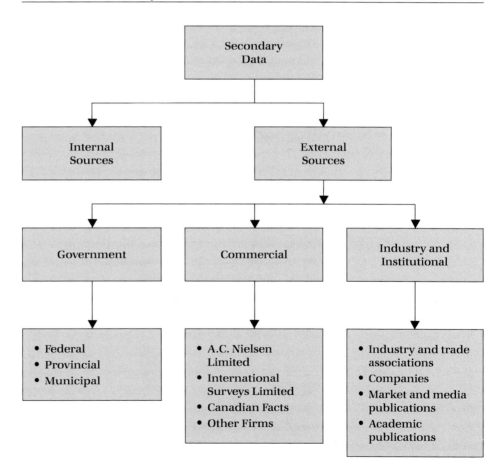

## Internal Data Sources

Internal data sources are those that are available within the organization. Certain information may be computerized and easily accessible to the manager who requires it. Such information includes sales analysis reports (e.g. sales by region, nation, customer, or product), inventory analysis, production reports, cost analysis, marketing budgets (e.g. actual spending versus planned spending), profit and loss statements, accounts receivables and payables. This information is usually compiled on a continuous basis for use in the planning and decision-making process. Refer to the discussion on marketing information systems, which appears later in this chapter, for more details.

## External Data Sources

An organization refers to external sources when internal information does not resolve the problem at hand. The primary sources of external data are governments, business, and academia.

Federal, provincial, and municipal governments have an abundance of information that marketing organizations can examine. The major source of government information is Statistics Canada (see chapter 4 for numerous data illustrations), which provides census information (population and household trends, income, education, and occupation trends), and information on all aspects of the economy (employment, inflation, interest rates, domestic production, international trade, to name a few). At the federal and provincial levels, the department or ministry involved with industry, trade, and commerce is the most common source of business information.

Basic data can also be obtained from a variety of commercial sources:

1. *Newspapers and Business Periodicals*   These focus specifically on business and commerce and include publications such as *The Globe and Mail*'s "Report on Business" and *Report on Business Magazine, Canadian Business, Financial Times of Canada, Financial Post* and the *Financial Post Moneywise* magazine.

2. *Handbooks and Surveys*   These sources usually provide information on consumer income and expenditures, employment, occupation and other relevant demographic data. Sources include *The Handbook of Canadian Consumer Markets* published by the Conference Board in Canada and the *Financial Post Survey of Markets*.

3. *Other Surveys and Directories*   A variety of information is included in this category, including company history and financial information, surveys on various industry sectors, and annual reports published by publicly-held companies. Specific examples include the series of *Financial Post* surveys which cover the industrial, oil, mining and investment industries. Dun and Bradstreet provides financial and credit information on businesses operating in Canada. Trade directories such as the *Canadian Key Business Directory, Canadian Trade Index,* and *Fraser's Canadian Trade Directory* provide statistical information and classification of companies by industry and by type of product manufactured.

4. *Industry and Trade Journals*   Most Canadian industries have a trade journal

which provides information on a particular industry. In the grocery trade, journals such as *Canadian Grocer, Food Store Magazine* and *L'épecier* provide information. In the aviation industry information is obtained from *Aerospace Canada, Aviation Trade* and *Canadian Aviation*. Typically, such journals contain industry trend information and articles on topical issues affecting the industry.

5. *Commercial Research Houses*   These firms conduct periodic and ongoing studies that are helpful to marketing organizations. The cost of obtaining information from these sources can be high, depending on the nature of the information. Information in this category is usually purchased on a subscription (contract) basis. Since other firms, including competitors, have access to the same information, the costs are shared by all purchasers and so are kept reasonable. A.C. Nielsen, a very large research company owned by Dun and Bradstreet, is an example of a company that sells information on a subscription basis. Their consumer index provides manufacturers of consumer packaged goods with information regarding market share trends, sales volume, inventory, distribution, pricing, media expenditures, and other variables. Their television index provides relevant data on viewing trends (e.g what the public watches, how long do they watch, etc.). Numerous other research services are provided by A.C. Nielsen.

6. *Industry Associations*   Associations serve as the promotion arm of particular industries and provide useful information to marketing organizations. To illustrate, Canadian media consumption data (data that shows the public's level of exposure to the different media) is available from associations such as the Television Bureau, the Radio Bureau of Canada, the Audit Bureau of Circulations, the Newspaper Marketing Bureau, and the Canadian Outdoor Measurement Bureau. Information available from these sources shows that they are effective in reaching the Canadian consumer. Such information is useful when an organization is developing advertising strategy.

## Advantages and Disadvantages of Secondary Data

Secondary data offers the marketing organization the following advantages:

1. Information from these sources is inexpensive or available at no cost. For information purchased on a contract basis, that is, purchased on a continuous basis, there are economies of scale, since costs are shared by many companies wanting the same information.
2. The information is readily available and regularly updated, often annually or monthly, or, as in the case of the government census data, every five years.
3. Very often, secondary sources are the only sources for certain kinds of information; data on birth rates are available only through the federal government census.
4. The information is useful for analyzing a situation in the exploratory research phase, so that problems can be pinpointed.

Some of the disadvantages of secondary data follow:

1. The data does not usually resolve a specific problem, due to such factors as incompleteness or false assumptions made in the collection of such data.

2. Since many research projects are not repeated, the reliability and accuracy of their data are questionable. The data was compiled originally for a situation that may not apply to the current problem under investigation. Also, the data could be incomplete.

3. If the information is outdated, its use in a rapidly changing marketplace is not practical.

For a summary of the pros and cons of secondary research refer to figure 5.5.

---

**FIGURE 5.5**    Secondary Data

---

### Advantages

1. Information is inexpensive or obtainable at no cost
2. Information is readily available
3. Possibly the only source of information (e.g., census data)
4. Useful in exploratory research stage where information is assessed to identify a problem area

### Disadvantages

1. The data does not resolve the specific problem under investigation (e.g., data was compiled for another problem or purpose)
2. Reliability and accuracy of data is questionable
3. Information can be outdated, even obsolete for the intended situation

---

## ⟩⟩⟩⟩ *Primary Research*

### Objectives and Hypotheses

**primary research**

If a problem has not been resolved by the previous steps, the research process moves to another stage: the collection of primary data. **Primary research** refers to the process of collecting and recording new data, called primary data, in order to resolve a specific problem, usually at high cost to the sponsoring organization. Primary research is custom-designed, with the focus on resolving a particular question or obtaining specified information. A procedure is developed and a research instrument designed to perform the specific task. In directing the primary research, the marketing organization identifies the precise nature of the problem, the objectives of the study, and the hypotheses associated with it. **Research objectives** are

**research objectives**
**hypotheses**

statements that outline what the research is to accomplish, while **hypotheses**, which are statements of predicted outcomes, are confirmed or refuted by the data collected. The outcomes of the research often lead to certain actions by the marketing organization. Refer to figure 5.6 for a summary of the steps involved in primary research.

To illustrate the concepts of objectives and hypotheses, let's assume that a marketer determines from extensive exploratory research that a problem exists with the

**FIGURE 5.6**   Primary Research Steps

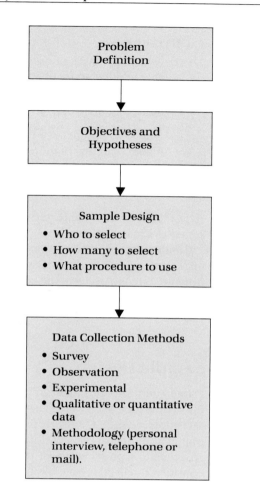

type of message that is directed at a target market. Let's further assume that a humourous television commercial was the primary method of communication. The problem, objectives, and hypotheses could be written as follows:

### Problem

To determine the relative effectiveness of humourous appeal techniques on a predetermined target market.

### Objectives

1. To determine if awareness levels of humorous messages compare favourably to other commonly used appeal techniques (e.g. positive benefit claims, the use of emotion, or the use of celebrities as product presenters).
2. To determine if message recall is higher with  humourous commercial messages than other styles of commercial messages.

In this case it has been determined that consumer awareness and recall are of primary importance to the marketing organization.

### Hypotheses

1. Awareness levels of humorous commercial messages will compare favourably to other styles of advertising.

   *Action:* If awareness levels fall within acceptable and comparable ranges, the humorous style of advertising will be maintained.

2. Due to its uniqueness, the message recall of humorous commercials will be higher than that of more traditional styles of advertising.

   *Action:* If recall is not higher, the use of humourous appeals will be re-evaluated.

Hypotheses of this nature serve as standards of action against which marketing activities can be evaluated.

Conducting a marketing research study is beyond the scope and expertise of most marketing organizations in Canada. Consequently, independent market research firms are hired to perform the task. Usually, a marketing research manager from the sponsoring organization is responsible for supervising the research study and working directly with the research consulting firm in designing the project.

## Sample Design

Prior to implementing a research study, the researchers identify the characteristics of the people they would like to have participate in the study. This process is referred to as sample design. A **sample** is defined as a representative portion of an entire population used to obtain information about that population. A sample must form an accurate representation of the population if the information gathered is to be considered reliable. Some basic steps have to be taken to develop a representative sample:

1. *Define the Population (Universe)*   It should be first pointed out that the terms *population* and *universe* are interchangeable in research terminology. Defining a **population** involves identifying its basic characteristics. For example, you might identify a population of male tennis players between the ages of 21 and 45 living in cities with over 500,000 residents, or female heads of households between the ages of 19 and 49. Proper research procedure will screen potential respondents for these characteristics.

2. *Identifying the Sampling Frame*   The **sampling frame** refers to a listing that can be used for reaching a population. The telephone directory could be used as a sampling frame. If Eaton's or Woodward's wanted to conduct research among present customers, they could use their credit card account holder list as a means of access.

3. *Determining the Type of Sample*   The researcher has the option of using a probability sample or a non-probability sample. If a **probability sample** is used, the respondents have a known chance of selection and are randomly selected

*Margin terms:*

**sample**

**population**

**sampling frame**

**probability sample**

non-probability
sample

from across the population. For example, the researcher may use a predetermined and systematic procedure for picking respondents through a telephone directory. The known chance of selection enables statistical procedures to be used in the results to estimate sampling errors, if such an estimation is required by the firm sponsoring the research. In a **non-probability sample**, the respondents have an unknown chance of selection, and their being chosen is based on factors such as convenience for the researcher or the judgement of the researcher. The researcher uses his or her experience to determine who would be most appropriate. For example, an independent retailer may conduct a survey by using a list of current customers or by approaching potential customers who visit the store.

4. *Determining the Sample Size*    Generally, the larger the sample, the greater the accuracy of the data collected and the higher the cost. The nature of the research study is a determining factor in the number of participants required. Some researchers use a 1 percent rule (1 percent of the defined population or universe), while others state absolute minimums of 200 respondents. The accuracy of the sample is usually calculated statistically and stated in the research report.

## Data Collection Methods

There are three primary methods a researcher can use to collect data: surveys, observation, and experiments (see figure 5.7), and the data collected can be qualitative or quantitative in nature.

### Survey Research

survey research

For **survey research**, data is collected systematically through some form of communication with a representative sample. The information is collected by means of a questionnaire that records responses. If the questionnaire is used for a large sample

**FIGURE 5.7**    Data Collection Methods

### Survey
- A systematic collection of data made by communicating with a representative sample, usually by using a questionnaire
- Disguised or undisguised, structured or unstructured formats are used

### Observation
- Behaviour of respondent is observed by personal, mechanical or electronic means

### Experiments
- The manipulation of variables under controlled conditions to observe respondents' reactions
- Good for testing marketing influences (e.g., product formula changes, package design alternatives, advertising copy tests, etc.)

**fixed response questioning**

it contains pre-determined questions and a selection of answers that are easily filled in by the respondent or interviewer. This technique is referred to as **fixed response questioning**. Survey research is implemented by personal interview, telephone or by mail.

A survey is usually designed to be disguised or undisguised, structured or unstructured. In a disguised survey, the respondent may not know the name of the product or service being researched or the purpose of the study. The intent is to eliminate any bias the respondent may have as a result of previous knowledge of the product. Conversely, in an undisguised survey, the product and purpose of the study are revealed to the respondent. For example, if Nescafé coffee was to test new package designs with its target market, a variety of clearly labelled jars would be used. Research to test the effectiveness of marketing-mix activities is usually of an undisguised nature.

In a structured survey, the questionnaire follows a planned format: screening questions at the front, central issue questions (those dealing with the objectives and hypotheses) in the middle, and classification (demographic) questions at the end. Closed-ended or fixed-response questions — that is, ones that, like multiple choice questions, include a list of possible answers to choose from — are most popular. They permit the data to be easily transferred to a computer for tabulation and subsequent analysis. Some sample questions used in survey research are included in figure 5.8.

### Observation Research

**observation research**

In **observation research**, the behaviour of the respondent is observed and recorded. In this form of research, participants do not have to be recruited; they can participate in a study without knowing it. To illustrate, the purchase behaviour of people in a supermarket can be observed in person or by electronic means. The behaviour of a shopper accepting or rejecting a product could be the focus of such a study. In other situations, respondents are usually aware of being observed, perhaps through a two-way mirror or by a hidden camera while being interviewed. The "people meter", a recent innovation developed by A.C. Nielsen, is an example of observation research. The people meter is an electronic device attached to Canadian television sets (a sample group of sets) which records who was watching television, what was watched, and for how long. The major weakness of observation is that it does not supply information about the attitudes underlying observable behaviour. Other devices used in observation research include 1) the psychogalvanator, which measures a person's emotional reaction to various stimuli by measuring changes in perspiration rate, and 2) the pupilometer, which measures changes in pupil size as a person is looking at an advertisement, package, or product design.[2]

### Experimental Research

**experimental research**

**test marketing**

In **experimental research**, one or more factors are manipulated under controlled conditions, while other elements remain constant, so that respondents' reactions can be evaluated. With this type of research, the test market is the acid test for a new product or service. **Test marketing** involves placing a product for sale in one or

**FIGURE 5.8**    A Survey using Fixed Response and Open Response Questions

## NISSAN
### Customer First

From:  Mr. Keith Tuckwell                                    E102432
       1 Portsmouth Avenue
       Kingston, Ontario
       K7L 5A6

### SURVEY

Your comments are important! Please answer the following
questions and return this survey in the enclosed postage paid
envelope.

1. I presently own the following vehicle(s):

| | 1st Vehicle | 2nd Vehicle | 3rd Vehicle |
|---|---|---|---|
| Make | _____ | _____ | _____ |
| Model | _____ | _____ | _____ |
| Year | _____ | _____ | _____ |

2. If you are not currently driving a Nissan, can you tell me why
   not? _____
   _____

3. When do you plan to purchase your next automobile?
   ( ) less than 3 months        ( ) 3–6 months
   ( ) 6–12 months               ( ) next year
   ( ) more than two years

4. What are the most important considerations for you when
   purchasing a new automobile? (please number in order of
   importance)
   ( ) reliability              ( ) price
   ( ) image                    ( ) warranty
   ( ) standard features        ( ) gas mileage

5. How much do you intend to spend on your next car purchase?
   ( ) under $9 999             ( ) $10 000 to $14 999
   ( ) $15 000 to $19 999       ( ) $20 000 to $24 999
   ( ) more than $25 000

6. I am interested in receiving more information on the
   following Nissan 1989 vehicles:
   ( ) Micra        ( ) Sentra        ( ) Stanza
   ( ) Pulsar NX    ( ) 240SX         ( ) Trucks
   ( ) Maxima       ( ) Pathfinder

*Courtesy*: Nissan Automobile Company (Canada) Ltd.

more representative markets to observe its performance under a proposed marketing plan. Good test marketing provides a marketing organization with three main benefits:

1. It allows the marketing organization to observe the reactions of consumers to the product.
2. It enables alternate marketing strategies to be evaluated; several test markets with different strategies can be arranged.
3. It provides experience prior to an expensive regional or national launch.

In contemporary marketing, the competition is so intense that many companies skip the test marketing stage, for it tips off the competitors as to what the firm is doing and gives them time to react. While skipping the test marketing stage involves a risk, companies that take this option argue that the costs associated with test marketing are steadily increasing and that they are unable to project national results from test markets. To illustrate, a test market in London, Ontario, may prove successful, but will the same product and marketing plan work in Halifax, Thunder Bay, or Regina, given the variations in economies and the demographic and psychographic differences between each city and area of the country?

## ⟩⟩⟩⟩ MARKETING IN ACTION

### WILL THAT BE CASH, CHEQUE OR DEBIT CARD?

The Royal Bank is the first of the major banks to introduce a debit card. Test marketing was conducted in London, Ontario, a market the bank judged to be demographically representative of the Canadian marketplace. A debit card provides an alternate to cash, cheques, and credit cards. In a transaction between the customer and the retailer, the debit card system electronically transfers funds from the customer's account to the merchant's account. Customers are charged 25 cents for each transaction, a savings of 20 cents over what it would cost them to write a cheque.

Retail outlets participating in the pilot project include Becker's, Miracle Food Mart, and Big V Pharmacies. Although acceptance of the debit card is still to be determined in the test market, the bank feels that retailers would benefit from faster customer service, and from the fact that the debit card would reduce costs from bad cheques and lower the cost of handling cheques and cash.

*The debit card system electronically transfers funds from the customer's account to the merchant's account*

Adapted from "Royal Bank tests debit cards for instant payment at stores", *Whig Standard*, October 5, 1988.

To compensate for some of these problems, a firm should be selective about the types of products they test market. For example, products with high financial risk should be tested initially. Products considered to be fads would not have time for testing before the financial opportunity would be lost. The firm should only use markets that are representative and normal — the market should not be dominated by one or a few industries, and the market should be demographically representative of the larger market that will eventually be pursued. Finally, the market should be large enough to provide meaningful results, but not so large that marketing costs are too high. For an illustration of test marketing in action, refer to the vignette "Will that be Cash, Cheque or Debit Card?"

## Qualitative Data versus Quantitative Data

According to the nature of the information sought, research data is classified as qualitative or quantitative.

### *Qualitative Data*

qualitative data

focus group

**Qualitative data** is usually collected from small samples in a controlled environment. It results from questions concerned with "why" and from in-depth probing of participants. Typically, such data is gathered from focus group interviews. A **focus group** is a small group of eight to twelve people with characteristics in common (e.g. a target market profile), brought together to discuss issues related to the marketing of a product or service. The word *focus* implies that the discussion concentrates on one topic or concept. Focus group interviews are generally conducted by professionally trained moderators. After answering questions, the participants interact more or less freely as the moderator probes for the reasons and motivations underlying their remarks. The major drawback of using focus groups concerns the reliability of the data. The sample size is too small to be representative of the entire population and, consequently, marketing decisions involving considerable sums of money are very risky if based on such limited research.

On the positive side, qualitative research is an excellent first stage in the collection of information. The results can be used to help form questions and questionnaires for quantitative research, and the responses from the qualitative research can be used as answers for closed-ended questions in a questionnaire. Qualitative research also reinforces the beliefs, attitudes, and convictions of marketing managers. For example, unsubstantiated beliefs or attitudes that a marketing manager may have had prior to the research (e.g., that the perceived quality of the product is not as high as expected) can be confirmed in the discussion among participants. Hearing responses in a focus group has greater impact than an impersonal and voluminous statistical study. To illustrate, in a recent study of cat owners

> women spoke with great affection about their pets, referring to them as a member of the family. The novice brand manager had no idea these feelings existed. This knowledge lead to the use of emotional advertising messages for a brand of cat food which capitalized on the relationships between cats and their owners.[3]

Focus groups help achieve responsiveness by fostering informal, uncensored consumer chit-chat about products and services.[4] Such discussions often reveal viewpoints that the marketing organization had not thought of, and they can be an early barometer of consumers' changing values and lifestyles.

### *Quantitative Data*

**quantitative data**

Research that generates quantitative data attempts to quantify feelings, attitudes, and opinions. As mentioned earlier, a quantitative study relies upon a structured procedure (questionnaire) and a large sample to obtain accurate and reliable data. **Quantitative data** provides answers to questions concerned with "how many", "how often" and "what". A brief comparison of qualitative and quantitative research is contained in figure 5.9.

## Survey Methodology

There are three primary means of contacting consumers when conducting surveys: telephone, personal interview, and mail. Each of these methods offers advantages and disadvantages for the market researcher (see figure 5.10).

### *Personal Interviews*

Personal interviews involve face-to-face communications with groups (e.g. focus groups) or with individuals through quantitative questionnaires. Popular locations for interviews are busy street corners, shopping malls, or the homes of respondents.

The first advantage of personal interviews is that they have higher participation rates than telephone or mail surveys, since it is harder to refuse participation in a face-to-face situation. The interviewer can also visually observe the respondent and provide guidance (e.g. explain questions) when the need arises. Also, personal interviews are flexible: visual aids can be included. Finally, personal interviews can produce large amounts of information when a structured questionnaire is used.

The disadvantages include cost, a reluctance to respond to certain types of questions and interviewer bias. Since interviewers must be paid for the time it takes them

---

**FIGURE 5.9**   Comparing Qualitative and Quantitative Research

#### Qualitative Research
- Is collected from a small sample (e.g., a focus group) by means of an unstructured question format
- Questions deal with why people act, do, purchase, etc.
- Small sample poses reliability (of data) problems

#### Quantitative Research
- Collection of data from a truly representative sample (e.g., 200–300 people who represent a specified target market)
- Data can be statistically reliable; degree of error can be calculated
- Structured format (e.g., questionnaire with pre-determined responses) is common

**FIGURE 5.10**    Survey Methodology for Collecting Quantitative Data

### Personal Interview

Advantages
- Higher rates of participation
- Visual observations possible by interviewer
- Flexibility (e.g. inclusion of visuals possible)
- Large amounts of data collected

Disadvantages
- Higher cost (time needed)
- Reluctance to respond to certain questions
- Interviewer bias is possible

### Telephone Interview

Advantages
- Convenience and control
- Costs less
- Timely responses
- Geographic flexibility

Disadvantages
- Lack of observation
- Short questions and questionnaire
- Can be viewed as an invasion of privacy

### Mail Surveys

Advantages
- Geographic flexibility in selecting target
- Cost efficient
- Large sample obtainable
- Respondent in relaxed environment
- Impersonality results in more accurate responses

Disadvantages
- Lack of control
- The time between distribution and return is long
- Potential for misinterpretation by respondent
- Low response rates

---

to fill in the questionnaires, and since several interview locations may be used to collect data, the cost of the personal interview method is high. Since respondents are not anonymous (face-to-face), many people are also reluctant to respond to controversial topics or to issue-related questions. Finally, interviewer bias can occur if the interviewer provides too much explanation. It is possible that an interviewer could lead respondents to provide answers that they believe to be acceptable, but that do not reflect their true feelings.

### *Telephone*

The advantages of using telephone interviews to collect survey information are convenience and control, time and cost. In terms of convenience the interviews are conducted from central locations (e.g. one central location can reach all Canadian markets), and, consequently, there is supervised control over the interview process. Such a procedure is fast, and, given modern technology, data can be transferred directly to a computer. The telephone is more economical than personal interviews, due to the time and control advantages.

The inability to make any visual assessment of the respondent is one of the disadvantages of telephone interviews. To hold the respondent's attention, the questionnaire must be short, thus limiting the amount of information collected. It is also easier for a potential respondent to reject the interview request over the telephone, as many view such requests as an invasion of privacy.

### *Mail*

Collecting primary research information by mail is a silent process. One of its advantages is geographic flexibility: it permits a highly dispersed sample to be used in a cost-efficient manner. The procedure is convenient since the survey is completed when the respondent is relaxed and in his or her own home environment. This system works well for time-pressed individuals (not so well for time-pressed companies in need of information). Finally, due to the impersonal nature of the method (there is no interviewer) the response to more difficult or controversial questions may be more honest and forthcoming.

The drawbacks of mail surveys center on the lack of control. Mail surveys require lots of time: there is usually a high degree of elapsed time between survey distribution and survey return. Follow-up procedures to remind respondents to complete and return surveys can be implemented, but at additional cost. Statistically, response rates tend to be low for mail surveys, a factor which is beyond the control of the researcher. The misinterpretation of a question by the respondent can lead to incorrect answers. A final disadvantage is that the mail survey competes for attention with other direct mail pieces delivered to Canadian homes.

The decision on which of these survey techniques to use is based on three factors:

1. *Nature of Information Sought*   The amount of information to be collected and the time it will take to complete the survey is a consideration. For example, if discussion is necessary to get the answers needed, personal interviews in a focus group may be best. If large amounts of information are required, the best option may be the mail.

2. *Cost and Time*   When time is critical, certain options are eliminated. The telephone is the best means of obtaining quick, cost-efficient information. Costs must also be weighed against benefits. The net financial gains expected to result from the research may determine which method is to be used.

3. *Respondent*   The selection of a methodology can be influenced by the location of the respondents and how easily they can be reached. For example, if the participant is to be reached at home, any methodology — personal interview, telephone or mail — can be used. In contrast, if the participant is to be reached in a central location such as a shopping mall, a personal interview is the only choice.

# 〉〉〉〉 *Data Transfer and Processing*

Once the data has been collected, editing, data transfer and tabulation occur:

1. *Editing*   Completed questionnaires are reviewed for consistency and completeness. Whether to include questionnaires with incomplete answers or answers that appear to be contradictory is left to the discretion of the researcher.

2. *Data Transfer*   On quantitative questionnaires, most questions are closed-ended (require fixed-response answers), and all answers are pre-coded to facilitate the transfer of the data to a computer.

3. *Tabulation*   As the results of the survey are entered into a computer, the different responses for each question are counted so as to arrive at a frequency distribution. This process is called **tabulation**. A frequency distribution shows the number of times each answer was chosen for a question. Numerous **cross-tabulations** are also made. These involve the pairing of certain answers. For example, a question dealing with brand awareness could be analyzed by age, sex, or income of respondents. Cross-tabulation allows for comparison and contrast among the answers of various sub-groups, or of particular sub-groups and the total response group.

**tabulation**
**cross-tabulation**

# 〉〉〉〉 *Data Analysis and Interpretation*

**data analysis**

**Data analysis** refers to the evaluation of responses on a question by question basis, which gives meaning to the data. At this point, the statistical data is reviewed for each question and the researcher makes observations about the data.

**data interpretation**

   **Data interpretation**, on the other hand, involves relating the accumulated data to the problem under review and to the objectives and hypotheses of the research study. The process of interpretation uncovers solutions to the problem. The researcher draws conclusions, which state the managerial implications of what the data means.

# 〉〉〉〉 *Recommendations and Implementation*

The recommendations outline suggested courses of action that the sponsoring organization should take in view of the data collected. Once a research project is complete, the research company will present its findings in a written report. Frequently, an oral presentation of the key findings is also made to the client. Very often, senior management is informed of research data as it becomes known so that they are better prepared for possible actions or changes in strategic direction. Preparing senior managers in this way is important, particularly if the proposed actions are in conflict with their personal views and feelings. Managers most likely to implement research findings are those who participate in research design, have the flexibility to make decisions, and see research findings that confirm their intentions.[5]

## ⟩⟩⟩⟩ *Benefits of Marketing Research*

There are several benefits of marketing research for an organization. These include the distribution of control information, planning information, the implementation of test markets, and sales forecasts.

### Control Information

Control information includes routine reports that indicate what has happened in an organization. Such information is continuously updated and distributed to managers through the management information system. Examples of control information include sales reports, inventory reports, budget and cost reports. The availability of this type of information will influence marketing strategy during the course of an operating year. For example, if raw material costs or packaging costs rise unexpectedly, a price increase will have to go into effect if profit levels are to be achieved. Sales-related statistics have a direct influence on other departments' operations as well. Those directly affected include Production, Purchasing, Distribution, and Human Resources.

### Planning Information

The availability of information collected by marketing research on matters such as economic, demographic, psychographic and geographic patterns is valuable for planning purposes. Such data should be integrated into the firm's database, and when it is combined with actual performance data, such as that concerning market share and sales, it forms a solid foundation for developing annual marketing plans.

management information system

Database information is retrieved from an organization's management information system (MIS). A **management information system** consists of the organization of people and equipment to provide a continuous, orderly collection and exchange of information (internal and external) needed in a firm's decision-making process.[6] A sample model of a management information system is contained in figure 5.11.

The electronic era has resulted in an information explosion that now allows for the storage and transfer of great amounts of business data in a short time. Consequently, the time involved in decision-making has been shortened. The access to information internally and externally, through computer terminals linked to other computers, enhances the strategic planning process. The flexibility and the many applications of microcomputer technology also allow small companies to enter the information age and to reap the advantages it offers. Managers can also access an "analytic system" that includes software programs such as Lotus 1-2-3 and many others, programs which can be used to adjust or manipulate the basic data. See the

**FIGURE 5.11**    Sample Model of a Management Information System

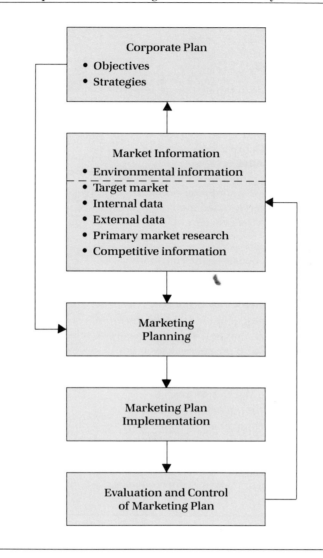

Marketing in Action vignette "Research has led to..." for an illustration of continuous information collection and use.

## Test Marketing

As a result of test marketing, a company may want to modify its marketing plan prior to expanding distribution to other markets. In effect, the test market provides a test of a product's performance and marketing plan. After reviewing test market results, a company has several options: withdraw the product (unsuccessful test), alter marketing strategies (any element of the marketing mix) and test again, or expand distribution beyond the test market (successful test).

## ⟩⟩⟩⟩ *MARKETING IN ACTION*

### *RESEARCH HAS LED TO...*

Due to a declining rate of population growth, the only way that supermarkets can now generate growth is by taking market share from competitors. In today's market, a clean, well-stocked and competitively priced store is not enough to ensure customer loyalty.

To counter strong competition, major chain stores are trying to make shopping easier through market research-based merchandising innovations. Some of the concepts being tested include:

1. Installation of keyboards, which customers can use to make inquiries about the availability and location of products. A computer voice directs the customer to the location.

2. Installation of ceiling monitors advertising in-store specials. Each message is repeated every six to ten minutes and produces an average sales increase of 36 percent over unadvertised products, according to statistics generated by A & P and Miracle Mart test stores.

3. To take advantage of the health and fitness craze, the Stop & Shop chain (Northeastern U.S.) uses yellow shelf tags to flag a "Facts about Food" program for foods low in calories, fat, sodium, and cholesterol. Such information allows consumers to make wise food choices.

*To facilitate price comparison by the consumer, Loblaws has installed Telepanels in some of its stores*

4. Canada Safeway has experimented with "singles nights" in order to encourage singles to spend more time shopping and meeting other singles. In major cities, the singles market represents a large, attractive target worthy of pursuit.

Adapted from Harlow Unger, "Store-level market research key ingredient", *Canadian Grocer*, January 1987, pp.22,23.

## Sales Forecasting

**sales forecast**

One of the most common uses of research data is sales forecasting. A **sales forecast** is a prediction of sales volume for a period of time. The accuracy of a sales forecast is important, since so many departments in an organization are affected by it. Long-term sales forecasts are primarily used in a firm's financial planning. For example, a five-year estimate of sales will be compared to costs to determine the stability of the firm over this extended period. Other departments, including Marketing, are concerned with short-term forecasts for one year and less. Marketing usually participates in quarterly financial reviews, at which time sales and cost estimates for a year are re-evaluated.

In developing a forecast, an organization commonly combines qualitative assessments with quantitative techniques. Input from sales managers, sales representatives, senior executives, and industry experts is combined with quantitative techniques. Some of the variables which influence a sales forecast include:

1. *Economic Conditions*  Gross national product figures, interest rates, unemploy-

ment numbers, inflation rates, income trends, and other measures of the economy affect forecasts.

2. *Industry Trends*   Are sales declining, flat, or increasing?

3. *Product Category Trends*   Is this market segment growing, and how well is the product selling in the segment?

4. *Marketing Mix*   What effect will a more aggressive or less aggressive marketing plan have on sales volume?

## Sales Forecasting Methods

### Trend Analysis

**trend analysis**

**Trend analysis** is a way of using fairly recent historical performance data to project sales for the forthcoming year. It is based on the assumption that the relationship between sales and time will remain constant. When using this method, the marketing executive considers variables such as the state of the economy, changing consumer preferences and competitive activity in relation to past performance. For example, consider the following:

**Sales Forecast, 1994**

|  | *Actual Sales* | *Growth* |
|---|---|---|
| 1991 | 100 000 units | + 10% |
| 1992 | 110 000 | + 10 |
| 1993 | 126 500 | + 15 |
| 1994 (estimate) | 144 210 | + 14 |

In this example, recent sales growth was quite good and the company concluded that, in view of the various economic and competitive factors, it should project a 14 percent increase for 1994. If a downturn in the economy was expected and if a new competitive product was anticipated, the same firm might project sales more conservatively, foreseeing, say, a 5 percent increase.

### Market Share Analysis

Market share analysis is similar to trend analysis except that market share figures are used as the base for projections. The firm has to project market growth (what size the total market will be), as it does when using trend analysis, and then calculate its sales volume according to the market share it expects to achieve in the year. Consider the following example where the 1994 market share objective is 22 percent.

|  | *Market Volume* | *Market Growth* | *Market Share* | *Volume* |
|---|---|---|---|---|
| 1991 | 1 000 000 units | +8% | 20% | 200 000 |
| 1992 | 1 200 000 | + 10 | 20 | 240 000 |
| 1993 | 1 300 000 | + 10 | 22 | 286 000 |
| 1994 | 1 400 000 | +8  (est.) | 22 | 308 000 |

As in trend analysis, factors such as the economy, the competition, and marketing activity should be considered when determining a market share objective. Regardless of which method is used, sales and marketing managers and other senior executives make qualitative assessments of the figures and introduce adjustments where appropriate. Once a sales forecast is approved, the figures are integrated into the plans of other operating departments.

### Simulation Model Analysis

simulation
model analysis

Given the current state of computer technology and the availability of software, the use of **simulation model analysis** is quite common. Simulation allows a company to enter data into a model using varying conditions (e.g. different economic conditions, competitive information, marketing mix activity, etc.). The complex links between these variables and sales performance are analyzed by the computer, and sales projections are made. For the manager, such figures are estimates only. Managers consult their intuitive judgement before committing to a computer-generated sales figure.

## ⟩⟩⟩⟩ S U M M A R Y

Marketing research must be viewed as a tool that assists the manager in the decision-making process. It is a systematic procedure that, if used properly, will produce reliable and useable data. There are several types of marketing research including exploratory research, descriptive research, performance evaluation research, and causal research.

The research process begins with a firm's becoming aware of a problem situation. From there, exploratory research is conducted to narrow the scope of the investigation. To do so requires the consultation of knowledgeable people and secondary data sources. If the problem is not resolved at this stage, the next step is primary research. Primary research gathers new data from a representative sample. The process requires the determination of who should participate and how many should participate in the sample.

Primary data is collected from surveys or through observation and experimental techniques. Survey data is qualitative or quantitative in nature and is obtained by focus-group interview or by personal interview, telephone, or mail. Once the data is secured it is computer processed for analysis and interpretation by the researcher. Primary data is often integrated with secondary information and other internal company information to form a database. The database is the nucleus of the organization's marketing information system. This system ensures the continuous and orderly flow of information to decision-makers, who use the information to develop marketing strategies.

Experimental research involves testing a marketing mix activity within a controlled situation in order to measure the effectiveness of the activity. Test marketing is an example of experimental research. In a test market, a product is placed in a representative market so that its performance under a proposed marketing plan can be observed.

In addition to providing information that assists in strategy development and test marketing, marketing research is a useful tool for providing data for sales forecasting. The organization uses several different methods of developing a sales forecast, including trend analysis, market share analysis, and simulation model analysis.

## >>>> KEY TERMS

| | | |
|---|---|---|
| marketing research | research objectives | qualitative data |
| basic research | hypotheses | focus group |
| applied research | sample | quantitative data |
| fact gathering | population | tabulation |
| exploratory research | sampling frame | cross-tabulation |
| descriptive research | probability sample | data analysis |
| performance research | non-probability sample | data interpretation |
| causal research | survey research | management information system |
| funnelling | fixed response questioning | sales forecast |
| situation analysis | observation research | trend analysis |
| secondary data | experimental research | simulation model analysis |
| primary research | test marketing | |

## >>>> REVIEW AND DISCUSSION QUESTIONS

**1.** Briefly explain the difference between the items in the following sets of terms:   **a)** basic research and applied research   **b)** exploratory research and causal research   **c)** secondary data and primary data   **d)** research objectives and hypotheses   **e)** observation and experimental techniques

**2.** What is a management information system? What are its uses?

**3.** What is the "problem awareness" stage of the marketing research process?

**4.** Visit the reference section of a library. Select any Canadian-based trade index and outline the nature and usefulness of the directory's content.

**5.** What are the advantages and disadvantages of secondary data sources?

**6.** Briefly explain the three steps in the sample design process.

**7.** What is a "focus group", and what are the benefits of focus group interviews?

**8.** Under what circumstances would you use the telephone for collecting survey data? Personal interview?

**9.** Explain the purpose and role of test marketing. Is test marketing a valid practice in today's competitive marketplace?

**10.** The trend to "information overkill" discourages the use of research data by managers. Discuss this statement.

**11.** "Information is the most important element of strategic marketing planning". Discuss.

**12.** "Decisions based on qualitative data are not risky". Discuss this statement.

## >>>> REFERENCES

1. "New Definition of Marketing Research Approved", *Marketing News*, January 2, 1987, p.1.

2. GEORGE KRESS, *Marketing Research*, 3rd Edition, (Englewood Cliffs, New Jersey: Prentice-Hall, 1988), pp.132-33.

3. JUDITH LANGER, "Getting to Know Your Customer through Qualitative Research", *Management Review*, American Management Association, April, 1987, pp. 42-46.

4. "Focus Groups Gain Wide Usage", *Wall Street Journal*, June 30, 1986, p.33.

5. ROHIT DESHPANDE, "The Organizational Context of Market Research use", *Journal of Marketing*, Fall 1982, pp.91-101.

6. GEORGE KRESS, *Marketing Research*, 3rd edition (Englewood Cliffs, New Jersey: Prentice-Hall, 1988), p.27.

⟩ ⟩ ⟩ ⟩ ⟩ **PART THREE**

# *Buying Behaviour*

# CHAPTER 6 〉〉〉〉

# Consumer Buying Behaviour

The behaviour of the Canadian consumer has changed dramatically in the past few decades, and will continue to change in the next century. The old expression that "the only constant in life is change" holds true here. It is this change that marketing organizations must recognize and act upon. Organizations must anticipate changes among consumers and develop appropriate marketing strategies to meet the challenges of a dynamic marketplace. The primary factors affecting behaviour change in the consumer market today include:

1. The growing presence of Canadian women in the workforce outside the home.
2. The formation of different sorts of households.
3. The emphasis among people on achieving a higher standard of living than was the norm in the past.
4. The aging population.

5. The growth of various ethnic groups in large urban centres.

This chapter will discuss the dynamics of consumer behaviour and illustrate how marketing organizations use behaviour information to develop marketing strategies.

# >>>> *What is Consumer Behaviour?*

consumer behaviour

**Consumer behaviour** is defined as "the acts of individuals in obtaining goods and services, including the decision processes that precede and determine these acts."[1] An organization must have a firm understanding of how consumers make purchase decisions, so that appropriate marketing strategies are planned and implemented. With the dominant role that market segmentation and target marketing play in the marketing of goods and services, there has been a considerable growth in research whose aim is to uncover information on consumer behaviour.

From a purely competitive viewpoint, marketers must have access to information on consumer buying motivation in order to develop persuasive strategies for getting members of the target market to buy or use a product. Consequently, large sums of money are allocated to marketing research in order to find answers to the following important questions:

1. Who makes the buying decision?
2. How do they buy?
3. Where do they buy?
4. When do they buy?
5. Why do they buy?

For any product, service, retail store, institution, or manufacturing company, the answers to these questions provide valuable input for developing a marketing strategy. Once the answers are known, they are used to design strategies that will motivate the market to buy. To gain a little insight into what Canadians buy and why they buy, read the Marketing in Action item "What Does the Typical Canadian Consumer Buy?"

# >>>> *Influences on Consumer Behaviour*

The purchase decisions of Canadian consumers are influenced by cultural, social, personal and psychological factors.[2] These influences cannot be controlled by the marketing organization. They simply occur and interact to form the dynamics involved in the consumer purchasing decision process. Knowledge of these influences, however, is essential, since an organization can use this understanding to maximize the effectiveness of the variables within its control, namely, those of the marketing mix: product, price, place and promotion.

## ⟩⟩⟩⟩ *MARKETING IN ACTION*

### *WHAT DOES THE TYPICAL CANADIAN CONSUMER BUY?*

The baby boom generation represents a very attractive market segment for manufacturers. This generation is getting married, having children, and buying homes. Consequently, they are making purchases for the home rather than for themselves as they did in their younger years.

The typical boomer living in suburbia probably drives a Ford Tempo, eats Kellogg's Corn Flakes for breakfast, enjoys a leisurely jog in Reebok running shoes, and cools down with a Coke or Diet-Coke. For entertainment, he or she more than likely watches "The Cosby Show" and probably saw *Who Framed Roger Rabbit?* the top grossing movie of 1988. Other predictable purchases might include the following brand leaders.

| Product or Service | Sales Volume or Market Share |
|---|---|
| Labatt's Blue/Blue Light | 18% |
| Campbell's Tomato Soup | 48 million cans annually |
| RCA Colour TV | 20% |
| IBM Personal Computer | 27% |
| Jockey Classic Underwear | 750 000 briefs annually |
| Maclean's Newsmagazine | 650 000 circulation |

Because of changing demographics, such as the aging of the population and the increase in the number of women working outside the home, the future will include make-it-snappy products (home-delivered groceries), place quality above all else (upscale appliances), and treat technology as toys (TVs with "surround sound" stereo). With the "wellness" trend continuing in the 1990s, fitness equipment will still be a big growth area. In a few years time the family recreation room could be replaced by a fully equipped gymnasium — and a whirlpool to ease the aches and pains after a workout.

On the food scene, "microwave-mania" will continue. With only half of Canadian households owning one, there is room for further penetration of the market. Food companies will still introduce new products for the microwave. Because of the importance of "wellness," the trend toward light products will also continue.

Nestlé Enterprises Limited

*Today's trend toward "light", "low-calorie" products is expected to continue*

Products described as "light," "low-calorie," and "less" will remain popular. Canadians will be smoking and drinking less.

And what about cars? In Canada, sales of the prestigious Jaguar have risen from 329 cars in 1978 to 2 154 in 1988. According to Jaguar Canada Inc., the average Jaguar buyer is a 45-year-old entrepreneur or professional earning about $200 000 annually. The best-selling model is the Sovereign Sedan which sells for $69 300 and the most popular colour is black. Ten years ago, metallic grey was the preferred colour. The list below shows the median household earnings of various buyers for some other cars:

| Make of Car | Median Household Earnings |
|---|---|
| Mercedes | $151 500 |
| Audi | 106 000 |
| Cadillac | 79 000 |
| Hyundai | 34 000 |
| Chevrolet Sprint | 29 000 |

Adapted from Barrie McKenna, "Leading the pack", *Financial Post*, September 12, 1988, p.17, *The Financial Post*, February 13, 1989, p.49, and *The Financial Times of Canada*, February 13, 1989, p.35.

# Cultural Influences

culture

**Culture** refers to behaviour learned from external sources, such as family and education, which influence the formation of value systems that hold strong sway over individuals. Over time, people's values can change. The "hippies" of the sixties became the "me generation" of the seventies, who in turn evolved into the "yuppies" and parents of the eighties. As each decade passed, individuals' values changed; they acquired different needs, different responsibilities, and different attitudes. We now live in a very materialistic society, and individuals constantly strive to possess more. Values are such that possession of a good quality house — a large house in comparison to those owned by parents and grandparents — or of a prestigious automobile suggest success. In previous times, social values dictated saving rather than spending, and in general life was simpler. Refer to figure 6.1 for a summary of some basic value changes which have occurred.

**FIGURE 6.1**    Some Basic Value Changes in Canadian Society

| Then | Now |
|---|---|
| Tendency to Save | Tendency to Spend |

Nowadays we live for today. Credit is readily available from banks and stores.

| Traditional Family | New Household Formations |
|---|---|

People are delaying marriage, and divorce rates remain relatively high. There are more single parent families and children living in two different households. Dual income families are now common and there are fewer children in the household.

| Husband Dominated Decision-making | Syncratic (shared) Decision-making |
|---|---|

The career and professional orientation of women and their greater presence in the work force outside the home has changed the roles and responsibilities of the sexes.

| Hard Work | Easy Life and Hard Work |
|---|---|

There is an emphasis on leisure time but, for both partners to obtain desired leisure and lifestyle, two jobs are often needed. Health club memberships and exotic vacations are now more popular than in previous times.

| Parent-Centered Households | Child-Centered Households |
|---|---|

Children play a more dominant role in the family. The growth of day care facilities means that parents see their children less. Parents spend more on their children than in previous times. Children decide what to do and where to go.

### Subculture

subculture

Existing within Canadian culture are many diverse subcultures. A **subculture** is a subgroup of a culture that has distinctive lifestyles based on racial, religious, or geographic factors, while retaining important features of the dominant culture. Canada's subcultures are evident in cities where parts of urban and suburban neighbourhoods contain large populations of one ethnic group. Very often, these ethnic groups are served by their own media, which provide marketers with an effective means of reaching them.

Prudent marketers are recognizing the opportunities that these markets represent. Census data from 1986 indicates that 60 percent of Toronto's population has ethnic origins other than English and French. In other major Canadian cities the corresponding figures are Vancouver (69 percent), Montreal (31 percent), Calgary (70 percent), and Edmonton (74 percent). The West Indian population in Toronto is as large as all of Regina, and the total population of ethnic groups other than English and French in Toronto is larger than the entire population of Vancouver.[3]

Not only the size but other characteristics of these groups make them attractive target-marketing opportunities:

1. *Size*   The urban population statistics of these ethnic subcultures make these markets worthy of unique consideration.

2. *Upward Mobility*   In recent years most Canadian immigrants have come from cultural groups other than French and English, and Canada has the second highest rate of upward mobility among immigrants in the world. It is estimated that 90 percent of immigrants won't remain in their parents' socioeconomic group.

3. *Education*   The immigrants who arrived between 1971 and 1981 are better educated and earn more money than native-born Canadians.

These factors make such ethnic groups as attractive as, and even more attractive than, some of the subgroups more commonly sought after by Canadian marketing organizations, such as those dubbed yuppies (young urban professionals), dinks (double income no kid families), and woofs (well-off older folks) in the 1980s. The key to attracting the various ethnic markets is to communicate with them in the language they speak and to recognize their cultural differences. Falling into stereotypical traps by using dubbed English commercials, for example, is a sure way to fail. Refer to the Marketing in Action feature, "Marketing to an Ethnic Mix", to see how the Sun Life Assurance Company of Canada developed a successful target marketing strategy aimed directly at Toronto's Chinese community.

Because of their unique characteristics and attitudes, adolescents, generally, can be said to belong to a subculture. Some adolescent groups differentiate themselves from the main culture more obviously than other groups do. The "punks" of the eighties differentiated themselves from the more traditional teenage groups through their taste in music, through the style of their clothing and accessories, and through their physical appearance. The products they purchased and the activities they participated in were different from those of the mainstream teenager.

Generally speaking, the adolescent market is status-conscious and brand name oriented. They buy what is "in", what is "right", and they are subject to a high degree

## ⟩⟩⟩⟩ *MARKETING IN ACTION*

### *MARKETING TO AN ETHNIC MIX*

Canada's subcultures are evident in cities where urban and suburban neighbourhoods are characterized by large populations of various ethnic groups. Sun Life Assurance Company of Canada recognized an opportunity when it realized that many of its leading agents were selling insurance premiums in their own ethnic communities. In 1987, Sun Life launched a targeted marketing strategy aimed directly at Toronto's Chinese community. In the planning stages, certain cultural differences were identified that would influence the nature of Sun Life's marketing activity. Of primary concern was the importance of family and the impact that older generations had on purchase decisions. Also, the language barrier had to be overcome.

The plan that Sun Life implemented included the following:

1. Respecting the importance of family, their television commercial deliberately included three generations: young adults (who were the potential purchasers), parents, and grandparents.
2. Television advertising was placed on channel 47, Toronto's multi-cultural and multi-lingual station.
3. Supporting promotional literature in Chinese, starting with a translation of the company name, was distributed. In Chinese characters, the company became Forever Bright Assurance Company.
4. To increase the profile of the company in the Chinese community, forty new agents were hired, which brought the total complement of Chinese agents to 75.

The plan was successful: it generated $20 million in premiums the first year. Based on this success,

*In 1987, SunLife launched a marketing campaign aimed directly at Toronto's Chinese community*

Sun Life expanded the program to Winnipeg and Vancouver the following year. In 1988, marketing plans were developed for Toronto's 360 000-strong Italian community.

Adapted from Gillian Pritchard, "Polyglot profits", *Canadian Business*, February 1988, pp.47-50.

of peer pressure. They are volatile and switch allegiances fast, so marketers have to be ready to react to rapid changes in tastes and preferences. As adolescents progress through their teen years, they gain independence but remain subject to peer pressures that dictate their behaviour, the fashions they adopt, their music, games, and food. Since many are employed in part-time jobs, they have money to purchase the "right" products. To attract this type of target, marketing communications must be fun and exciting; they must be in line with the lifestyle teenagers lead and can relate to, representing the image that the market wants. To illustrate, the advertising for products such as Certs (breath mints), Dentyne (chewing gum), and many diet soft drinks, appeal directly to the needs of active young people. They show socially active situations and leisure activities that teenagers are typically involved in, and they appeal to the adolescent belief that social acceptance follows from using a given product.

## Geographic Considerations

The geography of Canada has an influence on culture. The needs and attitudes of the Maritime fisherman will be quite different from those of the French-speaking Quebec farmer, which will be different again from those of the Calgary business executive. While all of these potential consumers may need the same products, the way in which the products are presented to each of them will vary. The influence of target marketing has led to a much greater use of regional marketing planning for national brand organizations. A common strategy in the past was to adapt English advertising for the French Canadian market. Today, more firms are recognizing the value of creating original advertising tailored to the French Canadian consumer.

## Social Class

**social class**

A person's social class derives from a system which ranks or classifies people within a society. **Social class** is the division of people into ordered groups based on similar values, lifestyles, and social history. This division into groups is based on variables such as income, occupation, education, and inherited wealth. In Western society, class groups are divided as follows: upper-upper, lower-upper, upper-middle, lower-middle, upper-lower, and lower-lower. Individuals can move in and out of the various social classes as they go through life. As an example, the young business executive on the rise in the corporate world could move rapidly from say, a lower-middle class background, to a lower-upper class level as he or she assumes more power, responsibility, and income in an organization. Conversely, a senior executive accustomed to a certain style of living and a certain social circle could suffer socially if his or her job were lost. The fallout would affect the social position of the entire family.

A person's place in the class structure influences his or her purchases of housing, automobiles, clothing, travel, and entertainment. The lower-upper class executive, if single, is likely to live downtown, to drive a trendy automobile that reflects achievement, to wear custom-designed suits, and to dine out frequently at "in" spots. Such purchases help create or maintain the image that goes with the corporate position. A description of the social class system is outlined in figure 6.2.

FIGURE 6.2   Social Class Structure

| Class Description | Characteristics |
| --- | --- |
| Upper-Upper | The social elite; those with inherited wealth; they live in exclusive neighbourhoods; own numerous residences; children attend private schools; money not an important factor in purchases |
| Lower-Upper | Those with earned wealth, professional occupations; they are socially mobile and materialistic; money not important in purchases; good education |
| Upper-Middle | Career-oriented professionals, managers; status based on occupation and income; fine home and clothing; good education; careful but conspicuous consumers |
| Lower-Middle | The average person; respectable, conscientious, and conservative; lower level white-collar occupations; price sensitivity influences purchases |
| Upper-Lower | Routine existence; blue collar occupation and lower incomes; lower education; job security a priority; purchase routine and regular items (eg. brand names); not status conscious |
| Lower-Lower | Live for today; low education; limited skills; low end occupations and incomes (possibly unemployed) |

*Source*:  Adapted from James Engel, Roger Blackwell and Paul Miniard, *Consumer Behaviour*, 5th edition (Hinsdale, Ill.: Dryden Press, 1985), pp. 346–47.

## Social Factors

The social factors that influence the purchase decision process stem from reference groups and the family, and from the role and status held by the individual within these groups.

### Reference Groups

reference group

A **reference group**, or peer group as it is often called, is a group of people with a common interest that influences the participants' attitudes and behaviour. Reference groups that people are commonly associated with include fellow students in a class, co-workers, sports teams, hobby clubs, civic and recreation associations, and fraternal organizations. A member of a group experiences considerable pressure to conform to the standards of the group, to "fit in". The participant's desire to fit in influences the type of products he or she will purchase. For example, the young man who joins a trendy downtown fitness studio may decide to purchase fashionable workout gear after his first visit to the club. During his first visit, he realizes that there are clothing norms. To fit in with the established crowd, he feels he must go out and buy the right attire. This type of behaviour is related to "lifestyle associations", which are now a strong influence on new members of any group.

By pinpointing the reference groups that affect consumers, a marketing organization can develop appropriate strategies for reaching them. Television commercials that show certain groups using specific products and services — sports teams (beer), successful professionals (automobiles, clothing, and accessories), or college students (casual clothing, entertainment, and travel) — are suggesting that these groups can be joined if such purchases are made.

### Family

The family influences buying when purchase decisions are shared among household members. The actual impact each member has on the decision depends on the type of product or service under consideration. In the past, the impact each person had on the purchase decision was related to the traditional roles of household members. For example, fathers were in charge of cars and household repairs, and mothers in charge of groceries. In recent times, the roles of family members have changed dramatically, and the distinction between the roles of the male and female heads of households are now vague. Among the elements contributing to the role changes are the increasing numbers of two-income families and of women working outside the home, as well as the growth of single parent families.

How have marketers reacted to this change? In the marketing of food, strategies are changing quickly. According to John Cassaday, president and chief operating officer of Campbell Soup Company Limited, "men have found their way into the grocery store. It could be hazardous to our bottom line if we don't pay attention to them."[4] Statistics show that at least once a month seven out of ten men now make the major grocery buying trip for their households, and that, overall, men account for 40 percent of grocery store expenditures.[5] In terms of their buying behaviour men shop for groceries differently than do their female counterparts. Cassaday went on to say that while male shoppers like to eat and cook just as much as women, they care less about unit pricing and nutritional information. Has grocery shopping dented the male ego? Quite the contrary: men who shop see themselves as more liberated, contemporary, considerate, ambitious, and achievement-oriented than men who don't buy groceries.[6] It would now appear that role sharing and sharing household responsibilities are part of the new way of life for both males and females.

The growing number of double-income families is a sign of another development affecting behaviour within the family: the pursuit of a high standard of living. As the cost of living rises, particularly in large cities, a conflict exists between the desire for more leisure time and the need to work more hours so that the desired leisure activities can be afforded. Not only are there two wage earners, but there is a recent trend toward individual workers holding multiple jobs. A recent Statistics Canada survey reveals that a half a million Canadians are holding down multiple jobs — and that the majority of these people are over the age of 25. Across the country there are another half a million people who are working full-time but looking for second jobs.[7]

For many people, the world now consists of the office, the road to the office, the day care center, the grocery store, a variety of local fast food restaurants, and bed. Leisure time is decreasing. As a society, Canada is busier than ever — this is not an illusion. A recent study, conducted by market researcher Louis Harris and Associates, found that leisure time actually decreased by 37 percent between 1973 and 1987. What factors are involved in this trend? Considering adjustments for inflation, hourly wages are less now than in 1973. Factory workers' hours were longer in the eighties than in the seventies, as manufacturers expanded production while holding hiring down. The same occurred in white collar jobs, resulting in longer working hours and less absolute income.[8] To maintain the standard of living to which we have grown accustomed, we must work more. It seems that we can no longer expect to have more material things as well as more leisure time. Marketing organizations have adopted strategies to meet the needs of this time-pressed society. Here are some examples:

1. VCRs, cellular telephones, and phone answering machines are appliances for people who need to do two activities at once. (e.g., watching one show while taping another, or calling a customer by automobile phone while on the way to the office).

2. Leisure activities such as golf and baseball have been speeded up. Speedy golf has emerged to move foursomes around the links faster, and major league umpires have been instructed to speed up the time between pitches.

3. Arts organizations now offer for sale smaller subscriber packages because patrons do not have time to attend all performances.

4. Many products have been developed to provide convenience — automated bank tellers, ten-minute lube jobs, microwavable products, and service organizations that perform routine household chores.

### Role and Status

The role and status of individuals within the family and the reference groups to which they belong also influence purchase decisions. For example, the female head of household may be a member of several groups: she may be mother and wife at home, an executive at work, and an active member of civic and recreation organizations. In each group she assumes a different role and level of status. The role of executive requires the purchase of certain styles of clothing. The role of wife and mother necessitates purchase decisions associated with motherhood, even though stereotypical roles are changing. Products in this area include household supplies and children's clothing.

The role of children also has to be considered by the marketer. As an example, the parents may decide to dine out at a restaurant, but the children may select the actual restaurant, which will be more in line with their tastes. To avoid conflict, and to have a reasonably enjoyable meal, parents will go along with such decisions; hence, the frequency of visits to restaurants such as McDonald's, Burger King, Harvey's, Wendy's, and Pizza Hut.

From a marketing viewpoint it is essential to determine who has the most influence within a family or group situation. In the family, is it the male head, the female head, or some combination of both, and is the decision made with or without the influence of children? Once this is known, strategies containing an appropriate message and using suitable media can be directed at the decision maker. Traditionally, purchase decisions were classified as husband-dominant, wife-dominant, or shared equally. Although roles are changing, there are still examples of product categories that are husband- or wife-dominated. Purchases of life insurance and other forms of investments, outdoor equipment, and garden supplies are still generally husband-dominated. Purchases of appliances, furniture, carpeting, and kitchenware are, even today, often wife-dominated. Both husband and wife may share in the purchase decision and in the use of any of these items, but one of the partners often has a greater interest than the other in certain of these products. Generally, the more expensive a product or service is, the greater the likelihood of a shared decision.

## Personal Influences

Personal influences affecting purchase decisions include the stage in the family life cycle, occupation, economic circumstance, lifestyle, and personality.

### Family Life Cycle

family life cycle

The **family life cycle** is a series of stages a person undergoes, starting with bachelorhood, progressing to marriage and parenthood, and ending in the stage of solitary survivor. Understanding the stages in the life cycle offers insight into household purchase decisions. Family life-cycle theory is based on the changing needs of a family as it progresses through the various stages. Such theory can be used by an organization to develop better target marketing strategies. The number of households in each stage can be determined through the study of demographic data.

Needs change in each stage according to variables such as age, income, marital status, and the presence of children. The purchase priorities of a young working family with children will be quite different from those of older married couples with no children living at home. Different types of buying occur in each stage. Generally, as individuals grow older, and as incomes rise, the overall financial burden eases. The traditional stages and characteristics of the family life cycle are illustrated in figure 6.3.

The original form of the family life cycle concept as shown in figure 6.3 is quite dated.[9] Demographic shifts in Canada are changing the nature of the life-cycle concept, and these changes must be considered during the development of contemporary marketing strategies. What has altered is the time an individual spends at each stage and the presence of more single parent families. It is quite clear that the family of the nineties is becoming very different from the family of the eighties and seventies, and very different, as well, from the family of the sixties, during which

FIGURE 6.3    An Overview of the Traditional Family Life Cycle
and Buying Behaviour

| Stage in Family Life Cycle | Buying or Behavioral Pattern |
| --- | --- |
| 1. Bachelor Stage: Young single people not living at home | Few financial burdens. Fashion opinion leaders. Recreation-oriented. Buy: basic kitchen equipment, basic furniture, cars, equipment for the mating game, vacations. |
| 2. Newly Married Couples: Young, no children | Better off financially than they will be in near future. Highest purchase rate and highest average purchase of durables. Buy: cars, refrigerators, stoves, sensible and durable furniture, vacations. |
| 3. Full Nest I: Youngest child under six | Home purchasing at peak. Liquid assets low. Dissatisfied with financial position and amount of money saved. Interested in new products. Like advertised products. Buy: washers, dryers, TV, baby food, cough medicines, vitamins, dolls, wagons, sleds, skates. |
| 4. Full Nest II: Youngest child six or over | Financial position better. Some wives work. Less influenced by advertising. Buy larger-sized packages, multiple-unit deals. Buy: many foods, cleaning materials, bicycles, music lessons, pianos. |
| 5. Full Nest III: Older married couples with dependent children | Financial position still better. More wives work. Some children get jobs. Hard to influence with advertising. High average purchase of durables. Buy: new, more tasteful furniture, auto travel, nonnecessary appliances, boats, dental services, magazines. |
| 6. Empty Nest 1: Older married couples, no children living with them, head in labor force | Home ownership at peak. Most satisfied with financial position and money saved. Interested in travel, recreation, self-education. Make gifts and contributions. Not interested in new products. Buy: vacations, luxuries, home improvements. |
| 7. Empty Nest II: Older married couples, no children living at home, head retired | Drastic cut in income. Keep home. Buy: medical appliances, medical-care products that aid health, sleep, and digestion. |
| 8. Solitary Survivor, in Labour Force | Income still good but likely to sell home. |
| 9. Solitary Survivor, Retired | Some medical and product needs as other retired group; drastic cut in income. Special need for attention, affection, and security. |

*Source*:  Phillip Kotler and Gordon H.G. McDougall, *Marketing Essentials* (Scarborough: Prentice-Hall Canada Inc., 1985) p. 110. Reprinted with permission.

decade the life-cycle concept was first developed. Figure 6.4 is a flowchart of a contemporary family life cycle which includes recent trends.

### Recent Demographic Shifts Affecting the Life Cycle Concept

Before the life cycle concept is to have an influence on contemporary marketing strategies, recent demographic shifts must be considered. These shifts were discussed in detail in chapter 4, but are worthy of quick review at this point:

1. *Smaller Family Size*  Families are smaller now than they were in past decades. This trend has developed because of the growing need for two incomes to survive, resulting in the necessity of placing children in expensive day care.

---

**FIGURE 6.4**  The Family Life Cycle Modernized

FAMILY LIFE CYCLE FLOWS

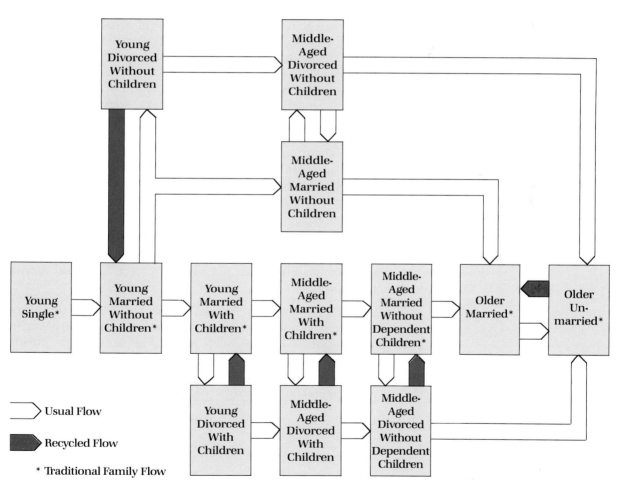

*Source*:  Patrick E. Murphy and William Staples, "A Modernized Family Life Cycle," *Journal of Consumer Research*, June 1979, p. 17. Reprinted with permission of The University of Chicago Press.

Further declines are expected in what was once referred to as the "traditional" household.[10]

For marketers, the decline of the traditional household means that positioning strategies must be re-evaluated. For example, due to the rapid increase in the number of women working outside the home, the prospects look good for the food service industry. Between 1963 and 1986, the food service industry doubled its market share from 18 to 35 percent as people have decided to eat fewer meals at home.[11] Grocery stores wanting to maintain their market share will have to stay in touch with the needs of the modern family, to focus on fresh foods, gourmet sections, microwave products, semi-prepared dishes and convenience items generally. Also, owing to lack of time, demand will increase for other commercial services that provide for household care (e.g. house cleaning, lawn and garden care, and painting. The influx of franchised maid services such as Molly Maid, Mini Maid, and Trend Tidy are examples of services related to the time-pressed family's needs.

2. *Greying Population* With birth rates declining and the baby boom generation aging, the population is getting older. In terms of the life cycle concept, the key groups in the nineties are becoming the Full Nest IIIs, Empty Nesters, and Survivors. Television programming has already recognized the importance of older age groups, as popular situation comedies are now about older families and are aimed at the more mature audience. Examples include The Golden Girls and Empty Nesters. Newspapers and specific interest magazines aimed directly at older audiences are also more common now. These older groups will influence marketing strategies the most in the nineties. Companies will launch new products geared specifically to mature targets, and reposition existing products to make them appeal to older people. Some pertinent population statistics are included in figure 6.5. This figure dramatizes the importance of elderly people as target markets to marketing organizations.

3. *Delay of Marriage* Young people are delaying marriage and, therefore, the single stage will be longer than in previous decades. Because of the career aspirations of couples, they are also having children later in life. The initial childless years of marriage are used primarily to reduce long-term financial burdens, such as mortgages.

4. *Single Parent Families* Marriage delays and a higher but stabilized divorce rate are contributing to new household formations in Canada. Single parent families are a fast-growing segment of households which, together with the growing number of two-career families, has helped to create a significant demand for day

FIGURE 6.5   The Changing Distribution of Canada's Population

| Age Group | 1961 | 1986 | 2011 | 2031 |
|---|---|---|---|---|
| 0–19 yr. | 42% | 29% | 22% | 21% |
| 20–44 | 35 | 41 | 33 | 32 |
| 45–64 | 17 | 19 | 29 | 25 |
| 65 + | 8 | 11 | 16 | 24 |
| All Ages (in thousands) | 18 238 | 25 310 | 30 659 | 32 430 |

*Source:* Adapted from information included in *The Royal Bank Reporter*, Winter 1989, p. 3.

care facilities. In addition, the daily needs of children (toys, clothing, and entertainment) are being met by divorced parents independent of each other.

### Occupation

The occupations of individuals are broadly classified into three categories: white collar, blue collar, or professional / managerial. Through the seventies and eighties, white collar occupations were relatively stable, while blue collar occupations declined and professional occupations increased. The growing use of electronic automation and robotics has caused a decrease in the number of blue collar occupations and an increase in professional / managerial jobs. In the professional / managerial sector the number of jobs increased by 700 000 between 1981 and 1987, an astounding 73 percent of Canada's net employment growth.[12] Growth in these jobs is due to the emergence of an information-oriented society, where businesses make their decisions based on elaborate computer data banks within organizations. This trend will continue through the 1990s. Automation will continue to affect white collar occupations in the nineties, and people who hold jobs in this category will be more productive because of technological advances.

Marketers use occupation in two basic ways for approaching customers. They may identify occupation groups that have an interest in their product or they may position a product so that it appeals to a certain group. While professional occupations are perceived to be the highest paying, marketers do not ignore the spending potential among high earning blue collar workers. Highly skilled blue collar workers earn more than some professionals, when overtime pay is taken into account.

### Economic Circumstances

Economic circumstances affect a person's purchase decisions. In recessionary economies, for example, where inflation, unemployment, and interest rates may be on the rise, the discretionary income of consumers may be low. Consequently, major purchases will be delayed, and consumers will make products they do have last longer; new purchases of items such as a larger house, a renovation, a car, or a major appliance may be placed on hold. Conversely, if the economy is booming, consumers are more likely to purchase goods and services.

The construction and housing industries are good examples of markets which roll with the economic shifts in Canada. When mortgage rates decline, the cost of carrying a mortgage drops; therefore, there is a frenzy as first-time buyers enter the market, and current homeowners consider trading up to larger accommodations, even though the steady demand forces the price of housing up.

Marketing organizations must be prepared to adjust marketing strategies as the economy enters various cyclical stages (refer to chapter 2). Generally, business organizations remain conservative in hard times and are aggressive in good times.

### Lifestyle

**lifestyle**

The importance of lifestyle considerations in marketing is the result of a growing use of psychographic research in Canada. A **lifestyle** is a "person's pattern of living as expressed in his or her activities, interests and opinions."[13] Marketing organizations try to determine who buys their product based on demographic variables such as age, income, sex, and education. Nevertheless, individuals with these variables in common, who even look alike and live side by side, can be entirely different in terms of their lifestyle. It is the psychographic profile, obtained through research, that indicates differences between people and why different people buy the products they do. Psychographic research determines the activities, interests and opinions of consumers (commonly referred to as their AIOs). Examples of questions used to collect psychographic information are included in figure 6.6.

Psychographics allow the marketing organization to position their products effectively in the marketplace. For example, messages can be communicated which link a product to a particular lifestyle. The beer industry in Canada is a heavy user of psychographic-based advertising in such campaigns as those for popular brands such as Labatt's Blue and Molson Export. Some brands are positioned to appeal to the blue collar male, while others are positioned to appeal to socially active young couples. Those potential users who are exposed to the message and who identify with the lifestyle presented in an advertisement may become receptive to the advertised brand. Refer.to figure 6.7 for an illustration of lifestyle marketing strategy.

---

**FIGURE 6.6**   Sample Questions for Collecting Psychographic Data

1. To collect information on likes, dislikes and attitudes of consumers (usually a scale of 1 to 5 is used with 1 being strongly agree and 5 strongly disagree)
   - I go out with friends a great deal of the time.
   - I generally achieve what I set out to do.
   - I like to think I'm a bit of a swinger.
   - An important part of my life is dressing smartly.

2. a) To collect information on principles, values and aspirations of consumers (a scale is used to rank statements based on degree of importance)
   - Getting married, having a happy marriage
   - Respect for authority
   - Commitment to the work ethic
   - Promotion of conservation and the fight against waste in society
   - College education

   b) To determine people's opinions (again, a scale is used to determine the strength of respondent's convictions)
   - Capital punishment should be reinstated.
   - It is important that children receive religious training.
   - A woman should not work outside the home unless her household needs the money.

3. To collect information on activities and participation (scales used to determine frequency of participation)
   a) How often do you personally participate in these activities?
   - Jogging/Running
   - Golf
   - Downhill skiing
   - Fishing
   - Gardening
   - Dancing
   - Entertaining at home
   etc.

---

**FIGURE 6.7    A Lifestyle Advertising Message**

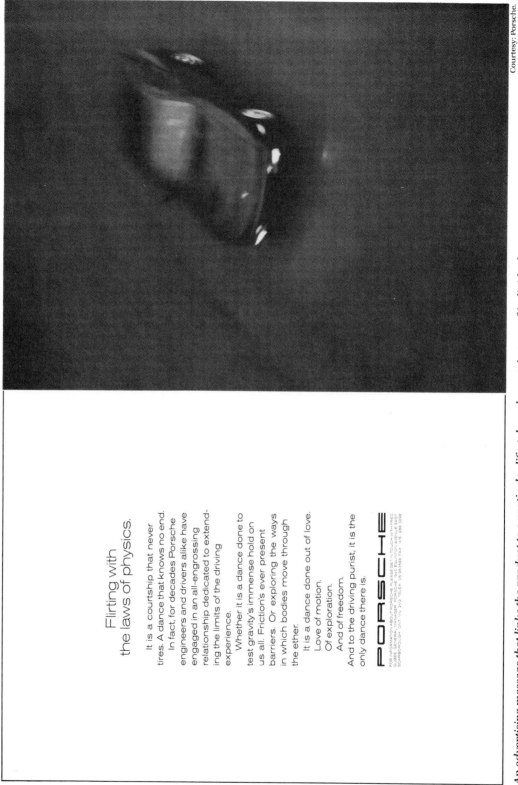

Flirting with
the laws of physics.

It is a courtship that never tires. A dance that knows no end. In fact, for decades Porsche engineers and drivers alike have engaged in an all-engrossing relationship dedicated to extending the limits of the driving experience.

Whether it is a dance done to test gravity's immense hold on us all. Friction's ever present barriers. Or exploring the ways in which bodies move through the ether.

It is a dance done out of love.

Love of motion.

Of exploration.

And of freedom.

And to the driving purist, it is the only dance there is.

PORSCHE

FOR INFORMATION ABOUT PORSCHE PLEASE GET IN TOUCH WITH FRED DUBEE, GENERAL MANAGER, PORSCHE, 1940 EGLINTON AVENUE EAST, SCARBOROUGH, ONT M1L 2M2. TELEX: 06-963598 FAX  416  288-3298

*An advertising message that links the product to a particular lifestyle and a certain type of individual.*

### *Personality and Self-Concept*

**personality**

**Personality** refers to a person's distinguishing psychological characteristics, those features which lead to relatively consistent and enduring responses to the environment in which that person lives. It is influenced by self-perceptions, which in turn are influenced by physiological and psychological needs, family, culture, and reference groups. Why would someone pay $50 000 for a Porsche when a less expensive automobile will perform the same task? Why do people buy designer label clothing at high prices and in upscale boutiques when low-priced items performing the same functions are available? Such purchases are based on the desired image we have of ourselves.

The self has four components: real self, self-image, looking-glass self and ideal self.[14]

1. *Real Self*   The real self is seen through an objective evaluation of the individual — it is you as you really are. The perception of this reality is distorted by the other selves.

2. *Self-Image*   This is how you see yourself. You might, for example, see yourself as a swinger, or an intellectual, even though you may be neither.

3. *Looking-Glass Self*   This concept derives from the way you think others see you.

4. *Ideal Self*   This is how you would like to be. It is your aspirations.

**self-concept theory**

Marketing organizations use this **self-concept theory** to advantage. Marketers know that, human nature being what it is, many important decisions are based on the looking-glass self and the ideal self. Goods and services that help to fulfill the ideal self are appealing to the consumer. The young business executive who is climbing the corporate ladder will have definite goals and aspirations to fulfill. Such an individual will purchase top quality business attire, perhaps designer-made; join prestigious clubs (golf, tennis, service); and probably drive an expensive sports car or luxury car (perhaps a European model). Purchase decisions like these are not based on where a person is but on where the person is going — in his or her own mind, at least. Marketing organizations accentuate the image-making appeal of their products in order to attract purchasers who buy with the ideal self in mind.

The importance of self-image in buying and marketing increased with the health and fitness craze of the eighties. People entered an era where "wellness" (both physical and mental) preoccupied their minds. People were increasingly conscious of what they were eating, and huge sums of money were being spent on health club memberships and personal workout equipment such as exercise bikes, light weights, and rowing machines. Such purchases were based on the desire to improve one's image — to look and feel better. Self-improvement leads to greater self-confidence, which in turn results in purchases in other product categories (e.g. new clothing, cosmetics, automobiles).

## Psychological Influences

The primary psychological characteristics that influence consumer behaviour and purchase decisions are needs, motives, perceptions, attitudes and beliefs, perceived risk, innovativeness, and the amount of time spent on the purchase.

### *Needs and Motives*

Let's clearly distinguish between needs and motives. The term **needs** suggests a state of deprivation or the absence of something useful, whereas **motives** are the conditions that prompt action to satisfy a need (the action stimulated by marketing activity). The relationship between needs and motives is direct in terms of marketing activity. Needs are developed or brought to the foreground of consumers' minds when product's benefits are presented to them in an interesting manner (e.g. in conjunction with a lifestyle the targeted people associate themselves with), so that they are motivated to purchase the product or service.

**Maslow's hierarchy of needs** and theory of motivation have had a significant impact on marketing strategies. According to this theory needs can be classified in an ascending order, from lower level to higher level. Two principles are at work in this hierarchy:[15]

1. When lower level needs are satisfied, a person moves up to higher level needs.

2. Satisfied needs do not motivate. Instead, behaviour is influenced by needs yet to be satisfied.

Maslow states that individuals progress through five levels of needs (see figure 6.8).

1. *Physiological Needs*   hunger, thirst, sex, clothing (basic survival needs).
2. *Safety Needs*   security, protection and comfort.
3. *Social Needs*   a sense of belonging, love from family and friends.
4. *Esteem Needs*   recognition, achievement and status, the need to excel.
5. *Self-Actualization Needs*   fulfillment, to realize one's potential (to achieve what you believe you can do).

**FIGURE 6.8**   Maslow's Hierarchy of Needs

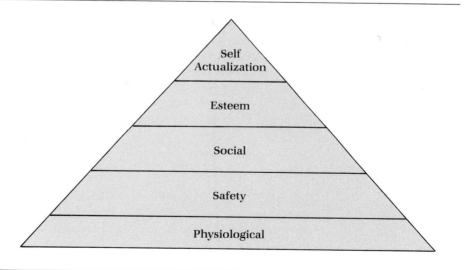

*Source*: ''Hierarchy of Needs'' from *Motivation and Personality, 2nd ed* by Abraham H. Maslow Copyright 1954 by Harper & Row, Publisher, Inc., © 1970 by Abraham H. Maslow. Reprinted by permission of the publishers.

Numerous examples can be cited to demonstrate how marketing uses the needs taken into account in Maslow's theory. Marketers bring attention to safety needs in order to motivate people to purchase automobile tires (e.g. the Michelin baby rotating in a tire sends out a safety message about the product to prospective buyers). The desire to be accepted by peers (social need satisfaction) is commonly used in the promotion of products like toothpaste, deodorant, and breath mints. Esteem needs are addressed in messages that portray people in successful business roles and occupations; a senior executive is shown travelling first class on an airline or purchasing an automobile symbolic of success, such as a Mercedes Benz, Porsche or Jaguar.

## *Perception*

**perception**

**Perception** refers to how individuals receive and interpret messages. Marketing knows that different individuals perceive the same product differently. Although their perceptions are influenced by the same advertising, pricing, packaging, and place of purchase, their perceptions differ because they are quite selective about the messages they receive. Selectivity is based on their level of interest and their needs. There are three levels of selectivity:

**selective exposure**

1. *Selective Exposure*   Our eyes and minds only notice information that is of interest.

**selective perception**

2. *Selective Perception*   We screen out messages and information that are in conflict with previously learned attitudes and beliefs.

**selective retention**

3. *Selective Retention*   We remember only what we want to remember.

For example, if a consumer is considering a purchase, let's say the purchase of an expensive camera or video recorder, that consumer will be interested in learning about the various products available, so that an informed decision can be made. He or she becomes receptive to messages about cameras and video recorders, while screening out other messages. This selective nature of perception helps explain why only some people respond to marketing activity; others quite simply do not notice it. The challenge for marketers is to penetrate the perceptual barriers — they must design messages and strategies that will command attention and compel the reader, listener, or viewer to take action.

## *Attitudes and Beliefs*

**attitudes**

Lets make the distinction between attitudes and beliefs. **Attitudes** are an individual's feelings, favourable or unfavourable, towards an idea or object (the product or service). **Beliefs** are the strongly held convictions on which an individual's actions are based.

**beliefs**

### *Acquiring and Changing Attitudes and Beliefs*
The variety of cultural, personal and social influences discussed in this chapter

determine an individual's attitudes and beliefs. The attitudes and beliefs people acquire about particular products promote or deter purchases. Marketers sometimes try to develop strategies to change negative attitudes and beliefs about products, since antagonistic outlooks discourage buying. Some situations, however, are beyond the control of the marketing organization. When people say "I'll never buy that again", whether the reason is valid or not, they usually mean it. A bad experience creates an attitude that no amount of marketing activity can overcome.

Marketers have generally found that it is expensive to try to change attitudes. Instead, they prefer to present products so that the products appear to fit attitudes already widely held by the target market. While it is difficult for a marketing organization to change attitudes, they can be reasonably successful in doing so by using the following strategies:

1. Making comparisons with other major brands, so long as the comparison is an accurate one, that show one's own product to be more to the target market's liking.

2. Identifying what the key attributes are to the market and stressing those attributes in their product offering. Ford uses the slogan "Quality is Job One" because quality is an important attribute to car purchasers, many of whom perceive North American quality to be lower than that of Japanese and European makes. Ford, therefore, decided to use such a slogan for a long period.

3. Emphasizing attributes formerly ignored. The fibre component and natural grain base of many cereals went unremarked by advertisers until the health and fitness craze of the eighties. Then, these features became the critical selling point that helped rejuvenate numerous brands. Established brands like Nabisco Shredded Wheat and Kellogg's Bran Flakes became popular once again. This trend also led to the development and marketing of new brands such as Kellogg's Pro-Grain, Kellogg's Common Sense Oat Bran, and Post Fruit 'n Fibre in a variety of flavour combinations.

See the Marketing in Action vignettes, "Women Purchase 40% of All Condoms" and "A Whiter Shade of Pale" for illustrations of how attitudes have affected marketing strategy.

The importance of attitudes can be quickly illustrated by the rivalry between Coca-Cola and Pepsi-Cola. The comparative taste tests between Pepsi-Cola and Coca-Cola demonstrated that when Coke drinkers tried both products in the tests, many of them preferred Pepsi. Advertising campaigns that showed the results of the tests were mounted to persuade Coke drinkers to try Pepsi. Consumers believed the message, and their attitudes changed. The number of Pepsi drinkers increased. This campaign, and the success that Pepsi had, was *one* of the factors leading to the now-famous changing of the original formula for Coca-Cola.

### Measuring Consumers' Attitudes

A firm evaluates the attitudes of its customers by using rating questions in its research. Different types of attitude rating scales are available to market researchers. One type, called a semantic differential, uses opposite descriptions of the attributes of a product or service to describe product or service attributes. The semantic

## ⟩⟩⟩ *MARKETING IN ACTION*

### *WOMEN PURCHASE 40 PERCENT OF ALL CONDOMS*

Some consumers still associate condoms with backseat sex and prostitutes, but in today's society, condom manufacturers are certainly trying to change that image. Fuelled by a rise in sexually transmitted diseases, including AIDS, the market for condoms has been rejuvenated for major manufacturers such as Julius Schmid and Ortho Pharmaceuticals.

As a result of the AIDS scare, condoms are now more in vogue. In 1987, sales increased 35 percent compared to 1986, but since that time, sales have sagged to the 5 percent range on an annual basis, and manufacturers do not fully understand why, since there is an urgent need for such a product. Media advertising in 1988 doubled to approximately $500 000 in the condom industry. Manufacturers thought that the investment would pay off, but admit that they are perplexed by the declining sales trends. It is a delicate and sensitive market limited by consumer attitudes.

There is, however, a sense of urgency in educating potential users, particularly young people, about the benefits of using condoms. Most people in Canada still use the condom primarily for birth control. Among new users, 75 percent are using condoms for protection against sexually transmitted diseases. For women, doctors do not prescribe the pill for smokers or for those over the age of thirty-five, and IUDs have caused pelvic infections. Consequently, women now purchase 35–40 percent of all condoms sold in North America. Such purchase patterns have influenced the marketing strategies of the manufacturers.

What about the marketing activity for condoms? The opportunities available for manufacturers have resulted in sportier condoms, which offer imaginative colours and provocative textures, stream-lined packaging, and package designs that use emotional relationships to advantage. As indicated earlier, promotional budgets have increased significantly. No longer are condoms tucked away behind the pharmacist's counter. They are in full view. Now you can even purchase condoms at the corner convenience store as manufacturers attempt to increase their share of the estimated $20 million Canadian market.

Adapted from "A very private product goes public," *Report on Business Magazine*, April 1987, pp.42 +, and "Condom sales slipping despite scare over AIDS," *The Globe and Mail*, January 24, 1989, p.B10.

*New purchase patterns have influenced the marketing strategies of condom manufacturers*

Julius Schmid of Canada Ltd.

## ⟩⟩⟩⟩ *MARKETING IN ACTION*

### *A WHITER SHADE OF PALE*

Do you remember the Coppertone tan, or how dark the Bain de Soleil model with the St. Tropez tan was? For tanning products, such advertising now belongs to the past. Fuelled by a fear that prolonged exposure to the sun's ultra-violet rays causes premature aging and skin cancer, the industry's leading brands have shifted their advertising strategies from "bronzed beauties" to "pale perfection". Today, advertising copy emphasizes protection from a deep dark tan.

Since tanning has become less desirable, the major brands, such as Coppertone, Paba-tan, and Bain de Soleil focus on the sun protection factor of SPF. Playing upon medical warnings that one bad burn as a child could cause melanoma, a potentially fatal skin cancer, an advertisement for Superblock (Elizabeth Arden) shows a lightly tanned woman emerging from a pool with a baby in her arms. The copy reminds readers that precious possessions demand the most protection. Following this changing social trend, all manufacturers stress that you can still enjoy the sun and do all you like to, while being protected and looking healthy.

Adapted from Laura Medcalf, "These days pale is preferable", *Marketing*, August 1, 1988, p.15.

*Today, advertising copy for tanning products emphasizes protection from the sun's ultra-violet rays*

---

differential scale determines the strength of the attitude held by the consumers. An illustration of the semantic differential is included in figure 6.9.

### *Perceived Risk*

**perceived risk**

Closely associated with attitudes and beliefs is the **perceived risk** associated with the purchase of a good or service. The risk factor is generally higher for first-time purchases or when the price of any purchase increases. Some risks that commonly play on the consumer's mind include the following:

1. Will the purchase cause embarrassment or social rejection rather than acceptance? If you purchased a Beta videocassette recorder, you probably faced the scorn of VHS purchasers. Purchase the wrong brand of microcomputer and see what your trusted friends say to you. Such a purchase leaves a person feeling uneasy.

**FIGURE 6.9** The Semantic Differential Scale

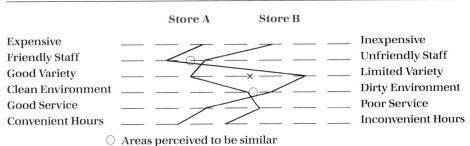

| | Store A | Store B | |
| --- | --- | --- | --- |
| Expensive | | | Inexpensive |
| Friendly Staff | | | Unfriendly Staff |
| Good Variety | | | Limited Variety |
| Clean Environment | | | Dirty Environment |
| Good Service | | | Poor Service |
| Convenient Hours | | | Inconvenient Hours |

○ Areas perceived to be similar
× Areas perceived to be different

The semantic differential is a rating scale that evaluates customer attitudes. The use of opposite descriptions at each end of the scale determines the strength of the attitude held by the customer.

Customers are comparing stores in the example above. The closer the lines are together for each store, the greater the similarity in customer perception. The farther apart the lines, the greater the difference in perception.

2. Will the product perform according to promises made? Children's toys often do not perform at the level shown in television commercials. This causes disappointment for both the child and the adult who purchased it.

3. Will the product be harmful? The purchase of products classified as hazardous creates a danger for anyone who may come into contact with the product.

Despite the attitudes and beliefs that may be associated with perceived risks in purchase decisions, marketers deal effectively with such situations. Marketing strategies include programs designed to reduce risk, such as trial coupons, money-back guarantees, extended warranties, annual sales, and the development of a reputation for good quality and service.

### Innovativeness

At the other end of the spectrum are consumers who revel in new and risky purchase decisions. They take risks because of their desire to be innovative and set the trends rather than follow them. While this group represents only a small percentage of the population, its members assist the marketer with their early adoptions of new products and services. Once a product is adopted by the masses, such individuals lose interest in it and move on to other products. The psychographic profile of innovators include descriptions like open-minded, venturesome, achievement-oriented, and status-conscious.[16] Very often, people like this are portrayed in the lead roles of commercial messages or pictured in print advertisements for products and services.

### Time Spent on the Purchase

The importance of the purchase plays a key role in the time and effort a consumer will spend searching the marketplace for a certain product. Purchase decisions are

**FIGURE 6.10**    The Purchase Decision Continuum

| Factors | Routine Decision | Limited Decision | Complex Decision |
|---------|------------------|------------------|------------------|
| Time | Low | Limited | Extensive (Rigid Process) |
| Evaluation | Minimal | Some | Significant |
| Preference | Existing Product | Open to New Product | Very Open to New Product Information |
| Purchase Frequency | Frequent | Moderate | Low |
| Risk | Low | Moderate | High |
| Experience | High | Some | Low |

classified as routine, limited, or complex. Routine purchases do not involve much money and take little time. Products that are routinely purchased include items subject to brand preference such as toothpaste, coffee, cigarettes, and deodorant. In contrast, decisions that are complex in nature — that is, that require lots of time, effort, money, and a proper evaluation of alternatives — make the consumer more receptive to advertising information. Products that fall into this category are housing, automobiles, televisions, audio-video equipment, and major household appliances. For example, the search for the most suitable registered retirement savings plan or the best stock market investment calls for complex decisions in the service sector. Refer to figure 6.10 for an illustration and explanation of the purchase decision continuum.

## 〉〉〉〉 *The Consumer Purchase Decision Process*

Knowing exactly how purchase decisions are made is difficult. While we know that certain variables influence behaviour, there are so many contributing variables that we cannot be certain of which ones actually trigger a response. Since consumer purchase decisions are based on a mix of cultural, personal, social and psychological factors, each consumer also presents a unique situation. Sometimes, too, a consumer may be governed by rational (logical) behaviour for one purchase, and at other times by irrational (emotional) behaviour.

Despite these difficulties a generic model of the buying decision process may be offered. This model assumes that behaviour is rational, however, and readers must

FIGURE 6.11    The Consumer Purchase Decision Process

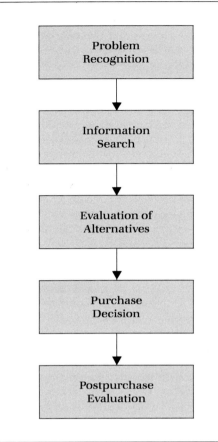

be aware that emotional responses can and do negate rational tendencies. Essentially, there are five steps in the consumer purchase decision process (see figure 6.11). These steps are problem recognition, information search, evaluation of alternatives, purchase decision, and postpurchase evaluation.

It should be pointed out that the purchase decision process can be terminated at any stage. Termination could be based on the perception that the good or service being evaluated is too expensive, or that it won't satisfactorily resolve the problem or need the consumer may have. Let's examine each step in the decision-making process in detail.

## Problem Recognition

The process begins with problem recognition. At this stage a consumer discovers a need, or unfulfilled desire; for example, the muffler goes on the family station wagon or one's squash racquet breaks. In each case there is a need to replace the product. As in Maslow's theory, the need leads to the motivation to fulfill it.

# Information Search

Once the problem or need has been defined the individual seeks the information needed to solve the problem. The extent of the search varies with the nature of the purchase (refer back to figure 6.11 on the purchase decision continuum). For a routine purchase, usually no information is sought, since the same product is automatically purchased again. For limited or complex decisions, time is taken for the search process. Generally, as the risk increases, the extent of the search for information also increases. To illustrate, let's assume that a family requires a new automobile. The purchasers (husband and wife) determine that what they want is a mid-priced family station wagon or similar vehicle. Having defined the need, they begin looking for ways to fulfill it. To do so, the family checks the following sources of information.

1. *Periodicals*  The husband and wife review advertisements in local newspapers and automobile magazines in order to become aware of the alternatives available.

2. *Consumer Reports*  They read the latest published reviews of the Consumers Association of Canada, which appear in the monthly magazine of the association.

3. *Reference Groups*  They seek the views of people they commonly associate with and whose views they trust.

4. *Showroom Visits*  Finally, the family visits the showrooms of car dealers to examine models. Here, they collect brochures and information for evaluation and comparison.

Now that the consumers have the appropriate information they move to the next stage in the buying process.

# Evaluation of Alternatives

At this stage the husband and wife have listed the alternatives that will satisfy the family's transportation needs. Let's say that after the vehicles were examined, the following short list prevailed:

1. Plymouth Voyageur or Dodge Caravan
2. Chevrolet Station Wagon
3. Ford Aerostar Van
4. Toyota Mini Van

Since each of these products would fulfill the basic transportation need, a rational consumer would evaluate each alternative for value; that is, he or she would try to determine which one offered the best combination of price and quality within a desired price range. In theory, consumers should identify the attributes that are most important to them and then rank the alternatives with reference to each of the attributes. In the case of the automobile purchase, the cars under consideration could be compared in terms of such characteristics as price, style, option packages and accessories, warranty, safety, reputation of the manufacturer, availability, and fuel economy. Since many attributes need to be considered, the family will have to rank the attributes in order of importance in order to make the comparisons meaningful. Because the purchase of a car is a high risk decision, these consumers may also seek the views of relatives or trusted associates. If the decision proves a difficult one, they may postpone it or sleep on it, or decide to collect information about alternatives overlooked initially. On the other hand, perhaps a clear decision can be made.

## Purchase Decision

Once the best alternative has been selected, a consumer is ready to make the purchase. In effect, he or she is ready to use cash, cheque, or credit card to obtain the item selected (ownership utility). Let's examine further the automobile purchase. The family, say, decides that the Plymouth Voyageur offers the best value in satisfying its transportation needs. Now, it must go through another decision-making process and evaluate variables such as place of purchase, price, availability of credit and service, and dealer reputation. Perhaps there are two or three dealers in the area who sell Plymouth Voyageurs. The family would visit all three and select the one offering the best deal based on the variables just mentioned. If no dealer appears satisfactory, the consumer could postpone the decision again and re-evaluate the situation.

## Postpurchase Evaluation

As indicated earlier, purchases involve risk, and the higher the cost of the purchase, the greater the risk for the consumer. Once the decision to purchase has been made, the delivery order signed, and the bank loan secured, certain common questions arise. Did I make the right decision? Do I feel good, bad, or indifferent about the purchase?

**cognitive dissonance**

The purchase of routine items is based on past experience and satisfaction; therefore, there is a positive, secure feeling after the purchase that says "I trust this product." Conversely, other purchases may result in dissatisfaction leading to brand switching, a process involving more purchases and evaluations. Such dissatisfaction is the result of **cognitive dissonance**, which is defined as the unsettled state of mind experienced by an individual after he or she has taken action. Cognitive dissonance is often referred to as postpurchase doubt. Its presence suggests that the consumer is not confident that he or she has made the right decision. The customer may begin to wish that another alternative had been chosen as the mind goes through numerous "what if" scenarios. The consumer can overcome cognitive dissonance by taking certain actions. In the example of the automobile purchase, a person could reread favourable consumer reports, get out the brochures again and review all of the positive attributes, or perhaps talk to a friend about the purchase. I can recall a personal situation that arose shortly after I purchased a foreign mini-van. Several passersby on the street stopped at my parked van and asked me how I liked it, since they were contemplating such a purchase. What I told them made me feel better about my purchase decision. The positive aspects of the purchase decision were reinforced in my own mind.

From a marketing perspective, the organization should initiate appropriate follow-up activities to put the consumer's mind at ease. In the automobile purchase decision, simply keeping in touch through service reminder notices may be all that is required.

## 〉〉〉〉 *Other Factors Affecting the Decision-Making Process*

In this chapter we have seen that many variables — cultural, social, personal, and psychological — combine to influence the decision-making process. The differences among these influences help explain why some consumers make the same decision, while others make quite different decisions. The knowledgeable marketer uses information about cultural, social, personal and psychological traits to develop target market profiles, which in turn are used to design effective marketing strategies.

Other factors, among them time and income, also affect an individual's decisions. A time-pressed person may make decisions hurriedly, whereas someone with lots of time to spend may choose to look around and carefully evaluate the alternatives before making the decision. Affluent shoppers may also make quick choices since there is little financial risk for them, while those with modest incomes are likely to proceed with caution.

In planning an effective marketing mix, an organization takes into account the behavioural factors discussed in this chapter. Here is a selection of some behavioural facts and information that could have a bearing on a firm's marketing strategy:[17]

1. The average Canadian adult of eighteen years of age and older watches 24.9 hours of television weekly; children aged two to eleven watch 21.9 hours weekly.
2. Ninety-nine percent of Canadian households have television sets and 54 percent have two or more sets.
3. Radio reaches 95 percent of all Canadian adults over the age of eighteen each week.
4. Newspapers are circulated to 65 percent of all households daily.
5. Studies show that satisfied new car buyers tell eight people of their experiences; dissatisfied buyers complain to about 25 people.
6. In 1988, Canadians spent over $100 million on exercise benches, light weights, exercise bikes, treadmills and rowing machines; a decade earlier the sales were less than $1 million.

## 〉〉〉〉 S U M M A R Y

Consumers, through their decision to purchase a product or service, determine an organization's success. Since organizations cannot control consumers, it is essential that they understand them so they can adapt strategies to consumers' thinking and behaviour.

This chapter discussed the dynamics of consumer behaviour and illustrated how marketing organizations can use behavioural information to advantage when developing marketing strategies. The study of consumer behaviour deals with why people buy the products and services they do and explains why two or more people behave differently or similarly. It has shown that purchase decisions are primarily based on four major influences, namely, cultural, social, personal, and psychological. Marketing organizations possessing knowledge of the influences on behaviour are adept at developing target market profiles and at using these profiles to prepare marketing strategies that trigger a response from the target markets.

The consumer decision-making process involves five distinct stages. These stages include problem recognition, information search, evaluation of alternatives, the purchase decision, and postpurchase behaviour.

## 〉〉〉〉 KEY TERMS

| | | |
|---|---|---|
| consumer behaviour | psychographics | selective perception |
| culture | personality | selective retention |
| subculture | self-concept theory | attitudes |
| social class | needs | beliefs |
| reference group | motives | semantic differential |
| family life cycle | Maslow's hierarchy of needs | perceived risk |
| greying population | perception | cognitive dissonance |
| lifestyle | selective exposure | |

## 〉〉〉〉 REVIEW AND DISCUSSION QUESTIONS

**1.** Compare and contrast your behaviour when making the following purchase decisions: **a)** a new business suit for an important job interview **b)** an audio component set **c)** a case of beer

**2.** Briefly discuss how decision-making is changing in Canadian households.

**3.** "Marketing strategies that appeal to our desires are more effective than those appealing to current needs." Discuss.

**4.** Briefly explain the difference between **a)** culture and subculture **b)** needs and motives **c)** selective exposure and selective retention

**5.** Briefly explain the four components of the self-concept theory, and illustrate how they have an influence on marketing strategy.

**6.** Examine the role of reference groups in the purchase of the following products: **a)** blue jeans **b)** personal computers **c)** chocolate bars **d)** cosmetics

**7.** "Presenting products according to widely held attitudes is preferable to other strategies, and almost always successful." Discuss.

**8.** What role does the family life cycle play in the development of a marketing strategy?

**9.** Using the 'lifestyle approach' in marketing is of questionable effectiveness since the consumer is told little about the actual product. Evaluate the validity of this statement, using examples of your own choice.

**10.** Provide some examples of how Maslow's hierarchy of needs and theory of motivation can be used in the practice of marketing.

**11.** Briefly explain the steps in the consumer decision making process.

## 〉〉〉 REFERENCES

1. JAMES F. ENGEL, DAVID T. KOLLATT, and ROGER D. BLACKWELL, *Consumer Behaviour*, 2nd Edition (New York: Holt Rinehart and Winston, 1973), p.5.

2. PHILIP KOTLER and GORDON McDOUGALL, *Marketing Essentials*, Canadian Edition (Scarborough, Ontario: Prentice-Hall Canada Inc., 1985), p.101.

3. Statistics Canada, "Population by Ethnic Background", *1986 Census Data*, (Ottawa: Ministry of Supply and Services Canada).

4. BARRIE McKENNA, "Food Firms Must Consider Marketing to Men", *Financial Post*, November 18, 1988, p.14.

5. Ibid.

6. Based on a marketing research study conducted by the Campbell Soup Company Limited, 1985.

7. FRANK GO, "Home and Work", *Canadian Hotel and Restaurant*, August 1988, p.24.

8. DAVE HAGE, "Americans Cram More Work into Less Time", *Whig Standard*, September 12, 1988, p.10.

9. WILLIAM D. WELLS and GEORGE GUBAR, "Life Cycle Concepts in Marketing Research", *Journal of Marketing Research*, November 1986, p.362.

10. CLARKSON GORDON/WOODS GORDON, *Tomorrow's Customers in Canada*, 20th edition, 1985, p.4.

11. FRANK GO, "Home and Work", p.24.

12. PATRICIA LUSH. "Shortage of Skills to Worsen in the Nineties", *The Globe and Mail*, January 23, 1989. p.B1.

13. PHILIP KOTLER, GORDON McDOUGALL and GARY ARMSTRONG, *Marketing*, Canadian edition (Scarborough, Ontario: Prentice-Hall Canada Inc., 1988), p.142.

14. JOHN DOUGLAS, GEORGE FIELD, and LAWRENCE TARPEY, *Human Behaviour in Marketing* (Columbus, Ohio: Charles E. Merrill Publishing, 1967), p.5.

15. A.H. MASLOW, *Motivation and Personality* (New York: Harper and Row Publishers, 1954), pp.370-396.

16. JAMES ENGEL, ROGER BLACKWELL, and PAUL MINIARD, *Consumer Behaviour*, 5th edition (Hinsdale, Illinois: Dryden Press, 1985), pp. 543-45.

17. Information obtained from *Canadian Media Directors Association Handbook*, 1988-89, BBM Bureau of Measurement data, and *Time* magazine.

# CHAPTER 7 ››››

# Business-to-Business Marketing and Organizational Buying Behaviour

*LEARNING OBJECTIVES*

After studying this chapter, you will be able to

1. Identify the types of customers comprising the business-to-business marketplace.

2. Describe the unique characteristics of the business-to-business market.

3. Explain the role of market segmentation in business-to business marketing strategy.

4. Outline the nature of organizational buying behaviour.

5. Identify the steps involved in the organizational buying decision process.

6. Describe the unique characteristics of the government market.

7. List the basic marketing mix decisions necessary for approaching the business-to-business marketplace.

Organizations marketing goods and services to other organizations is what business-to-business marketing is all about. Marketing strategies used in the business-to-business market are quite different from those used in the consumer market. Firms succeed in the business-to-business market when they fully understand the complex buying process that is involved and the different criteria that are used to evaluate purchase decisions.

The business-to-business market is comprised of business and industry, government, institutional, and professional segments. In serving these diverse markets, organizations must identify the unique demands and needs of each, and then develop responsive marketing strategies showing how their products or services will resolve a special problem or satisfy a particular need.

This chapter endeavours to illustrate the characteristics that influence the purchase decisions in the business-to-business market. It also outlines the role of market segmentation and the different buying behaviours in the various market segments.

# ⟩⟩⟩⟩ *Business-to-Business Markets*

business-to-business
market

The **business-to-business market** is comprised of individuals in an organization who are responsible for purchasing goods and services that the organization needs to produce a product or service, promote an idea, or produce an income.[1] The business-to-business market can be divided into four distinct buying groups: business and industry, governments, institutions, and professions. Figure 7.1 shows the diversity of the business-to-business marketplace.

## Business and Industry

Business and industrial organizations are grouped under the categories of users, original equipment manufacturers, dealers and distributor networks, and service businesses.

1. *Users*   These are organizations that purchase products to produce other products. For example, a firm purchases capital equipment such as equipment and machinery in order to produce products on an assembly line.

2. *Original Equipment Manufacturers (OEMs)*   These companies purchase industrial products that are incorporated directly into other products. General Motors would be classified as an OEM because it purchases finished radios, spark plugs, tires, and other products to install in its automobiles. As a producer, it makes a profit by creating and marketing form utility.

3. *Dealers (Retailers) and Distributors*   These are middlemen who purchase products to sell to other middlemen or to final users. Resellers make a profit by creating time, place, and ownership utility. The local General Motors or Mercury

**FIGURE 7.1** The Diversity of the Business-to-Business Market

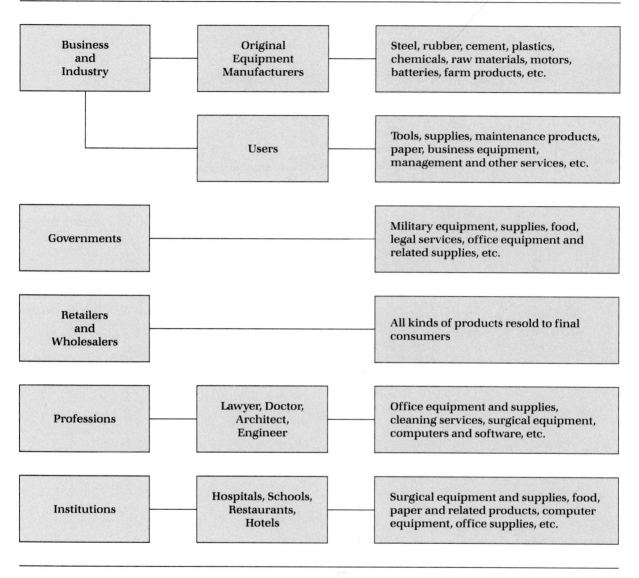

Marine outlet are examples of dealers, as are retailers such as Bata Shoes, Roots, and Lady Foot Locker.

4. *Service Businesses*  This category includes industries such as banks, insurance companies, real estate companies, and management or specialized service consultants, who collectively require a variety of goods and services in order to conduct their business operations. Figure 7.2 includes a list of Canada's leading business and industrial marketing organizations and customers.

FIGURE 7.2    Canada's Largest Companies

| Rank | Company | Sales (in thousands) |
|---|---|---|
| 1. | General Motors of Canada Limited | $  16 884 371 |
| 2. | BCE Inc. | 14 649 000 |
| 3. | Ford Motor Company of Canada Limited | 13 976 800 |
| 4. | Canadian Pacific Limited | 12 208 600 |
| 5. | George Weston Limited | 11 034 800 |
| 6. | Alcan Aluminum Limited | 9 012 822 |
| 7. | Imperial Oil Limited | 7 562 000 |
| 8. | Noranda Inc. | 7 343 566 |
| 9. | Chrysler Canada Limited | 7 246 800 |
| 10. | Provigo Inc. | 6 418 100 |

| Top 5 | Financial Institutions | Assets (in thousands) |
|---|---|---|
| 1. | Royal Bank of Canada | $ 102 170 201 |
| 2. | CIBC | 88 374 898 |
| 3. | Bank of Montreal | 84 227 721 |
| 4. | Bank of Nova Scotia | 71 429 739 |
| 5. | Toronto Dominion Bank | 54 525 475 |

| Top 5 | Energy Companies | Sales (in thousands) |
|---|---|---|
| 1. | Imperial Oil | $   7 562 000 |
| 2. | Ontario Hydro | 5 280 000 |
| 3. | Petro-Canada | 5 194 000 |
| 4. | Hydro-Quebec | 5 095 000 |
| 5. | Shell Canada | 4 819 000 |

| Top 5 | Forestry Companies | Sales (in thousands) |
|---|---|---|
| 1. | MacMillan Bloedell | $   3 134 500 |
| 2. | Abitibi-Price | 2 988 000 |
| 3. | Domtar | 2 567 800 |
| 4. | Consolidated-Bathurst | 2 261 300 |
| 5. | B.C. Forest Products | 1 400 427 |

| Top 5 | Merchandisers | Sales (in thousands) |
|---|---|---|
| 1. | George Weston Limited | $  11 034 800 |
| 2. | Provigo Inc. | 6 418 100 |
| 3. | Hudson's Bay | 4 845 178 |
| 4. | Steinberg | 4 491 385 |
| 5. | Sears Canada | 4 035 098 |

*Source*: "The Financial Post 500," *Financial Post Magazine*, Summer 1988.

## Governments

Collectively, the federal, provincial, and municipal governments form Canada's largest buying group. Governments tend to have a specialized buying procedure involving detailed order specifications and tender submissions from potential suppliers.

## Institutional Market

The third major buying group is the institutional market, which includes hospitals, restaurants, and educational establishments. These customers require a variety of products and services from potential suppliers. Hospitals and educational establishments operate on the basis of objectives other than profit, since they are funded by governments. Their motivation for buying is based on improving health care or quality of life.

## Professions

The professional market consists of doctors, lawyers, accountants, architects, engineers, and so on. The type of products that professionals buy usually improve the efficiency of their practice; for example, the purchase of a microcomputer and software enhances productivity in an accounting office.

It should be recognized that these four buying groups may require the same or similar products and services, but their needs are quite different. For this reason, marketing organizations must develop precise marketing strategies for each sub-market.

# ⟩⟩⟩⟩ *The Nature of Business-to-Business Markets*

Business markets are quite different from consumer markets (see figure 7.3). Their principal distinctions are that they have fewer buyers than consumer markets; the buyers tend to be concentrated near each other; the market presents different kinds

**FIGURE 7.3**  Some Differences between Consumer and Business-to-Business Marketing

| Consumer Marketing | Business-to-Business Marketing |
|---|---|
| **Product** | |
| Products are standardized, purchased frequently, and marketed by brand name. | Products are complex and marketed based on a combination of price, quality and service. Products are purchased less frequently. |
| **Price** | |
| Distributors are offered a list price and a series of discounts. Savings are passed on to consumers. | The same as consumer marketing, plus extensive price negotiation or contract bidding. |
| **Promotion** | |
| Mainly advertising, with support from sales promotion. Personal selling used in the channel of distribution. | Mainly personal selling, with support from sales promotion. Mass advertising is now more common than in previous times. |

*(continued)*

FIGURE 7.3    (continued)

**Place**

Mainly traditional channels — manufacturer to wholesaler to retailer to consumer.

Short, direct channels due to need for personal selling and high dollar value of transaction.

**Purchase Decision**

Made by an individual or household members.

Made by influence centers (users and non-users) and buying committees.

**Buying Behaviour**

Consumers more subject to emotional appeals that play on concerns about image, status, prestige.

Organizational buyers are more rational due to the formality of the purchase decision process.

---

of demand; purchase decisions involve many individuals; a formal buying process is used; and the time taken to make decisions is long.

## Number of Buyers

There are fewer buyers or customers in the business-to-business market than there are in consumer markets, but the few buyers have immense buying power. To illustrate, the "Big 3" in the automobile industry (General Motors, Ford, and Chrysler) dominate, as do two extremely large Canadian breweries (Molson and

FIGURE 7.4    Market Control by Leading Firms in Selected Industries, 1984

| Industry | Number of Enterprises | Percentage of Market Controlled by the Top 4 Enterprises |
|---|---|---|
| Motor Vehicles | 14 | 90.1% |
| Iron and Steel Mills | 37 | 76.8 |
| Smelting and Refining | 14 | 75.0 |
| Breweries | 8 | 98.9 |
| Tobacco Products | 10 | 97.7 |
| Electric Wire and Cable | 22 | 80.2 |
| Industrial Chemicals | 30 | 61.6 |

*Source*: Statistics Canada, *Canada Year Book 1988*, Ottawa: Supply and Services Canada, 1987, Cat. No. 11-402E/1987, p. 16–22. Reproduced with the permission of the Minister of Supply and Services Canada, 1990.

Labatt) in the beer industry. Firms like these are few in number but purchase incredible quantities of products. In the business market, the dollar value of individual purchases is much larger than it is in the consumer market (e.g., the value of a capital good like a computer compared to a consumer shopping good like a dress shirt). For this reason, marketing organizations will spend more to reach these customers. Depending on the industry, the cost of sales calls can range from $200 to $500; therefore, precise and effective communications are needed. Figure 7.4 shows how much control and buying power the top four firms have in a selected list of business markets.

## Geographic Concentration

The business markets tend to be concentrated geographically. Thus, the Quebec City-to-Windsor corridor encompasses 70 percent of all manufacturing establishments and 79 percent of all industrial employees in the manufacturing sector. This area is also the center of banking and financial services in Canada. Exporting to international markets is similarly concentrated: forestry products from British Columbia form Canada's fourth largest export, while Ontario accounts for a little over half of Canada's manufacturing export volume, and if Quebec is added, the figure reaches 65 percent.[2] Figure 7.5 includes some statistical information showing the nature of buying concentration in Canada.

The combination of three factors — fewer buyers, a high dollar value, and geographic concentration — makes personal selling an attractive and practical way to market goods and services to these markets despite the high costs of such activity. However, other promotional techniques such as direct mail and telemarketing are now playing an expanding role in helping firms penetrate the business-to-business marketplace.

**FIGURE 7.5**   Value of Shipment of Goods by Origin in Canada, 1984

| Region | Value (in thousands) | Percentage of Total |
|---|---|---|
| Maritimes | $ 10 147 000 | 4.4% |
| Quebec | 56 990 500 | 24.8 |
| Ontario | 121 726 400 | 52.9 |
| Prairies | 23 175 500 | 10.0 |
| British Columbia | 17 979 300 | 7.8 |
| Yukon and Territories | 51 300 | 0.1 |
| Canada | | 100.0 |

*Source*: Adapted from Statistics Canada, *Canada Year Book 1988*, Ottawa: Supply and Services Canada, 1987, Cat. No. 11-402E/1987, p. 16–21. Adapted with the permission of the Minister of Supply and Services Canada, 1990.

# Demand in the Business-to-Business Market

### *Derived Demand*

**derived demand**

There are two types of demand in the business-to-business market: derived demand and joint (shared) demand. **Derived demand** is a concept that states that the demand for products sold in the business-to-business market is actually derived from consumer demand, that is, from demand ultimately created by the final user. According to this notion, the less demand there is for the products a company sells, the less demand that company will have for the goods and services it purchases. To illustrate this relationship, let's assume that inflation is increasing along with interest and mortgage rates. As a result, the consumer demand for housing, automobiles, and major appliances decreases. Because of this drop in demand, there is, in turn, decreased demand for lumber, steel, plastics, rubber, glass, and other materials used in manufacturing automobiles, houses, and appliances. Less demand for products such as lumber and steel would also result in a diminished need for the transportation services used to move materials such as iron ore, and the equipment such as that used for milling, labour and so on. Conversely, increased consumer demand for certain products of companies leads to increased demand for certain products used by those companies. As beverage manufacturers like Coca-Cola, Pepsi-Cola, and Molson move to widespread use of the aluminum can, which consumers want, the manufacturer's demand for products produced by Alcan Aluminum increases dramatically. A change in consumer demand causes a corresponding change in demand in the business-to-business market. That means not only that Alcan's fortunes rise because of the movement to aluminum cans, but also that firms such as Consumers Glass (bottle manufacturer) and Stelco (steel processor providing sheet metal for canning manufacturers) are affected negatively.

As is the case in consumer marketing, environmental influences, particularly economic influences, must be considered in the strategic planning process of business-to-business marketing. Business marketers must recognize the conditions not only of their own market, but also of their customers' markets and of the markets of their customers. This process is very complicated for marketing organizations that operate in a variety of markets of which some offer favourable conditions, and others unfavourable.

### *Joint Demand*

**joint
(shared) demand**

**Joint** or **shared demand** occurs when industrial products can only be used in conjunction with others, when the production and marketing of one product is dependent upon another. This happens when the various parts needed for a finished product may arrive from various sources to be assembled at one central location. To manufacture Taster's Choice coffee, for example, the Nestlé Company would need coffee beans (probably imported from South America), plastic lids (from a plastics manufacturer who produces the lids to Nestlé's specifications), glass jars (from a glass manufacturer), paper labels (from a printing shop), and a cardboard shipping case (from another paper products supplier).

If any of these components is unavailable, demand for the other components will decrease, and the production and marketing of Taster's Choice will be adversely affected. Phenomena such as strikes and natural disasters that make certain items scarce can lessen demand for other items. For this reason, business marketers often have alternate sources of supply available.

## Purchase Decisions Involve a Number of Individuals

Numerous company departments including Production, Marketing, Accounting, Engineering, and Purchasing, have a say in a purchase decision. This situation often creates some conflict, even though the firm is supposedly trying to satisfy a common need or resolve a specific problem. The marketing organization, particularly the sales representatives who communicate with the buying organization, must figure out where to concentrate its efforts by determining who has the most influence on the decision.

## The Buying Process Can Be Formal

Organizations generally have specific policies and procedures to govern the buying process. For example, buying organizations specify their requirements, and potential suppliers submit bids based on them. To become the chosen supplier, the bidding organization may then have to go through further procedures. Purchase requisitions, invoices, and contracts (paperwork) are all used to specify the terms of sale of any transaction that is completed.

## The Decision Can Take a Long Time to Make

Since purchase decisions in business-to-business markets involve many individuals, buying behaviour is characteristically rational; that is, careful evaluations precede decision-making. For this reason the decision-making process is often long. To have a printing job done, price quotations may be solicited from a few reputable suppliers, and one of them chosen quickly on the basis of its quotation. In contrast, the purchase of a mainframe computer system generally involves extended evaluation and price negotiation between the seller and buyer. However, once a sale is closed, buyers usually remain loyal to the firm chosen, unless significant problems develop in the buyer-seller relationship as when, for example, the supplier is unreliable, provides poor service, or does not maintain product quality.

# 〉〉〉〉 *Market Segmentation and Business-to-Business Marketing*

The principles of market segmentation presented in chapter 4 also apply to business-to-business marketing. However, the variables considered when a segmentation strategy for business markets is being developed are quite different. In consumer

---

**FIGURE 7.6** Business-to-Business Market Segmentation

| Macro-Segmentation Variables | Micro-Segmentation Variables |
|---|---|
| 1. **Buying Organization** Size and location of customer and usage rate of product | 1. **Buying Motives** Rational motivation, with some emotional influence |
| 2. **Product Application** Standard industrial classification codes to identify potential customers | 2. **Purchase Strategy** Receptiveness of buyer to new sources of supply |
| 3. **Purchase Situation** Type of purchase and stage in purchase process | 3. **Importance of Purchase** Time (investment) required to complete transaction |
| | 4. **Personal Characteristics** The addition of emotional buying appeals to the marketing (message) mix |

---

market segmentation, markets are identified on the basis of groups of consumers with common needs and similar demographic characteristics and lifestyles. Target market profiles are developed according to demographic, psychographic, and geographic factors. Business market segmentation, on the other hand, is based on what are termed macro and micro variables; macro variables are primarily concerned with the nature of the buying organization and the purchase, while micro variables are concerned with the elements of the decision-making process (see figure 7.6).

## Macro-Segmentation

**macro-segmentation**

**Macro-segmentation** involves identifying a market according to the characteristics of the buying firm and the buying situation. It focuses on three areas: the basic features of the organization, product usage, and the nature of the purchase.

### Characteristics of the Buying Organization

The characteristics of an organization that marketing firms look at include size and location, the rate at which the organization might use the product, and the organization's purchasing procedure.

1. *Size* In considering the size of buying organizations, the marketing firm attempts to determine which customers offer the greatest potential for sales.

Should the firm pursue a small number of large organizations, where competition may be fierce, or a larger number of smaller customers where competition may be less intense? Should it go after specific industries like telecommunications, service companies, or health care institutions, or take a mass marketing approach to business and industry?

2. *Location*   Business and industrial markets can be divided into three distinct Canadian regions: East (Maritimes), Central (Quebec and Ontario), and West (Prairies and British Columbia). Besides these markets, there are the United States and international markets. As indicated earlier (figure 7.5), manufacturing is dominant in central Canada, while resource-based industries, such as agriculture, forestry and fishing, are dominant in other regions.

3. *Rates of Use*   Marketing firms analyze rates of use in order to determine where market potential is greatest. For example, will a small number of heavy users of a product be a priority, or will many light users represent equally attractive opportunities? The frequency of purchase is a factor a firm considers when identifying which customers to pursue.

4. *Purchasing Procedure*   Businesses exercise a high degree of caution when making decisions about purchases. Since the value of the transaction is high, organizations are beginning to use buying committees (collective decision-making) in purchasing. The buying committee is charged with evaluating carefully the product or service alternatives available.

All of these factors — size, rates of use, location, and purchasing procedure — affect the marketing activity of supply firms. Information about these is used to segment markets and to develop effective promotion, pricing, and distribution strategies, which stimulate awareness, preference, and, ultimately, action by the purchaser.

### *Product Usage*

**standard industrial classification (SIC)**

To identify and locate potential target markets, marketing firms also utilize the **standard industrial classification (SIC)** system. The SIC is a numbering system, established by the federal governments of Canada and the United States, that allows a supplier to track down customers who can utilize its goods and services (customers with buying potential) within an industry category. Each SIC category identifies customers by the number of firms in a classification, by sales volume, and by the number of employees in each firm.

The Canadian SIC system consists of twelve classifications ranging from agriculture to manufacturing, from transportation and communications to finance, insurance, and real estate. The system subdivides the main classifications into major industry segments; for example, it lists food and beverage manufacturers as a subcategory of the manufacturing classification. Within each subcategory, companies are identified by their product class and product line. The major benefit of the SIC system is that, by providing lists of the customers within a target market, it makes it

FIGURE 7.7   Standard Industrial Classification Codes: How the System Works

Standard industrial classification (SIC) codes provide the following information about potential customers:

1. The number of firms in an industry.
2. The sales volume of each firm.
3. The number of employees in each firm.

The classification system is intended to cover the entire field of economic activities. Included are

| Economic Classification | Characteristics |
|---|---|
| 1. Agriculture | Value of production |
| 2. Mining | Value of production |
| 3. Construction | Value of work done |
| 4. Manufacturing | Value of production |
| 5. Wholesaling and Retailing | Value of sales |
| 6. Finance, Insurance and Real Estate | Value of receipts or revenues |
| 7. Services | Value of receipts or revenues |
| 8. Public Administration | Employment or payroll |

Within each classification there are many sub-groups:

| Classification | Major Sub-Groups within Classification |
|---|---|
| Agriculture | 5 |
| Mining | 5 |
| Construction | 3 |
| Manufacturing | 20 |
| Transportation, Communications, Electric, Gas and Sanitary Services | 9 |
| Wholesale Trade | 2 |
| Retail Trade | 8 |
| Finance, Insurance and Real Estate | 8 |
| Services | 15 |
| Public Administration | 7 |
| Nonclassifiable | 1 |

To illustrate the use of the system, let's consider the retail trade classification. This classification has eight sub-groups that include

1. Building materials, hardware and farm equipment
2. General merchandise
3. Food stores
4. Automobile dealers and service stations
5. Apparel and accessories stores
6. Furniture, home furnishings and equipment
7. Eating and drinking places
8. Miscellaneous retail stores

*(continued)*

FIGURE 7.7  (continued)

Each major group has a two-digit code and, within each group, the firms are classified by industry on either a two-digit, three-digit, or four-digit code, according to the degree of detail of information provided. To illustrate, consider the manufacturing classification:

| Group | Manufacturing |
|-------|---------------|
| 20 | Food and kindred products |
| 25 | Furniture and fixtures |
| 34 | Fabricated metal products |
| 37 | Transportation equipment |

To illustrate the application of the two-, three-, and four-digit codes, here is an example of group 34 — Fabricated Metal Products:

| Industry Classification | | Products Manufactured |
|-------------------------|------|------------------------|
| Major Group | 34 | Fabricated metal products |
| Industry Group | 342 | Cutlery, hand tools and hardware |
| Specific Industry | 3423 | Hand and edge tools |
| | (2-digit) | |
| Product Class | 34231 | Mechanics and service tools |
| | (3-digit) | |
| Product | 342311 | Pliers |
| | (4-digit) | |

easier for the marketer to develop strategies for reaching the target market. How the SIC system is used is illustrated in figure 7.7.

## The Nature of the Purchase

The marketing organization is concerned with the nature of the purchase, for it has a bearing on how the sale opportunity is to be approached. A purchase classified as a new task will involve a lengthy and careful scrutinizing process set up by the buyer, and will entail, therefore, significant marketing costs for the marketer. For a reorder, on the other hand, only limited communication is needed to get the customer to take action.

In addition, the marketing firm will consider the stage in the purchase decision process at which the customer has arrived. Has the buyer just started to conduct a search for potential suppliers, or has the buyer already conducted a search and streamlined potential suppliers to a shortlist? This type of information allows a marketing firm to decide if a potential customer is worth pursuing. If the customer is too far along in the evaluation process, a marketing firm may find it financially preferable to seek other customers.

The Marketing in Action vignette ''Moore Corporation's Competitive Advantage'' illustrates how Moore benefits from macro-marketing segmentation.

## ⟩⟩⟩⟩ *MARKETING IN ACTION*

### *MOORE CORPORATION'S COMPETITIVE ADVANTAGE*

Keen competition and changing consumer needs fuelled Moore Corporation's decision to develop and execute better market segmentation strategies. The largest supplier of business forms in North America, the Toronto-based company wanted to maintain that position. Unlike consumer-goods marketers, many large business-to-business marketers are still novices in practicing market segmentation. The purpose of segmentation is to provide a firm with an understanding of the customer and the marketplace, so that marketing can be concentrated on targets representing attractive profit potential. Consumer-goods companies segment markets based on product use, demographic information, and attitude and lifestyle factors. In contrast, the Business Forms and Systems Division of Moore Corporation developed a five-year strategic plan based on a segmentation strategy that groups customer accounts by type of industry, size and location.

Recently, Moore has been consulting clients more than it did before, in order to uncover consumer needs, build on existing strengths, and penetrate promising segments. For example, Moore realigned its sales force to penetrate important markets better; and a new comprehensive training program for account managers helps them resolve problems in specialized industries.

How does Moore Corporation plan? By using a team approach, by drawing staff and management from all functional areas — Marketing, Sales, Research, Finance, and Manufacturing — the forms and systems division conducts a situation analysis to determine the company's strengths and weaknesses. This form of analysis includes an evaluation of potential threats and opportunities that will influence planning.

This planning system allows Moore to develop a more comprehensive, defined segmentation strategy. The markets it has targeted include health care, financial services and telecommunications, all growth areas now and for the future.

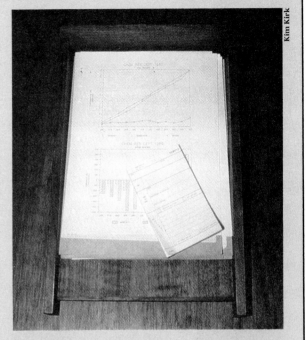

*Business forms produced by Moore Corporation may provide the health care industry, one of the market segments Moore is now targeting, with a means of streamlining record-keeping and admissions*

In health care, its business forms provide a system for streamlining record-keeping and admissions. In the financial services industry, it offers automated teller machine roll products, among many others.

Moore Corporation is a good example of a business-to-business marketing organization that recognized the value of segmentation strategies. This shift in planning philosophy saw Moore funnel financial and marketing resources into markets that were financially attractive. Such a strategy will prove beneficial to the Moore Corporation as it enters the 1990s.

Adapted from Kate Bertrand, "Harvesting the best," *Business Marketing*, October 1988, pp.46-50.

# Micro-Segmentation

Micro-segmentation variables are qualitative and relate directly to the decision-making unit (DMU). These variables include buying motives, purchasing strategy, importance of the purchase to the customer, and the personal characteristics of the buyer or of those who have influence on the buyer. These variables have a strong impact on the character and content of marketing strategies. The following section examines each variable.

## *Buying Motives*

As with consumer marketing, the identification of buying motives is imperative. Buying motives in business and industry are rational; that is, they focus on quality and price relationships, on service, and on continuity of product supply, and the evaluation process is much more consistent than it is in consumer buying, where emotions have a greater influence on buying. The greater a marketing organization's knowledge of customer buying motives, the greater its effectiveness in developing messages that appeal to these motives. A list of buying criteria is presented later in the chapter.

## *Purchasing Strategy*

It is common in buying-selling situations for customers to be unwilling to accept new suppliers. Their strategy is to retreat to the familiar and conduct business with current or past suppliers. Penetrating this type of buying organization is difficult for a sales representative. On the other hand, effective preparatory advertising and direct marketing communications may predispose buyers to new products and services. This predisposition may generate leads (through reply cards or toll free telephone numbers) and open up doors for sales representatives.

## *Importance of Purchase*

The importance of the purchase to the customer affects the way a marketing firm communicates with the customer. Purchasing a microcomputer may be quite significant for a small firm because of the investment required. Several sales calls in this case may be necessary to complete the transaction, although the seller must weigh the costs of the sales calls against the profit margin on the unit sale. For a much larger buying organization, the same decision may be relatively minor, and only a minimum of selling effort may be required. Less expensive forms of communication, such as advertising, may be equally effective in completing the transaction.

## *Personal Characteristics*

Business buyers are just as human as other consumers; thus, the more knowledge a marketer has about the specific buyer, the more impact the marketing message can have. To address the needs of certain personalities, emotional appeals centred on status and prestige may be included in overall marketing strategies, along with ordinary rational appeals.

# >>>> *The Buying Behaviour of Organizations*

**organizational buying**

When a marketing firm develops a marketing mix that it can use to approach business customers, it should understand the elements that influence the decision-making process in organizations. **Organizational buying** may be defined as the decision-making process by which firms establish what products they need to purchase, and then identify, evaluate, and select a brand and a supplier for those products. A number of characteristics distinguish this process. Typically, it involves a rational analysis of options that is aimed at ensuring optimal cost-effectiveness in the organization's purchasing; it takes a long time to complete; and it is influenced by many within the buying organization. The marketer must consider all of these elements, as well as the fact that each organization has unique needs and preferences. Let's look at each of these factors.

## Evaluation by Many Individuals

In many business organizations, one individual has the authority to sign the purchase order, but many other individuals may influence the purchase decision. There are two primary causes of this situation in modern business. First, businesses today often utilize buying committees, which bring together individuals to share the responsibility of making the purchase decision. Second, businesses may hold meetings of various informed groups of people in order to arrive at a purchase decision. This informal approach, involving several people in the organization, leads to what are called **buying centers**.

**buying centers**

1. *Buying Committees*   To illustrate the concept of a buying committee, we will assume that a firm is considering the purchase of a million-dollar piece of production-line equipment. Since the financial ramifications are significant, it is imperative that the firm make the best possible decision. Consequently, the firm appoints a committee consisting of key personnel from Production, Engineering, Finance, Marketing, and Purchasing, so that the decision can be evaluated from a variety of angles. Theoretically, such a decision-making process is very rational, and the participants are comforted to know that a costly purchase decision is a shared one.

2. *Buying Centres*   In buying centres, which are more informal than buying committees, the individuals involved have certain roles. Researchers have identified five specific roles:[3]

   • Users — those who use the product (e.g., a word processor is used by a secretary).

   • Influencers — those who assist in defining specifications for what is needed (e.g., an engineer designs a production line).

   • Buyers — those with the authority and responsibility to select suppliers and negotiate with them (e.g., a purchasing agent).

   • Deciders — those with formal or informal power to select the actual supplier (e.g., a high-dollar-value purchase of technical equipment may ultimately be the responsibility of a vice-president of Manufacturing).

- Gatekeepers — those who control the flow of information to others in the center (e.g., a purchasing agent may block certain information from reaching influencers and deciders).

From a marketing perspective, it must be determined who on the committee or within the buying centre has the most influence. Once that is known, the best means of communicating with the influence centre must be determined. What role should personal selling, sales promotion, and advertising have in the overall strategy, and what priority should each have?

## *Others Responsible for Buying*

### *Retail Buyers*

In large department stores such as The Bay, Eaton's, and Zellers, and in national chain stores like Tip Top, Shoppers Drug Mart, Canadian Tire, and Suzy Shier, retail buyers are responsible for buying merchandise. Each buyer is usually assigned responsibility for a type of product. For example, a hardware chain may divide buyers according to department: automotive parts, sporting goods, general merchandise, plumbing and electrical supplies, and so on. The department stores mentioned will also have buyers with narrowly defined responsibilities. In both cases, buyers are responsible for purchasing selected merchandise for all stores in their system. Marketing organizations refer to these types of buying organizations as **national accounts** and give them special attention, because of the volume they represent. In some industries — food and beverages, for example — it is quite common for national marketing organizations such as Kraft General Foods and Procter & Gamble to present a sales plan to their key account customers at the start of the year. At that time marketing support from the selling organization and volume commitments from the customers are negotiated and agreed to.

national accounts

Retailers are concerned with offering a balanced assortment of merchandise. **Assortment** refers to the variety of products, that is, the types, models, and styles of product that meet a retailer's target market needs. A buyer's willingness to purchase from a potential supplier is often dependent upon how well the suppliers product "fits in" to the merchandise mix. Retailers monitor their inventories closely and eliminate slow-moving merchandise quickly. Conversely, merchandise with high sales rates is carried in great quantity and variety.

assortment

### *Purchasing Managers*

In non-retail organizations, the purchasing manager (or purchasing agent) is usually responsible for the purchasing function. There can be more than one purchasing manager if the buying organization is large and requires a diversity of products and services. Such a manager is concerned with implementing company policy and procedure and is responsible for all documents involved in the purchase transaction. Although purchasing managers are responsible for making purchases, their authority in selecting brands and suppliers may be limited, for buying committees and buying centres have taken away some of their decision-making authority.

Purchasing managers are usually members of the Purchasing Managers Association of Canada (PMAC), an association formed to foster the professional development of its members. Individuals who take advantage of PMAC educational programs receive the designation of CPM — Certified Purchasing Manager.

# The Buying Criteria are Practical

In business and industry, the buying criteria tend to be practical and rationally pursued. Although impractical or irrational motives may sometimes be present, they generally play a small role. As earlier indicated, business organizations follow formal buying procedures to ensure that a good mix of quality and price is achieved. Quality, price, and a few other criteria form the basis for buying decisions in business and industry.

**vendor analysis**

Central to the buying procedures of organizations is a vendor analysis. A **vendor analysis** entails an evaluation of potential suppliers based on an assessment of their technological ability, consistency in meeting product specifications, overall quality, on-time delivery, and their ability to provide needed quantity. How well a supplier rates in these areas affects its chances of selection, but price also plays a key role in the decision. The buyer may request bids based on predetermined specifications or negotiate an acceptable price from a supplier that the vendor analysis indicates is acceptable, before signing a deal.

Let's examine these criteria in more detail:

1. *Price*   Price is usually evaluated in conjunction with other buying goals. The lowest price is not always accepted since the low-priced product may not satisfy other purchase criteria. Where the cash outlay is significant, cost is viewed from a long-term perspective. Potential long-term savings as a result of the purchase are weighed against the high purchase cost in the short term.

2. *Quality*   Business customers look for sources of supply that can provide the same unvarying quality with each order. Since a supplier's product becomes part of a new product during manufacturing, it could affect the quality of the final product if the supplier's product were inconsistent in quality. Generally, when business customers assess price-quality relationships, they do not sacrifice quality for price.

3. *Service*   Customers frequently review a supplier's reputation for keeping its current customers satisfied. They do so by contacting other customers to see how well the supplier performs the service function. The primary concern of the buying organization is that repair and replacement service be readily available when needed. The advertisements in figures 7.8 and 7.9 are examples of marketing organizations appealing to their customers on the basis of combinations of price, quality and service.

4. *Continuity of Supply*   Customers are concerned about the long-term availability of a product or service. They want to know how reliable the supplier is in meeting customer demand. To maintain a steady source of supply, customers often deal with numerous suppliers, knowing that factors such as strikes could halt the flow of product from any one supplier.

Among the less practical buying motives affecting business purchase decisions, two tend to stand out:

1. *Desire for Status and Recognition*   In this case the buyer may look for purchase transactions that provide short-term benefits to the organization. In essence, the buyer looks for deals that make his or her own performance look good, and

**FIGURE 7.8    An Advertising Message for the Rational Customer**

*This advertising message appeals to the rational motives of customers, emphasizing price, quality, and service.*

FIGURE 7.9    An Advertising Message for Business Customers

# What we do for passengers, we're doing for cargo.

### Wardair Cargo—because you care.

You probably fly frequently on behalf of your company, so you'll be familiar with all the things that make airlines like Wardair outstanding for their passenger service. Therefore, you won't be surprised to hear companies are shipping with Wardair Cargo, to gain the same advantages for their company's products as they've come to expect as passengers.

Wardair's high standards for air cargo ensure fast, efficient deliveries. And we offer dependable, frequent flights at convenient departure times between key destinations in Canada, the U.K., the U.S.A. and the Caribbean.

In addition, Wardair Cargo is equally diligent when it comes to all the finer details of cargo handling, tracking, and customer service.

We know you care, that's why Wardair Cargo goes the extra mile to meet your air cargo needs...give your shipments the kind of top flight service that brought us where we are today.

## *Wardair Cargo* We're there for you!

**Scheduled flights to:**
Vancouver, Calgary, Edmonton, Winnipeg, Toronto, Ottawa, Montreal, London (U.K.), Manchester, Prestwick, Birmingham, San Juan, Puerto Plata.
**Other flights to:** Honolulu, Tampa, Miami/Fort Lauderdale, Los Angeles, San Francisco, Barbados, Frankfurt.

**Sales Offices:**

| | | | |
|---|---|---|---|
| Vancouver | (604) 270-7611 | Toronto | (416) 676-4053 |
| Edmonton | (403) 955-8523 | Ottawa | (613) 521-2050 |
| Calgary | (403) 221-1616 | Montreal (Dorval) | (514) 631-9160 |
| Winnipeg | (204) 783-3210 | Montreal (Mirabel) | (514) 476-3896 |

*An advertising message that appeals to business customers' concern with service, speed of delivery, and dependability.*

ultimately lead to promotions within the organization. The buyer may not be accountable for the purchase decision when, at a much later date, its negative consequences emerge, and so he or she escapes criticism.

2. *Traditional Buyer Syndrome*   Here the buyer follows a purchase routine and is quite satisfied with current suppliers. Such situations suggest strong business relationships and possibly personal relationships with suppliers. Consequently, there is a reluctance to switch suppliers, even though there may be a real need to do so. This motive is quite contrary to the rational expectations of the buying organization; nonetheless, it exists and must be dealt with by new suppliers.

## Time Decision Process Takes a Long Time

Unlike consumer purchase decisions, which are frequently made spontaneously, after little consideration, the decision-making process in business can be tedious. The length of time taken to make a decision for a product such as a computer system is determined by the complexity of the decision, by the number of details to consider, and by the financial outlay the system requires.

## Centralized Purchasing

In today's economic environment, buying organizations are looking for the best possible prices and value for dollars spent. Consequently, many firms have developed centralized purchasing systems, in order to secure better price discounts based on volume purchases. For example, The Bay, Zellers, and Simpson's, all owned by The Hudson's Bay Company, have formed one large buying division that purchases for each retail division. In these situations, marketers must deal with just a few buyers, all at a high level of management.

## Customers Have Unique Needs

Business customers are looking for products and services that will resolve problems and satisfy needs specific to their company. Consequently, tailor-made presentations and demonstrations must be developed for selling. Since advertising messages usually focus on broadly-based needs important to a target market, generally the most they can do is open doors for the tailor-made sales presentations by showing concern for productivity and profit improvement. Together, advertising and selling can realize an effective marketing strategy for approaching business customers.

# ❭❭❭❭ *Types of Buying Decisions*

The types of buying decisions that business and industrial organizations face are classified according to time needed to make the decision, to the cost, and to the complexity of the product. There are basically three types of buying situations: new task, modified rebuy, and straight or full rebuy.

## New Task Purchase

new task purchase

What is called a **new task purchase** occurs when a business buys a product, usually an expensive one, for the first time. The organization lacks familiarity with the item, so it seeks information that will assist it in making the best decision. Since the product represents a high risk because of its great costs, numerous individuals often participate in the evaluation and decision, sometimes, for example, through a buying committee.

## Modified Rebuy

modified rebuy

In a **modified rebuy**, an organization purchases a product, usually of medium price, that it purchases infrequently. Typically, the organization is less than satisfied with the product it currently uses, and so searches the marketplace for a substitute that will perform better, one that will, for example, operate more efficiently and save the firm money. Savings in the long-term can be measured against any short-term cost increases.

## Straight or Full Rebuy

straight
(full) rebuys

**Straight** or **full rebuys** are used for inexpensive items bought on a regular basis. Essentially, they are routine re-orders requiring no modification, since the needs they fulfill remain relatively constant. Because the risks are low, the decision is a simple one, much like the routine purchase made by a consumer.

A summary of the key differences between the types of buying decisions is included in figure 7.10.

**FIGURE 7.10**   Types of Buying Decisions in Business-to-Business Marketing

| Type | Price | Risk | Knowledge | Involvement |
| --- | --- | --- | --- | --- |
| New Task | High | High | Limited. Must seek information on best alternatives. | Buying committee |
| Modified Rebuy | Medium | Some | Good. Seek out new information for better products. | Buying committee, buying centre influence, or purchasing agent. |
| Straight Rebuy | Low | Minimal | Good. Product considered acceptable. | Low. Routine order by purchasing manager. |

# ⟩⟩⟩⟩ *Steps in the Buying Decision Process*

Since business organizations and similar groups generally exhibit rational buying behaviour, the decision-making process tends to be clearly defined. The typical buying model has eight stages (see figure 7.11).[4] Let's examine each of these stages.

**FIGURE 7.11** A Typical Buying Decision Model in Business Organizations

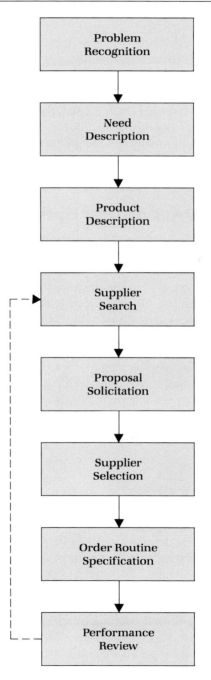

## Problem Recognition

In this initial stage, a change occurs in the organizational environment, which reveals a problem or a new need that must be resolved. For example, a computerized inventory system signals that it is time to reorder; plant personnel become dissatisfied with production capacity; Purchasing is not satisfied with some of the current suppliers because of their slow, unreliable delivery and lack of sufficient supplies; or marketing determines that an internal information and communications system more efficient than the present one is needed.

## Need Description

For the need description, the buying organization identifies the general characteristics and qualities of the needed item or service. In effect, it starts to look at potential solutions by reviewing alternatives that have been successful in the past.

## Product Description

With a general solution in mind, the buying organization now establishes precise descriptions or specifications of the item needed. The process of formally describing the characteristics of the product ensures that needs are clearly communicated both within the organization and to potential suppliers. The quantity required is usually stipulated at this time, which assists suppliers in submitting bids. Specifications may consist of blueprints for a new production line, documented copy quality and maximum run length for a photocopier, or stipulations on temperature tolerances for a machine tool. These specifications are key criteria against which potential supplier's products are evaluated. At this stage, too, the buying organization usually determines who will be responsible for deciding on the purchase. Will responsibility remain with the purchasing manager, or will a buying committee be formed? The marketing organization must be ready to identify those with the most influence and direct its communications appropriately.

## Supplier Search

During this step, the buying organization looks for potential suppliers. Usually, two key decisions need to be made in the purchase process: first, which product or service should the organization buy and, second, from what particular supplier should it buy. Buying organizations at this point search for and qualify acceptable suppliers, using the vendor analysis discussed earlier in this chapter. To qualify a supplier means that the buying organization has determined that the supplier can provide the product in a steady, reliable manner. At the same time, marketing organizations evaluate the prospective buyers. Potential sources of information for both organizations include trade indexes, internal records of any past dealings with the other organization, trade advertising journals and sales representatives. Trade indexes referred to frequently in Canada include the *Canadian Trade Index*, *Scott's Industrial Index*, *Canadian Key Business Directory*, *Fraser's Trade Index* and standard industrial classification codes (SIC codes).

To ensure that they are seriously considered, potential suppliers must make themselves known to buyers. They must be listed in trade indexes for the products and services they provide, and they must actively communicate with potential customers through some combination of promotion programs.

## Proposal Solicitation

The buying organization in the next step seeks and evaluates detailed written proposals from acceptable suppliers. Depending on the complexity of the purchase, the proposal could consist of a formal bid, a written quotation, or a price catalogue reference.

bid

1. *Formal Bid*   A **bid** is a written tender submitted in a sealed envelope by a specified deadline. There are two forms of bids:

closed bid

   * A **closed bid** is a written, sealed bid submitted by a supplier for review and evaluation by the purchaser on a particular date. The bid is based on specifications, or precise descriptions of what is required, published by the purchaser. Usually, the bid from the lowest "responsible" supplier is accepted, that is, one who is reputed to be dependable and stable.

open bid

   * An **open bid** is more informal in nature and may only involve a written or oral price quotation from a potential supplier. The quotation usually specifies how long the price is in effect. Typically, buyers and sellers negotiate a price during an open bidding process.

quotation

2. *Quotation*   A **quotation** consists of a written document, usually from a sales representative, which states the terms of the price quoted.

3. *Price Catalogue Reference*   In this situation the price is obtained by referring to a catalogue where all prices are listed. Buyers usually maintain current supplier catalogues on file. This procedure is common for routine orders of standardized products and supplies.

## Supplier Selection

At the supplier-selection stage, the buying organization evaluates the proposals of qualified suppliers and selects the one that matches its needs. Each proposal is assessed with reference to the purchase criteria. In a complex buying situation, the supplier's proposal might be judged on factors such as price, quality, delivery, technical support service, warranties, and trade-in policies.

While weighing these many variables, buyers usually attempt to negotiate a better price with the shortlisted suppliers. The bargaining process between buyers and sellers is now at its peak. The influence of buying centers (informal) or buying committees (formal) must be considered and their members addressed by the marketing organization during this phase. Another option for the buying organization is to select several sources of supply, for their own protection, assuming that there are equal alternatives to choose from.

For routine purchases, there is not much distinction between the solicitation and the selection stages. Where costs and risks are low, solicitation and selection can occur simultaneously.

## Order Routine Specification

After the supplier has been selected, the buying organization and marketing organization (the successful supplier or suppliers) agree on an order and re-order routine stipulating such matters as

1. The procedure for accepting orders.
2. Delivery times.
3. Return policies.
4. The quantities to be ordered.
5. Repair and service policies.
6. Any other factors judged important by the buyer.

This document constitutes a written contract or agreement between the buying and marketing organization.

## Performance Review

Since businesses are constantly looking for products and services to improve the efficiency of their operations, there is no guarantee that the relationship between a buyer and seller will be a lasting one. In fact, the relationship may only last as long as the last price quotation. Once the purchaser receives a lower quotation, a new supplier may replace the existing one even if the current supplier has been satisfactory. To ensure that their operations remain as efficient as possible, businesses develop means of reviewing the performance of suppliers.

Thus, as the final step in the buying process, the buying organization establishes a system of obtaining and evaluating feedback on the performance of the supplier's products. The purchasing manager will design an internal system for securing responses from user groups. Depending on whether the feedback is positive or negative, a decision to continue with or drop a supplier is made.

To marketers, this procedure demonstrates that the sale is never over. To avoid being dropped as a supplier, marketing organizations must accept criticisms and adapt their strategies when necessary to ensure that customers' needs are continuously satisfied. It has been shown that strong personal and business relationships develop when marketing organizations take fast, corrective action to resolve customer problems.

# ⟩⟩⟩⟩ *Some Special Considerations about the Government Market*

The government market is divided into three categories: federal, provincial, and municipal. Collectively, these governments represent tremendous opportunity for Canadian firms that are eager to have a piece of the government business. To put the extent of this opportunity into perspective, consider that in 1984 the actual expenditure of the federal government alone amounted to $113 billion.[5] Government purchases range from food to military equipment to office buildings to office supplies.

## How Does Government Buy?

Governments create the law in Canada, and by law all Canadian governments must solicit competitive bids before making their purchase decisions. The bids, usually submitted in writing, are based on specifications established by government buyers. In the federal government, the Ministry of Supply and Services is responsible for choosing among the bids on most brand name products for all federal agencies. This ministry gives preference to Canadian sources as long as a Canadian supplier can meet the purchase criteria. As they do in the business-to-business market generally, factors such as price, availability, quality, and performance play key roles in the selection process. The Ministry of Supply and Services operates out of its Hull, Quebec headquarters and regional offices strategically located across Canada. Provincial governments operate in a similarly centralized fashion.

**source list**

Canadian businesses in pursuit of government contracts must have themselves placed on a source list kept by the Ministry of Supply and Services. A **source list** includes the names, products, and services of all those companies that have expressed an interest in dealing with the federal government. To be considered as a potential source of supply, a firm should contact the ministry office in Hull or a regional office.

Despite the business potential that government markets represent, the red tape commonly associated with dealing with governments keeps potential suppliers away. Some negative aspects of dealing with governments are as follows

1. *The Concentration on Competitive Bidding*   The government bidding process emphasizes low price, despite the fact that there could be important trade-offs between higher price and product quality. Since the government stresses price, many Canadian businesses are reluctant to submit bids, as the venture could be unprofitable. For example, small suppliers are unable to compete with large suppliers, which can produce greater volume and therefore offer a lower cost.

2. *Extensive Paperwork Requirements*   Heavy paperwork involving forms and official documentation is customary when dealing with governments. The paperwork is extensive even for the routine ordering of standardized products like general office supplies. For custom-designed products and complex decisions, the paperwork problem is compounded.

On the positive side, the federal government, in particular, favours buying from Canadian sources. Giving business to small Canadian enterprises and to businesses located in economically depressed areas, even though costs of these purchases may be higher, is also a federal priority. In this regard, the government has a variety of purchase objectives. While it strives for efficiency by choosing the lowest bid most of the time, it is also concerned with social and economic issues. Its policies try to encourage employment in depressed areas and foster growth in the small business sector, an important sector for Canadian employment in the 1990s.

## ⟩⟩⟩⟩ *Marketing to the Business-to-Business Market*

In developing marketing strategies for approaching the business-to-business market, an organization must consider the buying motives typical of business, industry, and governments. Let's briefly examine the elements of the marketing mix as they apply to business-to-business marketing.

## Product

As indicated earlier, the business-to-business market buys all kinds of products and services. These range from ready-made standardized items — business equipment and supplies, paper products, hand power tools, and automobiles and trucks — to custom-designed items produced to satisfy only one customer, to business services such as accounting, or technical and management consulting.

To sell to this market, a marketing organization concentrates on the "value satis-factions" derived by a customer from a product or service. To illustrate, let's assume that an appliance manufacturer, such as Inglis or Maytag, purchases rolled sheet metal from Stelco (The Steel Company of Canada Limited). The purchaser estab-lishes the physical specifications of the product, but the features that make it buy are likely to include the product form, the technical advice offered by Stelco representa-tives, and promises of delivery dependability and of efficiency improvement. So the marketer concentrates on devising such features and communicating them to the purchaser. Generally, products that improve supplier operations — that is, that make them more productive or that provide savings with no sacrifice in quality — are more attractive to buyers.

## Distribution

The nature of the product and the location of the customer are the key factors influencing distribution strategy in the business-to-business market. The channels of distribution are either direct or indirect.

### *Direct Channel*

In the case of direct-channel distribution, the marketing organization sells directly to the purchaser. Such a channel is termed *short*. The company usually has its own highly trained sales force making direct customer contact. The customers tend to be large and centralized and high-level price negotiations are the major influence on the decision to buy. In effect, the marketing organization controls the channel, since no middlemen have an influence on marketing strategy. Companies such as IBM, Xerox, Canon, and Apple, which sell directly to industry, governments and institutions, fall into this category. For reaching other markets, including the consumer market, these same companies use longer indirect channels of distribution.

### *Indirect Channel*

In the case of indirect-channel distribution, the marketing organization sells through one or more middlemen or distributors. Therefore, the channel of distribution is called *long*. The marketing firm may or may not have its own sales force. The customers tend to be small and geographically dispersed in this situation; thus distributors provide better sales call coverage. In effect, middlemen have more control in the channel than the manufacturer. The middlemen used by manufacturers include agents and brokers. These groups do not take possession of the merchandise they sell, but complete the buy-sell transaction on behalf of the manufacturer for a commission. Such a practice is common in the food distribution business. The consumer goods division of Maple Leaf Mills Limited, a large agricultural company, uses brokers in small-volume regions such as the Prairies and the Maritimes, and its own direct sales force in Ontario and Quebec, where volume is much greater. Wholesalers and retailers that may be part of an indirect channel do take possession of a product and make their profit by reselling to the next channel member.

## Pricing

Among the buying criteria in the business-to-business market, price probably heads the list. Thus marketers must consider how purchasers evaluate price. Buyers do so using a cost-benefit analysis. A **cost-benefit analysis** is a procedure whereby all associated costs are measured against the benefits. The costs to the buying company include the base price of the product less any discounts, which are usually based on the volume purchased. The higher the volume ordered, the greater the discount and the lower the overall cost will be. Variables such as transportation, installation, and inventory costs are factored into potential costs.

**cost-benefit analysis**

The benefits refer to the "value derived" from the product or service. The value derived is based on the following variables:

1. *Functional Characteristics*   These are the physical characteristics of the product, namely its appearance and what it will do.

2. *Operational Characteristics*   These elements refer to the product's dependability, reliability, and consistency of quality.

3. *Financial Factors*   These concern the terms of sale offered by the supplier and the potential for cost savings.

4. *Personal Factors*   These factors concern the degree to which the person doing the buying perceives product improvement as linked to his or her position in the firm.

FIGURE 7.12    An Advertising Message Designed to Obtain Sales Leads

*Advertising messages of this type use a toll-free 800 phone number.*

It is these factors that the marketing organization must address in its promotion activities. As indicated earlier, the bidding process plays a key role in government business and in industries where custom-designed products and services are required, such as the construction industry.

## Promotion

Because of the characteristics of the business-to-business market, personal selling remains the dominant and most influential marketing tool. Although advertising also plays a role, especially in creating awareness and interest in a product or service, it is personal selling that wins customer preference and closes the sale. The focus of personal selling and advertising depends on the type of market a firm is approaching. For example, messages directed at private enterprise concentrate on how the product or service improves the buyer's operation or the quality of its end product. Messages aimed at professionals such as accountants emphasize convenience, saving time, and cost reduction. Effective advertising will secure leads for the sales force. Coupons, reply cards, and toll-free telephone numbers make it very convenient for a buying organization to seek more information about a product or service. Figure 7.12 contains an illustration that is designed to generate leads.

## ❯❯❯❯ S U M M A R Y

The business-to-business market is comprised of four primary buying groups: business and industry, governments, institutions, and the professions, all of which require a vast array of products and services. This market has fewer and larger buyers than the consumer market and tends to be concentrated in certain geographic areas.

Three factors distinguish the buying behaviour of businesses from that of consumers: in a business, the purchase decision often involves many individuals, commonly in the form of buying committees; the process tends to be formal, involving a bidding system; and the decision to buy may take a long time to make, primarily because of the financial risk involved and the complexity of the decision.

Segmentation strategies are employed in the business market. Marketing organizations identify macro- and micro-segmentation variables when developing strategies. Macro-segmentation variables include the size and location of customers, the use the customer will make of the product, and the nature of the purchase. Micro-segmentation variables include buying criteria such as price, quality and service, purchasing strategy, the importance of the purchase, and personal motives of buyers. Marketing organizations are also interested in the centralized purchasing procedures of many companies and the unique needs of each customer. Because of the need to address the uniqueness of the buyer, tailor-made presentations showing how products and services resolve specific problems are important.

New task, modified rebuy and straight (full) rebuy are the different types of purchases made by organizational customers. The basic buying process is a series of eight steps: problem recognition, need description, product description, supplier search, proposal solicitation, supplier selection, routine order specification, and performance review.

The challenge for marketers in approaching the business market is to consider the different buying behaviours in each of the major segments and then develop effective and efficient marketing mixes that will satisfy them. The approaches taken will vary from one segment to another.

## >>>> KEY TERMS

business-to-business market
derived demand
joint (shared) demand
macro-segmentation
micro-segmentation
standard industrial classification
   (SIC)

organizational buying
buying center
national account
assortment
vendor analysis
new task purchase
modified rebuy

straight (full) rebuy
bid
closed bid
open bid
quotation
source list
cost-benefit analysis

## >>>> REVIEW AND DISCUSSION QUESTIONS

**1.** What are the four major buying groups comprising the business-to-business market?

**2.** Briefly explain the major characteristics that distinguish the business market from the consumer market.

**3.** If interest rates and inflation were to rise and consumer demand for colour televisions declined, how would demand be affected in industries other than television production? Provide examples to illustrate your viewpoint.

**4.** How is buying behaviour in the business market different from that in the consumer market?

**5.** Identify and briefly explain the macro-segmentation variables that influence a business buy.

**6.** Identify and briefly explain the micro-segmentation variables that influence a business buy.

**7.** Who influences the purchase decisions of a business, and how do these people affect the strategy of marketing organizations?

**8.** Briefly describe the steps in the decision-making process that organizations follow to make purchases.

**9.** What are the unique characteristics of the government market that marketers must address?

**10.** "Effective business-to-business communications should only focus on the rational buying goals of the customer." Comment on this statement.

## 〉〉〉〉 REFERENCES

1. STUART HUSTED, DALE VARBLE, and JAMES LOWRY, *Modern Marketing* (Needham Heights, MA: Allyn & Bacon, 1989), p.125.

2. Statistics Canada, *Canada Yearbook 1988* (Ottawa: Supply and Services Canada, 1987, Cat. No. 11-402E/1987), p.16-19.

3. Adapted from FREDERICK E. WEBSTER and YORAM WIND, *Organizational Buying Behaviour* (Englewood Cliffs, New Jersey: Prentice-Hall, 1972), pp.78-80.

4. MICHAEL MORRIS, *Industrial and Organizational Marketing* (Columbus, Ohio: Merrill Publishing, 1988), p.86.

5. Statistics Canada, *Canada Yearbook 1988*, p.22-14.

# >>>> PART FOUR

## Прохладительные напитки

«Кока-кола», «Кока-кола лайт», «Спрайт» и «Фанта» в больших или стандартных стаканчиках

# *Product*

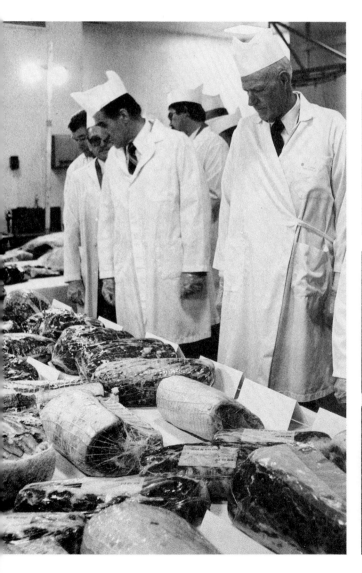

**PETRO·CANADA**

Pineapple Cup

Triple Berry Treat

Muffin Plate

Power Shake

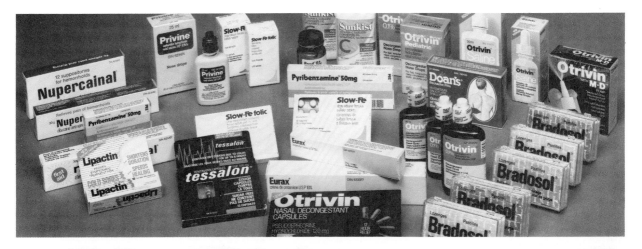

# Product Strategy

## LEARNING OBJECTIVES

After studying this chapter, you should be able to

1. Define the total product concept and explain the concept of the product mix.

2. Outline the classifications and subclassifications of products.

3. Distinguish between consumer goods and industrial (business) goods.

4. Describe the categories of consumer goods and industrial (business) goods.

5. Explain the role of branding and packaging decisions in the development of product strategy.

6. Characterize the various stages of brand loyalty.

7. Explain what the customer satisfaction mix is.

Product strategy is but one element of the marketing mix. This chapter presents the key decision-making areas for marketers when they are developing product strategy. The key elements discussed in this chapter include the product mix, product classifications, brand name and packaging considerations, brand loyalty, and the customer satisfaction mix.

# ⟩⟩⟩⟩ *The Total Product Concept*

**product**

A **product** is "a bundle of tangible and intangible benefits that a buyer receives in exchange for money and other considerations."[1] In effect, the consumer purchases much more than the actual object. Let's examine a couple of situations:

1. The purchase of, say, a washer or dryer is largely based on function. Thus, the question asked is "Will the appliance perform the task in a dependable, consistent manner?" The intangible factor of the availability of after-sales service may also be an important consideration. In this case, the consumer looks for dependable cleaning and reliable service.

2. The purchase of a Porsche is not based on transportation needs. It is a car you don't really need; you buy it in order to display your achievement and success. Such a purchase is concerned with the intangibles of prestige, status and image.

**total product concept**

These examples illustrate that a product is more than the actual physical object. There are several elements that a marketer can emphasize when attempting to attract consumers; those elements comprise the benefits that a buyer receives. This package of benefits is referred to as the **total product concept**. It includes the physical item, as well as the package, brand name, label, service guarantee, warranty, and image desired for the product.

## The Product Mix

**product mix**

The **product mix** is the total range of products offered for sale by a company. It is the collection of product items and product lines that a firm tries to market. Each of the products or product items in the mix appeals to a particular segment, and in a way that makes it distinct from the offerings of the competition. Most, if not all, large consumer-packaged-goods companies have a complete product mix, that is, they offer for sale a variety of different products that appeal to different user segments. An electrical parts manufacturer may offer for sale a variety of cables, switches, plugs and so on, all serving different customer needs.

**product item**

A **product item** is defined as a unique product offered for sale by an organization. The key word in this definition is *unique*. Marketers refer to the distinguishing product characteristic or primary benefit of a product or service as the **unique selling point** or **USP**. A USP is defined as the one feature that distinguishes a product from competing products. A product distinguishes itself from competing products on the basis of a particular feature. To illustrate, let's examine a few of the characteristics that products use to differentiate themselves:

**unique selling point (USP)**

| Product | Unique Characteristics |
|---|---|
| Toothpaste | Proven ability to reduce cavities |
| Ketchup | Thick texture (not runny) |
| Cargo Delivery | Speed and dependability of service |

Features such as these become a focal point in marketing the product. Any other distinguishing elements, such as the number of sizes, variety of colours or flavours, and price, are also used in marketing. Other characteristics, such as a range of

**product line**

available sizes and flavours, are not so much traits of a particular product as they are of a group of products called a product line. A **product line** is a grouping of product items with common characteristics.

The common characteristics may take several forms. A product line may consist of a similar type or classification, such as dry cereals, or of products whose only similarity is that they are distributed through the same channel of distribution.

**product line depth**
**product line width**

A firm's product line is described in terms of depth and width. **Product line depth** is the number of lines in the mix. **Product line width**, on the other hand, refers to the number of items in the line. All items and lines collectively form a firm's product mix (see figure 8.1). The depth and width of a product mix depend on the firm's overall marketing strategy. Packaged goods firms such as Procter & Gamble and RJR Nabisco, and industrial products companies such as General Electric and IBM have large product mixes, ones that are both deep and wide, because they want to balance risks, offset seasonal sales fluctuations, and address the various needs of customers. Other firms, pursuing different strategies, use small product mixes. The story featured in the Marketing in Action vignette "Wrigley's is Gum" shows the use of quite a different product-line strategy.

**FIGURE 8.1**   Mennen's Product Mix: A Selection of Personal Care Product Lines

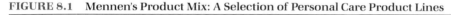

### ⟩⟩⟩⟩ *MARKETING IN ACTION*

#### *WRIGLEY'S IS GUM*

To be successful does not mean that a business organization must expand its product lines very widely, despite the fact that very large and successful organizations such as Kraft General Foods, Procter & Gamble, and others in the food-processing and household-products business have product lines that are both very deep and very wide.

Let's examine a different strategy, specifically the strategy of the William Wrigley Jr. Company, a company that does not play the food game by the same set of rules. The eighties were an era of merger mania in the food business. The big companies gobbled up other big companies and so became even bigger. Wrigley's was different. Unlike a lot of food companies, Wrigley's did not participate in merger mania and is debt free. As a result, numerous business analysts refer to the company as downright boring. Its financial results, however, are anything but dull.

Wrigley's success is shown by the following financial measures for 1987 (U.S. statistics).

| | | |
|---|---|---|
| Profit | $70.1 million | (double that of 1982) |
| Return on Equity | 23.9% | (14.2% in 1982) |
| Return on Assets | 17.5% | (more than most firms) |
| Market Share | 46.5% | (39.5% in 1982) |

*Among the new types of chewing gum Wrigley's has developed in recent years is Extra, a sugar-free gum that appeals to the sugar-conscious consumer and is available from many snack-food vending machines.*

Wrigley's is a company that knows its strength. Here's a company, famous for the "Doublemint twins" and the slogan "Double your pleasure, double your fun", that stays very close to a successful formula. Yes, they do experiment and market new varieties of gum. In fact, they have launched many new flavours as line extensions in an effort to grow in a weak, mature market. What is important, though, is the fact that the company has maintained a consistent focus on the gum business — on a single type of product. Such a strategy has created productivity gains in the areas of production and marketing. Not many brands or companies enjoy such status within their industries.

In recent years, the company has been successful in expanding the scope of its gum activity. Freedent, a product geared to denture wearers, is available in a variety of flavours; Extra, a sugar-free gum, appeals to the sugar-conscious consumer; and then there's sugar-based Hubba Bubba soft chunk bubble gum and Big League Chew (shredded gum) baseball-style gum for the kids. And of course, there are the old standbys — Juicy Fruit, Spearmint, and Doublemint — under the Wrigley's brand name. All in all, a formula for success.

Adapted from "Wrigley sticks to successful formula," *The Globe and Mail*, November 25, 1988, p.B16.

# >>>> *Product Classifications*

Products are divided in two basic ways. First, and most important, a product is classified according to who its customer is and what reasons he or she has for purchasing the product. Products are also categorized according to their durability and tangibility.[2] The categories based on how durable they are and whether or not they are tangible are as follows:

**nondurable goods**

1. **Nondurable goods** are tangible goods normally consumed after one or a few uses. Examples include everyday products like toothpaste, beer, coffee, milk, and detergent. These products are replenished frequently.

**durable goods**

2. **Durable goods** are tangible goods that survive many uses. Examples include automobiles, appliances, boats and motors, and entertainment equipment. These items are purchased infrequently.

**services**

3. **Services** are intangible; they are activities and benefits we take advantage of but do not take possession of. Examples include banking services, household care services (lawn and garden maintenance or painting and decorating), financial planning services, and repair services. The service industry marketing strategies are discussed in chapter 17.

Products are also broadly classified into two groups on the basis of who buys them and why; these groups are called consumer goods and industrial (business) goods.

**consumer goods**
**industrial (business) goods**

**Consumer goods** are products and services purchased by consumers for their own personal use or benefit. **Industrial (business) goods** are those products and services, purchased by business, industry, institutions, and governments, that are used directly or indirectly in the production of another good or service that is resold, in turn, to another user (possibly a consumer). In the classification of products, it is the intended use by the customer that distinguishes consumer goods from industrial (business) goods, but a product can be both. For example, a tire manufactured by GoodYear is a consumer good if sold by its retail outlet or an independent retail outlet to a consumer. It is an industrial good if purchased by the Ford Motor Company for installation on the assembly of an automobile.

## Consumer Goods

Consumer goods are generally classified into four categories: convenience goods, shopping goods, specialty goods and unsought goods (see figure 8.2).

### *Convenience Goods*

**convenience goods**

**Convenience goods** are those goods purchased frequently, with a minimum of effort and evaluation. Typical examples include bread, milk, daily newspapers, and a favourite brand of coffee. Convenience goods fall into the "routine" decision-making process discussed in chapter 6. For this reason, marketing organizations give priority to the following objectives in their strategies: making sure the product is readily available, predisposing the consumer to a brand through advertising messages, and setting up point-of-sale displays that are coordinated with a colourful packaging of the product.

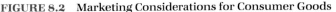

FIGURE 8.2    Marketing Considerations for Consumer Goods

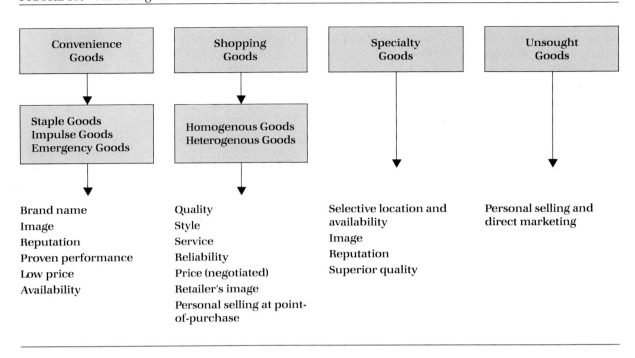

Convenience goods are subdivided into three categories: staples, impulse goods, and emergency goods.

**staple goods**

1.  **Staple goods** are products that are regularly needed or used, such as milk, bread, deodorant, and headache medicine. People buy many of these items by brand, remaining loyal to such names as Right Guard, Secret, Tylenol, and Advil.

**impulse goods**

2.  **Impulse goods** are goods bought because of a sudden need, without forethought: candy bars, chewing gum, and magazines are goods of this type. Availability and point-of-sales displays are critical; thus the items are often found at checkout counters.

**emergency goods**

3.  **Emergency goods** are purchased suddenly when a crisis or urgency arises; a snow shovel purchased at the first snow storm of the season, or a tensor bandage purchased when a muscle becomes strained are examples of emergency goods.

### *Shopping Goods*

**shopping goods**

**Shopping goods** are goods that the consumer compares on such bases as suitability, quality, price and style, before making a selection.[3] Other factors of concern to the shopper include dependability, service, functionality, guarantees, and warranties. Examples of shopping goods include automobiles, clothing, major appliances, household furnishings, decoration services, and major repairs around the house. It should be noted that, in the case of shopping goods, buying behaviour tends to be rational. The price of shopping goods tends to be higher than that of convenience goods. Marketing considerations deemed important for shopping goods include being located near competitive offerings where comparisons can be easily made; having a consistent and attractive image (proven performance has advantage over little known brands); and having effective communications so that awareness among consumers is high when their need for the product arises.

To illustrate, consider the automobile market. Competing dealerships are usually located within a reasonable distance of each other. Manufacturers such as Ford, General Motors and Chrysler also consistently advertise their corporate approach (e.g., "at Ford Quality is Job One") and their individual product lines. Individual consumers purchase these items infrequently, but someone is always buying them. Therefore, a company like Ford must constantly try to predispose consumers to their products. As another example, the "Idle Repairman" gives Maytag a competitive advantage in the appliance market. Such a consistent message over time has given Maytag an excellent reputation and a basis for comparison with other brands.

Shopping goods are divided into two categories: homogenous and heterogenous.[4]

### Homogenous Shopping Goods

Homogenous goods are goods that consumers perceive as the same and that, as a result, are bought on the basis of price or brand image. Comparable products or brands could be available at two different locations and the retailer with the best price gets the purchase. If a consumer was contemplating the purchase of a Toyota Celica or a Mazda RX-7 a difficult choice would be made. The consumer may accept either but will purchase from the dealer where the lowest price is negotiated or the best package of price and after-sales service is available. The same could be said of audio components, VCRs, and television sets.

### Heterogenous Shopping Goods

These are goods that consumers perceive to have different qualities and attributes. The brand name and the price are of less concern than they are with homogenous goods. In this case, the consumer gauges how well the product suits his or her needs. Examples include clothing or household furniture. In the case of furniture, factors such as construction and durability may dominate the decision, or how well the item fits in with the colour and decor of a room. In this situation, consumers are less concerned with price, and the retailer's ability to sell face-to-face definitely influences the decision to buy.

### Specialty Goods

specialty goods

**Specialty goods** are goods that consumers make an effort to find and purchase because the goods possess some unique or important characteristic. In effect, the consumer has already decided what item to buy. It is simply a matter of making the shopping excursion to buy it. Generally speaking, the marketing considerations that are important for specialty goods include the image and reputation resulting from communications and product quality; and that the goods be available in the appropriate stores, that is, available from the few specialty retailers that carry special lines or represent manufacturers that consumers will look for. A price, usually a high one in keeping with the product quality and the prestigious image created by other marketing activity, is also a consideration in marketing specialty goods.

Whether an item is a specialty good, a shopping good, or a convenience good depends on the behaviour of the consumer; what is a specialty good for some may be a shopping good for another. For instance, an individual who insists on wearing a sweatshirt that displays a brand name, such as Bennetton, Roots, Crossings, or Northern Reflections, looks for a store that sells the cherished brand and will travel to wherever it is located to purchase the sweatshirt. To this person the sweatshirt is a specialty good. Others may simply drop into the store, compare the merchandise with other brands they have seen, and then decide to purchase one of the sweatshirts. In this case the sweatshirt is a shopping good. Still another person on a suddenly cold fall day may rush into a retail outlet and buy the first sweatshirt that fits. This time the choice of clothing is a convenience good. With each successive situation, the degree of effort expended on the purchase decreases.[5] One good can be distinguished from another on the basis of how much effort consumers put into the purchase.

### Unsought Goods

**unsought goods**

**Unsought goods** are goods that consumers are unaware that they have a need of or that they lack knowledge about. Essentially, an unsought good is an item which, although useful or valuable, is of such a nature that the consumer lacks interest in purchasing it. Encyclopedias are the most cited examples of unsought goods. While the product has a clear educational value, people do not often try to buy it because the cost to them does not justify the purchase; they consider that the product is readily available in a library and not used that frequently. Life insurance is another example, as it is a product many consumers are uncomfortable discussing. It's a product many people postpone considering and purchasing.

Unsought goods are quite different from other categories of consumer goods. Given the nature of these goods, the primary influence on decisions to purchase is personal selling. Advertising will create awareness, but it is a consistent and persistent sales message that precipitates action by consumers.

## Industrial (Business) Goods

**industrial (business) goods**

By definition, **industrial** or **business goods** are products and services that have a direct or indirect role in the manufacture of other products and services. These goods are classified, not on the basis of behaviour, but by the function the good has in the production of another. The major marketing considerations for industrial goods are price (low price based on price negotiation and bidding), personal selling, the ability to meet customer specifications, and the reliability of supply when direct channels of distribution are used.

Typically, industrial (business) goods are subdivided into three categories: capital items, parts and materials, and supplies and services (see figure 8.3).

### Capital Items

**capital items**

**Capital items** are expensive goods with a long life span that are used directly in the production of another good or service. Whether an item has a direct or indirect role in the production process determines what type of capital item it is. There are two types of capital items.

#### Installations
These are major capital items used directly in the production of another product.

FIGURE 8.3    Types of Industrial Products and Services

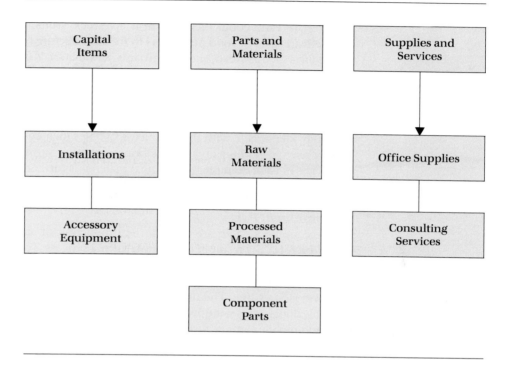

Examples of installations include buildings, production line equipment (e.g., robots in assembly plants), computer systems, and printing presses. These goods are characterized by their high price, long life, reliance on strong personal selling programs to gain customer acceptance, technical sales and support service, and direct channels of distribution. A lengthy and complex decision-making process confronts the marketer of installations.

### Accessory Equipment

These items are usually not part of a finished product, but they do facilitate a firm's overall operations, that is, their role is indirect. Typically, these goods are much less expensive than installations and include products such as microcomputers, photocopy machines, facsimile machines, typewriters, power tools, and office furnishings. These goods are characterized by their reasonably long life, the significance of price negotiation in the marketing process, unique features of the product that appeal to rational buying goals, and the use of direct and indirect marketing channels. As is the case with installations, personal selling plays a key role in marketing accessory equipment.

### Parts and Materials

parts and materials

**Parts and materials** are less expensive goods that directly enter another manufacturer's production process. These goods are an integral part of the customer's product and affect its quality. Parts and materials are subdivided into three categories: raw materials, processed materials, and component parts.

### Raw materials

Farm goods and other materials derived directly from natural resources are raw materials. Farm goods include wheat, livestock, fruits, vegetables, and milk, all of which are used by food processors in the manufacture of packaged consumer food products such as bread, cheese, and jams. Raw materials from other natural resources include crude oil, lumber, iron ore, and fish.

### Processed Materials

These are materials used in the production of another product, but which are not readily identifiable with the product. Examples include DuPont Nylon, a synthetic fibre used in clothing and other fabrics, and other yarns that become part of cloth fabrics. In each example, the original material is further processed or fabricated in the manufacturing process of another good, so that it changes form.

### Component Parts

These are goods that are used in the production of another product but do not change form as a result of the manufacturing process. Typically, these items are part of an assembly line process. Imagine the construction of an automobile: various components of the car are fitted together in sequence as the product automatically moves along a line. The tires, steel frame, seats, dashboards, engines, steering columns, doors, glass windows, radios, and other parts are classified as components to an automobile manufacturer. They arrive at a manufacturing facility ready for assembly. Price negotiation is an important consideration in the purchase of component parts. A buyer usually commits to buying large quantities if the source of supply is reliable. The contract states the length of the purchase period, which is usually one or more years.

## Supplies and Services

supplies and services    **Supplies and services** are those goods purchased by business and industry that do not enter the production process but facilitate other operations of the organization.

### Supplies

These are standardized products that are routinely purchased with a minimum of effort. Such products include items like paper, pens, pencils, typewriter and computer ribbons, fastening devices, and office stationary. Customers of such items look for quality at a good price. Purchasing agents also perceive service by sales representatives to be important.

### Services

These are the intangible offerings required to operate a business efficiently. Services are diverse both in nature and in cost. For example, repair services or ongoing maintenance contracts such as groundskeeping or janitorial services may be relatively inexpensive. By contrast, a management consulting service employed to analyze the management practices of a firm is expensive. In the case of ongoing services, variables such as price and service reliability are important to the buyer; for specialized, complex services, the reputation and quality of the people performing the service are important. Refer to figure 8.4 for a summary of the marketing considerations that apply to industrial (business) products.

FIGURE 8.4 Marketing Considerations for Industrial (Business) Goods

| | Installations | Accessory Equipment | Raw Materials | Processed Materials | Component Parts | Supplies | Services |
|---|---|---|---|---|---|---|---|
| Purchase Frequency | Infrequent | Infrequent but varied life span | Frequent unless contracted | Annual contracts | Infrequent | Frequent | Varied based on type |
| Purchase Motivation | Efficiency, Profitability, Service | Reliability, Standardized product, Service | Availability | Availability | Quality control, Availability | Service | Dependability |
| Supply Alternatives | Few | Several to many | Few, Usually large | Many | Several | Many | Few to many. |
| Product | Quality, Must meet customer specifications | Quality and Support Service | Quality (input for customer's product) | Quality, Consistent availability | Quality, Consistent availability | Quality at reasonable price, Assortment | Reputation |
| Price | Important, but not deciding factor | Important | Negotiated, Contract pricing | Important, Negotiated | Competitive | Important, Large quantities at low price | Important, but not deciding factor. |
| Promotion | Personal selling | Personal selling | Selling less important | Same importance | Personal selling Important | Personal selling Less important | Varies according to type |
| Place | Direct (short) channel | Short and medium channels | Medium to long channels | Short to medium channels | Short to medium channels | Medium to long channels | Short channels. |

## ⟩⟩⟩ *Branding and Brand Name Strategies*

How a consumer perceives a product largely depends on the brand name and what it stands for, that is, on the image marketing has developed for it over an extended period. For example, names such as Porsche or Jaguar suggest a certain quality and status. Obsession, a brand of perfume, suggests a mysterious, sexual image. Sanka is known as a decaffeinated coffee, and Maxwell House coffee is good to the last drop. Customers are accustomed to seeing brands and take them for granted. For the marketing organization, branding decisions are quite difficult. The basic decision is whether to proceed with individual brand names or family brand names, both of which are discussed in this section of the chapter.

Some key terms associated with branding decisions are as follows:

brand

1. A **brand** is a name, term, symbol or design (or some combination of them) that identifies the goods and services of an organization so that they can be differentiated from those of the competition.[6]

brand name

2. A **brand name** is that part of the brand that can be vocalized. Examples include names such as Colgate, Hertz, Seagram, Kellogg's, Betty Crocker, Huggies, Ritz, Scope, and so on.

brandmark

3. A **brandmark** is that part of a brand identifiable by a symbol or design. Examples include the Chrysler pentastar, which appears on dealer signs, promotional literature, and the front grill of Chrysler's automobiles; Nabisco's red triangle, which appears in the upper left corner of all of their packages; or Apple Computer's famous apple with a bite taken out of it. Brandmarks are referred to as logos (see figure 8.5).

**FIGURE 8.5** A Selection of Brandmarks

Courtesy: Nabisco Trademark is reproduced with the permission of Nabisco Brands, Ltd., Toronto, Ontario / Marque de commerce de Petro-Canada Inc. – Trademark / Domtar Inc. / Nissan Automobile Company (Canada) Ltd. / Ford Motor Company of Canada Ltd. / Journey's End Corporation.

trademark

4. A **trademark** is that part of a brand which is granted legal protection so that only the owner can use it. The letter *R* contained in a circle is the designation of a registered trademark. Trademarks include the brand names and symbols described above. They are effective for 15 years, and may be renewed as often as desired. Coke and Coca-Cola are registered trademarks of the Coca-Cola Company, and Pepsi and Pepsi-Cola are registered trademarks of the Pepsi-Cola Company.

copyright

5. **Copyright** is the exclusive right to reproduce, sell, or publish the matter and form of a dramatic, literary, musical or artistic work. Copyright protection is automatic, but copyrights are often designated by a *C* in a circle, which designates the work as being a registered copyright.

patent

6. A **patent** protects a manufacturing process or product design from being copied by competitors. It gives a manufacturer the sole right to develop and market a new product, process, or material as it sees fit. An industrial design registration protects appearance, while a true patent protects function. Under Canada's new Patent Act, which became effective October 1989, the maximum life of a Canadian patent is 20 years from the date on which the application is filed.

## The Benefits of Brands

Branding offers consumers and marketing organizations several benefits. Some of the benefits for the consumer follow:

1. Over time, the brand name suggests a certain level of quality. Consumers know what to expect; they trust and have confidence in a brand.
2. There can be psychological rewards for possessing certain brands. For example, purchasing a BMW automobile might suggest achievement to the owner, while wearing a suit with a designer label may make one feel stylish.
3. Brands distinguish competitive offerings, allowing consumers to make informed decisions. Names such as *Oat Bran*, *Fibre 1* and *Spoon Size Shredded Wheat* suggest clear messages or benefits about the product.

The marketing organization also enjoys benefits:

1. Branding enables the marketer to create and develop an image for a product or service. In most advertising a close relationship exists between a brand and slogan. Collectively they help form an impression in the consumer's mind. Here are a few examples, all from the same industry:

> Nissan — "Built for the human race"
> BMW — "The ultimate driving experience"
> Jaguar — "A blending of art and machine"
> Ford — "Quality is Job One"

2. Satisfied customers will make repeat purchases and ultimately stay loyal to a brand as long as it is available. This loyalty stabilizes market share and provides for certain economies of scale in production and efficiencies in marketing expenditures for a product.

# Brand Loyalty

brand loyalty

**Brand loyalty** is defined as the degree of consumer attachment to a particular brand of product or service. This degree of attachment can be weak or strong and varies from one product category to another. Brand loyalty is measured in three stages: brand recognition, brand preference, and brand insistence.[7]

brand recognition

1. *Brand Recognition* In the early stages of a product's life, the marketing objective is to create awareness of the brand name and package. With **brand recognition** achieved, and with the provision for incentives such as free samples or coupons, the consumer is tempted to make the first (trial) purchase.

brand preference

2. *Brand Preference* In the **brand preference** stage of a product's life, the brand is in the ballpark — that is, it is an acceptable alternative and will be purchased if it is available when needed. If it is unavailable the consumer will switch to an equal, competitive alternative. For example, if Coke is requested in a Burger King restaurant the order cannot be filled because the product is unavailable there. The consumer will usually accept the substitute, in this case, Pepsi-Cola.

brand insistence

3. *Brand Insistence* At the **brand insistence** point, a consumer will search the market extensively for the brand he or she wants. No alternatives are acceptable, and, if the brand is unavailable, the consumer is likely to postpone purchase until it is. Such a situation is a marketer's dream, a dream rarely achieved. Some critics insist that the original Coca-Cola product (now called Coke Classic) reached a level beyond brand insistence. So strong was the attachment that the product could not be changed. When it was, the backlash from the consumer franchise was so strong, the company had no alternative but to bring the original product back.

# Branding by Source of Product

Many types of brands exist and they can be distinguished according to who names them. Most of the brands mentioned in this section so far are manufacturer's brands or national brands. These brands are usually supported with their own marketing strategy to make them competitive and distinctive in the marketplace.

private label brand

A brand designated by a wholesaler or retailer is called a **private label brand**. These brands are usually produced by national brand manufacturers that also make similar products under their own brand names. These firms produce private label brands to the specifications of the distributor. Some examples of these brands follow:

| Company | Brand Name |
| --- | --- |
| Canadian Tire | Mastercraft |
| Sears | Kenmore, Diehard, Craftsman |
| The Bay | Beaumark |
| Shoppers Drug mart | Life Brand |
| Eaton's | Viking |

The presence of private label brands intensifies competition. Because shelf space is limited, the presence of private label brands makes it difficult for national brands to obtain space and causes slow-moving national brands to be quickly eliminated by the distributor, who uses computer technology to track product movement instantly. For the consumer, a private label brand offers reasonable quality at a low price, since marketing costs for such a brand tend to be significantly lower than those for national brands. In response to this form of competition, national brand manufacturers have introduced "fighting brands", or low priced national brands.[8] In this situation a national brand manufacturer may have two or more brands competing in the same market, but at different price and, probably, quality levels. For example, in the prepared cookie market — a market dominated by brand names such as Dare, Christie's, Dad's, and Colonial, among others — fighting brands play a key role in preserving total market share. Originally, Dare cookies were just Dare Cookies, but the competitive nature of the market forced Dare to reposition their original product. The original product became Dare Premium cookies and were priced at the high end of the market. Dare Classic cookies were positioned in the mid-price range and Dare regular cookies are at the bottom end. In effect, Dare competes in all segments or risks losing share to, say, Christie, a brand that also offers variety in each price segment. Such a strategy is becoming common among consumer packaged goods companies, particularly food processors and household-product marketers.

### Generic Brands

*generic brands*

Generic brands were a phenomenon of the early 1980s, particularly in supermarket chains such as Loblaws, Super Value, A&P, Safeway, and Dominion. A **generic brand** is a product without a brand name. Such a product has no brand name or identifying features. The packaging is kept simple; a minimum of colour is used and written words simply identify the contents. For example, "Corn Flakes" or "Fabric Softener." In Canada, it was Loblaws and its related supermarket chains, including Super Value and Zehrs, that popularized the use of generic brands. Through corporate advertising campaigns the grocery chain encouraged consumers to look for its "yellow label" products in the stores. Generic brands are common in such product categories as cereals, paper products, canned goods (fruits, vegetables and juices), and pet foods, among many others.

### National Brands

A national brand organization has two brand name options: an individual brand strategy or a family brand strategy, both of which offer advantages and disadvantages.

#### Individual Brand

*individual brand*

An **individual brand** is a means of identifying each product in a company's product mix with its own name. This brand name strategy is common among large household products manufacturers like Procter & Gamble, Canada Packers, and Lever Brothers. Some Procter & Gamble individual brand names are Scope (mouthwash), Tide (laundry detergent), Secret (deodorant), and Luvs (disposable diapers).

*multibrand strategy*

Very often a marketing organization operates in several market segments of a product category. In this case a **multibrand strategy** is used. The term multibrand refers to the use of a different brand name for each item a company offers in the same product category. To illustrate, Lever Brothers makes bar soap at different price levels, and each of its offerings has a different brand name — Dove, Lifebuoy, Caress, and Lux. Through advertising, each brand has acquired a different image among consumers. In effect, the brands compete against each other, but the revenues they generate all return to the same source.

An individual brand name is sometimes extended to an innovation in the market. For example, when Procter & Gamble launched a liquid laundry detergent it was to the company's advantage to use the Tide brand name. Such a marketing decision gives a brand instant credibility among distributors and consumers. For the same reason, Bounce fabric softener is marketed both in liquid and sheet form.

### Family Brand

**family brand**

A **family brand** exists when the same brand name is used for a group of related products. Family brand names are usually steeped in tradition and quickly come to mind because they have been on the market for a long time. Examples include names such as Heinz, Campbell's, Quaker, Nabisco, Jell-O, Christie, and Del Monte. These brand families take three different forms:

1. *Product Family*   In this case, a group of products holds its own family name. Jell-O dessert products, Post cereals, Ken-L-Ration dog food, Del Monte canned goods, and Tylenol cough and cold remedies are a few examples.

2. *Company Family*   Here the brand name is also the company name. Heinz (ketchup, juices, sauces, baby food, and other food products), Cooper (hockey and other sports equipment) and E.D. Smith (comparable product line to Heinz) are a few examples. Other popular company brand names include Polaroid, Kodak, Mennen, Philips, and General Electric.

3. *Company and Product Family*   In this case, the marketing organization combines both variables. The company name makes up part of the brand name, with another brand name making up the other part. Examples include:

| Company | Product |
|---------|---------|
| Kellogg's | Corn Flakes, Frosted Flakes, Special K, Bran Flakes, and Rice Krispies |
| Nabisco | Shreddies, Shredded Wheat, Ritz, Dad's Cookies, David Cookies |
| Gillette | Right Guard, Foamy, Silkience |

A family brand strategy offers two advantages to a marketing organization. First, promotional expenditures for one product will benefit the rest of the family by creating an awareness of the brand name, and, second, new products become accepted readily, since they capitalize on the success and reputation of the existing family products. Retailers and wholesalers like such new products because they come with additional promotion support and result in increased demand for the family of products. Consumers accept the product because of the reputation and performance of related products under the same brand name.

On the negative side, the failure or poor quality of a new product could tarnish the image of a family of products; for that reason, such products are usually removed

>>> *MARKETING IN ACTION*

### WHAT'S IN A NAME?

Just how important is a brand name in determining the success or failure of a product? Consider the following examples.

What is a Thixo-Tex? Right, you don't know. Thixo-tex is a superior rustproofing compound developed by the Matex Corporation. Sales of Thixo-Tex were averaging $2 million annually in the United States. Unsatisfied with growth prospects, Matex changed the name to "Rusty Jones" and created a trade character with the same name to promote the product. Within four years, sales reached $100 million.

The Toro Corporation, a name famous for snow removal products, introduced a snowthrower with the name "Snow Pup". The name was intended to imply that the unit was small and easy to use. Sales of Snow Pup were well below projections, and research conducted by the company traced the problem to the brand name. The perception of the name and the message it communicated were quite different from what the company had intended. Snow Pup implied that the product lacked power to do a good job — an

The name of a product is important, whether the product be a snow-blower or a rust-proofing compound

undesirable image for a product that removes snow from clogged walkways and driveways.

Adapted from "Cueing the consumer", *The Journal of Consumer Marketing*, Spring 1987, pp.23-27.

from the market quickly by the marketing organization. The importance of branding and brand-name strategies is illustrated in the Marketing in Action vignette "What's in a Name?"

### *Licensed Brand*

Brand image is a powerful marketing tool and a valuable asset to marketing organizations. The use of an established brand name or symbol by other firms on other products can benefit both firms financially. To make such an arrangement, the owner of the brand name or symbol enters into a licensing agreement with a second party. Licensing is a way of legally allowing another firm to use a brand name or trademark for a certain period (the duration of the contractual agreement); when a brand name or trademark is used in this manner, it is called a **licensed brand**. Clothing lines often adopt well-known brand names. A line of McKids clothing is available through Sears stores. The Coca-Cola brand name has appeared on running shoes, T-shirts, and sweatshirts. These arrangements provide moving advertisements for the owners of the brand name or trademark and ready-made promotion for the owners of the licensed product. In a licensing agreement the owner of the trademark is usually paid a royalty by the licensee.

**licensed brand**

**FIGURE 8.6    The Naming of a Brand or Company**

**Tridel Corporation**
This company is Canada's largest condominium developer. It was started by *three* brothers with the surname *Del*Zotto, hence the name Tridel.

**Mmmuffins Inc.**
The name for this storefront shopping-mall snack bar originated when one of the founding partners stumbled (stuttered) over the word muffin. The triple "m" became the trademark.

**Esso and Exxon**
Esso is the abbreviation of the company name Standard Oil. The parent name of Exxon stands for nothing.

**Bic**
The name for these popular pens came from the surname of the creator, Marcel Bich, from whose surname the "h" was dropped.

**Aquascutum**
These raincoats are from the Latin word meaning water shield.

**Coca-Cola**
The name comes from two original ingredients, cocoa leaves and cola nuts.

*Source*: Adapted from Bruce Gates, "Picking Name Often Based on Whim," *Financial Post*, September 26, 1988, p. 53.

In deciding what brand strategy to use, a company analyzes its own situation in relation to its corporate and marketing strategy. Firms have many ways of generating their brand names, even their company names. Figure 8.6 contains a few examples of how names originated.

## >>>> *Packaging and Labelling Strategies*

Packaging is often referred to as the "5th P" of the marketing mix, even though it is an integral part of product strategy. It is the combination of the package (which attracts the consumers' attention), the product (the quality inside the package) and the brand name that contributes to the image held by consumers. How important is the package? Just ask the makers of Nabob coffee. Prior to the introduction of a vacuum-sealed package, an innovation of Nabob Foods Limited, Nabob floundered in the ground coffee market with a 5 percent market share. Like other brands, Nabob was packed in the traditional paper bag style of package. But after introducing the new vacuum-sealed package, along with a convincing advertising presentation that dramatized the freshness benefit, Nabob surged into the lead in the marketplace, where it remains today. Nabob's current market share is 27.6 percent, compared to Maxwell House (the former leader) at 21.4 percent.[9] Today, 90 percent of all ground coffee sold in Canada is packed in vacuum-sealed packages.[10]

The package is what consumers look for when they are thinking of a purchase; thus marketers spend considerable time and money developing effective, functional, and eye-catching designs. **Packaging** is defined as those activities related to the

**packaging**

design and production of the container or wrapper of a product.[11] There are four basic components to a package:

primary package

1. *Primary Package*  The **primary package** contains the actual product (e.g., the jar containing the jam, the tube of toothpaste, the plastic bottle holding shampoo, or the box with cereal in it). Note that a product such as cereal will have an inner liner as part of the primary package to seal in freshness, but it is not visible until the product is opened by the user.

secondary package

2. *Secondary Package*  The **secondary package** is the outer wrapper that protects the product, often discarded once the product is used the first time. The box that tubes of toothpaste are packed in is an example. Even though these outer packages are discarded, they are important to the marketer as it is their design which attracts the customer's eye to the product.

labels

3. *Labels*  **Labels** are printed sheets of information affixed to a package container. A label can be wrapped around a jar of coffee, a can or cardboard canister, or glued to a flat surface at the front and back of a rigid surface.

4. *Shipping Carton*  Packages are packed in cartons, usually corrugated cardboard cartons, to facilitate movement from one destination or distributor to another. The shipping carton is marked with product codes to facilitate storage and transportation of merchandise. Today, more products are using a shrink-wrapping process, a plastic overwrap of product packed on cardboard trays. In the soft drink industry the 24 pack of cans are frequently packed with shrink wrapping.

## Packaging Decisions

In designing effective packages, marketers make decisions in two key areas. First, consideration is given to the basic functions of a package. Factors such as economy, marketing and merchandising, and safety are examined. Second, label design and any mandatory requirements for labels are considered.

### *Functions of a Package*

#### Protect the Product

This is the first of the four basic functions a package serves. Since a product may pass through many warehouses on its way to the consumer, even those products that are not fragile require protection. The degree of protection needed depends on how long the products will be in storage, what sort of transportation and handling they will experience, and how much protection from heat, light, and moisture they need.

#### Market the Product

The second function of the package is to sell the product at each stage of distribution. A retailer is concerned about the size and shape of the package since shelf space is limited, and whether or not enough information is on the package to resell the product. For example, will it provide adequate information for consumers who examine products in a self-serve store environment? The retailer may also consider the visibility of the product, because this may be an important influence on the consumer. For instance, some shampoos are packed in clear plastic packages to show their colour and consistency, while others are packed in packages that hide the appearance of the product. Over time, it is the package that establishes and helps maintain the product or brand image. For example, it can give a perfume or fragrance the quality look that is crucial in such a business.

Heinz Ketchup is a product with an interesting packaging dilemma. The product has been successfully positioned as the thickest brand of ketchup. Consequently, consumers shake, whack, and bang the bottle to get the ketchup out. In effect, consumers expect to go through this ritual when they use Heinz. However, when Heinz shifted from glass bottles to safer plastic bottles, their institutional customers filed some objections. While plastic bottles are safer, they do not have the same premium look. In addition, the ketchup sticks to the side walls of the plastic, according to regular customers buying for restaurants. Over a one-year period the accumulated ketchup loss was costly.[12]

### Provide Convenience to Consumers

The package should also allow consumers to use the product easily. It should be easy to carry, open, handle, and reseal. For example, if it is a liquid, it should pour without spills or drips. If the product is heavy or bulky, handles often become an important aspect of the design. Examples of the pursuit of convenience in packaging include resealable plastic lids for jars and cans, molded plastics that seal tightly (as if never opened), plastic carrying cases for large soft drink bottles, handles on beer cases, disposable diaper boxes, serving trays with frozen or microwave food products, and canned goods with molded bottoms that allow stacking.

The movement towards plastics has made products for the household (soaps, detergents, cleaners, etc.) more convenient and safer to use in comparison to glass and metal containers. On the negative side, plastics are not recyclable or biodegradable, a concern of consumer groups and governments.

### Meet Social Concerns

Product safety is a major concern of consumer groups and governments. Scares unforeseen by anybody, such as the scare resulting from the deaths in the mid-1980s linked to packages of Tylenol that had been tampered with, must be avoided at all costs. As a result of such scares, the pharmaceutical industry brought to market the concept of tamper-proof packaging. Most drug products now have extra seals on the inner and outer packages, and consumers are advised by manufacturers not to purchase a product if either of those seals is broken. Consumers are also concerned about unnecessarily extravagant packaging that adds to the cost of the product and its price, and about the excessive use of materials that are depleting Canada's natural resources. For instance, excessive use of paper products depletes forestry resources.

## Labelling

As stated above, labels are those parts of a package that contain information. A label serves three basic functions: it identifies the brand name and the owner of the brand; it provides essential information to the buyer; and it satisfies legal requirements where applicable. The typical components of a label are brand name, illustrations, directions, mandatory information, and optional information. Today labelling also generally includes a Universal Product Code.

1. *Brand Name*    This provides clear identification, usually in bold print or stylized printed form.

2. *Illustrations*    Sometimes an illustration, such as a photograph of the product, attracts attention (e.g., a cup of steaming hot coffee on a coffee label).

3. *Directions*    This is information on how to use or prepare the product and includes assembly instructions where necessary.

4. *Mandatory Information*    Size expressed in volume or weight, a list of ingredients ranking ingredients according to the amounts used in the product, company name, and mailing address must all appear by law on the label. For certain food categories — cereals, for example — the inclusion of nutritional information is also mandatory. For chemicals and for products containing drugs, safety warnings and instructions and precautions for users are required, along with appropriate symbols appearing prominently on the package.

5. *Optional Information*    Marketing information falls into this category. These messages usually appear in the form of a package "flash", that is, a temporary message announcing something new. Some products maintain a consistent product message, perhaps a slogan or a guarantee somewhere on the label. Some common examples of both types of messages are

"Win a trip to . . . . . . . . . . . . . . . . . . . . . . . ." See side panel for details
"New recipes . . . . . . . . . . . . . . . . . . . ." See reverse of label for details
"25% more . . . . . . . . . . . . . . . . . . . . . . . . . . ." Limited time offer
"Free Inside . . . . . . . . . . . . . . . . . . . . . . . . . . . . . . Collect all five"
"Satisfaction guaranteed or your money will be refunded"

Such information enhances the marketability of the product and is usually directly related to other marketing mix activities such as advertising and promotion. Ongoing messages such as money-back guarantees and refunds are included at the discretion of the manufacturer. Refer to the sample label in figure 8.7.

---

**FIGURE 8.7    A Sample Label Containing Mandatory and Optional Information**

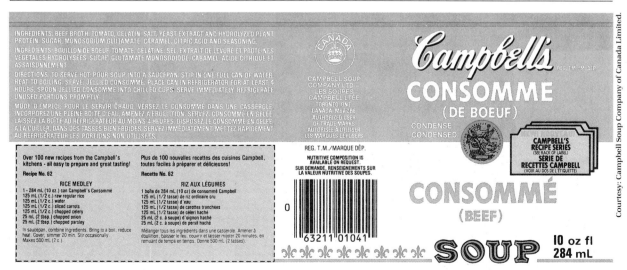

6. *Universal Product Code*   Another aspect of labelling is the now familiar series of black lines that appear on virtually all consumer packaged goods; these are called the Universal Product Code (UPC) symbols. These bars identify the manufacturer and product item (brand, size, variety, etc.). The UPC symbol is an essential labelling element, which allows for the use of electronic checkout stations in retailing organizations. The UPC symbol is read by a scanner, which automatically enters the item in the computer. The price is printed out and the item is taken out of inventory records. For retailers, the UPC symbol offers several benefits, namely, reduced labour costs, better records on product turnover (quicker and more informed decisions are made on what items to carry) and greater inventory control (automatic reorder points are established). For consumers, checkout time is reduced.

## What are Products Packed In?

Marketing organizations have numerous types of packaging alternatives to choose from. What type of material is used depends on the physical characteristics of the product or the product form. Some products are available in several different forms that necessitate different types of packaging (e.g., detergents in powdered and liquid form use cardboard and plastics in packages, while deodorants use metal spray cans and soft and rigid plastics). In other cases, such as margarine, molded plastics are suitable. Metallic paper materials are often used for snacks like candy bars and potato chips. Very often, packaging suppliers create innovations in package design that make new product forms available to the manufacturers they sell to.

In Canada, technology in the packaging industry is advancing rapidly, and new innovations are hitting the market constantly. The industry is also moving forward in terms of consumer appeal. In the past twenty years, the demand by consumers that products offer long shelf-life, convenience, and microwaveable containers has ensured steady growth in the packaging industry. It takes some $8 billion to wrap, can, bottle, bag, and box the products Canadians consume each year, yet packaging is so diverse, it has been referred to as one of the country's biggest non-industries. A breakdown of the total Canadian packaging industry reveals the following market shares for the various types of materials:[13]

| Type of Package | Market Share |
|---|---|
| Corrugated Boxes | 18% |
| Metal Cans | 16 |
| Folding Cartons | 14 |
| Glass | 9 |
| Plastics | 7 |

In the nineties, plastics will grow in importance. New types of plastic polymers are threatening glass and metal containers for numerous products, such as soft drinks. New York Seltzer, a maker of flavoured carbonated soda beverage, began test marketing plastic cans (polyethylene tetrephthalate) in 1988. Initial response to the test indicated that the cans were comparable to metal cans in their ability to maintain product quality. For the company, the motivation to use plastics is cost savings over traditional alternatives. The pros and cons of some of the various packaging materials are summarized in figure 8.8.

**FIGURE 8.8    The Benefits and Drawbacks of Packaging Materials**

| | Benefits | Drawbacks |
|---|---|---|
| Glass | • Strong protection barrier<br>• Quality appearance | • Breakage (safety)<br>• Weight, therefore higher shipping cost |
| Molded Plastic | • Aesthetic appeal of shape<br>• Quality impression<br>• Reuseable by consumer | • High tooling expenditure<br>• Production to high tolerance standards |
| Thermoformed Plastic | • Less expensive than glass<br>• Easier to fill, so offers production economies | • Negative impact on image<br>• Does not offer tight sealing against moisture |
| Flexible Packaging (Metallic Plastics) | • Maximum barrier properties<br>• Increased shelf life, therefore fresher product | • Product hidden (translucent not transparent)<br>• Higher start-up costs associated with production |
| Metal | • Good protection barrier<br>• Flexible metals are microwaveable<br>• Tensile strength for aerosols | • Not reuseable<br>• Can affect taste of product |
| Paper | • Good product display<br>• Microwaveable | • Less protection<br>• Degrades quickly |

## Package Innovation

Perhaps the most notable and recent innovation in consumer goods packaging has been the "Tetra Brik Aseptic" carton, developed by Tetra Pak Inc., which is used to provide ready-to-serve beverages of fruit and vegetable juices, milk, milkshakes, and alcohol-based coolers. This package is usually small and brick-like in appearance. For beverages sold in supermarkets, a straw is usually appended to the product, and the containers are often shrink-wrapped in sleeves of three units. This package format offers long shelf life without refrigeration, and, for consumers, the convenience outweighs the cost, which is high in comparison to products that come in more conventional package formats.

Another recent innovation is the development of vacuum-metallized films, which are lighter in weight and tougher than predecessors such as aluminum foil. Metallized film is now the favoured package material of such snack foods as candy bars, ice cream novelties, and potato chips; they have captured 70 percent of the market share in these product categories.[14] The metallized materials offer a better barrier to the various gases and the light that can harm the quality of the product. Snack food manufacturers say the new metallized plastics look better on the shelf and are easily transported, looking less shop-worn once they reach their destination.[15]

Innovation in packaging has not been all favourable. Pressure has been directed at the plastics industry, which is being urged by governments and consumer groups to develop biodegradable materials or use materials that provide opportunity for recycling.[16] Products packed in aerosol spray cans and products packed in foam-based packaging material (e.g., styrofoam egg cartons, hamburger containers, and coffee cups) have also proven harmful to the environment. They use CFCs (clouroflourocarbons), which are synthetic chemicals that destroy the ozone layer (refer to chapter 1), although these now appear to be on their way to extinction because of government legislation. The Ontario government, in February, 1988, was the first to announce a ban on the use of CFCs in products and packages. Soon thereafter, the federal government announced legislation that would phase out all fluorocarbons within a ten-year period.[17]

## ⟩⟩⟩⟩ *The Customer Satisfaction Mix*

**customer satisfaction mix**

The amount of attention an organization gives to customer service has a direct bearing on the level of satisfaction experienced by consumers. In this regard, it is important to point out that there is more to service than follow-up service programs after a sale has been made. Four distinct areas comprise the **customer satisfaction mix**: product-related variables, sales activity variables, after-sales variables, and corporate culture variables.[18] The coordination of this mix determines the degree of customer satisfaction realized (refer to figure 8.9).

### Product

Three product-related elements have an influence on the level of customer satisfaction achieved: the design of the product, the quality and source of raw materials and parts, and the production process itself. The Jaguar XJ-6 Sedan illustrated in figure 8.10 is an example of an automobile whose design has lasted much longer than expected. It was originally designed for the 1968 model. Over the years its reputation for quality parts, workmanship, and assembly has been undisputed. The Leica

FIGURE 8.9    The Customer Satisfaction Mix

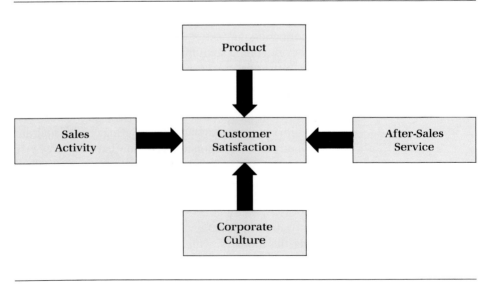

**FIGURE 8.10** An Advertisement for an Automobile

*This automobile has a reputation for quality, workmanship and assembly, features that constitute a key element of the customer satisfaction mix.*

M-series 35mm camera is a highly sophisticated model that was almost made obsolete in the sixties and seventies by the Nikon, which was simpler to operate. The survival of the Leica is due only to the unrelenting demand from professional photographers and serious amateurs. A manufacturer considers seriously the quality offered by its source of supply, for this variable has a direct impact on the quality of the manufacturer's product.

## Sales Activity

The messages about a product that are sent out by a marketing organization are the variables that condition customer attitudes and expectations before and during a sale. These messages are in the forms of advertising, sales literature, direct mailings, and the spoken word in sales presentations. Messages which "oversell" a product or service usually result in high levels of customer dissatisfaction. For this reason, IBM is an organization that firmly believes in not overselling. Their strategy is to: 1) create a set of expectations that the company can meet or even exceed when the product they sell is up and running, 2) screen out excessive and wrong expectations, even at the risk of losing customers, and 3) presell customers on the notion that IBM's approach is to work with customers to solve a problem, since customers want solutions. Such solutions are based on value rather than price.[19]

The attitudes and actions of those who communicate with customers also influence customer satisfaction. Positive, cheerful, helpful attitudes must be expressed by telephone receptionists, repair technicians, sales representatives, and anyone else who comes in contact with customers. Courtesy when dealing with inquiries and complaint calls, having the necessary product knowledge, and the expression of a sincere desire to meet customers' needs — all of these things will make customers feel satisfied.

## After-Sales Service

Ensuring a customer remains a customer is the responsibility of after-sales service. Sales-support activities reinforce loyalty, and, given the intense competitive environment that exists today, this is of primary concern to marketing organizations.

Contemporary organizations encourage customers to complain if dissatisfied with the products or services they have purchased, hoping that the complaints are directed to the company, not other customers. In this way the company has the opportunity to respond and to reinforce loyalty that otherwise would be lost. There is growing evidence that customer happiness shows up at the "bottom line", and it is the main reason why companies like General Electric, Coca-Cola, and British Airways invest millions of dollars to improve complaint-handling systems.[20]

Often referred to as "damage control" techniques, such sales support systems include toll-free 800 numbers, recall notices, liberal refund policies, repair and maintenance reminders, intensive staff training, training of customer service personnel, and warranties and extended warranties. For some specific examples of after-sales service programs, refer to the Marketing in Action vignette "Service and Satisfaction."

## ⟩⟩⟩ *MARKETING IN ACTION*

### *SERVICE AND SATISFACTION*

There's an old expression, "The sale never ends", and how true it is. In a world of intense competition and finicky consumers, disgruntled customers can prove costly to the best of marketing organizations. Astute organizations truly realize the value of customer service programs and their importance in the product mix. Here are some case histories demonstrating that importance.

The Coca-Cola Company (Atlanta, Georgia) installed a 1-800-GET-COKE line in 1983 to encourage customer feedback. Without the toll-free line, Coke might never have understood the error of its ways in replacing the old Coke with the new formula. Previously receiving an average of 400 calls per day, Coke received 12 000 calls per day when the formula was changed. The day after the announcement that old Coke would return as Coca-Cola Classic, 18 000 calls were received.

Toll-free phone lines offer additional benefits. The experience of Coca-Cola reveals that phone conversations are more personal and give a service representative a better opportunity to explain the company's position. This method of communication is also faster and, usually, less costly than other methods.

If telephones are used to handle complaints, the attitude of those company representatives on the phone is important, as these instances indicate:

1. Procter & Gamble trains new service representatives for four weeks in a classroom, teaching them how to diffuse anger and resolve problems.

2. American Express tracks the number of calls coming in from new card prospects and customers and the way their representatives talk to them.

3. Toyota ranks its representatives daily on the basis of their productivity in handling complaints from customers.

British Airways gives their customers the royal treatment, and then the chance to complain about it. When passengers disembark in London, they can visit a VideoPoint booth and record their

*Providing after-sales service is one means of keeping consumers satisfied*

complaints on tape. Customer service representatives review the tapes and respond to the customers as quickly as possible.

Sears Canada Inc. employs mystery shoppers who visit stores to assess service quality. They pose as shoppers, and their assignment is to evaluate the performance and behaviour of store personnel towards customers.

And what about after-sales service? It is quite common now for computer software suppliers to issue upgraded versions to registered owners — a nice touch indeed. Maytag does not let their customer down either: their parts inventory dates back some thirty years. That repairman really is lonely!

These examples demonstrate the importance of service — in every sense of the word. What separates winners from losers is the company's and the employee's intense interest in keeping customers happy.

Adapted from Karen Nickel, "How to handle customer gripes", *Fortune*, October 24, 1988, pp.88-100., and Milend Lele and Jagdesh Sheth, "Four fundamentals of customer satisfaction", *Business Marketing*, June 1988, p.80.

## Corporate Culture

The corporate values of an organization, its beliefs and attitudes, constitute the bond that holds together the product, sales, and after-sales variables. The organization that sincerely believes that maximizing customer satisfaction is necessary to long-term success will strategically combine these variables. The slogan of the John Deere Company, "Nothing runs like a Deere," states exactly what the values of the company are. Everything the firm does, from design to production to marketing to sales and service at the dealers, is designed to keep a customer's machine up and running. Customer-oriented cultural values are perhaps the most crucial, for if the culture does not support customer-focused attitudes, then all the investments in product design, marketing and sales programs, and so on is wasted.

## >>>> SUMMARY

A product is a combination of tangible and intangible benefits offered to consumers, and what marketing organizations develop and market is a total product concept. This concept includes the physical item, the image, the brand name, and the level of sales support and other activity.

The total range of products offered for sale is referred to as the product mix. Products are classified according to characteristics such as durability and tangibility. Products are also classified either as consumer goods or industrial (business) goods. Consumer goods are intended for the personal use of the customer, while industrial goods are generally used in the production of other goods and services. It is the use by the customer that distinguishes consumer goods from industrial goods.

Consumer goods are further subdivided into convenience goods, shopping goods, and specialty goods. These types are generally distinguished by price and by the time taken to purchase the item. Industrial goods are subdivided into three categories: capital items, parts and materials, and supplies and services.

How a customer perceives a product largely depends on the brand. Marketing organizations use branding as a means of identifying products and developing an image. Broadly speaking, an organization has two branding options: individual brands or family brands. Private label brands and generic brands are other strategies used by distributors of consumer goods. Consumers come to trust what the brand name stands for, and, if they derive satisfaction from the brand, to develop certain levels of brand loyalty. Loyalty is expressed in terms of recognition, preference, and insistence.

Packaging plays an integral part in the product mix. Decisions that must be made about packaging concern the type and nature of package to use and the labelling and shipping requirements. Packages selected must fulfill four basic functions. A good package protects the product, markets the product, provides the consumer with convenience in handling and using the product, and is environmentally safe.

An organization's product strategy and the success it yields is related to the development and implementation of a "customer satisfaction mix". A customer's level of satisfaction is related to how well an organization blends product, sales, after-sales and corporate-culture variables in putting the customer first.

## 〉〉〉〉 KEY TERMS

| | | |
|---|---|---|
| product | emergency goods | patent |
| total product concept | shopping goods | brand loyalty |
| product mix | specialty goods | brand recognition |
| product item | unsought goods | brand preference |
| unique selling point | capital items | brand insistence |
| product line | accessory equipment | private label brands |
| product line depth | parts and materials | generic brands |
| product line width | supplies and services | individual brands |
| nondurable goods | processed materials | multibrand strategy |
| durable goods | component parts | family brands |
| services | supplies | licensed brands |
| consumer goods | brand | packaging |
| industrial (business) goods | brand name | primary package |
| convenience goods | brandmark | secondary package |
| staple goods | trademark | labels |
| impulse goods | copyright | customer satisfaction mix |

## 〉〉〉〉 REVIEW AND DISCUSSION QUESTIONS

**1.** Explain what is meant by the "total product concept."

**2.** What is the difference between product line depth and product line width? Provide some examples other than those in the text to illustrate the difference.

**3.** What is the difference between a durable good and a nondurable good?

**4.** What are the basic characteristics that distinguish a convenience good from a shopping good and a specialty good?

**5.** What basic elements of the marketing mix are important to the marketing of shopping goods? Specialty goods? Briefly explain the difference.

**6.** Provide two examples of each type of industrial (business) good listed as follows: **(a)** installation **(b)** accessory equipment **(c)** component part **(d)** processed material **(e)** business service

**7.** What are the benefits of branding for consumers? For marketing organizations? Briefly explain your answers.

**8.** Distinguish between brand preference and brand insistence.

**9.** Provide examples of five different private label brand names other than those mentioned in the chapter.

**10.** "Family brand name strategies are more effective than individual brand name strategies." Briefly discuss this statement and support your position with appropriate examples.

**11.** Select two packages of your choice, one you think is good, one you perceive as not so good. Discuss the marketability of each package.

**12.** Briefly explain the four elements of the customer satisfaction mix.

**13.** "Brand loyalty, and how an organization maintains it, begins when the customer agrees to purchase." Discuss the relevance of this statement.

## ⟩⟩⟩ R E F E R E N C E S

1.  LAWRENCE RENY, DEREK NEWTON, NEIL BORDEN, and RALPH BIGGADIKE, *Decisions in Marketing* (Plano, Texas: Business Publications Inc., 1984), p.20.

2.  PHILIP KOTLER, *Principles of Marketing* (Scarborough, Ontario: Prentice-Hall Canada Inc., 1983), p.323.

3.  PHILIP KOTLER, GORDON McDOUGALL, and GARY ARMSTRONG, *Marketing*, Canadian Edition (Scarborough, Ontario: Prentice-Hall Canada Inc., 1988), p. 210.

4.  Ibid, p.323.

5.  STEWART HUSTED, DALE VARBLE, and JAMES LOWRY, *Principles of Modern Marketing* (Needham Heights, MA.: Allyn and Bacon,1989), p.210.

6.  Committee on Definitions, *Marketing Definitions: A Glossary of Marketing Terms* (Chicago: AMA, 1980), pp.8-10.

7.  DALE BECKMAN, DAVID KURTZ, and LOUIS BOONE, *Foundations of Marketing* (Toronto: Holt Rinehart and Winston, 1988), pp.316-317.

8.  HUSTED et al, *Principles of Modern Marketing*, p.217.

9.  *Financial Times of Canada*, October 31, 1988, p.13.

10.  "Who's on First?", *Financial Post*, October 23, 1988, p.A9.

11.  KOTLER, McDOUGALL, and ARMSTRONG, *Marketing*, p.221.

12.  "H.J. Heinz: Listening to Customers", *Foodservice and Hospitality*, October 1988, p.46.

13.  ROBERT ENGLISH, "Diverse Industry Faces Challenge," *Financial Post*, June 29, 1987, p.33.

14.  MICHAEL HARRISON, "The Snack-pack Revolution", *Financial Post*, June 29, 1987, p.34.

15.  Ibid.

16.  ENGLISH, "Diverse Industry", p.33.

17.  PETER GORRIE, "Ozone-destroying Products Banned", *Whig Standard*, February 21, 1989, p.1.

18.  MILEND LELE and JAGDESH SHETH, "Four Fundamentals of Customer Satisfaction", *Business Marketing*, June 1986, p.80.

19.  Ibid, p.82.

20.  "How to Handle Customer Gripes", *Fortune*, October 24, 1988, p.89.

# CHAPTER 9 〉〉〉〉

# *Product Management*

**LEARNING OBJECTIVES**

After studying this chapter, you will be able to

1. Describe the organizational systems for developing and managing products.

2. Explain the impact the product life cycle has on the development of marketing strategies at each stage of the cycle.

3. Describe the alternatives available to an organization for developing new products.

4. Identify and explain the steps in the new product development process.

5. Distinguish between product adoption and the diffusion process.

Product management concerns three key areas: 1) the internal organization structure for managing current products; 2) the allocation of resources for the development of new products; and 3) dealing with changing market needs, especially as products progress through their life cycles. In this third area, the firm must be aware of the need to change marketing strategies during the various stages of the product's life cycle. Organizations realize that demand for the products they offer for sale now will not last forever. The influence of technology in the past decade has resulted in many new products coming to market. The rapid changes expected to occur in the next decade will force managers to anticipate, plan for, and make some difficult product decisions, for example, on what products to add and what to delete. This chapter will look at the key areas involved in product management.

# 〉〉〉〉 *Organization Systems for Managing Products*

The variety of general management systems used in contemporary marketing organizations is discussed in chapter 3, "Strategic Planning". In this chapter, the focus is specifically on the product management system, or the roles and responsibilities of product managers, including some recent variations of this system.

The trend in contemporary marketing practice is to combine various organizational structures so that products may be developed and marketed more efficiently than before. The brand manager or product manager (referred to as the brand management system or product management system) usually represents the foundation of the organizational structure. Although such a management system is more typical of consumer-packaged-goods companies than of industrial product companies (business-to-business marketing organizations), industrial product companies are using brand managers more now than they did in the past. Other options available to the organization include the use of category managers, venture teams, and new product development committees. Each of the options will be discussed in the following section.

## The Product Manager

**product manager**

A **product manager** (brand manager) is an individual assigned responsibility for the development and implementation of effective and efficient marketing programs for a specific product or group of products. In large companies, a product manager is responsible for the marketing planning of one or a few brands. Typically, he or she reports to a marketing manager who does not have direct brand responsibilities, but is responsible for the overall marketing effort of the firm. In small companies a brand manager's portfolio of products can be greater in number, and the marketing manager may also have direct brand responsibility.

A product manager is responsible for developing the marketing mix that will lead to the growth in sales planned for a product. The manager is also often accountable for the profitability of the product. Usually, product managers work on established brands rather than new brands. Some organizations do, however, assign to product managers (or product development managers) the responsibility of overseeing new products.

## The Category Manager

**category manager**

A **category manager** is an individual assigned responsibility for developing and implementing the marketing activity for a group of related products or product lines. An individual in this position used to be called a group product manager. The current title appropriately suggests that the products for which the manager is responsible are closely related. For example, the products may belong to the same market segment (e.g., detergents, coffee, beverages, paper products, and other household items), or they may appeal to similar target markets (i.e., those of similar age, lifestyle, and purchase tendencies).

Some organizations employ both category managers and product managers. In such cases it is the interaction between the two managers that makes the system work. In these companies, the category manager often focuses on long term goals and strategies while the product manager focuses on short term, day-to-day operations. In organizations that use one or the other, the product or group of products receives the management attention they deserve from an individual whose only concern is the well-being of his or her product. This often fuels internal competition for financial resources, since each product has a certain status (e.g., products with large sales volume and profit contribution have a higher status) in an organization. Typically, aggressive brand managers and product managers aspire to have the marketing responsibility for the organization's number one brand (e.g., Labatt's Blue at Labatt's, Maxwell House Coffee at Kraft General Foods, or Crest at Procter & Gamble).

## Venture Teams

**venture team**

The purpose of a **venture team** is to bring together a group of individuals from the functional (operating) areas of the firm to devote all of their time to a product concept of high market potential.[1] A venture team operates independently of others in the organization. In effect, it consists of project managers or a project management group. Generally, a venture team is responsible for product design and development, capital expansion plans, if necessary, and the initial marketing planning for the new products, if they make it to market. Once the product is introduced, the day-to-day management is usually turned over to a product manager and the venture team is disbanded.

## New Product Development Committees

It is common to assign new product development to an individual or group of individuals because of the complexity and time associated with the task. Managers generally lack the time to combine new product development with their ongoing planning for existing products. Given the importance of both tasks, it is prudent for an organization to manage them independently. A new product committee will oversee a product from development to introduction and then turn over responsibility to a product manager. Unlike a venture team, a committee does not function autonomously; instead, it usually reports to someone such as the director or vice-president of marketing.

## Decisions of the Product Manager

Although the name may suggest otherwise, a product manager is responsible for all areas of the marketing mix. A product manager must establish profitable and fair prices and determine the policies and terms for price negotiation as well as for discounting. In the area of promotion, the manager must decide on the use of advertising, sales promotion, and publicity. Decisions also have to be made on where the product should be available, whether in selected places for a class market, or in a wide range of places for a mass market.

Let's be more specific about product decisions. Decisions and strategies about products may concern package design, making modifications to a product after its introduction, maintaining or withdrawing products from the marketplace, and adding new products to the product mix.

### *Product Modifications*

Changes in style are often implemented to give a product a contemporary look; automobiles and boats are redesigned to appeal to changing consumer tastes and preferences. Functional modifications are made widely: adding snap tops to beverage cans; affixing straws to small packaged juice containers; putting handles on bulky packages to make them easy to carry; or providing tamper-proof packaging for better safety — these are examples of functional modifications. Quality modifications include improvements such as making the product more durable (floor wax or furniture polish), improving the taste (a beverage or food product), improving the speed (a microcomputer) or making the product easier to use (an automatic camera). Refer to the Marketing in Action vignette "Standing Out in a Crowd" for an illustration of a unique product-package modification strategy.

## ›››› *MARKETING IN ACTION*

### *STANDING OUT IN A CROWD*

A health-conscious Canadian population, which is careful about the foods it eats and is active in recreation and sporting activity, has contributed to a spiralling growth in yogurt sales. Consequently, leading brands battle one another for the competitive edge.

The taste of the product is the major factor in determining brand loyalty, so marketing firms are constantly developing unique and innovative product ideas to tempt the palates of Canadians. Yoplait's latest answer is a "fruit-style" fruit-at-the-bottom yogurt that gives consumers a choice of eating their fruit and yogurt mixed or unmixed. While they can still enjoy the product in the traditional way (i.e., by eating it out of the container), the new idea allows consumers to turn the carton over so that, when the package seal is broken, the product slides out onto a serving plate and the fruit becomes a sauce on top of the yogurt.

No product can afford to stand still in a competitive market. This unique selling point, added to Yoplait's no-preservative, no-additive, real-fruit positioning, makes the brand a strong contender. Products such as "Fruit at the Bottom" are a means of penetrating the market in new areas. New product concepts are not new to Yoplait. In 1984, it introduced a yogurt drink to the Canadian market.

*Yoplait's new fruit-at-the-bottom yogurt gives consumers a choice of eating their fruit and yogurt mixed or unmixed*

Adapted from "Set yogurt served with fruit unmixed," *Food in Canada*, May 1987, p.26.

### *Product Mix*

As discussed in the previous chapter, product mix decisions concern the depth and width of a product line. The addition of new products and the creation of extended versions of existing products are the lifeblood of growth-oriented marketing organizations. To foster growth, a manager looks for gaps in the marketplace (perceived opportunities) and recommends developing products for the opportunities with the highest potential. For example, a company in the medium price range of a given market segment may decide to introduce a product either in the low price segment, to attract price-conscious shoppers, or in the high price segment, to attract shoppers primarily interested in quality. Such decisions are referred to as stretching. **Product stretching** is defined as the sequential addition of products to a product line so that its depth or width is increased. One type of stretching occurs when a product is marketed in a different format. A brand of deodorant may be introduced as an aerosol spray, but, gradually, roll-ons and stick formats may be offered as well. Various scents could also be added to each format.

*product stretching*

### *Maintenance or Withdrawal*

One of the toughest decisions facing a manager is whether or not to cut the lifeline of a product. Such a decision should be based on profit or loss, but other factors, such as sentiment and emotion (attachment to long established products), enter into the decision as well. It is unrealistic to think that products remain indefinitely, particularly in the fast-paced marketplace of today. A company can use two different strategies to withdraw unprofitable products from the market. First, it can end the product abruptly and sell old stock at fire sale prices, or it can gradually phase out products or product lines as they decline. The prudent marketing organization stays in touch with market needs so that as it phases out old products it introduces new products.

### *Packaging Decisions*

Packaging is an integral part of product strategy. It is common for consumer goods to undergo several package design changes throughout their lives. Similar to the periodic redesign of an automobile, package changes are intended to bolster the image of the product, provide a contemporary appearance, or fulfill some other product and marketing objective.

## ⟩⟩⟩ *The Product Life Cycle*

*product life cycle*

Products go through a series of phases known as the **product life cycle**. The term refers to the stages or path a product follows from its introduction to the market to its eventual withdrawal. Figure 9.1 provides an illustration of the product life cycle. According to life-cycle theory, a product starts with slow sales in the introduction stage; experiences rapid sales increases in the second, or growth, stage; undergoes only marginal growth or even some decline when it reaches maturity; and then enters the decline stage, where sales drop off at a much faster rate each year. The

**FIGURE 9.1**    Product life cycle

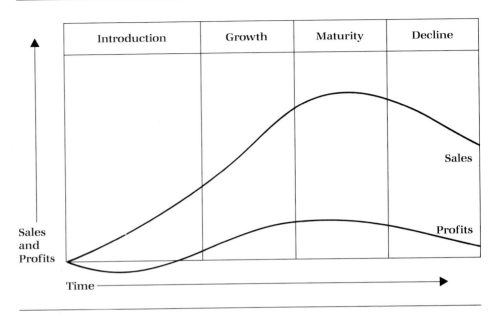

variables of age, sales, and profits are the determinants of a product's stage in the life cycle. The life-cycle concept is popular in strategic marketing planning. Since the conditions of each stage are quite different, the life cycle suggests that different strategies, or marketing mixes, should be utilized in each phase. This section of the chapter examines the four stages of the life cycle and discusses some of the marketing implications that each stage presents to the manager.

Although profit and time affect what stage an item is perceived to be in, sales is the primary indicator of what stage of the cycle a product has reached. Thus, the degree to which a market accepts a product determines how long the life cycle of that product will be. All products do not have the same life cycles; some are quite long, while others are quite short. A product may go "belly up" shortly after introduction, while products such as Quaker oatmeal, Betty Crocker cake mixes, and Cow Brand baking soda seem to stay on the market forever.

## Introduction Stage

introduction stage

The **introduction stage** is a period of slow sales growth, since the product is new and not yet widely known. Losses are frequently incurred in this stage because research and development expenses must be recovered along with the heavy investment in marketing that is needed to establish an awareness of the brand. This marketing investment is a reflection of the company's commitment to building a viable market position.

The immediate objective during the introduction stage is to create demand for the product. A sizeable budget is allocated to advertising and promotion to create awareness of the item and to get people to try it. It is common for advertising to include incentives such as coupons, which reduce the consumer's financial risk in making the first purchase. Widespread media coverage is also commonly used to communicate the product's benefits to the target market.

Setting prices high is common at the introduction stage (it's easier to lower prices later than to increase prices). Such a strategy is designed to offset development costs as quickly as possible. The firm attempts to secure as much distribution as possible by offering distributors allowances and discounts. Obtaining widespread distribution is difficult for new, unproven products.

The length of time a product stays in the introduction stage depends on the rate at which it is adopted by consumers or on the degree to which sales increase annually.

## Growth Stage

growth stage

As indicated by the sales curve in figure 9.1, the **growth stage** is a period of rapid consumer acceptance. Sales rise rapidly, as do profits. Several competitive brands generally enter the market at this stage, each seeking for itself a piece of the action; this means that aggressive marketing activity for the original product must continue in order to protect and build its market share.

The emphasis of the activity in this stage shifts from generating awareness to creating awareness and preference. Many of the activities implemented are designed to encourage consumers to prefer a particular product or brand. Depending on the degree of competition, the organization maintains or perhaps increases its marketing investment at this point. Advertising messages focus on product differentiation (unique selling points) and are intended to give consumers a sound reason why they should buy a particular product. Since, at this point, more information about the target market is known, messages and media selection become more suited to the target; therefore, the marketing activities tend to be more efficient at this stage. A greater variety of promotion incentives are also utilized, since it is important to get people to make both trial purchases (by generating awareness of the product) and repeat purchases (by engendering preference and loyalty). In addition to coupons, refund offers and contests are commonly used since they encourage multiple purchases by interested consumers.

Price strategies remain flexible, that is, they are often determined by competitive prices. The consumer's perception of a product and of the benefits it offers also plays a role in pricing strategy. Since consumer demand is higher in the growth stage than it is during the introduction stage, distribution is now easier to obtain. In effect, the combination of consumer demand and trade incentives offered by the manufacturer makes the product attractive to new distributors and helps move the product through the channel of distribution.

## Mature Stage

mature stage

In the **mature stage**, the product has been widely adopted by consumers. Sales growth slows, becoming marginal; eventually, a slight decline develops. The computer market as a whole, for example, should be seen as mature, for when we consider the sales of the various segments (mainframe, mini, micro, and laptop), we observe that high growth in the microcomputer segment is not enough to compensate for slow growth in the mainframe and minicomputer segments. Encouraging repeat purchases by loyal consumers is the key to maintaining a long and strong position in the mature stage of the life cycle. Many fringe brands are unable to cope and drop out at this stage, leaving the market to a core of competitors.

Some of the indicators that a product or entire market have reached maturity include:

1. Since sales only increase or decrease marginally each year, firms provide less marketing support to competing brands. However, depending on the level of competition and the desire to protect market share for specific brands, firms do not always provide less marketing support. Canada's beer market has shown stagnant growth for the past five years, but strong marketing support is maintained for certain popular brands in order to encourage brand switching.

2. Consolidations occur among rival companies (e.g., in the computer industry, Burroughs took over Sperry in 1986 and formed the Unisys Corporation). This takeover was largely due to slow growth and low revenues in the industry. Survival depended on consolidation.

3. A market starts to be dominated by foreign suppliers who often market imitations of products designed and developed locally. An abundant number of product alternatives in any market segment, be they domestic or foreign in origin, suggests a saturated, mature market.

Generally, most products remain in the mature stage for a long period of time, so product managers are accustomed to implementing marketing strategies for mature

**FIGURE 9.2**   Product Life Cycle and New Product Development

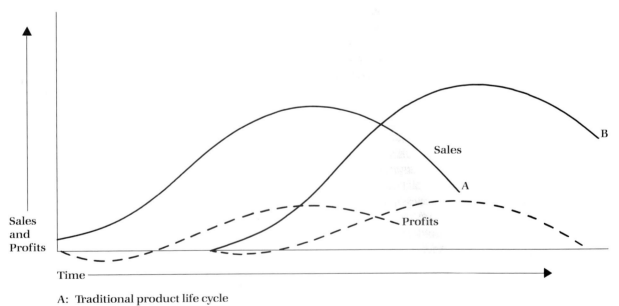

A: Traditional product life cycle

B: New product, traditional life cycle

Product A generates profits to support the development and marketing of Product B.

brands. The company's marketing strategy generally focuses on cost control at this point: programs to reduce product costs are investigated, and investment in promotion is decreased. The goal is to generate profits from mature products that can be reinvested in the development of new products (see figure 9.2).

An increase in the sales of a brand in a mature market can only be achieved if some of the market share is taken from competitors, since the market itself has ceased to grow. To avoid losing market share to others, organizations often implement marketing strategies that are defensive; many companies are concerned about protecting the consumer franchise they have for their brands. The emphasis in promotion strategies shifts from advertising to consumer promotion activity. Consumer promotions such as coupons, premium offers, cash refunds, and contests are critical because they encourage repeat purchases, which result in an increased degree of brand loyalty. To protect market share, prices are often dropped, which reduces profits. Distribution will remain reasonably stable if the organization continues to offer trade discounts and allowances to wholesalers and retailers. However, as sales move from a slight growth to an actual decrease, distributors start to eliminate the products and replace them with exciting product innovations.

Many product managers attempt to rejuvenate their brands, and extend their life cycles for as long as possible by employing a more offensive strategy in the mature stage. The three most commonly used strategies for extending the life cycle of a brand are to look for new markets, to alter the product in some way, and to experiment with new marketing mixes.[2] The effect of life-cycle extensions is illustrated in figure 9.3. Let's examine each of these options in more detail.

**FIGURE 9.3**    Life Cycle Extensions

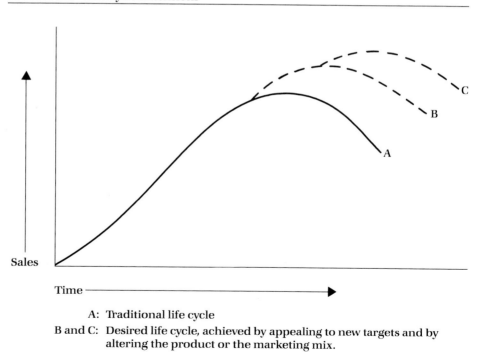

A:    Traditional life cycle

B and C:   Desired life cycle, achieved by appealing to new targets and by altering the product or the marketing mix.

## *Tap New Markets*

Increasing the number of product users can be accomplished in three ways: by attracting competitive users, by entering new segments, or by converting non-users to users.

### *Attract Competitive Users*

The soft drink and beer markets are good examples. Pepsi-Cola constantly strived to attract Coca-Cola drinkers by using the Pepsi Challenge advertising campaign of the early and mid-eighties. In the stagnant beer market, brands such as Blue, OV, Canadian, and others battle head-to-head to get established and loyal drinkers to switch brands. The manufacturers state that their advertising is not designed to encourage consumption, simply to encourage those who do drink to select a particular brand.

### *Enter New Market Segments*

This approach could involve geographic expansions (e.g., a regional brand expanding into other regions) or going after new demographic target markets (e.g., different age and income groups). Johnson & Johnson is the most cited example of a company that has used such a strategy; the company successfully repositioned their baby shampoo as a shampoo suitable for adults. The "gentle" characteristics of the product have proven to be an effective and unique selling point among adults.

### *Convert Non-Users*

It is not too late to attract new users at this point. Perhaps it is users of other products and services that provide the key to extended growth. For example, an individual may be persuaded to deal with more than one bank, in the search for the best interest rates for investments or loans. The business customer who has always relied upon the postal service to deliver packages may be an attractive prospect for air freight and overnight-courier-service companies.

## *Alter the Product*

In a product alteration strategy, the marketing organization changes the characteristics of the product to attract new users. Some rejuvenation strategies include making improvements in quality, features, and style in order to encourage customers to purchase more of the product.

### *Quality Improvement*

The marketing organization improves the primary benefit of a product, then presents the product as a "new and improved" item. For example, the product is made more durable than before, offers better colour than before, tastes better, or rides more smoothly along rough roads.

### *Feature Improvements*

The product is offered in new sizes such as bonus packs, which give more of the product for the same price (e.g., information such as "25 percent more" appears on the package); or in new formats (e.g., laundry detergents are introduced in liquid formats under existing brand names, or bleach is added to the powdered formula). Presenting a variety of new uses encourages current customers to purchase and use the product more frequently. Food companies that print recipes on their labels or that offer free recipe booklets through promotions on the label or through advertising are attempting to increase the frequency of use.

### Style Improvement

This strategy is appropriate for costly durable goods such as major appliances, home entertainment products, and automobiles. In the automobile industry, familiar names like Cadillac, Lincoln, Thunderbird, and Mustang remain, but the look, style, and appearance of these cars has changed considerably over the years. Many of these style changes were based on consumer research indicating that changes in tastes and preferences had occurred among buyers. Marketers also realize that they risk losing customers who may reject the new style.

## Change Other Marketing Mix Elements

### Pricing

Since products usually enter the market with a high price, the mature stage is the time to reduce price. The practice of price discounting encourages consumers to try different products. Instead of having its price lowered permanently, a product might frequently be offered to distributors at a discount and with allowances so that they can in turn offer price specials to consumers on a temporary basis.

### Advertising

Since sales volume in the mature stage is stable, marketers are prudent about expenditures, particularly where advertising is concerned. Emphasis is placed on controlling product costs and spending only enough on advertising to maintain the current market position. Copy (message) changes are made in line with product improvements, new features, or style changes. Alternate media mixes (the combinations of media used — radio, newspaper, television, etc.) are also considered.

### Sales Promotion

As stated earlier, the mature stage sees greater stress placed on sales promotion than on advertising. The use of promotions to get current customers to increase their purchases is crucial at this stage. Such promotions include cash refunds, contests, and premium offers (e.g., bonus items packed in a product, as when free toys are included in cereal boxes).

### Distribution

The combination of product improvements and lower prices makes the product more attractive to distributors that have not yet carried the product. Because of this the marketer seeks non-traditional channels of distribution. For example, marketers of food and snack food now sell some product lines through discount department stores such as Woolco, Zellers, and K-Mart. Selling such products at greatly discounted prices has proven to be an effective traffic builder for these retailers; that is, it draws customers into the store who have the potential to spend money on other items.

## Decline Stage

decline stage

In the **decline stage** of the product life cycle, sales begin to drop rapidly, and profits are eroded. Products become obsolete, as many consumers shift to innovative products entering the market. Price cuts are a common marketing strategy, as competing brands attempt to protect market share in a declining market.

Because costs of maintaining a product in decline are quite high, marketing objectives in the decline stage center on planning and implementing the withdrawal of the product from the market. Marketers cut advertising and promotion expenditures to maximize profit or minimize potential losses, and generate funds that can be invested in new products with greater profit potential. Since companies do not have

**FIGURE 9.4**  Product Life Cycle Characteristics and Strategic Marketing Focus

| Stage | Characteristics | Strategy |
|---|---|---|
| Introduction | • Low sales<br>• Negligible profits or losses<br>• No or few competitors<br>• Innovative customers | • Large budget needed to create awareness for new product<br>• Build distribution and expand market<br>• Usually a high price is established<br>• Promotion incentives for trial |
| Growth | • Rapid sales growth<br>• Profits grow rapidly and peak<br>• Mass market customers<br>• More competitors enter | • Market penetration<br>• Brand preference through advertising and repeat purchase incentives<br>• Product differentiation<br>• Large budget needed due to competition<br>• Intensive distribution<br>• Possibly lower price |
| Mature | • Marginal growth and then decline in sales<br>• Profits start to decline<br>• Mass market<br>• Many competitors | • A sustaining budget needed to protect current share position<br>• Emphasis on promotion instead of on advertising<br>• Repeat purchase incentives<br>• Intensive distribution<br>• Product improvements<br>• Possible price decrease |
| Decline | • Rapid decline in sales<br>• Product obsolete<br>• Low profit; potential loss<br>• Competition drops out<br>• Laggards purchase | • Cut marketing support<br>• Allocate profits to new products<br>• Price may rise<br>• Eventual withdrawal |

the resources to support all products equally, the wise ones have products at various stages of the product life cycle, so that the marketing strategies can be effectively managed within financial constraints (see figure 9.2).

Large drops in sales and in market demand often present difficult decisions for company executives. The decision to withdraw from a market or halt the production of a product at any manufacturing facility means plant closings, employee layoffs, relocation expenses, and new training, where applicable. In the wake of free trade with the United States, and because of the increasing importance of global trade, many firms are evaluating the number and location of their production facilities and marketing activities in North America. Firms such as Gillette and Dominion Textiles, both based in Montreal, announced plant closings in Quebec, and Inglis Limited of Toronto put 650 workers out of jobs when they announced the closing of their oldest Toronto production facility in 1989.[3]

A summary of the key marketing influences on the product life cycle is included in figure 9.4. Although the product life-cycle theory commonly forms a basis for the development of marketing strategies, it has certain limitations. As William Band states, "If you assume a business will inevitably mature, and then decline, rest assured that's exactly what will happen."[4] Band's statement is a reflection of a company's attitude: those companies that follow life-cycle planning too closely encourage a defeatist attitude among managers. Instead of assuming that maturity and decline are inevitable, managers should strive for innovation and generally play an aggressive role in ensuring future success — acting in the market rather than reacting to the market.

## The Length of the Product Life Cycle

All products do not follow the same life cycle. So far, this chapter has presented what may be called the traditional product life cycle so that marketing strategies associated with each stage can be described. Some of the variations in the length and shape of the product life cycle are illustrated in figure 9.5. Let's examine some of the common variations.

**instant bust**

1. The cycle of an **instant bust** applies to a product that a firm had high expectations of, and perhaps launched with a lot of marketing fanfare, but that, for whatever reason, was rejected by consumers very quickly. Examples include Ishtar, a highly promoted but very unsuccessful Hollywood movie, or the Edsel, Ford's classic blunder of the fifties.

**fad**

2. The cycle of the **fad** is reasonably short, perhaps one selling season or a few seasons, and usually financially successful for the organization. Perhaps a classic fad item was the Rubik's Cube of the early eighties and the Cabbage Patch Doll of the mid-eighties. Interestingly enough, the Coleco Toy Company went into receivership a few years after the Cabbage Patch success. This company had a high manufacturing overhead cost to cover and no successful products to follow the Cabbage Patch craze. The entire toy industry is generally influenced by fad life cycles. Competing companies like Hasbro, Mattel, Fisher-Price and Kenner-Parker invest heavily in hopes of developing that one big seller.

**fashion**

3. The cycle of a **fashion** is recurring. What is in style now will be out of style later,

**FIGURE 9.5**   Product Life Cycle Variations

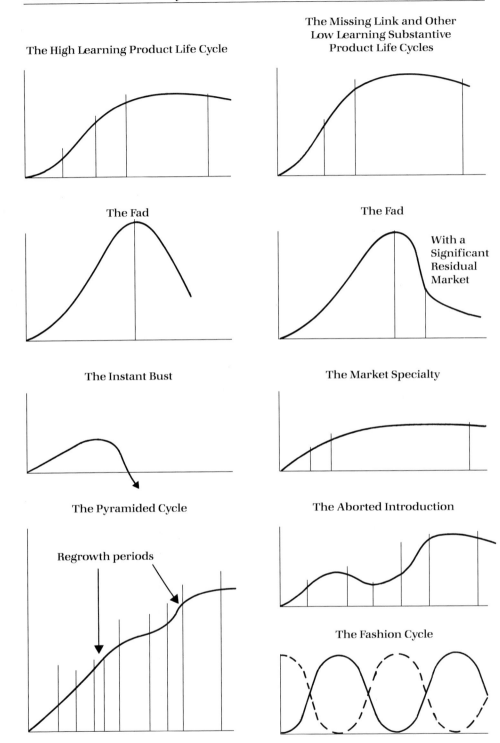

*Source*:  Chester R. Wasson, *Dynamic Competitive Strategy and Product Life Cycle*, 3rd ed. (Austin, TX: Austin Press, 1978), p. 13. Reproduced by permission of Lone Star Publishers.

and perhaps back in style at a later date. Product categories that are subject to fashion cycles include clothing (items such as business suits, skirts, and bathing suits), cosmetics, and automobiles.

These variations indicate that marketers must not be satisfied with passing through the various stages of the conventional product life cycle. Instead, strategies must be implemented that will initiate growth as the product matures, strategies that involve using the market and making changes to product and to marketing mix, as discussed in this chapter.

## 〉〉〉〉 *New Product Development*

new product

In the truest sense of the word, a **new product** is a product that is truly unique and that meets needs which have previously been unsatisfied. Advancing technology creates these unique opportunities. Advances in microcomputer technology are occurring so rapidly that the word "new" in this industry is relatively meaningless. Nonetheless, the major players such as IBM, Apple, Compaq, and Zenith, to name a few, are certainly investing heavily as they search for breakthrough products in this rapidly growing market segment.

Japan and electronics technology are synonymous with each other. High-tech Japanese firms are in the process of marketing EDTV receivers, extended definition televisions that are improved versions of digital televisions marketed in the mid-eighties. While these products are now on the market, the Japanese also have developed, high definition television (HDTV) systems known as Hi-Vision, an even more advanced technology than EDTV. Hi-Vision boasts a quality comparable to 35mm film.[5] Such technologies have to be placed on hold temporarily, because manufacturers cannot keep pace; that is, they cannot produce and market existing technologies quickly enough.

New products also include new versions of existing products. For example, electronic typewriters replaced electric typewriters, and word processors and microcomputers are replacing electronic typewriters. Athletic shoes for specific sports such as aerobics, running, squash, and tennis are constantly refined to meet the needs of a demanding customer. Products that "imitate", that copy the innovations of others, are also new, since they are new to the firm marketing them.

In Canada, new innovations can be protected by patent if the innovation is registered in accordance with the Patent Act, administered by Consumer and Corporate Affairs Canada. Some organizations choose to ignore patent protection laws and produce and market copies of patented products, though doing so is illegal. Technological products are especially prone to this practice. These look-alike products are referred to as "knock-offs". Such a practice is of major concern to the innovator because the life cycle of the product and therefore the opportunity to recover the development costs incurred by the innovation are shortened considerably.

Organizations basically have two options for developing new products: investing in research and development, and merging or acquiring other companies.

1. *Research and Development*  In this case the firm invests in the development of

its own new products. Research and development (R&D) is time consuming and very expensive and there are no guarantees of success once the product has been developed.

2. *Mergers and Acquisitions*   The firm invests in another firm that operates in financially attractive markets, acquiring the products of the bought company. BCE Inc. (formerly known as Bell Canada Enterprises) entered the financially attractive finance market by purchasing Montreal Trustco from the Power Corporation in 1989. Kraft Foods and General Foods merged in 1989 to form Kraft General Foods, the largest food company in North America. The parent company is the giant Philip Morris Inc., of the United States. Such strategies are increasing in popularity, particularly among very large firms, since they allow these top-end marketing organizations to seek and serve market niches they could not afford to serve independently. Have a look at the Marketing in Action feature "Joint Ventures" for some examples of mergers.

## The New Product Development Process

The development of innovative products involves seven steps: idea generation, screening, concept development and testing, business analysis, product development, test marketing and marketing planning, and commercialization (see figure 9.6). How the toy industry researches and develops new toy concepts is illustrated in

**FIGURE 9.6**   The New Product Development Process

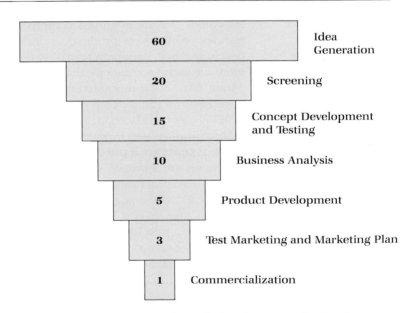

Number of product ideas or products left at the end of each stage in the development process.

*Source*: Adapted from Booz, Allen & Hamilton, *New Products Management for the 1980s* (New York, 1982), p.3.

## 〉〉〉 *MARKETING IN ACTION*

### *JOINT VENTURES*

*The Chevrolet Sprint is manufactured at the Cami Automobile plant in Ingersoll, Ontario, a joint venture between General Motors and Suzuki*

General Motors of Canada Limited

Survival and future success in the volatile world of automobile marketing is now contingent upon joint ventures between domestic and foreign automakers. Joint ventures involve cooperative efforts and shared investments by two firms wanting to take advantage of opportunities in the market. Frequently, such opportunities would be, due to cost, beyond the reach of the companies individually. A joint venture helps reduce costs and allows marketers to seek market niches they could not afford independently. Here are some recent joint ventures:

| Location | Joint Venture Group | Products |
|---|---|---|
| Ingersoll, Ontario | General Motors and Suzuki combine to invest $550 million in Cami Automotive Inc. | Chevrolet and GMC Tracker, Chevrolet Sprint, Pontiac Firefly and Suzuki Swift |
| Normal, Illinois | Chrysler and Mitsubishi invest equally to form Diamond-Star Motors Inc. | Plymouth Laser and Mitsubishi Eclipse |
| Freemont, California | General Motors and Toyota are equal partners in New United Motor Manufacturing Inc. | Chevy Nova |

#### Who Owns What?

1. Ford Motor Company owns 26 percent of Mazda
2. Chrysler owns 21.6 percent of Mitsubishi
3. General Motors own 5 percent of Suzuki

Adapted from Bruce McDougall, "More joint ventures as car firms cut production costs", *Financial Post*, February 13, 1988. p.44. and Michael Harrison, "Joint ventures blurring old nationalistic ideas", *Financial Post*, February 13, 1989, p.48.

>>>> *MARKETING IN ACTION*

*A STORY ABOUT THE LITTLE THREE*

What car company sells more cars than General Motors, Ford, and Chrysler combined? No, it's not a Japanese conglomerate. It's Matchbox Cars U.S.A., a company that sells 77 million vehicles annually.

Developing cars for the small set is big business, and both consumer research and product development are critical. Larry Wood used to design door handles and tail lights for Ford Motor Company in Detroit, but is now the leading designer of Mattel's Hot Wheels™, having designed most models since 1968. The main challenge for Woods is to anticipate what kids will want. He looks to different areas for inspiration for his designs, and he scans trade magazines to see what real cars are hot.

According to Matchbox, sports cars and military and construction vehicles are usually popular with the rug-running set; and there is a certain loyalty to what is seen in the streets or on television. The recent heavy hitter in the toy car market is Micro Machines (45 million units in U.S. sales in 1988) from upstart Lewis Galoob Toys Inc. The cars usually take nine months to move from concept to production. Before the cars go to mass production, kids are invited to play with and rate

*Larry Ford designed a Hot Wheels™ Version of the Mercedes 540K*

them. Vehicles that win their approval proceed to a company test track where executives make the final decision, and escape from the pressure of business. Life at the Big Three is not like this!

Adapted from Geoffrey Haynes, "No recalls, smog problems with Detroit's Little Three," *Toronto Star*, July 31, 1988, p.F2.

---

the Marketing in Action vignette "A Story About the Little Three". Let's examine each step in the development process.

### Idea Generation

All products stem from a good idea. Where do these ideas come from? Contemporary organizations are receptive to ideas from any source, whether it be customers, suppliers, employees, or marketing intelligence about competitors. Internally, a company may have a research and development department in place, which has the sole responsibility for researching and developing ideas. Other companies may schedule regular meetings of executives and cross-sections of employees to brainstorm for potential opportunities. The tone of such brainstorming sessions is generally positive and based on questions such as "What direction should the company be taking?" or "What products should we be offering five years from now? Ten years from now?"

There is now a famous story behind 3M's success with Post-it Notes. The paper has an adhesive strip on the back which can be affixed temporarily to virtually anything. An employee came up with the idea for the note paper when his place mark kept falling out of his hymn book at choir practice. Sales of Post-it Notes now exceed $100 million annually in North America.[6]

## Screening

The elimination of ideas begins with product screening. The purpose of screening is to eliminate quickly ideas that do not appear to offer financial promise for the company. Such a screening process is the responsibility of senior management, which must decide if the new idea is in line with the overall company strategy. So that new ideas may be compared, a rating checklist or scale might be used in screening ideas. Such a checklist would include criteria important to the company and would gauge each new product idea's compatibility with the overall company strategy. At the very least, this type of evaluation would give the company a ranking of new product ideas. Figure 9.7 presents a sample checklist. An important

---

**FIGURE 9.7   Sample Product Screening Checklist**

| General Criteria | Rating |
|---|---|
| 1. Patent protection | _____ |
| 2. Sales potential | _____ |
| 3. Market size and demand | _____ |
| 4. Existence or threat of competition | _____ |
| 5. Perceived risk (low to high) | _____ |

| Marketing Criteria | |
|---|---|
| 1. Compatability with current products | _____ |
| 2. Target market compatability | _____ |
| 3. Marketing investment required | _____ |
| 4. Anticipated life cycle (short/long) | _____ |
| 5. Degree of uniqueness | _____ |

| Production Criteria | |
|---|---|
| 1. Capital investment required (high/low) | _____ |
| 2. Expertise in production process | _____ |
| 3. Availability of labour, raw materials, processed materials | _____ |
| 4. Production cost competitiveness | _____ |
| 5. Time required for start-up | _____ |
| TOTAL SCORE | ═════ |

Rating Scale: 1–10 (1 = poor   10 = excellent)

This chart is intended to indicate some of the key variables examined in the screening process. Criteria used for evaluations vary from one organization to another and there tend to be more than are included here.

consideration in the screening process is the availability of patent protection, discussed earlier in the chapter.

### Concept Development and Testing

concept test

A **concept test** involves the presentation of a product idea in some visual form (usually a drawing or photograph) with a description of the basic product characteristics and benefits. The purpose of a concept test is to find out early how consumers react to the product idea. Typically, a consumer is provided with the product's picture, description, and price, and is then asked questions to determine his or her level of interest and the likelihood of the person purchasing the product. Such a step is a crucial one since this feedback determines whether the firm invests in prototype product development, an expensive proposition. Companies only proceed with ideas consumers perceive to be of high interest. To gauge the level of acceptability, a firm may show different information about the same concept. It may, for example, test different prices in order to determine what influence price has on the level of interest in the concept and to see at what point the concept becomes uninteresting. Such information is important for the sales and profit projections in the next stage.

### Business Analysis

business analysis

A **business analysis** entails a formal review of some of the ideas accepted in the screening stage. By this time the company is dealing only with product ideas that have been judged positively by potential customers. Consequently, the company must determine the market demand for the product and the costs of project production and marketing, and estimate revenue and profit. Such a review includes a thorough evaluation of competitive offerings and their marketing strengths and weaknesses. The purpose of business analysis is again to rank potential ideas and eliminate those judged to have low financial promise.

### Product Development

In this stage, the idea or concept is converted to a physical product. The purpose is to develop a prototype or several prototype models for evaluation by consumers. The **prototype** is a physical version of a potential product, that is, of a product designed and developed to meet the needs of potential customers. The prototype is refined based on feedback obtained in consumer research. In effect, the research and development department experiments with design and production capability to determine what type of product can be produced within the financial constraints placed on the project. These constraints were established in the business analysis stage.

prototype

Issues that must be resolved at this stage include

1. The type and quality of raw materials and processed materials available to use for manufacturing.

2. The method of production and any additional capital requirements.
3. The package configuration and its influence on production, shipping, and handling.
4. The time required for start-up (the time needed to have all equipment and materials in place, ready for production).

At this stage various functional areas of the firm must cooperate to ensure that the product produced is what the customer wants. What Production and Engineering can provide may not be what marketing wants. Therefore, these departments work together to coordinate their plans.

Product development is a very expensive phase of the development process. In addition to pure research costs, the firm has to pay to have the prototypes constantly tested for consumer reaction. Marketers develop brand names, identify the key benefits, develop a price, and perhaps provide consumers with samples of the prototype for their perusal and use. Many of the research techniques presented in chapter 5 are used to collect this information.

### *Test Marketing and Marketing Planning*

At this point the company develops an introductory marketing plan to support test marketing. The test market is the first real acid test for the product. It is the stage where consumers have the opportunity to purchase the product instead of simply indicating that they would purchase the product. The test market allows the company to gain feedback in a relatively inexpensive way. Many marketers view the test market stage as mandatory; without it, a significant financial risk is faced. Should a product be launched regionally, or should it be launched nationally, in which case the loss to the company would be great if the product should fail. The test market evaluates the product and the marketing plan so that further modifications to both can be made, if necessary, prior to an expensive full-scale launch. Others view it as a period that could be bypassed, since it tips off competitors to a firm's activity. It gives competitors time to react and develop imitations or plan defensive strategies for products already on the market. A firm may conduct several test markets in order to generate conclusive information to assist in the planning for market expansion.

### *Commercialization*

commercialization

**Commercialization** is the concluding step in the new product development process; the company puts together a full scale production and marketing plan for launching a product on a regional or national scale. All of the refining, adjusting, and tinkering with product design characteristics, production considerations, and marketing strategies is over at this point. The product is introduced in accordance with the information collected regarding consumer needs and expectations. Promotion materials acquaint distributors with the product and what it offers. The product has now entered the introduction stage of the product life cycle described earlier in this chapter, and is now subject to the costs and activities normally associated with that

**FIGURE 9.8**    Summary of New Product Development Process

| | |
|---|---|
| Idea Generation | Ideas solicited/accepted from all potential sources (customers, employees, suppliers, research and development department, etc.). |
| Screening | Executive evaluation used to eliminate ideas that are incompatible with company strategy. |
| Concept Development and Testing | Seek consumer perception and reaction to the product idea. Feedback and degree of interest determine further analysis and development. |
| Business Analysis | Analysis of market demand, production and marketing costs, and sales and profit projections. |
| Product Development | Physical product is developed. Prototype is produced and evaluated by consumers and altered accordingly. Production details examined in greater depth. |
| Test Marketing and Marketing Planning | Marketing plan is developed to support product testing in a real environment. Further input and experience obtained for future expansion. |
| Commercialization | Product launched regionally or nationally. Product accepted in marketplace. |

stage. The product will find future success only if the organization modifies strategies as the product and market segment matures. A summary of the new product development process is provided in figure 9.8.

# ⟩⟩⟩⟩ *Product Adoption*

The degree to which consumers accept or reject a product is the measure of its success or failure. Product adoption is concerned with two areas: adoption, or individual acceptance, and diffusion, or market acceptance.

## Adoption

**adoption**

Product adoption was discussed briefly in chapter 6, but it is worth reviewing in the context of new product development and the product life cycle. Let's examine each element of adoption. **Adoption** is defined as a series of stages a consumer passes through on the way to purchasing a product on a regular basis. The adoption process has up to five distinguishable steps (see figure 9.9). These steps include awareness, interest, evaluation, trial purchase, and adoption.

FIGURE 9.9    The Steps in the Adoption Process

| | |
|---|---|
| Awareness | Consumers learn of a product, but lack detailed knowledge of it. |
| Interest | Consumer seeks or accepts messages that provide product information. |
| Evaluation | Consumer evaluates benefits in relation to needs. |
| Trial | Consumer is motivated to make the first purchase. |
| Adoption | Consumer prefers product because of the satisfaction it provides. |

1. *Awareness*   In this stage, consumers learn about a product's existence, but lack detailed information about it.

2. *Interest*   Now aware of the product, the consumer seeks or accepts messages that provide essential information about the benefits of the product.

3. *Evaluation*   Here, the consumer considers the value offered by the product. The benefits offered are reviewed in relation to the problem to be solved or needs to be satisfied.

4. *Trial*   The first, or trial, purchase is the initial step in determining whether the product lives up to its promises. Techniques used to encourage trial purchase include coupons, samples in small or regular pack sizes, and availability at a convenient location. Such activities reduce the financial risk (for the company) and the inconvenience (for the consumer) associated with the first purchase of something new.

5. *Adoption*   This stage is reached when a customer uses and purchases a particular product regularly. The product satisfies needs to such an extent that it is made the preferred brand. The product itself is the key factor in holding consumers loyal to a given brand; its quality, reliability, and other characteristics generate loyalty.

## Diffusion

diffusion

The diffusion process concerns the acceptance of a product by the market generally. **Diffusion** refers to "the manner in which different market segments accept and purchase a product between product introduction to market saturation."[7] Everett M. Rogers has conducted intensive research into the diffusion process. His research indicates that

1. Individuals require different amounts of time to decide to adopt a product.

2. Consumers can be classified on the basis of how quickly or how slowly they adopt a product.

3. Five categories of adopters exist: innovators, early adopters, early majority, late majority, and laggards.[8]

A brief discussion of each adopter category follows. Refer to figure 9.10 for an illustration of the adopter categories and the proportion of the target market population each represents.

**innovators**

1. The **innovators** are the first group of consumers to accept a product. They are risk takers, ambitious, aggressive trend-setters who like to be apart from the mainstream. Eager to try new products, this group latches onto something as soon as it is available. Rogers' research indicates that this group only comprises 2.5 percent of a target market.

**early adopters**

2. **Early adopters** are more discrete in nature. They form a larger group of opinion leaders who like to try new products when they are new. They are strongly affected by the status and prestige of having an item early. This group represents 13.5 percent of a target market.

**early majority**

3. The **early majority** represents the initial phase of mass market acceptance. They follow the lead of early adopters and buy a proven commodity. This group represents 34 percent of a target market.

**late majority**

4. The **late majority** is the remainder of the mass market. This group is usually lower in social and economic status, tend to be older and only willing to try products that have been around for a while. They comprise 34 percent of a target market.

**laggards**

5. **Laggards** are the last people to purchase. Typically, they buy the same old things; that is, they do not like change. They are not influenced by advertising and brand image, but are influenced by price, especially a low price. Since the product is now at the point of late maturity or decline in the product life cycle, the laggards are not that important to the marketing organization.

**FIGURE 9.10**    Categories of Adopters

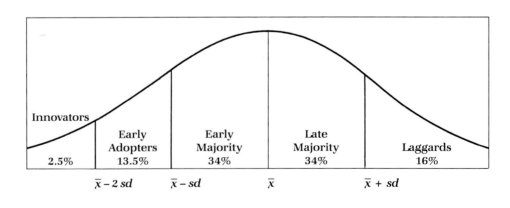

*Source*:  Reprinted with permission of The Free Press, a Division of Macmillan Inc. from *Communication of Innovations: A Cross Cultural Approach*, second edition, by Everett M. Rogers with F. Floyd Shoemaker. Copyright © 1971 by The Free Press.

It should be noted that innovators and early adopters have moved on to new innovations by the time that the mass market starts buying a product.

To illustrate the diffusion process, let's briefly examine the laptop microcomputer market. Research statistics indicate that the product segment grew by 63 percent in 1988 (54 000 units sold in Canada) and by 44 percent in 1989 (77 800 units sold). In the marketplace, the gap between laptops and desktops is disappearing, not to mention that the laptop is now a status symbol among contemporary business executives. This product was initially purchased by executives who saw themselves as innovators. Toshiba's venture into laptops was met with snickers and scepticism, initially, because critics could not see the business market accepting the product. However, as more and more executives purchased and used laptops (the early adopters and early majority), other firms started marketing similar products. Today, Toshiba dominates this market segment with more than a 50 percent market share in a $100 million market, and markets eleven different models ranging in price from $1800 to $17 000.[9] The other major players who have introduced laptops include IBM Canada Limited, Zenith Data Systems, and Compaq Canada Inc., a true reflection of market acceptance.

## 〉〉〉〉 S U M M A R Y

Product management concerns three key areas: the organization structure for managing products and services, the development of new products to stimulate growth in the organization, and the management of marketing strategies for products throughout their life cycles. The product management system is most typical of consumer packaged-goods companies, although an increasing number of business-to-business marketing organizations are also using it today. Alternatives to using product managers include the use of category managers, venture teams, and new product development committees. The latter two are responsible for converting ideas and concepts into marketable goods and services. The key decisions in product management concern product modifications, alterations to marketing mix strategies, and whether to keep a product in the market or withdraw it.

The product life cycle refers to the stages a product passes through from its introduction to its withdrawal from the market. The life cycle involves four stages: introduction, growth, maturity and decline. The marketing strategies employed by the firm vary considerably from stage to stage. Generally, products remain in the mature stage for the longest period; the variables of time, sales, and profit are the indicators of what stage a product is in. The length of the life cycle varies from one product or product category to another. Some cycles are short (fads), while others are long (fashion). Regardless of the length of the cycle, the primary objective of the organization is to generate profits. Profits are maximized in the late growth and mature stages of the product life cycle; hence organizations initiate strategies for extending these phases.

These strategies include tapping into new markets by attracting new seg-ments — competitive users or non-users; altering the product by making quality, feature, or style improvements; or changing the marketing mix.

New product development entails two basic strategies: creating products either through research and development or through mergers and acquisi-tions. There are seven steps in the research and development process for new products: idea generation, screening, concept development and testing, busi-ness analysis, product development, test marketing and marketing planning, and commercialization. The degree to which consumers accept a new prod-uct determines its success or failure.

Product adoption is concerned with a product's being accepted by individ-ual consumers, whereas diffusion is concerned with acceptance by a market. People are categorized according to how quickly or how slowly they adopt a product. There are five categories of adopters: innovators, early adopters, early majority, late majority, and laggards.

## ⟩⟩⟩⟩ KEY TERMS

| | | |
|---|---|---|
| product manager | decline stage | commercialization |
| category manager | instant bust | adoption |
| venture team | fad | diffusion |
| product stretching | fashion | innovators |
| product life cycle | concept test | early adopters |
| introduction stage | new product | early majority |
| growth stage | business analysis | late majority |
| mature stage | prototype | laggards |

## ⟩⟩⟩⟩ REVIEW AND DISCUSSION QUESTIONS

**1.** Briefly describe the role and responsibility of the product manager.

**2.** How do venture teams differ from new product development committees?

**3.** Briefly describe the characteristics of each stage of the product life cycle.

**4.** What factors determine the stage a product is at in the life cycle?

**5.** Briefly describe the marketing strategies an organ-ization uses to extend the life cycles of its products.

**6.** What factors influence the length of the product life cycle?

**7.** Briefly describe the seven steps in the new product development process.

**8.** What are the various stages in the consumer adop-tion process?

**9.** Identify and briefly describe the adopter catego-ries.

**10.** "Organizations that stick too close to product life cycle planning encourage a defeatist attitude". Discuss this statement.

**11.** "The decision to withdraw a product from the market should be based on profitability only". Discuss the merits of this statement.

## >>> R E F E R E N C E S

1. DON DUNN, "The Rise and Fall of Ten Venture Groups", *Business Horizons*, October 1977, pp.32-41.

2. WILLIAM BAND, "Achieving Success in Mature Markets Requires Careful Approach", *Sales & Marketing Management in Canada*, March 1987, p.16.

3. "Inglis Set to Close Factory in Toronto", *The Globe and Mail*, February 16, 1989, p.B1,B4.

4. WILLIAM BAND, "Don't Get Trapped in the Product Life Cycle", *Sales & Marketing Management in Canada*, September 1985, p.25.

5. STEVEN BRULL, "High Quality TV Shapes Video Future", *Financial Post*, October 10, 1988, p.19.

6. "Post-It Notes Click Thanks to Entrepreneurial Spirit", *Marketing News*, August 31, 1984, pp.21-22.

7. EVERETT M. ROGERS, *Diffusion of Innovations*, 3rd Edition (New York: Free Press, 1982), p.246 + .

8. Ibid.

9. Ibid.

 **PART FIVE**

# *Price*

# C H A P T E R 10 ❯❯❯❯

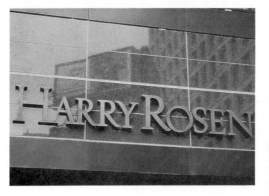

# Price Strategy and Determination

LEARNING OBJECTIVES

After studying this chapter you will be able to

1. Explain the importance of price in marketing strategy.

2. Describe the various types of economic markets that Canadian firms operate in.

3. Discuss how price elasticity of demand affects pricing strategy.

4. Describe the influences that various external and internal forces have on pricing strategy.

5. Differentiate among profit, sales, and competitive pricing objectives.

6. Calculate basic prices using a variety of pricing methodologies.

This chapter introduces some of the basic pricing concepts used in marketing strategy. The discussion initially focuses on the variety of markets that Canadian firms operate in and the implications these different markets have for pricing strategy. The external and internal factors influencing pricing strategy are then discussed. Finally, the issues of how pricing strategy is used to achieve marketing objectives and what specific methods are available for determining prices are addressed.

## >>>> *The Definition and Role of Price*

price

**Price** is defined as the exchange value of a good or service in the marketplace. The key word in this definition is "value". The value of a good or service is derived from its tangible and intangible benefits and from the perception a consumer has of it once he or she has been subjected to other marketing influences. Let's use an example to explain what tangible and intangible benefits are. A household decides to buy an expensive, top-of-the-line vacuum cleaner because of the product's superior capacity for and speed in picking up dirt from a rug. This is tangibility, a characteristic that can be experienced by the senses — in this case, a characteristic that can be seen. The vacuum is also purchased at a large reputable department store where the service and warranty are better than those offered by a small independent dealer. This is an intangible benefit, one that cannot be seen, and so will go unnoticed until the vacuum breaks down.

Prices take many forms and terms. Consider the following examples:

Price is . . . your college tuition fee
. . . a club membership
. . . the rate of interest on a loan
. . . admission charged at a theatre
. . . a donation to a charity
. . . rent charged for an apartment
. . . a fare charged by a bus or train
. . . a real estate commission

From a marketing organization's perspective, price is the factor that contributes to revenues and profits. In planning price strategy, the firm must consider a multitude of variables in order to arrive at fair and competitive prices in the marketplace while providing reasonable revenues and profits internally. It is only one element of the marketing mix, but it can be the most important. For example, retailers such as K-Mart and Zeller's rely on price to establish and maintain their image with consumers. Both chains are classified as discount department stores. Their strategy is to offer customers good value at reasonable price levels. At the opposite end of the scale are retailers like Creed's and Holt-Renfrew that practice prestige pricing. To their customers, price itself is unimportant in the purchase; it is the image that the high prices create that attracts their upscale clientele.

In a relatively free market economy like Canada, price is also a mechanism for ensuring adequate levels of competition. In a free and open market, where competition is strong, supply and demand factors influence price. Thus, when demand for a good increases, marketing organizations have the flexibility to increase price. When demand for a product drops, organizations tend to lower prices in order to entice consumers to continue to buy the product. It is this freedom to set prices in response to the marketplace that ensures competition will occur.

## >>>> *Controlling Price*

A firm's ability to control price depends upon the type of market it operates in. Many firms operate in different market economies, so their pricing practices vary from one market or product category to another. The four basic types of price markets are

FIGURE 10.1   Characteristics of Canadian Markets

| Factor | Pure Competition | Monopolistic Competition | Oligopoly | Monopoly |
|---|---|---|---|---|
| Competition and Product | Many sellers with same or similar product. | Many sellers with differentiated product. | Few large sellers with some product differentiation. | Single seller with unique product. |
| Price Decision Criteria | Price based on open market. How much should be produced? | Price based on competition and brand loyalty. How much should be produced and invested in marketing? | Price based on competition. Quick reaction to price changes. How much should be invested in marketing? | Price based on fair and reasonable profit for supplier. |
| Controls | None. Dictated by market dynamics. | Some. | Some (e.g., uniform beer pricing in retail outlets in some provinces). | By government or other regulatory body (e.g., CRTC). |

called pure competition, monopolistic competition, oligopoly, and monopoly (see figure 10.1).

## Pure Competition

**pure competition**

In a market environment of **pure competition**, there are many sellers and buyers marketing the same basic product; therefore, the firm has no choice but to charge the going market price. The firm's primary decision then is limited to determining how much to produce.[1]

**law of supply and demand**

The market in this situation controls the selling price. The basic **law of supply and demand** applies: an abundant supply and low demand lead to a low price, while a high demand and limited supply lead to a high price. Often it is simply expectations about supply or demand that have an impact on price. For example, if the supply of gasoline was expected to dwindle below normal demand, there would be a rush to buy the resource and its price would be driven up, at least temporarily. In other cases, it is the actual supply and demand that affect prices. As demand for houses rises, perhaps because of a swelling population or favourable interest rates, the price of houses increases. The demand for stocks on the stock market influences the rate at which they are traded. Other pure competition markets are those for food commodities such as fresh fruits and vegetables, sawn and planed lumber, household furniture, and clothing.

## Monopolistic Competition

**monopolistic competition**

**Monopolistic competition** exists when there are many competitors selling products which, though similar, are perceived to be different by consumers.[2] Marketing strategy, particularly product strategy, in these circumstances is to try to distinguish

>>>> *MARKETING IN ACTION*

### REBATES TO THE RESCUE

It's your move. Interest rates are rising, sales are slumping, you are producing at capacity, and inventory is everywhere. You need help . . . fast! Such occurrences are now commonplace in the automobile industry, an industry that rolls with the cyclical swings in the Canadian economy. So how do marketers of Canadian automobile companies react?

Rebates and related incentives such as discount financing, free air conditioning, automatic transmissions, and extended warranties are proven stimulators of short-term demand. General Motors, Ford, Chrysler, and even the Japanese manufacturers are obsessed with protecting market share. In a recent whirlwind of financing packages, General Motors announced a 9.9 percent interest rate for terms up to four years, at a time when banks were charging 15.75 percent. According to Paul Sullivan, assistant general sales manager of General Motors Canada, discount financing is "an attempt to kick-start the industry with interest rates being the hot button at this time." Reaction is fast in an oligopolistic market. Ford entered the fray with a 10.9 percent financing package over 48 months and lower rates for shorter terms.

As a marketing strategy, rebates and discounts meet several objectives. First, they pump up demand when production is high — preventing production cutbacks and layoffs, and, thus, protecting market share. Second, the incentive stimulates the customer to take immediate action — it gets the customer into a showroom to buy a vehicle. At the dealer level, the competition for scarce consumer dollars is just as fierce. In a buyer's market, no dealer can hold out for anywhere near the suggested list price.

For consumers, there is nothing but gain. The only problem is the intensive price analysis required so that competitive packages can be compared. Such comparisons make the consumer better informed about price, the real benefit.

Adapted from Adam Corelli, "The unwaxed realities of those fabulous rebates," *The Financial Times of Canada*, March 20, 1989, pp. 29-30, and Jim Daw, "Deals, freebies, rebates, subsidies," *Toronto Star*, March 19,1989, pp. F1-2.

*Automobile companies such as General Motors use rebates and related incentives to stimulate short-term demand (see opposite page)* ▶

---

one's own brand from the others. Variables such as service, style, function, and packaging are used to convey a difference to the consumer. The use of such elements is referred to as non-price competition, and it is their use that explains why leading brands such as Crest, Tide, and Scope are perceived to be better than other brands.

If the consumer thinks there are differences between the brands, brand loyalty can be created. Consumers that are brand loyal are less likely to be influenced by price; that is, they are willing to pay a little more for the brand of their choice than for other brands. Thus the brand loyalty created by product differentiation gives individual firms some power over price, more power than is possessed by firms in pure competition markets, where supply and demand is the only determinant of price.

In pure competition there are many small firms, so no single firm can dictate or offset the market. It is the market that controls the firm's price. In monopolistic competition, individual firms experience some independence of the market; they can capitalize on brand loyalty in setting prices and have little fear of counter measures from other firms. Generally, if a firm wishes to attract competitive users on the basis of price savings, those savings must be more important than the other reasons consumers buy products: reasons having to do with quality, image, and good service.

A good example of monopolistic competition is the desktop microcomputer market where consumers perceive IBM's product to be the industry standard. Competing brands such as Zenith, NEC, Compaq, Sanyo, and Hewlett-Packard must stress their compatibility with IBM to survive, while pricing their product lower and stressing other benefits such as ease of use. Other examples include the growing markets for videocassette recorders, portable photocopiers and facsimile machines — markets in which many firms are competing. In these cases, buyers face many options, for each competitor has a variety of models, features, and price ranges. The successful marketing strategy in these situations is to use price as only one among a variety of ways of differentiating the product in consumers' minds.

## Oligopolistic Market

**oligopolistic market**

An **oligopolistic market** is a market served by a few large sellers of a particular good or service. Industries traditionally associated with oligopolies are the automobile industry, dominated in North America by General Motors, Ford and Chrysler; and the brewing industry, dominated in Canada by Molson and Labatt. Other examples of oligopolies in Canada include the sporting goods industry, soft drink beverages, supermarket chains, banking and television broadcasting. In each industry a relatively small group of large companies maintains control.

In contrast to the situation that prevails in monopolistic competition, competitive actions are monitored closely in an oligopoly. The competition is so intense that if one firm raises or drops its price, other firms will quickly do the same. Similarly, if one automaker announces a cash rebate program, the competitors will very likely follow with a similar plan. This reaction is especially pronounced in markets where the products are basically the same (e.g., gasoline), but also occurs in markets where the products are different (e.g., automobiles). Refer to the Marketing in Action vignette "Rebates to the Rescue" (p. 290) for an illustration of strategic maneuvering in an oligopolistic market.

The prospect of increasing competition from Japanese car makers represents a great problem for domestic oligopolists. In the minds of North American consumers, the quality of Japanese cars is better. This impression is the result of a lot of advertising and marketing activity over an extended period of time. This quality image helps justify the higher price of Japanese automobiles, despite the high rate of the Japanese yen in relation to the dollar. This principle applies to all segments of the market that Japanese cars compete in: economy, mid-price, and luxury.

## Monopoly

**monopoly**

In a **monopoly**, the market is served by a single seller of a particular good or service for which there are no close substitutes. In Canada, monopolies are not common, but they do exist in the service industry sector. For example, Bell Canada and provincial power corporations like SaskPower and Hydro Quebec are monopolies in their markets. In Canada, monopolies cannot charge whatever they wish, since they are regulated by government or by some other body that must approve prices. Price changes are only allowed if the monopolist can justify the increase to the regulating body. Bell Canada and local suppliers of cable television service (which monopolize the local cable market) must seek approval for price increases from the Canadian Radio Television-telecommunications Commission (CRTC). In the case of utilities, prices are controlled by provincial governments.

# 〉〉〉〉 *Other Factors Influencing Price*

Besides the types of competition and of market, four other variables affect a firm's pricing strategies: consumers, governments, channel members, and costs. With the exception of costs, all influences are external to the firm, and even costs are affected by the price negotiated with outside suppliers (see figure 10.2).

## Consumers

The demand from consumers has a significant role in determining price. Two principles come into play:

**law of demand**

1. The **law of demand** states that consumers purchase greater quantities at lower prices.

**price elasticity of demand**

2. The **price elasticity of demand** measures the effect a price change has on the volume purchased (it shows the reaction to a price change).

**FIGURE 10.2**    Factors Affecting the Price of a Product

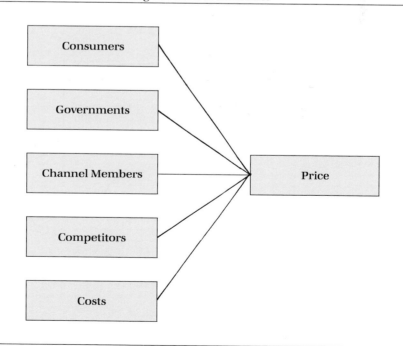

elastic demand

There are two types of demand: elastic demand and inelastic demand. **Elastic demand** is a situation in which a small change in price results in a large change in volume: for example, a 5 percent increase in price may result in a much higher percentage decrease in volume. If demand is elastic, the firm's total revenues go up as price goes down and revenues go down when prices go up. **Inelastic demand**, on the other hand, is a situation in which a price change does not have a significant impact on the quantity purchased. In this case total revenues go up when prices are increased and go down when prices are reduced. These demand concepts are represented in figure 10.3. For an illustration of how price affects demand, see the Marketing in Action story "Price Affects Entire Industry".

inelastic demand

In Canada's two most common markets, monopolistic competition and oligopoly, demand is based on the need in the marketplace and the availability of substitute products. If need (demand) for a product category is high, all competing firms can maintain high prices and reap the financial benefits. However, once a major competitor changes prices — say, it lowers the price significantly — demand in the market can change. Here are some examples of actions and reactions:

1. If Canadian Airlines announces a summer seat sale of 40 percent off fares to all Canadian destinations, Air Canada will likely follow suit. Both major airlines will temporarily reduce profit margins in an effort to attract seasonal flyers (in

**FIGURE 10.3    The Difference between Elastic Demand and Inelastic Demand**

If demand is elastic, consumers are price-sensitive. When price increases, demand goes down significantly.

In the illustration, when price increases from $500 to $750, revenue declined from $400 000 (800 units × $500) to $150 000 (200 units × $750).

If demand is inelastic, consumers are not price-sensitive. A large increase in price has a limited effect on sales volume.

In the illustration, when price increased from $750 to $1500, revenue increased from $225 000 ($750 × 300 units) to $300 000 ($1500 × 200 units).

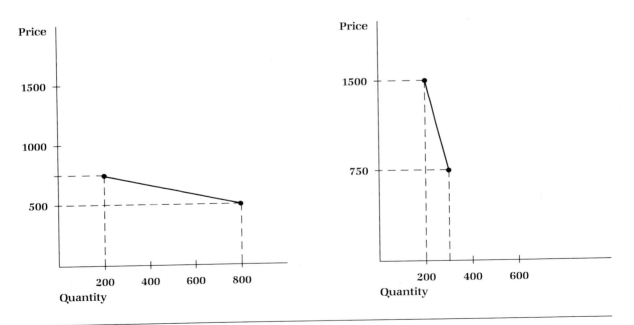

## ❯❯❯❯ *MARKETING IN ACTION*

### *PRICE AFFECTS ENTIRE INDUSTRY*

Most discussions of price and its effect on product demand are mainly concerned with competition. For example, they point out that if a product of equal quality and service has a better price, demand for it will increase until there is retaliatory action from competitors.

What happens, however, when the entire industry is perceived to have prices that are too high? Case in point — the Canadian toy industry. From 1985-1988, the entire toy industry experienced flat sales. It had experienced unexpectedly high growth in the early eighties, however, when the industry rode on the wave of trend-setting games and toys like Trivial Pursuit and Cabbage Patch Dolls.

Both of these items were expensive products, and their impact was so significant that the family toy budget increased. Now the industry is in turmoil because it has not been able to repeat the success of these products with new products. Coleco Industries, in particular, faced very high overheads due to the expansion created by the Cabbage Patch phenomenon, then experienced flat sales and lower profit margins when the bubble burst. In retrospect, the industry itself created the problem, as the major players expanded considerably to accommodate their bestsellers. In an attempt to maintain sales, Coleco Industries, the marketer of Cabbage Patch Dolls, bought out the distributor of Trivial Pursuit, well after the popular game's life cycle had peaked. The effort failed and Coleco filed for bankruptcy late in 1988.

From this experience, other toy companies have learned some valuable lessons:

1. Manufacturers must capitalize on the trend to inexpensive toys that is indicated by increasingly modest consumer buying behaviour. The ongoing success of affordable toys such as G.I. Joe and Barbie demonstrates that manufacturers need to make such an adjustment.

2. The industry cannot be led by marketing hype. Instead, emphasis should be placed on production efficiency and cost control — both variables which directly affect price strategy.

3. Emphasis should be placed on line extensions. Marketers must capitalize on the strength of popular toys and build from there. The development, production, and marketing investment required for this approach is much less than it is for a new product.

Seasonality has always been a factor in the toy industry. Typically, the eight-week period prior to Christmas accounts for as much as 70 percent of toy sales. Emerging marketing activities in retailing are attempting to change the seasonality factor. Toys "R" Us, a rapidly expanding chain, is pioneering efforts to stretch out the toy season over a full calendar. Their efforts have been successful, since the traditional selling season only accounts for 50 percent of their sales volume.

Adapted from "Toy industry plays new game as public balks at high prices", *Financial Post*, November 7, 1989, p.12.

*Toys "R" Us is pioneering efforts to make the toy season year-long*

Toys "R" Us

marketing terms, they are attempting to build market share). The lower prices boost demand for the seats; demand is elastic.

2. If General Motors announces an increase of 5 percent for all models in the forthcoming year, Ford and Chrysler will likely follow suit. If such an announcement is in line with consumer expectations, the increase is tolerated, and there will be little effect on demand in the market. In this case, demand is inelastic. In contrast, if the rate of increase is perceived to be too high, the consumer will decide to postpone buying until a time when conditions are favourable. Thus demand in the car industry and related industries will be definitely affected.

Consumer behaviour also has an impact on pricing strategy. A consumer may compare the price and quality of one product with other similar products; to other consumers, matters such as image, status, and prestige may be so important that the actual price of the product is ignored. In the first case, the consumer behaves rationally, so the price of the product is important. In the second case, the consumer acts less rationally and is influenced by other factors, so price is less important. Thus products aimed at status-seekers are apt to be priced high to convey prestige, while products targeted to the price-conscious would logically be priced low.

Elasticity of demand refers to how sensitive a product's sales volume is to changes in its own price. In competitive markets, however, most customers have several product alternatives to choose from, so that the demand for one product is also influenced by the price of another. **Cross-elasticity of demand** is "the degree to which the quantity demanded of one product will increase or decrease in response to changes in the price of another product."[3] It occurs in two circumstances: when substitute products are available and when complementary products are available.

**cross-elasticity of demand**

1. *Substitute Products*   Products that are easily substituted for each other have a high cross-elasticity of demand. If the price of Brand A is high, Brands B and C may see a boost in sales. For example, similar models of facsimile machines are available from suppliers such as Ricoh, Canon, Toshiba, NEC, Sharp, and Panafax. In the case of videocassette recorders, brands like RCA, Sanyo, Toshiba, Hitachi, Mitsubishi and JVC are almost interchangeable. In these cases, should one brand's price rise beyond a certain point, the demand for the other brands will climb.

2. *Complementary Products*   In this case, the sale of Product A directly affects the sale of Product B. If Kodak lowers the price of its cameras to boost sales, the sales of Kodak film will also increase even though the price for the film remains the same. The volume of film sold will compensate for the lower profit margins on cameras during the sale period. A sale of suits in a clothing store may similarly trigger a demand for dress shirts and neckties, which may not be on sale.

## Governments

The federal government oversees price activity in Canada. Through the Marketing Practices Branch of Consumer and Corporate Affairs Canada, it acts as a watchdog whose mandate is to ensure that pricing laws are followed. These laws cover such key areas as ordinary price claims, the use of the manufacturer's suggested list price, double ticketing, bait and switch selling, and charging prices above the advertised price.

## Ordinary Price Claims

A common practice among retailers is to quote sale prices using comparisons with the ordinary selling price of an article. For example, "Save up to 50 percent off the regular price." For the purposes of the law, no person or business shall

> make a materially misleading representation to the public concerning the price at which a product or like products have been, are, or will be ordinarily sold.[4]

The following general test can be used to determine whether an expression is in violation of the law:

> Would the use of the expression lead a reasonable shopper to conclude that the comparison price quoted is that at which the product has been ordinarily sold?[5]

When a comparison price is used to communicate the offer, it should be a recent and relevant price, that is, the price at which the product has normally been sold over an extended period of time.

## Manufacturer's Suggested List Price

**manufacturer's suggested list price**

It is common for manufacturers to suggest that retailers charge a certain price for their products; this amount is called the **manufacturer's suggested list price**. Such prices usually allow retailers adequate profit margins, but retailers can charge more or less if they want to. The laws on manufacturer's suggested list prices are somewhat vague. However, if a retailer has never charged the manufacturer's suggested list price, but uses it to suggest that a sale price offers a greater saving than it actually does, that retailer has broken the law. In this case, the message is misleading because the retailer has customarily sold the product at another price, a lower price. If both the regular selling price and the manufacturer's suggested list price are quoted in a sales message, the intent to mislead is less pronounced. A market research study by Ahmed and Gulas of Ottawa University concluded that using manufacturer's list price as a basis of comparison with a retailer's price can deceive many people, and that the comparison disregards the ordinary selling price.[6] Such deceptions could place a company in violation of the law.

## Double Ticketing

**double ticketing**

**Double ticketing** occurs when more than one price tag appears on an item. When this situation occurs, the product must be sold at the lower price. This provision of the law does not prohibit the practice, but requires that the lower of the two prices be collected from consumers.

## Bait and Switch

**bait and switch**

**Bait and switch** occurs when a company advertises a bargain price for a product that is not available in reasonable quantity. A customer arrives at a store expecting to buy one product, but is directed to another, often at a higher price. If the lack of supplies is beyond the control of the store or agent and this can be proven if challenged, the firm running this advertisement is not liable for penalty. Offering rain cheques is a way to avoid liability. A **rain cheque** guarantees the supply of the original product or a product of comparable quality within a reasonable time to those consumers requesting the product.

**rain cheque**

### *THE PRICE ISN'T RIGHT*

Every year the Marketing Practices Branch of Consumer and Corporate Affairs Canada prepares a comparative overview of the sentencing pattern in cases of misleading advertising and deceptive marketing, covered under the Competition Act. The following are actual cases that were tried under the Competition Act in 1988. These examples are good illustrations of the problems that businesses face when pricing their products or services.

*Company:*   Zellers Inc., Ottawa, Ontario

The accused, in promoting the sale of sewing machines, represented in their in-store flyers, "1/2 off manufacturer's suggested list price." Investigation revealed that this claim was untrue.

The accused pleaded guilty, and on July 4, 1988, was convicted and fined $5 000.

*Company:*   K-Mart Canada Limited, Sackville, Nova Scotia.

The accused, in promoting the sale of toys, represented by means of an in-store flyer that various models of the toy were available for $12.77 each. Investigation revealed that two of the illustrated models were not available at that price.

The accused pleaded guilty to one charge, and on September 19, 1988 was convicted and fined $10 000.

*Company:*   Centre de Distribution de la Piscine Trans-Canada Limited, Montreal, P.Q.

The accused, in promoting the sale of patio furniture, represented in newspaper advertising the

ordinary selling price at which the furniture normally sold. Investigation revealed that the representations were untrue.

The accused pleaded guilty to ten charges, and on August 22, 1988, was convicted and fined $2 000 on each charge, for a total fine of $20 000.

*Company:*  Video Source Direct Inc., and Philips Electronics Limited, Toronto, Ontario.

The accused, in promoting the sale of audio and video equipment in a "liquidation sale", represented in newspaper advertisements that substantial quantities of equipment were available. It was established that the representation was untrue.

The accused pleaded not guilty to one charge, but on March, 11, 1987 was convicted; the accused Video Source was fined $10 000 and the accused Philips was fined $20 000.

Some additional information on fines follows:

|  | 1984-85 | 1985-86 | 1986-87 |
|---|---|---|---|
| Total Number of Convictions | 130 | 128 | 131 |
| Total Fines | $771 695 | $676 800 | $747 670 |
| Average Fine per Case | $5 679 | $6 384 | $7 120 |

**Source:** Marketing Practices Branch, Consumer and Corporate Affairs Canada, *Misleading Advertising Bulletin*, Issue No. 1, 1988 and Issue No. 4, 1988.

*A brochure on questionable advertising and marketing practices distributed by Consumer and Corporate Affairs Canada*

misleads the public in one way or another about the product or service being advertised.

A misleading representation can also be made concerning the price at which the product or service is ordinarily sold. Jacking up the regular selling price of a product to make the sale price look like a real bargain, for instance, is prohibited.

• Double ticketing — In this instance, two or more prices may appear on the container or wrapper of a product. Though this in itself is not against the law, it is illegal for the retailer to insist that the purchaser pay the highest price. The product must be sold for the lowest price shown clearly on the product.

• Bait and switch selling — This occurs when a product is advertised at a bargain price by an advertiser who doesn't have a reasonable quantity of the product for sale. In other words, the bargain price is used as bait to get consumers into the store. It should be noted, however, that such a practice is not illegal if it can be established that the product was

unavailable due to circumstances beyond the advertiser's control, or if rain checks were offered when the supply of the product ran out.

This type of practice is prohibited except in instances where the advertised price was an error and steps were taken immediately to correct it.

Other misleading advertising and deceptive marketing practices provisions of the Combines Investigation Act relate to such things as performance claims, warranties, tests and testimonials, and pyramid and referral selling schemes. In addition, the Act covers promotional contests where the number and approximate value of the prizes are not disclosed, or where the distribution of prizes has been unduly delayed.

• Sale above advertised price — In this case, a product is sold by a retailer at a price higher than what is being advertised by the retailer at that time.

How to complain

Every year, a number of these illegal practices are brought to the attention of the courts as a result of work carried out by Consumer and Corporate Affairs Canada staff. However, most investigations into dealings of this type are undertaken following complaints from the public — by people who feel that an advertisement or

representation has been confusing, misleading or perhaps simply mistaken.

If you think the same has happened to you as a result of some questionable advertisement or business practice, or would like more detailed information concerning the misleading advertising and deceptive marketing practices provisions of the Combines Investigation Act, please contact the department through one of its regional or district offices, or write to:

Marketing Practices Branch, Bureau of Competition Policy, Consumer and Corporate Affairs Canada, Ottawa, Ontario K1A 0C9

Consumer and Corporate Affairs Canada

Consommation et Corporations Canada

### Selling Above the Advertised Price

The sale of any product by a retailer at a price higher than the price currently advertised is prohibited. Such action would include an element of "bait"; that is, the consumer would be attracted to the store by a certain price, but ends up paying more than expected. Such practice takes unfair advantage of consumers.

For some illustrations of organizations that have faced the wrath of the legal system for pricing practices, see the Marketing in Action account "The Price Isn't Right".

## Channel Members

The manufacturer of a product has virtually no control over the price at which a distributor resells the product. Once the title to the product changes hands, pricing is determined at the discretion of the new owner. Like manufacturers, however, the distributor (wholesalers and retailers) usually faces competitors and is primarily concerned with moving merchandise. Therefore, the prices it in turn charges its customers usually conform to a markup that is standard in the industry and provides for a reasonable profit margin.

To encourage channel members to charge prices that are in agreement with a manufacturer's overall marketing strategy, the manufacturer considers four factors:[7]

1. *Provision for Adequate Profit Margin*   Manufacturers suggest selling prices that cover the costs of shipping and handling, and other related marketing costs incurred by the distributor.

2. *Fair Treatment of All Customers*   Manufacturers assure all distributors that the prices quoted are the lowest available, that is, that the same list price is offered to all customers.

3. *Special Deals*   The manufacturing firm offers discounts for specified periods to encourage volume buying among distributors, who in turn pass on the savings to other distributors or to consumers.

4. *Impact of Price Increases*   When costs rise, manufacturers usually pass on price increases to distributors, who, in turn, pass them on to consumers. It is unrealistic for manufacturers and distributors to absorb all of these new costs. If the retail price has a strong impact on demand, the manufacturing firm must use its pricing experience to project the potential effects of a price increase. As an alternative, the manufacturer can explore ways to reduce costs.

## Costs

Costs that have a direct effect on price include the costs of labour, raw materials, processed materials, capital requirements, transportation, marketing, and administration. A common practice for firms is to establish a total product cost, taking into consideration these elements as well as a desirable and fair gross profit margin. The addition of the profit margin to the cost becomes the selling price to distributors. Such a practice is based on the assumption that the resulting retail price will be acceptable to consumers. The following provides a quick illustration of this cost procedure:

Product:  A case of cake-mix packed eighteen units to a shipping case.

| | **Costs:** | | |
|---|---|---|---|
| | Ingredients | | $9.22 |
| | Packaging | | 1.06 |
| | Shipping Case | | 0.40 |
| | Labour | | 0.90 |
| | Manufacturing | | 0.12 |
| | Warehousing | | 0.20 |
| | **Total Plant Cost** | | $12.00 |
| | *Add:* Freight Cost | | 0.80 |
| | **Total Product Cost** | | $12.80 |
| | *Add:* Gross Profit Margin | | 40% |
| | | | $5.12 |
| | **List Price** | | $17.92 |
| | *Add:* Retail Margin | | 25% |
| | | | $4.48 |
| | **Retail Case Price** | | $22.40 |
| | **Retail Price** (/18) | | $1.25 |

Additional explanations of how to determine selling prices, along with some examples, appear later in this chapter.

The pricing decisions of an organization become increasingly difficult as costs rise. If cost increases are gradual in occurrence and marginal in amount, a firm can usually plan its strategy effectively; it can build prices around projected cost increases for a period of time, using, say, a one-year planning cycle. Unforeseen increases (those which happen quickly and unexpectedly) are a different matter. In such cases, a firm may choose to absorb the cost increases and accept lower profit margins, at least for the short term, in the hopes that the situation will correct itself. If it does not, there is little alternative but to pass the increase to channel members in order to ensure long-term profitability. Another option available to the organization is to search for and implement **cost reductions**; price increases are not always the solution to protecting profit margins. Examples of some cost reduction measures follow:

**cost reductions**

1. *Improving the Efficiency of the Means of Production*  Automation will increase costs in the short term due to the capital outlay required, but the improvement in efficiency will, in the long term, lower the cost of each unit produced.

2. *Using Less Expensive Raw Materials of Similar or Equal Quality and Performance*  Ingredients in the processed foods we eat are frequently subject to this type of change. If the change is undetected by product users, it has a positive effect on profit margin.

3. *Using Less Expensive Packaging*  Perhaps a thinner gauge cardboard is as effective and less costly per unit.

Refer back to the cost example in this section. If the company implemented some of these cost reduction programs and managed to save $0.10 on each unit of production, and assuming they sold 500 000 cases annually, the cost savings would amount to $50 000. This amount would drop to the bottom line, that is, would become net profit.

Generally, a firm tries to combine cost reductions with reasonable price increases. It will remain competitive and move prices when necessary to protect the profitability of the firm. Should costs actually decline, the company has the option of lowering prices or taking advantage of higher profit margins. The nature of the market and the battle for market share will play a role in this decision. As an example of a situation where this has occurred, the advancing technology of microcomputers has lowered prices within the industry. The lower prices in turn have resulted in expansion of the entire market so that all competitors have benefited.

# ⟩⟩⟩ *Pricing Objectives*

In a pure business environment, the primary goal of the organization is to produce the highest possible rate of return to the owner (shareholder, partners, sole proprietor, etc.). Pricing strategies must be in line with this overall company strategy. Chapter 3 noted that pricing strategy is a part of marketing strategy which, in turn, is a part of corporate strategy.

A firm is not locked into one particular pricing strategy. In fact, each product or product line (market) will be assessed independently, and appropriate objectives will be established for the product in question. Organizations strive to achieve three basic objectives in pricing: profit maximization, sales volume maximization, and establishing competitive position.

## Profit Maximization

profit maximization

The goal of **profit maximization** is to achieve a high profit margin, a high return on investment, and a recovery of the capital invested. In this case, an organization sets some type of measurable and attainable profit objective based on their situation in the market. Consider the following profit objective statement:

**Objective:**
To achieve a net profit contribution of $2 000 000 and a return on investment (ROI) of 30 percent in fiscal year 19XX.

While we cannot assess how conservative or how aggressive this objective is, it is certain that the organization will implement a marketing strategy to accomplish it. At the end of the year the degree of success can be measured by comparing actual return to planned return. The profits obtained are redirected into new product development projects, which facilitate the organization's expansion into new markets (refer to chapter 9). Historical trends pertaining to such ratios as a firm's return on investment or return on sales are also a factor in attracting potential new investors to the firm.

## Sales Volume Maximization

The objective of **sales volume maximization** is to increase the volume of sales each year. A firm strives for a growth in sales that exceeds the growth in the size of the total market so that its market share increases. As you recall, market share is defined as a firm's product volume divided by the industry volume; market share is expressed as a percentage of the total market. An example of a sales volume objective follows:

> To increase sales volume from $15 000 000 to $16 500 000, an increase of 10 percent, in 19XX.

> To increase market share from 25 percent to 27.5 percent in 19XX.

Sales levels, as we have seen, are affected by price; an increase in price can result in a decrease in demand and, therefore, a reduction in the quantity sold. In figure 10.4 we see that when price goes down (P1 to P2), volume goes up (Q1 to Q2); when prices go up, volume goes down.

An organization also develops the appropriate marketing strategies, including price strategy, for achieving sales objectives. In establishing these objectives, a firm considers the type of market it operates in and its elasticity of demand. Generally,

FIGURE 10.4   Relationships between Price and Quantity

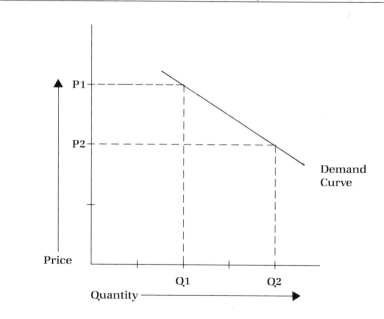

brand leaders have the most flexibility in establishing sales and market share objectives. Brands with a small share of the market tend to follow the trend established by the leader. To achieve market share objectives, a firm often sacrifices profit, at least temporarily.

## Establishing a Competitive Position

competitive pricing

The aim in this case is to minimize the effect of competitive actions and provide channel members with reasonable profit margins. The strategy is often termed status quo pricing, or simply **competitive pricing**. To attain such an objective, an organization assesses the competitive situation, including its own position in the market, and adopts a strategy that puts its prices above, equal to, or below those of competitors. In effect, each competitor uses a pricing strategy to position itself in the consumer's mind.

### Above Competition

To have its price set above those of the competition, a product must be perceived as being of a higher quality than the competitors' products or must offer customers an intangible benefit like prestige or status. Such a strategy provides a higher profit margin on each unit sold. Examples of such products include established market leaders such as Toshiba laptop computers (36.5 percent market share) and Xerox photocopiers (30 percent market share).[8] Both of these products have a reputation for quality, service, and dependability which justifies the higher price. Upscale automobiles and exclusive retail shops like Harry Rosen's and Chadwick's also fall into this category.

### Equal to Competition

A firm that uses this strategy adopts a conservative position because it does not want to be caught in price wars. In effect, the company is satisfied with its volume, market share, and profit margin, and is content to follow the lead of others.

### Below Competition

Here a firm uses price to secure and hold a certain position in the market. To accomplish this objective, the company must accept lower profit margins (unless it is producing so efficiently that profit margins are maintained despite the reduction in price). If the volume of sales rises significantly because of the low prices, production efficiency will increase, which will produce, in turn, lower costs and better profit margins. When Japanese automobiles were originally marketed in Canada, they offered good quality at a low price, an enviable combination compared to domestic alternatives. With the value of the Japanese yen so high now, their price advantage has been lost, but their reputation for a quality product, for proven performance and for excellent after-sales service (non-price strategies) has kept them a dominant factor in the market.

## 〉〉〉〉 *Pricing Methods*

A firm may use one or any combination of three basic methods in calculating prices for the products and services it markets: cost-based pricing, demand-based pricing, and competitive-based pricing (see figure 10.5).

## Cost-Based Pricing

**cost-based pricing**

In the case of **cost-based pricing**, a company arives at a list price for the product by calculating its total costs and then adding a desired profit margin. The costs usually included in this calculation follow:

**fixed costs**

1. **Fixed costs** are those costs that do not vary with different quantities of output (e.g., equipment and other fixed assets such as light, heat, and power).

**variable costs**

2. **Variable costs** are costs that do change according to the level of output (e.g., labour and raw materials). Variable costs rise and fall depending on the production level — up to a point. Generally, the more a firm is producing, the greater the quantities of raw materials and parts it buys, and this increased volume leads to lower unit costs; therefore, the variable costs should be lower.

For an illustration of these cost concepts, refer to figure 10.6. In the long-term, the firm must establish prices that recover total costs (that is, fixed costs plus variable costs). An organization that is using cost-based pricing to do so has a few options: full cost pricing, target pricing, and break-even pricing (break-even analysis). All three consider the variables of costs, revenues, and profits (see figure 10.7 for illustrations).

**FIGURE 10.5**  Pricing Methods

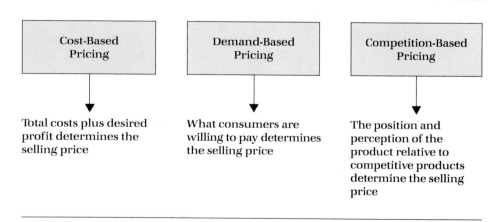

| Cost-Based Pricing | Demand-Based Pricing | Competition-Based Pricing |
| --- | --- | --- |
| Total costs plus desired profit determines the selling price | What consumers are willing to pay determines the selling price | The position and perception of the product relative to competitive products determine the selling price |

**FIGURE 10.6**   The Concept of Fixed and Variable Costs

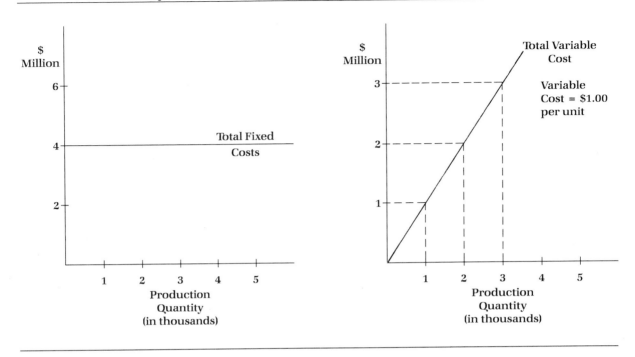

## Full Cost Pricing

full cost pricing

In **full cost pricing** or cost-plus pricing, a desired profit margin is added to the full cost of producing a product. This method considers both fixed and variable costs, calculating price using the following formula:

$$\text{Price} = \frac{\text{Total Fixed Costs} + \text{Total Variable Costs} + \text{Profit}}{\text{Quantity Produced}}$$

   In such a system, profits are based on costs rather than on revenue or demand for the product. Since profit is added to costs, there is little incentive to reduce costs to achieve a higher profit margin. Other weaknesses of this method include its failure to consider the following: competitors' prices, the stage in the product life cycle the product is in, consumer demand, and other factors that typically influence price. On the positive side, this method does generate a reasonable level of profit for the firm (see figure 10.7).

## Target Pricing

target pricing

**Target pricing** is designed to generate a desirable rate of return on investment (ROI) and is based on the full costs of producing a product. For this method to be effective, the firm must have the ability to sell as much as it produces. The formula for calculating target return pricing is

$$\text{Price} = \frac{\text{Investment Costs} \times \text{Target Return Investment \%}}{\text{Standard Volume (Quantity)}} + \text{Average Costs}$$

**FIGURE 10.7**  Pricing Methods: Examples

### 1. Cost-Plus Pricing

A manufacturer of colour televisions has fixed costs of $100 000 and variable costs of $300 for every unit produced. The profit objective is to achieve $10 000 based on a production of 150 televisions. What is the selling price?

Price 

$$= \frac{\text{Total Fixed Costs} + \text{Total Variable Costs} + \text{Projected Profit}}{\text{Quantity Produced}}$$

$$= \frac{\$100\ 000 + (\$300 \times 150) + \$10\ 000}{150}$$

$$= \frac{\$150\ 000}{100}$$

$$= \underline{\underline{\$1\ 550}}$$

### 2. Target Pricing

A manufacturer has just built a new plant at a cost of $75 000 000. The target return on investment is 10%. The standard volume of production for the year is estimated at 15 000 units. The average total cost for each unit is $5 000 based on the standard volume of 15 000 units. What is the selling price?

Price 

$$= \frac{\text{Investment Costs} \times \text{Target Return on Investment (\%)} + \text{Average Total Costs (at Standard Volume)}}{\text{Standard Volume}}$$

$$= \frac{\$75\ 000\ 000 \times 10\% + \$5\ 000}{15\ 000}$$

$$= \underline{\underline{\$5\ 500}}$$

### 3. Break-Even Pricing

A manufacturer incurs total fixed costs of $210 000. Variable costs are $0.15 per unit. The product sells for $0.45. What is the break-even point in units? In dollars?

Break-Even in Units 

$$= \frac{\text{Total Fixed Costs}}{\text{Price} - \text{Variable Costs (per unit)}}$$

$$= \frac{\$210\ 000}{\$0.45 - \$0.15}$$

$$= \underline{\underline{700\ 000}}$$

Break-Even in Dollars 

$$= \frac{\text{Total Fixed Costs}}{1 - \dfrac{\text{Variable Costs (per unit)}}{\text{Price}}}$$

$$= \frac{\$210\ 000}{1 - \dfrac{\$0.15}{\$0.45}}$$

$$= \underline{\underline{\$314\ 843}}$$

The major drawback of this method is that demand is not considered. If the quantity produced is not sold at the target price, the objective of the strategy, to achieve a desired level of ROI, is defeated (see figure 10.7).

### Break-Even Analysis

break-even analysis

Break-even analysis has a greater emphasis on sales than do the other methods, and it allows a firm to assess profit at alternate price levels. **Break-even analysis** determines the sales in units or dollars that are necessary for total revenue (price x quantity sold) to equal total costs (fixed plus variable costs) at a certain price. The concept is quite simple. If sales are greater than the break-even point (B.E.P.), the firm yields a profit; if the sales are below the break-even point, a loss results (see figure 10.8). The formulae for break-even are

$$\text{B.E.P. (Units)} = \frac{\text{Total Fixed Costs}}{\text{Price - Variable Costs (per unit)}}$$

$$\text{B.E.P. (Dollars)} = \frac{\text{Total Fixed Costs}}{1 - \dfrac{\text{Variable Costs (per unit)}}{\text{Price}}}$$

---

**FIGURE 10.8   Standard Break-Even Chart**

#### Example Calculation and Chart

| Assumption | : | Total Fixed Costs | = | \$50 000 |
|---|---|---|---|---|
| | | Total Variable Costs | = | \$15.00 per unit |
| | | Selling Price | = | \$25.00 |

$$\text{Break-Even in Units} = \frac{\text{Total Fixed Cost}}{\text{Price - Variable Cost}}$$

$$= \frac{50\ 000}{25 - 15}$$

$$= \underline{\underline{5\ 000}}$$

$$\text{Break-Even in Dollars} = \frac{\text{Total Fixed Cost}}{1 - \dfrac{\text{Variable Cost}}{\text{Price}}}$$

$$= \frac{50\ 000}{1 - \dfrac{15}{25}}$$

$$= \underline{\underline{\$125\ 000}}$$

*(continued)*

**FIGURE 10.8** (continued)

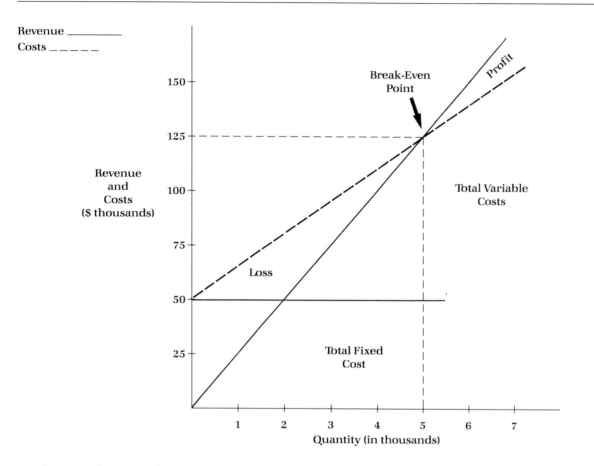

Break-Even is the point where total revenues equal total costs

Like the other cost-based pricing options, break-even analysis has several limitations. First of all, it neglects to consider demand: the method assumes that the quantity sold can vary while the price remains the same, which is very unlikely given market conditions and any degree of competition. It also assumes that variable costs remain constant, but as production becomes increasingly efficient, such costs can actually decrease so that prices can be lowered and the firm still break even for a certain quantity.

## Demand-Based Pricing

demand-based pricing   As the name **demand-based pricing** suggests, it is the price that customers will pay that influences this pricing method the most. The firm calculates the markup needed to cover selling expenses and profits, and determines the maximum it can spend to produce the product. Very often, the product cannot be produced for the costs determined using this method (that is, by working back from the price the consumer will ultimately pay). Many new product projects are cancelled at an early stage because of this cost analysis process.

To utilize the demand-based pricing method, a firm requires information from three areas: 1) research to determine the quantity that is purchased at various price levels, 2) knowledge of the elasticity of demand, or how sensitive to price changes the quantity is, and, 3) knowledge of the consumers' willingness to pay, or whether the product quality is perceived to be in line with the price charged. The two most commonly applied methods of demand-based pricing are demand-minus (backward) pricing and chain markup pricing.

### Demand-Minus (Backward) Pricing

**demand-minus pricing**

Under the **demand-minus pricing** method, an organization determines the optimum retail selling price that consumers are willing to accept and then subtracts the desired profit margin and marketing expenses (markup) to arrive at the costs for which the product should be produced. This practice is more common in cases where the company sells directly to consumers. The formula for this cost calculation is (see figure 10.9):

$$\text{Product Cost} = \text{Price} \times [(100 - \text{Markup \%}) / 100]$$

### Chain Markup Pricing

**chain markup pricing**

Following the **chain markup pricing** method, the firm considers the profit margins of its distributors. The calculations start with the final retail selling price and work back to the manufacturer's selling price. The markup that each channel member takes is incorporated into the calculation. If we assume that a traditional channel of distribution is used, which includes a wholesaler and retailer, the formulae for this calculation are:

$$\begin{array}{l} \text{Maximum Selling} \\ \text{Price to} \\ \text{Retailer} \end{array} = \begin{array}{l} \text{Final} \\ \text{Selling} \\ \text{Price} \end{array} \times [(100 - \begin{array}{l} \text{Retailer's} \\ \text{Markup} \end{array}) / 100]$$

$$\begin{array}{l} \text{Maximum Selling} \\ \text{Price to} \\ \text{Wholesaler} \end{array} = \begin{array}{l} \text{Selling} \\ \text{Price to} \\ \text{Retailer} \end{array} \times [(100 - \begin{array}{l} \text{Wholesaler's} \\ \text{Markup} \end{array}) / 100]$$

$$\begin{array}{l} \text{Maximum Product} \\ \text{Cost to} \\ \text{Manufacturer} \end{array} = \begin{array}{l} \text{Selling} \\ \text{Price to} \\ \text{Wholesaler} \end{array} \times [(100 - \begin{array}{l} \text{Manufacturer's} \\ \text{Markup} \end{array}) / 100]$$

In another form of chain markup pricing, a firm establishes its costs and then adds a markup for each channel member. In this case it is presumed that the ultimate selling price is acceptable to consumers. Examples of these demand-based price calculations are included in figure 10.9.

FIGURE 10.9    Demand-Based Pricing Methods

### 1. Demand-Minus (Backward) Pricing

A record and tape distributor has determined that people are willing to spend $30.00 for a 3 record/tape set of classic rock 'n roll tunes. The company estimates that marketing expenses and profits will be 40% of the selling price. How much can the firm spend producing the records and tapes?

| Product Cost | = | Price × [(100 – Markup %)/100] |
|---|---|---|
| | = | $30.00 × [(100 – 40)/100] |
| | = | $30.00 × (60/100) |
| | = | $18.00 |

### 2. Chain Markup Pricing

A manufacturer of blue jeans has determined that consumers will pay $40.00 for their product. The company sells the jeans through wholesalers who in turn sell to retailers. Each distributor requires a markup of 20%. The manufacturer needs a markup of 25%. What price will the wholesaler and retailer pay? What is the maximum amount the jeans will cost to make?

a) Maximum Selling Price to Retailers
= Final Selling Price × [(100 – Retailer's Markup)/100]
= $40.00 × [(100 – 20/100)]
= $40.00 × 0.8
= $32.00

b) Maximum Selling Price to Wholesalers
= Selling Price to Retailer × [(100 – Wholesaler's Markup)/100]
= $32.00 × [(100 – 20)/100]
= $32.00 × 0.80
= $25.60

c) Maximum Cost to Manufacturer
= Selling Price to Wholesaler × [(100 – Manufacturer's Markup)/100]
= $25.60 × [(100 – 25)/100]
= $25.60 × 0.75
= $19.20

## Competitive-Based Pricing

A company that uses this approach bases its pricing decisions on the degree of competition in the market or where it would like to position the product in terms of price. If in the mind of the consumer the product has a prestigious image and is of an appropriate quality, it could be priced high, perhaps at a leadership level. Conversely, a discount image may be the goal, in which case a lower price than those of the competitors is set. Zellers advertises that its prices will be lower than the competitors' and that, if they are not, it will match the competition for any comparable offering. Competitive bidding and price negotiation between buyers and sellers is another form of competitive-based pricing.

## Price Leadership

In markets where numerous brands compete, there are brand leaders and brand followers. The market share of each brand helps determine whether it is a leader or a follower. The brand leader usually provides leadership in pricing. When its prices go up, the competitors follow suit, since the followers recognize that the risks of a price increase (e.g., rejection by the customer) are now less. Companies that follow the example of a brand leader in their market adhere to a type of competitive-based pricing; that is, their pricing is based on what the competition is doing. Brand leaders are generally products that are firmly entrenched in their markets, occupy the leading market share position, and command the respect of their competitors. The following are examples of such brands, classified by industry:[9]

| *Industry* | *Brand* | *Market Share* |
|---|---|---|
| Portable Computers | Toshiba | 40.0% |
| Mainframe Computers | IBM | 68.6 |
| Desktop Computers | IBM | 24.1 |
| Hand Held Vacuum | DustBuster | 81.8 |
| Detergents | Tide | 33.0 |
| Hockey skates | Bauer | 46.5 |
| Camera Film | Kodak | 75.0 |

## Competitive Bidding

competitive bidding

As we have seen in chapter 7, **competitive bidding** involves two or more firms submitting to a purchaser written price quotations based on specifications established by the purchaser.

Due to the dynamics of competitive bidding and to the size, resources, and objectives of potential bidders, it is difficult to explain how costs and price quotations are arrived at. For example, let's assume several firms are submitting bids for the opportunity to construct a new building. There could be great variation among price quotations if one firm considers all of its costs and then adds a profit margin, while another firm sets its price at the breakeven point. The objectives of firms submitting bids differ: some businesses simply want to win the contract, while others expect to earn a certain profit. Thus, if a firm builds in a high profit margin, the likelihood of its being accepted by the purchaser diminishes.

## ⟩⟩⟩⟩ SUMMARY

Price refers to the exchange value of a good or service in the marketplace. Prices are offered in many different forms, including fares, commissions, interest rates, and fees. In the Canadian economy, an organization's control over price is determined primarily by the type of market it operates in. The four basic markets are pure competition (where no control exists, since prices are controlled by the market), monopolistic competition (where firms have some control, but are mainly directed by the competition), oligopoly (where organizations also have some control but where pricing is directed even more by competition — a sort of follow-the-leader type of approach), and monopoly (where pricing is controlled by governments or some government-designated body).

Four major variables affect a firm's pricing activities: consumers, who dictate the level of demand in the market; governments, which ensure that pricing laws are not violated; channel members, whose profit margins are considered in a firm's estimation of the final price; and finally, costs, which affect the ability of a company to produce and market a product that will yield an adequate and reasonable profit margin for the firm and fair prices for customers.

The prices established by an organization are part of an overall marketing strategy that is designed to achieve specific objectives. The three basic pricing objectives are profit maximization (improving owners' return on investment), sales volume maximization (improving growth rates and market share), and establishing competitive position (maintaining adequate profit margins so that all companies that sell the product remain satisfied).

Specific methods for calculating price include cost-based pricing, demand-based pricing, and competition-based pricing. The method used is chosen by a firm according to the nature and degree of competition in the markets it operates in.

## 〉〉〉〉 KEY TERMS

| | | |
|---|---|---|
| price | cross-elasticity of demand | cost-based pricing |
| pure competition | manufacturer's suggested | fixed costs |
| law of supply and demand | list price | variable costs |
| monopolistic competition | bait and switch | full cost pricing |
| oligopolistic market | double ticketing | target pricing |
| monopoly | rain cheque | break-even analysis |
| law of demand | cost reductions | demand-based pricing |
| price elasticity of demand | profit maximization | demand-minus pricing |
| elastic demand | sales volume maximization | chain markup pricing |
| inelastic demand | competitive pricing | competitive bidding |

## 〉〉〉〉 REVIEW AND DISCUSSION QUESTIONS

**1.** Briefly explain how operating in an oligopoly and a monopolistic competition market affects the pricing activity of an organization.

**2.** "Are monopolistic markets in the best interests of the average Canadian citizen?" Discuss this question providing examples of your choice.

**3.** What are the differences between elastic demand and inelastic demand?

**4.** How does cross-elasticity of demand affect the pricing strategy of an organization?

**5.** Briefly describe the importance of the competition to a firm's pricing strategy.

**6.** What is the difference between a profit maximization pricing objective and a sales volume maximization pricing objective?

**7.** Explain the difference between fixed and variable costs.

**8.** Given the following information, calculate the unit price using the cost-plus-pricing method:

| | | |
|---|---|---|
| Fixed Costs | = | $350 000 |
| Variable Costs | = | $65.00 per unit of production |
| Profit Objective | = | $29 500 based on a production level of 600 units. |

**9.** Calculate the break-even point in units and dollars, given the following information:

| | | |
|---|---|---|
| Fixed Costs | = | $300 000 |
| Variable Costs | = | $0.75 per unit |
| Selling Price | = | $2.50 per unit |

**10.** A book publisher determines that the consumer will pay $29.95 for a reprint of a classic bestseller. They estimate that marketing expenses and profit margin will consume 60 percent of the selling price. Using the demand-minus pricing method, calculate how much the publisher can spend on producing the book.

## ⟩⟩⟩ REFERENCES

1. ALEXANDER MACMILLAN and BOHUMIR PAZDERKA, *Microeconomics*, 3rd Edition, (Scarborough: Prentice-Hall Canada Inc., 1989), p.107.

2. Ibid., p. 181.

3. PETER D. BENNETT, *Marketing* (New York: McGraw Hill, 1988),p.461.

4. Marketing Practices Branch, Consumer and Corporate Affairs Canada, *Misleading Advertising Bulletin*, 1984, p.34.

5. Ibid.

6. SODRUDIN A. AHMED and GARY M. GULAS, "Consumers' Perception of Manufacturer's Suggested List Price", University of Ottawa, 1979.

7. JOEL EVANS and BARRY BERMAN, *Principles of Marketing*, 2nd Edition, (New York: MacMillan Publishing Company), p.373.

8. "Who's on First", *The Financial Times of Canada*, October 31, 1988, pp. A12-13.

9. "Who's on First", *The Financial Times of Canada*, October 31, 1988, pp. A6, A10, A12, and A13.

# CHAPTER 11 〉〉〉〉

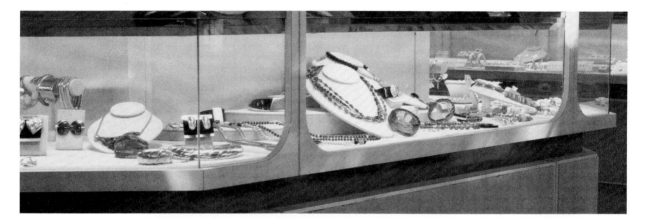

# Price
# Management

*LEARNING OBJECTIVES*

After studying this chapter, you will be able to

1. Describe the various pricing policies practiced by Canadian marketing organizations.

2. Outline the various discounts and allowances offered to customers by marketing organizations.

3. Characterize the alternative pricing strategies used in the course of the product life cycle.

4. Explain what the role and benefits of leasing are as a pricing strategy in the marketplace.

This chapter will focus on the management of pricing activity. The various pricing policies a firm may adopt are discussed, and the variety of discounts commonly offered in the marketplace are explained. The influence of the product life cycle on price management is also presented. Discussion in this area centers on the pricing of new products and the pricing changes that are implemented throughout the product life cycle. Finally, the use of leasing as an alternative to selling goods outright is examined.

# ⟩⟩⟩⟩ *Pricing Policies*

Pricing policies are the basic rules about pricing that enable a firm to achieve its marketing objectives. The policy options available are classified into four primary categories: psychological pricing, promotional pricing, geographic pricing, and flexible pricing. A firm may use one or any combination of these price policies, depending on the objectives established for the product or the nature of the market that the product competes in (refer to figure 11.1).

## Psychological Pricing

**psychological pricing**

In the case of **psychological pricing**, the organization appeals to tendencies in consumer behaviour other than rational ones. It is a practice used more often by retailers than by manufacturers. Psychological pricing influences the purchasing patterns of the final consumers. There are several types of psychological pricing strategies:

### *Prestige Pricing*

**prestige pricing**

**Prestige pricing** is strongly associated with luxury goods. The fact that the price is high contributes to the image of the product and the status of the buyer. For example, a mink coat that sells for $10 000 carries prestige that is inherited by whoever buys it. The price of the mink has been set high enough to create the image of quality and status. A consumer seeking such prestige may be attracted to a very expensive perfume, and forget that the scent of the perfume should probably be the primary consideration. When prestige pricing has been effective in creating the desired image, demand for certain products actually decreases if the price is reduced.

**FIGURE 11.1   Some Typical Pricing Policies**

| | | |
|---|---|---|
| Psychological Pricing | *Strategy* | Appeal to customer emotionally |
| | *Example* | Prestige, odd-even, price lining, unit pricing |
| Promotional Pricing | *Strategy* | Lowering prices to attract customers |
| | *Example* | Loss leaders, multi-unit pricing |
| Geographic Pricing | *Strategy* | Pricing based on who pays freight (seller or buyer) |
| | *Example* | F.O.B. pricing, zone pricing, uniform delivered pricing |
| Flexible Pricing | *Strategy* | Price negotiation between sellers and buyers |
| | *Example* | Purchase offers and price dickering |

### Odd-Even Pricing

odd-even pricing

For psychological reasons, an odd number is more effective with consumers than a rounded-off number. Thus, a colour television is priced at $399.00 because it is then not seen as costing $400.00. Research has shown that consumers register and remember the first digit more clearly than they do subsequent ones (in this case the *3* which puts the price in the $300 range).[1] For this reason, prices are set below even-dollar amounts. Such a strategy, called **odd-even pricing**, is popular with retailers and explains the widespread use of prices such as $19.95, $99.95 and $199.95. Sales tax in most provinces puts the price into the next range, over the "even barrier," but it does not have a major influence on purchases because consumers are accustomed to this mandatory addition to most of the items they purchase.

### Price Lining

price lining

**Price lining** refers to the adoption of price points for the various lines of merchandise a retailer carries. Thus, in the case of a clothing store, the retailer establishes a limited number of prices for selected lines of products rather than price the items individually. For instance, price ranges for business suits could be set in the $200 range ($299), the $300 range ($399) and the $400 range ($499). Customers entering the store are directed to the assortment of suits that fall within their price range, once it is known. In each range, the retailer may have purchased suits from different suppliers at different costs, but is satisfied with an average markup within each price range because it saves the consumer from confusion over price. Assuming the retailer understands the needs and expectations of the clientele, and how much they are willing to pay, it can establish its price lines (price ranges) accordingly.

### Customary Pricing

customary pricing

**Customary pricing** matches a buyer's expectations: the price reflects tradition or is a price that people are accustomed to paying. For example, chocolate bars of average size and weight are expected to have the same price, regardless of the different brand names. Other examples are the costs of daily newspapers, which increase only marginally in price from time to time, and transit fares for buses and subways. In the candy business, consumers started some years ago to balk at the continual price increases of chocolate bars, and the industry was faced with flat sales. As an alternative to increasing price, manufacturers decided to reduce the weight of the bars. This option was more acceptable than raising the price — and less fattening! It also led to the creation of a new, more expensive category of chocolate bar, the thick bar, which appealed to those consumers who would pay more for a large bar.

### Unit Pricing

unit pricing

**Unit pricing** is a policy adopted by retailers, particularly food retailers, who are anxious to let shoppers compare the prices of similar products and who are aware that the tagged prices make comparisons difficult. The difficulty occurs because the different brands are in different-sized packages. In the case of food items, a shelf sticker states the retail price, the size or weight of the item, and the cost per unit of measurement (e.g., cost per gram, cost per millilitre). Although unit prices were originally designed to assist low-income groups, research has shown that well-educated income groups of the middle and upper-middle classes refer to them most often.[2]

## Promotional Pricing

*promotional pricing*

**Promotional pricing** is defined as the lowering of prices temporarily to attract customers (offering sale prices). In a retail environment, the objective of this practice is to attract people (build consumer traffic) to the store; retailers know that while the customers are in the store they could purchase other merchandise at regular prices. Common types of promotional pricing used by retailers include loss leaders and multi-unit pricing strategies.

### Loss Leaders

*loss leaders*

**Loss leaders** are products offered for sale at or slightly below cost. The consumer recognizes the item as a true bargain and is attracted to a store by the offer. Honest Ed's department store in downtown Toronto is famous for daily "door-crasher" specials. So successful are these door crashers that people line up hours before the store opens to get a shot at the specials, a phenomenon that occurs with unusual regularity.

### Multiple-Unit Pricing

*multiple-unit pricing*

When **multiple-unit pricing** is followed, items are offered for sale in multiples (pairs are quite common), usually at a price below the combined regular price of each item. Such a practice is quite common in food retailing. Stores such as Safeway, Loblaws, Super Value, Sobey's, and Dominion offer such deals in their weekly flyers (e.g. soup at 2 / $ 0.99). Other variations include deals such as "two for the price of one" specials or "buy one get one free" or "buy one at regular price and get the second at half price". These types of offers are more frequent in other segments of the retailing industry such as clothing and hardware stores.

For an example of how the Canadian hotel industry uses promotional pricing to its advantage, refer to the Marketing in Action vignette "Flexible Rate Structures Bolster Weekend Traffic."

## Geographic Pricing

*geographic pricing*

The question "Who is paying the freight?" is what **geographic pricing** is all about. Does the seller pay the freight costs of delivering the merchandise to the buyer, or does the buyer absorb these charges? Are freight charges averaged to all customers and included in the price? These are geographic pricing questions, and their answers

#### ⟩⟩⟩⟩ *MARKETING IN ACTION*

##### *FLEXIBLE RATE STRUCTURES BOLSTER WEEKEND TRAFFIC*

What does a downtown urban hotel do to attract guests in the dead of winter? Generally speaking, the major hotel chains do well during the week by catering to the needs of business travellers. However, occupancy rates dip considerably on weekends. According to Robert Cornell, vice-president of Marketing for Four Seasons Hotels & Resorts Limited, "the key to successful winter strategy is overall flexibility in rates, combined with a creative twist to planning events".

The Four Seasons is generally satisfied with occupancy rates in the peak tourist season, but in January the occupancy rate dips to 60 percent from 90 percent in August. The off-season is November to March. To lure business its way, the Four Seasons cuts room rates by as much as 30 percent and often offers additional incentives — theatre tickets, car rentals, and, to attract families, complimentary breakfasts.

The Four Seasons has found weekend package plans for families extremely popular. Their Toronto hotels offer cross-country skiing in nearby parks and supply skates for courtyard rinks. They have also found that mom and dad want time away from the kids. Inn Kids, a supervised children's program of swimming, baking, and arts and crafts is popular with adults and children.

Target groups for these packages include double-income families, which possess the income for weekend getaways. Because of their hectic lifestyles, such families need many breaks, and downtown hotels offering the right value make the city an attractive vacation spot even in the coldest period of winter.

Adapted from Gayle MacDonald, "Winter can be cold for hotels", *Financial Post*, October 1, 1988, pp.27-28.

**In Toronto, families come first at the only resort in the city.**

Winter Weekend Special

From **$89*** per night

At the Inn on the Park we cater to your every notion of the perfect winter weekend retreat. Discover cross-country skiing and tobogganing for the whole family on 600 acres of neighbouring parkland. There's also an indoor pool and our free "Inn Kids" program for children aged 5 to 12.

In January, kids will have a ball with our "Inn Kids" *Winter Magic* theme of indoor and outdoor activities. They'll build snow forts and win prizes for the most original snowman.

In February, families can choc-a-lot of fun into every moment with our *Families Luv Choklit* activities.

*Price per family, per night includes two adults. Children under 18 sharing the same room stay free
• Valid Fridays, Saturdays and Sunday nights until April 30, 1990, based on availability.

**Four Seasons Inn on the Park** TORONTO

For reservations call your travel agent or 1-800-268-6282. In Toronto call (416) 444-2561.

*Four Season/Palmer Bonner Inc.*

*To lure business its way during the off-season, the Inn on the Park, a Four Seasons hotel located in Toronto, offers this weekend package plan to families*

are largely based on the practices of the industry in which the firm operates. In some industries, the seller customarily pays, while in others the buyer generally pays. A choice by a seller not to pay the costs in an industry where the sellers usually do pay would have an adverse effect on sales, even though the product might otherwise be the preferred choice. Several geographic pricing possibilities exist, including F.O.B.

FIGURE 11.2    Who Pays the Freight?

| | | |
|---|---|---|
| F.O.B. Origin, or Plant | *Buyer* | The buyer takes title when the product is on a common carrier (e.g. a truck). |
| F.O.B. Destination, or Freight Absorption | *Seller* | The seller pays all freight necessary to reach a stated destination. |
| Uniform Delivered Price | *Buyer* | The buyer's price includes an average freight cost that all customers pay regardless of location. |
| Zone Pricing | *Buyer* | All customers within a designated geographic area pay the same freight cost. |

pricing (free on board pricing), uniform delivered pricing, and zone pricing (see figure 11.2).

## F.O.B. Pricing

Under this classification are two sub-categories based on who pays the freight.

### F.O.B. Origin (Plant)

**F.O.B. Origin**

In a **F.O.B. Origin** arrangement, the seller quotes a price that does not include freight charges. The buyer pays the freight and assumes title (ownership) of the merchandise when it is loaded onto a common carrier — a truck, train, or airplane. This practice is satisfactory to local customers, but distant customers are disadvantaged. Under such a pricing system, a customer in Vancouver would pay much more for merchandise shipped from Montreal than would a customer in Toronto.

### F.O.B. Destination (Freight Absorption)

**F.O.B. Destination**

To counter the impression that distant customers are being penalized, the seller under the terms of **F.O.B. Destination** agrees to pay all freight charges. How much of the charges the seller actually absorbs is questionable, however, since the freight costs are built into the price charged the buyer. In any event, the title does not transfer to the buyer until the goods arrive at their destination, the buyer's warehouse. Such a strategy is effective in attracting new customers in distant locations.

## Uniform Delivered Pricing

**uniform delivered pricing**

In the case of **uniform delivered pricing**, the price includes an average freight charge for all customers regardless of their location. To develop a uniform delivered price, a firm calculates the average freight cost of sending goods to the various locations of its customers. This practice is more attractive to distant customers than to nearby customers, who pay more than they would under a different pricing system. Local customers pay "phantom freight" or the amount by which average transportation charges exceed the actual cost of shipping for customers near the source of supply.[3]

**FIGURE 11.3**   Geographic Pricing Strategies

| F.O.B.: | Maritimes | Quebec | Ontario | Prairies | B.C. |
|---|---|---|---|---|---|
| F.O.B. Origin (Toronto) | $10.00 | $10.00 | $10.00 | $10.00 | $10.00 |
| *Add*: Profit Margin and Freight to Each Customer | 2.75 | 1.75 | 1.10 | 2.00 | 3.25 |
| Customer Pays | 12.75 | 11.75 | 11.10 | 12.00 | 13.25 |
| | | | | | |
| **Zone Price:** | | | | | |
| F.O.B. Origin (Toronto) | $10.00 | $10.00 | $10.00 | $10.00 | $10.00 |
| *Add*: Profit Margin (40%) | 4.00 | 4.00 | 4.00 | 4.00 | 4.00 |
| | 14.00 | 14.00 | 14.00 | 14.00 | 14.00 |
| *Add*: Average Freight to Each Region | 2.50 | 1.50 | 1.00 | 2.50 | 3.00 |
| Zone Price for Each Customer | 16.50 | 15.50 | 15.00 | 16.50 | 17.00 |
| | | | | | |
| **Uniform Delivered Price:** | | | | | |
| Zone Price | 16.50 | 15.50 | 15.00 | 16.50 | 17.00 |
| *Multiply by*: Volume Importance of Each Region | 5% | 25% | 40% | 15% | 15% |
| Uniform Delivered Price | | | $15.72 | | |

### *Zone Pricing*

zone pricing

In the case of **zone pricing**, the market is divided into geographic zones and a uniform delivered price is established for each zone. For these purposes, the Canadian market is easily divided into geographic zones: the Atlantic Provinces, Quebec, Ontario, the Prairies, British Columbia, and the territories. Each of these zones may be sub-divided further. The Ontario zone could be divided into Northern Ontario, Eastern Ontario, South-Central Ontario, and Southwestern Ontario. For an illustration of geographic pricing strategies and calculations, see figure 11.3.

## Flexible Pricing

flexible pricing

**Flexible pricing** means charging different customers different prices. While such a practice initially seems unfair, its actual effect is to allow buyers to negotiate a lower price than that asked by the sellers. It means that the price is open to negotiation. Such negotiations are typical in the purchase of something expensive: of a house, say, or of an automobile. In the case of a car purchase, negotiations are commonly referred to as "dickering". The salesperson and the buyer dicker back and forth until a mutually agreeable price is arrived at, usually a price well below the "sticker price".

## ⟩⟩⟩⟩ *Source Pricing and the Offering of Discounts*

**list price**

Part of price management involves offering discounts to customers. The firm first establishes a **list price**, which is the rate normally quoted to potential buyers. Then, a host of discounts and allowances, which provide savings off the list price, are commonly offered to customers. In effect, price discounts and allowances become part of the firm's promotional plans for dealing with trade customers — wholesalers, for example — who in turn pass on all or some of the savings to their customers, to other wholesalers, or to retailers. Very often, it is the combination of allowances that convinces customers to buy in large volumes. The list price is rarely paid by a buyer. Typically, a buyer is eligible for at least some, but not all, of the discounts given by a manufacturer. Various types of discounts exist (see figure 11.4).

### Cash Discounts

**cash discounts**

**Cash discounts** are granted when a bill is paid promptly, within a stated period. An example is 2/10, Net 30. In this case the buyer may deduct 2 percent from the invoice price if the charge is paid within ten days of receipt of the invoice. The account is due and payable within 30 days at invoice price. While this discount appears to be small, it adds up to considerable savings for such mass merchandisers as Canadian Tire, Safeway, and The Bay.

### Quantity Discounts

**quantity discounts**

**Quantity discounts** are offered on the basis of volume purchased in units or dollars, and can be offered non-cumulatively (i.e., during a special sale period only)

**FIGURE 11.4    Types of Discounts**

| | |
|---|---|
| Cash Discount | Discount for Prompt Payment |
| Quantity Discount | Discount based on volume purchased. Usually follows a scale which increases with volume. |
| Trade Discounts<br>a) Off-Invoice Allowance | Temporary allowance off list price to encourage volume selling. There is a variety of formats (e.g., dollars off invoice price, bill-backs, and free merchandise). |
| b) Performance Allowance | Discount for performing a merchandising function (e.g., display or feature price). |
| Seasonal Discount | Discount for off-season or pre-season purchases. |
| Rebates | Discounts offered consumers by the original source of the product, after the product is purchased and paid for at the dealer's |

FIGURE 11.5    A Quantity Discount Schedule

**Schedule Based on Volume Purchased over One Year**

| Volume | | Discount |
|---|---|---|
| Units | Dollars | |
| 100 – 1000 | 200 000 – 2 000 000 | 10% |
| 1001 – 2000 | 2 000 001 – 4 000 000 | 15% |
| 2001 – 3000 | 4 000 001 – 6 000 000 | 20% |
| 3001 – 4000 | 6 000 001 – 8 000 000 | 25% |

or cumulatively (i.e., so that they apply to all purchases over an extended period, say a year). Normally, eligible purchases are recorded in an invoicing system and a cheque from the supplier is issued to cover the value of the discounts earned by the buyer at the end of the discount period. Refer to figure 11.5 for an illustration of a quantity discount schedule.

## Trade or Functional Discounts

There are two basic types of trade discounts:

### *Off-Invoice Trade Allowances*

off-invoice allowance    An **off-invoice allowance** is a temporary allowance that is deducted from the invoice at the time of customer billing. The invoice indicates the regular list price, the amount of the discount, and the volume purchased. Consider the following example:

| | |
|---|---|
| Product × (24 units in case) | $36.00 per case |
| Off-Invoice Allowance | $7.20 per case |
| Net Price | $28.80 per case |
| Volume Purchased | 10 cases |
| Amount Due | $288.00 |
| Terms: | 2/10, Net 30 |

Such discounts are offered by manufacturers to stimulate volume-buying in the short-term and to encourage distributors to pass on the savings to their customers; in the example above, as much as $0.30 per unit ($7.20 / 24 units) could be passed on. Such price reductions take the form either of a pre-determined dollar amount that is deducted from the list price (as in the example above) or of a free-goods offer (e.g., buy ten cases, get one case free).

Instead of allowing for such discounts on the invoice, a manufacturer sometimes offers them on the basis of a bill-back, in which case the manufacturer keeps a record of the volume purchased by each customer and issues cheques at a later date to cover the allowances earned over the term of the offer.

## Performance (Promotional) Allowances

performance allowance    A **performance allowance** is a price discount given by a manufacturer to a distributor that performs a promotional function on the manufacturer's behalf. These discounts are frequently made available in conjunction with off-invoice allowances so that greater savings can be earned by wholesalers who purchase in large volumes. The performances that qualify for the allowances may take some or all of the following forms:

1. There is guaranteed product distribution to all stores served by the distributor (e.g., Safeway agrees to ship a certain quantity of product to each of its stores in a certain region), rather than a system whereby the distributor waits for individual stores to place orders.
2. In-store displays are set in a prominent location.
3. A product is mentioned in retail advertising flyers or in newspaper advertisements that announce weekly specials.

Performance allowances are usually negotiated between a manufacturer and a distributor, and an agreement is signed. The distributor is paid upon proof of performance at the end of the term of the offer. Refer to figure 11.6 for an illustration of promotional discount calculations that a manufacturer may use to promote its product and of their effect on the price customers pay.

**FIGURE 11.6   List Price and Discount Calculations**

Information:

| | |
|---|---|
| Cost of Product | $40.00 per case |
| Trade Discount | $4.00 per case |
| Quantity Discount | 2% for each 100 cases |
| Performance Allowance | 5% |
| Cash Discount | 2/10, N30 |
| Customer Purchases | 500 cases |

Calculation of Price to Customer:

| | | |
|---|---|---|
| List Price | | $40.00 |
| *Less*: Trade Discount | | 4.00 |
| | | 36.00 |
| *Less*: Quantity Discount (2% × 5) | | 3.60 |
| | | 32.40 |
| *Less*: Performance Allowance (5%) | | 1.62 |
| | | 30.78 |
| *Less*: Cash Discount (2%) | | .62 |
| Net Price | | 30.16 |
| Total Discount | | 9.84 |
| Total Percentage Discount ($9.84/40.00) | = | 24.6% |

## Seasonal Discounts

seasonal discounts

**Seasonal discounts** apply to off-season or pre-season purchases. They are typical of products and services that sell strongly only in a certain season or during certain times. Some examples are as follows: (1) downtown hotels are busy during the week with business travellers, but require family package plans to attract customers on weekends; (2) resorts and vacation retreats often offer 10–20 percent discounts before and after their prime season; and (3) swimming pool contractors often encourage sales with promotions such as "Buy in the winter months at last summer's prices." See the Marketing in Action account "Flexible Rate Structures Bolster Week-end Traffic" for an illustration of the use of seasonal discounts.

## Rebates

rebates

**Rebates** are temporary price discounts that take the form of a cash return made directly to a consumer, usually by a manufacturer. Periodically, car and appliance manufacturers offer cash rebates to customers who buy their models. Frequently, the rebate program becomes the focal point of advertising campaigns. Such programs are commonly used to reduce inventories or to stimulate sales in traditionally slow selling seasons.

An automobile manufacturer offers rebates, and its dealers offer "trade-ins." In the case of a trade-in, the dealer establishes a value for the customer's current car and deducts this amount from the price negotiated for the new car.

Figure 11.7 shows rebate advertising and other forms of promotional price advertising.

**FIGURE 11.7**   Examples of Promotional Pricing and Incentives

## ⟩⟩⟩⟩ *Pricing and the Product Life Cycle*

There are basically two strategies for pricing a new product: skimming and penetration.[4] Which strategy is used depends on the objectives established by the firm at the introduction stage and at subsequent stages of the product life cycle. Generally, higher prices are associated with the early stages, when the firm is trying to recover product-development costs quickly; lower prices are associated with the latter stages, when more competition exists.

### Price Skimming

price-skimming

A **price-skimming** strategy involves the use of a high entry price, which enables a firm to maximize its revenue early. Some of the conditions that encourage the use of a skimming strategy follow:

1. The product is an innovation or is perceived to be significantly better than competing products. Such a situation justifies a higher price.

2. If competing products exist, they are few in number and are generally weak. New products that carry strong and popular brand names face little risk in using a skimming strategy.

3. The product is protected by patent; the resulting lack of direct competition allows a product to recover its development costs quickly by using this strategy.

A skimming strategy should only be used in cases where the marketing organization has a thorough understanding of the target market's behaviour. If price is an important consideration for consumers, a skimming strategy will not encourage new buyers to try a product, and the adoption and diffusion process will be slow. A possible hazard of skimming is that competitors who see a product enjoying high profit margins, mainly due to the lack of competition and a skimming pricing strategy, are likely to bring similar products to the market very quickly.

The following are some well-known brands that have successfully used a skimming pricing strategy:[5]

1. While Michelin tires are not the market leader (they rank fourth in market share in Canada), they have an image of having the highest quality and safest performance (their advertising is quite convincing). Consumers' perception of Michelin tires as exceptionally safe justifies their being higher-priced than other well-known brand names, several of which have a larger market share.

2. Advertised as the ball used more frequently by professionals than other brands, Titleist golf balls sell for more than Wilson and Dunlop, their major competitors. Titleist is the brand leader in Canada, due in part to the consumer's perception that the ball performs better, since it is used by professionals who demand performance. This justifies the higher price in the consumer's mind, thus allowing the company to use a skimming strategy.

3. Kodak's dominant share of the film market (75 percent) allows the company to charge a higher price for the product. Kodak faces only limited competition from Fuji, which has 10 percent of the market, and from some private label brands. If Kodak's market share were closer to that of Fuji, the variation in price between the two would probably be much less.

4. The Westin and Four Seasons hotels are both positioned as upscale hotels that appeal to a selective target market. They offer clients extra services and amenities and have created, through advertising, an image of quality, elegance, and prestige. Their image of superior quality allows them to charge more for rooms than do other hotel chains such as Sheraton or Holiday Inn, which have a different image.

5. Duracell batteries, the "coppertop" batteries, known for reliability and durability, cost more than the Energizer (the closest competitor), Eveready, or Mallory batteries. Consumers perceive the product to be better and longer lasting and so will pay the higher price charged for it.

## Price Penetration

price penetration

A **price penetration** strategy establishes a low entry price in order to gain wide market acceptance for the product quickly. The objective of price penetration is to create demand in a market quickly, to build market share, and to discourage competitors from entering. Generally, low prices are attractive to larger numbers of customers, so demand and market share objectives are achieved more rapidly. Potential competitors who analyze the market situation may think twice about entering it if they see that the profit margins of existing competitors are low and their market shares large. Under such circumstances, the opportunity to recover development costs, especially in a short time, diminishes. Certain conditions are favourable to the use of a penetration strategy:

1. The market or market segment is characterized by elastic demand, that is, demand that goes up if prices are low — buyers tend to be price-sensitive.

2. The marketing organization has the ability to keep production costs down. Either costs are low initially, allowing a satisfactory profit margin to be achieved with the low-price strategy, or the firm banks on improved production economies — resulting from the volume-selling the strategy encourages — to reduce costs.

3. The market is clearly divided into segments on the basis of price, and the low price or economy segment is large enough to justify entrance or accommodate competition among several brands (see figure 11.8).

The shortcoming of a penetration strategy is that it generally takes a long time to recover the costs of development and marketing, including the high costs of introducing products, because a high volume of sales is necessary in order to do so. If volume sales are not produced as quickly as anticipated, the realization of any profit may be delayed.

**FIGURE 11.8** Penetration Pricing in the Economy Segment of the Lodging Industry

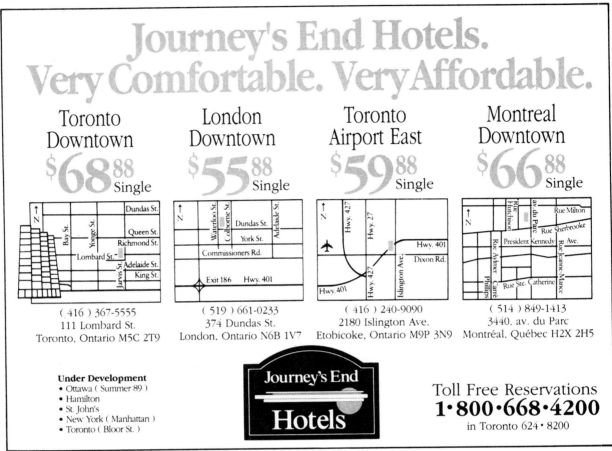

The following are examples of products and services which have used a penetration strategy with success:[6]

1. Journey's End motels have captured 2.5 percent of the total lodging market in Canada and are now the established leader in the thriving budget lodging segment. Refer to the Marketing in Action vignette "Big Bucks in Budget Lodging" for an illustration of an effective product-and-pricing marketing mix.

2. What helps make private label brands and generic brands successful is their low price in relation to national brands they compete against. In Canada, the number-one-selling brand of refrigerator, oven, washer, and dryer is Kenmore, a private label brand marketed by Sears. Kenmore's price advantage, as well as the fact that its products are perceived to be of good quality by consumers, enables it to compete successfully against well-known national brand names like Maytag, Hot Point, Inglis, Admiral, and many more in these product categories.

3. In the desktop computer market, the only way that brands such as Epson, Tandy (Radio Shack), Zenith, and Olivetti have survived is by offering a significant price advantage over the firmly entrenched leading brands like IBM and Apple. Their selling proposition is performance at a low price. Using a penetration pricing

## 〉〉〉 *MARKETING IN ACTION*

### *BIG BUCKS IN BUDGET LODGING*

Can you name the lodging chain that leads Canada's budget, limited-service accommodation segment? If you said Journey's End, you are correct. Started in 1978 by Maurice Rollins and Joseph Basch, the chain has grown from a single 60-unit motel in Belleville, Ontario, to a chain of over 130 motels, hotels and all-suite hotels and 14 000 rooms located throughout Canada and the northeastern United States. According to Chairman Rollins, the success of Journey's End is due to its dedication to quality. Its formula is hard to beat — a large, well-equipped, superbly clean room, and pleasant service at an affordable rate. That could be described as real value for the consumer. Today, this value translates into one of the highest chain-wide occupancy rates in North America — 79 percent in 1988 — which is ten to fifteen points higher than the national average.

At Journey's End, quality is paramount. Each property manager inspects at least 15 percent of the rooms daily, and a quality control supervisor checks all rooms frequently. The lodging chain also prides itself on employee training and realizes the importance that front-line staff play in satisfying customer needs. New managers attend a comprehensive six-week management training program at the company's training center in Mississauga, Ontario, where they sharpen their front-desk skills and learn about housekeeping procedures and human resources practices.

Journey's End has no plans to become a full service operation. Rollins wants to stick with what they do best — offering good accommoda-tions at affordable rates. According to Rollins, "As soon as you add amenities you start adding overhead. The next thing you know you've lost touch with your original intent and lost your place in the market." However, with revenues in 1989-90 of $140 million, expansion into certain areas has been inevitable. On the immediate horizon is an aggressive expansion of their award-winning no-frills concept to hotels. The flagship hotel was opened in downtown Toronto in 1988; room rates at Journey's End Hotels are offered for as low as $56.88. Additional Journey's End Hotels have opened in Toronto, London, and Ottawa, Ontario; Montreal and Anjou, Quebec; and St. John's, Newfoundland. A 189-room, 29-storey Journey's End Hotel at 40th Street and Fifth Avenue in midtown Manhattan opened in July 1990, marking the company's first entry into a major U.S. hotel market. Future plans also call for an expansion of their all-suite product line, Journey's End Suites, where each suite includes a bedroom and a sitting room with executive work area. This segment is a growth area in the lodging industry, which particularly caters to the needs of business travellers. Regardless of the direction that Journey's End will take, their basic philosophy will remain — offer the customer quality accommodations at a reasonable price.

Adapted from Lori Boland, "The achievers", *Canadian Hotel and Restaurant*, August 1988, p.59., and Michael Brodshaw, "Journey's End, just the beginning", *Leisure-ways*, August 1989, pp.32-35.

*Journey's End Motels, such as this one in Cambridge, Ontario, strive to offer quality at an affordable rate*

Journey's End Corporation

FIGURE 11.9    New Product Pricing Strategy

|  | Price Skimming | Price Penetration |
|---|---|---|
| Strategy | High entry price | Low entry price |
| Objective | Maximize revenue, and recover research, development, and marketing costs quickly | Gain market acceptance fast, expand the market, and build market share |
| Suitable Market Characteristics | Inelastic demand and markets where customers are less price-sensitive | Elastic demand and markets where customers are price-sensitive |

strategy has enabled Tandy and others to enter and establish themselves in the microcomputer market.

Figure 11.9 contains a brief summary of new-product pricing strategy and objectives.

## ⟩⟩⟩⟩ *Unfair Pricing Strategies*

predatory pricing

Periodically, an organization employs a pricing strategy that is judged to be unfair because it violates the spirit of competition. One such negative practice is **predatory pricing**, which occurs when a large firm sets an extremely low price in an attempt to undercut all other competitors and place them in a difficult financial position.

The ultimate objective of predatory pricing is to drive the competition out of business so that the price predator can then raise its prices. When Hyundai Motor Company introduced the Pony to the Canadian market, it experienced immediate acceptance and success. The car was perceived to be of better quality than domestic products and was available at a much lower price. Japanese automakers marketing cars in Canada felt the impact of Pony sales also. The domestic automakers and their parts suppliers complained, suggesting that the Pony was being dumped into Canada and sold at prices below cost. In essence, they accused Hyundai of a kind of predatory pricing. However, the charge was never substantiated, and in 1988 Hyundai discontinued the sale of the Pony in Canada.

Marketing organizations must be careful about how they offer discounts and allowances to their channel customers. Customers must be treated fairly; that is, if discounts are offered, the same offer must be made to all customers. For example, if coffee is offered at $10.00 off per case for a four week period, all customers must receive this discount. In the case of a volume discount, the rate is graduated to accommodate both the small and large customer (refer to figure 11.5). In this situation, a manufacturer like Nabisco Brands or General Mills offers a higher discount to Safeway or A&P than it does to a local independent grocer because the national chain stores buy in much greater quantity. The size of the customer is usually determined by the volume of product purchased from the manufacturer. The volume discount scale is in proportion to the size of each customer or buying group. Discounts of this kind are legal.

# ⟩⟩⟩⟩ *Leasing as a Pricing Option*

In recent years, certain industries have increasingly used leasing in place of buying and selling. When considering the purchase of expensive capital equipment, buyers now frequently assess the lease option. Industries in which manufacturers frequently lease their products are those of the computer, the automobile, office equipment and furnishings, and aircraft.

The leasing industry in Canada has grown significantly in the past few years. As of 1988, the industry was estimated to be worth between ten and eleven billion dollars.[7] Figure 11.10 illustrates the growth in this industry. Leasing is becoming increasingly widespread in Canada, but the extent of its use still lags well behind that of the United States. In Canada, leasing accounts for 10–12 percent of the total value of equipment purchases compared to 25–30 percent in the United States.

Leasing is particularly attractive to computer-marketing organizations. As of 1989, IBM estimated that 25 percent of its computer hardware was leased. Statistics for 1987 show that IBM leased $590 million worth of equipment in a total market of $2 billion. In response to the growth in the leasing of computer hardware, IBM established IBM Canada Leasing in 1988 to serve this market segment effectively. In the

**FIGURE 11.10**   The Canadian Leasing Industry

| | Value of Lease Receivables* (in billions) | Growth Rate |
|---|---|---|
| 1984 | $ 5.2 | |
| 1985 | 6.6 | +27% |
| 1986 | 7.8 | +18 |
| 1987 | 9.2 | +18 |
| 1988 (est) | 10.5 | +14 |

* Value of assets leased by all sources.

*Source*:  Adapted from "Major Expansion Coming in Canadian Leasing," *The Globe and Mail*, June 23, 1989, p. B9.

photocopier market, Xerox Canada Financing Inc. holds about $1.5 billion in leasing assets.[8]

## Benefits of Leasing

A leasing arrangement offers certain advantages to the marketing organization and the buying organization. The advantages for the marketer include the following:

1. A lease option may secure a sale that otherwise would be lost if the purchaser had to buy the product.
2. The lease provides the same amount of money, but it is received over a longer period, usually 4 to 5 years.
3. The infusion of monthly payments from leases assists in cash flow. In the wake of changing technology, the need for research and development has grown, and such infusions are needed to sustain it.

For the buying organization, advantages also exist:

1. The balance sheet looks better, since it shows none of the large outstanding debt usually associated with a major capital purchase.
2. Valuable working capital is preserved for investment in other areas.
3. Often the equipment suppliers issue leases at fixed rates; this protects the lessee from the cyclical rates of traditional lenders such as banks and trust companies.

## Composition of the Leasing Industry

The leasing industry is divided into four broad categories: a financial services group, original equipment manufacturers, independents, and lease transaction brokers:[9]

1. *Financial Services Group*  This group includes leasing subsidiaries of large Canadian banks, trust companies, and insurance companies. These organizations provide loans for leases that are readily available at competitive rates.

2. *Equipment Manufacturers*  Although the manufacturer's primary objective is to sell the equipment, if the customer prefers to lease it, the manufacturer will lease it. In this case, the manufacturer is responsible for providing complete service to customers, since ownership rights are retained by the manufacturer.

3. *Independents*  These are independent companies, publicly traded companies, and individuals who provide funds for leases or who lease equipment themselves. Leasing is their principal business activity. Compared to the first two groups, these organizations are much smaller. To survive in the leasing market, and to avoid confrontations with the big companies, such organizations use niche-marketing strategies.

4. *Lease Transaction Brokers*  These are also independent leasing companies who

work for a fee paid by the lessor. The broker presents the requirements of equipment users (potential customers) to the various lessors in the industry.

〉〉〉〉 S U M M A R Y

The pricing policies of an organization are the rules it establishes for setting prices that will enable it to achieve marketing objectives. Price policies are generally divided into four categories: psychological pricing (pricing concerned with tendencies in consumer behaviour), geographic pricing (pricing that takes into account freight and shipping costs and whether the seller or the buyer is to absorb such costs), promotional pricing (pricing concerned with the availability of discounts and allowances for attracting potential customers), and flexible pricing (charging different prices to different customers).

In managing price strategy, an organization starts with a list price and then offers discounts and allowances to potential buyers. The discounts commonly offered to distributors include cash discounts for prompt payment; quantity discounts, which are meant to encourage volume purchases; functional discounts, which are paid to customers for performing a promotional function; and rebates, which are temporary discounts intended to stimulate demand.

When a firm introduces a product, it chooses between price skimming and price penetration. Price skimming involves the use of a high entry price, which maximizes revenue and recovers development costs as quickly as possible. It is a strategy suitable for innovative products or for products perceived as offering better value. It is also used in markets where a brand leader has a dominant market share. In the case of price penetration, the organization employs a low price in order to gain wide market acceptance for a product and to discourage potential competitors from entering the market. In this situation, it takes longer for the company to recover research and development costs and marketing costs. In markets where one or a few brands dominate, other competing brands use penetration price strategies in order to attract customers that are more sensitive to price.

Implementing price strategies can be a problem for an organization, which must be careful to stay within the laws. In advertising price, an organization must make fair and reasonable representations. All discounts offered must be made available to all competing distributors and must be offered, where applicable, on a proportionate basis; that is, distributors must be treated fairly in accordance with their size.

Finally, leasing is becoming a popular pricing strategy in the Canadian marketplace. Certain industries — computer, automobile, and aircraft, for example — now frequently use leasing in order to generate new business. For the marketer, the primary advantage of leasing is that it preserves a sale that would have been lost had the lease option not been available. Leasing enables the lessee to avoid the debt load that would result from buying. When expensive state-of-the-art capital equipment is purchased on a lease basis, funds can be redirected into other areas of the company.

## ⟩⟩⟩⟩ KEY TERMS

psychological pricing
prestige pricing
odd-even pricing
price lining
customary pricing
unit pricing
promotional pricing
loss leaders
multiple-unit pricing

geographic pricing
F.O.B. Origin
F.O.B. Destination
uniform delivered price
zone pricing
flexible pricing
list price
cash discounts

quantity discounts
off-invoice allowance
performance allowance
seasonal discounts
rebates
price skimming
price penetration
predatory pricing

## ⟩⟩⟩⟩ REVIEW AND DISCUSSION QUESTIONS

**1.** Identify and briefly explain the various types of psychological pricing.

**2.** What is a loss leader, and what role does it play in pricing strategy?

**3.** Briefly explain the difference between uniform delivered pricing and zone pricing.

**4.** Is it fair to charge different customers different prices? Discuss.

**5.** Briefly explain the nature and role of: **(a)** quantity discounts **(b)** trade discounts **(c)** performance allowances

**6.** Briefly contrast a price-skimming strategy with a price-penetration strategy. Is one strategy better than the other?

**7.** What is predatory pricing and why does it occur?

**8.** What factors do you think will contribute to continued growth in the leasing business? Is leasing a desirable pricing option for marketing organizations?

## ⟩⟩⟩⟩ REFERENCES

**1.** GABRIELLE A. BRENNER and RAUVEN BRENNER, "Memory and Markets, or Why You Pay $2.99 for a Widget", *Journal of Business*, Vol.55, No.1, 1982, pp.147-58.

**2.** BRUCE F. McILROY and DAVID A. HACKER, "Unit Pricing Six Years after Introduction", *Journal of Retailing*, Fall 1979, pp. 45-47.

**3.** DALE BECKMAN, DAVID KURTZ, and LOUIS BOONE, *Foundations of Marketing* (Toronto: HBJ Holt Canada Limited), 1988, p.865.

**4.** KENT B. MONROE, "Techniques for Pricing New Products", *Handbook of Modern Marketing* (New York: McGraw Hill, 1986), pp. 32-1 to 32-8.

**5.** Data obtained from "Who's on First?", *The Financial Times of Canada*, October 31, 1988.

**6.** Ibid.

**7.** JOHN CRABB, "Major Expansion Coming in Canadian Leasing Business", *The Globe and Mail*, June 23, 1989, p.B9.

**8.** CARL STIEREN, "Fast-changing Computer Industry Rediscovers Leasing", *The Globe and Mail*, June 23, 1989, p.B9.

**9.** DAVID WAGNER, "Leasing Industry Involves Players from Different Fields", *The Globe and Mail*, June 23, 1989, p. B10.

# >>>>> PART SIX

# *Place*

# C H A P T E R 12 〉〉〉〉

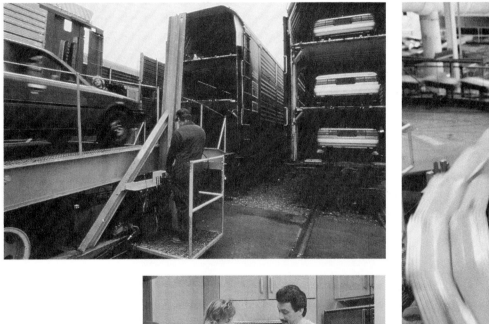

# Distribution Planning and Physical Distribution

**LEARNING OBJECTIVES**

After studying this chapter, you will be able to

1. Define distribution planning and describe the different types of channels and functions of channel members.

2. Describe the factors considered in selecting channels of distribution.

3. Outline the conflicts present in a channel and the strategies used to reduce conflict.

4. Explain the concept of integrated marketing systems.

5. Define physical distribution and describe the various components of physical distribution.

The third element of the marketing mix is place or distribution. Distribution involves all of the functions and activities related to the transfer of goods and services from one business to another or from a business to a consumer. Given the competitive nature of the market today, business organizations constantly strive to improve the efficiency of their distribution systems. Very often the goal of an organization is to reduce the costs of distribution and thereby improve profit margins, or to find new channels of distribution and thereby gain a competitive edge.

# ⟩⟩⟩⟩ *Distribution Planning*

distribution planning

**Distribution planning** is "a systematic decision-making process regarding the physical movement and transfer of ownership of goods and services from producers to consumers."[1] The physical movement and transfer of ownership includes activities such as transportation, storage, and customer transactions. These activities are carried out among members of the channel of distribution, which is comprised of organizations and people commonly referred to as wholesalers, retailers, agents, brokers, and manufacturer representatives. In marketing terminology, these organizations are called channel members, intermediaries, or middlemen.

## Basic Role of Intermediaries

intermediary

An **intermediary** offers producers of goods and services the advantage of being able to make goods and services readily available to target markets. A manufacturer located in Winnipeg, Manitoba, would have difficulty contacting retail customers in all parts of Canada if it did not have a direct sales force of its own, and even if it did have such a sales force, it would not be able to contact customers very frequently. To address this difficulty, the manufacturer sells to a wholesaler that in turn contacts and supplies the product to retail customers. The manufacturer gives up control of a marketing function (distribution) in order to improve its efficiency, as figure 12.1 indicates. In option A of this figure, sixteen transactions occur when four different manufacturers attempt to reach four consumers. In option B, where a middleman is used, the transactions are reduced to eight. Option B provides a more economical transfer of goods.

## Functions of Intermediaries

The functions of intermediaries in the channel of distribution include not only distribution but also marketing research, buying, promotion, consumer services, product planning, and pricing.

### Marketing Research

Because they are positioned between producers and users in the channel of distribution, intermediaries are closer to the final users than are manufacturers; therefore, they provide insight into the needs and expectations of consumers. By passing this information to manufacturers, they assist them in strategic market planning. For example, they convey to manufacturers product improvement suggestions, as well as reasons for customer dissatisfaction.

### Buying

Intermediaries buy goods from manufacturers and other supply organizations. When they do, a variety of payment options are available to them. For example, the

**FIGURE 12.1    Economies of a Distribution System**

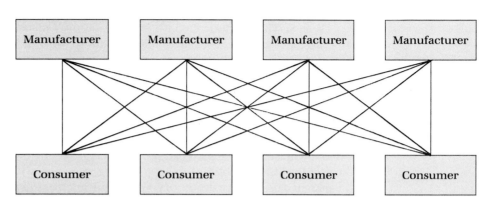

Option A.   With no distributor, sixteen transactions occur

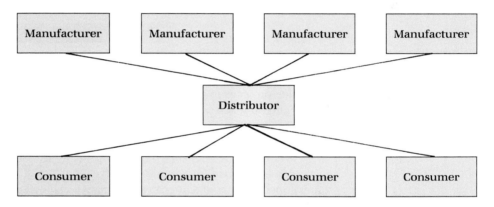

Option B.   The inclusion of one distributor reduces the number of transactions to eight.

net payment terms could be 30 days or 60 days, and there may or may not be a cash discount for prompt payment. Regardless of the system used, each level of the channel must agree to a price and pay within stipulated terms in order to ensure good cash flow at each level.

## Promotion

Producers offer their middlemen trade discounts, performance allowances, and cooperative advertising assistance. Middlemen use all or a portion of these funds to promote the product among their customers. These funds help push the product through the channel of distribution by enabling retailers to offer sale prices and by providing retail advertising support at the local market level.

### Customer Services

Retailers offer their customers various services to assist in the transaction process. These services include credit purchases, layaway plans, free delivery, guarantees, warranties, product exchange, and refunds. The size and the financial position of a retail organization influence the number of services it makes available. Mass merchandise operations such as The Bay or Sears offer a complete range of services, whereas small independent stores only provide selected services.

### Pricing

As ownership of the merchandise transfers from one channel member to another, each member establishes its own pricing structure, which is based on the profit margin it desires, the degree of competition, and considerations of what is fair to the next channel member. Manufacturers cannot control the price of merchandise as it moves through the channel of distribution. Therefore, the manufacturer must establish an initial price that generates the profit it wants and results in fair and competitive prices for consumers at the other end of the channel.

### Product Planning

How fast merchandise sells often determines how willing a channel member will be to carry, support, and maintain a product. Therefore, middlemen offer manufacturers advice on ways to improve the sale of products, on how to improve product quality, and on when to discontinue products.

### Distribution

As already mentioned, distribution involves transportation, warehousing, and customer contact. A manufacturer's representative may sell products to a retailer or to a group of retailers; the amount sold would be shipped to the retailer and the remaining supply stored in the wholesaler's warehouse. The retailer also performs the three activities involved in distribution. It encourages transfer to consumers by having goods available in quantities adequate to meet demand, and available at a convenient time and location. Customer contact is provided by a trained sales staff, which assists customers in making the right decisions. An effective inventory management system, another responsibility of the retailer, is essential for ensuring sufficient supply is available to meet demand.

## Distribution and the Sorting Process

**sorting**

Intermediaries provide assistance to manufacturers in the sorting process. **Sorting** is the accumulation, allocation, classifying, and assorting of merchandise.[2] The purpose of the sorting process is to reconcile the different objectives of manufacturers and consumers. Manufacturers like to produce and market a limited variety of items in large quantities and with as few transactions as possible. Such a system keeps their costs down and profit margins up. In contrast, consumers prefer a selection of merchandise that is wide in terms of brand image, colour, size, and price range, and they want products to be available in a variety of locations and in quantities that meet the needs of their replacement purchase cycles. They also prefer to deal with retailers that provide additional services, such as free delivery or the opportunity to purchase by credit card. For the manufacturer, this system forces costs up and squeezes profit margins, because a variety of products may have to be produced in small production runs. The sorting process, along with the other functions that intermediaries provide, helps to bridge the gap between the expectations of consumers and the capabilities of manufacturers. Let's examine each stage of the sorting process.

accumulation

1. Wholesalers purchase and store quantities of merchandise that come from many producers, and then redistribute the merchandise in small quantities among the retailers they serve; this process is termed **accumulation**.

allocation

2. **Allocation** is a wholesaler and retailer function that involves dividing the goods available from a producer among the various wholesale and retail customers. In times of great supply, customers can order the quantity they need and be confident of receiving the required amount. In times of high demand and short supply, a producer would have to allocate goods among its various wholesalers, who in turn would do the same for the retail customers. This situation could occur during a labour strike, when goods may not be readily available, or when there is unprecedented demand for a product. The Cabbage Patch doll craze in the mid-eighties was a good example of short supply and forced product allocation by the manufacturer.

3. The wholesaling and retailing function of separating or classifying merchandise into grades, colours and sizes is itself sometimes called sorting. It involves, for example, grading canned fruit as choice or fancy; categorizing eggs as grade A small, medium, large, and extra large; and classifying fashion apparel into small, medium, and large sizes.

assorting

4. The retailing function called **assorting** involves making sure that the merchandise is available to consumers in an adequate variety of brand names, features, and price ranges.

# >>>> *The Structure of Distribution Systems*

## Types of Distribution Channels

direct channel
indirect channel

Channels of distribution are either direct or indirect. A **direct channel** is a short channel, and an **indirect channel** is a long channel. Longer channels have more middlemen, who are responsible for reselling goods to other channel members (see figure 12.2).

**FIGURE 12.2** The Channels of Distribution

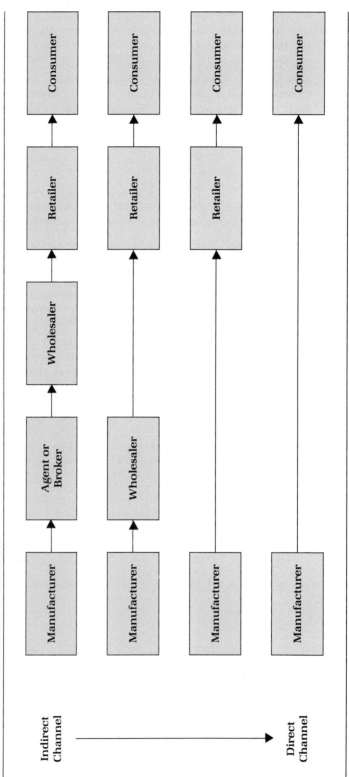

## Manufacturer to Consumer

The manufacturer-to-consumer channel of distribution is a direct channel in which manufacturers themselves contact and distribute to the final users. It may take the form of a business-to-business transaction or of a transaction in which a business sells directly to a consumer. Companies such as Avon, Mary Kay, and Creative Kids operate on a direct selling basis. In the case of an organization like Mary Kay, the sales force is responsible for stocking inventory directly from the producer and selling to customers in their local community. Financial services companies like Canada Life, London Life, or The Mutual Group sell directly through their head office or regional branch offices to consumers, using their own sales force.

## Manufacturer to Retailer to Consumer

The inclusion of a retailer makes the channel somewhat indirect. The retailer provides consumers with convenient access to goods. Apparel manufacturers such as Levi Strauss (blue jeans and leisure wear), Cluett and Peabody (Arrow Shirts), and Tan Jay (ladies fashions) sell directly to retail buyers of department stores and corporate chain stores. Retailers often store the merchandise in their own central warehouses so that it can be distributed to retail stores at a later time.

## Manufacturer to Wholesaler to Retailer to Consumer

The system in which products move from manufacturer to wholesaler to retailer to consumer is indirect and complex, since the number of transactions has increased with the addition of wholesalers. Such a channel is commonly used for products that are sold through a large variety of retail outlets. It is impractical for manufacturers to contact and deliver goods efficiently to many retailers; so wholesalers are used in the distribution of the goods. Convenience goods in such product categories as food, household cleaning products, personal care products, pharmaceuticals, and sundry supplies use this distribution channel (see figure 12.3). A manufacturer like

**FIGURE 12.3    An Indirect Channel of Distribution in the Grocery Products Industry**

| Manufacturer | Wholesaler | Retailer | Consumer |
|---|---|---|---|
| Procter & Gamble | Kelly Douglas | A & P/Dominion | Final |
| Kraft General Foods | Oshawa Group | Loblaws | Users |
| Natural Sea Products | National Grocers | Safeway | |
| Kimberly Clarke | M. Loeb Limited | Super Value | |
| Nabisco Brands | Bolands | IGA | |
| McCain Foods | | Food City | |
| Bristol Myers | | Steinberg's | |
| | | Provigo | |
| | | Sobey's | |
| | | Mac's | |
| | | 7-Eleven | |

## ⟩⟩⟩⟩ *MARKETING IN ACTION*

### *WHO NEEDS A WAREHOUSE?*

In the food distribution industry there is a definite trend toward very large superstores or warehouse type operations. All of Canada's major grocery chains rely on efficient warehousing and distribution systems to improve profit margins. Major retail chains such as Safeway, Loblaws, and A & P are all supplied by fully automated central warehouses.

In Toronto, an independent operation called Knob Hill Farms competes directly against the major chains quite effectively. Knob Hill operates on a grand scale. The owner, Steve Stavro, refers to the stores as food terminals. They are big, so big that they eliminate the need for a warehouse; merchandise is transferred directly from the truck to the selling floor.

Knob Hill's latest terminal is located near the intersection of Weston Road and the Macdonald-Cartier Freeway, in the suburbs of west Toronto. Approximately one million people reside within ten minutes of the terminal. How big is the store? The gross structure is 325 000 square feet (30 194 m²), with 125 000 square feet (11 613 m²) devoted to retailing space. The meat counter is over 500 feet (153 m) long and the production and cutting areas are behind the counter, in full view of customers. There are 0.75 km of coolers and freezers. Frozen food occupies 13 000 square feet and produce 20 000 (1 208 and 1 858 m² respectively). There are seventeen loading docks to handle incoming inventory and 42 checkouts to handle the outflow. Originally a small fruit vending operation, Knob Hill has come a long way.

Perhaps the most unique feature is the 80 000 square feet (7 432 m²) of indoor parking and a rail

One of the special features of Knob Hill Farms is its meat counter, which is over 500 feet long; behind it, in full view of customers, are the production and cutting areas

siding directly through one side of the retailing floor. Rail cars or truck-trailers can be unloaded for storage on one side or taken directly to the retailing floor on the other, where special carload promotions are commonly offered customers.

Is the store successful? Knob Hill Farms claims that the Weston Road location is the busiest store in the world given its location and size, a claim that is hard to prove or disprove.

Adapted from "The jewel of Knob Hill Farms", *Canadian Grocer*, August, 1986, p.96,98.

Colgate-Palmolive (personal care products) or S.C. Johnson (waxes and household cleaning products) ship their goods to wholesalers such as Bolands in the Maritimes, who in turn ship the goods in smaller quantities to the IGA stores they serve. Refer to the Marketing in Action feature "Who Needs a Warehouse?" for an example of an exception to the use of traditional wholesalers.

## *Channels that Include Agents and Brokers*

The inclusion of agents and brokers makes the channel very long. Typically, an agent or a broker represents a host of small manufacturers who do not have the resources to sell through the channel themselves. In this system, the agent or broker represents the manufacturer to the wholesale and retail trade, and earns a commission based on the sales generated. Since the manufacturer is not in direct contact with the customer, it has less control in marketing its product. Such a channel is commonly used to distribute food among small manufacturers who do not employ their own sales force.

It is not essential that agents sell through wholesalers and retailers. For example, in the financial services market, independent insurance agents operating out of storefront locations or home locations represent many of the small Canadian insurance companies directly to consumers.

# Factors Considered in Developing a Channel

Which type of channel a firm uses depends on which markets it would like to reach and what objectives are to be achieved. A number of questions must be answered: What levels of customer satisfaction are necessary? What functions will middlemen perform? What degree of coverage is desired? Organizations consider the following characteristics when making channel decisions.[3]

## *Customer Characteristics*

A manufacturer that wants to reach a large, geographically dispersed customer group requires long channels; the costs would be excessive if they were to directly contact and transport goods to widely dispersed customers. Reaching a few customers that need lots of service requires short channels.

## *Product Characteristics*

Perishable goods like fruits and vegetables require direct channels, or channels whereby the goods are transferred quickly to avoid spoilage. Products requiring installation and frequent maintenance, such as photocopiers and plant machinery, also require direct channels. Companies like IBM, Canon, and Xerox use a variety of channels, but they ship directly to other business organizations. The technical information communicated by their own sales force to potential buyers necessitates the direct approach. For frequently purchased, inexpensive convenience goods such as confectionery products and household cleaning supplies, indirect channels are used.

## *Competitive Characteristics*

It is appropriate to employ the same channels as competitors, and to employ channels that are common to a particular industry, but a firm gains a competitive advantage by developing a new channel of distribution. Having a product available in a non-traditional environment results in new purchases by consumers. For example, making motor oil available in supermarkets, or making snack food items available in department stores or stores like Beaver Lumber and Canadian Tire, could result in a consumer's making an unplanned purchase simply because the item was there. Movie videos distributed via vending machines are a new source of competition for retail video chains like Major Video and Movie Movie.

## Company Characteristics

Size and financial resources determine which marketing functions a firm can and cannot handle. Small firms with customers located coast to coast generally need to transfer the distribution function to intermediaries, who can perform the task with greater efficiency. Large companies have more flexibility and can employ their own direct sales force or use a combination of direct and indirect channels, depending on the customer segments they are going after.

## Characteristics of Intermediaries

The different functions performed by the various kinds of middlemen also influence what sort of channel is selected. For example, a sales agent does not take possession and ownership of goods. An agent only sells; therefore, the producer is responsible for inventory management. Independent manufacturer's representatives such as self-employed insurance brokers contact customers, but represent many general insurance companies; therefore, the amount of attention given any one manufacturer's product line is difficult to monitor. Wholesalers provide inventory and distribution functions, but the time they allocate to selling goods to retailers — the next link in the channel — could be less than desirable from the producer's viewpoint. These situations can cause conflict between producers and wholesalers, so every attempt is made by a producer to find the right wholesaler, one that will serve as many of their needs as possible.

## Product Life Cycle

The stage a product has reached in the product life cycle also affects what channel is used. An attempt is made to use a channel that offers the service and adds the value suitable for the particular stage a product has reached and for the rate of growth in the overall market.[4] The service and value provided by channel members before, during, and after a transaction occurs are taken into account. Considered are such factors as warehousing (e.g., the ability to maintain adequate inventory) and selling (e.g., customer contact and after-sales service). How the stages in the life cycle influence channel strategy is as follows (see figure 12.4).

1. *Introduction*  In this stage, when innovators and early adopters comprise the market, growth is very modest, so buyers have heavy support needs (buyers like detailed product information and expect a high degree of after-sales service). Products, therefore, are sold through specialists who spot trends, screen and select the best new products, and act as a communications link between manufacturers and leading-edge consumers (those who like to try new products when they first arrive on the scene). Microcomputers were originally sold by specialty

FIGURE 12.4    How Product Age Influences Marketing Strategy

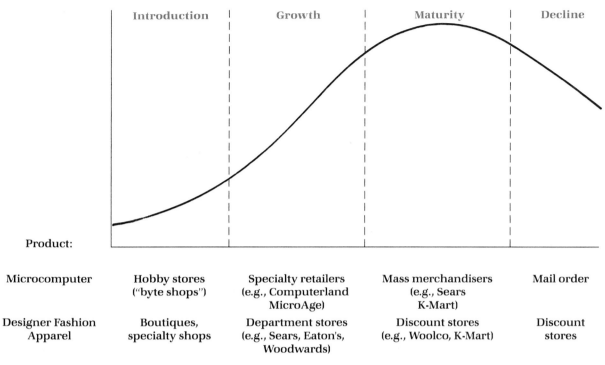

| Product: | Introduction | Growth | Maturity | Decline |
|---|---|---|---|---|
| Microcomputer | Hobby stores ("byte shops") | Specialty retailers (e.g., Computerland MicroAge) | Mass merchandisers (e.g., Sears K-Mart) | Mail order |
| Designer Fashion Apparel | Boutiques, specialty shops | Department stores (e.g., Sears, Eaton's, Woodwards) | Discount stores (e.g., Woolco, K-Mart) | Discount stores |

What stage a product has reached in its life cycle has an influence on what type of store the firm chooses to market the product.

stores that focused on only that product line. Stores like MicroAge and Computerland served the needs of the market initially, but today they face other forms of competition.

2. *Growth*    The buyers at this stage are comprised of the early majority, and market growth is rapid. The producer requires new channels with members that offer a different sort of value than is required during the introduction stage. The channel must now be able to handle the tremendous influx in volume. Typically, mass merchandisers — large wholesaling and retailing operations like Sears, The Bay and Woodwards — enter the distribution picture at this stage to capitalize on a popular product trend.

3. *Maturity*    During this phase, purchases are made by the late majority, and market growth is marginal or flat. Generally, the motivation for making a purchase is price (i.e., low price), so value-added services such as store guarantees, free delivery, and return policies are much less important. Discount retailers are more important than mass merchandisers like department stores. Junior department stores like Kresge's and Woolworths may carry the product, as might discount retailers such as Bi-Way, Army & Navy Stores, and Bargain Harold's.

4. *Decline*    In this stage, purchases come from laggards, and the market shrinks

**FIGURE 12.5**  A Checklist for Rating Potential Distributors

1. Does the distributor have the respect and confidence of its customers?
2. Does the distributor handle conflicting product lines?
3. Are the employees of the distributor, particularly the sales staff, well-trained?
4. Is the distributor a profitable operation?
5. Will the distributor be interested and enthusiastic about your product line (i.e., will the distributor give it the marketing attention it deserves)?
6. How effective is the distributor's coverage of sales territory?
7. Will the distributor cooperate in implementing marketing strategies?
8. Does the distributor provide its customers with good service?

quickly. Therefore, channels adding little value to the product start to dominate. Direct marketing through direct mail programs is a good example of the type of channel used. Mail programs simply communicate that a product is available and that it can be distributed directly to the customer at a certain price. Services normally associated with retailing are not important.

For an additional list of the factors considered when a company selects a channel of distribution, refer to Figure 12.5.

## Channel Length and Width

When trying to develop an appropriate channel, a producer must consider two characteristics: length and width. **Channel length** refers to the number of intermediaries or levels in the channel of distribution. As indicated earlier, channels are direct (short) or indirect (long). Long channels contain many intermediaries and are commonly used for inexpensive, frequently purchased convenience goods. As products increase in price, sell less frequently, and require more direct forms of communication to keep customers informed, the channels become shorter and contain fewer intermediaries. The direct communication of accurate, often technical product information between a seller and a buyer is more important under these conditions.

channel length

As channels become longer, control shifts from the producer to others in the channel. When this situation occurs, the producer implements "pull" strategies (advertising and promotional messages directed to final users) to assist in moving a product through the channel.

channel width

**Channel width** refers to the number of intermediaries at any one level of the channel of distribution. The width of the channel depends on how widely available a producer wants its product to be. Convenience products such as milk, bread, tobacco, candy and gum, toothpaste, and deodorant have wide channels of distribution at both wholesale and retail levels. Shopping goods such as clothing, furniture, and appliances require a narrower or more selective list of retailers to sell to consumers. Wholesalers may or may not be used in these markets. Specialty goods are generally available in only one location for any particular geographic market, since one is all that is required. For example, how many Jaguar dealers would Regina, Saskatchewan or Kitchener, Ontario need?

In wide channels, the producing organization has little control. For example, retailers who compete for customers of the same merchandise may do so on the basis of low prices. Such a strategy could be in conflict with that of the supplier of the good, who may want to create an image of quality by keeping prices high in retail stores. The different objectives of the channel members create conflict. The topic of conflict is discussed later in this chapter.

Manufacturers and other suppliers of goods and services are not restricted to any one channel. Manufacturers such as Xerox, Canon, or IBM market their products to industrial, institutional, professional, and dealer-network markets, using different channels to reach these targets. In effect, these firms use multiple channels (see figure 12.6). A **multiple channel** is a type of distribution for which different kinds of intermediaries are used at the same level in the channel of distribution. A

**multiple channel**

**FIGURE 12.6** Using Multiple Channels

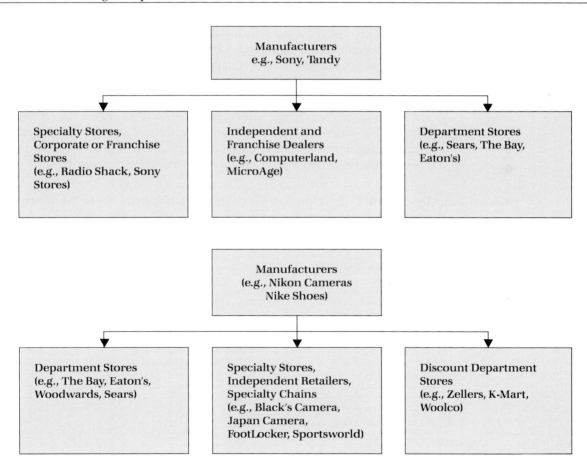

manufacturer of household cleaning products may sell directly to large supermarkets through a customer's head-office buying division, but use wholesalers to reach small, independent customers. A direct sales force may be employed to contact concentrated markets, while agents and brokers may be used to contact distant markets. The combinations that are possible describe the concept of multiple channels.

## Intensity of Distribution

In planning distribution and developing an appropriate type of channel with the proper length and width, a producer has to consider what sort of coverage of the market is needed. The degree of market coverage or the availability of a product concern what is termed intensity of distribution. Distribution coverage is either intensive, selective, or exclusive (see figure 12.7).

intensive distribution

1. An **intensive distribution** is used by those who want as wide a channel of distribution as possible so that they can reach as much of the population as possible. This usually applies to low-priced, frequently purchased, branded, convenience goods requiring no service or limited service. Producers continually search for new wholesale and retail outlets to sell through.

selective distribution

2. A **selective distribution** is suitable for medium-priced shopping goods that are purchased less frequently. With this type of distribution, the product is available in only a few outlets in a particular market. Selective distribution is often appropriate for consumer shopping goods and for industrial accessory equipment, where consumers may have preferences for particular brand names.

exclusive distribution

3. An **exclusive distribution** is sought for high-priced shopping or specialty goods that offer the purchaser a unique value. Typically, the product is purchased infrequently and is associated with prestige and status. In any given geographic area, only one dealer or retail outlet exists, a circumstance which helps protect the producer's image.

FIGURE 12.7   Intensity of Distribution

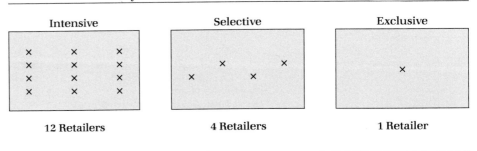

| Intensive | Selective | Exclusive |
|:---:|:---:|:---:|
| 12 Retailers | 4 Retailers | 1 Retailer |

# >>>> *Channel Conflict and Cooperation*

All channel members have the same basic objectives of making a profit, providing efficient distribution, and keeping customers satisfied. However, the strategies used by the different members in a channel often lead to problems or conflict between members. Much of the conflict derives from the differences in the functions that they perform and from their desire to maintain as much control of their strategies as possible.

In the Canadian marketplace of today, the balance of control or power has shifted from manufacturers to retailers, due to the growth of retailing chains and private label merchandise. This is particularly true of the fashion-apparel and food markets. Huge retailing chains in the grocery business, such as Safeway in western Canada, Loblaws and A & P in central Canada, Provigo and Steinberg in Quebec, and Sobey's in the Maritimes, all have significant buying power. A manufacturer that does not have its product available in these outlets suffers competitively. Retail clothing chains such as Dylex (which includes such stores as Tip Top, Thrifty's, Fairweather, Big Steel, and Suzy Shier) now cover the nation with stores located in major malls across the country. Such coverage has counterbalanced the national coverage of manufacturers, who in the past sold to regional and independent operations.

## Types of Conflict

Developments such as those just mentioned have tended to increase conflict or at least certain forms of it. Three types of channel conflict are common: horizontal, intertype, and vertical.

### *Horizontal Conflict*

horizontal conflict

**Horizontal conflict** stems from competition between similar organizations at the same level in the channel of distribution. For example, if Sears and The Bay are selling the same make of camera to the same target market, each store may strive to have the better or more attractive price policy. But if one store constantly has the lower price, the store with the higher price may begin to question the manufacturer, inquiring whether the other retailer is receiving preferential treatment. Were better discounts offered the store with the lower price? Such competition between similar firms is an example of horizontal conflict, which can flare into frustrations and resentments.

### *Intertype Conflict*

intertype conflict

**Intertype conflict** arises from competition between different types of middlemen at the same level of distribution. For instance, Mac's (a convenience store) competes with Loblaws (a supermarket), and 7-Eleven (a convenience store) competes with Safeway (a supermarket) for the sale of the same merchandise. In these cases, competition exists even though the two types of store meet different consumer needs. Mac's and 7-Eleven provide convenience, while Safeway and Loblaws offer lower prices and greater product selection.

### *Vertical Conflict*

vertical conflict

**Vertical conflict** occurs when a channel member feels that another member at a different level is engaging in inappropriate conduct. For example, if wholesalers do not pass on discounts that are offered by manufacturers to retailers, friction between the wholesaler and retailer will develop. A manufacturer may pressure a wholesaler or retailer to keep prices at a certain level, but the action desired by the manufacturer may be contrary to the profit objectives of the distributors; conflict is the result. If certain channel members delay payment for merchandise received, they could affect the cash flow of the supply source in the transaction.

## Achieving Cooperation in the Channel

channel captain

Securing cooperation in the channel of distribution is the task of the channel captain. A **channel captain** is a leader that integrates and coordinates the objectives and policies of all other members. The manufacturer is usually the first link in the channel, but is not always the one that controls the channel. Depending on the conditions present, leadership and control can be held by the manufacturer, the wholesaler, or the retailer.

### *Manufacturer Control*

When the manufacturer is in control, the channel is usually a direct one (i.e., one consisting of a producer distributing directly to the industrial user or to consumers). Companies such as IBM, Bell Canada, and McDonald's have control in their respective channels. A pizza business delivering directly to consumers exercises a form of manufacturing control. See the Marketing in Action vignette "Delivery — The Key to Success" for an illustration of manufacturer control.

### *Wholesaler Control*

When a group of wholesalers controls the channel, the only way for manufacturers to gain access to the retailers is through the wholesaling operation. For example, all products sold in IGA stores across the country pass through franchised wholesalers. These wholesalers include H.Y. Louie Company Ltd. in British Columbia, Horne & Pitfield in Alberta, The Codville Company in Manitoba and Saskatchewan, and The Oshawa Group in Ontario. These franchised wholesalers operate twelve major supply depots in Canada from which IGA retailers order stock. The headquarters of IGA operations acts as a coordinating body and service operation for the IGA distribution system in Canada, with the headquarters being owned by its franchised wholesalers.[5]

### *Retailer Control*

Sometimes a select group of retailers control the process of selling to consumers a wide variety of manufacturers' products. The regional supermarket chains such as

⟩⟩⟩⟩ *MARKETING IN ACTION*

### DELIVERY — THE KEY TO SUCCESS

If you were in the pizza business, your primary objective would be to have a product quality that competes with the best of them. This was Pizza Pizza's objective, but it went one step further. It promised either to deliver pizza to consumers within 30 minutes or give them the pizza for free. It also provided a convenient central phone number. Now the business is the owner of such a famous phone number, 967-11-11, that the number alone is an advertising message in Toronto, and it is a registered trademark of the company. Pizza Pizza has grown from a small business to a very successful franchised operation.

Pizza Pizza does not only make pizza. It realizes that it is in the transportation business. Its central phone number system allows it to take orders and coordinate efficient delivery; the pizza is made and delivered from the outlet closest to the point of order. The combination of a good quality product and efficient delivery lets Pizza Pizza stand out in a very competitive pizza market. Its

*A Pizza Pizza delivery man rushes pizza to a waiting car*

promise of delivery within 30 minutes is quite a promise in view of the traffic congestion in a city like Toronto.

Safeway, Provigo, Steinberg's, and Sobey's exercise such retail control. A few chains control a major proportion of the volume of merchandise sold through their retail outlets. In Ontario, A&P/Dominion, Steinberg's/Valdi/Miracle Food Mart, Loblaws and IGA control 62.4 percent of the grocery volume. In Saskatchewan, Loblaws, Co-op, Safeway and IGA control 88 percent of the grocery volume.[6] Retailers with significant control in other markets include Shoppers Drug Mart and Pharma Prix in drug and related sundry supplies, and Canadian Tire in automotive and general household supplies.

## Factors Encouraging Cooperation in the Channel

To illustrate how cooperation is achieved, let's consider a situation where the manufacturer is the channel captain. The channel captain motivates channel members to accomplish specific objectives or perform certain tasks by providing good service, attractive pricing policies, advertising and promotional support, and sales training (see figure 12.8).

**FIGURE 12.8   Conflict and Cooperation in Channels**

| Channel Conflict Types | Channel Cooperation |
|---|---|
| *Horizontal*<br>Conflict and competition between similar organizations at the same level of the channel<br><br>*Intertype*<br>Conflict between different types of middlemen at the same level of distribution<br><br>*Vertical*<br>Conflict between channel members at different levels of the distribution system. | A manufacturer encourages cooperation by:<br>1. Providing distributors with adequate and proper service in all facets of marketing and distribution support.<br>2. Providing fair and equitable pricing policies to all distributors.<br>3. Providing advertising and promotion support to encourage reselling and merchandising support.<br>4. Providing all dealers and retailers with adequate sales training so that all will benefit. |

## Service

To provide good service, to ensure dealers' orders can be filled quickly, the manufacturer maintains adequate inventory. Car dealers in Canada, for example, can obtain original replacement parts within one day of the request, in many cases. Advancing computer technology has certainly assisted in processing orders; orders can now be accepted, processed, and delivered much more quickly than before.

## Pricing Policies

Manufacturers recognize that every member of the channel must make a fair and competitive profit margin. Therefore, they establish list prices and offer discounts and allowances that permit members to make a reasonable profit. Movement of merchandise is a concern to middlemen; therefore, manufacturers must allow for higher margins on slow-moving items and lower margins on fast-moving items so that, on balance, the middleman maintains a reasonable level of profit.

## Advertising and Promotion

Another way to coordinate the different objectives of channel members is through cooperative advertising, which involves sharing of advertising expenses between manufacturers and distributors, and the manufacturer's providing copy and illustrations to be integrated into the distributor's advertising. This arrangement allows the manufacturer to promote its product, while giving the distributor the opportunity to promote itself. Incentives such as sales contests and dealer premiums can also spark interest in a manufacturer's products, at least temporarily, and help gain distributors' support in increasing sales or in acquiring new accounts. Information about such programs is communicated through a direct sales force or through designated sales agents.

### Sales Training

Manufacturers that train their customers in how to sell the product gain the interest of their customers. Any training provided, particularly to the distributor's sales staff, encourages cooperation. Companies such as IBM and Apple spend time training the sales staff of dealers' computer stores. Detailed training in hardware and software, which provides crucial product knowledge, is the key to success at this stage in the distribution process. The training is mutually beneficial; without it, dealers might be unable to persuade consumers or businesses to buy, and the dealer and the manufacturer would both suffer.

## >>>> *Integrated Marketing Systems*

In order to gain control of a channel of distribution or to foster cooperation among its members, a firm will pursue the development of a planned integrated marketing system. There are two categories of integrated marketing systems: vertical marketing systems (or vertical integration) and horizontal marketing systems (or horizontal integration).

## Vertical Marketing System

vertical marketing
system

In a **vertical marketing system** (VMS), channel members are linked at different levels in the marketing process to form a centrally controlled marketing system where one member dominates the channel. A channel captain has control in a vertical marketing system, whether the captain is the manufacturer, the wholesaler, or the retailer. There are three types of vertical marketing systems: administered, contractual, and corporate.

### Administered

In an administered VMS, the organization with the greatest economic influence has control. In the computer market, IBM is a manufacturer to whose marketing programs dealers adhere closely if they wish to remain dealers. Due to the economic clout and high market share of IBM, it is in the dealers' best interests to follow IBM programs. At the retail level, organizations such as Sears and Canadian Tire have control, since they contract with suppliers for a large portion of the suppliers' output. Canadian Tire arranges contracts for the supply of their Mastercraft product lines; Sears makes contracts with suppliers for Kenmore product lines.

### Contractual

As implied by the name, this vertical marketing system is governed by a legal agreement that binds the members in the channel. Three forms of contractual vertical marketing systems are possible: retail cooperatives, wholesale-sponsored voluntary chains, and franchises.

retail cooperative

### Retail Cooperatives

**Retail cooperatives** are composed of retailers that join together to establish a distribution center that performs the role of the wholesaler in the channel. It is a system that is initiated by retailers, and designed to allow them to compete successfully with chain stores. The cooperative enables the retailers to take advantage of the lowered prices that manufacturers offer to dealers that purchase in large quantities. Each retailer owns a share of the operations and benefits from the economies.

voluntary chain

### Wholesale-Sponsored Voluntary Chains

A **voluntary chain** is initiated by the wholesaler and consists of a group of independent retailers organized into a centrally controlled system. Retailers agree to buy from the designated wholesaler. As in the case of the retail cooperative, the increased buying power results in lower prices for all retailers.

---

## >>>> MARKETING IN ACTION

### GOURMET COFFEE A HIT

The entrepreneurial spirit is alive and well in the retail coffee business. Tom Culligan and a partner started The Second Cup coffee chain in 1978 with little more than a good idea. By 1987, sales were estimated at $45 million. How did it all happen?

Tom Culligan entered the world of business by working for a shopping mall developer in Ontario. In one particular mall, he helped a tenant open up a coffee bean kiosk. From there, a partnership developed with Frank O'Dea, and the pair opened another Second Cup location in the Scarborough Town Centre, one of Toronto's very busy suburban shopping malls. Sales in the first year were $69 000, and each partner was taking home a weekly pay cheque of $25.00. Undaunted by a slow start, the partners decided to try selling cups of coffee in addition to packaged beans. Without the benefit of plumbing, they sold coffee by the cup, using water from a pair of five-gallon (23 l) containers. The aroma of the coffee was an immediate hit with passers-by in the mall.

By 1979, thirteen stores had opened, and competition had entered the market. To support future growth potential, the partners decided to franchise operations. In the process, Culligan bought out O'Dea's half of the business partnership. As of 1987, there were 100 stores in existence, each averaging $260 000 in annual sales.

*After a slow start selling packaged coffee beans, the founders of The Second Cup decided to offer consumers cups of coffee, as well*

Plans for forty new outlets were on the drawing boards. For potential investors who may be attracted by the aroma of fresh-brewed coffee, the cost of a turnkey operation runs around $125 000.

Adapted from Wayne Lilley, "Designer beans", *Report on Business Magazine*, April 1987, p.51,53.

The difference between a retail cooperative and a wholesale-sponsored voluntary chain is that the system of ownership is different for each. Oshawa Wholesale (part of the Oshawa Group Limited) is a voluntary chain. The wholesaling operation supplies grocery products to Food City and IGA stores in Ontario. Home Hardware is a retail cooperative; all retail franchise owners own a share of the Home Hardware wholesaling operation.

### Franchises

franchise

In a **franchise** agreement, the franchisee (retailer), in exchange for a fee, uses the franchiser's name and operating methods in conducting business. The success of franchises is based on the marketing of a unique product or service concept, and on the principle of uniformity, according to which franchisees conduct business in a manner consistent with the policies and procedures established by the franchiser. Refer to the Marketing in Action vignette "Gourmet Coffee a Hit." Regardless of their location, franchise operations such as McDonald's, Budget Rent-A-Car, and Midas Muffler offer goods and services as well as a quality level that customers are familiar with. Franchising is discussed in detail in chapter 13.

### Corporate

A corporate VMS is a tightly controlled arrangement in which a single corporation owns and operates each level of the channel. The ownership and control of the channel can be located at either end; that is, manufacturers may own wholesalers, and retailers or retailers may own the source of supply. The direction of control is forward or backward. In **forward integration**, manufacturers have control; in **backward integration**, retailers have control. Wholesalers can integrate either forward or backward. Refer to figure 12.9 for an illustration of a corporate VMS.

**FIGURE 12.9**    A Vertical Marketing System: Loblaws Companies Limited

| Region | Buying and Wholesaling Operation | Retail Stores |
| --- | --- | --- |
| Maritimes | Atlantic Wholesalers | Save Easy<br>Save Easy Warehouse Stores<br>Real Atlantic Superstores<br>Capitol Stores |
| Ontario | Loblaws Supermarkets Ltd.<br>National Grocers<br>Zehrmart Ltd. | Loblaws<br>Loblaws Warehouse Stores<br>No Frills Stores<br>Ziggy's Gourmet Shop<br>SuperCentres<br>Zehrs<br>Mr. Grocer (franchises) |
| Western Canada | Kelly Douglas & Company Ltd.<br>West Fair Foods | OK Economy<br>Real Canadian Superstores<br>Super Value<br>Numerous independents |

To illustrate the forward integration concept, let's consider the purchase of Thrifty Rent-A-Car by Chrysler Corporation in 1989 at a cost of $263 million. Thrifty has 650 retail locations worldwide and an average fleet size of 33 000 vehicles. They are the fifth largest auto rental company in North America.[7] Owning Thrifty, Chrysler now has the ability to introduce a large number of potential customers to its cars through rentals. Satisfied renters could decide to purchase a Chrysler product. In the same market, Ford owns 55 percent of Hertz Rent-A-Car, and General Motors owns a minority interest in National Car Rental System Inc.

## Horizontal Marketing Systems

**horizontal marketing system**

In a **horizontal marketing system**, many channel members at one level in the channel have the same owner. Such a situation is common at the manufacturer or retailer level. In the late 1980s, many mergers occurred, and this led to the establishment of a number of horizontal marketing systems among manufacturers, all of which resulted in greater control for the manufacturer or source of supply. In the industry concerned with the exploration and distribution of oil and gas, for instance, Imperial Oil purchased Texaco Canada at a cost of $5 billion; in the chemical industry, Nova purchased Polysar Chemical Corp. for $1.9 billion; and in the brewing industry, Molson purchased Carling O'Keefe for $1.6 billion.

At the retail level, a corporation such as Dylex attempts to secure extensive control of fashion-apparel distribution through its corporate chain stores, which include Harry Rosen, Big Steel, Fairweathers, Tip Top, Braemar, Thrifty's, Suzy Shier, and Bi-Way. Because of the variety of merchandise that Dylex offers to different market segments, it has a direct influence on the manufacturers it buys from and on the nature of the product bought. In effect, Dylex, because of its size and power, can dictate the type of product a source supplier is to provide if it wants Dylex business. In the convenience store industry, Silcorp Limited is a major integrated marketer operation, with 1168 retail stores in Canada under the names Mac's, La Maisonnée, and Mike's Mart. They also own 200 Baskin-Robbins Ice Cream stores and fifteen Yogurty's Yogurt Discovery stores in Canada.[8] Look at the Marketing in Action account "Fitness Spawns New Franchises."

## ⟩⟩⟩⟩ *Physical Distribution*

**physical distribution**

**Physical distribution** encompasses "the range of activities involved in the delivery of raw materials, parts, semi-finished products, and finished products to designated places at designated times, and in proper condition."[9] The components of physical distribution include customer service, warehousing, transportation and transportation coordination, and inventory management.

## Customer Service

Determining how much customer service to provide and how much to spend on this service are the major considerations for a company that is developing a physical-

## ⟩⟩⟩⟩ *MARKETING IN ACTION*

### *FITNESS SPAWNS NEW FRANCHISES*

Changing lifestyles in Canada, specifically the movement toward health and fitness, has provided development opportunities for some new franchise concepts. A product in demand is yogurt, a low-fat milk-based product which is now being sold by operations that are set up like ice cream parlours.

TCBY, which stands for The Country's Best Yogurt, is a joint venture between Mother's Restaurants (a pizza chain) and TCBY Enterprises Inc. of the United States. The joint venture company currently has thirteen outlets in Ontario. Other competitors in this burgeoning market include Silcorp Limited of Toronto (of Mac's Milk and Baskin-Robbins fame), who have opened twenty Yogurty's Yogurt Discovery outlets. Zack's Famous Frozen Yogurts, a third entrant to the market, has seventeen outlets in Ontario, with aggressive expansion plans for other provinces on the drawing board.

Not to be outdone, one of the old standbys, Dairy Queen, is test-marketing a line of frozen yogurt products in the U.S. Success in the U.S. will lead to the availability of a yogurt product in Dairy Queen's Canadian outlets. As the franchisers make the pitch to the health-conscious consumer, what benefits do they offer? It's very simple — frozen yogurt is up to 98 percent fat-free and has about half the calories of ice cream.

*A Yogurty's Yogurt Discovery publication parodies a popular magazine*

It's a product you can enjoy without feeling guilty. Sounds like a can't-fail concept, doesn't it?

---

distribution strategy. To provide good service, suppliers of goods develop an order-processing system, designed to maximize frequency (how often orders are received), speed (the time it takes to process orders) and consistency (the correct and punctual filling of orders). They also provide warehousing when necessary and develop emergency shipping policies.

To prevent the loss of customers, an organization often sets service standards for its physical distribution activities. The maintenance of these standards helps ensure satisfaction among customers. These standards could be as follows:

1. To fill 80 percent of orders from existing inventory.
2. To handle all customer complaints the day they are received.
3. To reduce the level of damaged goods in transit to 5 percent.

In providing good distribution service, a firm evaluates costs against opportunities. Usually the alternatives with the lowest costs, which are preferable to the organization, are not the best for the customer. Therefore, to encourage sales, firms choose higher cost options. To illustrate, a producer might want to ship by rail, but loading and unloading at various points might slow delivery. The customer might want prompt, direct shipment by truck transport, a method which could cost the producer more. To meet the service needs and expectations of customers, the firm may decide to ship by truck, despite the extra expense.

### Transportation

Five basic modes of transportation are available for the delivery of goods: truck transport, rail, air freight, waterways, and pipeline. Air freight is the largest carrier of freight in Canada (see figure 12.10).

### Truck Transport

Truck transportation is used to make small shipments over short distances; deliveries within a local area or a certain region are made by truck. Truck transportation is also used for very long hauls, when time is not a consideration. The main advantages of truck delivery are that it can serve a number of locations, particularly distant and remote locations that other modes can't reach, and that it can make shipments frequently and speedily in local markets. On the negative side, damages to goods tend to occur often, and costs are relatively high.

### Rail

Railways commonly transport bulky items over long distances. They ship heavy items such as farm equipment and industrial machinery that trucks cannot accommodate. The benefits of trains are that they can carry a wide range of products and that they serve a large number of locations. The disadvantages include a relatively high potential for lost or damaged goods and a low frequency of shipment.

---

**FIGURE 12.10**    Cargo Volume by Mode of Transportation (1984)

|  | Value of Cargo in Kilograms |
|---|---|
| Air Freight | 464 088 |
| Water (cargo loaded and unloaded) | 381 986 |
| Rail | 254 581 |
| Motor Carrier (truck) | 162 039 |
| Pipeline | 14 147* |

\* thousand cubic metres

---

*Source*: Statistics Canada, *Canada Year Book 1988*, Ottawa: Ministry of Supply and Services Canada, 1987, Cat. No. 11-402E/1987. Adapted with the permission of the Minister of Supply and Services Canada, 1990.

### Air Freight

The speed of air transportation is its primary advantage. Air carriers commonly carry expensive items that can absorb the high freight costs. It is also common to ship perishable goods and urgently needed goods by air. Its appeal lies in its fast delivery and in the number of markets it serves, particularly major urban markets in Canada and around the world. Its high cost is its major disadvantage (see figure 12.11).

**FIGURE 12.11**     Stressing the Benefits of Air Transportation

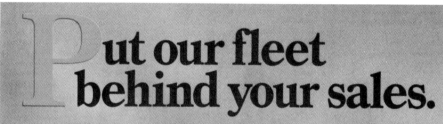

Courtesy: Air Canada Cargo.

### *Waterways*

Shipping by waterways involves the movement of goods by ocean tankers and by inland freighters. In Canada, waterway shipping through the St. Lawrence Seaway and the Great Lakes is common. The use of water transportation is widespread for bulky items such as coal, iron ore, gravel, grain, and chemicals. High value finished goods from overseas are also shipped by water. For example, automobiles from Japan and South Korea arrive in Vancouver by water carrier.

Water transportation is attractive because it allows a wide range of products to be moved at low cost, with only a small amount of loss or damage. On the other hand, movement by water is slow; water carriers can only reach certain places; and shipments tend to be infrequent.

### *Pipeline*

Pipelines can deliver only certain products, namely natural gas and petroleum-based products. Their advantage lies in their smooth, uninterrupted delivery. Delivery is continuous, and there is a minimum of loss and damage. The drawbacks of a pipeline are that it can serve only a limited number of destinations (e.g., pipelines do not reach all residential neighbourhoods and deliver natural gas to them) and that only a narrow range of products can use such a mode of transportation.

### *Other Transportation Services*

In order to meet the needs of business customers, other transportation services have emerged. Some companies offer a combination of travel modes in their attempt to deliver goods quickly and dependably. The combination of air and truck transportation is common for cargo carriers such as UPS (United Parcel Service), Emery, Federal Express, and Air Canada Cargo. These companies combine truck fleets for ground travel with air cargo for overnight delivery to distant locations. Other delivery service companies include: 1) Canada Post, which offers an overnight service — Priority Post — that is popular for small items and documents, and 2) local delivery companies, which generally pick up and deliver, using two-way radio communications between a local dispatch office and a fleet of small delivery vehicles.

## Transportation Coordination

containerization

To increase efficiency, more and more firms are employing a combination of transportation modes to ship their products. When several modes of transportation are used, containerization plays a key role. **Containerization** entails the grouping of individual items into an economical shipping quantity that is sealed in a protective container for intermodal transportation to a final customer. These loads are easily transferred from one mode of transportation to another as they reach different destinations. Since containers are marked and sealed, and remain in that state until delivery to the customer, loss and damage is kept to a minimum.

piggybacking

Containers have enabled companies to combine various transportation modes and thereby make use of the service and cost advantages offered by each mode. The most common form of intermodal transportation is called piggybacking. **Piggybacking** is a system in which the entire load of a truck trailer is placed in a rail flatcar for movement from one place to another. The railway performs the long haul, and the truck performs the local pick-up and delivery. Other combinations for intermodal transportation are possible, such as the combination of trucking and water. For example, ferries are used to transport goods from Vancouver Island to the mainland, and from Newfoundland and Prince Edward Island to the mainland, then trucks are used to complete the delivery of goods.

freight forwarder

In a situation where only small quantities of goods are to be shipped, the services of a freight forwarder may be required. A **freight forwarder** is a firm that consolidates small shipments — shipments that form less than a carload or truckload — from small companies. Freight forwarders are essential to firms that do not meet the minimum requirements of such traditional carriers as the railway and trucks. The forwarders prosper because the common carrier charges them the carload or truckload rate, while they in turn charge their customers a higher rate to pay for their service and to generate a profit.

## Inventory Management

inventory management

**Inventory management** is a system that ensures a continuous flow of needed goods by matching the quantity of goods in inventory to sales demand so that neither too little nor too much stock is carried. It is the system of balancing supply with demand in such a way that the costs of carrying inventory are kept to a minimum, while enough inventory is maintained to meet the demands of customers. If inventories become too low, customers face shortages. If inventories are too high, carrying costs increase, as does the potential for goods to go stale, and working capital becomes tied up.

just-in-time (JIT)<br>inventory system

Many firms in Canada and the United States have now adopted a **just-in-time (JIT) inventory system**, a system of Japanese origin. The objective of a JIT inventory system is to reduce the amount of inventory on hand by ordering small quantities frequently. This is the opposite of past practice, which was to order large quantities at low costs and thus to save money in purchasing rather than in storing. A JIT inventory system has become increasingly feasible because of the growing presence of computers in inventory planning and in other forms of business planning. All three North American automakers — General Motors, Ford, and Chrysler — as well as durable-goods and high-technology companies such as General Electric, IBM, and Hewlett Packard, have implemented such systems.

In any inventory system, the key decisions concern the reorder point and the economic order quantity.

### *Reorder Point*

reorder point

A **reorder point** is an inventory level at which new orders must be placed if normal production operations are to be maintained or demand for finished products to be satisfied. Factors considered in reordering include lead time, usage rate, and safety stock.

1. *Lead Time* This is the amount of time that elapses between the placing of an order and the receiving of it (i.e. the point at which it is available for use).

2. *Usage Rate* This is the rate at which a product is used (in production) or sold (by a wholesaler or retailer) on a daily basis.

3. *Safety Stock* Safety stock is the extra merchandise kept on hand (in inventory) to prevent out-of-stock predicaments. Such situations can occur when there is unexpected demand, increased production, or delivery delays from suppliers.

The formula for calculating the reorder point is:

$$ROP = (\text{Order Lead Time} \times \text{Usage Rate}) + \text{Safety Stock}$$

Assuming that the lead time is five days and the usage rate is 100 per day, and a minimum of 100 is kept as safety stock, the calculation would be:

$$
\begin{aligned}
ROP &= (5 \text{ days} \times 100/\text{day}) + 100 \\
&= \quad 500 + 100 \\
&= \quad 600
\end{aligned}
$$

The firm must decide how much to actually order when the reorder point is reached. In doing so, it must take into account such matters as the discounts offered by suppliers, the resources of the buying firm, the rate of inventory turnover, the order-processing costs and the inventory-carrying costs. To illustrate, if a firm reorders a large quantity, it qualifies for special discounts, but the savings that result could be offset by inventory carrying costs if stock turnover is low. Conversely, if not enough stock is purchased, and if inventory turnover is high, the firm may suffer out-of-stocks, production downtime, and lost sales.

### Economic Order Quantity

Establishing an economic order quantity is important in inventory planning. The economic order quantity is the order size that minimizes the total cost of ordering and carrying inventory. Costs involved in ordering inventory are purchasing and receiving costs, while carrying costs include the costs of storage, handling, and insurance. Therefore, the **economic order quantity** is the amount of goods that will strike a balance between the cost of ordering goods and the cost of carrying goods in inventory.

**economic order quantity**

It is calculated by means of the following formula:

$$EOQ = \frac{2\,DS}{IC}$$

where: D = demand or usage rate

S = cost of placing order

I = inventory carrying cost (percent of unit cost)

C = unit cost of item

$$\text{For example: } D = 3\ 000$$
$$S = 3$$
$$I = 20\%$$
$$C = \$1.00$$

$$EOQ = \frac{2\ DS}{IC}$$
$$= \frac{(2)(3\ 000)(3)}{(0.20)(\$1)}$$
$$= \frac{18\ 000}{0.20}$$
$$= 90\ 000$$
$$= 300$$

## Warehousing

The role of a warehouse is to receive, sort, and redistribute merchandise to customers. There are two types of warehouse: storage warehouses and distribution warehouses.

1. *Storage (Public) Warehouse*  This warehouse stores merchandise for manufacturers or distributors for moderate periods of time. Generally, these facilities are not specialized; they handle a variety of items such as tires, equipment, appliances and other hard goods, as well as case goods. Very often, a storage warehouse stores manufacturer inventory that the manufacturer cannot handle in its own storage facilities.

2. *Distribution Warehouse*  This warehouse receives inventories and then redistributes merchandise to customers, usually in smaller quantities than those it receives. A variety of goods ordered by a customer are assembled into a truckload by the distribution warehouse for shipment to the customer. Loblaws warehouses receive shipments from a variety of manufacturers (see figure 12.9). These warehouses store, assemble, and redistribute the same merchandise in smaller quantities to their retail locations.

## ⟩⟩⟩⟩ S U M M A R Y

Distribution planning entails making decisions regarding the physical movement of merchandise and its transfer between producers and consumers. A channel of distribution is comprised of organizations known as middlemen, intermediaries, or channel members. The role of such middlemen as wholesalers, agents, brokers, and retailers is to facilitate the transfer of merchandise in an efficient, economical manner.

Intermediaries are active in market research, buying, promotion, consumer services, product planning, pricing, and distribution. Since manufacturers ship large quantities while retailers and consumers purchase in small quantities, wholesalers provide a sorting function. Sorting refers to the accumulation, allocation, classifying, and assorting of merchandise.

Channels of distribution are either direct (short) or indirect (long). Short channels are commonly used to distribute expensive capital goods under circumstances where communications between the producer and buyer are crucial. For goods that are less valuable and purchased more frequently, long channels of distribution are used. The elements a firm considers when designing channel strategy include the product, the competition, the company, the middlemen, the characteristics of the consumer, and the product life cycle.

Channel length refers to the number or levels of middlemen in the channel of distribution. Channel width is the number of middlemen at any one level of the channel. Usually, a channel becomes wider as the product moves toward the point of purchase (that is, the retail level where consumers buy). Distribution can be intensive, selective, or exclusive, depending on the marketing objectives of the producing firm.

Within any channel, conflict between members occurs. Conflict can be horizontal (i.e., between similar members at the same level), or vertical (between members at different levels), or intertype (between different types of middlemen at the same level of distribution). The channel captain implements strategies that encourage cooperation between channel members. These strategies include providing good service, fair pricing policies, advertising and promotional support, and sales training programs.

Integrated marketing systems are a means of gaining increased control over channel operations. Basically, two types of integrated marketing systems exist. In a vertical marketing system, control is held by a manufacturer, wholesaler, or retailer. These vertical systems are: 1) administered, in which case the member with the most economic influence holds control; 2) contractual, in which case control is maintained through a legal agreement; and 3) corporate, in which case one company operates at each level of the channel. In a horizontal marketing system, one firm has many members at one level of the channel.

Physical distribution refers to the activities involved in the delivery of merchandise. The major components of physical distribution include customer service, warehousing, transportation, and inventory management.

## >>>> KEY TERMS

| | | |
|---|---|---|
| distribution planning | intensive distribution | forward integration |
| intermediary | selective distribution | backward integration |
| sorting | exclusive distribution | horizontal marketing system |
| accumulation | horizontal conflict | physical distribution |
| allocation | intertype conflict | containerization |
| assorting | vertical conflict | piggybacking |
| direct channel | channel captain | freight forwarder |

| | | |
|---|---|---|
| indirect channel | vertical marketing system | inventory management |
| channel length | retail cooperative | JIT inventory system |
| channel width | voluntary chain | reorder point |
| multiple channel | franchise | economic order quantity |

## ⟩⟩⟩⟩ QUESTIONS FOR REVIEW AND DISCUSSION

**1.** What is the basic role of intermediaries in the channel of distribution?

**2.** Identify and briefly describe the functions of intermediaries.

**3.** What is the sorting process?

**4.** Briefly describe the factors a firm considers when designing a channel of distribution.

**5.** What type of channel of distribution would you recommend for: **a)** a daily newspaper **b)** cellular telephone **c)** desktop photocopier **d)** canned fruits and vegetables

**6.** What is the difference between channel length and channel width?

**7.** Under what conditions are the following types of distribution appropriate? **a)** intensive **b)** selective **c)** exclusive

**8.** What is a channel captain and where is the captain located in the channel?

**9.** Briefly explain the difference between vertical integration and horizontal integration.

**10.** Briefly describe the functions of physical distribution.

**11.** What are the primary advantages of each mode of transportation?

**12.** What advantages and disadvantages do you see for a JIT inventory system?

## ⟩⟩⟩⟩ REFERENCES

1. JOEL EVANS and BARRY BERMAN, *Marketing*, 3rd Edition (New York: Macmillan Publishing Company, 1987), p.324.

2. WROE ANDERSON, *Marketing Behaviour and Executive Action* (Homewood, Illinois: Irwin, 1957), chapter 7.

3. WILLIAM BAND, "Successful Distribution Channel Strategies", *Sales and Marketing Management in Canada*, April 1987, pp. 11-12.

4. MILIND LELE, "Matching Your Channels to Your Product's Life Cycle", *Business Marketing*, December 1986, p.61.

5. "The Chains", *Canadian Grocer*, August 1988, p.55.

6. "Top Four Distributors", *Canadian Grocer*, May 1987, p.39.

7. "Chrysler Pays $263 million for Thrifty Rent-A-Car", *Globe and Mail*, May 19, 1989, p.B6.

8. Silcorp Limited, *Annual Report*, 1988, p.1.

9. JOEL EVANS and BARRY BERMAN, *Marketing*, 3rd Edition (New York: Macmillan Publishing Company, 1987), p.337.

# CHAPTER 13 ❯❯❯❯

# Wholesaling and Retailing

## >>>> Wholesaling and Its Functions

**wholesaling**

**Wholesaling** is the process of buying or handling merchandise and subsequently reselling it to organizational users, other wholesalers, and retailers. As discussed in the previous chapter, the wholesaling role is performed either by manufacturers themselves or by independent channel members. Not all independent wholesalers, however, perform every wholesaling function, so individual manufacturers have to select the channels and channel members that will carry out the functions needed to distribute their particular products. The following list is a description of the basic functions that wholesalers may perform.[1]

1. *Covering the Market*  Manufacturers produce in and market from one location or a few regional facilities; otherwise, the product is imported from foreign markets and stored in a central warehouse in Canada. Yet manufacturers' customers are geographically dispersed, a circumstance which makes it difficult to reach many of them. Wholesalers make it easier to reach these customers, providing the market coverage needed and distributing goods to retailers from their warehouses.

2. *Providing Sales Contact*  Manufacturers who use wholesalers to reach all or a large portion of their customers reduce the costs of direct selling, for their direct sales force has to call only on a small number of wholesalers rather than a large number of customers.

3. *Holding Inventory*  In many cases, the title to the merchandise is transferred to the wholesaler, who then holds the goods in inventory. For the manufacturer, this reduces the financial burden of carrying inventory and improves its cash flow to other operational costs.

4. *Order-Processing*  Wholesalers represent many manufacturers of similar products. Unlike manufacturers, wholesalers ship small quantities of a variety of merchandise to their customers. Not only do wholesalers process orders for the manufacturers' products, they also spread the costs of the order-processing across all of the manufacturers' products they represent.

5. *Performing Market Intelligence*  Since wholesalers are in frequent contact with their customers, they have a good understanding of customer needs (e.g., product requirements, service expectations, price, etc.). This information is passed to manufacturers to assist in improving marketing strategies.

6. *Offering Sales Support*  After goods have been transferred to the next level in the channel — to another wholesaler, retailer, or organizational customer — the wholesaler provides after-sales service, addressing any problems that arise. Such service takes the form of returns or exchanges, installations, adjustments, general repairs, technical assistance, and training users in how to use equipment.

7. *Providing Assortment*  Wholesalers carry a wide variety of manufacturers' products. The amassing of various items is called assortment. The assortment function simplifies customers' ordering tasks. In certain cases, customers can order from one wholesaler instead of from many. A few general-line wholesalers can provide customers with most of the products they need.

**breaking bulk**

8. *Breaking Bulk*  **Breaking bulk** refers to the delivery of small quantities to customers. Very often, customers do not meet the minimum shipping-weight

requirement established by the transportation companies that deliver the goods. Therefore, wholesalers buy in large quantities from manufacturers and break the "bulk" orders into small quantities, so that their customers may buy in the quantities they need.

# ⟩⟩⟩⟩ *Types of Wholesalers*

Wholesaling merchants account for about 84 percent of the total volume of trade and in 1984 had sales estimated at $158.9 billion. Agents and brokers accounted for $33.6 billion in the same period.[2] As figure 13.1 indicates, the Canadian wholesaling market covers many industries, including those of food, coal, coke and petroleum products, machinery, motor vehicles and accessories, and lumber and building materials. Within Canadian industries, wholesalers belong to one of three main categories. They are manufacturer wholesaling, merchant wholesaling, and agents, brokers and commission merchants (see figure 13.2).

**FIGURE 13.1**  Wholesale Volume by Trade Group, 1984

|  | Wholesaling Merchants (in millions) | Agents and Brokers (in millions) |
|---|---|---|
| Farm Products | $ 19 770 | $ 7 850 |
| Coal, Coke, Petroleum | 27 851 | 5 026 |
| Paper, Paper Products | 3 790 | 367 |
| General Merchandise | — | — |
| Food | 28 721 | 7 257 |
| Tobacco Products and Drugs | 5 035 | 150 |
| Apparel and Dry Goods | 3 242 | 1 669 |
| Household Furniture and Furnishings | 1 952 | 612 |
| Motor Vehicles and Accessories | 13 301 | 576 |
| Electrical Machinery, Equipment | 12 330 | 1 615 |
| Farm Machinery | 14 933 | 99 |
| Machinery and Equipment | 15 767 | 518 |
| Hardware, Plumbing, Heating Equipment | 5 000 | 1 575 |
| Lumber and Building Materials | 12 384 | 910 |
| Scrap and Waste Metals | — | 18 |
| Wholesalers, n.e.s. | 16 787 | 2 054 |
| Total All Trades | 180 162 | 33 600 |
| Percentage of Wholesale Trade | 84.2% | 15.8% |

*Source*: Statistics Canada, *Canada Year Book 1988*, Ottawa: Ministry of Supply and Services Canada, 1987, Cat. No. 11-402E/1987, p. 17–21. Adapted with the permission of the Minister of Supply and Services Canada, 1990.

**FIGURE 13.2**   Types of Wholesalers

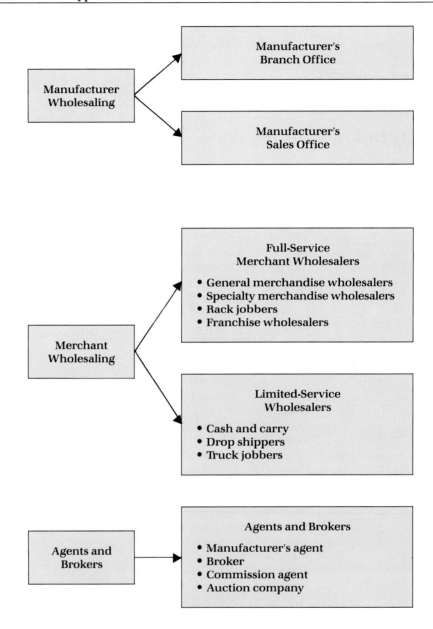

## Manufacturer Wholesaling

manufacturer
wholesaling

In the case of **manufacturer wholesaling**, the producer undertakes the wholesaling function because the firm feels that it can reach customers (retailers and organizational customers) effectively and efficiently through direct contact. Examples of such firms include auto-makers (e.g., General Motors, Ford, and Chrysler) that ship cars and trucks directly to their own dealers; technology-based customers such as IBM and Xerox, which may ship directly to other organizational customers; and snack-food manufacturers such as Hostess Foods and Frito-Lay, which use their own delivery trucks to ship directly to retailers. In each case, the manufacturer stores the merchandise itself and delivers it directly to the customer. Auto-makers store product at the point of manufacture or at designated regional locations and ship it directly to dealers by truck transport, by rail transport, or by some combination of the two modes. IBM and Xerox have the option of either selling their products directly to organizational customers or selling through dealer networks. For food items prone to damage and spoilage, manufacturers find it economical to deliver to local market customers directly. Such deliveries are often done on a daily basis to high-volume customers, to ensure the food remains fresh.

Manufacturers often conduct wholesaling activities through a branch office or a sales office. Let's distinguish them from one another.

1. *Branch Office*  This office usually includes a warehouse facility from which goods are delivered to customers in a specified geographic area. For example, the Prairie region may be served by a branch office of a national company.

2. *Sales Office*  This office is usually located near the customers, but it does not carry inventory. A sales office accepts orders that are processed elsewhere (e.g., a branch office or regional warehouse). In Canada, it is quite common for a manufacturer like Procter & Gamble or General Mills to have centralized production and warehousing facilities and regional sales offices in key areas such as the Atlantic Provinces, Quebec, Ontario, the Prairies, and British Columbia.

## Merchant Wholesaling

Merchant wholesalers perform the traditional functions of wholesaling. They buy goods and take both title to and possession of them, then resell them to other customers in the channel. The two classifications of merchant wholesalers are full-service wholesalers and limited-service wholesalers. Each of these classifications encompasses several variations. The difference between the two classifications lies in the number and extent of services each provides.

### Full-Service Merchant Wholesalers

**full-service merchant wholesaler**

**Full-service merchant wholesalers** assemble an assortment of products in a central warehouse and offer their customers a full range of services, including delivery, storage, credit, and support in merchandising and promotion and in research and planning. Full-service merchant wholesalers, who work closely with the manufacturers they represent, are common in certain industries: pharmaceuticals, grocery products, tobacco, and hardware supplies. There are many varieties of full-service merchant wholesalers.

### General Merchandise Wholesalers

**general-merchandise wholesaler**

A **general-merchandise wholesaler** carries a full line or wide assortment of merchandise that serves virtually all of its customers' needs. Such wholesalers can be found in the automotive and electrical businesses and in those dealing with plumbing and hardware supplies.

### Specialty Merchandise Wholesalers

specialty-merchandise
wholesaler

A **specialty-merchandise wholesaler** carries a limited number or a narrow line of products, but offers an extensive assortment within these lines (i.e., a wide selection of colours, sizes, features, and price ranges). Specialty wholesaling, for instance, is used in the frozen-food, health-food and seafood industries. The storage and distribution capability of the frozen-food wholesaler would, of course, be quite different from that of a packaged-goods food wholesaler.

### Rack Jobber

rack jobber

**Rack jobbers** are responsible for stocking merchandise-display racks, which they own and which display products they carry. Rack jobbers typically supply non-food items to the supermarket trade, such as health and beauty aids, cosmetics, magazines, and stationary supplies. Rack jobbers sell on a consignment basis; that is, the retailer pays the jobber after the items are sold, and the jobber takes back unsold merchandise.

### Franchise Wholesalers

franchise wholesaling

In **franchise wholesaling**, or wholesale-sponsored voluntary chains, retailers affiliate with an existing wholesaling operation and agree to purchase merchandise through them. The operation of the affiliates is standardized in accordance with a legal agreement: the franchises operate under a certain name, use the same purchasing system, have similar store designs, and advertise cooperatively. Home Hardware, Pro Hardware, IGA Food Markets, IDA Drug stores, Color Your World, and St. Clair Paint and Wallpaper follow a system of franchise wholesaling. The Marketing in Action vignette ''Home Hardware's Billion Dollar Operation'' provides an illustration of such an operation.

## Limited-Service Merchant Wholesalers

limited-service
merchant wholesaler

In contrast to full-service wholesalers, **limited-service merchant wholesalers** are selective about the functions they perform. They exist in three main forms: cash-and-carry outlets, drop shippers, and truck distributors.

### Cash-and-Carry Outlets

cash-and-carry
outlet

In a cash-and-carry operation, the customer comes to the wholesaler to purchase small quantities of goods. A **cash-and-carry outlet** serves small independent retailers such as convenience stores, corner grocery stores, and hardware stores. These establishments do not provide credit, delivery, promotion support, or selling assistance. Industries in which cash-and-carries are common include the industries for grocery products, automobile supplies, electrical supplies, and construction materials.

### Drop Shippers

drop shipper

A **drop shipper** purchases goods from manufacturers but does not take possession of them. It buys the item and leaves it with the manufacturer. Then it contacts

---

### 〉〉〉〉 *MARKETING IN ACTION*

#### *HOME HARDWARE'S BILLION DOLLAR OPERATION*

Home Hardware, a billion dollar operation, has its roots in the tiny village of St. Jacobs, Ontario, a Mennonite farming community with a population of 450. Started by Walter Hachborn as Hollinger's Hardware store, the business has grown to over one thousand stores coast to coast in Canada. In his travels to the United States in search of new products and supplies, Walter noticed that the trend among independent stores was to band together in buying and marketing groups to take advantage of economies of scale.

In 1963, he proposed that such a relationship be established among 122 independent hardware-store owners in Ontario who were buying merchandise from Hollinger's wholesale division. In 1964, 108 dealers bought the operation, named Hachborn president, and emerged under the new name of Home Hardware.

There are 922 owners of 977 stores, in every province and territory in Canada. Now famous for their slogan, "Home Hardware — Home of the Handyman", the company has a one-million-square-foot (92 903 m²) computer-controlled warehouse that stores the over 30 000 items sold through Home Hardware every year. A fleet of 350 tractor-trailer trucks delivers merchandise from the warehouse to the retail stores.

The central warehouse computer is linked by satellite to distribution centers in Nova Scotia and

*Home Hardware's central distribution center in St. Jacob's, Ontario*

Alberta, which send in a continuous flow of orders. With the advances in computer technology, the firm is planning satellite communications with individual stores in the future.

Adapted from Pat Brennan, "Hardware has 1 000 stores but it stays close to home", *Toronto Star*, August 8, 1988, p.B6.

---

customers and puts together carload quantities that can be delivered. Although drop shippers arrange direct shipment from the supplier to the user (usually an organization), they do not offer any promotional assistance to their customers. Drop shippers are prevalent among the raw-materials (e.g., coal and iron ore), and building-materials (e.g., lumber and related building supplies) industries.

#### *Truck Jobbers*

**truck jobber**

A **truck jobber** is a specialty wholesaler operating mainly in the food distribution industry. The jobber distributes well-known brands of semi-perishable goods and perishable goods such as candies, tobacco products, potato chips, and dairy products. Voortman Cookies delivers fresh product to its retail customers by means of a local delivery truck jobber. This wholesaler may call on an account several times a week to ensure that fresh products are available. A truck jobber sells and delivers merchandise during the same sales call, supplying the retailer with fresh product on short notice. Since the orders tend to be small, the costs to truck jobbers are high; consequently, the prices retailers pay for the items are high. The store weighs these high costs against the convenience of instant delivery when deciding whether and how much to purchase.

## Agents and Brokers

Agents and brokers provide a variety of wholesaling functions but do not take title to the goods that are sold. They represent the seller in the transaction and work for commissions paid by the selling organization. The main difference between an agent and a broker is in the relationship with the seller. An agent is more likely to be used on a permanent basis whereas a broker is usually used on a temporary basis. The main types of agents and brokers are manufacturers' agents, brokers, commission merchants, and auction companies.

### Manufacturers' Agents

**manufacturers' agent**

A **manufacturers' agent** carries and sells similar products for non-competing manufacturers in an exclusive territory. Such agents are commonly associated with particular industries: machinery, electronics, automotive parts, clothing, and food. They also carry and sell complementary goods to wholesalers and dealers in these industries, so they can stock a complete line of products for their market area. The commission arrangements for these wholesalers are attractive to small manufacturers, who could not afford the cost of directly contacting the same customers themselves. The agents' primary task is selling, and they do so based on pricing policies established by the manufacturers they represent.

### Brokers

**broker**

A **broker** plays a key role in the negotiations between buyers and sellers. Depending on the industry and the nature of the selling situation, the broker's relationship with the supply organization can be permanent or temporary. For example, food brokers who represent suppliers (usually small manufacturers) to the wholesale and retail food trade generally have long-term relationships. One reason they can maintain the relationships is that they represent manufacturers of non-competing products to avoid conflict of interest. Food brokers are paid a commission, and their agreement with the supplier is usually outlined in a contract that clearly defines the length and terms of the arrangement. A commission rate of 5 percent is common in the food industry.

Temporary relationships are commonly found in the real estate industry, where brokers are used for individual transactions. The broker may represent many different vendors (sellers) at any one time, but the relationship with each one ends when the sales transaction is complete. A commission rate of 6 percent of sales is common in real estate transactions, though this rate is subject to negotiations between the seller and the broker.

### Commission Merchants

commission merchant

A **commission merchant** works with small manufacturers or suppliers that require representation to reach customers in centralized markets. The merchant receives and sells goods on consignment. Typically, the supplier lacks marketing resources, so the commission merchant arranges shipment of the product to a market, completes the sale, and returns the collected funds less the commission earned to the supplier. Dairy and produce farmers rely on merchants to sell their products in urban markets, since the farmer cannot accompany each shipment of goods to the city. In this sort of market, the product is sold at the market price, which is based on supply and demand at the time of sale.

### Auction Companies

auction company

An **auction company** brings buyers and sellers together at a central location to complete a transaction. The supply and demand for the merchandise at auction time determines the selling price. Auctions play a key role in markets such as those for livestock, tobacco, and used automobiles. Auction companies are usually paid a flat fee or a commission for the service provided.

## >>>> Retailing and Its Functions

retailing

**Retailing** refers to those activities involved in the sale of goods and services to final consumers for personal, family, or household use. It is the last stage in the channel of distribution. As of 1985, the value of the Canadian retail market amounted to $129.4 billion. On a provincial basis, and because of demographic predominance, Ontario was the largest retail trade market with 38 percent of retail sales in 1985, followed by Quebec at 24.6 percent, and British Columbia at 11.1 percent (see figure 13.3).[3]

**FIGURE 13.3**    Distribution of Retail Trade by Province, 1985

|  | Percentage of Canada |
|---|---|
| Newfoundland | 1.7% |
| Prince Edward Island | 0.4 |
| Nova Scotia | 3.5 |
| New Brunswick | 2.5 |
| Quebec | 24.6 |
| Ontario | 37.9 |
| Manitoba | 4.0 |
| Saskatchewan | 3.6 |
| Alberta | 10.4 |
| British Columbia | 11.1 |
| Canada | 100.0 |

*Source*: Adapted from Statistics Canada, *Canada Year Book 1988*, Ottawa: Ministry of Supply and Services Canada, 1987, Cat. No. 11:402E/1987, p. 17-2. Adapted with the permission of the Minister of Supply and Services Canada, 1990.

**FIGURE 13.4   The Functions of a Retailer**

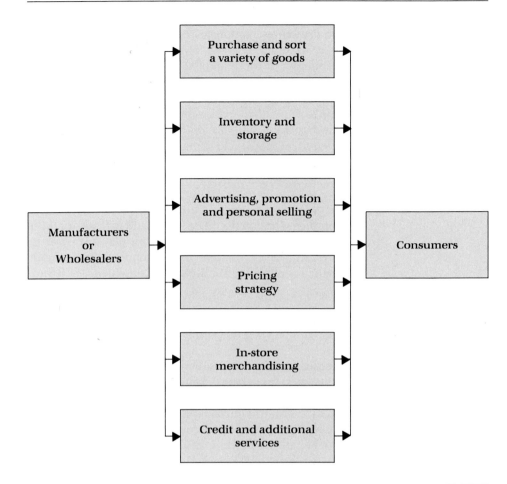

Generally, a retailer performs four main functions (see figure 13.4)

1. Retailers are part of the sorting process: the store buys an assortment of goods and services from a variety of suppliers and offers them for sale.
2. They provide information to consumers through advertising, promotion, and personal selling.
3. They store merchandise, establish retail selling prices, and place items on the sales floor.
4. They complete a transaction by offering credit terms, convenient hours and store locations, and other services such as credit-purchasing and delivery.

Much as he or she has a choice among products, a consumer usually has a number of retailers to choose from when shopping. A retail store is chosen on the basis of factors such as

1. Store image
2. Hours of operation

3. Availability of parking
4. Quality of products carried
5. Helpfulness of sales staff
6. Additional services offered
7. Store location
8. Store layout and facilities
9. Customer service policies

**retailing mix**

In planning a strategy, retailers consider the factors listed above and develop a **retailing mix**, which is much like the marketing mix in that its goal is to attract customers to the store. Customers shop at certain stores as a result of both rational and irrational motivations, and retailers look at both types when developing their strategies. For example, Holt-Renfrew and Creeds carry the latest in designer fashion and merchandise, and their extremely high prices appeal to the woman who seeks status and prestige. These are stores where successful, monied people shop. In contrast, a discount department store such as Zellers or K-Mart uses low price as their primary marketing strategy. At Zellers, the low-price themes are backed by price guarantees; it promises to match any regular or advertised sale price in Canada, employing the phrase "the law of prices" to promote its policy. The policy grew from a concept that was started and successfully implemented in Zellers' toy department.[4] These two examples present a contrast in retailing strategy. Stores such as Creeds and Holt-Renfrew appeal to the "classes", while stores like Zellers, Woolco and K-Mart appeal to the "masses".

# 〉〉〉〉 *Types of Retailers*

Canadian retailers are classified into three primary groups according to size, form of ownership, strategy mix, and non-store operations. It is possible for a store to fit into several of these classifications. Mac's, 7-Eleven, and Circle K are convenience stores, chain stores, and franchise stores. The Bay is a chain store and a department store. The different types of stores have different characteristics, and, therefore, diverse marketing strategies.

## Size

In Canada, most retailers are small; a high percentage of establishments do less than $1 million in annual sales. In contrast, a relatively few large chains have a significant influence on retail sales. The largest three categories of retail trade are motor vehicles ($26 billion or 20.1 percent of total retail trade), combination food stores ($23 billion or 18.4 percent), and department stores ($12 billion or 9.3 percent).[5] George Weston Limited, which includes Loblaws, Real Atlantic Superstores, and Real Canadian Superstores, and other companies such as Provigo, Steinbergs, The Oshawa Group (Food City and IGA) and Safeway dominate the food-distribution industry. Hudson's

FIGURE 13.5    Canada's Top Ten Retailers

| Rank | Company | Sales (in thousands) |
|------|---------|----------------------|
| 1 | George Weston Limited | $10 831.2 |
| 2 | Provigo | 7 387.5 |
| 3 | Hudson's Bay Company | 4 671.7 |
| 4 | Steinberg Inc. | 4 584.6 |
| 5 | Sears Canada Inc. | 4 327.2 |
| 6 | Oshawa Group | 4 274.5 |
| 7 | Canada Safeway | 4 041.6 |
| 8 | Canadian Tire | 2 640.7 |
| 9 | Metro Richelieu | 2 200.2 |
| 10 | A & P | 2 198.3 |

*Source*: "Merchandising", *The Financial Post 500*, Summer 1989, p. 28.

Bay, which owns The Bay, Zellers and Simpsons, dominates in department-store merchandising, and Canadian Tire dominates automotive-supplies and general-merchandise retailing. All of these companies are established leaders in their respective areas of retailing (see figure 13.5).

# Ownership

The three most prevalent forms of ownership are chain stores, independent retailers, and retail franchises.

### Retail Chain Stores

retail chain store

A **retail chain store** is an organization operating four or more retail stores in the same kind of business under the same legal ownership. Chain stores are a dominant and growing presence in the Canadian retail marketplace. Although their domination varies from one product to another, they tend to dominate in supermarkets, general merchandise stores, variety stores, clothing and retail shoe stores (see figure 13.6). As of 1985, the value of retail trade through chain stores amounted to $54 billion or 42 percent of retail sales. Examples of large chain store operations include Bowrings, Bata, The Brick, Shoppers Drug Mart, Peoples Jewellers, Woolworth's and the Foot Locker.

### Independent Retail Stores

independent retailer

An **independent retailer** is a retailer that operates one to three stores, even if the stores are affiliated with a large retail organization. Independent retailing is dominant among domestic- and imported-car dealers, pharmacies, automotive-parts

**FIGURE 13.6**   Chain Stores: Share of Market by Type of Business, 1985

|  | Share |
|---|---|
| Combination Stores (Meat and Grocery) | 64.5% |
| Grocery, Confectionery, Sundry Stores | 30.4 |
| Department Stores | 100.0 |
| General Merchandise Stores | 78.7 |
| General Stores | 41.8 |
| Variety Stores | 87.2 |
| Automotive Parts | 7.7 |
| Men's Clothing | 53.3 |
| Family Clothing | 67.1 |
| Specialty Shoe Stores | 52.7 |
| Household Furniture | 27.7 |
| Furniture, Television, Appliances | 50.1 |
| Pharmacies | 29.1 |
| Books and Stationery Stores | 57.9 |
| Sporting Goods | 15.8 |

*Source*: Statistics Canada, *Canada Year Book 1988*, Ottawa: Ministry of Supply and Services Canada, 1987, Cat. No. 11-402E/1987, p. 17-14. Adapted with the permission of the Minister of Supply and Services Canada, 1990.

dealers and locally owned food stores. Total sales among independent retailers in 1985 were $75.1 billion or 58 percent of the total retail trade in Canada.[6]

Independent retailers contrast greatly with chain stores. To enter the independent retailing business is relatively easy, since many kinds of retailing require low initial investments and little technical knowledge. Because it is easy to get started, many retailers fail, particularly in the first year of operation, often as a result of poor management skills and inadequate financial resources. Competing with large chains is difficult. The chain store is a large-scale operation, and because it buys in large quantities it can offer customers lower prices than the independent retailer can (although chains do not always choose to offer low prices). The risk of financial loss is also spread across many stores in a chain operation; successful stores compensate for the unsuccessful. The Marketing in Action vignette "Action in Superstore Videos" provides an illustration of competition between chains and independent retailers.

### *Retail Franchising*

retail franchise

A **retail franchise** is a contractual agreement between a franchiser — a manufacturer, wholesaler or service sponsor — and a franchisee — the retailer. In a franchising arrangement, the franchisee agrees to conduct business under a certain name and to subscribe to a certain set of rules and business practices. For example, the franchiser may require that certain suppliers be used, depending on whether an agreement has been established between the franchiser and the supplier; the franchiser requires that the product be prepared a certain way; and management practices and accounting systems must be consistent among all franchises. The typical franchise arrangement involves an initial franchise fee and a percentage of sales being returned to the

>>>> *MARKETING IN ACTION*

*ACTION IN SUPERSTORE VIDEOS*

*Major Video is one of the new mass-merchandise video retailers now dominating the market*

Major Video Canada, Inc.

The latest trend in video retailing is the shift to superstores that stock anywhere from 5 000 to 10 000 titles. The industry is going through the growing pains associated with maturity. The small, mom-and-pop (i.e., independent) operators that dominated in the early mid-eighties are gradually diasappearing. The result is a battle between the mass merchandise superstore and the niche-marketing independent.

The Canadian video market is estimated to be worth $1 billion, and market surveys show that in 1989, 62 percent of households owned a VCR, while in 1986 only 31 percent owned one. Each household rents an average of two films a week.

Retailers such as Jumbo Video, Rogers Video, Giant Video, Major Video, and Movie Movie are now dominating the rental market. According to Jim Lemgre, a Rogers vice-president of operations, the move to superstores is a response to the consumers' demand for greater selection. Movie Movie's strategy confirms this; it is voluntarily closing all the small stores within an area and replacing them with one large superstore.

Independent operators counter the mass market approach by stressing customer service. The independents acknowledge that the superstore grabs the customer's attention, but add that the expanded selection is comprised primarily of B-movies, a fact which leaves consumers unsatisfied. Their "service with a smile" approach is a contrast to the poor, or rather impersonalized, service offered by superstores.

Also affecting the entire video industry are automated video vending machines in grocery stores. They now account for 6 percent of the market and are expected to reach 20 percent by 1995. The growth of vending machines and the marketing strength of the superstores leave the struggling independents in a perilous position.

Adapted from Mark Evans, "Big getting beautiful in video world", *Financial Post*, March 27, 1989. p.20.

franchiser. Franchisees also contribute to a pool of advertising funds, which is spent by the franchiser in markets where franchises exist (see figure 13.7).

The benefits of owning and operating a franchise are similar to those associated with being part of a large chain. Franchises have a great buying capability, and each franchisee benefits from the image of the total franchise system. If the franchise is a success in the marketplace, the new franchisee has instant recognition and may capitalize on that recognition and reputation. However, becoming part of a franchis-

**FIGURE 13.7** Examples of Franchise Agreements in Canada

| Franchise | Parent Company | Franchise Fee | Start up Costs | Royalty Fee | Advertising Fee |
|---|---|---|---|---|---|
| Goodyear Tire Centre | Goodyear Canada Inc. | none | $ 200 000 | 3% | $900–2 000/mo. |
| Marlin Travel | The Marlin Travel Group Inc. | $ 5 000 | 3 000–5 000 | 0.75 | 0.5% |
| Swiss Chalet | Cara Operations Limited | 75 000 | 2 000 000 | 5 | 5% |
| Tim Horton Donuts | Tim Donut Ltd. | 15 000 | 200 000 | 3 | 4% |
| Pizza Pizza | Pizza Pizza Ltd. | 20 000 | 170 000 | 6 | 6% |

*Source*: Adapted from "Canada's Top 75 Franchises", *Financial Times*, 1988.

ing concept, especially a new one, is a risky venture, much like opening an independent small business. Very often a large initial investment is required, and there is little scope for innovation for the franchisee. Figure 13.8 presents a list of Canada's top five franchises.

In Canada, franchises can be found in retailing, food operations, personal services, automotive operations, business services, and miscellaneous operations. Some of the more common names in Canadian franchising include McDonald's, Burger King, Harvey's, Dairy Queen, MMMarvellous MMMuffins, Tim Horton Donuts, Boston Pizza, First Choice Haircutters, Marks Work Wearhouse, Color Your World, and Hertz Rent-A-Car.

In the late 1980s, some new franchising trends emerged in Canada. Retail chains such as Consumers Distributing started converting existing outlets to franchises. This "branchising" process allows Consumers Distributing to increase productivity and sales by getting more entrepreneurial commitment from managers. It also raises capital to fuel growth. In the food service industry, a trend known as "piggybacking" started. In this system two different franchises are located under the same roof. Common locations have been in highway restaurants where combinations such as Kentucky Fried Chicken and Tim Horton's, or Wendy's and Tim Horton's appeared.[7]

**FIGURE 13.8** Canada's Top Five Franchises, 1988

| Rank | Franchise | Gross Revenue (in thousands) | Average Sales Location (in thousands) | Parent | Type of Business |
|---|---|---|---|---|---|
| 1 | Shoppers Drug Mart | $2 000 000 | $3 500 | Imasco Ltd. | Pharmacy |
| 2 | McDonald's | 1 500 000 | 2 800 | McDonald's Restaurants of Canada Limited | Fast Food |
| 3 | Beaver Lumber | 902 000 | 4 580 | Molson Companies Limited | Building Materials |
| 4 | Goodyear Tire Centre | 695 534 | n/a | Goodyear Canada Inc. | Auto Service |
| 5 | Kentucky Fried Chicken | 500 000 | 652 | Pepsi Cola Canada Limited | Fast Food |

*Source*: Adapted from Financial Times of Canada Limited, 1988.

# Strategy Mix

Retail stores classified by strategy mix or by type of operation include convenience stores, supermarkets, superstores or hypermarkets, specialty stores, variety stores, department stores, discount department stores, and catalogue showrooms (see figure 13.9).

### Convenience Stores

convenience store

A **convenience store** is a food and general merchandise store situated in busy areas of communities selling limited numbers of lines over long hours. Frequently, convenience stores operate on a 24-hour basis. Consumers use these stores frequently to purchase snack foods, reading materials, and to replace needed goods quickly at odd hours. Popular items carried by convenience stores include milk, bread, soft-drink beverages, and tobacco products. Convenience store operations in Canada include Mac's (781 stores), Becker's (778), 7-Eleven (550), Bonisoir (233), Provi-Soir (230), Kwik Way (210), and Irving Stores (112).[8]

**FIGURE 13.9**   Stores by Type of Operation

| Type of Store | Description | Example |
|---|---|---|
| Convenience | Small food-oriented stores in local communities | Mac's, 7-Eleven, Bonisoir |
| Supermarket | Departmentalized food stores (dairy, meat, produce, frozen, and packaged food) | Safeway, Sobey's, Miracle Mart |
| Discount Supermarket | Limited-line supermarket offering fewer services and lower prices | Valdi, Save-On, No Frills |
| Superstores | Diversified supermarkets carrying a broad range of products | SuperCentres, Real Atlantic Food Stores |
| Specialty Stores | Stores selling a single line or limited line of merchandise | Bretton's, Radio Shack, A&A Records, Bata Shoes |
| Variety Stores | Stores carrying a wide range of staple merchandise | Bi-Way, Kresges |
| Department Stores | General-line retailers offering a variety of products in many price ranges | The Bay, Eaton's Woodwards |
| Discount Department Stores | Stores carrying a full line of products at popular prices (fewer services than department stores) | Woolco, K-Mart, Zellers, Towers |
| Catalogue Showroom | Discount retailing operation where customers buy from a catalogue | Consumers Distributing |

## Supermarkets

supermarket

A **supermarket** is a departmentalized food store selling packaged grocery products, produce, dairy, meat, frozen food, and general merchandise. Supermarkets offer consumers low prices (compared to convenience stores), for they are usually part of large chain-store operations where large volume buying at low prices is common. Supermarkets offer consumers the convenience of one-stop shopping as a result of the large number of lines they carry and their convenient locations. Some major Canadian supermarkets include Safeway, Loblaws, A&P, Steinberg, Provigo, and Sobey's.

Supermarket marketing has changed significantly in the past decade to meet the needs of consumers who want more convenience, fresher merchandise, and lower prices than before. To remain competitive and still generate profits, many of the established chains have cut prices by reducing services, opening no-frills stores, and providing generic brands. Chain-stores have also expanded the size of their stores and their product assortment. Superstores were created to cater to both the food and the non-food needs of consumers. These trends towards discount supermarkets and superstores are the marks of supermarket operations today.

## Discount Supermarkets

discount supermarket

A **discount supermarket** or warehouse store, as it is often referred to, is a type of supermarket that offers limited lines of merchandise, a limited assortment of brands (less selection), few services, low margins, and low prices. The products are usually displayed in their shipping cartons and stacked on heavy steel shelving units. Such a "no frills" concept is very attractive to the price-conscious food shopper. These stores also sell national brands, thereby ensuring quality. The labour saved by the no-frills strategy and by the consumer's buying in bulk helps lower prices. Examples of discount supermarkets include Save Easy Warehouse Foods in the Maritimes, Loblaws Warehouse stores and No Frills (also a Loblaws operation) in central Canada, Econo-Mart in the Prairies, and Save-On Foods in British Columbia.

## Superstores

superstore

A **superstore** is a diversified supermarket that sells a broad range of food and non-food items. A superstore is much like a supermarket, but it caters to an expanded list of needs. In addition to a full line of traditional supermarket items, the superstore carries merchandise such as garden supplies, hardware items, clothing, and household appliances. George Weston Limited owns and operates superstores called SuperCentres, Real Canadian Superstores, and Real Atlantic Superstores.

The concept of the superstore originated in France where it is called a *hypermarché* (hypermarket). The first hypermarket or superstore in Canada opened in suburban Montreal in the mid 1970s and was owned and operated by Oshawa Group Limited of Ontario. Such operations are an attempt to combine under one roof the product mixes of food stores with those of department stores, a strategy suited for one-stop shopping. The superstore is usually twice the size of the traditional supermarket and does three times the normal volume of sales. Superstores generate profits by combining higher margin non-food items with lower margin food items. For a

## ⟩⟩⟩ *MARKETING IN ACTION*

### *HYPERMARKET, OR JUST PLAIN HYPE?*

Imagine shopping in a store that occupies the space of six or seven football fields. Anyone for exercise? The latest invasion of North America has occurred in retailing, where a French company, Carrefour, is in the process of establishing hypermarkets, the first of which opened in Philadelphia, Pa.

What is a hypermarket? A hypermarket is an extremely large store carrying a selection of merchandise that includes groceries, apparel, and general merchandise. While only a few hypermarkets are in operation, their potential impact could change the ways consumers shop for everything from soup to television sets. Certainly, hypermarkets will throw a scare into established department stores and discount department stores. Statistics from the United States reveal that volume in a hypermarket is twice that of a large discount department store such as K-Mart.

Hypermarkets were created by French merchants following World War II, during a period in which there was a need to build a new and efficient distribution system in France. Now, with the European market saturated, French companies like Carrefour and Auchan have expanded to North America. Hypermarkets battle department stores, discount department stores, and grocery superstores for customer allegiance, combining the best elements of each under one roof. Among the unique features of a hypermarket are high ceilings with shelves that do not rise above eight feet, a feature which gives the store a vast, see-it-all look. There are fifty to sixty checkout lanes

in the average hypermarket, a testament to its sales potential.

The strategy of the hypermarket is to carry products that represent 80 percent of the consumers' regular needs and to avoid slow-moving items in all product categories. Consequently, a hypermarket concentrates on popular brands and avoids carrying product lines that have a low turnover rate. Hypermarkets give the impression that they are discount stores, but they are not. In fact, the merchandise they carry is tailored more to middle- and upper-income targets. For example, they carry brand-name shirts (e.g., Arrow) and Levi jeans, but price them slightly lower than do their competitors.

The primary drawing card of a hypermarket is the bargain price of food. Food occupies about 40 percent of the space but generates 60 percent of revenue and only takes a margin of 10 percent, about half that of an average supermarket. It is estimated that a busy hypermarket attracts 50 000 customers a week, almost triple the traffic of a supermarket. The reaction of competitors in the U.S. has been fast. Established supermarkets are opening fewer, but much larger, stores. Discount department stores like K-Mart are doubling the size of their stores in anticipation of the bigger-is-better trend — the trend that is shaping the face of retailing.

Adapted from Bill Saporito, "Retailers fly into hyperspace", *Fortune*, October 24, 1988, pp. 148.

*In the average hypermarket there are 50 to 60 lanes, and the combination of high ceilings and low shelves gives customers the sense of having a vast, "see-it-all" perspective*

Carrefour

perspective on superstores, see the Marketing in Action vignette "Hypermarket, or Just Plain Hype?"

### Specialty Stores

specialty store

A **specialty store** is a store that sells a single line or limited line of merchandise. Specialty stores appeal to a narrow target market by offering a unique product assortment, a well-trained sales staff, and good customer service. They appear, for example, in the retailing of leather goods, fashion apparel, leisure sportswear and equipment, electronics, and toys. Sports World, Foot Locker, and Lady Foot Locker sell training shoes and sports clothing while Radio Shack, Canary Island, Toys "R" Us, Elk's, and Lewis Craft carry other specialized lines. Bretton's is a specialty clothing chain offering the latest men's, women's, and children's fashions for upscale consumer segments. Their stores have merchandise organized in departments much like a department store, but on a smaller scale.

### Variety Store

variety store

A **variety store** is a store that handles a wide range of staple merchandise (i.e., products that are bought often and routinely, without much effort) at low or popular prices. These stores are often referred to as "dime" stores because of the low-priced merchandise they originally offered. Lines carried include housewares, light hardware, confectionery products, clothing, stationery, and giftware. Some of the large variety store operations in Canada are chains: F.W. Woolworth, Kresge's, Bi-Way, Stedman's, and Metropolitan.

### Department Stores

department store

A **department store** is a large general-product-line retailer that sells a wide variety of merchandise in a variety of price ranges. Department stores are usually organized into departments for the purposes of buying, promotion, service, and control. They carry products from furniture to fashion apparel, sporting goods, dry goods, and jewellery.

A department store serves a broad range of people and usually makes available an extensive list of customer services such as credit shopping, layaway plans, delivery, installations, and alterations. Typically, department stores are located in suburban and regional shopping malls, where they function as the anchor stores. An anchor store is usually located at the end of pedestrian traffic routes in indoor malls, hence the reference to anchor. Their presence in malls in downtown or suburban locations is a major drawing card from which all other merchants in the mall benefit. Many Canadian department stores belong to chains, the largest of which is Hudson's Bay Limited, which owns The Bay, Simpsons, and Zellers. Woodward's in British Columbia, and Ogilvy's and Robinson's in Ontario are other examples of regional department store chains.

### Discount Department Stores

discount department store

A **discount department store** is a store that carries a full line of merchandise at low prices while offering consumers limited customer service. These stores stock lines similar to those found in department stores. What distinguishes a department store from a discount department store is price and service. Prices of well-known national brands are lower in discount department stores, while services are fewer. A

## >>>> *MARKETING IN ACTION*

### *MERGERS AND CONVERSIONS: A RETAILING TREND*

As the retailing business progresses through the 1990s, retailers will become leaner and more tightly controlled, better equipped to respond quickly to consumer needs and market changes. Retailing in the eighties underwent widespread mergers, buyouts, and streamlining, and this trend is expected to continue in the nineties. Perhaps the biggest example of merger mania was Robert Campeau's much-publicized takeover of the Federated Stores and Allied Department Store chains and their retailing subsidiaries in the United States in 1988.

Following are some other trends that will affect retailing in the nineties:

1. Fewer corporations will own a larger number of stores.

2. Store sizes will decrease, except in the case of hypermarkets.

3. Small regional chains will face even stiffer competition from national chains.

4. Specialty stores will continue to target markets but will not focus exclusively on a specific trend or lifestyle. Rapid change presents too much financial risk.

5. Department stores, if corporately controlled, will merge or be grouped together, because sharing operations improves efficiency.

The merging of department stores is already occurring in Canada. In 1986, Hudson's Bay converted eight Montreal and Toronto Simpsons stores to Bay stores. Its retailing operations were a collective source of financial woe for Hudson's Bay in the 1980s. In 1988, all remaining Simpsons stores in Montreal were converted to Bay stores. These moves were an attempt to correct an ailing financial situation, since Simpsons was not a profitable unit of the company.

*One of the few remaining Simpsons stores in the Toronto area*

The conversion of Simpsons stores to Bay stores is part of an overall marketing strategy. In terms of market segmentation, the Simpsons stores that remain in the Toronto area only appeal to fashion-conscious, upscale consumers. The Bay is targeted at middle-income earners and Zellers appeals to discount shoppers. The store mix of Hudson's Bay reaches a broad cross-section of the Canadian population.

Adapted from "Lessons of the '80s to make retailers leaner for the '90s", *Marketing News*, May 22, 1989, p.37.

discount department store generally operates on a self-serve basis, providing few floor staff for personal assistance. Its services tend to be restricted to cheque cashing and credit purchases.

Discount department stores attract the price-conscious segment of the market. The store atmosphere is suggestive of the prices offered (e.g., bright fluorescent lighting, loud speakers, and large signs announcing sales). The image presented is a "discount" image. Customers concerned with upscale image and status do not usually shop in this type of store. But since the consumer market today is increasingly worried about price, these stores have been very successful and have expanded rapidly in the past decade. Retailers in this category include Zellers, Woolco, and K-Mart. Zellers is the most profitable retailing operation in The Hudson's Bay group of stores. The Marketing in Action vignette "Mergers and Conversions: A Retailing Trend" describes some of the happenings within the Hudson's Bay retailing empire.

### Catalogue Showroom

**catalogue showroom**

A **catalogue showroom** is a form of advertising often used in discount retailing whereby a store lists its merchandise in a catalogue and displays selected lines of merchandise in a showroom where customers come to place their orders. At the showroom, the consumer selects items from the catalogue, fills in an order form, processes the order through a central cash register, and waits for the item to be retrieved from a backroom warehouse. The benefit of catalogue retailing is that it offers low prices on a limited selection of brand-name merchandise in product categories such as jewellery, small household appliances, household furnishings, sporting goods, toys, and games. To keep prices down, it generally only offers the customer credit and merchandise-return services. Consumers Distributing is the largest catalogue showroom operation in Canada.

## Non-store Operations

This form of retailing does not use traditional store facilities. The traditional retailer is bypassed by manufacturers, importers, and wholesalers so that the final consumer is reached directly. Such retailing includes vending machines, direct home retailing, and direct marketing.

### Vending Machines

We do not usually think of a vending machine as a form of retailing, but it is. Vending machines often sell cigarettes, soft drinks, and confectionery products. The machines are usually owned and operated by the retail stores, restaurants, and service stations where they are located. In other arrangements, space in retail locations may be leased by vending machine operators, or the retailer and vending machine operator may strike a deal to share profits in return for the space granted by the retailer.

As of 1984, over seven hundred firms in Canada were operating over 141 000 vending machines, generating $379 million in sales revenue. In 1988, vending machines became a means of distribution for videocassette rentals. The strengths of vending machines are their convenience and 24-hour sales capability.

### Direct Home Retailing

**direct home retailing**

Often referred to as in-home retailing or party-plan selling, **direct home retailing** is the selling of merchandise by personal contact in the home of the customer. Several variations of direct home selling exist, covering a wide variety of product lines from cosmetics to vacuum cleaners, newspapers, and toys. Some of the selling alternatives include:

1. *Cold Canvas* In this case, a salesperson without notice knocks on doors in a neighbourhood in search of customers. Electrolux and other vacuum cleaners, as well as Fuller Brush products, are sold in this manner.

2. *Referral* In this approach, visits with customers are planned. A salesperson secures names of potential customers from satisfied customers and makes an initial contact by telephone to arrange a time for a face-to-face meeting. A company such as Avon operates in this way.

3. *Party* In this situation, one person acts as a host and invites friends to his or her home for a sales demonstration. Tupperware products are the merchandise best-known for being sold on a party-plan basis. Creative Kids, a company selling educational toys, also uses this approach successfully.

The impact of direct home retailing is clear from the sales it generates. In 1985, Canadian households spent $2.5 billion on goods bought through these methods. Sales for major commodities handled by direct sellers include newspapers ($348 million), dairy products ($320 million), books ($245 million), cosmetics and personal care products ($190 million), and household electrical appliances ($180 million).[9]

### Direct Marketing

In the case of direct marketing, a sales message reaches consumers through the media — television, radio, newspaper, and magazine — or consumers are contacted directly by telephone or mail. In delivering merchandise to consumers, the supplier ships them directly (i.e., the normal channel of distribution is bypassed). The operating costs of direct marketing are low for manufacturers, and companies can use it to reach a geographically dispersed consumer market efficiently. With the growing number of two-income families, reaching consumers in person has become increasingly difficult, since householders are often away from the home. In Canada, Sears is probably the largest direct marketing organization, selling goods directly through the Sears Catalogue. Direct marketing is an increasingly important strategy in marketing activity. Chapter 16 discusses it in detail.

## ⟩⟩⟩⟩ *Elements of Retail Planning*

The major considerations in retail planning are site location, atmosphere, merchandise assortment, and merchandise control (see figure 13.10).

### Site Location

Many experts suggest that two factors contribute to the success of a retail operation: location and location! A good location in a high traffic area gets people into a store. Once they are inside, the quality of the product and the service will determine

FIGURE 13.10   Elements of Retail Planning

| Subject | Concerns |
|---|---|
| Site Location | Where to locate (e.g., in the central business district, regional shopping mall, strip mall, or in the inner city or the suburbs) |
| Atmosphere | Physical characteristics required to establish and maintain the store image desired (e.g. store exterior, sign, layout of store, in-store displays) |
| Merchandise Assortment | Determining the breadth and depth of product selection, the relationships between product lines and stock balance |
| Merchandise Control | Implementing controls that measure the correspondence between actual performance and planned performance (e.g., analyzing stock turnover) |

whether and how often the customers return. Various types of shopping location are commonly identified in large and small cities alike: central business districts, secondary shopping districts, neighbourhood shopping districts, strip clusters, freestanding stores, and planned shopping centers.[10]

## Central Business District

The central business district is normally the hub of retailing activity in the heart of the downtown core (i.e., in the main street and busy cross-streets of a centralized area). The area usually contains the major financial, cultural, entertainment and retailing facilities of the city. The retailing store mix in these areas generally consists of department stores, specialty stores, independent stores, and convenience stores.

The growth of suburbia in the sixties and seventies, as people and households moved out of the cities, led to a decrease in downtown store volume, since people preferred to shop where they lived. The late seventies and eighties, however, saw a rejuvenation of the inner city. There was a trend toward downtown redevelopment that involved growth in high-rise apartments and condominiums, and the redevelopment of old neighbourhoods. In many instances, rundown neighbourhoods were refurbished to appeal to a different type of person. Such neighbourhoods attracted an upscale group of people. Retailers also undertook to revitalize their stores through remodelling, while developers built downtown indoor malls to get people to shop there again. The Eaton Centre in Toronto, Rideau Centre in Ottawa, Pacific Centre in Vancouver, and Scotia Square in Halifax, all downtown malls, are now among the busiest shopping centres in their respective markets. The factors that deter people from shopping downtown are traffic congestion and the lack of adequate parking facilities, both factors that retailers cannot control.

## Secondary Shopping Districts

A secondary shopping district is usually bounded by the intersection of two major streets and located beyond the central downtown core but still within the city. These districts usually developed as residential areas and expanded outward from the city core. In Toronto, shopping districts have emerged at key intersections of Yonge Street, the main north-south traffic artery. These intersections contain a combination of developments — office, commercial, and residential — and generally draw most of their customers from those who work or live in the immediate area.

### Neighbourhood Shopping Districts

A neighbourhood district is usually a small cluster of stores that serve the convenience needs of the immediate residential area. Such a shopping district is generally composed of a supermarket, a drug store, a variety store, a dry cleaners, a bank, a hair stylist, and other similar service operations. When the stores are clustered or attached together (i.e., leased from the same building), the collection of storefront operations is referred to as a strip mall.

### Strip Clusters

**strip cluster**

A **strip cluster** usually exists along a major traffic artery. The volume of business is dependent upon the flow of traffic that passes by. The retail operations found in strip clusters include fast food restaurants, motels, car dealerships, and entertainment establishments. Strip clusters are very common on the main routes in or out of cities and towns.

### Free-Standing Store

**free-standing store**

A **free-standing store** is an isolated store usually located on a busy street or highway. The nature of the business often influences the location of such a store. Consumers will travel beyond their immediate area for the products and services these stores provide. Examples include furniture stores and factory outlets, garden supply centers, restaurants, and convenience stores. The problem facing these types of retailers is that they must attract their customers without assistance from other retailers.

### Planned Shopping Malls

**planned shopping mall**

A **planned shopping mall** is a shopping facility that is centrally owned, managed, planned, and operated, and comprised of a balanced mix of retail tenants and parking space for customers. The Campeau Corporation and large real-estate development companies like it own malls throughout Canada. They lease space to a balanced mix of tenants; in other words, the stores that comprise the malls offer a wide range of products and services to the area they serve. The stores in a planned mall complement each other in terms of quality and variety. There are three types of planned shopping malls: regional malls, community malls and neighbourhood malls or plazas.

#### Regional Shopping Mall

This is a large mall containing as many as 100 or more stores and several large department stores. Customers will travel great distances to shop at a regional mall. The stores carry shopping goods and include the established retail specialty chains, such as Fairweather, Atlantic Video, Northern Reflections, Roots, and Shoppers Drug Mart. Department stores usually anchor the mall, as do large supermarkets.

The latest trend in regional malls is the super shopping mall. The opening, in 1981, of the West Edmonton Mall, the world's largest indoor mall, created new meaning for shopping malls. The mall contains 5.2 million square feet (483 098 m²), which is the equivalent of 115 football fields, and includes over 800 stores and services, 110 eating establishments, and five amusement areas, including a wave pool and rides for the children, a hockey rink, and many other attractions.

### Community Shopping Mall

A medium-sized mall that serves an immediate geographic area, a community shopping mall contains convenience goods as well as shopping goods operations. The typical store mix includes a grocery store, a drug store, a variety of specialty shops, and a discount department store such as Towers or Woolco.

### Neighbourhood Shopping Mall

The neighbourhood shopping mall is the "strip mall" referred to earlier. The mall or plaza contains a row or strip of stores, mainly selling convenience items and services. It typically houses a drug store, a hardware store, a variety store, a bake shop, a hair stylist, and a convenience store. The anchor store is usually a small grocery store or a large drug store.

## Atmosphere

atmosphere

**Atmosphere** in retailing refers to the physical characteristics of a retail store or of a group of stores that are used to develop an image and attract customers.[11] The image of a store has an impact on the type of customer that shops there, so retailers give their stores looks that will attract the sort of patrons they want. The appropriate image is created by the exterior appearance, interior appearance, store layout, and the interior merchandising and display practices.

1. The exterior appearance encompasses signage (store sign and lighting), store visibility, the ease with which the store can be entered, and the display window.
2. The interior appearance consists of lighting, fixtures, aisle width, colours, dressing facilities, dress code for the sales staff, and cash register placement.
3. The store layout involves the division of space for customers (e.g., aisle space for traffic flow), selling space, and storage space.
4. The interior merchandising display includes the use of racks, bins, mannequins, and other point-of-purchase displays, including in-store advertising signs and video monitors that promote selected merchandise.

The image and merchandising activity of a discounter such as K-Mart will be quite different from that of an upscale clothing merchandiser like Bretton's. To illustrate, consider that K-Mart uses bin displays (i.e., self-standing display tables on which sale merchandise is stacked); lots of colourful signs that focus on price; centrally located cash registers at exits; shopping carts, and minimal personal service. On the other hand, Bretton's uses the latest in merchandising display racks; customers pay for goods in the area of purchase; store surroundings are elegant; and a well-trained and plentiful sales staff serves the customer.

# Merchandise Assortment

To ensure that adequate supply of goods is available to meet customer demands, retailers take into account three merchandising components: the breadth and depth of the selection, assortment consistency, and stock balance. To understand what these components mean, let us first examine some of the merchandise terms that retailers employ:

**merchandise assortment**

1. *Merchandise Assortment* The **merchandise assortment** is often also cited as the product mix; it is the total assortment of products a retailer carries. Retailers perform an "assorting" function, described in chapter 12 with regard to distributors, whereby they consolidate diverse goods and services in one location.

2. *Merchandise Group* This is a store product line, that is, a broadly related assortment of goods (e.g., sporting goods, furniture, and appliances). Large department stores organize separate departments around merchandise groupings.

3. *Merchandise Class* Such a class is a sub-group or narrow product line within a merchandise group (e.g., camping equipment, small household appliances).

4. *Merchandise Category* This refers to specific goods within a merchandising class (e.g., sleeping bags, tents, microwave ovens, toasters).

## *Breadth and Depth of Selection*

**breadth of selection**

The width or **breadth of selection** concerns the number of goods classifications a store carries. For example, a department store carries fashion apparel, furniture, appliances, toys, sporting goods, home furnishings, mens wear, ladies wear, linens, dry goods, and many more sorts of goods. A drug store stocks cough and cold remedies, personal care products, cosmetics, tobacco products, confectionery goods, and a mixture of general merchandise.

**depth of selection**

The **depth of a selection** is the number of brands and styles carried within each classification. A grocery store or drug store may sell three different brands of potato chips and several flavours and pack sizes of each brand. The type of retailer an operation is (e.g., department store, convenience store, or variety store) and the needs of the customers it serves determine the breadth and depth of product assortment.

## *Assortment Consistency*

**assortment consistency**

**Assortment consistency** refers to product lines that can be used in conjunction with each other or that all relate to the same sorts of activities and needs. An example of such consistency is a general-line sporting-goods retailer that stocks equipment for the various popular sports — baseball, hockey, basketball, and running, for example — as well as clothing and accessories to complement these sports. An automotive supply store sells batteries, tires, antifreeze, mufflers, and other related automobile supplies. Basically, consistency is achieved when the customer finds in the particular store only those products that he or she expects to see.

**scrambled merchandising**

In the 1980s, a certain amount of assortment inconsistency emerged in retailing. Called **scrambled merchandising**, it arises when a retailer begins to carry products and product lines that seem unrelated to the products it already carries. Thus, a supermarket may add a large pharmacy section, or a convenience store (e.g., Mac's) may add a self-serve counter selling coffee and light sandwiches, or a drug store might start selling toys. Such a practice stemmed from consumers' growing demand for convenience. The demand led to a one-stop shopping concept. The benefit to the retailer is that scrambled merchandising can increase traffic and profit. The retailer does, however, face additional forms of competition.

In today's competitive marketplace, supermarkets and drug stores have become experts in scrambled merchandising. Their objective is to stock anything that will sell in volume and include a cross-section of merchandise. Items added by these stores include motor oil, photography supplies, magazines, pantyhose, and garden supplies.

### *Stock Balance*

**stock balance**

**Stock balance** is the practice of maintaining an adequate assortment of goods that will attract customers while keeping inventories of both high demand and low demand goods at reasonable levels. This is not an easy task, but such factors as profit margin, inventory carrying costs, and stock turnover have a direct impact on cash flow and profitability. In addition, the retailer must know the market and tailor the product mix accordingly. Thus, decisions are made regarding what assortment of name brands and private-label brands to stock, what variety of price ranges to offer, and what mix of traditional (established) products and innovative (new) products to stock.

## Merchandise Control

There is a direct link between merchandise planning and merchandise control. The best of plans can go astray if proper controls are not implemented to measure the relationship between actual performance and planned performance. Deviations from the plan are dealt with by instituting new marketing strategies or by making adjustments in budgets.

**stockturn**

The concept of **stockturn** or stock turnover is a key measure of retail control. Stockturn is the number of times during a specific time period that the average inventory is sold. The period for calculating stockturn is usually one year, though the period can be shorter. Stockturn considers two figures: the total value of retail sales in dollars and the average value of inventory the store carries. It is calculated using this formula:

$$\text{Stockturn} = \frac{\text{Retail Sales}}{\text{Average Inventory at Retail}}$$

Therefore, if retail sales were $1 000 000 and the average inventory at retail were $200 000, the stockturn would be

$$= \frac{\$1\ 000\ 000}{\$200\ 000}$$

$$= \quad 5$$

Retailers often find it more meaningful to calculate stockturn on the basis of costs or units (see figure 13.11).

Knowing the stockturn rate allows the retailer to plan inventory (i.e., to match supply with demand) effectively. It also enables the retailer to compare the current turnover with past turnovers, to compare one department with another, and to compare the turnover of different stores in a chain operation. Stockturn is a guideline for planning. To illustrate, if a retailer has a stockturn of four and the average of other stores is six, it indicates that some action is required: perhaps prices are too high, the selection of merchandise is poor, too much inventory is being held, or

**FIGURE 13.11   Stockturn Rates Based on Sales, Costs and Units**

| Retail Sales | Stockturn | = | $\dfrac{\text{Retail Sales}}{\text{Average Retail Inventory}}$ |
|---|---|---|---|
| | | = | $\dfrac{2\ 000\ 000}{200\ 000}$ |
| | | = | 10 |
| Costs | Stockturn | = | $\dfrac{\text{Cost of Goods Sold}}{\text{Average Inventory at Cost}}$ |
| | | = | $\dfrac{1\ 500\ 000}{300\ 000}$ |
| | | = | 5 |
| Units | Stockturn | = | $\dfrac{\text{Total Units Sold}}{\text{Average Inventory (Units)}}$ |
| | | = | $\dfrac{1\ 500}{300}$ |
| | | = | 5 |

promotion is ineffective. Conversely, if stockturn is higher than average, some action may be needed since price may be too low. Regardless of the situation, stockturn rates do trigger changes in marketing strategy.

Placing too much emphasis on stockturn rates can, however, lead to problems. For example, it is unrealistic for a national chain to expect each store to approximate a national average. Each store is unique, and regional and local market conditions (i.e., economy, employment, income) account for differences in stockturn rates. Similarly, a retailer that carries a narrow and shallow assortment of merchandise will have a higher turnover than a store with a wide and deep assortment. Stores that only carry popular lines have higher stockturn rates; therefore, retailers must be cautious in how they use comparable stockturn figures in the planning process.

## >>>> SUMMARY

This chapter introduces some of the key elements of wholesaling and retailing activity. Wholesaling involves buying and handling merchandise and reselling it to organizational users, to other wholesalers, and to retailers. The functions of a wholesaler include providing direct sales contact, holding inventory, processing orders, supplying market intelligence, offering sales support, enabling assortment, and breaking bulk.

There are three main categories of wholesalers. In a manufacturer's wholesaling operation, product is sold directly to customers through branch offices and sales offices. Merchant wholesaling consists of full-service wholesalers and limited-service wholesalers. Full-service wholesalers include general-merchandise wholesalers, specialty-merchandise wholesalers and franchise wholesalers. Cash-and-carry outlets, drop shippers, and truck jobbers are limited-service wholesalers. The agent and broker category encompasses manufacturers' agents, brokers, commission merchants, and auction companies.

Retailing is the activity involved in selling goods and services to final consumers. The primary function of a retailer is assortment (i.e., bringing together a wide selection of merchandise to one location to meet the needs of customers). Many types of retail operations exist in Canada, and the businesses fall into various classifications depending on the nature of their ownership and strategy mix and on whether they use store facilities or not.

When classified according to the nature of their ownership, stores are categorized as retail chain stores, as independent stores, or as retail franchise stores. When classified according to their strategy mix categories, stores are classified as convenience stores, supermarkets, discount supermarkets, superstores, specialty stores, variety stores, department stores, discount department stores, or catalogue showrooms. Non-store retailing includes vending machines, direct home retailing and direct marketing.

Planning in retailing operations centers on store location, merchandise assortment, the store environment, and merchandise control.

## ⟩⟩⟩⟩ K E Y   T E R M S

wholesaling
breaking bulk
manufacturer wholesaling
full-service merchant wholesaler
general-merchandise wholesaler
specialty-merchandise wholesaler
rack jobbers
franchise wholesaling
limited service wholesaler
cash-and-carry outlets
drop shipper
truck jobber
manufacturers' agent
broker

commission merchant
auction company
retailing mix
retail chain store
independent retailer
retail franchise
convenience store
supermarket
discount supermarket
superstore
specialty store
variety store
department store
discount department store

catalogue showroom
direct home retailing
central business district
strip cluster
free-standing store
planned shopping mall
atmosphere
merchandise assortment
depth of selection
breadth of selection
assortment consistency
scrambled merchandising
stock balance
stockturn

## ⟩⟩⟩⟩ R E V I E W   A N D   D I S C U S S I O N   Q U E S T I O N S

**1.** Describe the basic functions associated with who-lesaling.

**2.** What is the difference between a manufacturer wholesaling system and a merchant wholesaling system?

**3.** Identify and briefly describe the types of full-service merchant wholesalers.

**4.** Differentiate between a drop shipper and a truck jobber.

**5.** Under what circumstances are agents and brokers likely to be used by a manufacturing organization?

**6.** What are the four basic functions performed by a retailer?

**7.** How are each of the following types of retailers different? For each type, provide two examples that are not mentioned in the textbook.   **(a)** chain store   **(b)** retail franchise   **(c)** convenience store   **(d)** discount supermarket   **(e)** specialty store   **(f)** discount department store

**8.** Visit a department store in your local market, then present a brief analysis of your perception of the store's image as conveyed by the atmosphere consid-erations discussed in this chapter.

**9.** Why is direct home retailing such a successful form of retailing in Canada?

**10.** What is the best location for the following types of stores in the market nearest your college or univer-sity? Explain your choice?   **a)** photography equip-ment and supply store   **b)** specialty dress shop   **c)** leisure sportswear store   **d)** car dealership   **e)** convenience store   **f)** audio component store   **g)** sports memorabilia store

**11.** What is the difference between breadth and depth of merchandise in retailing? Describe what is meant by breadth and depth as it applies to stores like Northern Reflections, Crossings, Beaver Canoe, and Kettle Creek Canvas Company.

**12.** Why has franchising become such a successful retailing concept in Canada?

## ⟩⟩⟩⟩ R E F E R E N C E S

1. Adapted from Bert Rosenbloom, *Marketing Chan-nels: A Management View*, 3rd Edition (New York: Dry-den Press, 1987), pp.44-46.

2. Statistics Canada, *Canada Yearbook 1988*, (Ottawa: Ministry of Supply and Services Canada, 1987), Cat. No. 11-402E/1987, p.17-6.

3. Ibid., p.17-1.

4. JIM McELGUNN, ''Putting on the Ritz'', *Marketing*, August 22, 1986, p.2.

5. Statistics Canada, *Canada Yearbook 1988*, p.17-1.

6. Ibid., p.17-2.

7. CLARKSON GORDON/WOODS GORDON, *Tomorrow's Customers*, 22nd Edition, 1989, p.20.

8. ''Convenience Store Groups'', *Canadian Grocer*, August 1988, p.48.

9. Statistics Canada, *Canada Yearbook 1988*, p.17-4.

10. JOHN BEISEL, *Contemporary Retailing* (New York: Macmillan Publishing Company, 1987), p.121.

11. JOEL EVANS and BARRY BERMAN, *Marketing*, 3rd Edition (New York: Macmillan Publishing Company, 1987), p.389.

> > > > > **PART SEVEN**

# *Promotion*

On your next vacation cross the border between art and reality.

Introducing Tetley Tapestry of Teas

# C H A P T E R   14   〉〉〉〉

# Promotion Strategy I
## Advertising and Public Relations

*LEARNING   OBJECTIVES*

After studying this chapter, you will be able to

1. Describe the marketing communications process and the role of the promotion mix in that process.

2. Identify the factors that influence the size of a marketing budget and list the methods for determining a budget.

3. Characterize the various types of consumer and business-to-business advertising.

4. Explain the role of advertising agencies in the communications process.

5. Identify the types of creative strategies commonly used in advertising.

6. Describe the roles media planning has in the advertising process.

7. Outline the measurement techniques used for evaluating advertising effectiveness.

8. Explain what role public relations has in the communications process.

# ⟩⟩⟩⟩ *The Promotion Mix*

**promotion mix**

The **promotion mix** is comprised of five main elements: advertising, public relations, sales promotion, personal selling, and event marketing and sponsorships. Each of these elements, as well as their relationship to each other, is examined in this and the next chapter. Prior to examining each element of the promotion mix, the reader should have an understanding of marketing communications and the use of the promotion mix in communications. **Marketing communications** is the process of sending an understood message from a marketer (business organization) to another business organization or consumer. The process begins with a sender (the marketing organization), which develops a message (a mixture of words, pictures, music and gestures) in the form of a print advertisement or broadcast commercial. This message is transmitted by the media (television, radio, magazine, newspaper, transit advertising, and so on) to a receiver (a business organization or final user). Refer to figure 14.1 for an illustration of a marketing communications model.

**marketing communications**

In marketing communications, various elements of the promotion mix are combined to send out messages that are designed to inform, persuade, and remind people or other businesses of a product or service.[1]

1. *To Inform*   All forms of promotion provide basic information about a product, service or company. For example, an advertisement for a downtown hotel may stress the hotel's quality service, convenient location, or the amenities it provides. An advertisement for a large industrial corporation may stress the quality of its people or the diversity of its operations. Dofasco advertises how they work together with customers to develop better products for the future (see figure 14.2).

2. *To Persuade*   Persuasion is the part of the message that moves the receiver close to taking action. In all forms of communication, the marketing organization links the benefits of its product to the needs of the target market. The goal is to do it in such a convincing way that the customer perceives the product to be a better alternative than the competition. Thus IBM says, "Why buy a product that compares itself to IBM, when you can have an IBM?"

**FIGURE 14.1    The Communications Process**

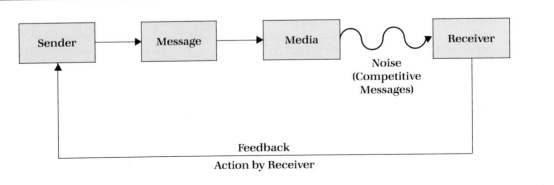

**FIGURE 14.2** Advertising to Inform

---

FIGURE 14.3    Some Roles of Promotion Communication

- To create and maintain company, product or brand image
- To inform the public of benefits offered by a product or service
- To position or reposition the perception of a product in the customer's mind
- To encourage merchandising support from distributors
- To stimulate trial purchase
- To announce a sale or special event
- To create a perception of competitive advantage
- To justify the price of a product

---

3. *To Remind*    Generally, such messages are used late in the product life cycle to remind customers that a certain product is still available. The phrase "drink Coca Cola", which is seen frequently in point-of-purchase messages, is an example of reminder advertising. Once a product is firmly established on the market, a company has the flexibility to reduce promotion support so that adequate marketing funds are available for new products. Refer to figure 14.3 for a summary of some specific roles of marketing communications.

Given that the role of marketing communications is to inform, persuade, and remind a target market about a product or service, marketers realize that competitors are sending out similar messages to attract the same customers. In effect, the target market is exposed to many messages for competing products. This influx of messages is referred to as "noise" in the communications channel. If the message of one product can break through the clutter or the noise of competing messages, and if the product is relevant to the receiver (i.e., if the benefits satisfy a need), then the product may become a preferred alternative. The marketer sees product purchases as positive feedback. If the message does not break through the clutter or noise — because it is dull, makes inappropriate appeals, or is misunderstood — there is little chance that the product will be purchased. A lack of purchases amounts to negative feedback for the marketer.

# ⟩⟩⟩⟩ *Promotion Planning*

promotion planning

**Promotion planning** is the process of making systematic decisions regarding what elements of the promotion mix to use in marketing communications; the process by which objectives and strategies are outlined. Promotion planning is only one element of company planning, though, due to the nature of advertising, it is the most visible. A company develops its promotion plans in accordance with the direction provided by corporate and marketing plans. The promotion plan complements other marketing-mix plans, such as those for pricing, product, and place, and together they form the company's marketing plan or a plan for a specific product or service.

In developing the promotional component of a marketing plan, the organization establishes the role and importance of each element of the promotion mix, then devises an overall promotion strategy that is in keeping with the corporate and marketing plan. Each element of the promotion mix is given objectives and strategies.

## Promotion Objectives

Like any other element of the marketing mix, promotional activity must complement the total marketing effort. That is to say, its objectives must fulfill the overall corporate and marketing objectives. Thus, each element of the promotion mix is assigned a goal based on what it is capable of contributing to the overall plans. These objectives are supposed to meet the following criteria. They should be

1. Realistically achievable.
2. Quantitative in nature (for measurement purposes).
3. Directed at a carefully defined target market.
4. Capable of being evaluated and modified when necessary.[2]

Whether such goals are achievable can be easily assessed during the evaluation and control stage of the marketing planning process. The relationships between corporate objectives, marketing objectives, and promotion objectives are summarized in figure 14.4 by means of examples.

**FIGURE 14.4**    The Relationships of Objectives at Different Levels of Planning

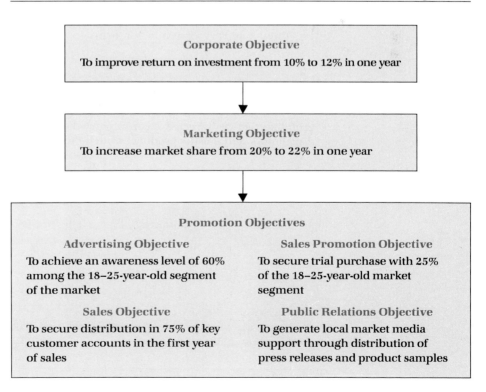

**Corporate Objective**
To improve return on investment from 10% to 12% in one year

**Marketing Objective**
To increase market share from 20% to 22% in one year

**Promotion Objectives**

**Advertising Objective**
To achieve an awareness level of 60% among the 18–25-year-old segment of the market

**Sales Promotion Objective**
To secure trial purchase with 25% of the 18–25-year-old market segment

**Sales Objective**
To secure distribution in 75% of key customer accounts in the first year of sales

**Public Relations Objective**
To generate local market media support through distribution of press releases and product samples

## Promotion Strategy

Promotion strategy is the battle plan that outlines the means of achieving the objectives. While objectives state what is to be accomplished, strategy describes how they are to be achieved. There are two basic types of promotion strategy: push and pull.

### Push Strategy

**push strategy**

In a **push strategy**, the organization creates demand for a product by directing promotional efforts at middlemen who in turn promote the product among consumers. Push strategies tend to rely on a mixture of personal selling and sales-promotion techniques to create demand. The use of trade discounts and allowances, cooperative advertising, and other such activities mentioned in chapters 11 and 13 are examples of the techniques employed.

### Pull Strategy

**pull strategy**

In a **pull strategy**, the organization creates demand by directing promotional efforts at consumers or final users of a product (i.e., at the business user or buyer in an organization). Pull strategies tend to rely on mass media advertising and direct marketing techniques, supplemented by consumer promotion activities. In recent years, event marketing (the sponsorship of particular events by organizations) has also played an important role in pull strategies. These activities cause consumers to search for the product in stores; by asking for the product, they put pressure on the retailer to carry it. This strategy "pulls" the product through the channel (see figure 14.5).

Most firms feel that attention must be given to both channel customers and final users; thus, it is very common for firms to combine push and pull promotion

**FIGURE 14.5**    The Flow of Push and Pull Promotion Strategies

**Pull**

• Promotion activity directed at consumers who in turn request the product from distributors, and pull the product through the channel

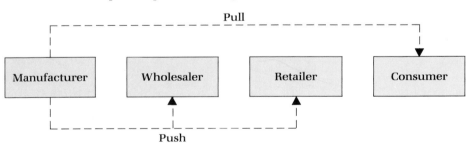

**Push**

• Promotion activity directed at distributors who resell the product, and push the product through the channel

strategies. Companies such as Kraft General Foods, RJR Nabisco, Canon, and Xerox all advertise their product heavily to end-users while their sales forces promote the products among business customers or channel members.

# Promotion Budgets

In order to develop a promotion budget, the manager responsible analyzes several factors, each of which has an impact on the amount of funds required.

### The Customer

Managers must consider what type of customer is targeted as they decide on the nature of the promotional activity and the size of the promotion budget. Consumer products directed at mass markets rely on advertising, while industrial and business-oriented products, which have a more narrowly defined and geographically-centered audience, rely more on personal selling. Budgets are allocated for promotional activities when a company determines the most effective means of reaching its targets.

### Degree of Competition

A firm monitors the amount of money its competitors invest in promotion as well as the effectiveness of these investments. How much its competitors spend provides a useful guideline when a firm is planning a budget. Firms that do not keep pace with others risk a loss in sales. For instance, now that the Canadian beer market is dominated by only two breweries (Molson and Labatt), industry analysts project that the battle for market share between the two could be won or lost by the promotional support they offer. In many markets, the competition is so intense that competitors force other companies to spend more on promotion than they would like. This is the reason Coca-Cola and Pepsi-Cola advertise so heavily to protect market share. As of 1988 in Canada, Coca-Cola led with a market share of 21.1 percent compared to Pepsi-Cola with 19.9 percent.[3]

### Stage in the Product Life Cycle

The amount of money required for promotional support varies with each stage of the product life cycle. In the introductory stage, the objective is to create demand along with product- and brand-awareness. To achieve these goals, companies generally provide large budgets for promotion, allocating funds to numerous push and pull strategies. While attempting to establish a product in the market during the introductory phase, a firm usually incurs short-term financial losses on the product. In the growth stage, the emergence of competition keeps the promotional investment at a high level. It is a period when a product must firmly establish a presence in a growing market, or risk falling behind competitors that are more aggressive. To establish this presence, to foster brand preference, organizations employ strategies that differentiate products from each other. Since the market is growing, firms strive for additional market share, an objective that also requires high degrees of promotion.

The focus in the mature phase shifts from brand development to profit maximization. Rather than spending money on promotion, companies try to recover money wherever possible, thereby improving its profit margin. Profit is a priority during the decline period, as well. Since new products have taken over the market, promotion budgets for old products are cut significantly or withdrawn entirely.

# Budgeting Methods

An organization can use a variety of budgeting methods: percentage-of-sales, industry-averages, the arbitrary allocation method, and the task, or objective, method.

### Percentage of Sales

For the percentage-of-sales method, the usual procedure is to forecast sales volume in dollars for the forthcoming year and allocate a predetermined percentage of those sales to marketing. This predetermined percentage may be a figure traditionally used by the organization. The shortcoming of this system is that the budget is derived from projected sales; but promotion, as the wise manager realizes, can result in sales. The popularity of this method is due to its simplicity and to the fact that it at least connects promotion expenditures with sales. If this approach is used, the budgetary effects are predictable: if sales increase, the budget goes up, and vice versa.

### Industry Averages

Some marketing organizations try to base their promotion budgets on what competitors are spending. Depending on the performance objectives established for a product, the company may choose to lag behind, to equal, or to exceed the spending of competitors. Using average historical expenditures for the industry as a starting point, companies attempt to forecast competitive spending for the next year, then position their budget accordingly. For example, if an industry historically spends from 5–10 percent of their sales on promotion and marketing activities, such a figure would be a good one to start with. However, the influence of other planning objectives, such as the desire to grow or build market share, often forces the firm to modify this "starting point" budget.

### Arbitrary Allocation

The arbitrary-allocation method is popular with small firms that lack the resources for much promotional support and do not have a formal budgeting process. Relying on his or her own knowledge and experience, the owner or manager analyzes cost and profit trends and then assigns an arbitrary amount to cover promotion expenses. Because the amount allocated is an arbitrary one, the effects of promotion as a marketing stimulus are not considered in the case of this method.

### Task (Objective) Method

The budgeting methods discussed so far fail to acknowledge that promotion is a means of achieving marketing objectives. The task method, on the other hand, assumes that promotion has an impact on sales. For each element of the promotion mix, the company sets specific objectives and develops strategies for achieving them. Then it calculates a cost for each activity. The sum of these costs becomes the promotion budget.

# >>>> *Advertising and its Role*

advertising

**Advertising** is any paid form of nonpersonal sales presentation and promotion of goods and services by an identified sponsor.[4] While advertising is designed to accomplish specific tasks (e.g., raising the public's awareness of a product or service or getting people to try a product or service), its basic role is to influence the behaviour of a target market in such a way that those targeted view the product, service, or idea favourably. Once a favourable attitude develops, the role of advertising is to motivate the purchase of a specific brand of product.

Studies have been conducted on how advertising messages influence behaviour. Such studies try to determine what effect advertising has on the stages involved in making a purchase decision. One such study, DAGMAR (Defining Advertising Goals, Measuring Advertising Results), conducted by Richard Colley, concludes that

> advertising's job, purely and simply, is to communicate to a defined target audience information and a frame of mind that stimulates action. Advertising succeeds or fails on how well it communicates desired information and attitudes to the right people at the right time and cost.[5]

The DAGMAR model is based on the premise that an individual passes through several behavioural stages when in the process of deciding to buy a product. These stages are:

1. *Awareness*  In this stage, the customer learns of a product or service for the first time. Such a realization can occur when the individual is exposed to an advertisement, a situation that the marketing organization plans for and seeks to control. The awareness can also come from word of mouth, a situation that is beyond the control of the organization.

2. *Comprehension*  By this stage, interest has been created. The individual perceives the advertising message to be relevant and the product to be useful. The product has become part of the customer's frame of reference; in other words, it is now included as a possible option among other options when the customer considers what to purchase.

3. *Conviction*  The customer evaluates the product benefits presented in the advertising and decides he or she would like the item. The buyer views the product as satisfactory and preferable and may be sufficiently motivated to buy it. A purchase will occur when the product is needed.

4. *Action*  In this stage, the desired active response occurs: a customer visits a car dealer's showroom or clips out a coupon in a magazine for later use, or a business

FIGURE 14.6   Leading Customers to Action

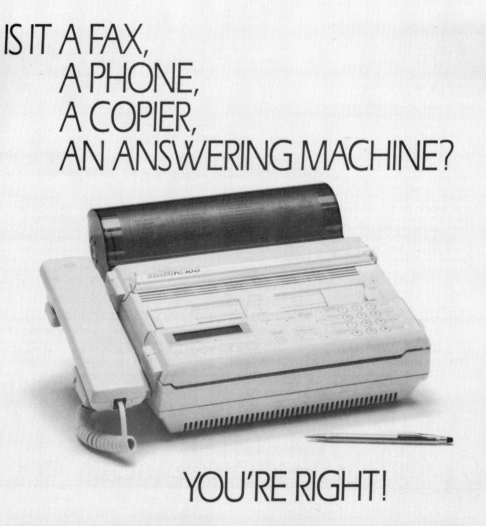

IS IT A FAX,
A PHONE,
A COPIER,
AN ANSWERING MACHINE?

YOU'RE RIGHT!

Introducing Mita's multi-talented, "long-distance copier." **It's a fax** that sends and receives copy-perfect documents, citywide or worldwide, in just seconds. All for the cost of a telephone call.

With "fine resolution" and "16 levels of grey scale", copy quality is clean and clear at the receiving end.

Convenient speed dialing lets you program 50 frequently "faxed and phoned" numbers for quick and easy access. Intelligent fax/phone logic lets you use just a single telephone line for both fax and phone. When a document is loaded, the fax number is automatically dialed. Otherwise the phone number is dialed.

With "delayed transmission", you can transmit documents after hours when long-distance rates are lowest. **It's a full-featured business phone** that does everything from speed dialing to automatic redialing when you've reached a busy number.

**It's a personal copier too,** able to reproduce convenient copies in seconds – letter or legal size.

**It's an answering machine** that delivers your message or greeting, then records those 'can't afford to miss' phone messages while you're away from your office. When the incoming message is a fax, it automatically receives the document.

Check our line of multi-talented, easy to use fax-copiers. On your desk top or in your fax room, **Mita's "long-distance copiers" deliver the efficiency that will change the way you do business.**

**All we make are great copiers.**

Mita Copystar Canada Ltd., 6120 Kestrel Road, Mississauga, Ont. L5T 1S8  Tel: (416) 671-4425  **1-800-268-4735**

**FIGURE 14.6**    (continued)

*Mita presents its unique benefits and provides consumers with a convenient way of responding to its message.*

sends back a reply card from an advertisement, requesting information about a product. All are desired forms of action.

The advertisement for the Mita facsimile machines, presented in figure 14.6, illustrates how advertising can lead a customer through these stages. This advertisement creates awareness by appearing frequently in prominent business magazines read by potential buyers, and it conveys the information that potential buyers need in order to understand the product and reach a conviction or decision about it. It does this by presenting the major benefits to the user. The reply card represents an attempt by the advertiser to build upon conviction and stimulate action.

## ›››› *The Forms of Advertising*

### Consumer Advertising

Like marketing generally, advertising is classified into two broad categories: consumer advertising and business-to-business advertising. Consumer advertising can be further subdivided into four types: national advertising, retail advertising, end-product advertising, and direct-response advertising.

#### *National Advertising*

national advertising

**National advertising** is the advertising of a trademarked product or service wherever the product or service is available. The term *national* here refers to the brand name rather than to a geographic area. National advertising messages identify a brand name, the benefits offered, and the availability of the product or service. The advertising messages for products such as Coca-Cola, Campbell's Soup, Good Year tires, General Motors automobiles, Royal Bank, and Holiday Inn are examples of national advertising.

#### *Retail Advertising*

retail advertising

**Retail advertising** refers to advertising by a retail operation to communicate image, store sales, and the variety of merchandise carried. Retail advertising includes advertising by large department stores, which typically use full-page advertisements in local newspapers or distribute flyers through the local newspapers to announce sales. The advertising of weekly specials by food distributors and the advertising produced by specialty stores are also examples of retail advertising.

#### *End Product Advertising*

end-product advertising

**End-product advertising** is advertising that promotes an ingredient of a finished product. Advertising of this nature encourages consumers to look for a particular component when buying a final product. For example, a consumer takes his or her film to a retailer to get it processed into a picture (the finished product). Kodak encourages consumers to visit a shop that displays the Kodak paper sign (the customer's guarantee of quality prints). Kodak paper is part of that finished product. The manufacturer of NutraSweet encourages consumers to look for their designation on products that use it as a food and beverage ingredient.

#### *Direct-Response Advertising*

direct-response advertising

**Direct-response advertising** involves advertising directly to consumers and so bypassing traditional channels of distribution (wholesalers and retailers). The special record and cassette-tape offers commonly seen on television, and other offers received through direct mail campaigns, are examples of direct response advertising.

### Business-to-Business Advertising

business-to-business advertising

**Business-to-business advertising** occurs when a business advertises its products, its services, or itself to other business organizations. Among the major types of business-to-business advertising are trade advertising, industrial advertising, advertising to professionals, and corporate advertising (see figure 14.7).

**FIGURE 14.7** **Business-to-business Advertising**

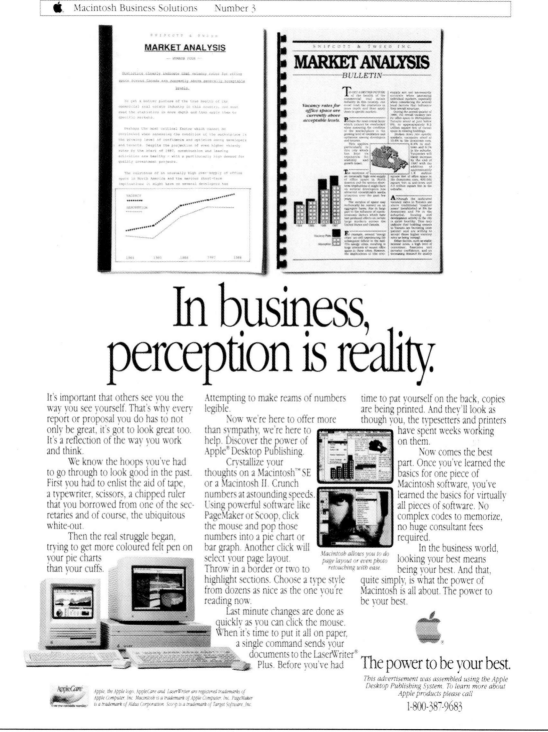

*Apple appeals to business users by presenting some business applications of its product.*

### Trade Advertising

trade advertising

**Trade advertising** originates from a source supplier, such as a manufacturer, and is directed at members of a channel of distribution. The goal of trade advertising is to encourage distributors to carry and resell a product. The message is communicated to distributors in trade publications such as *Canadian Grocer* (food distribution trade), *Hardware Merchandising* (building-supply and related retail trade), and *Foodservice and Hospitality* (food-service and restaurant trade).

### Industrial Advertising

industrial advertising

**Industrial advertising** is advertising by industrial suppliers that is directed at industrial buyers. For raw materials, processed materials, and accessory equipment, advertising generally conveys two messages, one to create initial product awareness and the other to develop sales leads. Leads are developed through the action taken by a prospective customer. For instance, the customer may return a reply card or call a toll-free telephone number for more information. Many specialized magazines aimed at specific industries, such as *Heavy Construction News*, *Canadian Packaging*, *Canadian DataSystems*, and *Materials Management and Distribution*, provide a vehicle for industrial advertising.

### Advertising to Professionals

Manufacturers direct advertising to professional groups in order to increase awareness and communicate detailed product information. Drug manufacturers, for example, address the medical profession through a number of publications, including *The Medical Post* and *MD* magazines. As of 1989, the Canadian Medical Association's list of member physicians became available, so direct marketing can now be made part of an advertising strategy. The legal profession can be reached through magazines such as *Canadian Lawyer* and the *Lawyer's Weekly*. Those who would want to reach the legal profession through advertising include producers of accounting systems, legal software systems, and business equipment.

### Corporate Advertising

corporate advertising

**Corporate advertising** is advertising designed to convey a favourable image of a company among its various publics. The intent of corporate advertising is varied. It may attempt to create or improve a company image by showing the strength of the people employed by the firm (see figure 14.8). It may communicate a company's stance on an issue which affects them or society directly, or it may promote goodwill. For example, a firm may advertise its support of a clean, safe environment. Procter & Gamble's advertising for its enviro-packs is an example of such advertising. The contents of enviro-packs are poured into the rigid plastic container originally purchased by the consumer. This form of packaging is used for several of Procter & Gamble's household products such as Tide, Ivory, and Mr. Clean, all products that are marketed in a liquid form.

**FIGURE 14.8** Corporate Advertising

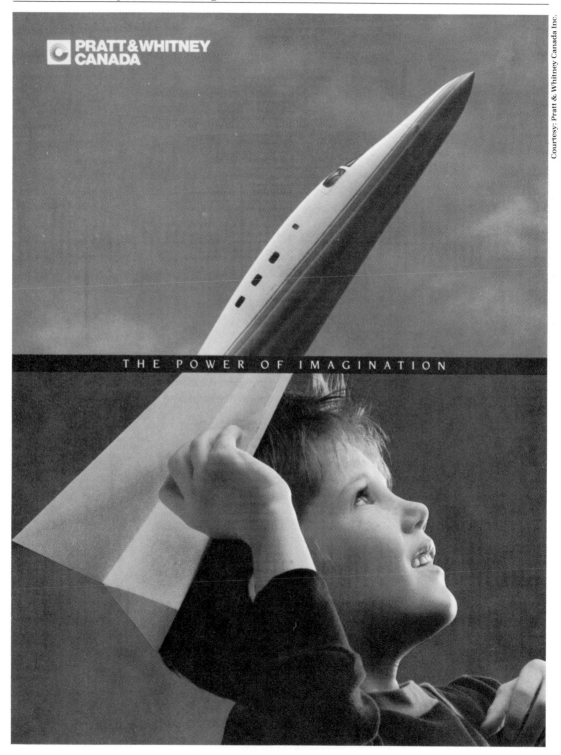

## >>>> *The Canadian Advertising Industry*

To put the financial significance of advertising into perspective, consider that the Canadian advertising industry generated gross revenues of $8.5 billion in 1988.[6] This figure represents all revenues generated by expenditures with the traditional mass media. The advertising industry is comprised of three primary groups: the advertisers, advertising agencies, and the media.

### Advertisers

Canadian advertisers include manufacturers, retailers, service firms, governments, and non-profit and charitable organizations. The largest advertiser in Canada is the federal government, which spends considerably more on advertising than does private enterprise. The largest private sector advertiser is Procter & Gamble (see figure 14.9).

### Advertising Agencies

**advertising agencies**

**media billings**

**Advertising agencies** are service organizations responsible for creating, planning, producing, and placing advertising messages for clients (the advertisers). The largest advertising agency in Canada is MacLaren:Lintas Inc. as of 1989. Canadian advertising agencies are ranked in size based on their media billings (see figure 14.10). **Media billings** are the total dollar volume of advertising time and space handled by an agency in a one-year period. Advertising agencies are classified into three groups according to the nature of services they provide to clients: full service agencies, creative boutiques, and media-buying services.

#### *Full-Service Agencies*

**full-service agency**

**Full-service agencies** have a strong appeal for large advertisers that need the full range of services these agencies offer, including product and marketing research,

FIGURE 14.9   Canada's Leading Advertisers

|  | | Amount Spent (in millions) |
|---|---|---|
| 1 | Government of Canada | $76.0 |
| 2 | Procter & Gamble | 61.4 |
| 3 | General Motors | 55.7 |
| 4 | Unilever | 47.0 |
| 5 | John Labatt Limited | 44.7 |
| 6 | Kraft General Foods | 44.2 |
| 7 | Cineplex Odeon | 43.3 |
| 8 | Paramount Communications | 42.5 |
| 9 | McDonald's | 34.8 |
| 10 | RJR Nabisco | 33.5 |

*Source: Marketing*, March 26, 1990, p. 4.

**FIGURE 14.10**   Canada's Largest Advertising Agencies

|   |   | Billings (in millions) |
|---|---|---|
| 1 | MacLaren-Lintas Inc. | $220.0 |
| 2 | Cossette Communication-Marketing | 215.4 |
| 3 | FCB/Ronalds-Reynolds Ltd. | 202.0 |
| 4 | J. Walter Thompson Company Ltd. | 195.0 |
| 5 | Young & Rubicam Limited | 193.8 |
| 6 | McCann-Erickson Advertising Ltd. | 190.9 |
| 7 | McKim Advertising Ltd. | 185.3 |
| 8 | Ogilvy & Mather (Canada Ltd) | 185.0 |
| 9 | Saffer Advertising Inc. | 180.0 |
| 10 | Vickers & Benson Advertising Ltd. | 169.1 |

creative planning (message development), media planning and placement, sales promotion, direct marketing, and public relations. Such agencies are traditionally divided into three functional areas: account management, creative services, and media. The account management group works with its clients, its members acting as consultants and coordinators who 1) advise clients on a variety of strategic marketing and financial issues, 2) identify and motivate the correct agency resources, particularly the creative and media personnel who develop the advertising concepts and media plans to build the client's business, and 3) coordinate the involvement of both agency and client in project assignments.[7] Such projects include advertising research, plans for new product introductions, and contingency planning for anticipated competitive developments in the marketplace.

The creative department develops advertising ideas and concepts. A copywriter converts marketing information into a persuasive sales message composed of a headline, body copy, and slogan, while the art director develops a visual presentation that works with the copy in gaining an interested response from the target audience. Copywriters and art directors usually work as a team, collaborating on client assignments to impart a certain continuity and consistency to the advertising effort.

The media department is responsible for planning and arranging the placement of advertisements; it schedules and buys advertising time (broadcast media) and space (print media), usually over a one-year period. The media department prepares a document that shows all the details of how a client's budget is spent to achieve advertising objectives. In scheduling, they strive to achieve maximum exposure at the lowest possible cost.

### Creative Boutiques

creative boutiques

**Creative boutiques** specialize in the development and execution of creative ideas for clients' advertising campaigns. Using the client's marketing objectives and strategies as guidelines, the creative boutique develops and designs the most important component of the campaign — the advertising message. This design and development process covers copy, artwork, music, themes, and slogans, all common elements of the message.

### Media Buying Service

media-buying service

A **media-buying service** specializes in planning and purchasing the most cost-efficient time and space in the media for a client. These agencies claim that, as specialists, they are able to generate cost savings for the client at a rate greater than that of a full-service agency-media department. Such cost savings can be reinvested in the creative product. Full-service agencies argue that they can handle both creative and media services equally well for their clients.

### Other Specialist Agencies

Agencies can develop reputations for particular specializations. The growth of direct-response advertising in today's marketplace has resulted in an increased number of agencies that specialize in this area. Most large full-service agencies have formed direct-response subsidiaries in response to the demand. JWT Direct is a subsidiary of J. Walter Thompson, and V&B Direct Response is a subsidiary of Vickers & Benson Advertising. Retail agencies have also emerged to serve the unique needs of retail advertisers while applying concepts similar to those used by national-brand advertisers. Their task is to position the retailer within the competitive environment by creating a suitable and attractive image, as well as to communicate specific features such as sales and special events. Canada's largest retail advertising agency is Saffer Advertising Inc., based in Toronto.

## ⟩⟩⟩⟩ *Creating the Advertising Message*

## Creative Objectives

creative objectives

Setting creative objectives is the first stage in developing an advertising message. It is followed by planning a creative strategy and, finally, by outlining how to perform the creative execution. **Creative objectives** state what information is to be communicated to a target audience. They usually contain 1) a key benefit statement, which conveys the basic idea, service, or benefit the advertiser is promising the consumer, and 2) a support-claims statement, which verifies or provides proof of the promise. An example of these statements occurs in the Michelin Tire advertisements, which pledge "safety" (the promise) based on the advanced tread design and tire durability (the proof).

## Creative Strategy

creative strategy

The **creative strategy** specifies how a message is to be communicated to the target audience. It pinpoints the personality and image that an agency should strive to create for its client's products and services through the mood, tone, and style of the advertising.

## Creative Execution

creative execution

**Creative execution** refers to the formation of more precisely defined strategies for presenting the message. In this stage, strategies are converted into a physical presentation that expresses the desired image, mood, and personality. The goal is to find the best or most convincing way to present a product so that the customer will be motivated to take the desired action. A unique and successful creative strategy and execution is discussed in the Marketing in Action vignette that appears on the next page: "Doing it Differently — The Black Label Way".

## Types of Advertisements

### Humorous

In humorous advertisements, the promise and proof is presented in a light-hearted manner. Fibreglas Pink Insulation uses humour when it shows a middle-aged husband and wife making bizarre additions to their house — a second story consisting of a tiny sewing room, or a yard full of pink flamingos — with the savings they enjoy from purchasing the insulation. While humorous commercials can be successful, the value of humour is often questioned: a campaign can suffer from premature wearout once the humour becomes familiar. Fibreglas Pink avoids this problem by employing a series of different commercials, each one presenting a different home improvement.

### Comparative

In comparative advertisements, the promise and proof are shown by means of comparing the attributes of a given product to those of competing products. To avoid misleading the public, the competitor must be identified fairly and properly, and the advertiser must be able to substantiate its claims with independent marketing research. When using the comparative technique, regulations advertisers are governed by the Canadian Advertising Foundation through its Advertising Advisory Board. Such advertising can present a convincing argument to consumers. In the mid-1980s, comparative advertising peaked in Canada with campaigns dubbed the "Cola Wars" (Pepsi-Cola vs Coca-Cola) and the "Burger Wars" (Burger King vs McDonald's and others). That the gap between market share for Pepsi-Cola and Coca-Cola narrowed was partly due to the comparative advertising campaign used by Pepsi.

### Emotional

Emotional advertisements concentrate on creating a mood and conveying the message in a manner that arouses the feelings of the audience or shows that psychological satisfaction is gained by using the product. The Michelin Tire advertisement that shows a baby rotating in a tire as the parents discuss safety appeals to the emotions of the audience.

### *Lifestyle*

Some advertisers attempt to associate their brand with the lifestyle of a certain target audience. This type of appeal is demonstrated in the Pepsi-Cola advertising that employs actors and contemporary rock musicians who endorse the drink. The use of such personalities and of such slogans as "The choice of a New Generation" or "A Generation Ahead" combine to appeal to a certain lifestyle, in this case a more youthful target market. The Marketing in Action vignette "Doing it Differently — The Black Label Way" discusses another instance of lifestyle advertising.

---

## ⟩⟩⟩⟩ *MARKETING IN ACTION*

### *DOING IT DIFFERENTLY — THE BLACK LABEL WAY*

As we live in an age of sophisticated graphic presentations where technology is rapidly advancing the quality of colour, why would Carling-O'Keefe develop black and white advertisements?

Launched in such publications as *Now*, *Graffiti*, and *Croc* and in a television spot entitled "Images," the campaign was used to relaunch and reposition Black Label beer in the Ontario market. Black Label was popular in the fifties and early sixties but had taken a back seat to trendier brands in the seventies and eighties. The ads are daring and offbeat, appealing to those who see themselves as hip, trendsetting, and individualistic. The television commercial was shot in black and white and then transferred to reverse polarity to make it look like a film negative. It conveyed a kind of night-time, street feel.

Bruce McCallum, the creative director at Palmer Bonner Inc., Carling's advertising agency, said that initially "this one scared a lot of people" and that some thought "this may be going too far." The creative strategy was to be unique, that is, totally different from mainstream beer advertising. The use of reverse imagery tied in with the concept of "legendary, mysterious, and temporary". Robin Milward, Carling's vice-president of Advertising, felt that a different campaign would make gains for the company. And gains they made. Even though the brand started from a small base, market share doubled in Ontario, and sales were up so much that the product was often sold out in retail beer outlets.

Paul Hains, associate creative director of Palmer Bonner Inc., was the man behind the campaign. His pool of commercials have made Black Label a popular brand among a lifestyle group that does not want to be characterized as mainstream beer drinkers. Black Label was successfully repositioned as an innovative, leading-edge beer for an ultra cool, non-conformist, urban-oriented target group or for those who like to think of themselves that way. Hain's analysis of beer advertising was quite simple. What every other beer commercial had been in the past, his commercials weren't going to be. His goal was to communicate an attitude rather than a hard sell. The campaign was acknowledged as innovative and has won numerous Canadian advertising awards.

Adapted from Jim McElgunn, "Black Label tries reverse approach", *Marketing*, August 15, 1988, p.2, Constance Draganes, "The hot minds behind cool ads", *Flare*, March 1989, pp.74, 175, and Steven Manners, "The black and white world of Paul Hains", *Applied Arts Quarterly*, Summer 1989, pp. 25-29.

*Black label advertisements appeal to those who see themselves as hip, trendsetting, and individualistic.* ▶

**FIGURE 14.11    A Third-Party Endorsement**

# The PC you might not think of first... just came first.

PC Magazine, December 22, 1987 issue, put nine 386-based PCs through their paces. And, although they all had their strengths, the 'Editor's Choice' among the nine reviewed was the NCR PC916. His reasons included: "...NCR Corp. has always gone a bit further in originality... . The PC916 brings the same refreshing spirit to the realm of high-performance 80386-based PCs." "...its faithfulness to PC compatibility is beyond reproach — but the cosmetics and implementation of the PC916 show a wonderful freshness combined with top performance." "The German-made PC916 uses 70-nanosecond dynamic RAM chips that allow the 80386 micro-processor to rip along at a full 16 MHz without wait states." Plus, "The speed of the PC916 is entirely programmable ... from 2.65 MHz all the way up to top speed."

"The bus-oriented design makes the PC916 amazingly upgradable. Pull out one board and plug in another, and the computer can change its demeanor entirely — from 80286 to 80386, potentially from 16 MHz to 20 or 25 MHz — all while maintaining most of your hardware investment."

"Nevertheless, the NCR PC916 rates among the fastest and best desktop computers ever made, and that's high praise indeed."

"Its excellent upgradability and the reputation of its maker make it a formidable competitor and one of the best choices for an 80386-based PC."

If you'd like to put the PC916, or any of our family of surprising PCs, high-performance workstations or other networking products to your own test, call NCR CANADA LTD at 1-800-387-8489.

*EDITOR'S CHOICE*

*"The speed leader among these newest 80386-based PCs is clearly NCR Corp.'s PC916. It also rates highly for its innovative design, styling, and execution. In fact, it earns higher honors than even the original 16-MHz Compaq Deskpro 386.*

*Compared with the first batch of 80386-based PCs we evaluated, the NCR PC916 does amazingly well, too."*

Creating value

### Testimonial

In the case of testimonial advertising, a typical user of the product or an apparently objective third party describes the benefits of the item. Such testimonials can enhance the credibility of the message, since the claims made are not directly attributed to the advertiser. Refer to figure 14.11 for an illustration of a third party endorsement.

### Celebrity Endorsements

An endorsement is a testimonial by a celebrity or "star", whose popularity the advertiser attempts to capitalize on. Stars from television, movies, music, and sports form the nucleus of celebrity endorsers (e.g., Coca-Cola's use of Wayne Gretzky and Kodak's use of Bill Cosby). While the use of celebrities can be beneficial, advertisers must be very careful about who they use to present their message. After Ben Johnson was stripped of a gold medal at the 1988 Seoul Olympics, many firms reevaluated their use of stars, suddenly aware of the potentially damaging publicity they could face in certain situations. For an example of an effective use of celebrity endorsement read the Marketing in Action feature that appears on the next page: "The Greatest of Them All."

### Reason Why

Reason-why advertisements explain what a product does and what benefit it can offer to the potential consumer. The messages are factual in nature and may have either a positive or a negative tone. Advertisements for American Express traveller's cheques are good examples of messages of this kind that have a negative tone. Often American Express advertisements show situations in which vacationers' cheques have been stolen. The fear and anxiety of the traveller are quickly put to rest when he or she finds out how easily the cheques are replaced.

### Slice-of-Life

The slice-of-life advertisement shows an ordinary person or persons presenting a message in an everyday, common setting. Commonly used situations are the family around the dinner table, parents bathing a child, or children playing and smudging their clothes. In each case, the product is shown to quickly satisfy a need or resolve a problem. Tide detergent has used this technique effectively for years, and it has helped to attain its leading position in the marketplace.

## >>>> Media Planning

## Media Objectives

media planning

**Media planning** begins with a precise outline of media objectives, a media strategy, and the media execution, and culminates in a media plan that recommends how advertising funds should be spent to achieve the previously established advertising

### ⟩⟩⟩⟩ *MARKETING IN ACTION*

#### THE GREATEST OF THEM ALL

To athletes who experience a sudden rise to stardom, the advertising world beckons. Sponsors are constantly looking for an ideal role model to pitch their product or service to the Canadian public. A leading product that is associated with a sports star or entertainment personality is often unbeatable.

In Canada, Wayne Gretzky fits the mold. The former Edmonton Oiler left Canada for Hollywood in one of the biggest sports trades ever. His hockey contract with the Los Angeles Kings is reportedly worth $2 million a season over eight years. Prior to the trade, it was estimated that Canadian advertising endorsements earned Gretzky another $1 million a year; the larger U.S. market may raise that figure.

It has been said that Wayne Gretzky possesses an unbeatable combination for a successful endorser: looks, talent, personality, and success. His image in the United States is a tougher sell, though, since hockey takes a back seat to football and basketball in that country. Stars such as Michael Jordan (of basketball fame) are much more popular with advertising executives. On Gretzky's side, however, is that "all-American" image that makes advertisers stop for a look, and, yes, he is popular in the United States. A survey by USA Today asked 10 000 sports fans for the greatest athlete in history. Gretzky ranked fourth behind Babe Ruth (baseball), Jim Thorpe (Olympian), and Muhammad Ali (boxing). Verification of Gretzky's popularity is the fact that Coca-Cola USA was the first national advertiser to sign him to an advertising contract.

Adapted from Adam Mayers, "Great One's a scoring ace in ad world", *Toronto Star*, October 8, 1988, pp.B1,B8.

*Lloyds Bank Canada is one of a number of companies to have associated its product with Wayne Gretzky*

objectives. Its role is to devise an effective plan for placing the message produced by the creative department in the available media.

**media objectives**

In defining **media objectives**, the first consideration is the target market. The target market is defined in terms of demographic, psychographic, and geographic variables. The desired physical presentation of the message (print or broadcast) influences the actual media (newspaper or magazines, radio or television) that is selected to communicate with the target. Next, geographic market priorities are established, a selection process usually influenced by the size of the media budget.

The final thing to be considered is what is the best time to reach the target: the best time of day, day of week, or period of weeks during the year.

## Media Strategy

media strategy

A **media strategy** describes "how" the media objectives will be accomplished: how many advertisements or commercials will run; how often, and for what length of time, they will appear. A media strategy presents recommendations regarding what media to use and details why certain media are selected and others rejected.

### Matching the Target Market

Essentially, the task of an advertising agency's media department is to match the advertised product's target-market profile with a compatible media profile such as the readership profile of a magazine or newspaper, or the listenership of a radio station. Three common target-market media strategies are as follows:

profile matching

1. In the case of **profile matching**, the advertising message is placed in media where the profile of readers, listeners, or viewers is reasonably close to that of the product's target market. For example, advertising in *The Financial Post* or *The Globe and Mail's Report on Business* reaches one type of person; an advertisement in *The Hockey News* reaches another type of person.

shotgun strategy

2. In the case of a **shotgun strategy**, general-interest media are selected to reach a broad cross-section of a market population. For example, television may be chosen to make contact with diverse age groups, from young children to teens to adults; newspapers may be used to gain access to a broad cross-section of adult age groups.

rifle strategy

3. In the case of a **rifle strategy**, the target market is defined by a common characteristic, such as being employed in a certain industry or participating in a leisure activity. Media that appeal specifically to this common characteristic are then used. For example, *Ski Canada* magazine is used to reach skiers and *Hotel & Restaurant* magazine to reach people in the hospitality industry.

### Reach, Frequency, and Continuity

reach

During the development of a media strategy, the organization must decide on the reach, frequency, and continuity needed to fulfill the media objectives for an advertising message. These factors interact with each other. **Reach** refers to the total audience potentially exposed, one or more times, to an advertiser's schedule of messages in a given period, usually a week. It is expressed as a percentage of the target population in a geographically defined area. Assume a television station was seen by 30 000 households in a geographic area of 150 000 households. Reach is calculated by the formula:

$$\text{Reach} = \frac{\text{Number of Households Tuned to Station}}{\text{Number of Households in Area}}$$

$$= \frac{30\ 000}{150\ 000}$$

$$= 20\%$$

frequency

**Frequency** refers to the average number of times an audience is exposed to an advertising message over a period, usually a week. The airing of a television commercial three times on a station during a week would represent its frequency. In media planning, a balance must be struck between reach and frequency. A common dilemma faced by a media planner is whether to recommend more reach at the expense of frequency, or vice versa.

continuity

**Continuity** refers to the length of time required to create an impact on a target market through a particular medium. Continuity concerns the duration of the campaign. For example, an advertiser may schedule television commercials in eight week flights, three times a year, thus covering a total of 24 weeks of the calendar year. A **flight** or **flighting** refers to the purchase of media time and space in planned intervals, separated by periods of inactivity.

flight (flighting)

impressions

The combination of reach, frequency, and continuity is expressed in terms of **impressions** made on a target audience. Impressions refer to the total audience delivered by a media plan. Often referred to as total exposures, impressions are calculated by means of multiplying the number of people reached by the average number of times they are reached in the total schedule.

## Market Coverage

coverage

**Coverage** refers to the number of geographic markets where the advertising is to occur for the duration of a media plan. In deciding the extent of coverage, the advertiser could select national, regional, or particular urban markets, depending on its marketing and advertising objectives. Factors such as budget, sales volume by area, and level of distribution by area affect the selection.

## Timing

Determining the best time to reach a target market may center on either the time of day, the week, or the year. The best time to advertise a product or service is the time at which it will have the most impact on the consumer's buying decision. Decisions about some products and services tend to be made at particular moments in the day, week, or year (e.g., decisions about groceries tend to be made in the middle of or late in the week, just before paycheques are received, whereas decisions about snowmobiles are made in the fall). The advertisements should reach the buyers at the time they are making the buying decision. That time is just before a product is normally used most. For instance, people shop for and purchase lawnmowers during the few weeks just prior to the time of year when the lawn first needs cutting.

## Media Alternatives: The Pros and Cons

In conjunction with other strategic factors, the advantages and disadvantages of the various media are considered (see figure 14.12). Rarely can an advertiser use all media. In keeping with budget constraints, and in consideration of the habits of the target market and of variables such as reach, frequency, and continuity, specific media are chosen. For example, advertising for automobiles is concentrated in television and print (magazines and newspapers). Television creates awareness and a sense of excitement about an automobile, while print creates awareness and gives readers more specific details about the automobile.

**FIGURE 14.12**   Media Selection Considerations

| Advantages | Disadvantages |
|---|---|

**Television**

| Advantages | Disadvantages |
|---|---|
| 1. Impact — it combines sight, sound, and motion | 1. Cost — high cost of time and commercial production |
| 2. Reach — very high among all age groups | 2. Clutter — commercials are clustered together, reducing impact |
| 3. Demonstration — product can be shown in use | 3. Fragmentation — the audience has many stations to choose from |

**Radio**

| Advantages | Disadvantages |
|---|---|
| 1. Targeting — it reaches a selective audience based on type of music | 1. Retention — it offers only short, single-sense messages |
| 2. Reach and Frequency — the message reaches the same audience frequently, at reasonable cost | 2. Fragmentation — many stations in large markets reduces impact |

**Newspaper**

| Advantages | Disadvantages |
|---|---|
| 1. Coverage — good local market reach for local and national advertisers | 1. Life Span — very short, a one-day medium |
| 2. Flexibility — the message can be inserted quickly and altered quickly | 2. Target Market — it reaches a broad cross-section; not appropriate for reaching specific targets |
|  | 3. Clutter — many ads in each edition |

| Advantages | Disadvantages |
|---|---|

**Magazine**

| Advantages | Disadvantages |
|---|---|
| 1. Target Marketing — specialized magazines reach defined demographic groups | 1. Clutter — each issue contains too many advertisements |
| 2. Environment — the quality of the surrounding editorial enhances the advertising message | 2. Frequency — low message frequency in case of monthly publication |

**Outdoor and Transit**

| Advantages | Disadvantages |
|---|---|
| 1. Reach and Frequency — frequent message sent to same target audience (based on assumption of daily travel patterns) | 1. Message — small size in transit; short messages in outdoor |
| 2. Coverage — available on a market-by-market basis | 2. Targeting — reaches the broad cross-section of a market's population |

**Direct Marketing**

| Advantages | Disadvantages |
|---|---|
| 1. Targeting — it reaches a preselected and defined audience | 1. Image — low (e.g., junk mail) image; hard-sell approach required to solicit orders |
| 2. Control — advertising expenditure can be evaluated directly for effectiveness |  |

## Media Execution

Media execution is the final stage of media planning. It is the process of fine-tuning strategy into specific action plans. Such action plans are divided into the following areas: evaluating cost comparisons so that one particular medium may be selected over another; scheduling of specific media in a planning format (i.e., establishing a media calendar of activity); and developing budget summaries that show how advertising funds are to be spent. For example, if magazines are the chosen medium, the decision regarding which magazines to use and how often advertisements will appear in the magazines is made. To reach a business executive, an advertiser such as Mercedes Benz or Jaguar may decide to use a combination of magazines such as *Financial Post Moneywise*, *The Globe and Mail's Report on Business Magazine* or *Canadian Business*. Depending on the budget available, these advertisers could use all or any combination of the magazine alternatives. Appendix A, "The Ontario Tourism Marketing Plan", includes some good illustrations of media strategy and execution concepts.

## ⟩⟩⟩⟩ *Evaluating Advertising Effectiveness*

Advertisers spend a considerable amount of money on evaluating the effectiveness of their advertising messages. Research is conducted at two different stages: pretesting and post-testing. **Pretesting** involves evaluating — prior to final creative production and media placement — an advertisement, commercial, or campaign in order to determine the strengths and weaknesses of the message. **Post-testing** is the evaluation of an advertisement, commercial or campaign, during or after its implementation.

**pretesting**

**post-testing**

The basic purpose of pretesting is to gauge initial reaction and make changes where necessary, while post-testing provides new input for future advertising planning. One of the options available for collecting this information is the personal interview questionnaire, where the consumers is asked to view some ads and respond to a series of questions, or is brought to a facility to view commercials and respond to a series of questions.

Two common techniques for measuring the effectiveness of a message are recognition testing and recall testing. A **recognition test** is a test of consumer awareness. Respondents are asked if they can remember an advertisement or any specific points made in it about a product or service. A **recall test** is a method of measuring consumers' comprehension following exposure to a message in a test or a real situation. Respondents are asked to recall specific elements of an advertisement or commercial (e.g., specific selling points, slogans, characters, and presenters of the message). Recall information is normally collected by questionnaire. Two of the more common methods for measuring recognition and recall are the Starch readership test (in print media) and the DAR or day after recall test (in broadcast media).

**recognition test**

**recall test**

## Starch Readership Test

**Starch readership test**

A **Starch readership test** is a pretest or post-test readership procedure applied to both newspaper and magazine advertisements. The objectives of a Starch test are to measure how many readers have seen an ad, and what percentage of those who saw it actually read it. After the test, the results are quantified and data is classified into three areas of measurement:

1. *Noted*   This refers to the percentage of readers who remember seeing the advertisement.

2. *Associated*   The associated category includes that percentage of readers who saw any part of the advertisement and could recall the brand or advertiser.

3. *Read Most*   The percentage of readers who read more than half of the written material form this group.

### Day After Recall Test

**day after recall**

As the name implies, **day after recall** testing is conducted the day after the audience is exposed to a commercial message. Using a telephone survey technique, a sampling of the advertiser's target market is asked a series of questions so that their exposure to and recall of a particular commercial message can be determined.

The quantified measures obtained through a day after recall test are of two dimensions: intrusiveness and impact. Recall refers to the percentage of the audience who claim to remember the test commercial, and are also able to provide some description of the commercial.[8] The higher the percentage, the more intrusive the message is said to have been. In a DAR test, the advertiser learns the level of brand-name recall and the impact its message has had on the audience by examining the quality and quantity of message playback by respondents in the test.

## ⟩⟩⟩ *Public Relations*

**public relations**

**Public relations** consist of a variety of activities and communications that organizations undertake to monitor, evaluate, influence, and adapt to the attitudes, opinions, and behaviours of groups or individuals who constitute the organization's publics.[9] These publics include shareholders, employees, suppliers, the government, channel-member customers, and consumers. Communications with these publics may entail the transfer of financial information about the company and about its developments (e.g., acquisitions and mergers), its expansion plans, appointments, and layoffs of its personnel. Public relations is distinguished from advertising in two ways:

1. Advertising is controlled and paid for by a sponsor, whereas public relations is a form of communications controlled by the media and not paid for directly by the company the media story concerns. The media determines the amount and content of the message, constrained only by the known facts of the situation presented. Organizations, however, can and often do include paid advertising as part of their public relations activity.

2. While advertising is primarily concerned with product image, public relations is primarily concerned with corporate image.

**publicity**

At the product level, publicity is used to help promote goods and services. **Publicity** is one aspect of public relations; it is the communication of newsworthy information about a product, service, company or idea, usually in the form of a press release. Examples of a press release and of a public relations advertisement for a corporate program are given in figure 14.13. Typically, publicity attends the launch-

**FIGURE 14.13** Public Relations Communications

130 Winges Rd.
Suite 201
Woodbridge, Ontario
L4L 6B9
(416) 856-2252

## Di$count

### CAR AND TRUCK RENTALS

FOR IMMEDIATE RELEASE   -   ATTENTION SPORTS/BUSINESS EDITORS

THURSDAY MAY 11, 1989 - 11:15 A.M.

DISCOUNT CAR AND TRUCK RENTALS ANNOUNCES GYMNASTICS SPONSORSHIP

Discount Car and Truck Rentals today announced a four-year,
$160,000 "support" sponsorship of the Canadian National
Gymnastics and Trampoline Championships, beginning in 1989 and
culminating in 1992.  This national sponsorship is in addition to
the annual support given to gymnastics in Ontario which amounts
to $35,000 - a grand total of $300,000 over the next four years.

Discount Car and Truck Rentals will be the "support category"
sponsor of the Nationals, along with the title sponsor - Philips
Electronics Ltd.  The sponsorship is comprised of a significant
cash allotment as well as the provision of complimentary vehicles
to the organizing committee for use during the event.  With this
four year, $160,000 pledge, Discount builds on its previous
sponsorships of the '88 Nationals and Four Continents
Championships.

"As a family-oriented sport, gymnastics provides Discount with
the opportunity to reinforce our commitment to our customers and
to the community as a whole," said Herb Singer, President and
Founder of Discount Car and Truck Rentals....

"Discount's unique national/regional marketing program has
greatly benefited both the Canadian and Ontario Gymnastic
Federations", remarked Lester Wood, President of The Ontario
Gymnastic Federation.  "We work together as a team to maximize
the return for all parties involved."

Discount Car and Truck Rentals is riding the wave of the future -
expanding through franchising opportunities in its quest for
increased growth.  Beginning with one outlet in 1980, the company
currently operates in 73 locations across the country.

According to Singer, "We celebrate individuals who go the extra
mile.  We hope our sponsorship of gymnastics will provide the
thousands of gymnasts across Canada with an opportunity to
achieve excellence, at a variety of skill levels."

Contacts:    Morgan H. Groen, Marketing Manager
             Discount Car and Truck Rentals
             (416) 856-2252

             Lawrence J. Moran, Executive Director
             The Ontario Gymnastic Federation
             (416) 495-4110

*A press release announcing news of a company.*

**FIGURE 14.13** (continued)

## Bravo.

 Proud sponsors:
May 18–21, 1989, University of Alberta Pavilion, Edmonton.

Dedication. Heart. Guts.
You'll never see any of these accurately reflected on a scoreboard.
Yet they're the qualities that can make the joy of victory possible. And the agony of defeat endurable.

More important, they're the attributes that make the athletes of this country so commendable.
The people at Discount salute our athletes. Not for winning or losing. But, once again, for playing the game so admirably.

We want your business.
And we'll come right to your front door to get it.

*A corporate advertisement used in conjunction with sponsorship.*

ing of a new product, the opening of a new store, a technological breakthrough, or the achievement of some milestone. Since publicity is usually not paid for by the sponsor, the sponsor accepts whatever media coverage it receives. For an illustration of the impact that publicity can have, see the Marketing in Action vignette "Beware, Ice Cream Addicts. . . Here's an Ice Cream as Good as Sex."

Public relations is also a vital form of communication for a company during a

# ⟩⟩⟩⟩ *MARKETING IN ACTION*

### *BEWARE ICE CREAM ADDICTS. . . HERE'S AN ICE CREAM AS GOOD AS SEX*

A pair of Toronto entrepreneurs, Hart Melvin and Gary Soren, believed there was an untapped niche in the high end of the ice cream market, dominated by products of premium quality and high price. They claim that their product is like no other. It has great taste, great texture, and a low fat content, a combination that should win the hearts and stomachs of Canadians.

From a stand-still start, the product obtained distribution in gourmet shops in Toronto, in sixteen local Loblaws stores, and in 20 Marks & Spencer stores across Canada. The product called Gelato Fresco is sold in small 500-ml tubs and retailed for $3.89 when introduced.

What made Gelato Fresco a success was its high quality and some good fortune along the way. Joanne Kates, food critic for *The Globe and Mail*, reviewed the product. She wrote that Gelato Fresco was at least as good as sex with a loved one, and that it was to ice cream what truffles were to chocolates. At the same time, Loblaws agreed to test the product in six Toronto stores. With such favourable publicity from *The Globe and Mail*, the product sold out in 24 hours.

Loblaws and other retailers liked the pricing structure (small item, high profit margin). Gelato Fresco is really an indulgence for the discerning ice cream buyer.

Gelato Fresco now faces a problem common to other local firms that want to expand nationally. How to expand (produce enough) nationally while maintaining the quality they have locally. A new $300 000 plant opened in 1989 that produces 4 000 half-litres a day, ten times their local production. Another limiting factor is the size of the market. Positioned as a super-premium ice cream, one that has only 10 percent air content, it

*Gelato Fresco offers the consumer a combination of great taste, great texture, and low fat content*

faces a segment that comprises less than one-half of one percent of the Canadian market. Average consumers are attracted to lower-priced budget and premium-priced brands. Undaunted by this barrier, the business is moving forward. Under consideration is the development of an elegant and sophisticated ice-cream-parlour concept for potential franchising opportunities.

Adapted from Tracy Nesdoly, "The Ice Cream Men Cometh", *Canadian Business*, July 1988, p.21.

crisis. When facing adverse public reaction to a product because of its poor perform-ance or danger to health or safety, a company often responds through public rela-tions. The final outcome of such a crisis often depends on how effectively a firm manages its public-relations activity. For instance, a drug manufacturer may face an angry public when a certain drug is discovered to create health problems. Lawsuits brought against the company and media coverage of the public's concern is a significant problem that the company must deal with. In an unusual case, MacNeil Laboratories, a division of Johnson & Johnson, faced a potentially disastrous loss of customer loyalty in the early 1980s when some bottles of Tylenol were deliberately tampered with and caused deaths. The combination of advertising and public-relations communications based on trust (e.g., users of the product made statements in commercials about how they have trusted the name and quality of Tylenol over time) helped restore Tylenol to its leading market position. The scare also resulted in new, safer packaging throughout the drug industry, a move spearheaded by Tylenol.

Since public relations, publicity, and advertising are all components of the promo-tion mix, the use of each is carefully considered by a marketing organization. Many advertising agencies offer all of these services to their clients.

## >>>> SUMMARY

Promotion is any means of communications used by marketing organizations to inform, persuade, or remind potential buyers about a product or service. To fulfill these tasks, an organization employs a promotion mix comprised of advertising, public relations, sales promotion, personal selling, and programs for event-marketing and sponsorship. A company can also use two types of promotion strategy: push and pull. In the case of a push strategy, the firm directs promotional efforts at the channel members or intermediaries, while in a pull strategy it directs efforts at final business users or consumers. Often a firm will use a combination of push and pull strategies in the promotion mix.

In developing a promotion budget, a business considers many factors, including the type of customer sought for the product, the degree of competi-tion that exists, and the stage of the product life cycle the product has reached. Several different methods of determining the actual size of a budget are available to the firm.

The primary role of advertising is to influence the behaviour of a target market in such a way that its members view the product, service or idea favourably. In developing print and broadcast messages, the creative team (copywriter and art director) consider the behavioural stages an individual passes through prior to making a purchase decision.

Advertising is classified into two different forms: consumer advertising and business-to-business advertising. Those involved in the Canadian advertising industry comprise three primary groups: advertisers, advertising agencies, and media. Advertisers evaluate the services provided by agencies and decide on using a full-service agency or some type of specialist. Specialist agencies include creative boutiques, media-buying services, retail agencies, and direct-response agencies.

In advertising planning, there is clear division between creative and media functions. On the creative side, creative objectives (what to communicate) are established and a creative strategy (how to communicate) is developed. The quality of the message is evaluated through a variety of pretest and post-test research techniques. The media plan is divided into three sections: media objectives, media strategy, and media execution. A well-conceived media plan will utilize the right media to gain maximum exposure for the message developed by the creative department.

Public relations refers to the communications a firm has with its various publics. Controlled by the media, it is a form of communication for which the organization does not pay, but it is based on information supplied by the organization. Public relations plays a role in developing an organization's image and is an important means of communication in times of crisis. At the product level, publicity is used to promote goods and services.

## ⟩⟩⟩⟩ KEY TERMS

| | | |
|---|---|---|
| promotion mix | advertising agencies | frequency |
| marketing communications | full-service agency | continuity |
| promotion planning | creative boutiques | flight/flighting |
| push strategy | media-buying service | impressions |
| pull strategy | creative objectives | coverage |
| advertising | creative strategy | pretesting |
| national advertising | creative execution | post-testing |
| retail advertising | media planning | recognition test |
| end-product advertising | media objectives | recall test |
| direct-response advertising | media strategy | starch readership test |
| business-to-business advertising | profile matching | day after recall |
| trade advertising | shotgun strategy | public relations |
| industrial advertising | rifle strategy | publicity |
| corporate advertising | reach | |

## ⟩⟩⟩⟩ QUESTIONS FOR REVIEW AND DISCUSSION

**1.** What is the difference between advertising and public relations?

**2.** Briefly describe the five elements of the promotion mix.

**3.** Briefly explain the difference between a push strategy and a pull strategy. Provide two examples of products that use each of these strategies.

**4.** What factors influence the size of an advertising budget?

**5.** What impact does DAGMAR have on the development of advertising messages?

**6.** Describe the role of the three functional areas of a full-service advertising agency.

**7.** Provide examples of commercials or campaigns which use the following creative appeals: **(a)** humour **(b)** emotion **(c)** lifestyle **(d)** testimonial Which commercial or campaign has the most influence on you? Briefly explain why.

**8.** Explain the basic elements of media objective-statements.

**9.** Explain the following media-strategy concepts: reach, frequency, and continuity.

**10.** "When a new product is being introduced, the objective is reach, at the expense of frequency." Discuss this statement.

**11.** "Advertisers who use celebrities to endorse their products are guaranteed success." Discuss the merits of this statement.

**12.** Which media are best suited for a profile-matching strategy? shotgun strategy? Provide some specific examples.

**13.** What is the difference between pretesting and post-testing, and how is each concept used in the creative planning process?

## >>>> REFERENCES

1. PETER D. BENNETT, *Marketing* (Toronto: McGraw-Hill Ryerson, 1988), p.511.

2. RICHARD E. STANLEY, *Promotion* (New York: Prentice-Hall, 1977).

3. "Brand Leaders", *Playback Strategy*, September 11, 1989, p.36.

4. American Marketing Association, "Definition of Marketing Terms", n.d., p.1.

5. RUSSEL H. COLLEY, *Defining Advertising Goals* (New York: Association of National Advertisers Inc., 1961).

6. "Fight Getting Fiercer for Ad Revenues", *Financial Post*, February 13, 1989, p.1.

7. Institute of Canadian Advertising, *So. . . You Want to be in an Advertising Agency*, n.d., p.2.

8. CHERIE HILL, "In Defense of DAR Testing", *Stimulus*, June 1984, p.28.

9. DOUG NEWSOM, ALAN SCOTT, and JUDY VANSLYKE TURK, *This is PR* (Belmont, California: Wadsworth Publishing Company, 1989), p.509.

# CHAPTER 15 ›››››

# Promotion Strategy II

## Sales Promotion, Personal Selling, Event Marketing and Sponsorships

---

### LEARNING OBJECTIVES

After studying this chapter, you will be able to

1. Describe the various types of consumer and trade promotion activities.

2. Identify the role of sales promotion in the promotion mix.

3. Describe the roles of sales representatives and the types of selling that occur in a business organization.

4. Outline the steps in the selling process.

5. Explain the importance that event marketing and sponsorships have in contemporary marketing.

6. List the unique considerations involved in planning event-marketing programs.

---

This chapter examines the remaining elements of the promotion mix: namely, sales promotion, personal selling, event marketing, and sponsorship programs. These activities, along with advertising and public relations, complement one another and the total marketing effort of the organization. Collectively, these activities influence the consumer's decision to buy products and services.

## 〉〉〉〉 Sales Promotion

In Canada, the value of sales promotion activity is estimated to be $7 billion.[1] Such a high investment is indicative of the important role sales promotion plays in the

FIGURE 15.1    Marketing Budget Expense Allocations

Percentage of budget allocated to:

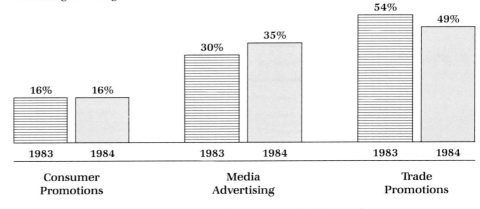

Funds allocated between consumer and trade are basically equal

*Source*: Nielsen Promotion Services. Reprinted with permission of A.C. Nielsen Company of Canada Ltd.

**sales promotion**

marketing of goods and services. **Sales promotion** is an activity that provides special incentives to bring about immediate action from consumers, distributors, and an organization's sales force; in other words, it encourages the decision to buy. The expression "advertising appeals to the heart, and sales promotion to the wallet" shows the distinction between the two types of activity. For instance, advertising tells us why we should buy a product, whereas sales promotion offers financial or other incentives to purchase a product. A cents-off coupon, for example, is a form of sales promotion; by lowering the price of a brand-name product, it provides the consumer with a financial inducement to make a purchase. Two principal kinds of sales promotion exist: consumer promotion and trade promotion. Figure 15.1 indicates how spending is distributed among consumer promotion, trade promotion, and advertising by manufacturers in the food, household, and personal-care-product industries.

# ⟩⟩⟩⟩ *Consumer Promotion*

**consumer promotion**

**Consumer promotion** is any activity that promotes extra brand sales by offering the consumer an incentive over and above the product's inherent benefits. These promotions are designed to pull the product through the channel of distribution by motivating consumers to make an immediate purchase. The sorts of purchases the promotions are used to foster are as follows:

1. *Trial Purchase*   When introducing a new product, marketers want customers to make a first purchase right away so that product acceptance can be secured quickly.

2. *Repeat Purchases*   Marketers protect loyalty to established products by offering incentives for consumers to buy the item repeatedly. Including coupons with a

product that can be redeemed on the next purchase of the product is a way of holding loyalty.

3. *Multiple Purchases* Promotions of this nature "load the consumer up." For example, a contest may be run to spur many entries and purchases, or cash refunds may offer savings that increase with each additional purchase of an item. For instance, a $1.00 refund may be available on one purchase and a $3.00 refund on two purchases.

The major types of consumer promotion are coupons, free samples, contests, cash refunds, and premiums.

## Coupons

coupons

The first major type of consumer promotions is that of **coupons**. They are defined as price-saving incentives offered consumers by manufacturers and retailers which stimulate an immediate purchase of a designated product. The basic elements of a coupon are shown in figure 15.2. In Canada, coupons are distributed in mass

**FIGURE 15.2**   Sample Coupon Design

A coupon should:

- Be immediately recognizable as a coupon
- Clearly state the offer terms
- Show a picture of the featured brand
- Give clear instructions to the retailer
- Contain a unique Smartscan offer code
- If used, have the expiry date printed in the recommended location.

This coupon example contains the most important coupon design elements, including a Smartscan code in the required location.

Source: A.C. Nielsen Company of Canada Limited, *A Marketer's Guide to Couponing*. Reprinted with permission.

**FIGURE 15.3**   The Number of Coupons Distributed and Redeemed in Canada

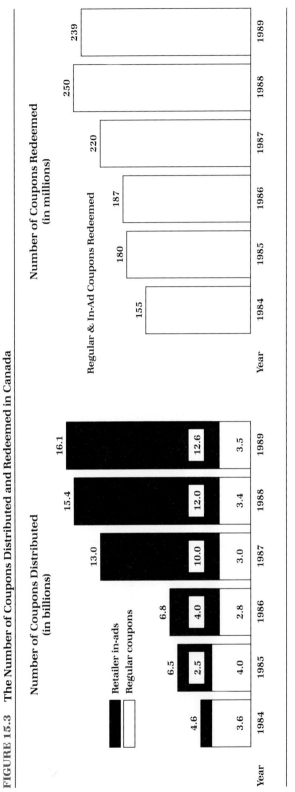

## Number of Coupons Redeemed
### (in millions)

Regular & In-Ad Coupons Redeemed

| Year | 1984 | 1985 | 1986 | 1987 | 1988 | 1989 |
|------|------|------|------|------|------|------|
|      | 155  | 180  | 187  | 220  | 250  | 239  |

## Number of Coupons Distributed
### (in billions)

■ Retailer in-ads
□ Regular coupons

| Year | 1984 | 1985 | 1986 | 1987 | 1988 | 1989 |
|------|------|------|------|------|------|------|
| Retailer in-ads | 4.6 | 6.5 | 6.8 | 13.0 | 15.4 | 16.1 |
|  |  | 2.5 | 4.0 | 10.0 | 12.0 | 12.6 |
| Regular coupons | 3.6 | 4.0 | 2.8 | 3.0 | 3.4 | 3.5 |

*Source:* A.C. Nielsen Company of Canada Limited, *A Marketer's Guide to Couponing.* Reprinted with permission.

**redemption rate**

quantity. As of 1989, the total number of coupons distributed by manufacturers and retailers amounted to 16.1 billion, of which 239 million were redeemed (see figure 15.3).[2]

The effectiveness of a coupon campaign is determined by the **redemption rate**, or the number of coupons returned to an organization expressed as a percentage of the total number of coupons in distribution for a particular coupon offer. Figure 15.4 shows the average redemption figures for different kinds of coupons. Among the factors that influence the rate of redemption are the method of distribution, the face value of the coupon in relation to the retail selling price, the frequency of product purchases, the brand's market share, the availability of the product, the terms of the offer (e.g., the number of purchases required), and the coupon design.[3]

Coupons are delivered to consumers in three different ways: through such media as newspapers, magazines, and direct mail; in or on the package of the product; and in-store, through display centers, handouts, or coupon-dispensing machines.

### Coupons Delivered by Product

**product-delivered coupons**

One kind of **product-delivered coupon**, in-pack self-coupons, are redeemable on the next purchase of the same product. The package is usually "flagged" somehow to draw attention to the coupon included inside the package. They are distinct from the two types of on-pack self-coupons: 1) regular on-pack coupons usually appear on the back or side panel of the package or behind a label and are valid for a future purchase of the same product; and 2) instantly redeemable coupons are valid when the product carrying the coupon is bought and the coupon is removed from the package. Other variations are in-pack or on-pack cross-coupons, which are valid on the purchase of a different product. Such coupons encourage the consumer to buy complementary products. For example, a tea or coffee brand may carry coupons for a brand of cookies and vice versa.

**FIGURE 15.4** Coupon Redemption Rates by Method of Distribution

| Media | Range | Median |
|---|---|---|
| Cooperative Direct Mail | 2.2% – 17.7% | 7.2% |
| Free-Standing Inserts (FSI) | 1.7 – 9.7 | 4.0 |
| Magazines | 0.4 – 9.2 | 2.7 |
| Newspaper (RoP) | 0.4 – 5.5 | 1.9 |
| Selective Direct Mail | 4.8 – 42.8 | 17.5 |
| In-Store Display Center/Entrance | 0.3 – 40.2 | 14.2 |
| In-Store Shelf | 10.3 – 51.9 | — |
| In-Store Handout | 9.2 – 60.5 | 27.1 |
| Retailer Coupon Booklets/Calendars | 0.1 – 3.5 | — |
| In-Pack Self | 5.2 – 47.2 | 21.8 |
| On-Pack Self | 3.2 – 50.7 | 15.7 |
| Instantly Redeemable Coupons | 15.5 – 91.8 | 45.9 |
| In-Pack Cross | 2.8 – 20.2 | 7.7 |
| On-Pack Cross | 0.8 – 15.7 | 4.4 |

*Source*: A.C. Nielsen Company of Canada Limited, *A Marketer's Guide to Couponing*. Reprinted with permission.

### *Coupons Delivered by Media*

**media-delivered**
**coupons**

Included in the category of **media-delivered coupons** are cooperative direct-mail coupons, which are distributed directly to households along selected postal walks in the form of unaddressed mail. The Carole Martin envelope is a good example of a cooperative direct-mail package; it is delivered numerous times each year and contains coupons for a range of non-competing products made by different companies. Each product shares in the cost of distributing the envelope, hence the name cooperative direct mail.

Another common type of coupon is the free-standing insert. These coupons are distributed as special supplements inserted in newspapers. Usually, the inserts are printed by means of a full-colour process, on quality paper, and they contain coupons for a variety of products. Free-standing inserts are marketed by distribution organizations that use such names as "The Coupon Clipper" and "Shop and Save". Advertisers also distribute coupons through newspapers and magazines, including them as part of their advertising copy.

### *Coupons Delivered In-store*

**in-store delivered**
**coupons**

The category of **in-store delivered coupons** includes coupons distributed by in-store display centers and dispensing machines usually located near the store entrance; by handout, as the customer enters the store; or on the reverse side of cash register tapes that customers receive after paying for their merchandise.

The objectives behind a coupon promotion affect the way coupons are delivered. These objectives are often related to the stage in the product life cycle that the item has reached. In the introduction and growth stages, getting people to make a trial purchase is the main objective, so coupons are predominantly delivered by media. As a product moves into maturity, coupons are frequently distributed in or on products, because prompting current consumers to continue purchasing is vital to preserving market share. When the objective is to make competitive users switch to one's own brand regardless of the stage of the life cycle, delivering coupons through the media is effective.

## Free Sample Distribution

**sample**

Another form of consumer promotion is the **sample**, a free product distributed to potential users either in a small trial size or in its regular size. Sampling is commonly practised when a company is introducing a new product, a line extension of a new product, or a product improvement such as a new flavour, taste, blend, or scent. It is an effective way of getting the market to try some item because it eliminates the financial risk of a purchase. It is, however, considered to be less efficient than coupons in converting trial users to regular users, and it is an expensive proposition because of the costs of the product and its packaging and distribution.[4] Often a manufacturer will combine samples and coupons to encourage consumers to try or continue using a product (see figure 15.5).

**FIGURE 15.5**   Combining Samples and Coupons

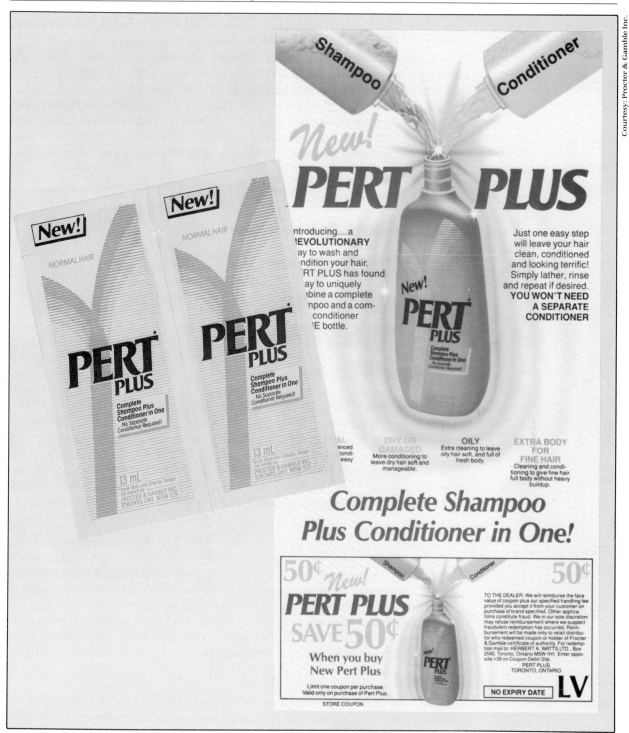

*To secure trial purchase, Procter & Gamble distributes a free sample and coupon for a new product by cooperative direct mail.*

Samples are most frequently distributed in stores, mainly because of reduced costs. They can also be delivered by cooperative direct mail, so long as the sample is small and light enough to be accommodated in a mailing envelope, or they can be delivered directly to households by independent delivery organizations.

Some variations in sampling occur. Sometimes, product demonstrations are combined with sampling. For instance, a display table with product samples is set up in a supermarket so that shoppers who pass by can try a new product. At other times, instead of distributing free products, small trial sizes that replicate the regular package and product are offered for sale. Free samples may also be given away with another product, a practice called **cross-sampling**. An example of cross-sampling would be a regular-size package of Kellogg's Corn Flakes carrying a sample size of Special K inside.

**cross-sampling**

## Contests

Contests are designed to create short-term excitement about a product. A contest usually provides an incentive to buy an item, requiring, for example, the submission of a product label or symbol and an entry form that is included with the product. Consumers are encouraged to enter often and thereby improve their chances of winning a prize. This results in many purchases. While contests tend to attract the current users of a product, they are less effective in inducing trial purchases than are coupons and samples. Consequently, contests are most appropriate in the late stages of the product life cycle, when the aim is to retain the present market share. Among the elements that influence the success of a contest are the type and value of the prizes offered; these features affect consumers' perception of the contest, the odds of winning, and the complexity of the contest. Generally, the easier it is to enter, the more favourable the reaction of the customer. The Marketing in Action vignette "Do Promotions Work?" (see page 452) illustrates how effective contests can be. Sweepstakes and instant wins are two major types of contests.

**sweepstakes**

1. In a **sweepstakes** contest, prizes such as cash, cars, homes, and vacations are given away. Consumers enter contests by filling in a blank entry form, usually available at the point-of-purchase or through print advertising, and submitting it along with a proof of purchase to a central location where a draw is held to determine the winners. Usually, an independent organization selects the winners on behalf of the sponsor company. A study conducted by Nielsen Promotion services showed that prizes of automobiles, cash, and vacations produced more than the average number of entries among the contests they analyzed (see figure 15.6).[5]

**instant wins**

2. In **instant wins**, packages contain winning certificates to be redeemed for prizes. Variations of this type of contest include collect-and-wins, match-and-wins, and small-prize instant-wins combined with a grand-prize contest.

FIGURE 15.6    Prizes Affect Consumer Participation in Sweepstakes

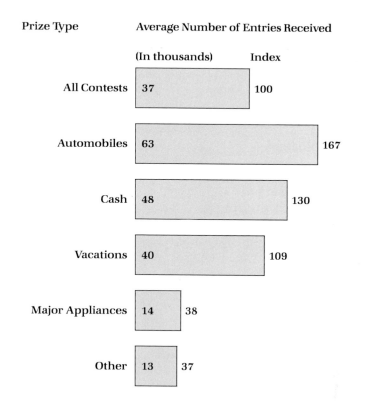

This chart shows how consumer participation varied according to the type of prizes which were offered in sweepstakes managed by Nielsen Promotion Services.

*Source*:  A.C. Nielsen Company of Canada Limited, *A Marketer's Guide to Couponing*. Reprinted with permission.

Contests are governed by laws and regulations, and any company that runs one must publish certain information:

1.  How, where, and when to enter.
2.  Who is eligible or ineligible to enter.
3.  The prize structure, value, and number of prizes.
4.  The odds of winning and the selection procedure.
5.  Conditions that must be met before a prize can be accepted (e.g., a skill-testing question must be answered).

## >>>> *MARKETING IN ACTION*

### *DO PROMOTIONS WORK?*

Marketing organizations are spending more money on consumer promotions than ever before. One of the arguments in favour of promotional spending is that the results or effectiveness of the promotion can be measured, whereas the effectiveness of media advertising cannot. By way of illustration, here is a consumer promotion used by Air France:

*Promotion Objective:* To increase bookings from selected metropolitan areas.

*Promotion Strategy:* The Air-France "Fly-Free" sweepstakes was developed, which offered consumers the opportunity to "win one of 115 round trips to Paris on a Concorde."

*Promotion Execution:* Entry forms were located in travel agency offices to build their traffic flow. Newspaper and radio advertising were used to support the promotion and generate consumer interest.

*Results Achieved:* Air France's average passenger load increased from 62 percent in 1986 to more than 80 percent in the promotion year 1987. A further benefit was that these gains were achieved without fare-cutting, a popular but unprofitable practice used by competitors.

Sheila McMeekin

*With its "Fly-Free" sweepstakes, which were developed to increase bookings from selected metropolitan areas, Air France gave consumers the opportunity to win one of 155 round trips to Paris on a Concorde*

Adapted from "Six promotions earn the top awards", *Marketing*, August 15, 1988, p.40.

## Cash Refunds

**cash refund (rebate)**

A **cash refund**, or **rebate** as it is often called, is a predetermined amount of money returned directly to the consumer by the manufacturer after the purchase has been made. For companies in the packaged-goods industry, cash refunds are useful promotion techniques in the mature stage of the product's life cycle, for such activity reinforces loyalty. Refunds encourage consumers to make multiple purchases and stock their pantries (see figure 15.7). The most common type of refund is the single-purchase refund, given when, for example, the consumer is promised that he or she will "get $1.00 back" for the purchase of a specified product. However, refunds are designed to achieve different objectives; hence, they can be offered in several formats.

FIGURE 15.7  Combining Sweepstakes and Cash Refund

*Courtesy: Beatrice Foods, Inc.*

*Beatrice Foods Inc. uses a combination of a sweepstakes contest and a cash refund offer to encourage multiple purchases.*

### Refunds of Escalating Value

In the case of refunds of escalating value, the refund increases with each additional purchase; the refund is greatest when the consumer takes maximum advantage of the offer. For example, the offer could be structured as follows:

> Buy one and get $1.00 back
> Buy two and get $2.50 back
> Buy three and get $5.00 back

### Multi-Product or Family Refund Offers

In this case, a company plans a promotion involving many of their products. For example, a company like Procter & Gamble may designate brands from various product categories to be part of such a refund offer (e.g., Pampers, Scope, Duncan Hines, Crisco, Crest). If the consumer takes advantage of the entire offer, significant cash savings are possible. A common and popular format is a bingo-card approach, where a certain dollar amount is returned for any single line, a greater amount for two lines, and an even greater amount for a full card.

**slippage**

In the case of such refund offers, slippage generally occurs, which increases the efficiency of the manufacturer's promotion. **Slippage** happens when a consumer starts collecting proofs of purchase for a refund offer, but neglects to follow through and submit a request for the refund. In effect, the manufacturer does not pay for the purchases induced by the promotion. Slippage is a significant factor. In a 1986 survey of grocery shoppers, it was found that one half of all refund participants sometimes neglect to submit a request for a refund even after they have bought the product with the intention of using the refund offer.[6]

Rebates are now popular among manufacturers of durable goods like cars and major appliances. Rebates accomplish such objectives as the liquidation of inventory prior to the introduction of new models, and the generation of sales during traditionally weak periods or at times when interest rates on loans are high.

## Premium Offers

premium

A **premium** is an item offered free or at a bargain price to consumers who buy a specific item. For an illustration of the impact of premium offers on purchase patterns, refer to the Marketing in Action vignette "Premium Offer Helps The Bay." Although premiums can take different forms, they are principally offered in two ways, either as a mail-in, or as an in-pack or on-pack promotion.

### ⟩⟩⟩ *MARKETING IN ACTION*

*PREMIUM OFFER HELPS THE BAY*

In 1986, The Bay encountered a problem with its credit-card accounts. Too many of its credit accounts were inactive. The Bay had worked hard at attracting cardholders, but the infrequent use of the cards in a very competitive mass-retailing market posed a dilemma. The solution was an attractive premium offer to encourage credit-card use. Here's a brief summary of the consumer promotion.

*Problem:* High incidence of inactive credit cards.

*Promotion Objective:* To encourage card use and build traffic flow in Bay stores.

*Promotion Strategy:* Establish a reasonable minimum purchase requirement for credit-card users which would allow them to receive "free" a bonus premium.

*Promotion Offer:* For the premium, The Bay made a special purchase of 60 000 Silverstone frying pans, which were non-stick and had a red enamel outer covering. For a purchase of $10.00 or more, the consumer was entitled to a free pan.

*Promotion Tactics:* The offer was communicated through The Bay's credit-card data base. Inactive accounts (those not used in the last six to eighteen months) received a direct mail package. An envelope resembling a wrapped gift encouraged the recipient to "tear open the package to discover your bonus gift!" Inside were the promotion details and the full story on the merits of a Silverstone frying pan.

*Results:* The Bay had to order more frying pans; 25 percent of those who received the mailing

*In another consumer promotion, the Bay offered consumers a free Sport Watch with any Bay Card purchase*

responded. This response level exceeded that generated by any previous Bay premium offer. Many cardholders also purchased much more than the $10.00 minimum. That's where the promotion really paid off.

Adapted from Rick Muldoon, "Out of the fire and into the frying pan", *Sales & Marketing Management in Canada*, February 1988, pp.6-7.

### *Mail-In Premiums*

*mail-in premium*

**Mail-in premiums** are items that are made available free or at a much lower cost than the retail price to consumers who send away for them. A premium that a consumer pays for is called a self-liquidating premium; in effect, what the consumer pays covers the marketing costs of the offer. For example, in offering a coffee mug with a brand name or slogan printed on it for $1.95 and two proofs of purchase, a coffee company could recover the cost of the mug, appropriate sales taxes, and a handling charge. To the consumer this may still look like a good offer. Such promotions encourage multiple purchases and reinforce brand loyalty; hence, they are used most frequently in the mature stage of a product's life cycle.

### *In-Pack or On-Pack Premiums*

*in-pack or on-pack premiums*

**In-pack or on-pack premiums** are free items placed inside the package or attached to a package and over-wrapped for protection and security. Common examples include the small toys and games packed in cereal boxes, towels packed in detergent boxes, and samples of dental floss packaged with toothbrushes.

## ⟩⟩⟩⟩ *Trade Promotion*

*trade promotion*

Consumer promotion activities work best as part of a balanced marketing plan that combines pull strategies with trade-promotion activities, which are designed to push a product through the channel of distribution. **Trade promotion** is promotional activity directed at distributors; it is designed to increase the volume purchased and encourage merchandising support for a manufacturer's product. Along with trade discounts and performance allowances (discussed in chapter 11), the most commonly used trade promotion activities are cooperative advertising, in-ad coupons, dealer premiums, collateral materials, dealer display materials, and trade shows.

## Cooperative Advertising

*cooperative advertising*

In the case of **cooperative advertising**, manufacturers allocate allowances to pay a portion of a retailer's advertising. The weekly specials advertised by major supermarket chains, for example, are partially paid for by the manufacturers participating in the advertisements in any given week. In some cases, the manufacturer may agree to pay half of the retailer's cost of advertising, and frequently the manufacturer provides advertising illustrations and artwork that are integrated into the retailer's advertising message.

## Retail In-Ad Coupons

*retail in-ad coupon*

A **retail in-ad coupon** is a coupon printed in a retailer's weekly advertising, either in the newspaper or in supplements inserted in the newspaper. These coupons are redeemable on national brands and are usually paid for by the manufacturer. Retailers pay for coupons redeemable on private-label brands. The programs for national brands are developed by manufacturers' sales representatives and retail buyers. Usually, the funds to cover such coupons are derived from a trade-promotion budget; thus they are included as a trade-promotion activity.

## Dealer Premiums

**dealer premium**

A **dealer premium** is an incentive offered to a distributor by a manufacturer to encourage a special purchase (i.e., a specified volume of merchandise) or to secure additional merchandising support from a distributor. Dealer premiums are usually merchandise, and the value of the premium generally increases with the amount of product bought by the distributor. Their use is often controversial. Some distributors forbid their buyers to accept premiums because they feel only the individual buyer, rather than the organization, benefits. Such a situation may lead the buyer to make unnecessary purchases and ignore the objectives of the distributor.

## Collateral Material

To help itself in the personal-selling process, the sales force uses collateral materials supplied by the manufacturer to provide information to customers. These materials include price lists, catalogues, sales brochures, pamphlets, specification sheets, product manuals, and audio-visual materials (see figure 15.8).

## Dealer Display Material

**point-of-purchase material**

**Point-of-purchase material** consists of self-contained, custom-designed merchandising units, either permanent or temporary, that display a manufacturer's product. It includes posters, shelf talkers (small posters that hang from shelves), channel strips (narrow strips containing a brief message attached to the channel face of a shelf), advertising pads (tear-off sheets that usually explain details of a consumer promotion offer), display shippers (shipping cases that convert to display bins or stands when opened), and permanent display racks. The use of such displays and materials is at the discretion of retailers, whose space they occupy. The role of a manufacturer's sales representative is to convince the retailer of the merits of using the display.

## Trade Shows

Trade shows typically are organized by an industry association annually to demonstrate the latest products of member manufacturers. There are, for example, toy shows, automobile shows, and appliance shows. The unique value of a trade show is that it allows buyers and other decision-makers to come to a central location to secure the most recent product information from potential suppliers. For manufacturers, it is an important opportunity to develop a prospect list that the sales force can follow up. Thus, participants compete for the visitors' attention at the show, usually investing considerable sums to build unique and alluring display exhibits.

**FIGURE 15.8    Collateral Sales Material**

**BEATRICE WILL PUT YOUR 1989 YOGOURT SALES INTO HIGH GEAR WITH THIS DYNAMIC CONSUMER PROMOTION**

*Your customers can receive $2 back, and be eligible to win a hot, new 1989 GMC Tracker!*

 Along with an easy-to-complete entry form, all they have to do is submit proofs of purchase (foil lids): 8 from any 125g/175g Beatrice Yogourt *or* 4 from any 500g size.

 All you have to do is ensure you have plenty of Beatrice Yogourt on hand to meet the accelerating demand!

*A power-packed promotion.*

 The Beatrice "Four For The Road" Promotion will be supported by:
- An exciting F.S.I. distributed to 1.7 million households in Ontario and Manitoba on January 25, 1989.
- Impactful in-store point-of-sale including entry form/ad pads, and an eye-catching two-sided ceiling dangler.

*Two Fast-Track Performers.*

 Beatrice is the N°.1 Brand of Yogourt in Ontario and Manitoba (A. C. Nielsen 12 months ended, Aug./Sept. 1988) on the strength of our Fruit Bottom™, La Crème, Light, and new Swiss Style brands.

 Beatrice Yogourts continue to generate the highest level of stockturns per year in Ontario, (69 annual turns) which means more profit for you.

 General Motors has just introduced the new GMC Tracker for 1989. The subcompact 4 × 4 is built for family fun, on or off the road.

Beatrice is committed to maintain its N°.1 rank in the Yogourt Market, and to profitably build your Yogourt business.

**DON'T LET THIS OPPORTUNITY "PASS YOU BY".
ACCELERATE YOUR YOGOURT SALES WITH BEATRICE.**

We put good taste into everything we make

# ⟩⟩⟩⟩ *Personal Selling*

**personal selling**

**Personal selling** is face-to-face communication that involves a seller presenting the features and benefits of a product or service to a buyer for the purpose of making a sale. It is an integral component of the promotion mix, for it is the activity that in many cases clinches a deal. Advertising and sales promotion create awareness and interest and get the customer to come to the point of purchase. From there, personal selling takes over. The interaction between the seller and the buyer, along with a demonstration of the product, creates the desire for the product which leads to action on the part of the buyer. While the purpose of selling is to make the sale, the role of the sales representative goes beyond this task.

## The Role of the Contemporary Salesperson

### *Gathering Market Intelligence*

In a competitive marketplace, salespeople must be attuned to the happenings of their particular industry. They must be alert to what the competitor is doing, to its new product projects and to its advertising and promotion plans, and they must listen to feedback from customers regarding their own products' performances. All the data they collect from the field is reported to the company's head office for review by the appropriate managers.

### *Problem Solving*

The only way a salesperson can make a sale is to listen to what a customer wants and ask questions to determine his or her real needs. Asking, listening, and providing information and advice that is in the best interests of the customer is what consulta-

**consultative selling**

tive selling is all about. **Consultative selling** is the form of selling most prominent in today's marketplace.

### *Locating and Maintaining Customers*

Salespeople who locate new customers play a key role in a company's growth. A company cannot be satisfied with its present list of customers because aggressive competitors attempt to lure them away. To prevent shrinkage and to increase sales, salespeople actively pursue new accounts. Their time is divided between finding new accounts and selling and servicing current accounts.

### *Follow-Up Service*

The sale is never over. Once a deal has been closed, numerous tasks arise: helping with financing; providing installation and technical assistance; and handling any customer problems that emerge during and after delivery.

# Types of Selling

## *Business-to-Business Selling*

Business-to-business salespeople either sell products for use in the production and sale of other products or sell products to channel members who in turn resell the product, as in the following examples: a Xerox sales representative sells photocopiers to another business for use in its daily operations; a representative from Nike may sell a new line of running shoes to the head office of a group of specialty retailers such as The Foot Locker or Sports World, who in turn distribute the running shoe through their retail locations; a Uniroyal sales representative may secure a long-term contract to supply tires for certain lines of new Chrysler automobiles assembled in Windsor, Ontario.

## *Retail Selling*

Retail selling is the sale of merchandise or services to final customers for personal use. Such salespeople are often referred to as sales clerks and are employed by department stores, specialty stores, and other types of retailing firms. Anyone employed by these types of stores who comes in contact with a customer has a direct or indirect influence on the sale of merchandise or the level of customer satisfaction and, therefore, should have some basic training in sales and customer service.

The current trend in retailing is to reduce the number of employees responsible for selling. The market is shifting towards self-service and a reliance on visual merchandising and price promotions to make the sale. Self-service stores contain centralized checkouts intended to process sales quickly and efficiently. The Bay, Sears, and Canadian Tire are leaders in this merchandising direction.

## *Direct Selling*

### *In-Home Selling*

in-home selling

**In-home selling** is popular today, due in part to the decline of personal services offered by retailers. In-home selling uses a network of local people to sell products in their communities, often at home "parties". These selling practices take advantage of the social setting, where there is less pressure to buy. Companies that operate in this way include Mary Kay (cosmetics), Avon (perfumes, cosmetics, and a variety of personal care products), Tupperware (plastic goods for the household) and Creative Kids (educational toys).

### *Telemarketing*

telemarketing

**Telemarketing** is a discipline that makes advanced telecommunications technology part of a well-organized and well-managed marketing program.[7] It employs highly trained people and data-based marketing techniques to seek and serve new customers. Telemarketing improves productivity because it reduces direct selling costs. Advertising campaigns such as the one Bell Canada has used in Ontario and Quebec have been very successful in promoting the role of telemarketing in

Canadian business practice. In response to the escalating costs of selling, many firms use telemarketing to perform the following sales functions:

1. Screen and qualify incoming sales leads before passing them on to the sales force.
2. Generate sales leads from directories and mailing lists.
3. Call present customers regularly to secure orders, offer additional service, or determine the level of customer satisfaction.[8]

## The Steps in the Selling Process

### Prospecting

prospecting

Seven steps are commonly associated with personal selling (see figure 15.9). The first step is **prospecting**, which is a systematic procedure for developing sales leads. If salespeople do not allocate enough time to finding new customers, they risk causing a decline in sales for their company. If their income is geared to the value of the business they produce, they risk the loss of personal compensation also. Potential customers, or prospects, are identified by means of published lists and directories such as the Scott's Industrial Directory, Fraser's Canadian Trade Directory, and the Canadian Key Business Directory. The salesperson also seeks referrals from satisfied customers or tries to find new customers by cold canvass, the process of calling on people or organizations without appointments or advance knowledge of them. As indicated earlier, telemarketing now plays a key role in prospecting.

**FIGURE 15.9**   The Steps in the Selling Process

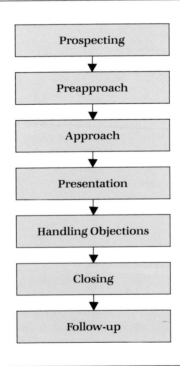

## *Preapproach*

preapproach
qualifying

Customers are qualified in the **preapproach** stage. **Qualifying** a customer is the procedure for determining if a prospect needs the product, has the authority to buy it, and has the ability to pay for it. There is little sense in pursuing customers who lack the financial resources or have no need to make the business relationship successful. Besides screening possible customers, the preapproach allows sales representatives to gather information about the qualified customer that assists them in making the sales presentation. This information may concern the buyer's likes and dislikes, personal interests and hobbies, buying procedures, and special needs and problems. Potential sources of such information include secretarial staff in the buyer's organization and other sales representatives who have called on the buyer.

## *Approach*

approach

The **approach** is the initial contact with the prospect, usually a face-to-face selling situation. Since buyers are usually busy, little time should be wasted in the approach. In the first few minutes of a sales interview, the salesperson must capture the attention and interest of the buyer so that an effective environment is created for the presentation of the product's benefits.

## *Presentation*

presentation

The actual sales **presentation** consists of a persuasive presentation and demonstration of a product's benefits. An effective sales presentation shows the buyer how the benefits of the product satisfy his or her needs or help resolve a particular problem. The wise salesperson uses to advantage the customer knowledge derived from the preapproach, focusing on benefits that are most important to the buyer. What benefits are deemed important varies from situation to situation, but, typically, the critical elements include low price, the durability of the product, the dependability of supply, the performance of the product, and the availability of follow-up service, guarantees, and warranties.

Since buyers have different needs and different problems, salespeople develop alternate strategies for selling the same product. They do so by asking questions and listening to customer responses. Effective sales presentations rely on good two-way communication between sellers and buyers. A salesperson listens to and analyzes what buyers are saying, then uses what he or she has discovered when presenting the appropriate benefits. The ongoing dialogue between sellers and buyers is what was earlier designated as consultative selling.

When presenting the appropriate benefits, the salesperson must do more than speak about them. The spoken word is not enough to sell a product. It is the combination of words and visuals that keeps the attention of buyers and increases their retention of key points. Therefore, effective salespeople carefully plan the presentation and integrate visuals wherever suitable. These may include demonstrations on videocassette tapes, sales brochures and pamphlets, price lists, and the product itself. A useful tactic in the presentation is to let the buyer handle the product and the materials relevant to it. This action results in a feeling of ownership and helps in the decision-making process.

## Handling Objections

**objections**

Handling objections involves dealing with the buyer's resistance to purchasing a product. An **objection** is an obstacle that the salesperson must confront and resolve if the sales transaction is to be completed. Prospects almost always express resistance when contemplating the purchase of a product. An objection is a cue for more information. The buyer is suggesting that the presentation of a product has not revealed how the product will satisfy a particular need. The objection, therefore, is feedback that should be analyzed and used. It may enable the salesperson to discover another benefit in the product, a benefit that can then be presented to the buyer.

Objections come in many forms. A buyer may complain that the price is too high, that the quality is poor, that the variety in sizes or colours is too limited, that the delivery arrangements are unacceptable, that the service is too infrequent, or that the products available from competitors are better. Whatever the objection, the salesperson's response to it determines whether the sale is made. The salesperson must remain calm and not take objections personally, recognizing that they are the normal reactions of a buyer. Instead, the salesperson should ask questions of the buyer to confirm his or her understanding of the situation, then answer the objection, and then move on to the next benefit or attempt in order to close the sale.

## Closing

**closing**

**trial close**

Does the buyer voluntarily say "Yes, I'll buy it"? The answer is no! Getting the buyer to say yes is the entire purpose of the sales interview, but this task is only accomplished if the salesperson asks for the order. **Closing** consists of asking for the order, and it is the most difficult step in the process of selling. Salespeople are reluctant to ask the big question, even though it is the logical sequel to a good presentation and demonstration. In fact, a good salesperson attempts a close whenever a point of agreement is made with the buyer. If the buyer says no, the close is referred to as a **trial close** (an attempt to close that failed). The salesperson simply moves on to the next point in the presentation.

Timing a close is a matter of judgement. Good salespeople know when to close — it's often referred to as the "sixth sense" of selling. The salesperson assesses the buyer's verbal and non-verbal responses in an effort to judge when he or she has become receptive, and at a precise moment asks the big question. When the time to close arrives, the seller may employ one of these commonly used techniques:

1. *Assumptive Close*   In the case of this close, the salesperson assumes the prospect has already decided to buy. The representative makes a statement such as "I will have this model delivered by Friday", or asks a question such as "What is the best day for delivery?" An agreement or answer confirms the assumption that the customer has chosen to buy.

2. *Alternate-Choice Close*   Here the seller also assumes the sale has been made and simply inquires which option is preferable. For example, the representative may ask, "Would you prefer the metallic blue or cherry red colour?"

3. *Summary-of-Benefits Close*   The salesperson using this close summarizes the key benefits that the buyer acknowledged during the presentation, such as the favourable credit terms, the dependability of the product, the availability of frequent service, and the prompt delivery. When the summary is complete the

representative then poses a direct closing question like "Do we have a deal?" or "When would you like delivery?"

4. *T-Account Close*   In this case, the prospect evaluates the pros and cons of the purchase. The salesperson lists the positive and negative points in a manner suggesting that the positive points outweigh the negative. In doing so, he or she leads the prospect to the decision that now is the time to buy.

### Follow-up

follow-up

Joe Girard, one of the most successful sellers of automobiles in North America, is claimed to have made the following statement — "I hope something goes wrong with the car so I can prove to you how good I really am." This statement epitomizes the importance of **follow-up** after the sale is made. The sale does not end with the close. In fact, in many cases it just begins.

Keeping current customers satisfied is the key to success, for their satisfaction dictates the amount of repeat business that a company will enjoy. Effective salespeople keep in touch with customers to ensure that the delivery and installation of the goods are satisfactory, and that promises are kept, and that, generally, the expectations of the buyer are met. When problems do occur, the salesperson is ready to take action to resolve the situation.

## >>>> *Event Marketing and Sponsorships*

Event marketing and sponsorships are fast becoming important elements of the promotion mix. Some firms and certain industries have been quick to realize the benefits of this form of promotion. Prior to discussing this promotion activity, let's define some basic terms.

event

1. An **event** is a theme activity created by a special-interest group (e.g., an Indy-style race through the streets of Toronto). In this case, the race is the activity and the interest group is the city of Toronto, which benefits from the influx of tourist dollars during the race week.

event marketing

2. **Event marketing** is the process, planned by a sponsoring organization, of integrating a variety of communication elements behind an event theme (e.g., Molson's coordination of advertising, public relations, and sales promotion activities for the Molson Indy car race).

event sponsorship

3. **Event sponsorship** is a situation where a sponsor agrees to support an event financially (e.g., an auto race, theatre production, or a marathon road-race) in return for advertising privileges associated with the event. Usually, sponsorships are offered by the organizer on a tiered basis. For instance, if the sponsor pays the maximum amount stipulated by the organizer, that sponsor receives the maximum amount of advertising privileges. Sponsors that pay lesser amounts receive fewer advertising privileges. In the case of the Molson Indy (an auto race held in Toronto each summer), Molson's is classified as a primary sponsor and receives the maximum rights and privileges offered by the organizing body. Other sponsors, classified as secondary sponsors, support the race financially, but since they contribute less, their advertising privileges are also less than those accorded Molson.

In Canada, marketing organizations spent $1.5 billion in 1987 sponsoring sports, entertainment, and cultural events, the three main areas of event marketing.[9] Some of Canada's largest corporations are involved in event marketing. These corporations include the two major breweries, Molson and Labatt's, the Royal Bank of Canada and the Canadian Imperial Bank of Commerce, Imperial Tobacco Limited, Coca-Cola Limited, Pepsi-Cola Limited and Joseph E. Seagram & Sons Limited. To assess the impact of event marketing, let's examine some activities in each of the three main areas.

## Sports Sponsorship

Sports sponsorship occurs at amateur and professional levels. According to Leo Lefaive, President of the Sports Marketing Council, amateur sports in Canada receives direct contributions of $15 million annually from Canadian corporations. He also states that companies acquiring sponsorship rights invest $3.00 in promoting the event or activity for every $1.00 they spend on acquiring those rights; therefore, the total contribution to amateur sport is $60 million annually.[10]

Generally, sports sponsorships are dominated by oil companies such as Petro-Canada, Shell, and Texaco; automobile manufacturers such as General Motors, Ford, and Chrysler; breweries such as Molson and Labatt's; and tobacco manufacturers, Imperial Tobacco and Rothman's (see figure 15.10). How effective is the investment in sports sponsorship? A key indicator of success is the effect the association with a sponsored event has on consumers' awareness of a brand or company. A recent marketing study among men in the Montreal area revealed that[11]

1. Seventy-eight percent knew that Molson was the principal sponsor of the Montreal Canadiens; among respondents interested in hockey, the figure was 87 percent.

**FIGURE 15.10**   Canada's Leading Sports Sponsors

| Company | Sponsorship Activity |
|---|---|
| Labatt Brewing Company | Toronto Blue Jays (ownership)<br>Montréal Expos (broadcast rights)<br>Canada Cup Hockey |
| Molson Companies | Montreal Canadians (ownership)<br>Hockey Night in Canada<br>Molson Indy<br>Men's Alpine Ski Team |
| Rothman's Inc. | Auto racing, equestrian events, and thoroughbred racing |
| Imperial Tobacco Limited | Player's Challenge Tennis<br>Canadian Open Golf (du Maurier) |
| Imperial Oil Limited | Hockey Night in Canada |
| Canadian Imperial Bank of Commerce | Toronto Blue Jays (ownership)<br>Women's National Alpine Ski Team<br>Numerous amateur sports |

2. Thirty-two percent of respondents identified Labatt's as the principal sponsor of Montreal Expos (in the first year of sponsorship), while 28 percent answered O'Keefe (the previous sponsor for many years). Of the respondents interested in baseball, 53 percent identified Labatt's as the principal sponsor.

For a further illustration of the benefits of event marketing, refer to the Marketing in Action vignette "The Molson Indy."

---

## >>>> *MARKETING IN ACTION*

### *THE MOLSON INDY*

Roger Samson, Molson's vice-president of Marketing, Sports and Entertainment Properties, has stated that the firm's decision to sponsor the Molson Indy was a major business decision, since the size of the investment was to be considerable and on-going.

Sponsorship of the Molson Indy, a race through the streets of Toronto, was started by Molson in 1984. Involvement in an event of this nature calls for tremendous amounts of strategic planning and promotional activity by the sponsor if it is to capitalize on all of the rights and privileges it has secured as a result of its association with the event. In Molson's case, this involves a full range of marketing activity — research, network advertising, public relations, merchandising promotions, and post-event research.

Name-recognition is the key issue in event sponsorship, and it is something that is measurable at the end of the event. To build name-recognition, Molson strategies include using television advertising to promote the race, using shopping mall exhibits, supplements in newspapers, collateral sales materials, outdoor advertising, and point-of-purchase material.

According to Samson, events such as the Molson Indy capture the imagination of those involved, who get more and more caught up in making the event happen. He cautions that prospective firms contemplating sponsorship programs should maintain their business perspective. In a business sense, then, how has Molson benefited from the Molson Indy?

Molson's benefits consist in the fact that it reaches its consumers by an alternate means, going outside the forms of media advertising traditionally used in the beer industry. Molson

*The Molson Indy represents Molson's attempt to reach beyond the forms of media advertising traditionally used in the beer industry*

can reach its consumer through leisure-time activity; in this case, Molson knows that beer drinkers who favour motorsport consume more beer than any other sports fan. More quantitative measures were taken after the event. The recognition of Export as the brand associated with the event was 53 percent, up 11 percent from the first year of the sponsorship. Also, 20 percent of the adults polled after the event indicated that there was a strong likelihood they would purchase Molson brands as a result of their attendance at the race.

Generally, the sponsorship can be viewed as a success; the statistics on brand recognition, corporate identification, and intention to purchase have reinforced Molson's commitment to using the sponsorship of motorsport as a long-term marketing strategy.

Adapted from Roger Samson, "Sponsoring a major event has long-term benefits", *Sales & Marketing Management in Canada*, November 1987, pp.10–11.

## Entertainment Sponsorships

Canadian corporations invest huge amounts of money to sponsor concerts and secure endorsements from high-profile personalities in the hope that the celebrity-company relationship will pay off in the long run. According to Bill Gray, a vice-president of Rockbill International Limited, pop music sponsorship alone cost four companies (Coca-Cola, Pepsi-Cola, Molson and Labatt's) $15 million in 1988.[12] All of these firms are interested in targeting messages at youth and young adult segments; thus, they are naturally interested in pop-music and youth-lifestyle marketing strategies. Many benefits are sought from this form of sponsorship.

1. Sponsorships in pop music identify the given brand with a particular lifestyle or demographic group (e.g., a certain age category). For example, Pepsi-Cola sponsored tours by Tina Turner, Michael Jackson and David Bowie in hopes of appealing to youth segments.
2. Pop-music sponsorships engender brand loyalties that can last for a lifetime. Securing loyalty at an early age is beneficial.

In the case of Pepsi-Cola, the first company to recognize the value of rock celebrities in commercials, the strategy has been to use celebrities that project the leading-edge image the company desires. Thus it has linked the "Pepsi Generation" theme and slogans like "The Choice of a New Generation" and "A Generation Ahead" with the latest celebrities (e.g., Don Johnson, Michael J. Fox, Lionel Richie, Madonna, and Michael Jackson in the 1980s).

The Ford Motor Company entered into music sponsorship with their "Anne Murray Tracer Tour" in 1987. Ford saw an ideal correspondence between the singer's tour and the Mercury Tracer, since the target market of the Tracer was similar to the profile of Murray's audience, 25–49 years of age and 65 percent female. The Tracer appeals to business women and families that require a second car. According to Gary Marsh, Ford's Merchandising Manager, "music sponsorship and other event-marketing programs are likely to join cash-back deals, low-interest financing and other incentives as a new weapon in the increasingly competitive auto industry."[13]

## Cultural Event Sponsorships

Canada's arts industry is a force in the economy. It is an $11-billion-a-year industry that includes dance, film, literature, music, painting, sculpture, and theatre. Among Canada's biggest arts supporters, apart from federal and provincial governments, are Imperial Tobacco Limited, IBM Canada Limited, Alcan Aluminum Limited, and Joseph E. Seagram & Sons Limited. The primary benefit these companies gain by sponsoring the arts is goodwill. Most firms view this type of investment as part of their corporate citizenship objectives; by contributing to the arts, a company maintains the reputation of being a good, contributing member of society. Unlike Coke and Pepsi's use of rock music, this form of support is not promotional activity per se (i.e., promotion intended only to increase sales). For instance, BMW Canada Limited has been a constant supporter of the Toronto Symphony Orchestra. According to company President, Victor Doolan, "it's our contribution to helping certain cultural organizations prosper and develop. The Toronto Symphony Orchestra appeals to the same sort of people that are drawn to our cars."[14]

# Factors to Consider for Participation in Event Marketing

Companies enter into sponsorships in an effort to create a favourable impression with their customers and target groups. For this to be accomplished, the "fit" between the event and the sponsor must be a good one. For instance, Xerox sponsors national squash championships as well as local squash tournaments since they recognize that squash is a popular sport among business decision-makers who have the potential to purchase Xerox products. The association of a brand of beer with motor sports represents another good fit. Generally, event sponsorship is a vehicle for enhancing the reputation of a company and the customer's awareness of a brand. It is seen to be less self-serving than other forms of promotion and marketing activity. The most effective sponsors adhere to the following principles when considering participation in event marketing.

1. *Use Sponsorships to Complement Other Promotional Activity* The role that advertising and promotion will play in the sponsorship must be determined first. Sponsorship of the proper event will complement that other promotional activity. For example, a brand of margarine may sponsor the Heart Fund because the relationship of the two is in keeping with the health image that is communicated by the advertising for the brand.

2. *Choose the Target Carefully* Events reach specific targets. For example, while rock focuses on youth, symphonies tend to reach audiences that are older, urban, and upscale. As suggested earlier, it is the "fit" or matching of targets that is crucial.

3. *Select an Event with an Image that Sells* The sponsor must capitalize on the image of the event and perhaps the prestige or status associated with it. Sponsorship works best when the attraction to a brand is affected by such irrational considerations. A luxury car such as the Cadillac may be a suitable sponsor for a significant arts or cultural event, or a major national golf championship. The prestigious image and status of such events have an impact on the sale of products that project a comparable image (in this example, the image and status that come with ownership of a Cadillac).

4. *Select an Event with the Right Personality* Events do have personalities. Sports, for example, are exciting, young, and healthy, and therefore they are attractive events for beer and tobacco companies that want to portray this type of lifestyle in their advertising. Cultural events tend to be upscale, refined, and status-oriented, and they attract, therefore, a different type of sponsor. Typical sponsors of cultural events include corporations such as Imperial Oil, Texaco Canada Limited, General Motors and IBM.

5. *Establish Selection Criteria* In addition to using the criteria cited above, companies evaluating potential events for sponsorship should consider the long-term benefit such sponsorship offers compared to the costs in the short term. For example, being associated with an event that is ongoing, popular, and successful is wise, as there is less risk for the sponsor. Before committing financial resources to an event, a company should also consider whether it is likely to receive communications exposure through unpaid media sources, and whether it will be able to administer the event efficiently.

An instance of how these principles are applied is given in the Marketing in Action vignette "Year of the Coach: A 3M Press Release", which concerns a major sponsorship program of 3M Canada Inc.

## Measuring The Benefits of Sponsorship

One reason many companies are reluctant to enter into sponsorship programs is that results are difficult to measure. Large sums of money are spent at one time for a benefit that may be short-lived. Companies conduct marketing research in order to

---

### ››› *MARKETING IN ACTION*

#### *YEAR OF THE COACH: A 3M PRESS RELEASE*

Toronto, December 6, 1988: 3M Canada Inc. announced today, at a news conference held by the Coaching Association of Canada, that it would be supporting coaching development through the National Coaching Certification Program (N.C.C.P.) in 1989.

The executive vice-president of Marketing and Public Affairs for 3M Canada, Alf Cordell, made the announcement jointly with the Minister of State for Fitness and Amateur Sport, the Honourable Jean Charest.

Cordell said that the company was a world-wide sponsor of the Olympics last year and that a portion of each sales dollar in 1988 went to Olympic coaching in Canada. "The very positive experience we had at that time with all the people in the Coaching Association of Canada and the things that they are attempting to do, led us to continue our support of coaching but in a slightly different way," he stated.

"With this new program, we intend to focus our support on coaches at the local level. Right on the coach that works with your son or daughter. Our intention is to provide recognition, support and tangible help to that person who can be so important to our children today, the coach," Cordell said.

3M will sponsor the National Coaching Certification Program, a five-level educational program run by the C.A.C. It involves more than 50 sports and extends across the country. Many sports organizations require their people to take the N.C.C.P. course before they involve themselves

with coaching. It is 3M's desire to increase the number of coaches going through this coaching education program.

"Just about everybody comes in contact with a coach at some time in his or her lifetime, whether as a child, a parent or in a coaching role itself. These people help shape the physical, the moral and the psychological make-up of our children, and if we can provide them with the best tools available, then our efforts will have been truly worthwhile," said Cordell.

"The certification program helps produce the kind of coach that every parent hopes for," he said. "Coaches who have the insight and understanding to make life's hard lessons a little easier to take and who can inspire leadership and the will to be a better citizen for Canada's future are what we hope will be the result of this partnership."

3M Canada also announced that it was implementing a recognition program consisting of awards for the outstanding coaches of the year. 3M Canada "Coach of the Year" awards will go to the top female and the top male individual coach as well as one award each to the top female and top male team coach in Canada.

Coaches at all levels, for all disciplines, including the disabled will be eligible, as long as they meet the high standards set out in the criteria.

The four winners will each receive a monetary award to further their education in coaching, a trophy and several other useful and tangible prizes.

determine the impact that sponsorship association has. The following indicators, many of which are obtained from research, are used to measure the benefits of sponsorship.

1. *Awareness*   How much awareness of the event within each target group is there, and how well do people recall the brand or product name that sponsored the event?

2. *Image*   What change in image and what increase in the consumer perception of leadership or credibility result from the sponsorship?

The executive vice-president of Marketing and Public Affairs for 3M Canada, Alf Cordell, announces 3M's plans to sponsor the Coaching Association of Canada

The criteria for the awards include:

- Showing respect for officials, opponents, parents, and espousing a philosophy of fair play.
- Demonstrating concern for the all-round development of the athlete and providing guidance as to responsible conduct beyond the athletic arena.
- Presenting a positive public image of coaching and the role of the coach.
- Regular participation in the National Coaching Certification Program.

- Application of relevant training theory and coaching practice.
- Demonstrating a proven capacity to improve competitive performance.

"3M recognizes the need to guarantee qualified coaches for Canadian youth, which in turn will ensure a more positive sport experience for the athlete. Furthermore we realize the important leadership role they play in the development of sport and of our youth," says Cordell.

"We feel also that this program is an excellent 'fit' for 3M. The coaching and leadership philosophy which is part of the company's corporate culture has been instrumental in the invention and bringing to market of a large number of well-known 3M products. We hope that our support of coaching will likewise bring great positive results to the youth of our country."

The public will be involved in the coach-recognition process through a broad television advertising and public relations campaign which 3M Canada is planning for 1989 and beyond. It will feature the coach and emphasize how important he or she is in the development of the young athlete and the young person.

More 3M involvement with the C.A.C. and with coaching will be announced early in the new year, according to a 3M Canada spokesperson.

This news release is reproduced by permission of 3M Canada Inc.

3. *New Clients*   How many new clients were generated as a result of the company's sponsoring an event?

4. *Sales*   Do increases in sales or market share occur during post-event periods?

5. *Specific Target Reach*   Do the events deliver constituency? Carefully selected events reach specific targets that are difficult to reach by conventional communications. For example, pre-teens and teens are difficult to reach through conventional media, but can be reached effectively through sponsorship of rock concerts and music tours.

6. *Media Coverage*   What value was derived from editorial coverage? Did the sponsorship result in free publicity for the sponsor?

## ⟩⟩⟩⟩ SUMMARY

Sales promotion activity can be divided into two categories. The first is consumer promotions. These are designed to pull the product through the channel of distribution and prompt purchases (trial, repeat, or multiple) of the product. Such promotions may take the form of coupons, free samples, contests, cash refunds, and premiums.

Trade promotions, the second kind of sales promotion, are designed to push the product through the channel of distribution and secure product listings among distributors, build sales volume, and gain merchandising support. Trade discounts, performance allowances, cooperative advertising, retail in-ad coupons, dealer premiums, collateral materials, point-of-purchase (or dealer) displays, and trade shows are among the types of trade promotion that occur.

Personal selling refers to face-to-face communication between sellers and buyers. The role of the salesperson is to locate customers whose needs can be satisfied or problems resolved through the use of a company's products or services. The selling process involves seven distinct steps: prospecting, preapproach, approach, presentation, handling objections, closing, and follow-up.

Event marketing and sponsorship programs are now an important element of a firm's promotion mix, particularly among large Canadian corporations. Sponsorship is popular in three areas, namely cultural events, sports, and entertainment. Unlike other promotion-mix elements, these types of programs have an indirect impact on product or company performance. The benefits are received in the form of goodwill and increased awareness as opposed to measurable increases in sales or market share.

## ⟩⟩⟩⟩ KEY TERMS

| | | |
|---|---|---|
| sales promotion | premium | prospecting |
| consumer promotion | mail-in premium | preapproach |
| coupons | in-pack or on-pack premiums | qualifying |

| | | |
|---|---|---|
| redemption rate | trade promotion | approach |
| product-delivered coupons | cooperative advertising | presentation |
| media-delivered coupons | retail in-ad coupon | objections |
| in-store delivered coupons | dealer premiums | closing |
| sample | point-of-purchase material | trial close |
| cross-sampling | personal selling | follow-up |
| sweepstakes | consultative selling | event |
| instant-wins | in-home selling | event marketing |
| cash refunds (rebates) | telemarketing | event sponsorship |
| slippage | | |

## >>>> QUESTIONS FOR REVIEW AND DISCUSSION

**1.** What are the objectives of consumer promotions and trade promotions?

**2.** Explain how the product life cycle affects the use of media-delivered coupons and product-delivered coupons.

**3.** "Contests and sweepstakes are more appropriate for products in the mature stage of the product life cycle." Comment on this statement.

**4.** Briefly describe the following terms:
**(a)** redemption rate **(b)** self-liquidating premium
**(c)** slippage **(d)** refund (rebate)

**5.** "The use of dealer premiums is an unethical practice in contemporary marketing." Discuss this statement.

**6.** List and briefly describe the seven steps in the selling process.

**7.** What is meant by the term "direct selling" ?

**8.** If you were the marketing manager for Nike or Reebok, what events would you sponsor? What benefits would you derive from these sponsorships? Be specific.

## >>>> REFERENCES

1. JO MARNEY, "Sales Promotion: A $7 Billion Enigma", *Marketing*, June 8, 1987, p.14.

2. "A Coupon Blizzard is Growing", *Globe and Mail*, June 30, 1988, pp. B1, B5.

3. Nielsen Promotion Services, *A Marketer's Guide to Consumer Promotion*, 1988, p.7A.

4. JO MARNEY, "The Basics of Promotion", *Marketing*, February 6, 1989, p.28.

5. Nielsen Promotion Services, *A Marketer's Guide*, p.5D.

6. Ibid., p.4C.

7. "Telemarketing Glossary of Terms", *Telemarketing*, December 1983, p.34.

8. EARL HITCHCOCK, "Suddenly Marketers are Calling Up America", *Sales & Marketing Management*, June 4, 1984, pp.34-35.

9. BRUCE GATES, "Who's Who in Sports Sponsorship", *Financial Post*, May 23, 1988, p.36.

10. Ibid.

11. GAIL CHIASSON, "Benefits of Sports Sponsorship", *Marketing*, April 3, 1989, p.9.

12. MIRIAM CU-UY-GAM, "Music Marketing Hits Profitable Note", *Financial Post*, April 3, 1989, p.44.

13. IAN TIMBERLAKE, "Headline Billing for Anne and Ford", *Marketing*, June 8, 1988, p.10.

14. KARA KURYLLOWICZ, "TSO in Tune with Sponsors," *Financial Post*, April 3, 1989, p.45.

>>>>> **PART EIGHT**

# Emerging Directions in Marketing

# C H A P T E R  16  〉〉〉〉〉

# Direct Marketing

This chapter introduces the reader to some fundamental concepts of direct marketing strategy and activity in Canada. Often a neglected area of discussion, the impact and importance of direct marketing should not be underestimated. Direct marketing has become the largest single source of advertising revenue in Canada, a clear indicator of its value to contemporary marketing organizations. Terry Belgue, the

## ❭❭❭ *MARKETING IN ACTION*

### *THE OLYMPIC TORCH RELAY*

One of the biggest promotional efforts ever made in Canada was Petro-Canada's Olympics promotion. The company paid $5.5 million for the rights to organize and sponsor the Olympic Torch Relay. This figure also includes the actual cost of staging the event. Additional advertising funds were used for media advertising to generate excitement over related promotions.

To ensure maximum benefit from its association with the Olympics, Petro-Canada started these promotions well ahead of the February 1988 Olympics. In October 1986, glassware became available at a low price to customers buying gas at retail outlets. The campaign was supported heavily by media advertising. According to company officials, the glasses embossed with Olympic symbols were quite successful as a promotion. Amateur sport in Canada also benefitted; 10 percent of the consumer purchase price was set aside in a special fund for amateur sport. Well over $1 million was generated for amateur sport in Canada.

The Olympic Torch Relay was a very large event in terms of planning and implementation. It involved the single largest non-government direct mailing (9.5 million mailings) to Canadian households ever. The mailing included the details on how Canadian citizens could apply to become torch carriers in the course of the flame's journey across Canada prior to the 1988 Olympics. The torch was passed from one runner to another along the route. When it arrived at its Calgary destination, it was used to ignite the Olympic cauldron. Petro-Canada was pleasantly surprised by the incredible response from the Canadian public — a total of seven million people applied for 6 500 positions in the relay.

Was the promotion worthwhile? Promotions of this nature are hard to measure quantitatively, but several benefits are mentioned by company officials. First, the relay captured the hearts and imagination of Canadians coast-to-coast, as throngs of people showed up to salute the torch as it passed from one community to another. This

*A total of seven million people applied for positions in the Olympic Torch Relay organized by Petro-Canada*

resulted in an unmeasurable amount of free and positive media coverage for the company. Second, retail traffic at Petro-Canada outlets picked up considerably. The decision to collect applications at a retail outlet was responsible for traffic building. Third, an enormous amount of company goodwill was generated. The promotion created a warm feeling in the minds of the public, a task which is difficult, at best, for any large company to accomplish.

On the quantitative side, *Southam News* conducted some research through Angus Reid Associates, two months prior to the start of the Olympics in Calgary. They found that 63 percent of Canadians could name just one sponsor. The highest recognition went to Petro-Canada, which was named by 23 percent of respondents. Such a response rate was a very good sign that Petro Canada's investment in advertising and promotion was paying off.

Adapted from Randy Scotland, "Petro-Canada's Olympic triumph", *Marketing*, June 8, 1987, pp.9, 27.

president of the Canadian Direct Marketing Association, gives a reason for its significance: "The intrusiveness of direct marketing is why it is so powerful."

Many firms today are integrating direct marketing techniques into multi-media campaigns. Petro-Canada, responsible for the "Share the Flame" campaign for the Calgary Winter Olympics in 1988, solicited applications for the Olympic torch relay, using direct mail, newspapers, radio, television, and outdoor posters. It was the largest non-government mail drop in Canadian history, with mail going to 9.5 million households and providing 6.6 million leads.[1] Direct marketing is now and will continue to be an integral part of marketing strategy and corporate business strategy in Canada. The Marketing in Action vignette, "The Olympic Torch Relay," illustrates the concept of integrated marketing strategy and shows how direct marketing helps generate action among customers.

# 〉〉〉〉 *Direct Marketing*

**direct marketing**

Direct marketing is different from other types of marketing in that it attempts to satisfy customer needs directly, without the use of intermediaries. **Direct marketing** is an interactive marketing system, fully controlled by the marketer, who develops products, promotes them directly to customers through a variety of media, accepts orders directly from customers, and distributes products directly to customers. Some distinctions must be made between several terms that are all related to direct marketing and that are often confused with each other.

**direct advertising**

1. **Direct advertising** is advertising delivered directly to prospects by mail, salespeople, and dealers (e.g., direct mail, door-to-door flyers, and telemarketing).

**direct mail**

2. **Direct mail** is a form of direct advertising communicated to prospects through the postal service.

**direct-response advertising**

3. **Direct-response advertising** presents a message that prompts immediate action; for example, it may come with a clip-out coupon, a response card requesting more information, or an order form. Such advertising is commonly distributed through direct mail or through conventional mass media (see figure 16.1).

Direct marketing often involves media advertising. For instance, figure 16.1 is an advertisement placed in prominent Canadian business magazines. It is classified as direct-response advertising, since the effectiveness of the advertisement can be measured by the number of responses generated by the reply coupon. Since no middleman is used in the distribution of goods ordered, direct marketing also includes order processing, order fulfillment, list preparation, and list brokering.

Other forms of direct marketing include catalogues such as the Sears Catalogue or those of specialty retailers such as L.L. Bean or Tilley Endurables; direct home shopping, a service provided through the Canadian Home Shopping Network on cable television stations; and telemarketing, the use of the telephone in a sales capacity by business organizations. Telemarketing, as indicated in the previous

**FIGURE 16.1    Securing Responses**

# When you can't get face to face get fax to fax.

Let's face it. Sometimes you just can't afford the time or money to get face to face. Get fax to fax. With Toshiba's new desktop facsimile transceivers.

Set up is easy. And you can operate it with your little finger. Speed dial up to 50 frequently called destinations.

Send an 8½″ x 11″ letter around the world in as little as 11 seconds. Got more to say? A Toshiba fax will transmit 30 pages. And send it after hours to save money on telephone rates.

From our new 9 lb. TF-111 personal facsimile to the very latest TF-451 bond paper facsimile, we've got one to keep any size office busy.

Our new facsimiles can take it as well as dish it out. With the dependability that comes from Toshiba's 110 year heritage of quality.

The message is clear. Getting fax to fax with Toshiba is good business. Let's talk about how I can: • Cut courier costs right out of my business. • Deliver information in seconds. • Be sure it got there.

Name

Address

City                          Prov.

Code                         Phone (    )

Mail coupon to: Toshiba of Canada Limited, Facsimile Systems
Division, 191 McNabb St., Markham, Ontario, L3R 8H2
Or call 1-800-263-1618

## TOSHIBA

**WE MEAN BUSINESS**
FACSIMILE SYSTEMS DIVISION

ROBM0289

*Responses to this direct-response advertisement result in leads for the advertiser.*

chapter, is the use of telecommunications to promote the products and services of a business.

## The Uniqueness of Direct Marketing

In terms of the 4Ps, direct marketing is quite different from traditional marketing practice. Let's examine each variable briefly.

### *Product*

Direct marketing generally cannot handle impulse purchases, inexpensive items, or items requiring demonstration, though the use of videos is beginning to make direct marketing possible for the last group of products. The use of videos in direct marketing is discussed in detail later in the chapter. Handling impulse and inexpensive items has traditionally been avoided because the high distribution costs of direct marketing would further reduce the small profit margins on such items. Selecting the right product for direct marketing is a key decision area. Basically, the product must be unique, must be perceived as offering good value, and must not be readily available at retail outlets.

### *Price*

Products selected for direct marketing usually carry competitive prices, but higher prices are acceptable if the item has high perceived value and is not readily available through traditional channels. For a campaign to be financially successful, the price must cover the costs of production, promotion expenses, order processing, administration, delivery, and profit margin.

### *Place*

Normal channels are eliminated. Buyers and sellers communicate directly through personal mail and impersonal media, and the merchandise is shipped directly to the customer (e.g., through Canada Post). Distribution is the one area where direct marketing differs most from traditional marketing.

### *Promotion*

Promotion strategy, including media selection and creative strategy for communicating an offer, is crucial. The creation of a convincing message is perhaps the most critical aspect of planning the campaign, for the message must do all of the selling, without support from other marketing sources. Messages often come with incentives — whether free goods, premiums, special trial orders, or price discounts — to get the customer to take action. Using all of these incentives is common among magazine publishers searching for new subscribers. How many orders result usually depends upon how effective the campaign was in reaching a designated target

FIGURE 16.2   The Differences Between Advertising and Direct Marketing

| Advertising | Direct Marketing |
|---|---|
| Potential target-market capability within limits of media selected | Precise target-market capability |
| Effectiveness is measured by awareness and recall | Effectiveness is measured by dollars (bottom-line profit) |
| Attitudes and preference are influenced by multiple exposure | Action is influenced by one exposure |
| Short copy and emotional appeals are used | Long copy and rational appeals are used |
| Media-driven | Database driven |
| Competes for attention with other messages | Gets attention via personal approach |
| One-way communication | Two-way interactive communication |

audience. If the message is off-target, sales will fall below expectations and losses will occur. Figure 16.2 describes some specific differences between advertising and direct marketing.

## Functions of Direct Marketing

The ultimate purpose of direct marketing is to solicit action. However, the applications of direct marketing extend beyond this task. Direct marketing performs three main roles. It builds sales, cultivates customers, and provides information and support to dealers.

### Building Sales

Direct marketing bolsters sales in many ways.

1. *Securing Leads*   Response cards that are returned to obtain additional information supply leads that are passed to sales staff for follow-up.

2. *Contacting Customers*   Direct marketing may provide the first contact with a customer. It can create interest in the product and lower buyers' resistance to a personal sales presentation. It can also serve as a reminder after a sales presentation has been made.

3. *Covering Territory*   Direct marketing is an efficient means of reaching customers in territories where personal contact is too expensive to arrange. It can also supply a means of dealing with small customers whose volume of sales, being low, does not justify personal sales contact on a regular basis.

4. *Securing Direct Orders*   This is the primary objective of direct marketing, and it is often achieved. An order form is always part of a mailing, and details on how to

order are clearly communicated if broadcast media are used to convey the offer. In eliciting orders, the sales message (creative strategy) moves through many of the same steps as are involved in the selling process, from the stage of initial contact (the approach) to that of asking for the order (the close). Typically, a direct mail offer includes a personalized letter that serves as the approach, pamphlets and promotional materials that present the benefits, and a reply card or an order form that asks for the order.

5. *Sampling of New Product by Customer* Direct marketing is an effective way of inducing people to make a trial purchase. Packaged-goods companies use cooperative direct mailings to distribute trial coupons and sample sizes of a product. A cooperative direct-mail package usually contains coupons and other offers for a variety of different products. No direct competitors are included in the same mailing, so each product has exclusiveness in a mailing. Cooperative direct mail has proven to be an effective way to get people to try packaged goods. The response rate or percentage of coupons returned from a mailing is in the range of 8 percent.[2]

6. *Selling Other Items* Direct marketing is, finally, a way of introducing new products cheaply, while maintaining focus on the attributes of an established product. Such introductions are accomplished when information about a new product is enclosed with a related product that has already been ordered, or with an invoice. Retailers such as The Bay or Eaton's announce upcoming sales events on the bottom of credit-card statements mailed to customers, or include direct-marketing offers with the invoice envelope each month.

How direct marketing builds sales is shown in the Marketing in Action vignette, "Timex Uses Direct Marketing to Build Premium/Incentive Business."

## Cultivating Customers

Direct marketing also performs several roles in maintaining customers.

1. *Welcoming New Customers* To those who have made a purchase in response to a direct-marketing campaign, a thank-you letter may be sent to consolidate the relationship and plant seeds for another purchase.

2. *Reviving Inactive Accounts* Sending out a series of messages is an economical way of getting past customers to buy again.

3. *Collecting Accounts* A series of diplomatic collection letters will keep accounts up to date and leave the recipient in a friendly frame of mind.

## Providing Dealer Support

Finally, direct marketing can be used to assist dealers and to establish productive relationships with them.

1. *Merchandising* Printed messages can forcefully present merchandising plans and show dealers how to put promotion plans to work.

2. *Information and Education* Since most selling situations are competitive, the

## ⟩⟩⟩ *MARKETING IN ACTION*

### *TIMEX USES DIRECT MARKETING TO BUILD PREMIUM/INCENTIVE BUSINESS*

Timex Canada first entered the premium/incentive business in 1984 when clients began to request their products for this use. During the next few years this phase of business grew steadily until, in the fall of 1987, the company decided to test ways of increasing sales.

In December of that year, Hull Direct Marketing prepared a direct marketing plan for 1988 with the objective of achieving sales of 14 000 units at a defined margin level. Secondary objectives were to measure the effectiveness of direct marketing amongst different key target groups as an order-generating vehicle, and to create broader awareness of Timex as a supplier of quality premiums.

The campaign tested two mediums — a solo-addressed mail package to a targeted audience using purchased lists and the company's house list, and direct-response on-page advertising with a coupon to generate leads in appropriate business magazines.

The targeted audience included advertising, marketing and sales promotion/incentive companies, large manufacturing companies, banks, insurance and financial institutions, large restaurant chains, sports clubs, and newspapers.

By the end of the first half of the year, premium/incentive business was 72 percent ahead of the same period the previous year, and the company expected that its year-end objective would be exceeded.

Analysis of the program results have helped to further define target groups and offers, and a further test program that will also include telemarketing, is scheduled to be introduced this year.

From *Sales & Marketing Management in Canada*, January 1989, p.7. Reprinted with permission of Sanford Evans Communications Ltd.

*A solo-addressed sales-generation package, one of the two mediums tested by Timex in its 1988 campaign*

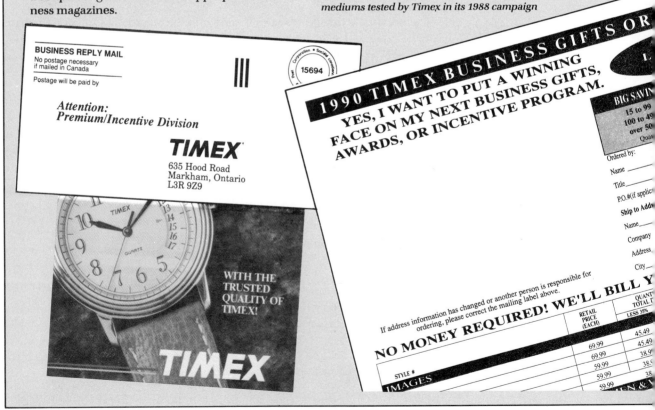

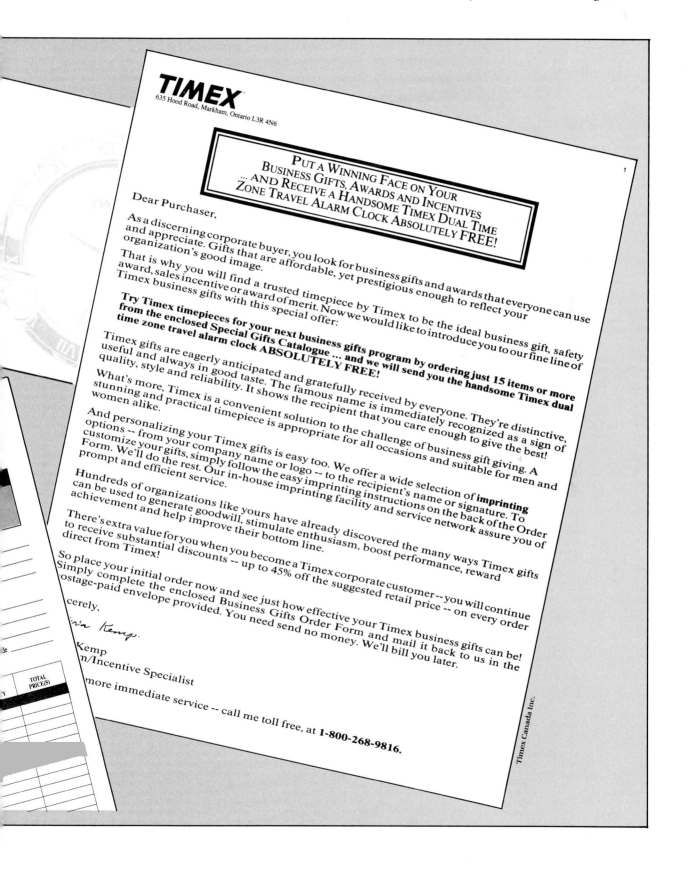

**TIMEX**

635 Hood Road, Markham, Ontario L3R 4N6

> **PUT A WINNING FACE ON YOUR BUSINESS GIFTS, AWARDS AND INCENTIVES ... AND RECEIVE A HANDSOME TIMEX DUAL TIME ZONE TRAVEL ALARM CLOCK ABSOLUTELY FREE!**

Dear Purchaser,

As a discerning corporate buyer, you look for business gifts and awards that everyone can use and appreciate. Gifts that are affordable, yet prestigious enough to reflect your organization's good image.

That is why you will find a trusted timepiece by Timex to be the ideal business gift, safety award, sales incentive or award of merit. Now we would like to introduce you to our fine line of Timex business gifts with this special offer:

**Try Timex timepieces for your next business gifts program by ordering just 15 items or more from the enclosed Special Gifts Catalogue ... and we will send you the handsome Timex dual time zone travel alarm clock ABSOLUTELY FREE!**

Timex gifts are eagerly anticipated and gratefully received by everyone. They're distinctive, useful and always in good taste. The famous name is immediately recognized as a sign of quality, style and reliability. It shows the recipient that you care enough to give the best!

What's more, Timex is a convenient solution to the challenge of business gift giving. A stunning and practical timepiece is appropriate for all occasions and suitable for men and women alike.

And personalizing your Timex gifts is easy too. We offer a wide selection of **imprinting** options -- from your company name or logo -- to the recipient's name or signature. To customize your gifts, simply follow the easy imprinting instructions on the back of the Order Form. We'll do the rest. Our in-house imprinting facility and service network assure you of prompt and efficient service.

Hundreds of organizations like yours have already discovered the many ways Timex gifts can be used to generate goodwill, stimulate enthusiasm, boost performance, reward achievement and help improve their bottom line.

There's extra value for you when you become a Timex corporate customer -- you will continue to receive substantial discounts -- up to 45% off the suggested retail price -- on every order direct from Timex!

So place your initial order now and see just how effective your Timex business gifts can be! Simply complete the enclosed Business Gifts Order Form and mail it back to us in the postage-paid envelope provided. You need send no money. We'll bill you later.

cerely,

*ria Kemp.*

Kemp
n/Incentive Specialist

more immediate service -- call me toll free, at **1-800-268-9816**.

Timex Canada Inc.

merits of a product need to be reinforced constantly among dealers. Knowledgeable sales staff at the point of purchase are crucial to the sale of any product. Videos provided by manufacturers' sales-training programs, and detailed product literature, now play a prominent role in educating retail salespeople.

## ⟩⟩⟩⟩ *Planning Direct Marketing*

Planning for a direct-marketing program is guided by the overall marketing strategy or marketing plan of the firm. Within a large corporation like IBM or Xerox, direct marketing is but one component of the marketing strategy. Since the basic elements of marketing planning and corporate business planning are discussed in chapter 3, this section focuses on planning the direct marketing effort itself. This process involves a series of eight steps (see figure 16.3)

**FIGURE 16.3**    The Steps for Planning Direct Marketing

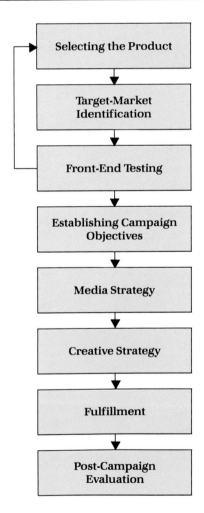

# Selecting the Product

Direct marketing is hardly a means of disposing of unwanted or slow-moving merchandise. The merchandise sold in this manner has to be carefully selected; companies must determine which items are suitable for this strategy. For instance, the items sold through direct marketing should not be very heavy or break easily when handled during the distribution process. The marketer must also consider the availability of the merchandise, that is, whether supplies can be re-ordered if demand exceeds expectations (see figure 16.4). In addition, consumers must perceive the value of the product to be high. The product must be unique, or unlike those items generally available in a retail store, to attract the customers' attention.

Some of the characteristics and sorts of products that sell well through direct marketing are as follows:[3]

1. *Bargains*  Products that sell well at retail also sell through direct mail, especially if consumers perceive that direct mail entails a significant price advantage.

---

**FIGURE 16.4**  Checklist for Evaluating Products and Services for Direct Marketing

1. Industry Sales
   - What is the present and projected market size?
   - What is the rate of market growth?
   - What factors contribute to growth?

2. Competition
   - Is there room for another entry?
   - How many and how strong are competitors?

3. Customer Profile
   - Who buys the product?
   - Why, where, and when do they buy?
   - Can they be reached efficiently by lists or direct-response advertising?

4. Uniqueness
   - Can something unique be offered or is it a "me-too" product?

5. Comparative Value
   - Can greater value be offered?
   - Is a price advantage possible?
   - What will the prospect's perception of value be?

6. Customer Service
   - Can fulfillment be handled quickly and efficiently?
   - Is there an internal system for order processing, packing and delivery, and inventory management?

7. Repeat Business
   - Will sales lead to repeat business for other products?

8. Profit Margin
   - What is the potential profit?
   - Is the margin adequate to justify investment?

---

2. *Exclusives*   Products that are widely available but are offered by mail in a unique and exclusive way are preferred. For example, a pre-packaged offer of photography equipment (camera, lenses, film, and carrying case) may be perceived as unique compared to the items sold separately at retail. Perhaps the price of the combination offer was lower than that available through retailer stores, adding to the uniqueness of the offer.

3. *Specialty Items*   Products that meet the needs of special market segments are appropriate for direct marketing, assuming that market segment can be reached through a mailing list. Thus products aimed directly at new mothers, teachers, lawyers, accountants, and engineers are marketed in this manner, since these special interest groups can be easily reached through lists that direct marketers can purchase.

4. *Standardized Items*   For inventory control and planning purposes, products that are available only in a limited range of formats (e.g., a limited range of colours and sizes) are appropriate for direct marketing. Such limitation allows inventories of the product to be kept at reasonable levels. Offering a wide variety of items poses inventory problems and cuts into the profit margin of the offer.

5. *Items that are Delivered Easily*   Since shipments are made by mail, only merchandise that can be mailed at a reasonable cost and that is not likely to be damaged during the mailing process can be marketed. This restricts the size and weight of direct-mail merchandise.

6. *Items of Reasonable Cost*   Generally, items with an average value of $20 are appropriate for direct marketing.[4] Products offering value in this price range include books, records and tapes, magazine subscriptions, garden supplies, hobby and craft supplies, and unique gift products.

The type of buyer who takes advantage of such offers is different from the consumer who purchases from retail. Such a shopper is willing to wait, say, 4 to 6 weeks for product delivery, whereas the retail shopper seeks instant gratification.

## Target Market Identification

The primary advantage of direct marketing is its ability to reach a targeted audience. To reach the desired market, the firm first develops a target profile, then determines if the target can be reached efficiently. Once the target profile has been completed, the firm reviews the various sources of information that can be used to reach these customers. Internal customer records are the most likely source of information for identifying prospects for new offers. These current customer records, combined with published lists (e.g., subscription lists), form a significant data base for direct-marketing organizations. Success in direct marketing depends on the presence of accurate and reliable information in a data bank. Data-base marketing involves analyzing purchased or collected information in order to develop the most effective direct-response marketing possible to elicit orders, sales leads, donations, or in-building traffic. Further discussion of database marketing is included later in this chapter, in the discussion of recent trends in direct marketing.

In direct marketing, the best prospect is often someone who has bought the given product in the past. The more recently the customer has purchased and the greater the value of the order, the greater is the likelihood that he or she will make another purchase. This shows that an organization needs to keep accurate lists of names from past campaigns or to gain access to new lists compiled by external sources. Such lists are available through Canada Post or through list brokers.

### *Postal Information*

Canada Post supports direct marketing not only by carrying messages to potential customers, but also by providing information that is vital to the accurate targeting of messages. A good mailing list is a critical factor in a campaign's success, and an integral part of a list is the postal code. To illustrate, a code can isolate small geographic areas — say, a city block — and can then be married with census data to provide relevant statistics regarding the ages and incomes of homeowners in the area, and whether children are present in households. Such data can be matched with information regarding consumer expenditures to reveal how a particular group of people spend disposable income.

### *List Brokers*

**list broker**

A **list broker** is a specialist who makes all the arrangements for one company to use the list or lists of another company. A marketing firm provides such a broker with a profile of the target customer, and the broker supplies a list of possible prospects at a cost that ranges from $0.03 to $0.50 per name, depending on the quality of the list. Generally, high quality lists are developed on a computer through a merge/purge process, whereby numerous lists are purchased, combined, and stripped of duplicate names. There are several types of lists available including response lists, circulation lists, and compiled lists. Internal customer lists are called "house lists".

#### *Response Lists*

**response list**

A **response list** identifies mail-order buyers. They are expensive to obtain but well worth the return. Such lists itemize people who frequently buy from the Book-of-the-Month Club, people who are subscribers to Maclean Hunter business publications, or people who order from Carole Martin packages or those of other cooperative direct-mailing firms. These are people who are receptive to direct-marketing promotional materials.

#### *Circulation Lists*

**circulation list**

**Circulation lists** are moderately priced magazine subscription lists that target potential customers by an interest or activity (see figure 16.5). A publishing company, for example, might sell its lists of subscribers to all of its consumer magazines. As figure 16.5 shows, Equinox subscribers are described as intelligent, enquiring, and upscale types that are interested in science, geography, and travel. Such a list may be of interest to an organization that promotes travel to exotic destinations.

**FIGURE 16.5** Mailing Lists Available to Direct Marketing Organizations

## Menu of Lists

**Canadian Living** 368,000 ACTIVE CANADIAN
SUBSCRIBERS . . . . . . . . . . . . . . . . . . . . . . . . . . . . **$80/M**
This tantilizing list is served with a mixture of career
women and homemakers in the prime of their buying
lives. With interests in fashion, crafts, cooking and
beauty, this list will whet your response hunger!

**TV GUIDE** 450,000 ACTIVE CANADIAN
SUBSCRIBERS . . . . . . . . . . . . . . . . . . . . . . . . . . . . **$75/M**
The chefs' specialty!
One large dose of entertainment,
A dash of who's hot and who's not,
An oodle of informative articles,
A pinch of timely gossip.
Mix with movie reviews and recipes of today's biggest
stars and add only the freshest, responsive Canadian
subscribers, MMM . . . response!

**EQUINOX** 136,000 ACTIVE CANADIAN
SUBSCRIBERS. . . . . . . . . . . . . . . . . . . . . . . . . . . . **$100/M**
The Equinox list is made only with intelligent,
enquiring, upscale subscribers with an interest in
science, geography and travel. These readers will
satisfy your hunger for response!

**Harrowsmith** 116,000 ACTIVE CANADIAN
SUBSCRIBERS . . . . . . . . . . . . . . . . . . . . . . . . . . . **$100/M**
Devoted to a quality conscious lifestyle. This beautiful
magazine is comprised of Canadians with interests
ranging from home renovation and gardening to
environmental preservation. Country fresh response
with big city sophistication!

**CAMDEN HOUSE BOOK BUYERS**
28,000 BOOK BUYERS . . . . . . . . . . . . . . . . . . . . . **$90/M**
New, new, new. These book buyers have proven
interests in home service, the environment, the
garden and **your** offer!

**SELECT HOMES & FOOD**
125,000+ ACTIVE CANADIAN SUBSCRIBERS . . . . . **$85/M**
An incredible combination! Readers are prime
prospects for your home service offers as well as
fundraising campaigns and much, much more!
This list is haute, haute, haute!

**TV GUIDE/TELEMEDIA MULTIS**
47,000 MULTI SUBSCRIBERS . . . . . . . . . . . . . . . . **$90/M**
The best of all worlds! These readers are TV Guide
subscribers who also subscribe to one or more
Telemedia publications. Multi response . . . MMM!

**Canadian Living Craft/Book Buyers**
46,000 BUYERS . . . . . . . . . . . . . . . . . . . . . . . . . . . **$80/M**
Proven mail order responders from the pages of
Canadian Living. Cookbook buyers, Craft buyers . . .
and waiting to hear from you!

All above lists are served in your choice of 1600 BP,
magnetic tape, 4-up cheshire labels or pressure
sensitive labels.

These highly responsive lists will satisfy your response
cravings in;

- Fundraising campaigns
- Home and garden offers
- Financial offers
- Travel offers
- Book and tape offers
- Fashion and beauty offers

For a full menu review call Postal Promotions at
(416) 752-8100

Courtesy: Postal Promotions Ltd.

*Marketers can select a subscription list whose reader profile resembles their target market.*

*compiled lists*

### Compiled Lists

**Compiled lists** are prepared from public sources of information (e.g., government, census, telephone, and warranty). They are the least expensive of the lists and are not always personalized. For instance, a business firm may be identified on the list but not the appropriate contact person within the firm. For business direct marketing, names of firms are listed by Standard Industrial Classification codes (e.g., by size, type of product, or location) and can be found through a variety of industrial trade indexes such as Fraser's Canadian Trade Index or Scott's Industrial Directory. Lists of such professionals as physicians, lawyers, accountants and teachers are also available through the provincial and national associations of which such professionals are members.

## Front-End Testing

*front-end testing*

**Front-end testing** measures the effectiveness of direct-marketing activity on a sample of the market, thus determining whether it is feasible to extend the activity to the rest of the market. If the test results are positive, a rollout campaign is imple-

*rollout*

mented. A **rollout** is the process of distributing an offer to the remaining names on a mailing list after a portion of that list has been successfully tested.

Two types of front-end testing are possible: product testing and comparative

*product testing*
*comparative testing*

testing. In the case of **product testing**, the viability of the product or service is evaluated to see how acceptable it is to the target market. In the case of **comparative testing**, one component of the proposed campaign is altered, and the effect of this change on the acceptability of the offer is gauged. For example, various prices or different incentives are tested for the same product to determine which one performs best.

To illustrate, let's consider an organization that is using comparative testing to determine how best to sell a $20 denim jacket by mail (see figure 16.6 for comparative figures). The intention is to offer a booklet premium to buyers of the jacket in a rollout mailing to one million potential customers. The organization must determine if the number of jackets sold justifies the cost of the premium. In the test, one-half of a sample mailing receives the premium (Offer A) while the other half does not (Offer B). Comparing the results shows that the premium is justified: an additional profit of $1.17 per jacket is generated when the booklet premium is offered, and sales volume rises from 30 000 to 40 000 jackets.

The purpose of such testing is to establish what is the best offer for the rollout campaign, while eliminating the financial risk of a rollout. Sales and profit achieved in the test are projected to the rollout campaign. To avoid wasting money on needless tests, the rule of thumb in the direct marketing industry is to test only for variables that might have a dramatic impact on profit and loss. Since price is often a key variable, it is common to test an offer at a variety of price levels before making rollout decisions.

A statistical approach can be taken for front-end testing. Generally speaking, a 4 percent response rate, which means that 4 percent of the people on a mailing list place an order for the product, qualifies as a successful test. In the industry, a common practice is to ensure that at least 200 responses are obtained in a test

**FIGURE 16.6**   The Costs, Sales, and Profits of a Direct-Mail Marketing Campaign

### DENIM JACKET TEST MAILING

|  | Offer A (includes premium) | Offer B (no premium) |
|---|---|---|
| **Test:** | | |
| Number of Mailings | 20 000 | 20 000 |
| Mailing Cost ($200/M) | $4 000 | $4 000 |
| Number of Replies | 800 | 600 |
| Response Rate | 4% | 3% |
| Advertising Cost per Response | $5.00 | $6.67 |
| Premium Cost per Response (includes fulfillment) | $0.50 | n/a |
| Total Cost per Response | $5.50 | $6.67 |
| | | |
| **Rollout:** | | |
| **Revenue** | | |
|   40 000 jackets × $20 | $800 000 | |
|   30 000 jackets × $20 | | $600 000 |
| | | |
| **Cost** | | |
| Direct Product Cost | | |
|   40 000 × $10 | 400 000 | |
|   30 000 × $10 | | 300 000 |
| Promotion Cost | | |
|   40 000 × $5.50 | 220 000 | |
|   30 000 × $6.67 | | 200 100 |
|   Total Cost | 620 000 | 500 100 |
|   Profit | 180 000 | 99 900 |

In this example, the data obtained from a test mailing of 4 000 was used to project sales, costs and profits for a rollout mailing of 1 000 000. The response rate achieved in the test was 4 percent for Offer A and 3 percent for Offer B.

situation. For instance, in a properly conducted test, one that generates 200 purchases, a list of 5 000 names would be required to achieve the desired response rate of 4 percent.[5] More sophisticated marketing organizations refer to probability tables to determine optimum sample size for testing.

## Establishing Objectives

This phase of the planning process entails specifying in quantifiable terms the sales and profits the firm wants to accomplish. The data collected in the test situation is used as a basis on which to project the sales and profits for the rollout campaign. For instance, a bank may use computerized lists of graduates at certain colleges to determine how many will apply for a credit card after being exposed to a direct mailing. The test data is used to project how many mailings would have to be made to achieve a desired quantity — say, 10 000 new applications — in a rollout. Financial planning is an important element of a direct-marketing campaign, just as it is of other business activities. All revenues, including cash and accounts receivable, and all costs, such as those of the product, premiums, promotion, and order processing, have to be considered to ensure that financial goals can be achieved.

## Media Selection

Selecting the most effective advertising media is the next step in planning a campaign. Various media are tested and evaluated to determine which ones generate the highest rate of response in the market segment, and the greatest opportunity for profit. The media alternatives commonly used in direct marketing campaigns are 1) direct mail, (used in conjunction with available lists); 2) conventional mass media (i.e., directing advertising messages through newspapers, magazines, television or radio); 3) interactive media, where sellers and buyers communicate directly with each other by telephone (telemarketing); 4) certain television venues, such as The Canadian Home Shopping Network; and 5) miscellaneous media, including cooperative direct mailings, bill enclosures, statement stuffers, take-ones, and card decks.

In addition to considering which media reach the most prospects, the firm must take into account certain creative and other factors when deciding what media to use:

1. *Demonstration*   If a persuasive demonstration is crucial to selling a particular product, television becomes an obvious media choice (e.g., small kitchen appliances such as the veg-o-matic are quickly and convincingly demonstrated in television commercials). Direct mail is also a possibility because it may contain many colour photographs to demonstrate the product.

2. *Personalization*   A prospect's name is important since it is one of several positive influences on response rates. If a name is available it should be included in the communication, particularly if telephone or direct mail is the media choice. Computer technology has enabled the form letters used in direct mail campaigns to be personalized.

3. *Length of Message*   In contrast to other forms of print advertising, direct-mail campaigns are copy-oriented. In other words, they rely less on visual illustrations and more on copy to present benefits and to ask continually for the order. The inclusion of preprinted inserts such as reply cards and order forms increases the probability of getting a response. The use of such inserts makes it necessary that mail be used as the medium in many direct marketing campaigns.

4. *Contract*   If a signature is needed to close the sale, media that can distribute order forms must be used. For instance, the signature of a new or returning subscriber must be included on an order form when the subscription is purchased by means of a credit card. Under such circumstances, print is the only possible medium for delivering the message.

5. *Coverage*   The mass coverage of a geographic area is often achieved through cooperative direct mailings, especially when targeted audiences are sought. These mailings are distributed on postal routes by mail carriers to selected postal codes in any designated region of the country. If a general cross-section of the population is sought, the conventional mass media can be used, but they tend to be less effective in generating response.

## Creative Strategy

Successful direct mail campaigns have rules for copy, layout, and design that are different from the rules followed in other forms of print advertising. Long copy and factual information are common elements of direct mail. In support of long copy, David Ogilvy, a founder of Ogilvy & Mather Advertising, states that "long copy sells more than short copy, particularly when you are asking the reader to spend a lot of money."[6] Since direct mail is the most prominent form of direct marketing communication, let's examine briefly some of the design elements of these messages:

1. White space is unimportant, and every line should communicate details.
2. A coupon or reply card is mandatory because such cards are used by companies for measurement and evaluation.
3. Copy tone should be "upbeat" (i.e., positive) all the time, and illustrations must serve a specific purpose.
4. Copy should close continually. Because the interest of readers fades quickly, the copy, like an effective salesperson, must ask for the order early and often.

Refer to figure 16.7 for an example of some of these creative considerations. Regardless of the medium used, the message must contain combinations of the following content elements so that it entices consumers to take action:[7]

1. *Free Home Trial*   Such a strategy gets the product into the hands of the prospect, who will then, hopefully, want to keep it. Payment is required when the trial period expires.

2. *Free Sample*   A trial-size sample is delivered so that product claims can be verified.

3. *Free Premium*   This provides the customer with an added incentive to buy (e.g., a free pen or calculator may be offered with a magazine subscription).

4. *Limited-Time Offer*   Such an offer is an incentive to respond quickly (e.g., the first 1 000 respondents receive a sports bag free).

5. *Sweepstakes*   Sometimes a contest giving the prospect a chance to win cash or merchandise is instituted.

6. *Satisfaction Guaranteed*   Offering a full refund gives the prospect confidence in the product.

**FIGURE 16.7**   Contents of a Typical Direct Mail Campaign

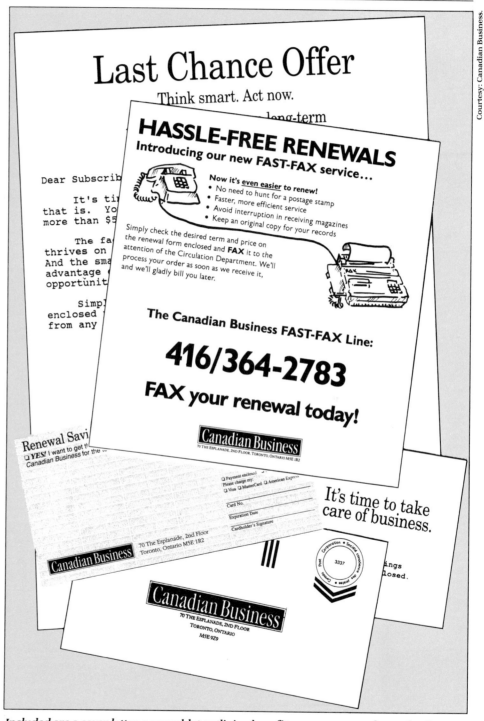

*Included are a cover letter, a pamphlet outlining benefits, a response card or order form, and a postage paid return envelope.*

**FIGURE 16.8    A Free-Standing Direct-Response Advertisement with an Order Form**

*Courtesy: The Bradford Exchange.*

"The Grizzly Bear"
Actual diameter: 8½ inches (21.6 cm)
©1988 Dominion China®

### A definitive portrait of the king of the Canadian wilderness...
### a Bradford Exchange recommendation

Few men have come this close to a grizzly bear and lived to tell about it. So real are the bear and his surroundings in this stunning portrait that we can almost feel the frosty chill in the early November air and hear the loud crunch underfoot as this giant pads its way through the snow.

"The Grizzly Bear" is issued in an edition limited to a maximum of 150 firing days. Since exceptional first issue collector's plates have increased dramatically in value— as much as 1,000%—anyone wishing to obtain this plate at its $37.80 issue price is urged to act as quickly as possible. *Send no money now.* You will be billed when your plate is shipped.

*Just use the order form at right.*

**Buy-Order Form**

The Bradford Exchange
P. O. Box 5290
40 Pacific Court
London, Ontario N6A 9Z9

Please respond by:      August 26, 1989

**YES.** Please enter my buy-order for "The Grizzly Bear," first plate in the *Wild and Free: Canada's Big Game* series. *Limit: one plate per customer.*

I understand that I need SEND NO MONEY NOW. I will be billed the $37.80 issue price, plus $2.79 for postage and handling, with shipment. (Ontario residents will be billed 8% sales tax.)

X _____                          Date _____
Signature

_____                ( _____ ) _____
Name (Please Print)                                 Telephone

_____
Address

_____
City                                      Province              Postal Code

Please respond promptly. Plates are produced in a limited edition, and we can guarantee availability at issue price only until the edition closes.

Fill out this form and drop it in the mailbox. No postage necessary.

Kingston Whig-Standard          July 15, 1989          3371-151001

*This particular advertisement was distributed as an insert in daily newspapers.*

positive action

7. *Positive Action*   When **positive action** is required, customers must take action to receive the offer: they may, for example, have to sign and return a response card prior to obtaining the merchandise (see figure 16.8).

negative action

8. *Negative Action*   In some circumstances, **negative action** is necessary. In these cases, the customer agrees that unless he or she replies to a notice by refusing to accept a shipment, the product will be sent. This is a fairly common practice with book and record clubs.

free ride

9. *Free Rides*   A **free ride** is an extra offer that comes free (i.e., "piggybacks") with a primary offer. For example, a mailing may include a second circular outlining an additional offer, along with an order form for this additional offer.

bounce back

10. *Bounce Backs*   A **bounce back** is an offer that rides along with a product shipment or with an invoice from a previous order. In this case, one order leads to another, and the same prospect is reached at a very low cost.

Practitioners of direct marketing acknowledge that there is no magic formula for assembling offers. The key to continued success is testing new concepts that will improve results. Generally, direct marketing organizations test only those ideas that are fundamentally unique, since only these have the potential for eliciting significant differences in response. Ideas for minor modifications to offers would merely bring about slight changes in results and therefore are not worth the time and money invested in testing.

## Fulfillment

fulfillment

Once the customer responds to the offer, the marketer's focus shifts to fulfillment. **Fulfillment** concerns the processing of an order, an information request, a premium, or a refund. The processing of an order embraces numerous activities:

1. Addressing and mailing promotion pieces.
2. Establishing new accounts.
3. Setting up billing procedures.
4. Addressing and mailing invoices.
5. Receiving, recording, and depositing credit payments.
6. Handling all customer transactions (e.g., address changes, complaints, and cancellations).
7. Inventory control.
8. Compiling statistics for financial and marketing analysis.

It should be noted that, unlike retailers, direct marketers are unaware of a prospect's credit rating and ability to pay. Direct marketing reaches the "unknown" customer who often orders and receives goods before he or she has paid for them. Consequently, it encounters higher rates of returned merchandise, more bad debts and more requests for more information than does retailing. These occurrences increase fulfillment and other costs and have to be considered in financial planning, since they do affect an offer's profitability.

Companies contemplating the use of direct marketing must have a system to handle the projected volume of orders and all the related customer requirements. It should also be computerized to accommodate the needs of financial and marketing planning. For firms new to direct marketing, the use of established fulfillment houses, which specialize in all fulfillment tasks, eases the burden of implementing such a system.

## Post Campaign Evaluation

**back-end testing**

Once the direct marketing campaign is over, it is evaluated by means of back-end testing. **Back-end testing** measures the degree of a campaign's success or failure. The organization at this stage wants to determine if the actual sales and, especially, the profits were close to what was planned. Profit is measured in three ways: absolute dollars, percentage-of-sales and percentage-of-promotion expenditures. The promotion described in figure 16.9 produces a profit of $50 000. This figure may be quite acceptable to the firm; however, the firm might have a predetermined goal for each promotion it implements. For example, if the profit margin expressed as a percentage of sales had been 5 percent instead of 10 percent (the goal), the same promotion might have been judged a failure. Other indicators of success or failure include the following.[8]

**cost per response (CPR)**

1. **Cost per response (CPR)** is the actual cost of filling a single order, with lower costs being the more acceptable.

**response rate**

2. The **response rate** refers to the number of responses received, expressed as a percentage of the total distribution.

**conversion rate**

3. The **conversion rate** is the ratio of orders delivered as a percentage of the enquiries received.

---

**FIGURE 16.9  A Post-Campaign Evaluation**

A book offer at a price of $20.00 per book

| | |
|---|---:|
| Mailing Quantity | 1 000 000 |
| Response rate | 2.5% |
| Number of Orders | 25 000 |
| Revenue at $20.00 per book | $500 000 |
| | |
| Costs | |
| Direct Product Cost at $10.00 per book (includes fulfillment) | 250 000 |
| Promotion Cost at $200.00 per M | 200 000 |
| Total Cost | 450 000 |
| Profit | 50 000 |
| Profit Margin (% of Sales) | 10% |
| Margin (% of Promotion Investment) | 25% |

---

4. Returned merchandise is expressed as the percentage of the merchandise shipped to the customer that is returned to the supplier as unwanted.
5. Cancellations concern the number of members or subscribers who cancel their memberships or subscriptions.
6. Repeat business refers to the percentage of buyers who are sold other products at a later date.

## ⟩⟩⟩⟩ *The Canadian Direct Marketing Industry*

As of 1987, advertising expenditures in Canada on direct marketing activity amounted to $1.8 billion or 22.6 percent of all advertising revenue.[9] According to the Maclean Hunter Research Bureau, advertising expenditures on direct marketing are second only to those spent on advertisements in daily newspapers (24.4 percent). Sales revenue that has resulted from direct-marketing advertising has grown significantly, from $1.7 billion in 1981 to $6.4 billion in 1987. Sales generated by direct mail, the largest category of direct-marketing activity, was estimated to be $3.6 billion or 56 percent of direct-marketing sales.[10]

### History of Direct Marketing

Direct-mail marketing was first introduced into North America to meet the needs of isolated rural communities of the American midwest in the 1870s. The lack of retail stores serving the farming population was an opportunity for the catalogue mail-order business. The first mail-order catalogue was established in 1872 by Montgomery Ward, a Chicago-based retail organization. Catalogues came to be used extensively across both the United States and Canada, with the goods being transported by rail from station to station. The use of the post office and of parcel-post delivery started in 1914.

The first mail-order house in Canada was Eaton's. Its first store opened in Toronto in 1869, and the mail-order business started in 1884. Catalogue operations were a new form of competition for general stores in rural areas, and the competition was significant, for catalogues offered greater product selection at lower prices.

The period spanned by the 1920s and 1930s was a very busy era for catalogue merchandising, since a large proportion of Canada's population lived in small towns and rural areas. In the 1940s and 1950s, better rail and truck transportation and mail service improved direct mail activity by reducing the delivery time required for goods ordered to reach consumers. More recently, computer technology has been adapted to direct marketing to facilitate the preparation, segmentation, and use of mailing lists.

Direct marketing is no longer confined to mail order. Today, all forms of media are used to communicate directly with customers. Direct home shopping by consumers through shopping channels on cable television, and the use of telemarketing techniques by businesses, are examples of contemporary direct-marketing activity. Some of the heaviest users of direct marketing include magazine publishers, petroleum

FIGURE 16.10    Major Uses of Direct Marketing in Canada

| Industry | Use |
|---|---|
| Magazines | To obtain new, renewal and gift subscriptions |
| Book and Record Clubs | To obtain or extend memberships |
| Petroleum Companies | To encourage use of credit cards; to sell products and services the credit can be used for |
| Department Stores | To deliver catalogues, pamphlets, promote sales and encourage use of credit cards |
| Industrial Manufacturers | To provide information, generate sales leads, and obtain orders |
| Packaged Goods Companies | To distribute trial coupons and samples |
| Colleges and Universities | To promote seminars and conferences; fundraising |
| Fundraisers | To solicit funds for philanthropic agencies, political parties, etc. |

companies, department stores, colleges, and universities (see figure 16.10). The future looks bright for direct marketing. Despite the urbanization of the population, even catalogue ordering from the Sears catalogue and specialty mail-order organizations like L.L. Bean and Tilley Endurables are growing, in effect, following the shift in population location. Specialty mail-order houses advertise the availability of their catalogues, which customers request and then order from.

## Recent Trends in Direct Marketing

Is direct marketing the future of marketing? Many in the direct marketing industry think so as more and more firms incorporate direct marketing techniques into their marketing strategies. Innovations in direct marketing present even further opportunities for marketers. Among the recent innovations are the resurgence of catalogue shopping and the use of telemarketing, video brochures, and direct home shopping.

### Catalogue Shopping

The distribution of catalogues by direct marketing organizations in the United States is big business. In Canada, such activity is in its infancy. The established leader in catalogue shopping is Sears Canada Inc. Its catalogue is available free of charge to established catalogue shoppers, or sold at a nominal price to new prospects through Sears retail outlets. Catalogues containing specialized lines of merchandise are now more commonplace and are very often targeted at people with particular interests. For example, catalogues containing home furnishings and accessories, leisure sportswear, sporting goods, outdoor gear, and computer supplies are now available. The Marketing in Action story ''Shopping by Magalogue'' illustrates the growing importance of catalogue shopping.

⟩⟩⟩⟩ *MARKETING IN ACTION*

## *SHOPPING BY MAGALOGUE*

Did you know that home shopping now accounts for 10 percent of all retail sales in the United States? The figure in Canada is not as high, but there is a definite trend toward more home shopping. In the United States, 20 to 25 billion direct-marketing publications are distributed annually by over 10 000 firms.

What they distribute are not the standard catalogues you may be familiar with. The new catalogues are called "magalogues" and are slick, sexy, and sophisticated. They tend to be seasonal in nature and are directed to carefully defined "upscale," (i.e., higher income) groups.

Why is there a resurgence in catalogue retailing? Several factors have effected their renaissance. One is the growing number of women working outside the home, a circumstance which has reduced the shopping time available to families. Personal shopping can also be inconvenient for other reasons today. Gasoline and parking must be paid for, and buyers are often exposed to poorly trained sales personnel, incompetent service people, and the presence of "mall-brats." Rather than face these aggravations, consumers are staying home, leisurely reviewing their glitzy catalogues, and dialing a toll-free number when the urge to buy strikes. The first marketer of

*Courtesy of Sears Canada Inc.*

*To avoid the aggravation of shopping expeditions, many consumers are staying at home, leisurely reviewing their catalogues, and dialling a toll-free number when struck by the urge to buy*

magalogues across Canada, not surprisingly, is a U.S. operation which sees great potential here. The company is L.L. Bean, an aficionado of outdoor gear.

Adapted from Ryszard Dubanski, "Let the fingers do the walking", *The Globe and Mail*, December 20, 1988, p.A7.

Catalogues offer the marketing organization the ability to target customers with special interests and provide ample space for presenting products. In addition, their quality can play a key role in developing an image and identity for a product line. Their disadvantages include the expense of colour production and the long lead time needed for preparation. Carrying a wide variety of product lines also poses inventory problems for catalogue-marketing organizations. Historically, only limited variations of products have been carried so that inventory carrying costs could be kept to a minimum.

### *Telemarketing*

inbound telemarketing Two categories of telemarketing exist: inbound and outbound. **Inbound telemarketing** refers to the reception of calls by the order desk, customer service inquiry, and direct-response calls, often generated through the use of toll-free 800

outbound
telemarketing

numbers. **Outbound telemarketing**, on the other hand, refers to calls a company makes to a customer in order to develop new accounts, generate sales leads, qualify prospects, and conduct marketing research.

With the employment of well-trained personnel, telemarketing can fulfill a variety of sales functions. The training and preparation of telemarketing representatives needs to be as comprehensive as it is for personal selling if its maximum benefits are to be realized. The primary advantage of telemarketing is that it can complete a sale for less cost than is needed to complete a sale using face-to-face sales calls.

### Video Brochures

video brochures

**Video brochures**, or video presentations of a product, are now an integral component of the salesperson's presentation strategy. For marketers, the advantage of the video is in the presentation since material can be presented in a planned and orderly sequence. Also, certain actions and situations can be shown that would not be possible through speech or slide-presentation techniques. General Motors used videos to introduce the Cadillac Allante. In its direct-marketing program, affluent and influential people were selected to receive a video presentation of the car. In a similar program, Air France, in order to entice prospects to fly to France, mailed to potential customers videos that vividly illustrated what it is like to be dining in luxury restaurants in Paris and that showed famous scenes from the French countryside.[11]

### Direct Home Shopping

direct home shopping

**Direct home shopping** is a service provided by cable television stations across Canada. Called the Canadian Home Shopping Network, the stations offer products for sale by broadcast message. Messages to prospects are presented in the form of still photographs and graphics accompanied by a voiceover describing the product. Details on how the customer places an order are frequently broadcast throughout the product presentations. It is not a very exciting medium in its current presentation format, but it does offer the shopper convenience. It is very likely that home shopping presentations will move to a live-action format, much like conventional product commercials seen on television, in the near future. Live action messages are now commonplace on the home shopping channels in the United States.

### Telefocus Marketing

Progressive marketing organizations now combine the best elements of several direct-marketing techniques into an integrated campaign. Such integration, described as telefocus marketing, combines telemarketing, direct mail, and video brochures into one direct-marketing campaign.[12] The integration of these techniques adds to the cost of a campaign, but sometimes such programs are justified. The telefocus marketing campaign is ideal for situations where

1. The product is a "high ticket" (expensive) item.
2. The personal selling process is long and complicated.
3. Numerous demonstrations are necessary to many individuals involved in the buying decision (a business buying situation).
4. Prospects are not that accessible (distant locations).
5. The prospects are classified as "upscale."

The Cadillac Allante campaign implemented by General Motors, referred to earlier, is an example of an integrated campaign. Direct mail and video brochures presented the benefits of the product and generated awareness and interest in potential customers. The customers viewed the video in the relaxing surroundings of their own home. Telephone and direct mail were used as follow-up to encourage potential customers to visit a dealer showroom for a test drive.

## Factors Affecting the Growth of Direct Marketing

### *Domination of the Channel of Distribution*

In Canada, six supermarket chains and five department stores dominate the grocery and department store markets. These businesses, therefore, have a great influence on the relationship between a source supplier (manufacturer) and the consumer. The retailer has control over the items carried in the channel and over the merchandising support given to national manufacturers. Direct marketing puts control back into the hands of manufacturers, since the middleman is bypassed entirely in the communications and delivery process.

### *Targeting Capability*

Direct marketing can focus on a target market that is precisely defined by demographic, psychographic and geographic segmentation. This is a significant benefit in a country where regional and local differences in markets abound. For example, one in four Canadians is French; one out of every seven retail dollars is spent in the Toronto area; and only three cities represent one-third of all commercial activity in Canada.[13] Statistics such as these indicate what target areas to concentrate on. Direct marketers can purchase lists (e.g., magazine subscribers lists) that mirror the target group they want to appeal to with their products. This capability adds an element of efficiency to their marketing programs.

### *Database Marketing*

**database marketing**

**Database marketing** involves analyzing the data concerning customers and prospects that is contained in a database, with a view to identifying new markets and selling opportunities and to preparing marketing programs targeted to the customers most likely to buy.[14] Advancing computer technology allows marketing organizations to accumulate, analyze, and use customer information for direct marketing purposes. Using list information that can be purchased from a variety of sources, the marketer can prepare and segment potential prospects and reach them efficiently through direct marketing. The type of information collected includes the names of customers and prospects, where they live, what they buy and do, and how often they buy.

The advantage of a database is that it changes and evolves as new information is added, and therefore generates an effective list for targeted direct-mail marketing programs. Banks and trust companies use their customer files to target different customers according to their known financial resources. This allows the bank to target specific services to the groups most likely to use them. Retailers effectively use their lists of credit card holders to build store traffic by sending the listed holders promotional material through the mail. They also employ the lists to establish mail-order distribution channels.

### Socioeconomic Influences

Some basic changes in society, such as the greater number of women working outside the home and the increasing use of credit cards, have benefited direct marketing. Women and families now have much less time for personal shopping, a circumstance that makes the convenience of direct mail and catalogue shopping attractive. By using these vehicles, people may shop at their leisure in a relaxed environment. The impersonal environment and ill-trained sales staff of many retailers, as well as the traffic and parking problems in urban shopping areas, have also prompted people to turn to direct marketing as a welcome alternative.

### Customer Contact Cost

In business-to-business situations, the cost of a personal sales call is now estimated to be between $200 and $250 and it takes five calls on average to close a sale.[15] Because of these escalating costs, marketing organizations are finding direct marketing an attractive option. It can be used to generate leads, to qualify customers, and, in many cases, to sell the product. Direct marketing either complements the personal sales call or even replaces it. Telemarketing campaigns, and the use of 800 numbers to handle enquiries from customers, are cost-efficient direct-marketing activities.

### Advertising Accountability

Unlike traditional advertising, where success is measured in terms of recognition and recall, direct marketing is measured for effectiveness at the bottom line. For instance, an organization can measure the number of orders received as a result of direct marketing by tracking responses from specific campaigns. This assists an organization in planning, as actual experience can be used to forecast sales and profits for new campaigns. Marketing organizations like to know precisely how effective their advertising investment will be.

## Canadian Direct Marketing Association (CDMA)

**Canadian Direct Marketing Association (CDMA)**

The Canadian Direct Marketing Association (CDMA) is a non-profit association comprised of a cross-section of industry members. Members of the CDMA include magazine and book publishers, record and book clubs, banks and insurance companies, fundraisers and political parties, retail stores, catalogue houses, heavy manufacturing industries, distributors, printers, lettershops, list brokers, and Canada Post.

The role of this organization is to promote the use of direct marketing and to govern the operations of members, ensuring that they adhere to established standards of practice. Through the development of Operation Integrity (see figure 16.11) and the Code of Ethics and Standards of Practice, the CDMA aspires to make certain that member organizations who employ direct marketing to sell products to Canadians do so in an ethical and professional manner. In keeping with its mandate, the

**FIGURE 16.11    Ensuring Standards of Conduct in Direct Marketing**

# Operation Integrity

The symbol above is the registered hallmark of the Canadian Direct Marketing Association. Its use is restricted to merchants and marketers registered as members of the CDMA.

When you see this official CDMA symbol on advertising mail, or in mail order ads in publications, or used as an imprimatur on catalogues and sales brochures, you know that the sales message is from a marketer you can trust. When this symbol is displayed in an ad, it is a guarantee that you'll receive exactly what the advertiser promises.

To gain the privilege of using this symbol in their ads, merchants must become a member of the Canadian Direct Marketing Association. As one of our members, we insist that they abide by a tough, exacting Code of Ethics (see next page), and maintain the highest standards of business practice. If they fail to do so, they are kicked out of the Association, and denied the right to use the integrity symbol.

Our members work for publishers, mail order catalogues, book clubs, fund raisers, department stores, financial institutions, insurance firms, schools, departments of government, and many other merchants and manufacturers who use mail order to offer their goods and services to the public.

In all, our members represent about 80% of the Direct Marketing Industry.

But we are aware that there are a few mail order people who don't always treat their customers fairly. To rid our industry of these, the Canadian Direct Marketing Association has set up a task force to rigorously investigate customer complaints.

If you've received poor treatment from a mail order seller, *after trying to resolve the problem with the seller*, write to us about your experience. Give us as much information as possible. Whether they are members of our Association or are not, we'll go after them for you. Our 'Operation Integrity' will do its best to resolve whatever problems you may have encountered.

Write to:
Operation Integrity,
CDMA,
1 Concorde Gate
Suite 607
Don Mills, ON
M3C 3N6

12

CDMA also maintains an ongoing relationship with the Department of Consumer and Corporate Affairs, the Consumers Association of Canada, and other provincial government agencies and consumer protection associations to foster a mutual understanding between direct marketing organizations and consumers.

## ⟩⟩⟩⟩ SUMMARY

Direct marketing is an interactive system that is fully controlled by the marketing organization. The primary differences between direct marketing and traditional marketing concern place and promotion. In direct marketing, middlemen are bypassed because the organization communicates with and ships merchandise directly to customers. Direct marketing is now a proven technique for building sales, developing better relationships with business customers, and providing information to dealers.

The direct marketing process involves a series of eight interrelated steps. These are product selection, target-market identification, front-end testing, setting objectives, media selection, creative strategy, fulfillment, and post-campaign evaluation.

Direct marketing techniques play an increasingly important role in the marketing strategies of Canadian businesses. Among the reasons for their growing popularity are the domination of distribution channels by selected retailers, the targeting capabilities of direct marketing, the trend to database marketing, certain socioeconomic influences, the high costs of personal selling, and the need to have accountable promotional expenditures. Some of the more recent innovations and activities that will play a prominent role in the future of direct marketing include the resurgence of catalogue shopping, telemarketing, video brochures, and direct home shopping through cable television.

## ⟩⟩⟩⟩ KEY TERMS

| | | |
|---|---|---|
| direct marketing | product testing | response rate |
| direct advertising | comparative testing | conversion rate |
| direct mail | positive action | inbound telemarketing |
| direct-response advertising | negative action | outbound telemarketing |
| list broker | free ride | video brochure |
| response list | bounce back | direct home shopping |
| circulation list | fulfillment | telefocus marketing |
| compiled lists | back-end testing | database marketing |
| front-end testing | cost per response | CDMA |
| rollout | | |

## ⟩⟩⟩⟩ REVIEW AND DISCUSSION QUESTIONS

**1.** Briefly explain the primary advantages of direct marketing compared to traditional forms of promotion strategy.

**2.** How does direct marketing differ from traditional marketing in terms of the 4Ps?

**3.** Briefly describe the ways in which direct marketing can increase sales for an organization.

**4.** What role does testing play in the direct marketing process?

**5.** What types of products are suitable for direct marketing campaigns? Provide some specific examples.

**6.** "The success of a direct mail campaign depends on the quality of the list used." Discuss.

**7.** Under what circumstances should comparative testing be undertaken?

**8.** What is an "offer", and what types of offers are commonly used in direct marketing?

**9.** What activities are involved in the fulfillment stage of direct marketing?

**10.** What evaluation mechanisms determine the success or failure of a direct-marketing campaign?

## ⟩⟩⟩⟩ REFERENCES

1. Direct Marketing in Canada, *Canadian Direct Marketing Association of Canada Newsletter*, n.d.

2. Nielsen Promotion Services, *A Marketer's Guide to Consumer Promotions*, 1988, p.8A.

3. *Canadian Direct Marketing Association Handbook*, Chapter 2, p.13.

4. Ibid., Chapter 1, p.13.

5. *Canadian Direct Marketing Association Handbook*, Chapter 8, p.13.

6. DAVID OGILVY, *Ogilvy on Advertising* (Toronto: John Wiley and Sons Ltd., 1983),p.146.

7. Ibid., Chapter 2, p.23.

8. Canadian Direct Marketing Association, *Glossary of Terms*.

9. KEN RIDDELL, "Ad Revenue Tops $7 Billion", *Marketing*, February 8, 1988.

10. Figures supplied by the Canadian Direct Marketing Association.

11. RICHARD BENCIN, "Telefocus Marketing", *Sales and Marketing Management in Canada*, May 1989, p.16.

12. Ibid.

13. LEONARD KUBAS, "Direct Marketing Is Siphoning National Budgets", *Marketing*, June 8, 1987, p.26.

14. STEPHEN SHAW, "New Era Dawning for Direct Mail", *Marketing*, July 10, 1989, p.24.

15. RICHARD BENCIN, "Building a Telemarketing Blue Print", *Sales and Marketing Management in Canada*, August 1988, p.8.

# C H A P T E R 17 〉〉〉〉

# Service and Nonprofit Marketing

## LEARNING OBJECTIVES

After studying this chapter, you will be able to

1. Identify the factors that have contributed to the growth of services marketing.

2. Outline the characteristics of services marketing and distinguish between service and product marketing.

3. Describe the elements of the service-marketing mix.

4. Explain what the nature, scope, and characteristics of nonprofit marketing are.

5. Describe the types of nonprofit marketing and the role of the marketing mix in nonprofit environments.

## >>>> Services Marketing

The service economy in Canada is diverse and includes many of the country's largest corporations. The market encompasses venture-capital firms, investment dealers, banks, trust and insurance companies, professional firms of accountants and management consultants, real estate companies, advertising agencies, and hotel and food-service businesses. All of these industries, and the companies that compete within them, are actively involved in marketing.

Services have multiplied in the last several years to the point where they represent 61 percent of the Canadian gross domestic product and 69 percent of employment. The service sector now employs nine million Canadians.[1] Through the 1970s and 1980s, community, business and personal services grew significantly. The number of people employed by the hotel and restaurant industry, for instance, increased by 21 percent in the years 1983 to 1986, twice the rate of the service sector as a whole.[2] Much of Canada's growth in the 1990s is expected to come from the service sector.

## Factors Contributing to Growth in Services

### Competition and Regulatory Change

The rising level of competition today has led manufacturers to use service to differentiate themselves from competitors. Thus, automobile manufacturers offer extended car warranties and low- or no-cost maintenance packages. Computer-supply firms offer deals on software, installation, finance, and maintenance to distinguish their product offerings. In an effort to attract customers, firms in these industries and others are emphasizing benefits beyond what the physical product provides itself. More than ever, they are stressing value-added services in an attempt to differentiate their products. This is particularly true of the financial services market, where products and services offered by banks, trust companies, insurance companies, and independent financial planners are so similar. For example, they all offer retirement savings plans, educational savings plans, annuities, and other forms of financial investments.

### Technology

Technological developments have also spurred the service sector. Advancing technology both creates and erases jobs. The introduction of automatic tellers in banks and of personal computers in business has eliminated many clerical positions, while the use of robotics in automobile assembly plants has eliminated manufacturing jobs. In both cases, however, the lost jobs are offset to some extent by the creation of service jobs which are needed to operate, service, and support the machines.

### New Marketing Orientation

Professionals in the service sector have become aware of the usefulness of marketing. Practitioners are leaving their offices for storefront operations in order to be closer to their customers: Tridont, Inc., is a chain of franchised dental clinics located in malls across the country, and lawyers now offer storefront legal aid. Lawyers can now use advertising in a limited way to promote the services they offer. Many of the dental and medical clinics are franchises of national or regional chains, a trend which is expected to continue well into the 1990s.

### Time Pressed Consumers

Although many dual-income households have ample disposable incomes, they tend to have too little time to perform routine chores. Consequently, such Canadians are buying many services, such as maid and cleaning services, lawn and garden care, home decorating, and personal financial planning. Services that are expected to grow in the 1990s are indicated in figure 17.1.

**FIGURE 17.1**    Services Expected to Grow in the 1990s

| Product | Rationale |
| --- | --- |
| Electronic Database Services | The demand for financial, credit, corporate, and marketing information is likely to spur growth of this industry, but much of the expenditure will ultimately flow to U.S. service providers, where this will be a $3.6 billion industry in 1987. Referral databases which bring together buyers and sellers will experience strong demand in various industry sectors over the next ten years. |
| Temporary Employment Agencies | Companies do not need to make long-term, expensive commitments to people, and employees obtain variety and control over working hours not possible in some routine jobs. Temporaries could increasingly be provided in skilled professional areas, and long-term employee leasing could emerge to reduce fringe benefits while keeping labour costs more variable than traditional employment allows. |
| Home Shopping | The store is now as far away as the living room TV. Home shopping can be expected to gain sales in areas where products are low-risk purchases requiring minimal on-site inspection for size, quality or fit. |
| Mega Stores | Stores of over 100,000 square feet are expected to flourish as consumers appreciate the selection of foods, drugs, furniture, and other products they offer. Smaller stores offering local convenience should not be adversely affected by the growth in these operations, but medium sized supermarkets could experience sales declines unless they offer added service, like home delivery or extended hours of shopping. |
| Financial Supermarkets | The "merging of pillars" represented by the insurance, brokerage, banking, and trust companies could lead to cross-selling of services available from sister firms under one roof. However, consumers are likely to appreciate variety and independence, and perhaps more personal service, setting the stage for the growth of separate financial-service "boutiques" in close proximity to one another. |

*Source*: Clarkson Gordon/Woods Gordon, *Tomorrow's Customers*, 21st Edition, 1988. Reprinted with permission.

# Characteristics of Services

service

A **service** is defined as the benefits provided by an organization that satisfy the buyers' needs without conferring ownership of tangible goods.[3] There are four characteristics that distinguish services from products: intangibility, inseparability, quality variability, and perishability of demand.

## *Intangibility*

Services cannot be seen, heard, or touched. For example, a life insurance policy may be worth $500 000, but its true benefit is the security it imparts, and security cannot be seen or touched. Similarly, the advice given by a financial planner has neither colour nor odour; while advice may save money, in itself it cannot be experienced by the senses. This type of product is quite different from something like coffee, whose aroma can be smelled and whose flavour can be tasted. Thus services are said

intangibility

to be intangible or have **intangibility**.

Intangibility is something of a problem for marketers of services. To deal with it, marketers attempt to express the value of the service in tangible terms. For example, they may use the testimonials of well-known personalities when advertising a service in an attempt to give a visual and audible expression to the satisfaction the service provides. The advertisement for Federal Express shows the tangible or material consequences of not using their delivery service (e.g., the financial hardship that can result from missing a business deadline). Brand names help establish images that convey the material effects of a service. London Life's "Freedom 55" campaign for retirement planning suggests the leisurely enjoyment that could result from the plan. The names of firms such as Budget Rent-A-Car and Discount Car and Truck Rentals suggest that these firms offer price savings that competitive services do not offer. Hotels sometimes offer free newspapers and light snacks in rooms as a way of creating tangibility. In the marketing of a service, a company finds it helpful to elaborate the material consequences of the service, rather than just the service itself.

## *Inseparability*

To say that services are *inseparable* is to say that they have a one-of-a-kind quality; it is to say, in effect, that a service is performed uniquely by each supplier and cannot be duplicated by any other. People feel this way about their doctor, their lawyer, or even their hair stylist. While apparent substitutes are available, the buyer feels more comfortable with his or her preferred and regular source of supply. A close relation-

inseparability

ship, or **inseparability**, exists between the service and the supplier. Thus the channel of distribution for services is short, or direct.

Because of peoples' tendency to identify a service with a particular supplier, expansion in a service business is difficult. Any given supplier can only service so many customers. Therefore, to enlarge its clientele, a business must reduce the tendency to identify a service with a particular person or supplier; it must convince the market that others can supply the identical service. A business accomplishes this task by training others to perform the service at the desired level; in other words, the business standardizes the performance of many suppliers of the service. Franchising enables this uniformity to be established; franchisees are all trained to execute the service in the same way, at the same level. In this manner, the service becomes identified with the franchising company and name rather than with the individual operator, and the business is able to expand by opening more franchise outlets. Because franchising facilitates growth, it has increased in popularity in the service sector. In the lawn-care business, firms such as The Weedman (90 franchises), Bobby Lawn (30 franchises) and Lawn-A-Mat (26 franchises) prove that the inseparability factor can be overcome.[4]

### *Quality Variability*

To customers, a quality service is one that meets their expectations, is available when needed, and is administered in a consistent manner. The supply and consistency of tangible products is assured by mass production. By contrast, services are offered by many different people even within the same organization. All Sun Life insurance agents perform the same service, but they approach and deal with their customers differently, and some are much more attentive to their clients' needs than others. This **quality variability** causes problems and challenges for marketers.

**quality variability**

Quality in services can be controlled through standardization programs. The growth of franchises and their acceptance by consumers is, as indicated above, due to their offering of a uniform quality throughout the franchise system. McDonald's motto of quality, service, and value, and the intensive training program all its employees and managers must undergo demonstrate how food products can be prepared and delivered in a standardized way.

Consistency can be maintained through quality-control programs. Reacting to customer feedback is a key aspect of maintaining consistency. Surveys, placed in hotel rooms or at the tables in restaurants, are used to monitor the quality of service in individual locations of a chain operation.

### *Perishability of Demand*

**perishability**

Services suffer from a high degree of demand **perishability**, that is, demand for them varies over a given period. Demand for a service may diminish, but the facilities offering the unwanted service still remain. To understand the concept of uneven demand, consider that hotel rooms sit idle during weekends, when business travel is less frequent, and that theatre seats are often vacant on weekdays and full on weekends. In both cases, the building must be large enough, or have sufficient rooms or seats, to accommodate crowds during peak demand. In the financial-services market, the services of tax specialists such as H&R Block peak in the January-to-March period, since that is when consumers are preparing to submit their annual tax forms.

In the case of service enterprises, marketing's goal is to counter the perishability of demand. Thus marketers offer reduced rates for hotel rooms on weekends, discounted phone rates in non-business hours, and low airline fares for late-night travel. With these measures, they try to increase the use of services during times of low demand. Businesses also attempt to prolong or spread the demand of peak periods by adding related services. For example, patrons of a restaurant are encouraged to visit the bar while waiting for their table, and members of a fitness club are encouraged to use the training room while waiting for their squash court. These schemes extend the demand on the main facilities by retaining the interest of the customers for a longer period than idle waiting would. The use of part-time labour by fast-food restaurants at peak moments is another answer to demand-perishability. Service is maintained at the same level during both fast and slow periods, even though the volume of production varies; by this means, customer dissatisfaction is avoided and demand is kept high.

## Differences Between Services Marketing and Product Marketing

As our industrial economy matures, most of Canada's economic growth is expected to come from the service sector. Yet the experience of most marketing practitioners is in the marketing of industrial and packaged goods; their education and work experience has largely been concerned with tangible products. Without retraining, practitioners find it difficult to shift from tangibles to intangibles and from products to services. Many of the strategies used in packaged-goods and industrial marketing are transferrable to services marketing, but some differences exist (see figure 17.2). In terms of the 4Ps, the major differences are as follows:

1. *Product*  Tangible products serve customer needs through the marketing of standardized goods. In marketing services, a firm analyzes customers' needs or

**FIGURE 17.2**  Some Differences between Market Planning of Goods and Services

| Variable | Goods | Services |
|---|---|---|
| Philosophy | Products satisfy needs | Services resolve problems |
| Research and development | A lengthy, costly, high-risk process; patent protection possible | Conceptual orientation; little lead time and investment; concepts easily copied |
| Capital investment | Extensive investment in land, plants, and machinery | People are the principal investment |
| Production | Centered on facilities to make, store, and ship tangible goods | Centered on training and support of people dealing with customers |
| Promotion | Focus on brand name, benefits, packaging, pricing, and distribution; aimed at channel members and end-users | Focused directly on client and based on intangibles such as reputation and image; referrals are important |
| Pricing | Based on costs and subject to discounts and allowances | Based on value derived by the user; less discounting |
| Distribution | Long channels due to use of middlemen | Short channels due to direct contact with customers |
| Control | Standardized products controlled at point of manufacture | Based on the performance of people; can be inconsistent |

attempts to resolve customers' problems, often discovering a unique problem that can only be resolved by customizing the service. For example, an independent financial consultant or a stockbroker representing a large brokerage firm will analyze a customer's financial situation, his or her financial resources and investment objectives, and then tailor specific recommendations to meet those objectives.

2. *Pricing*   In product marketing, the emphasis is on costs, on being competitively priced, and on providing discounts and allowances that will stimulate purchase. In services marketing, prices are based on benefits and on what customers perceive to be the value of the service offered. Referring to the financial-planning example cited above, we see that it is difficult to put a direct cost on the time a stockbroker spends in consultation with a client (i.e., what is the hourly cost of the service or advice the stockbroker provides?), whereas in a manufacturing environment, direct costs can be assigned to all materials and labour.

3. *Distribution*   In product marketing, goods are stored and redistributed by middlemen; in services marketing, the channel between the seller and the buyer is direct. Consequently, the service-marketing organization has much more control in the channel.

4. *Promotion*   Promotions for tangible products are directed both at distributors (so that the product is pushed through the channel) and at consumers (so that the product is pulled through the channel). By contrast, marketers of services aim the promotional effort only at the user.

# The Services-Marketing Mix

## *Service as a Product*

The marketing mix for services consists of the same elements as are found in the mix for tangible goods. As a "product", however, a service differs from other products inasmuch as its selling attributes are intangible (see figure 17.3). With services, the customer is interested not so much in ownership or physical qualities as in certain conveniences, uses, or effects. Following is a list of some of the intangible qualities that sell a service:

1. *Consistency*   Federal Express's promise to deliver "when it absolutely, positively has to be there" is a good example of a service firm promoting consistency. The company markets its ability to deliver a parcel on time, all of the time.

2. *Attitude*   The attitude of those providing the service may be a selling point. Thus, the staff of a restaurant acknowledge customers by name and ask the customers whether the quality of service they have received is satisfactory.

3. *Completeness*   Some organizations provide a range of conveniences to attract customers. A hotel may offer an express checkout service for busy business travellers, accept credit cards as a means of payment, and provide other amenities (e.g., mini-bars in the rooms) to distinguish itself from competitors.

FIGURE 17.3    The Services Marketing Mix

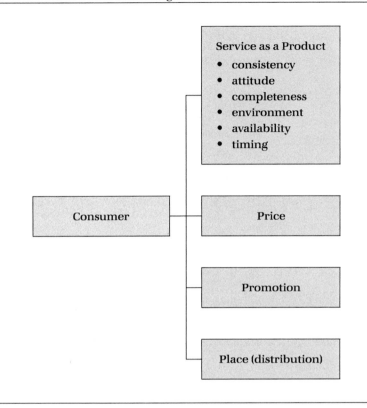

4. *Environment*   Clean rooms in a hotel, non-smoking rooms in a hotel, and non-smoking sections in restaurants are environmental attributes that customers look for.

5. *Availability*   An airline or busline that offers frequent and convenient departure times, or ease of entry and accessibility for the disabled, is selling availability.

6. *Timing*   Being available at the time it is needed may be a selling attribute for a service. For example, a cleaning service may be prepared to assist during emergencies in a hotel, or a restaurant may make a point of serving the main course of a meal at precisely the "right" time, not too early and not too late.

Refer to figure 17.4 for an illustration of CN's commitment to customer service, which commitment entails using many of these intangible attributes.

### The Service Mix

service mix

The **service mix** is the listing of all services that a supplier offers. A company will often market a primary service and then supplement the basic offering with peripheral services.[5] For example, the primary service supplied by a luxury hotel is clean lodging. Yet a hotel can distinguish itself from competitors by offering toll-free

**FIGURE 17.4**    Advertising the Intangible Aspects of a Service

reservation service, free parking, recreation facilities, bathrobes and other amenities within rooms, as well as free transportation to and from airports. For an illustration of how Holiday Inns of Canada uses this service mix to respond to the needs of its customers, refer to the Marketing in Action vignette "The Holiflex Fitness System."

The addition of peripheral services does increase the amount that a firm must invest in its operations; however, consumers like to choose among services that are clearly differentiated, just as they do with tangible products. Differentiating the

---

## ⟩⟩⟩ *MARKETING IN ACTION*

### *THE HOLIFLEX FITNESS SYSTEM*

Commonwealth Holiday Inns of Canada was the first hotel chain to truly recognize the fitness trend, and itdecided to become a market leader in providing fitness facilities and instruction for business travellers. The hotel chain answered the fitness challenge by introducing a professional systematic approach to health, fitness, and fun. This approach is called the "Holiflex Fitness System", a program which offers variety to accommodate the needs of consumers. There are individually prescribed programs, aerobic classes, and a complete needs-analysis and fitness evaluation for serious clients. There are also running programs, fitness seminars, and swimming programs in hotels that can accommodate these clients.

*Holiflex fitness centers are available to both hotel guests and Holiflex members*

Commonwealth Holiday Inns has gone after corporate clients who see the benefits of having their thousands of travelling employees continue their fitness regimens while on the road. The company pointed to research to justify this marketing strategy. It is expected that, by 1990, most major corporations will have a health-and-wellness program of some nature. This will lead to greater numbers of fitness participants and greater numbers of people looking for fitness facilities while travelling.

The Holiflex program, offered in 25 inns across the country, was developed by Brian Townsend, the hotel's director of fitness. In developing the program, Townsend wanted to cater to the fitness market in a serious way and do it better than anyone else. The fitness facilities are now used as a marketing tool.

The system was developed by fitness profes-

sionals who were concerned with making fitness challenging, satisfying, and fun. The fitness directors at each hotel, carefully selected and trained in the Holiflex System, are qualified to assist club members and guests to set, reach, and maintain their health and fitness goals.

Townsend admits that Holiday Inns have invested heavily in the Holiflex System and that it is difficult to measure the financial returns on such expenditure. The hotel feels that the biggest return is in the form of guest satisfaction. For the business traveller or the vacation traveller, the chain offers the best coordinated system of fitness facilities in the Canadian hotel industry.

Adapted from a variety of Holiday Inn press releases dated January 21, 1987.

service through the service mix can ensure that the service attracts its target market. In the case of the hotel, consumers can compare room rates and additional services before selecting the one that they view as offering the best value.

The number and level of services offered influence the purchase decisions of consumers. Therefore, a company must quickly address any problems that customers have with the number or level of the services; otherwise, the customer loses confidence in the company, whose credibility and reputation suffer accordingly. Perhaps the best example of a service company that promotes confidence among consumers is American Express. Its commercial messages show travellers losing their traveller's cheques and becoming fearful and anxious as a result. The company's offer to replace the cheques within 24 hours represents an attempt to inspire confidence and peace of mind among customers.

## Pricing

The various types of services require various pricing strategies from the supplier. Prices can be determined by regulation, tradition, or negotiation.

1. *Regulated Pricing*   In the case of utilities, telephone service, and cable television, the services provided are regulated by government agencies. The suppliers of the service must present and defend rate increases to the agency prior to changing prices.

2. *Traditional Pricing*   Some services have prices that are established or have become traditional. It could be an established hourly rate for a service provided by an auto mechanic, electrician, or plumber. Advertising agencies work on a fixed commission rate of 15 percent, with the rate based on the amount of media time and space purchased on behalf of their clients. Brokers in the food-distribution business work on a commission rate of 5 percent, and the payment is obtained from the manufacturers they represent.

3. *Negotiated Pricing*   Fees for the services of lawyers, financial-planning companies, real estate companies, and marketing-research and management consultants are often negotiated. In the case of marketing-research consultants, the supplier provides the client with a price quotation based on specifications set by the client. Many competitive firms may bid on the same job. The buyer in such situations analyzes each quotation and selects one supplier, often after further decreases in price have been negotiated.

## Distribution

In the service sector, where the relationship between the supplier and the client is close, the distribution channels tend to be direct. Because services are intangible and cannot be stored, there is often no need for middlemen. Even if intermediaries are used, and in some businesses they commonly are (e.g., numerous small insurance companies are represented by independent insurance agents), their role is to create demand rather than perform the traditional functions of middlemen. Much personal contact is necessary to sell services such as life insurance, real estate, or financial investments.

### Promotion

Promotion strategies focus on the primary service, detailing what it is and what it does for the customer. Frequently, the nature of the service is to resolve a problem; in such a case, personal contact with customers is an important element of promotion strategy. Sales-promotion techniques are also now a part of successful services marketing. Financial institutions that once frowned upon the use of promotions for fear they would tarnish their image, now use them as a means of attracting consumers to their facilities (see figure 17.5). For an example of the new promotion strategies in the banking industry, read the Marketing in Action feature that appears on page 520: "A New Style of Banking."

**FIGURE 17.5**   Using Sales Promotion to Attract Consumers to a Financial Institution

# Buying Behaviour in Services

Few significant differences in buying behaviour exist between consumers of goods and consumers of services. What differences do exist concern attitudes, needs, and motives, and the different considerations that each type of consumer takes into account when making the purchase decision.

## *Attitudes*

When deciding whether to purchase a good or a service, customers are obviously influenced by their attitudes. Since services are intangible, the impression that a customer has of the service and of the supplier is probably a strong influence on his or her decision to purchase the service. It is also much easier for a customer to express dissatisfaction with a service, because of the personal nature of a service offering. The expression of dissatisfaction definitely affects repurchase of a service or the purchase of other services from the same supplier.

A customer's dissatisfaction with a service may stem from an unfriendly ticket agent, baggage handler or flight attendant (in the case of an airline), or from the telephone receptionist who is the business's initial point of contact. It is the people who come in contact with customers that influence consumers' attitudes, and, as Jan Carlzon, president of Scandinavian Airlines, has observed, one bad impression may erase many good ones: " A customer's experience with a company is made up of many moments of truth, and in the eyes of the customer, one bad moment can easily defeat ten good ones."

## *Needs and Motives*

Both goods and services satisfy needs and motives, often the same ones. Thus one could satisfy the need to repair a roof either by buying shingles and laying them oneself or by hiring a contractor to provide and lay the shingles. Both purchasing the goods and purchasing the service address the same requirement. Yet in addition to satisfying the need for a repaired roof, the service could also cater to another need of the customer — the need for personal attention. By customizing the service for a particular customer and treating him or her as an individual with unique needs, the service could give the customer the feeling that he or she is receiving personal attention. People often feel that such personalization is lacking in their time-pressed, hectic lives, in which personal needs sometimes get overlooked. The provider of services also offers the customer convenience and expertise in getting the task performed.

## *Purchase Behaviour*

A customer must decide what to buy, when to buy it, and whom to buy it from. The purchase of many services is seasonal. Household improvements are commonly made in the spring and summer; retirement plans sell heavily in the winter, and vacation travel peaks in the summer months. Whatever the time of year, selecting a service takes longer than choosing goods because it is difficult for a buyer to assess the quality and value of a service due to its intangibility. In making a decision, buyers of services are often more influenced by the attitudes and opinions of other people

>>>> *MARKETING IN ACTION*

### *A NEW STYLE OF BANKING*

Can the promotion tactics of packaged-goods marketers work in the banking and financial services industry? Yes!, say the bankers. Canada Trust of London, Ontario, is the established leader in using promotion strategy. One of its more famous and newsworthy promotions is a "mortgage-burning" contest (a $100 000 prize limit) in which a customer gets to burn his or her mortgage papers in a special ceremony. Other Canada Trust promotions have included car contests for opening new accounts and "double your interest rate" contests for RRSP (retirement savings plans) holders. The contests are unique and innovative.

The traditional banking indistry is quite conservative, so the move toward promotion strategy is seen as a major shift in strategic thinking. In the past, the banks felt that promotions would tarnish their image, but this thinking has vanished. Product innovation is important in banking, but all banks offer a myriad of similar services. The new promotion strategies attempt to add spark to their customer presentation and attract attention to the services of a particular bank. Another reason for the increase in promotion spending is the competition among banks, trust companies, life insurance companies and other financial planning organizations. For those who do not participate, what's at stake are markets of $335 billion in personal saving deposits, $175 billion in residential mortgages, and $70 billion in personal loans.

Over the past decade, traditional banks such as The Royal Bank of Canada, Bank of Montreal, Toronto-Dominion, Scotia Bank, and CIBC have been losing ground to trust companies with respect to savings deposits and retirement savings plans. To counter the competition, banks have significantly increased their advertising and promotion expenditures.

Competitive banks laughed at the Bank of Montreal in 1977 when it was the first bank to enter the promotion battle with a $100 000 Dream Home contest. Now, if a bank is not in the promotion business, it is the exception. One of the more recent and innovative promotions is from CIBC, which offered discount mortgage coupons in packages of Post Fruit 'n Fibre cereal, Maxwell House Coffee, and Tang flavoured-drink crystals, all Kraft General Foods Inc. products. The coupons are redeemable on a six-month mortgage and could save the customer a maximum of $156 on a $150 000 mortgage over the period. A grand prize draw of $50 000 attracts people to the promotion.

The use of such promotional strategies is new to the banking industry, and traditional banks may be uncomfortable offering contests and sweepstakes. Nevertheless, such programs are now almost mandatory for banks that hope to keep pace with trust company competitors.

Adapted from Barrie McKenna, "Breakfast-table pitch typifies new banking era", *Financial Post*, February 27, 1989, p.15.

*An advertisement issued by Canada Trust of London, Ontario, a leader in the use of promotions among banks and trust companies* ▶

— be they friends, neighbours, or relatives — than are buyers of tangible products. Since buyers cannot, in most cases, try the service or see it demonstrated before purchasing it, they have to rely on the views of those who have tried it, a fact that shows how important it is for providers of services to ensure that their customers are satisfied. A negative word-of-mouth network is very harmful to service organizations. Statistics verify this point:[6]

1. For every complaint received, the average company actually has 26 customers with problems.
2. The average customer who has a problem tells nine or ten others about it.

## ⟩⟩⟩⟩ *Nonprofit Marketing*

nonprofit marketing

**Nonprofit marketing** refers to the marketing effort and activity of nonprofit organizations. These organizations operate in the best interests of the public or champion a particular idea or cause, and they do so without seeking financial profit. The goals and objectives of these groups are quite different from those of profit-based enterprises.

## Nature and Scope of Nonprofit Marketing

Not only do nonprofit organizations market goods and services, but they also market people, places, ideas, and organizations. One major goal of nonprofit marketing is to promote a social consciousness. The use of marketing to increase the acceptability of social ideas is referred to as **social marketing**. There are social marketing programs in the service of pollution control, recycling, the preservation and conservation of natural resources, and the pro- and anti-abortion campaigns, to suggest a few.

social marketing

Nonprofit organizations that now use marketing strategies effectively include colleges and universities, political parties and politicians, the Canadian Armed Forces, Red Cross, Canadian Cancer Society, Canadian Heart and Stroke Foundation, and the YMCA of Canada. This brief cross-section of organizations indicates that marketing achieves different objectives. It is used to recruit personnel, to raise funds to support causes, and to encourage the public to volunteer time and to make other contributions, such as giving blood to the Red Cross.

## Characteristics of Nonprofit Marketing

There are many similarities between marketing in a nonprofit environment and marketing in a profit environment. In both situations, the customer must choose between competing organizations. A person must decide which charitable groups to support and how much support to give, just as he or she must determine which car to buy and how much to pay for it. People also experience varying levels of satisfaction or dissatisfaction with the activities and performance of both types of organizations.

Yet differences between nonprofit and profit-based marketing also exist, especially in the areas of philosophy, exchange (what is exchanged), objectives, benefits, and target groups (see figure 17.6).

### *Philosophy*

Nonprofit marketing is concerned with the promotion and support of people, causes, ideas, and organizations. It raises funds to support a cause or promote a concept. In the case of profit-based marketing, the goal is to generate a financial return on investment.

FIGURE 17.6   Differences Between Nonprofit and Profit Marketing

| Characteristic | Nonprofit Marketing | Profit Marketing |
|---|---|---|
| Philosophy | Emphasis on people, causes, ideas and organizations | Emphasis on goods and services |
| Exchange | Money, time, expertise, or other forms (e.g. votes in elections) | Money for goods purchased |
| Objectives | Financial targets (e.g. fundraising goals) and nonfinancial (e.g. changing attitudes) | Financial: sales, profits, and return on investment |
| Benefits | Many contribute, but few benefit directly | Buyers benefit directly |
| Targets | Donors (givers) and clients (recipients) | Clients only |

## Exchange

In profit marketing, money is exchanged between buyers and sellers for the product or services provided. While money may exchange hands in nonprofit marketing, it does so under different circumstances. What people receive for their money cannot be quantified; they give, for example, for the psychological satisfaction of supporting a cause they believe in. In the political arena, the exchange may take the form of a vote given in return for the promise of a better government.

## Objectives of the Organization

Profit-oriented companies establish objectives in terms of sales, profit, return on investment, and market share. In nonprofit organizations, the objectives are not always quantifiable and measurable. They establish targets for fundraising, but these are subordinate to other non-financial objectives. The Canadian Cancer Society attempts to find a cure for a disease, as do similar organizations. The Red Cross encourages people to give blood when the blood supply is low. Other groups attempt to change the public's attitudes or to get the public to agree with a certain position. Examples include Greenpeace, the Non-Smokers Rights Association, Mothers Against Drunk Driving, and many others.

## Benefits Derived

In an exchange made for profit, a buyer benefits directly from the good or service supplied by the selling firm. In a nonprofit environment, only a small portion of "buyers" or supporters ever receive any material benefits from the supported association or institution. For instance, funds to aid health organizations are solicited from the general population, but only a relatively small number of people contract a particular disease or use the services of any given health clinic each year. In such cases, financial support may come from the general population, but few contributors would benefit directly from their contribution.

### *Targets*

Nonprofit organizations must serve two groups: clients and donors. Clients are those to whom the service is provided. Donors are those from whom the resources are received. The resources they donate may be in the form either of money or of time. Donors are concerned about the availability of goods and services, about whether or not the resources they provide are spent well in the provision of service, and generally about receiving recognition for their contribution.

## Types of Nonprofit Marketing

### *Organization Marketing*

**organization marketing**

**Organization marketing** is the first of four categories of nonprofit marketing (see figure 17.7).[7] It is marketing that seeks to gain, or maintain, acceptance of an organization's objectives and services. Colleges and universities engage in such marketing; they turn to fundraising campaigns as a survival tactic in the wake of government restraints on funds for education. Churches, art galleries, and museums also practice this type of marketing. In all of these examples, the organizations not only want the public to accept their goals, but also to use their services. Colleges and universities promote the concept of "life-long learning", and they seek to have organizations use their facilities for business training, seminars, and conferences.

### *People Marketing*

**people marketing**

**People marketing** refers to the process of marketing an individual or a group of people in order to create a favourable impression of that individual or group. Marketing of this nature usually centers on politicians and political parties, leading business executives who influence the business community at large, and sports and entertainment personalities.

The growing sports market in Canada is estimated to be worth $7–8 billion annually, and the use of sports personalities as presenters for corporations is quite commonplace. To take advantage of endorsement opportunities, sports and entertainment personalities employ agents and marketing consultants who seek and secure contracts for them. Undoubtedly, one of Canada's best known but selectively

**FIGURE 17.7**   Types of Nonprofit Marketing

| | |
|---|---|
| Organization Marketing | Strives to gain acceptance of an organization's objectives and services |
| People Marketing | Tries to create a favourable impression of an individual or group |
| Place Marketing | Attempts to foster a favourable attitude toward a destination |
| Idea Marketing | Endeavours to win public acceptance of a viewpoint |

used sports endorsers is Wayne Gretzky (Coca-Cola, Lloyds Bank, and others). According to Paul Baily, vice-president of Marketing at Lloyds Bank, the reason for using the hockey star is quite simple: "It's profile. Wayne is the best in the world at what he does."[8] As Lloyds knows, choosing the "right" sports hero is crucial and requires strategy. The right choice can mean instant recognition for the company and significant gains in profit. At Lloyds Bank the use of Wayne Gretzky increased the number of callers to its "Silver Service" personal banking hotline by 8000 percent.[9]

Politicians, aware that they are created or destroyed by their images, also use people marketing. They recognize that, where the public is concerned, perception is reality. Therefore, in the age of the electronic media, politicians call upon image makers to fine tune their personal and presentation style. In preparation for political debates on television, all participants are carefully prepared by consultants so that their strengths will be portrayed in the heat of battle.

The objective of people marketing is to create or maintain a positive impression or image of an individual among a target group. A person can be said to have made an impression if people are aware of, and hold certain attitudes about, that person. As in services marketing, attitudes play a large role in people marketing. It is thought that a target market acts in accordance with its opinion of the endorser. For instance, if people have a high opinion of a spokesperson, they will buy a product that he or she endorses, or vote for him or her in an election. For more insight into people marketing, see the Marketing in Action vignette, "The Power of Image."

### Place Marketing

place marketing

**Place marketing** draws attention to, and creates a favourable attitude toward, a particular place, be it a country, province, region, or city. Places are marketed in much the same way as products. The benefits and advantages of the location are the focal points of advertising and promotion campaigns. Themes and slogans are developed for long-term use to provide continuity in advertising. Examples of such campaigns include "Ontario Incredible" for the Ontario Ministry of Industry Trade and Tourism, and "Super, Natural" for the British Columbia Ministry of Tourism. The campaign that has had the most impact on place marketing originated in New York State in the late 1970s. Using the slogan "I Love New York", and a combination of lush scenery and upbeat music and lyrics, the campaign was extremely successful in attracting visitors from out of state. The campaign became a model for the marketers of other U.S. states and for marketers of Canadian provinces, who analyzed it to determine why it was so successful.

In place marketing, promotion is the principal strategy, for it creates the image for the destination. In the sample marketing plan included in Appendix A, note the emphasis on promotion.

### Idea Marketing

idea marketing

**Idea marketing** encourages the public to accept and agree with certain issues and causes. The campaigns aimed at convincing people of the need to wear seatbelts, to avoid drinking while driving, to exercise regularly, to maintain a balanced diet, and to stop smoking are instances of idea marketing. Idea marketing is social marketing,

>>>> *MARKETING IN ACTION*

## THE POWER OF IMAGE

In sports, politics, and business, image is extremely important, as was demonstrated by the fall of Ben Johnson after the drug scandal at the 1988 Seoul Olympics. If you were asked to identify some of the most recognizable faces in Canada, the names of Brian Mulroney, Wayne Gretzky, and Ben Johnson would certainly be mentioned. You might not think Lanny McDonald, former winger with the 1988 Stanley cup champion Calgary Flames, had such a face.

Yet, according to Mike Barnett, the agent for both Gretzky and McDonald, only Gretzky makes more on endorsements than McDonald among NHL players. Why is there such interest in McDonald? The answer is image. McDonald's tireless volunteer work with children with exceptionalities and the Special Olympics, as well as his successful hockey career, make him a valuable commodity among commercial corporations. McDonald has been a pitch man for Swanson Hungry Man dinners and Bauer Skates, to name two products. He also continues as volunteer spokesperson for the Special Olympics in television commercials.

What about politicians? They turn to image-makers and media gurus who are capable of turning political slovens into dapper, articulate presenters. In a political debate, the big event prior to a federal election, the participants are well-prepared by image advisors who fashion their style and appearance. If the consultant is good, the winner is chosen not by what was said, but by how it was said and how the person looked saying it.

Why the focus on image? In the case of politicians, the answer is television. Nearly 70 percent

Photo courtesy of Dave Chidley, Calgary Sun, and of Canadian Special Olympics, Inc.

*Due to his tireless volunteer work for children with exceptionalities and to his successful hockey career, Lanny McDonald has one of the most recognizable faces in Canada. He is shown here with Mila Mulroney, participating in the 1986 Canadian Special Olympic Summer Games*

of Canadians get their primary news from television. If a politician wants to make an impression, he or she must do so quickly, during each and every interview with the news media. The person must be consistent in style and presentation even in the heat of a controversy.

Business executives are not immune to public scrutiny either. Very often they are in front of television cameras in a damage-control situation. When they are in the news . . . it's bad news! Ill-prepared executives can worsen a crisis. To be ready for such occasions, corporations are seeking the advice of consultants and sending key executives on media courses so that they will feel comfortable in front of cameras.

Adapted from Canadian Press, "Lanny, aka The Endorser", *The Globe and Mail*, July 17, 1989, p.A14., and Jamie Hubbard, "Votes can hang on the image-maker's skill", *Financial Post*, October 10, 1988, p.13.

and its ultimate objective is to induce the majority of the population to accept a given idea, cause, or way of thinking. Like place marketing, idea marketing uses promotion as its key strategy for communicating with the public (see figure 17.8).

**advocacy advertising**      **Advocacy advertising** is a form of idea marketing practiced by corporations and associations that are concerned about issues or legislation that affect them. It is designed to communicate a company's position on a particular issue. Steel mills may

NaNr n

**FIGURE 17.8** Addressing an Issue of Public Interest in an Advertising Message

# We're spending 500 million dollars on something we'd all like to see.

## Clean air.

As the Western World's largest nickel producer, we're best known for our work underground.

But in the latter half of this century, we've focussed much of our effort on the sky, reducing the sulphur dioxide emissions that contribute to acid rain.

Since the mid-60's, we've cut emissions from our Sudbury smelting complex by 70% – the largest tonnage reduction by any organization on the continent.

And now we're about to go one giant step further. We're spending half a billion dollars to implement major changes in the way we process our sulphur-rich ore, changes which will drastically reduce emissions over the next 5 years.

The end result is clear. In 1994, we will contain fully 90% of the sulphur before it can ever reach the atmosphere.

Obviously the problem is global in scope, and calls for a concerted effort worldwide. A healthier environment is in everyone's interest. At Inco, we're doing our part.

And it's worth every nickel.

**STRONGER FOR OUR EXPERIENCE**

Courtesy: Inco.

use this form of advertising to tell the public what they are doing about pollution control. General insurance companies advertise why their rates must increase. Their message is countered by consumer groups who advertise the opposite viewpoint. From these few examples it can be seen that ideas and causes often generate controversy, since viewpoints differ. Advertising tries to get the public to adopt the outlook of one side or the other.

## The Marketing Mix in a Nonprofit Organization

A comprehensive marketing strategy is crucial to the success of any nonprofit group today. Many organizations still practise marketing quite haphazardly, as they remain unclear on the merits of implementing a well-conceived strategy. Some of the weaknesses of current nonprofit marketing strategies are as follows:

1. Many organizations have persisted in using a mass marketing approach rather than a segmentation approach. Campaigns by charitable organizations that are more targeted and reach higher income groups, or groups of proven donators, might yield a greater return for the organization. Increased recognition and improved use of direct marketing tactics is necessary.

2. Competition is not acknowledged in a significant way. Members of the public are bombarded with literature urging them to give generously to various institutes and associations; there is no consideration of the fact that any one particular income group can only give so much. Therefore, individual associations need to devote more time and effort to creating attention-grabbing and convincing messages that will win for their particular cause the resources donors have to give.

3. Marketing research is under-utilized. Nonprofit groups do not understand the motivation of their publics, particularly those publics that are predisposed to donate. An exception has been the U.S. Army, which successfully used research to increase recruiting effectiveness. Its successful "Be-all-that-you-can-be" campaign evolved from research indicating that, in its advertising messages, military aspects should be given less attention and training, particularly in high-technology fields, more attention.

What aspects of the 4Ps are stressed in nonprofit marketing? As suggested earlier, promotion plays a prominent role, but all elements of the mix are given due consideration. This section briefly examines the contribution of each P to the strategic market planning of nonprofit organizations.

### *Product*

Product strategy in a nonprofit organization is virtually the opposite of the strategy employed by a firm driven by the profit motive. Nonprofit bodies believe from the start that they provide what the public needs. Very often they feel that others only have to be made aware of a certain viewpoint regarding an idea, cause, person or place, for it to become widely accepted. These groups begin with an already formulated concept and try to show the public how it accords with their needs or desires.

Campaigns against drunk driving exemplify this strategy. Profit-based organizations, on the other hand, start by trying to discover what needs the consumer has and then formulate a concept — a product or a service — to satisfy those needs. Despite the difference, contemporary nonprofit organizations, like companies that operate for a profit, find it effective to develop a product mix that includes identification (e.g., logos), a package (membership cards to acknowledge contribution) and other product variables.

### Price

In a nonprofit organization, money is not necessarily the only form of exchange. Sometimes no money changes hands; instead, time or expertise is volunteered in return for the psychological satisfaction of helping or knowing society will be made better. Even if money is involved, the nature of the exchange is different from an exchange made for material profit. While long-term profit is the goal of the profit-based organization, a short-term gain is all a nonprofit organization seeks. Special events are frequently a means of generating revenue for nonprofit organizations.

### Distribution

Because nonprofit entities deal in intangibles, channels tend to be direct, that is, the organization tends to work directly with the donors. If intermediaries — a professional fundraiser, for example — are used, they act on behalf of the organization. They do not assume any responsibility or control.

### Promotion

Promotion is the most visible aspect of nonprofit marketing, and advertising, direct marketing, and personal selling form the nucleus of an organization's promotional effort. Public service announcements, a low-cost form of advertising, may be used to point out the benefits of contributing to a cause or charitable foundation. People marketing uses advertising to create and maintain an image for a person or group. Very often a charitable organization will use a known personality as its spokesperson. Personal selling is common: the Heart Fund, for instance, uses local residents to solicit funds door-to-door in their neighbourhoods. Such campaigns are undertaken annually and are supported with advertising to build awareness of the fundraising project.

## 〉〉〉〉 SUMMARY

The service sector in Canada is a rapidly growing segment of the economy and includes many large corporations in a cross-section of markets. Increasing competition, arising partly in response to regulatory change, advancing technology, the use of modern marketing strategies by service companies, and the growing number of time-pressed consumers, has contributed to the expansion of this sector.

Services have certain characteristics that distinguish them from products. A service is intangible; it cannot be seen, heard, or touched. It is inseparable from the source of supply since each supplier is unique, despite competitive attempts to imitate a service. The quality of a service also varies, even within a single organization, where different people perform the same service in different manners. Finally, demand for certain services is perishable; in other words, demand is uneven, in some cases seasonal, and this creates a problem for marketers of services.

Since services are intangible, their price is derived more from the value they provide consumers than from direct costs. The channels of distribution are direct, and promotional efforts are aimed directly at the final user. Service marketers do employ all elements of the marketing mix, but the main planning concern is that the firm understand exactly what it is that the customer is buying. Once it establishes what the primary service is, a firm develops a complete service mix. A service mix includes those additional elements that differentiate one service from another in the minds of consumers. Promotional projects are then developed to communicate the benefits to the target market.

Nonprofit marketing is used by organizations whose goals do not center on financial gain. Such organizations operate in the best interests of the public or advocate a particular idea or cause. Nonprofit groups have unique characteristics and different objectives. Their objectives are to promote 1) people, by fostering certain attitudes toward particular persons; 2) ideas, by gaining acceptance for a way of thinking; 3) places, by encouraging visits to a country, province, or city; and 4) organizations, by raising funds, cultivating an image, or persuading people to use the facilities. Rather than aim for financial targets, nonprofit bodies attempt to change attitudes. In doing so, they must consider two distinct targets: the clients who use and derive the benefits of the organization; and the donors who provide the organization with resources.

Planned marketing among nonprofit organizations is just beginning, though these organizations do employ other proven tactics used by profit-based enterprises. As more nonprofit organizations become aware of the merits of strategic marketing, their marketing efforts will be more carefully planned and targeted. A strategic focus will produce convincing messages and promotion campaigns that will achieve the goals of the organization.

## ⟩⟩⟩⟩ KEY TERMS

| | | |
|---|---|---|
| service | perishability | organization marketing |
| intangibility | service mix | people marketing |
| inseparability | nonprofit marketing | place marketing |
| quality variability | social marketing | idea marketing |

## >>>> QUESTIONS FOR REVIEW AND DISCUSSION

**1.** What factors have contributed to the growth of the service economy in Canada?

**2.** Briefly describe the characteristics that distinguish services from products.

**3.** A service is an attribute or series of attributes offered to consumers. What does this statement mean?

**4.** How is pricing a service different from pricing a product? Whatare the different pricing strategies used in services marketing?

**5.** How important a role do customers' attitudes play in their decisions to purchase a service?

**6.** If you were in the home-decorating business (painting and wall papering), how would you convince "do-it-yourselfers" to use your service?

**7.** Briefly describe the various types of nonprofit marketing.

**8.** Describe the basic differences between marketing for profit and nonprofit organizations.

**9.** What strategies would you recommend to:
**a)** The Canadian Red Cross for encouraging people to give blood?
**b)** The Boy Scouts of Canada for encouraging the public to make a financial contribution?
**c)** A city symphony orchestra for encouraging corporations to make a financial contribution?
**d)** The local YMCA for encouraging more adults to participate in fitness programs?

## >>>> REFERENCES

1. CLARKSON GORDON/WOODS GORDON, *Competing for Tomorrow's Customers*, 21st Edition, 1988, p.17.

2. Ibid.

3. S. HUSTED, D. VARBLE, and J. LOWRY, *Modern Marketing* (Needham Heights, Ma.: Allyn and Bacon, 1989), p.609.

4. BARRIE McKENNA, "Lawn and Garden Business Blooms with House Boom", *Financial Post*, May 2, 1988, p.11.

5. J. EVANS and B. BERMAN, *Marketing*, 3rd Edition (New York: Macmillan Publishing Company, 1987), p.623.

6. Statistics obtained from Technical Assistance Research Programs Inc., Washington, D.C.

7. PHILIP KOTLER, *Marketing for Nonprofit Organizations* (Englewood Cliffs, N.J.: Prentice-Hall, 1982), p.481.

8. "Looking for Mr. Goodjock to Bolster the Bottom Line", *Financial Times*, May 29,1989, p.7.

9. Ibid.

# CHAPTER 18 〉〉〉〉

# Global
# Marketing

*LEARNING OBJECTIVES*

After studying this chapter you will be able to

1. Identify the role that the federal government plays in assisting the global marketing effort of Canadian business.

2. Give the reasons why a growing number of firms are active in seeking global market opportunities.

3. Outline the factors a firm considers when planning to enter foreign markets.

4. Describe the marketing strategies commonly used by firms entering foreign markets.

5. Explain the role of the marketing mix in implementing global marketing strategies.

The next decade will be a challenging one for Canada and Canadian business, as a new era of global marketing beckons. A global market already exists for products such as automobiles, consumer electronics, computers, and soft drinks. Honda, General Motors, Boeing, IBM, Coca Cola, and McDonald's are examples of global corporations. For Canadian firms, the bilateral trade agreement with the United States, and the unification of the European Economic Community into a true common market in 1992, represent new opportunities and challenges.

Canada has many world-class marketing organizations. Olympia and York is a prominent real-estate development firm; Noranda is a leading mining operation; and

Northern Telecom is a world leader in telecommunications technology. In the 1990s, opportunities for the development of Canadian firms will come about as a result of niche marketing programs that build on the strengths of Canada's resources. Firms that do not expand aggressively into world markets could become acquisition targets for European, Asian, and United States businesses that want to invest in this country.

## 〉〉〉〉 *Canadian International Trade*

As of 1987, the value of imports to Canada amounted to $117.8 billion and the value of exports to $129.5 billion. The merchandise trade surplus (i.e., the value of exports over imports) was $11.7 billion.[1] By far, Canada's largest trading partner is the United States, which accounts for 69.5 percent of the value of Canadian imports and 77.6 percent of Canadian exports (see figure 18.1). Canada's other major trading partners include the United Kingdom, the European Economic Community, and Japan. With these countries, the value of Canadian imports exceeds exports. Clearly, it is trade with the United States that creates Canada's trade surplus.

Automotive products form the largest import item in Canada, followed by machinery and equipment, and industrial goods and materials. Canada's largest exports are automotive products, industrial goods and materials, machinery and equipment, and forestry products (see figure 18.2).

### Role of the Federal Government

Global trade has a significant impact on the Canadian economy. External Affairs and International Trade Canada are responsible for maintaining and encouraging an international trading climate favourable to Canadian exporters, and for implemen-

**FIGURE 18.1**  Canadian Trade By Trading Area, 1987

| | Imports | | Exports | |
|---|---|---|---|---|
| | **(In thousands)** | **(Percentage of total)** | **(In thousands)** | **(Percentage of total)** |
| United States | $ 79 609 | 68.0% | $ 91 756 | 75.5% |
| United Kingdom | 4 339 | 3.7 | 2 850 | 2.3 |
| Other European Economic Community (EEC) Countries | 9 182 | 7.9 | 6 259 | 5.2 |
| Japan | 7 550 | 6.5 | 7 036 | 5.8 |
| Other Countries | 16 097 | 13.9 | 13 560 | 11.2 |
| | 116 237 | 100.0 | 121 461 | 100.0 |

*Source*: Statistics Canada, *Canada 1989 Facts*, Investment Canada. Adapted with the permission of the Minister of Supply and Services Canada, 1990.

FIGURE 18.2   Canadian Imports and Exports by Commodity, 1986

| Classification of Goods | Imports | Exports |
|---|---|---|
| Automotive Products | 30.2% | 28.5% |
| Machinery and Equipment | 28.3 | 15.6 |
| Industrial Goods and Materials | 17.6 | 19.0 |
| Other Consumer Goods | 10.8 | 2.8 |
| Agriculture and Fishing Products | 6.5 | 9.0 |
| Energy Products | 4.6 | 9.4 |
| Forestry Products | 1.4 | 14.6 |

*Source*: Statistics Canada, *Canada Year Book 1988*, Ottawa: Ministry of Supply and Services Canada, 1987, Cat. No. 11-402E/1987, p. 21–28. Reproduced with the permission of the Minister of Supply and Services Canada, 1990.

ting policies and programs to safeguard and advance Canada's trading interests. The Ministry of External Affairs is the primary contact with foreign governments and with international organizations that influence trade.

## Services of External Affairs

Since competition among industrialized nations is intense, and since knowledge of customs and tariffs is both necessary and hard to acquire, exporting to foreign markets is difficult. Good products, efficient production, aggressive and intelligent marketing, and government support are the ingredients of successful global trading. Some of the more prominent programs delivered by External Affairs to assist the marketing effort include the Program for Export Market Development, the Technology Inflow Program, and the Cost-Recoverable Technical Assistance Program (see figure 18.3).

FIGURE 18.3   Marketing Assistance Programs Offered by External Affairs and International Trade Canada

### Program for Export Market Development (PEMD)
By sharing the financial risks of entering foreign markets, this program encourages Canadian enterprises to participate in export promotion activities. For example, funds are available for participating in trade fairs or trade missions to foreign countries.

### Technology Inflow Program (TIP)
This program promotes international collaboration on technological innovation. New Canadian products are developed by merging foreign and domestic technology.

### Cost Recoverable Technical Assistance Program (CRTAP)
This program tries to generate export opportunities for technical goods and services through intra-government technical assistance projects, and through secondment of public-sector expertise in support of private-sector development projects.

Within External Affairs, certain departments play important roles in developing global trade:

1. *Trade Relations Bureau*   This department administers import and export controls through the Export and Import Permits Act. It implements policies concerning the imports of many commercial products, including textiles, clothing, footwear, and agricultural products, and concerning the exports of military and strategic goods.

2. *Trade Policy Bureau*   This department formulates and implements Canadian trade policy regarding the activities of the General Agreement on Tariffs and Trade (GATT), and regarding the trade aspects of domestic, industrial, and agricultural policies.

3. *Trade Commissioner Service*   This department promotes Canadian export trade, in part by representing and protecting commercial interests abroad. It also provides consultation on matters of international marketing, acts as a link between foreign buyers and Canadian firms, and recommends programs for developing new markets for Canadian products. Part of its mandate is to attract investment and the transfer of technology to Canada. To fulfill this role, it encourages countries to exchange information for the joint development of products, or to share an area of expertise.

External Affairs is organized into five branches, each headed by an Assistant Deputy Minister. The branches are Europe, Asia and the Pacific, Africa and the Middle East, Latin America and the Caribbean, and the United States. Each branch is responsible for international trade strategy, market development programs, and improving the access of Canadian products to export markets.

### Export Development Corporation

The Export Development Corporation (EDC) is a federal Crown corporation that provides insurance to exporters, guarantees to banks, and financing to foreign buyers of Canadian goods and services. The services of the EDC are available to all firms that market products of 60 percent Canadian content. Export credit insurance protects firms against up to 90 percent of their losses if foreign customers are unable or unwilling to pay because of political events, exchange blockage, or insolvency. Export financing is provided to Canadian firms as a means of encouraging foreign buyers to purchase capital goods and services. The Crown corporation and the Canadian company agree to the rates and terms when a contract is signed between the foreign buyer and the Canadian supplier.

## ⟩⟩⟩⟩ *The Movement to Global Markets*

Firms are placing an increasing emphasis on global marketing opportunities for many reasons. One reason is that domestic markets, where most opportunities have been exhausted, furnish only mediocre prospects for expansion. The growth of some markets is slow; others are saturated with competition; others are too small.

Another reason for the emphasis on global marketing is the formation of common markets or trading blocks. In the next decade, the free trade agreement, which encourages open trade between Canada and the United States, will affect other countries and companies wanting to trade with these two nations. Similarly, the unification of the European Community in 1992 will provide new opportunities for the marketing of North American goods in those countries.

When deciding to market in a foreign country, a firm looks at the absolute advantage or comparative advantage that can be gained.

## Absolute Advantage

**absolute advantage**

**Absolute advantage** occurs when only one country provides a good or service, or when one country produces a product at significantly lower cost than others. Thus Hong Kong and other Asian countries where labour costs are lower than they are in North America can manufacture products such as toys, clothing, and electronic goods much less expensively than can North America. As a result, goods can be sold in North America at prices lower than those of similar, domestically produced products.

## Comparative Advantage

**comparative advantage**

A **comparative advantage** derives from producing and marketing an item more efficiently or abundantly, as well as more cheaply, than other countries. It allows a country to become a market leader in a certain area, as Canada is in forestry products, where resources are plentiful. Japan and the United States are leaders in technology; hence both enjoy comparative advantage in certain markets: computers, automobiles, electronics, and aircraft. In the case of technology, Japan and the United States have invested heavily in research and development to ensure that they stay ahead of other countries. In theory, a country might want to export products where it enjoys a comparative or absolute advantage and import products where others enjoy such an advantage. In fact, countries do exchange goods and services in which they have advantages for those in which they have disadvantages.[2] Yet they do impose some limitations on this process. The constant importing of items in markets where they experience a disadvantage could undermine the domestic production of these items, thus reducing employment at home. Consequently, countries guard against importing too heavily in markets where they are vulnerable. Tariffs and quotas are established to protect local industries that could be hurt by unlimited importing.

## Canada – United States Free Trade Agreement

The free trade agreement between Canada and the United States came into effect January 1, 1989. The agreement established a framework for bilateral free trade that allowed trade barriers to be phased out over ten years. The agreement changed the competitive environment in North America and presented new opportunities for Canadian and U.S. firms to gain competitive advantage. In essence, the market is

## >>>> *MARKETING IN ACTION*

### *FREE TRADE AND NEW OPPORTUNITIES*

A comparative advantage is definitely available to some Canadian businesses wishing to take advantage of the opportunities created by the free trade agreement between Canada and the United States.

Two strategic directions have emerged as a result of the deal. Some large corporations, operating in Canada but controlled by U.S. headquarters, are examining the number and the location of all their North American plants, trying to determine whether they are meeting the needs of the North American market efficiently. To achieve their efficiency goals, firms are, where necessary, closing plants, expanding plants, or even building new plants. If fewer plants can serve the larger market more efficiently, the decision to close some has justification. Will U.S.-based firms close Canadian plants or U.S. plants? Both types of closing are occurring. Some U.S. companies are dismantling plants in Canada; others are keeping them open but changing their role.

Gillette Canada Inc., a subsidiary of the U.S.-based Gillette Company, decided to close its Toronto and Montreal plants in 1989, laying off 600 employees. Gillette's Boston plant only operated at 65 percent capacity and with a 10 percent tariff removed under free trade; thus the decision by Gillette was a sound one. They were looking at their production facilities from a continental perspective.

In other cases, U.S. parent companies are avoiding Canadian layoffs by encouraging Canadian subsidiaries to develop specialized products for niche markets around the world. Plants will only produce one product or a few, instead of many.

*Du Pont is aiming to make inroads into the North American market with its plastic products for foods and beverages*

Du Pont Canada Inc. is investing $187 million in capital expansion in Canadian locations. Their strategy is to invest in businesses that can serve the full North American market, and in those products that are now, and will become, competitive with the best in the world. The investment in Canada gives Du Pont easier access to the U.S., the world's largest market. Du Pont is aiming to make major inroads in plastic production — in, for example, the liquid packaging process by which plastic bags for food products are made. This system, familiar to the Canadian market in the packaging of milk products, is a concept that is to be marketed for the first time in the United States.

Adapted from David Estok, "Firms restructuring for global market", *Financial Post*, January 9, 1989, p.11.

more open than before and prompts Canadian firms to market its products and services in the United States. Large manufacturing concerns can now rationalize their operations, that is, they can examine their manufacturing facilities on a continental basis and phase out locations that do not serve the market efficiently.

The open North American market will force Canadian business to expand manufacturing facilities and improve the efficiency of their operations in order to supply the volume of product necessary to meet the needs of a much larger market. The elimination of tariffs presents an opportunity for companies to increase their market share, particularly in resource industries and related manufacturing industries. The agreement also encourages U.S.-based businesses to make further investments in their Canadian operations so that these operations can be expanded to serve the North American market. Some firms may also choose to close down Canadian manufacturing facilities, particularly if U.S. locations can produce adequate volume for the North American market. For more information on how firms have reacted to the free trade agreement, consult the Marketing in Action feature, "Free Trade and New Opportunities."

## Multinational Corporations

multinational
corporation

A **multinational corporation** is a firm that operates in several countries and usually has a substantial share of its total assets, sales, and labour force in foreign subsidiaries. Although multinationals are all large and successful — Seagrams, Abitibi-Price, Noranda, Alcan and Northern Telecom are examples — they have different operating philosophies, marketing strategies, investment opportunities, and locations. All of them, however, are likely to be aggressive in exploiting new global market opportunities.

Commonly, a company exports goods to a foreign country initially, and then, if conditions are right, establishes a manufacturing and marketing operation in that country, using a mixture of local labour and management, along with corporate management from the home country. This was the practice of the Japanese automakers, Toyota and Honda, and of Hyundai of South Korea, when they opened plants in Canada. This practice allows the multinational to familiarize itself quickly with the customs, preferences, and business practices of the country it is entering.

## >>>> *Analyzing Global Marketing Opportunities*

When a firm considers the global market, it must assess several elements before deciding which country or environment to enter. The economy, culture, and politics of the area, the technology available and the existing competition must all be taken into account.

## Economic Environment

From nation to nation, economies vary considerably. The economic character of any country is shaped by its natural resources, its population, income distribution, employment, systems of education, and by the way its goods are marketed. Four basic types of economy exist: subsistence, raw-material exporting, industrializing, and industrialized.[3]

1. *Subsistence Economy*  A subsistence economy is based on land and agriculture and consumes most of what it produces, a circumstance which leaves the country

**countertrading**

few opportunities for trade. Nepal and Bangladesh fit this category. What is available after satisfying its own needs is generally used for countertrading or bartering. **Countertrading** is a system of exchange whereby something other than currency or credit is used as a form of payment.

2. *Raw-Material Exporting Economy*   Countries with this sort of economy usually have one rich natural resource or a few natural resources that can be exported, but lack many manufacturing industries. These economies are attractive to companies that export equipment, technology, and transportation and communications expertise — all products that can be used in the extraction of the natural resource. Examples of resource-based nations include Saudi Arabia (oil), Malaysia (rubber) and Cuba (sugar).

3. *Industrializing Economy*   These places have a skilled or semi-skilled workforce and a growing manufacturing base. Their populations are shifting into middle and upper classes. Mexico and South Korea have economies of this kind. Such countries import the goods and services needed to facilitate their industrial development.

4. *Industrialized Economy*   These countries have a highly skilled workforce and a strong manufacturing and technological base. They export manufactured goods, services, and investment funds. Their extremely large middle class makes them a good target for imported consumer goods. Canada, the United States, Japan, and members of the European Economic Community are all industrial nations.

## Cultural Environment

Segmenting markets on the basis of culture is important in global marketing, since the values and beliefs held by people vary from nation to nation. While businesses must think globally, they must act locally. Failing to recognize cultural differences has resulted in marketing blunders by even the biggest corporations.

To illustrate the importance of being alert to cultural differences, let's consider a problem that Procter & Gamble encountered in marketing Camay soap in Japan. Camay is a toilet soap for facial and bath use and looks the same in all the countries where it is marketed. It is positioned everywhere as an elegant product, feminine in character and fragrance, and good for the skin; it is known as a "soap for beautiful women." Many of Camay's commercials include men, for the product is intended to make a woman feel more attractive to men. This strategy failed in Japan: Procter & Gamble did not recognize Japanese notions of good manners and politeness, according to which it is bad manners for a husband to intrude on a wife when she is bathing.[4] Products and promotion strategies must be adapted to local customs and preferences if the company is to be successful in a foreign country.

In support of global marketing strategies, however, a cluster of five distinct consumer classes crossing national borders and cultural differences has emerged from a study of global consumer attitudes. The study found that the attitudes prevailing in the United States, United Kingdom, Japan, and Canada were almost identical (see figure 18.4).

FIGURE 18.4   Some Commonalities in Global Consumer Market Segments

In a major study of 15 000 adults in fourteen countries, conducted by Baker Spievogel Bates Worldwide, five consumer segments emerged. In terms of attitude, it was found that traditional values are breaking down and materialism is emerging as a dominant force as society moves into the next century. The five consumer segments are:

**Strivers (26% of population)**

These are young age groups in their twenties and thirties leading active lives and working hard to succeed. They lack time, energy, and money, and face much stress. They value convenience and instant gratification.

**Achievers (22%)**

These are affluent and assertive groups who set trends with respect to opinion and style. They are the same age as strivers but they value status and quality in what they buy.

**Pressured (13%)**

These are mostly women facing economic and family pressure. They have little time for pleasure and recreation due to their roles and responsibilities in the family unit.

**Adapters (18%)**

These are older consumers, living comfortably, who are receptive to a changing world and new ideas. They will try new products and activities.

**Traditionals (16%)**

These are older consumers who resist change. They prefer routine and purchase familiar products.

---

*Source*: Adapted from Stan Sutter, "Materialism Will Reign Supreme in Third Millenium", *Marketing*, August 7, 1989, pp. 1, 3.

## Political Environment

The political environments of foreign countries can shape trading policy. Political changes in the USSR, for example, made that country increasingly open to western influence and trade in the late 1980s, when new relationships with the west were seen as a means of spurring a sagging internal economy. The Chinese also became more open to western economic practice and trade opportunities in the eighties. The size and potential of these two markets presented a tremendous opportunity for foreign businesses. In sharp contrast, countries and companies divested South Africa of their business interests during the last quarter of the century due to that government's racial policies. Trade opportunities are particularly affected by two aspects of political environment: nationalism and trade barriers.

## Nationalism

nationalization

It is common for less developed countries to accept multinational companies into the fold. The companies invest directly in establishing manufacturing facilities and provide assistance in a country's development. These relationships are often temporary and are influenced by the state of the country's government. In countries where political unrest prevails, nationalization of an industry can occur. **Nationalization** is a form of expropriation where the government of a country takes control of the operations of a foreign company operating in that country.

## Trade Barriers

protectionism

The purpose of a trade barrier is to protect a country from too much foreign competition within its borders. Trade restrictions are based on the premise that domestic companies and industries need some form of protection. Such practice is common in industrialized nations such as Canada, the United States, France, and West Germany. The free trade agreement between Canada and the United States was negotiated at a time when many American politicians were pressing for more protectionism. **Protectionism** is a belief that foreign trade should be restricted so that domestic industries can be preserved. To restrict trade, governments use tariffs, quotas, embargoes, and local-content laws.

tariff

1. A **tariff** is a tax or duty imposed on imported goods. In Canada, prices for domestically produced goods and services tend to be high due to the high costs of labour, raw materials, and parts. In comparison, goods from Asian countries, in markets such as toys, clothing and electronics, are produced at much less cost. To balance the price differences between imported and domestic products in these industries, Canada imposes a tariff on incoming foreign goods. The advantage of a tariff is that it can be specific in nature and protect particular industries when needed. Both Canada and the United States impose tariffs on foreign produced automobiles to protect the position and employment levels of domestic automakers, the largest manufacturer in both countries.

quota

2. A **quota** is a specific limit on the amount of goods that may be imported into a country. In Canada, precise quotas are placed on Japanese automobiles each year to restrict their penetration of the domestic market. In the late 1980s, several Japanese producers built Canadian production facilities as a means of circumventing quotas. All automobiles must contain a specified level of Canadian parts.

embargo

3. An **embargo** disallows entry of specified products into a country. Concerns related to politics, health, and morality are frequently cited as the reasons for imposing embargoes. Canada customs is responsible for screening various products — pharmaceutical, chemical, food and many others — as they enter the country. Products that do not meet standards are rejected. For example, many toys from abroad, which do not meet Canadian safety standards, are rejected at the border.

   Some items are placed under an embargo because the majority of the population or its government finds them morally objectionable. The Canadian government does not allow the entry of sexually explicit materials, though what is acceptable and unacceptable is often the focus of debate among citizens and governments.

Organizations and groups can also impose embargoes in the form of a boycott. A boycott is an organized refusal to buy a specific product. The best known case of a boycott was directed against the Swiss-based Nestlé Company. A combination of labour, religious, and health organizations encouraged a boycott of all Nestlé products in the belief that Nestlé sold infant formula in some countries without considering whether it could be used safely. Nestlé eventually succumbed to pressure and changed its marketing practices for this product.

**local content law**

4. A **local content law** is another way of protecting local industry and employment. In this case, a foreign-based manufacturer is required to use a specified amount of locally produced components. The goal of such laws is to promote domestic employment in related industries. All automobile manufacturing plants producing cars in Canada must abide by such a law. This stimulates employment in the Canadian auto parts industry.

## Technological Environment

The technological environment in a country is bound up with what type of economy it has. A company that plans to organize a technologically based manufacturing operation in a non-industrialized country must do so with caution, for the available workforce may not have the education and skills required to run it. The foreign firm may have to commit to extensive training and development, which adds to the cost of operations. When the Japanese and South Korean automobile manufacturers built facilities in Canada, they had to deal with this situation to a certain extent. While Canada was knowledgeable in automobile manufacturing and its labour force was skilled, the foreign firms had to educate their Canadian employees in their management style and their way of doing business. Such integration of Canadian and foreign influence allowed the foreign organization to learn about Canadian culture, trade, consumers, and ways of doing business.

Of concern to Canadian companies is the increasing sophistication of technology, the speed at which technology is developed, and the fact that new technology, like competition, can originate from many places. It is expected that the Far East will have significant impact on the North American economy by the mid 1990s.

## Competitive Environment

Firms that market globally are aware of the developments that affect the global economy generally. These influences include cartels, orderly market agreements, and common markets.

### Cartels

**cartel**

A **cartel** is a group of firms or countries that band together and conduct trade in a manner similar to a monopoly. The purpose of a cartel is to improve the bargaining position of members in the world market. The world's most influential cartel in recent times has been the Organization of Petroleum Exporting Countries (OPEC), which is comprised of thirteen oil-producing nations from around the world. OPEC countries can restrict the supply of oil, a resource which is in high demand in other nations, thereby forcing the price up. For importing countries, the higher prices affect their economies because any increase in oil price is added to the cost of manufacturing in the importing country. This means that consumers ultimately pay more for the products they purchase.

### Orderly Market Agreement

**orderly market agreement**

An **orderly market agreement** is an agreement by which nations share a market, eliminating trade barriers between the two nations. The free trade agreement between Canada and the United States is an example of an orderly market agreement because it allows the markets to become open to industries on both sides of the border. Formal in nature, the agreement formed a bilateral free trade area (see figure 18.5).

### Common Markets

**common market**

A **common market** is a regional or geographical group of countries that agree to limit trade barriers among its members and apply a common tariff on goods from non-member countries. The European Economic Community is the best known common market. Originally formed in 1958, it now includes the United Kingdom, Ireland, Belgium, France, Italy, Denmark, Greece, West Germany, Luxembourg, the Netherlands, Spain, and Portugal. Gradually removing trade barriers that existed among its members, the community decided all trade barriers would be eliminated in 1992. Companies and countries wishing to enter this market began developing strategies in the 1980s so as to be ready for the change. Some North American companies acquired European facilities as a means of securing European sales, while others developed new marketing strategies. For an example, read the Marketing in Action account "Buying an Italian Brewery."

---

**FIGURE 18.5**   Highlights of the Canada-U.S. Free Trade Agreement

1. All tariffs on Canada-U.S. trade will be phased out or eliminated.
2. Domestic content preferences in some government purchases are to be relaxed.
3. Binational panels will be established to help settle trade disputes.
4. Auto Pact benefits will be restricted to existing participants; duty remissions for non-auto pact members will be phased out; a higher North American content rule will apply.
5. Discriminating practices affecting trade in magazines, wines, distilled spirits, plywood, used aircraft and cars, and lottery materials are to be phased out.
6. Restrictions on U.S. access to Canadian energy will be relaxed; the potential for future increases in U.S. trade barriers to Canadian energy will be reduced.
7. Canada retains the right to subsidize selected regions and industries, but could face the imposition of countervailing duties in the United States.

---

>>>> *MARKETING IN ACTION*

### BUYING AN ITALIAN BREWERY

Labatt Breweries of Europe, a subsidiary of John Labatt Limited, based in London, Ontario, formed a joint venture with an Italian brewery, Birra Moretti SPA, which is Italy's seventh largest brewer. Labatt's owns 70 percent of the new company. The intent of this deal was to help position Labatt's strategically for the unification of the European Economic Community in 1992. The new venture gave Labatt's a 10 percent market share of Italy's $8.8-billion beer market. Growth of beer sales in Italy averages 3 percent to 5 percent annually; it is one of the few developed countries in the world experiencing growth in beer sales.

In Canada, the merger of Molson Companies Limited and Carling O'Keefe Breweries of Canada Limited, owned by Elders IXL Limited of Australia, also had global market implications. A need to ship beer out of Canada exists because the domestic beer market has been persistently stagnant. The merger of Molson's and Carling O'Keefe resulted in job losses in Canada, as several outdated plants were closed. On the positive side, the move has given Molson's access to a tremendous distribution system world-wide, particularly in Australia and the United Kingdom, where Elders

*Birra Moretti, Italy's seventh largest brewer, has embarked on a joint venture with Labatt Breweries of Europe*

is a dominant beer marketer. In addition, the merger makes the new company the sixth largest in North America. It is now a North American company, not a Canadian company, whose objective is to penetrate the $20 billion U.S. beer market in the nineties.

Adapted from Philip de Mont, "Getting a toe in the boot", *Financial Times of Canada*, June 5, 1989, p.8, and Leonard Zehr, "Labatt sees benefit in brewery merger", *Globe and Mail*, January 19, 1989, pp.B1,B4.

---

## >>>> *Strategies for Global Marketing*

Companies pursuing international opportunities must decide how to enter the various markets. Some of the strategies for doing so include direct investments and acquisitions, joint ventures, and exports.

### Direct Investment and Acquisitions

Direct investment refers to a company's financial commitment in a foreign country whereby the investing company owns and operates, in whole or in part, the manufacturing or retailing facility in that foreign country. Foreign investment in Canada has increased from $37 billion in 1975 to $93 billion in 1986. Canadian direct investment abroad for the same period increased from $34 billion to $146 billion. Statistics Canada estimates that foreign control of Canadian corporations was 23 percent in 1985 and that the United States controlled 72 percent of Canada's foreign-controlled firms.[5]

Canadian companies have recently increased investment in the United States. Between 1975 and 1986, investment increased from $6 billion to $25 billion. Some of the biggest investment acquisitions were made in the late 1980s. Seagram's purchased Tropicanna Products Inc. for Cdn $1.4 billion and Campeau Corporation acquired Allied Stores and Federated Department Stores and their subsidiaries (see figure 18.6). Canadian investment in the U.S. has grown at three times the rate of U.S. investment in Canada over the past decade.[6] Acquisition strategies allow a firm quick entry into a foreign market. By purchasing all or part of an established and viable operation in a foreign country, a company avoids the cost of developing new products and the need to invest heavily in marketing to create an awareness of new products in that country.

On a worldwide scale, there have been acquisitions of many prominent U.S. companies. In 1989, Sony of Japan acquired CBS Records, and Grand Metropolitan of the United Kingdom acquired Pillsbury, which in turn controls Burger King. These acquisitions indicate that global markets will become priorities for organizations that are searching for opportunities to grow in the next decade. See the Marketing in Action vignette "Mega Mergers in Food Land" for other details on acquisition strategies.

**FIGURE 18.6** Canadian Acquisitions Activity

### Top Five Canadian Acquisitions Abroad

| Rank | Acquiring Company | Acquired or Merged Company | Date | Percentage of Stock Acquired | Purchase Price (in millions) |
|------|-------------------|----------------------------|------|------------------------------|------------------------------|
| 1 | Campeau Corp. | Federated Department Stores | 1988 | 100.0% | $6 600 |
| 2 | Campeau Corp. | Allied Department Stores | 1986 | 97.5 | 5 004 |
| 3 | Seagram Co. | du Pont (U.S.) | 1981 | 20.0 | 3 120 |
| 4 | Northern Telecom Ltd. | STC PLC, Britain | 1987 | 28.0 | 1 009 |
| 5 | Olympia & York | Sante Fe Southern Pacific Corp. (U.S.) | 1987 | 10.0 | 914 |

### Top Five Foreign Acquisitions in Canada

| Rank | Acquiring Company | Acquired or Merged Company | Date | Percentage of Stock Acquired | Purchase Price (in millions) |
|------|-------------------|----------------------------|------|------------------------------|------------------------------|
| 1 | Allied Lyons PLC, Britain | Hiram Walker-Gooderham & Worts | 1986 | 100% | $2 600 |
| 2 | CFCL Acquisitions Corp. | Cadillac Fairview Corp. | 1987 | 100 | 2 600 |
| 3 | Superior Oil, Houston | Canadian Superior Oil Ltd. | 1979 | 51 | 537 |
| 4 | Fletcher Challenge Ltd., New Zealand | B.C. Forest Products Ltd. | 1987 | 69 | 753 |
| 5 | Union Faith Co., Hong Kong | Husky Oil Ltd. | 1987 | 43 | 484 |

*Source*: Adapted from *The Financial Post 500*, Summer 1988.

## >>> *MARKETING IN ACTION*

### *MEGA MERGERS IN FOOD LAND*

In October 1988, New York-based Philip Morris announced a bid to take over Kraft Inc. for U.S. $11 billion ($90 per share). This bid was the largest non-oil corporate takeover offer on record until Ross Johnson, the president of RJR Nabisco, announced he was spearheading a U.S. $17.6 billion management buyout of his company. Shortly thereafter, KKR joined the buyout binge by announcing a $21.6 billion buyout of RJR Nabisco. Does this sound confusing? Why are all the mergers and takeovers occurring?

Global merger-mania has had little impact on Canadian branch plants so far, but the frantic takeover activity shows the marketability of food companies, particularily those with established, international brand names. Nabisco's products include Oreos, Planter's Nuts, Christie's Cookies, Life Savers, and many more popular brands. Top brands at Kraft include Kraft Dinner, Cracker Barrel Cheese, Philadelphia Brand Cream Cheese, and Parkay Margarine.

Many industry executives realize that it costs less to purchase established brand names than to create and market brand names. Furthermore, brand leaders are cheaper to maintain on an ongoing basis. These are some of the reasons for the interest in takeovers, but there are others.

Philip Morris, for example, is interested in Kraft because of Kraft's strong penetration in Europe (56 percent of Kraft's international sales were in Europe), and because the European Economic Community becomes one large free market in 1992.

Philip Morris already owns General Foods, which is the maker of Maxwell House coffee, Tang Beverages, Jell-o Desserts, and many other well-known food products. Should they be successful in acquiring Kraft, huge economies of scale can be realized in distribution, commodity buying, and advertising. Generic advertising for brand-name products can be adapted for use all over the world, and larger discounts are available to the volume purchasers of media time and space. Supermarkets also demand considerable funds from suppliers in return for prominent shelf space. A Philip Morris group that combined the brand-name muscle of General Foods and Kraft might be able to shift the power base back to the manufacturer, which would then have more control of its marketing programs.

Adapted from Frances Phillips, "Food business feels bite of global takeover trend", *Financial Post*, October 22, 1988, pp.1,10.

*Some of the brands now controlled by the Philip Morris company*

Kraft General Foods Canada, Inc. These are registered trademarks of Kraft General Foods Canada Inc.

# Joint Ventures

joint venture

In a global context, a **joint venture** is a partnership between a domestic and foreign company. Such an arrangement allows a company to produce and market in a foreign country with less cost and with less risk to itself than would be the case if it undertook a venture on its own. Pursuing global markets is a financial challenge for the largest of today's corporations because the world is so large and so competitive. The foreign partner can take advantage of the domestic company's knowledge of the domestic culture, lifestyles, and business practices. Texas Instruments has struck many joint ventures with companies such as IBM, General Instrument, Fujitsu, National Semiconductor, and Hitachi. The partnership of General Motors and Toyota, producing small cars in a California production facility, is another instance of a joint venture between two large multinational corporations.

Sharing technologies and investing cooperatively with partners provides mutual benefit. Global strategic alliances are founded on the premise that each party has something unique to contribute. For example, the technology of one partner is combined with the marketing expertise of another. Successful joint ventures require that the power and control be shared by each of the partners; such sharing represents a new experience for North American business executives.

Among other forms of shared enterprises are licensing, franchising, and contract manufacturing.

## *Licensing*

licensing

**Licensing** is a temporary agreement allowing a company (the licensee) to use the trademark, patent, copyright, or manufacturing process of another company (the licensor). In this type of agreement, the licensee assumes most of the financial risk. In return for the license, the source company is paid a royalty. Designer clothing firms use this strategy to gain access to foreign markets. Firms such as Levi Strauss, Jordache, Gloria Vanderbilt, Ralph Lauren, and Calvin Klein have such agreements for their products in many countries. While the investment risk is minimal for licensors that adopt this strategy, they lack control over operations.

## *International Franchising*

International franchising is the same as domestic market franchising, except that it is done in other countries. Major fast-food chains such as McDonald's, Burger King, Wendy's, Bonanza, and others have franchise networks in numerous nations. In many cases, the products have to be adapted to conform to local tastes if the company is to be successful. In other cases, the consumers in foreign countries gradually accept the taste of the original food.

## *Contract Manufacturing*

contract
manufacturing

**Contract manufacturing** occurs when a manufacturer stops producing a good domestically, preferring to find a foreign country that can produce the good according to their specifications. Typically, the original firm will seek a nation where raw-material and labour costs are lower. In most cases, such initiatives are taken because the costs of manufacturing in the domestic country are too high. Even though the good is produced elsewhere, the same brand name appears on the product.

Using this strategy, the company avoids any direct investment in the producing nation, while capitalizing on, say, its low labour rates. Sporting goods manufacturer Cooper Canada manufactures many of its products in offshore locations such as Asia and the Caribbean. Its goods can be manufactured in, exported and marketed from these countries less expensively than would be the case in Canada.

### Indirect and Direct Exporting

**indirect exporting**

There are two forms of exporting available to a company: indirect exporting and direct exporting. The difference is in the distribution strategy each form entails. A company that uses **indirect exporting** employs a middleman or trading company that specializes in international marketing. It is an attractive option for firms that are new to the global market scene. The middlemen establish a distribution network for the goods of the foreign company. Generally, the intermediary works for a commission. In terms of control, the foreign company has very little.

**direct exporting**

A company using **direct exporting** faces a greater risk than does a company pursuing indirect exporting, but it has greater control over the distribution process. The foreign company usually strikes agreements directly with local market companies that would be responsible for distribution in that country. Basically, the company itself performs the role of the intermediary. An export division or export sales force often becomes part of an organization's structure and is responsible for developing the distribution network.

## 〉〉〉 *The Global Marketing Mix*

How do firms use the marketing mix in the international marketplace? Do they develop specific strategies for each country, or do they use a common strategy in all countries where their products are available?

**global strategy**

In the past, the tendency has been to specialize by giving consideration to the unique characteristics and tendencies of local markets. The 1980s saw a growing movement toward the use of global marketing strategies, a trend that is expected to continue during the nineties. When it uses a **global strategy**, the company markets the product in essentially the same way, whatever the country, though some modifications to particular elements of the marketing mix are often necessary.

**country-centered strategy**

While there is no guaranteed formula for success, a common practice among marketers is to assess each international market and then decide what marketing mix it will employ in that market, whether a standard (global) mix or one customized for that particular country. The growing popularity of global marketing strategies suggests that advancing technology in communications and transportation has created markets for standardized products; everyone everywhere wants the same thing. The global approach enables a company to enjoy economies of scale in production and marketing expenditures, particularly in the areas of advertising, distribution, and management. By contrast, a company using a **country-centered strategy** (i.e., developing unique strategies for each country) may find its strategies are more effective, but also more expensive. The Marketing in Action feature "Is McDonald's a Global Marketer?" gives some insight into that restaurant's marketing strategy.

>>>> *MARKETING IN ACTION*

### IS McDONALD'S A GLOBAL MARKETER?

Does McDonald's practise global marketing? Clearly the corporation operates on a global basis, but the answer to the question of whether it uses a global marketing strategy is *yes and no*, according to Gary Reinblatt, the company's vice-president of marketing in Canada.

According to Reinblatt, the multinational company markets itself globally, internationally, nationally, regionally, and locally. McDonald's does not lock itself into one marketing approach. The one marketing approach it does adhere to is that of customer marketing. In Canada, marketing programs are designed to encourage more Canadians to come to McDonald's, but promotions designed for one market can be utilized elsewhere if they make a correct fit. One example is the "Mac Tonight" campaign, originally developed in Los Angeles for use in the United States.

This campaign was eventually used in Canada and many other countries.

Even though McDonald's in Canada can tap into other campaigns that run internationally, the company is, more than anything, a local marketer. Marketing programs developed by local-market franchise operators, the presence of Ronald McDonald at a local school, a new opening of a restaurant — these are part of the overall strategy. The advantage of being part of a global operation is that the Canadian company can consider adapting ideas used elsewhere to the Canadian marketplace.

Adapted from "For McDonald's, being multinational is more a matter of being multi-local", *Marketing*, May 23, 1988, p.7.

*Moscow-McDonald's opened on January 31, 1990*

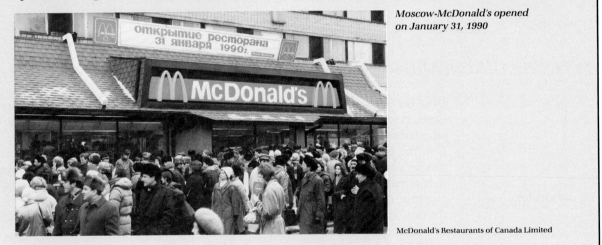

McDonald's Restaurants of Canada Limited

What decision is made regarding whether to use a global strategy or a country-centered strategy depends on answers to the following questions.

1. *How does market development differ from one country to another?* A company will consider the type of economy a foreign country has, the prospective size and growth potential of the country's market, and the stage of the life cycle its product would be in when marketed in that country. For instance, if a mature product such as fast food, which originated in the United States and Canada, were being marketed in the Far East, the strategic impetus of marketing activity would be different from what it is in Norht America. In Canada and the United States,

maintenance of position (protecting share of market) would be the primary consideration, whereas marketers in the Far East would seek to create awareness of the company name and of the food services provided. A company would also consider local eating habits, in order to avoid alienating potential customers.

2. *Is the product acceptable in the country?* A business will also look at the preferences of the local consumer. It needs to analyze factors such as demographics and psychographics in order to develop an understanding of the type of person it is marketing to and of what products and attributes this person will find attractive. For example, the average camera user in Japan likes a complex camera, while in Canada the average camera user wants a camera that is of good quality, but simple to operate.

3. *Do the needs and wants of consumers differ from one country to another?* The firm further considers the appeal of a standardized product in relation to needs and attitudes. The product may be acceptable, but the positioning strategy for it may have to be adapted to the target market. The Camay experience in Japan, described earlier in the chapter, is a good example of this assessment.

## Product

When it comes to product strategy, a company has three options: to market a standardized product in all markets, to adapt the product to suit local markets, or to develop a new product.

Using standardized products in all markets can be a successful strategy. Products such as Coca-Cola (the formula is consistent everywhere), Polaroid Cameras (the film-developing process is uniform) and John Deere farm equipment (farm equipment is farm equipment) are examples of successfully marketed standardized products.

Adapting a product to local tastes and preferences is common in the fast-food industry. Different ingredients may be used to make a fairly uniform product more attractive to local customers. Companies such as Kentucky Fried Chicken and McDonald's alter their products somewhat, since the taste preferences of consumers in, say, Japan are different from those of Canadian consumers.

The final alternative, that of developing a new product, is the most costly. A company only employs such a strategy when its market analysis indicates the existence of a sizable market opportunity. This strategy presents a high degree of risk because the company may not fully understand the needs and customs of the local market in different countries. Very often the assistance of local marketing consultants is sought to ensure that development is heading in the right direction.

To illustrate the uniqueness of needs in different countries, let's consider the situation that Pampers faced in Japan. The name Pampers is synonymous with disposable diapers in the North American market. In Japan, the product was not initially a big hit. Pampers were perceived by Japanese consumers to be too bulky and only appropriate for mothers who left them on their children for long periods. Once Procter & Gamble realized that Japanese mothers change their babies' diapers twice as often as North American mothers do, a thinner, more compact design was developed. The result, a product one-third the thickness of regular Pampers, was highly acceptable. Market share went from 7 percent to 28 percent in thirty months. This product is now called Ultra Pampers and is marketed in many countries around the world.[7]

## Price

dumping

Among the factors affecting price are local competition, dumping, tariffs, and the value of currency and inflation. **Dumping** is the practice of selling goods in a foreign market at a price lower than they are sold in the domestic market. Used as a means of penetrating foreign markets, it is judged by most countries to be an unfair practice, since it can undermine domestic companies and the work force they employ. To protect themselves against such undermining and to maintain a reasonable level of competition between foreign and domestic marketers, countries impose tariffs. Tariffs are sometimes imposed on products in industries that require protection. For example, Canada imposes tariffs on textiles entering the country so that the domestic industry can maintain a certain level of production and employment. The imposition of tariffs is only one among a number of factors affecting the levels of production and employment, and the price of the goods in an industry. Market demand is a much stronger influence on price.

The value of the Canadian dollar in relation to foreign currency also has an impact on the level of demand for Canadian goods. When its value is low in relation to the U.S. dollar, the prices for our goods are more attractive to U.S. buyers; therefore, demand for Canadian goods increases, and exports to the U.S. increase. Conversely, if the Canadian dollar rises in relation to the U.S. dollar, the prices of our goods are less attractive than those of U.S. products or other foreign products; therefore, demand for Canadian goods decreases.

If the rate of inflation in a foreign country is high in comparison to that of Canada, the price of Canadian goods in that country is appealing. Conversely, goods produced in foreign countries, where the labour rates are low, could cost much less than similar items made in Canada. Such goods, when imported to Canada, may be priced for much less than comparable domestic ones.

## Promotion

While a product may be suited for world-wide distribution, it is very difficult to promote it in a uniform manner everywhere. In similar markets, such as Canadian and U.S. markets, a uniform promotion can be successfully implemented, but regional differences will often dictate that alternate strategies be used. For example, French Canadian consumers are unique among North American consumers and generally require promotions customized to suit them. On a world-wide basis, differences in language and culture also often make the use of different or adapted promotion strategies necessary. Standardized advertising is only effective if consumers think, act, and buy in the same manner. From one country to another, rarely is that the case.

Language poses the main threat to global advertising. In Canada, McDonald's advertising for Big Macs became an embarrassment when it was discovered that in Quebec the phrase "Big Mac" is slang for big bust. The name of the product was changed. To avoid language problems, it is in the best interests of the outside firm to use the services of a local advertising agency. Today, there is a movement toward globalization in the advertising industry, since most large advertising firms now have offices or subsidiaries around the world to help multinational clients adapt their advertising to local ways.

When entering foreign countries, a marketing organization has to analyze cultural distinctions and legislative differences — the norms and laws that govern advertising — so that it is aware of what it can and cannot say about its products. Pirelli Tires is a good example of a company that had communication problems when it entered the Canadian market. Pirelli is a market leader around the world, whose reputation derives largely from its involvement with Formula One racing. Throughout the world, its advertising reflects its racing heritage. In Canada, however, the company is little known, so it concluded that a different strategy was needed to crack the mainstream tire market. To suit the Canadian environment, a campaign highlighting how their tires handled severe road conditions was developed. This campaign was not used anywhere else in the world.[8]

## Place

Firms generally secure distribution in international markets in two ways. Either they use existing channels, employing middlemen, or they introduce new channels; their choice depends on the needs of the marketing organization. If it chooses existing channels, a firm may employ a trading company in the home country, making it responsible for distributing goods to other distributors and to final users in the foreign country. A company may also decide to use a specialized sales force of its own that sells directly to existing foreign-market agents, distributors, or final users (see figure 18.7). On the other hand, new channels of distribution can be developed.

**FIGURE 18.7**  **Potential Global Marketing Channels**

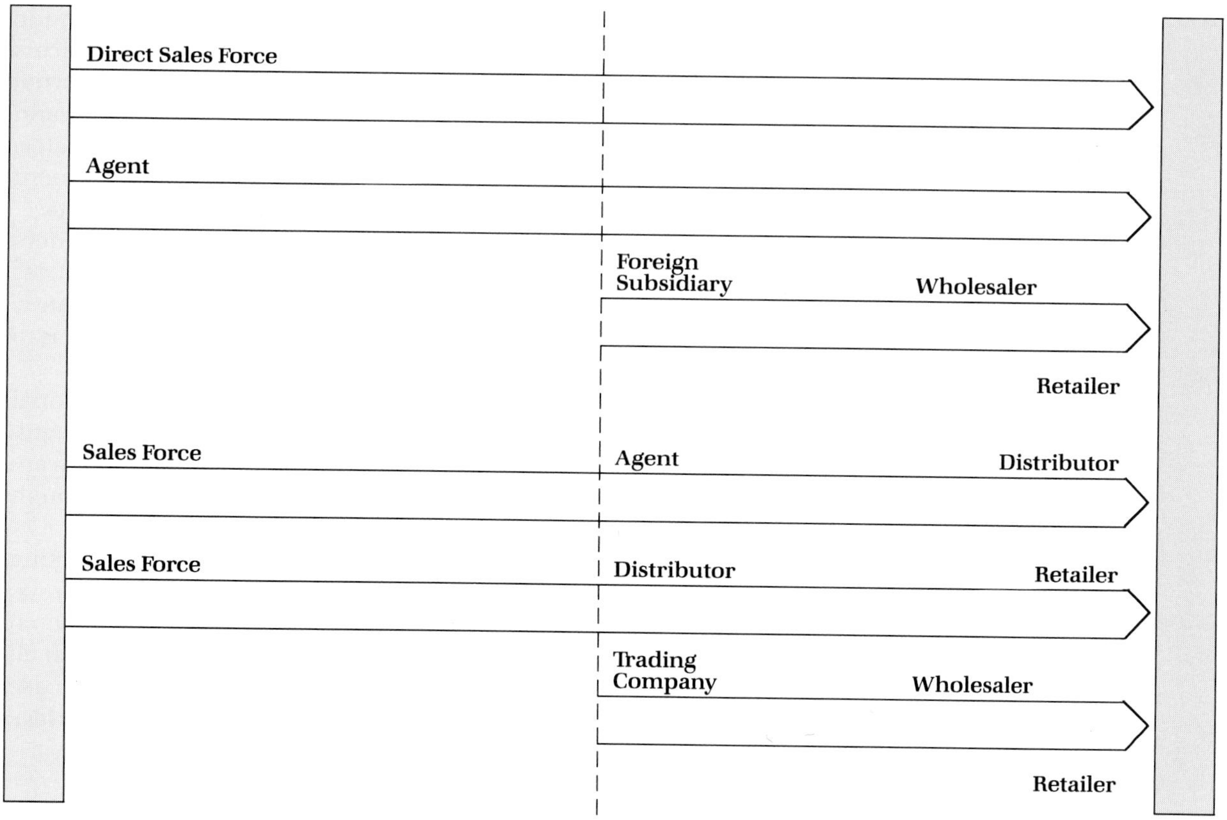

To illustrate, two North American fast food outlets, McDonald's and Kentucky Fried Chicken, have successfully extended their distribution strategies into the European and Asian markets. The acceptance of hypermarkets in the United States and Canada is an example of European distribution systems working in North America.

Since shipping overseas involves water transportation, the port facilities of foreign market destinations is an important consideration in distribution planning. For instance, some ports are unequipped to load and unload containerized ships, a circumstance which makes water transportation impractical for some countries. Distribution capabilities must be evaluated when a company is considering marketing products in other countries.

## ⟩⟩⟩⟩ SUMMARY

As Canada and Canadian businesses move further into the 1990s, more and more emphasis will be placed on global marketing. Factors such as the Canada–United States trade agreement and the unification of the European Economic Community represent new challenges for Canadian marketing organizations.

The federal government, through External Affairs and International Trade Canada and its various departments, provides assistance to Canadian firms seeking global markets. Essentially, the five operating branches of External Affairs extend to all parts of the world: Europe, Asia and the Pacific, Africa and the Middle East, Latin America and the Caribbean, and the United States. Their role is to develop international trade strategy and market development programs, and to improve access for Canadian products to export markets.

To analyze global market opportunities, a marketing organization considers the economy, culture, political environment, and technology of countries where apparent markets exist, as well as the level of the competition there. Before entering a foreign market, a firm must understand that market if it is to develop appropriate marketing strategies for penetrating it.

Several options are available to a firm that is going into an international market. Among the more common strategies are direct investment and acquisition, and such joint ventures as partnerships, licensing agreements, franchising, and contract manufacturing. Exporting goods indirectly, through middlemen, or directly, by oneself, are other options.

As it does in domestic marketing, a company that is developing a marketing strategy for a foreign market employs the elements of the marketing mix: product, price, promotion and place. The company can either use a global strategy (i.e., a standardized product is marketed in a uniform manner in all markets where it is available), or a country-centered strategy (in which case the marketing mix is tailored to the specific needs of individual countries). Often a firm combines the best elements of both strategies.

## 〉〉〉〉 KEY TERMS

absolute advantage
comparative advantage
multinational corporation
countertrading
nationalization
protectionism
tariff

quota
embargo
local content law
cartel
orderly market agreement
common market
joint venture

licensing
contract manufacturing
indirect exporting
direct exporting
global strategy
country-centered strategy
dumping

## 〉〉〉〉 REVIEW AND DISCUSSION QUESTIONS

**1.** Briefly describe the role of External Affairs and International Trade Canada in global trade.

**2.** What is the difference between an absolute advantage and a comparative advantage?

**3.** How does knowledge of a nation's stage of economic development assist a global marketer?

**4.** "Because of the cultural differences that exist from nation to nation, promotion strategies must be tailored to each country." Discuss the validity of this statement.

**5.** Why do countries impose trade barriers? Briefly describe the three types of barrier imposed.

**6.** What is the difference between a cartel and an orderly market agreement?

**7.** Are Canadian corporations likely targets for takeover by foreign-based multinationals? Present your view on this statement.

**8.** What is a joint venture, and what benefits does it provide participants?

**9.** If you were marketing a soft drink such as Pepsi-Cola or 7-Up in Latin America, what factors would you consider when developing a marketing strategy? Would you use a global strategy or a country-centered strategy?

## 〉〉〉〉 REFERENCES

1. Investment Canada, *Canada Facts 1989*, p.27.

2. JOEL EVANS and BARRY BERMAN, *Marketing*, Third Edition (New York: Macmillan, 1987), p.585.

3. PHILIP KOTLER, GORDON McDOUGALL, and GARY ARMSTRONG, *Marketing*, Canadian Edition (Toronto: Prentice-Hall Canada Inc., 1988), p.424.

4. EDWIN ARTZT, "Winning in Japan: Keys to Global Success", *Business Quarterly*, Winter 1989, p.14.

5. CLARKSON GORDON/WOODS GORDON, *Tomorrow's Customers*, 22nd Edition, 1989, p.18.

6. Ibid.

7. EDWIN ARTZT, "Winning in Japan: Keys to Global Success", *Business Quarterly*, Winter 1989, p.13.

8. DANIEL ROBINOWICZ, "Globalization Casts a Shadow", *Marketing*, May 9, 1988, p.42.

# Tourism Marketing Plan

## Ontario Ministry of Tourism and Recreation

This marketing plan demonstrates the practical application of various components of a typical marketing plan. Readers must view the plan as a sample model only, since plans vary from one organization to another in length, content, and format.

The initial sections of this marketing plan present the overall picture, focusing on background information, marketing objectives, and the geographic priorities of interest to Tourism Ontario. This is *not* the complete plan. The original and complete plan contained detailed strategies for reaching Ontario residents as well as residents of Quebec, Manitoba, and the northern United States. This plan only includes the strategies for encouraging Quebec residents to travel in Ontario.

Readers should analyze the plan and determine the relationships between the various sections. For instance, review the influence that marketing objectives and strategies have on creative and media objectives and strategies.

# INTRODUCTION

In 1986, the Ministry of Tourism and Recreation (MTR) changed direction from an image approach to marketing tourism in Ontario, to a more product-specific approach. The Ministry's marketing efforts had succeeded in growing the awareness of "Ontario" in the traditional markets of Ontario and border U.S. States, and the next step was to convert this high awareness into even more sales with a more specific, tactical program.

Competition for world wide tourism expenditures have grown 15% annually since 1979. Budgets of U.S. State Tourism Offices have increased steadily, with one third of the current allocations accounted for by Ontario's primary border state competitors. Many of these states and most Canadian provinces have targeted Ontario as a source of market growth, including Michigan and New York State.

To respond to these challenges, research on all key markets was initiated in 1986. As the marketing program evolved, consultations with the tourism industry and independent research on market segments have begun to reveal what Ontario's customers are seeking in a vacation so that we can market more effectively to them and capture a greater share of their travel dollar.

Toward this end, a tracking system has been established to measure the impact of MTR's advertising to provide benchmarks to help reach our objectives.

Continuous segmentation studies and scans of market trends and competitive activity will help identify products and benefits sought by each type of customer in different regions of the province. This will be on-going to ensure that the activities on strategy, and that the strategy remains correct and current.

This plan sets strategic objectives for each *market* and *trip type*, as well as *sales objectives* to help increase business.

This plan is the result of the most information that has ever been gathered on our markets. Continued research is needed to ensure that our marketing is increasingly "customer focused".

# SITUATION ANALYSIS AND OUTLOOK

Following several years of sustained gains in travel volume and spending, growth in North American markets was mixed in 1988:

- U.S. travel to Ontario is down 3.1% in the year-to-date (Jan.–Oct 1988–87), reversing an upward trend during recent years.

- Ontarians' travel to the U.S. rose 18.3%, fueling growth of the province's travel deficit.

- Preliminary indications are that Ontario residents' travel within the province may be up over 13% for 1988. This is also mirrored by a shift in share of travel enquiries by market towards Ontario callers.

These signs and others suggest that the high growth since 1982 may be more difficult to sustain without more marketing and more strategically targetted marketing in the future.

Significant changes in market demand characteristics are also occurring.

The volume of overnight U.S. visitors to Canada has leveled off, and Ontario's border market particularly has become mature. By "mature", we mean little new growth in the travel market can be expected and Ontario has reached saturation point in the market. Little new sustained growth can be expected from traditional U.S. markets.

As the "baby boom" generation ages, the North American market generally grows older. While disposable income has increased, the recent growth in short-term travel and dual-income households suggests more constrained leisure time.

This market includes more experienced travellers than ever before and they are used to a wide range of choice in any product they purchase. The pressure will be on all destinations to offer unique and interesting products and excellent service in order to attract this sophisticated market.

Growth in household income shows signs of slowing as female participation rates peak. Future gains in household income are less likely to come from increased work force participation, but from longer-term, structural changes in the economy.

Emerging claims on disposable income may dampen demand for travel, in the short-term, where housing and related costs are rising faster than household incomes. Competition for what remains of disposable income continues along with a broadening of personal horizons, higher expectations of quality, better service and product diversity.

These changes also suggest opportunities. The growth of specialty markets, and the means of tailoring vacations to specific market segments, reflects an opportunity to promote Ontario's wide diversity of scenery, cultures, and facilities.

The decreased size and changing nature of families may reduce obstacles of time and cost, provided marketers can capitalize on the demand for flexibility of choices. For example, more frequent trips of shorter duration may be more popular.

Threats to North America's natural environment, and the steadily growing awareness of the need for fresh air, water and open space suggest Ontario is well-positioned to offer its superior outdoors to meet this emergent demand. In time, trends would also indicate that the market will be more interested in traditional family values, family activities, natural and fresh images and products. This makes "Ontario" even more desirable.

These requirements will shape Ontario's positioning in all markets and trip segments, presenting a clear image of the province as a travel destination offering high quality and superior service in a natural setting.

## Advertising Tracking 1987/88

To provide data which will enable the Ministry to set out strategic directions, an advertising tracking study was conducted throughout the 1988 campaign.

The key findings on the new campaign in 1986 and 1987 were:

- The advertising created a significant growth in spontaneous awareness of Ontario as a travel destination in Ontario and Quebec, and a directional (non statistical) increase in the U.S. test cities of Ontario as a travel destination.

- Awareness of Ontario vs. its competitors was high in all markets. In Ontario, awareness topped all major competitors by a margin of approximately 40%. In the U.S., Ontario's recognition was less than New York and Florida, but higher than Michigan, New England and Quebec.

- After advertising was placed, no apparent shift in likelihood of Ontario residents to travel within the province occurred, but a significant increase in likelihood of U.S. residents to visit Ontario did.

- Spontaneous awareness of Ontario trip types was greatest for *city* and *outdoor* trips among Ontarians. U.S. residents cited city trips most frequently. Quebeckers cited city trips and touring trips, and a rising knowledge of outdoor trips.

- Ontario's vacation image is strongest among provincial residents, who rated Ontario highest in terms of appeal to families, outdoor trips, different cultures, and wilderness adventure.

- Ontario's image among U.S. residents focused on charming towns, arts/culture, city trips, shopping, friendliness, and history. But results showed a less clear image of Ontario for U.S. residents than Ontarians.

- Ontario's image in Quebec was greatest for roads/highways and lowest for cities/nightlife. Outdoors/wilderness rated highly among Manitobans.

- The tracking results indicate that the campaign has been working well but, that a clearer image of "Ontario" is required especially in the U.S. and Quebec and more product specific (unique and different) information is needed in all markets.

## MARKETING OBJECTIVES AND MARKETING PRIORITIES

Marketing objectives are comprised of *sales objectives* and *strategic* (positioning) *objectives*. More specific objectives are set for each market. Sales targets are for 1989 only, but the strategic direction is for at least 3 years.

### Sales Objectives:

1. To increase *total trips* from U.S., Ontario, Quebec and Manitoba markets by: 5.5% (1989)

2. To increase *real expenditures* from U.S., Ontario, Quebec and Manitoba markets by: 5.5% (1989)

3. To increase *yield*, expressed as an increase in real spending per person night in U.S. and Ontario markets by: 4% (1989)

4. (a) To increase *seasonal* visitations, in shoulder and winter seasons.
   (b) To increase the monthly share of telephone enquiries in shoulder and winter seasons.

5. (a) To increase overnight *pleasure* travel volume by: 2% in Ontario (1989)
   (b) To maintain *pleasure* travel volume in the U.S. in 1989. (by 1991 we will target growth in the U.S. investment markets)
   (c) To increase *pleasure* travel volume by: 2% in Manitoba and 1% in Quebec by 1990 over 1988.

### Strategic Objectives:

1. Ontario's advantage is being perceived by all markets as especially good for outdoors, having the ultimate in natural settings. Ontario is also perceived as having a population that respects the environment. On the other hand, Ontario is not perceived to have the ultimate in amenities.
   We will position Ontario in all markets for all trip types as a place that

respects its *natural environment*, has high quality *amenities* in these natural settings and is easily *accessible*. This will be a unifying element in the creative approach for each trip type.

2. "Soft Outdoors" vacations will be introduced as a key trip type that you can only experience in Ontario. This will capitalize on Ontario's strong, outdoor image and respond to the lack of knowledge of Ontario's amenities. It will distinguish Ontario from its competition.

3. For each market and trip type, specific objectives and strategies will be developed.

4. Spontaneous awareness of Ontario will be increased versus major North American competitors in all markets throughout the 1989 campaign and reflected in tracking studies.

5. The most appropriate trip types will be matched with target audiences and market areas in the highest potential season(s).

## Market Priorities:

The following summarizes the priority markets for Ontario tourism. A percentage of effort is indicated. Effort represents the amount of activity which will be undertaken in the market and does *not* indicate a budget allocation. In some cases, relatively few dollars will be spent but significant staff time will be spent in public relations and sales. The measure of effort is simply an indicator of priority.

Dollar allocations will remain fairly constant with some budget being shifted to investment activities. New funds will be targetted at investment markets or growth trip types.

| Market | Effort | Summary |
|---|---|---|
| Ontario | 30% | – maintain traditional trip types<br>– invest in new trip type which is a secondary, short holiday |
| U.S. Traditional | 30% | – maintain traditional trip types<br>– invest in off season trips<br>– invest in secondary, short trip types |
| U.S. Investment | 20% | – invest in growth potential<br>– U.S. market areas with city trips and soft outdoor trips |
| Quebec | 15% | – continue investment |
| Manitoba | 2% | – maintain activity but sell only N.W. Ontario |
| International | 3% | – invest in key overseas markets that are growing rapidly (see Overseas Strategy) |

# QUEBEC MARKETING PLAN

## Market Description

Quebec is the largest Canadian market for Ontario and it has increased significantly over the last four years from 1 564 000 person trips in 1984 to 2 997 000 person trips in 1987, an increase of 92%.

The main target audience for Ontario is urban dwellers – both French and English speaking — who are looking for a city trip to Toronto or Ottawa or for a tour which includes cities, Niagara Falls and attractions.

No significant differences have been reported on the subject of vacationing between anglophones and francophones in Quebec.

In general, the travellers from Quebec to Ontario are better educated/higher income earners and those travelling to Ontario are significantly more likely than average to have taken a family trip.

The average pleasure trip for Montrealers would seem to last 4–9 nights. Summer trips to Ontario were of longer duration (6.3 nights) than trips to Ontario that were taken in the spring (5.0 nights).

About 50% of Quebec person-nights were spent with friends and relatives, followed by 21% camping. The average length of stay was 4.04 nights. This represents a higher than average number of travellers who do not stay in commercial roofed accommodations.

The two most frequently visited areas by Montrealers in Ontario are Metro Toronto and Eastern Ontario followed by Niagara and Mid Western Ontario.

For Quebec travellers, the most popular activities participated in focused on general activities such as shopping, visiting friends and relatives, restaurant dining, etc.

Quebec travellers to Ontario spent $264 million dollars in 1986. In 1986, the average expenditure per trip per visitor from Quebec was $92 and per day it was $57.

## Industry Trends

### Economy and Consumer Spending

| | Economic Indicators (% Change) | | |
| --- | --- | --- | --- |
| | 1988 | 1989 | 1990 |
| Real Gross Domestic Product | 4.8 | 2.2 | 2.9 |
| Unemployment Rate | 9.4 | 9.1 | 8.8 |
| Consumer Price Inflation | 4.2 | 5.1 | 4.7 |
| Personal Disposable Income | 6.7 | 8.9 | 6.7 |

Source: The Conference Board of Canada

The superheated growth in Quebec's economy will continue through 1988 (i.e. in real Gross Domestic Product), but is expected to slow down over the next two years to a rate approximating the national average. The unemployment rate will probably remain above the national average. Some short term gains should be realized in personal disposable income.

Stage one of the federal tax reform will see a continuance of the 1988 personal tax cut into 1989, however, a regression in consumer spending is anticipated over the next two years as a result of increasing interest rates and deteriorating debt-to-income ratio.

### Number of Travellers

|  | Quebec | % Change From Previous Year |
|---|---|---|
| 1982 | 1 895 000 | – 9.3% |
| 1983 | 1 900 000 | 0.3 |
| 1984 | 1 564 000 | –17.7 |
| 1985 | 1 580 000 | 1.0 |
| 1986 | 2 882 000 | 82.4 |
| 1987 | 2 997 000 | 4.0 |
| 1988P | 3 307 000 | 10.3 |

P = Preliminary

Source: Tourism Canada, *Canadian Travel Survey, 1982*, 1984, 1986, 1988 – all other years estimated by Tourism Canada and MTR.

The strong economic performance and the satisfaction of pent-up demand since the recession of the early eighties were in large part the main factors behind the recent significant growth which has occurred in travel from Quebec to Ontario. In 1986, 76% of Quebec travellers to Ontario were on overnight trips.

Quebec travellers spent $264 million (current $), in Ontario in 1986. It is estimated that about 96% of this expenditure was on overnight travel only. In 1986, the average expenditure per trip per traveller from Quebec was $92.

### Seasonality of Travel

|  | Calendar Quarter, 1986 | | | |
|---|---|---|---|---|
|  | Q1 | Q2 | Q3 | Q4 |
| Quebec | 21.2% | 26.1% | 32.3% | 20.4% |

Source: Tourism Canada, *Canadian Travel Survey, 1986*

For Quebec, there may be a current trend towards decreased travel during the third quarter, and an increase in the fourth.

A double income household has created a situation, whereby, although there may be no children involved, other constraints such as holiday schedules are now obliging couples to travel for shorter periods of time and more often. A common trend is the Friday to Monday weekend trip.

Condominium and chalet skiing vacations and cottage vacations are gaining popularity and Quebeckers are looking at more foreign destinations than ever before.

## Problems and Opportunities

### Problems — Quebec Specific

- Negative perception of Ontario — must convince there is lots to see and do.
- Lack of advertising, PR and travel trade activities over last years.
- Very few private sector partners in Quebec.
- Difficulty to break traditional North-South travel patterns.
- Need to be able to service the Quebec market with literature/sales aids etc. in French.
- Lack of Ontario knowledge other than the corridor.

### Opportunities — Quebec Specific

- Opportunity to build on successful 1986–87 "Venez Voir" campaign.
- Opportunity to build on the fact that 86.7% Quebeckers visited in 87 — larger base exposed to Ontario.
- Visiting friends and relatives traffic from Quebec to Ontario is high.
- Ontario attractions and organizations increased their marketing activities in Quebec.

## Marketing Objectives

The hard hitting campaign "VENEZ VOIR COMME L'ONTARIO A CHANGE/ COME SEE HOW ONTARIO HAS CHANGED" has been very successful for the past three years. While the advertising tracking study indicates a high awareness of the campaign in Quebec there is also a higher than average negative response about vacation opportunities in Ontario. It is time now to give more specific product information.

In 1989, the campaign will develop a more definitive statement about Ontario. While new qualitative research will provide the insight required to determine our creative and media approach to Quebec, it is known that Quebec travellers need to be informed and convinced that Ontario can deliver those unique activities and attractions they may be seeking in a holiday.

The growth in travel from Quebec to Ontario during the past 2 years has been significant. Indications are that this growth will slow in 1989. Our communication effort in this market must, therefore, be "break through" in order to sustain market share gained.

City trips and touring will be the primary trip types used to influence this market.

### Sales Objectives:

Due to the data collection schedule, objectives for Quebec will be carried out over 2 years. Most data will not be available until 1990.

1. To increase trip volume from Quebec by 1% by 1990 over 1988.

2. To increase real expenditures from Quebec by 4% by 1990 over 1988.

3. To increase overnight pleasure travel volume by 1% by 1990 over 1988, particularly at commercial accommodation.

4. To increase yield (real spending per person per night) from Quebec visitors by 3% by 1990 over 1988.

5. To shift share of French language telephone enquiries to off-season months.

## Strategic Objectives:

1. For the fiscal year 1989–90, Ontario will concentrate its efforts on the Montreal market. A considerable increase in expenditure would be required to extend beyond the Montreal Market.

2. Quebeckers indicated an above average interest in receiving "value for money", e.g., inexpensive accommodation and meals are important. There is more emphasis on ambience and shopping rather than on accommodation and meals.

3. Packaging is important in this market. Therefore, an inventory of existing packages will be undertaken. The Ministry will work with the travel trade, city bureaux, and associations to promote existing packages and develop more.

4. Aggressive sales programs will be developed for group and independent travel.

5. Research will be utilized to determine special interests within the city trip and touring categories.

6. "Fun, food, and lots of attractions" in Ontario will be the emphasis.

7. Efforts will be concentrated on spring, summer and fall business.

## Trip Types – Detailed Descriptions

## City Trips

A city trip is a short holiday to a city which can be taken by car, airplane or train. The city trip averages 2–3 days.

Strolling around, dining, shopping, viewing sights, visiting museums and galleries are activities undertaken.

This trip could be planned less than a month before and it could be taken spontaneously.

This trip-type appeals to all groups, but is probably more common for couples than families.

### Positioning Statement

Ontario cities that offer excitement in a safe and friendly environment in which to stroll around and enjoy cultural activities and a variety of experiences.

### Competition

In this category our competition is New York and New England destinations. Also competing are trips to sun destinations such as Florida, Caribbean and

South Carolina. Other purchases such as high tech appliances (VCR, computers), fitness clubs and involvement in sports can also compete for vacation dollars.

### Timing

All seasons offer potential for travellers of this trip type. In summer, spring and fall this could be part of a touring trip but in winter generally the city would be the end destination.

### Opportunities

Ontario cities still have the image of not having much to see and do. The challenge is to continue to change this image and to make Quebeckers aware of the atmosphere and the variety of amenities available and the wide selection of things to see and do.

### Desired Results

Ontario cities are relaxing, hospitable cities suitable for strolling, shopping and have an excellent variety of cuisine.

## Touring

### Product Description

Touring is a vacation by car, train or motorcoach where usually couples or families go through areas of scenic beauty, historical, or general interest. Purpose of the trip is to visit friends and family, see interesting sights, visit attractions, cities, and small towns. It is a combination holiday which involves a mix of vacation experiences.

### Positioning Statement

Nearby Ontario offers a network of scenic routes as an ideal way to explore a wide variety of major sites, attractions in a friendly environment where Quebeckers can feel comfortable.

### Competition

Competition is getting more intense for the Quebec market. New Brunswick, P.E.I., Nova Scotia, New England, New York and The Virginias are all active in Quebec. The emphasis in these competitors' ads is on sun, beaches and friendliness. Also a factor to be considered in 1989–90 is the domestic advertising planned by Tourism Quebec. The most frequently visited tourist regions visited by Quebeckers are Montreal, the Laurentians, Quebec City and the Eastern Townships.

### Timing

Spring, summer and fall offer potential for travellers of this trip type.

### Opportunities

Ontario is a friendly nearby destination offering a wide variety of things to see and do on a touring vacation. Ontario has the product in place for this trip type.

*Desired Results*

There are many sites and attractions, things to see and do in Ontario. You can meet old friends, meet new people and share new experiences. Ontario is fun and vibrant.

## Target Audience

The primary target audience for the spring/summer/fall can be defined as follows:

> Quebec residents, 18 years or older, with specific emphasis on adults 18–49, living in the greater Montreal market with disposable income for travel and planning a vacation in 1988.

Within primary target audience further segmentation can be made as follows:

1. Young Couples without Children: Mid to upper income individuals who want a short travel experience that will fill their leisure time with a unique quality experience.

2. Families: People who are looking for a quality vacation experience, either a long vacation or a two to three day touring experience. Value for money is important for this group. They want to have a great time but don't have a large amount of money to spend.

3. Singles: Working people who are looking for short travel experience.

## Creative Strategy

In 1988, the evolution of the Ministry's tourism communication activities will continue. Our advertising will address the two main vacation types: touring vacations and drive/stay vacations.

## Tone:

The tone and style of our communications will convey that Quebec is informative, insightful, friendly, cheerful.

## Anticipated Response:

Our messages to the vacationing public will be designed to elicit the following responses from Quebeckers who see them:

> There are many sites and attractions, things to see and do in Ontario that are different from anywhere else. I'm travelling there to visit old friends, meet new people, discover new sites and share new experiences.

## Creative Direction

In order to generate these anticipated responses, it is important to have the proper tone, communicate the messages that will prompt a sale and to package the province in such a way as to make the purchase easy and desirable. Based on our experience in 1986 and 1987, as well as conversations with the Travel Associations, the following messages or topics will be used in our communications.

## Media Strategies

### Media Objectives

Direct media support to Montrealers in order to increase and maintain high levels of awareness of the numerous exciting vacation possibilities within Ontario.

Ensure that all residents are aware of and can easily access the Minister's toll-free telephone number (1-800-268-3736).

### Media Strategy

#### *Target Group*

Direct media to residents of Greater Montreal area defined as:

- Adults 18 + who are pre-disposed to vacation travelling. They include singles/couples without children and families with an average or higher income and Senior Citizens.

*Rationale:* All residents of Montreal are potential travellers to Ontario.

- Adults 18–49 are more likely to have school aged children. The segment is targeted for its "Family Vacation" potential.
- Adults 18–49 with a high propensity for travel will still have to be motivated to travel to Ontario.

#### *Regionality/Market Selection*

Direct media support to Montreal (E.& Fr.) market.

*Rationale:* The Montreal market offers the best potential for Ontario vacation travelling.

#### *Timing*

Provide media support throughout the April through October period with emphasis on April/May, August/September, and October.

*Rationale:* Short duration vacations will be promoted throughout the season.

- April/May is the planning period for the main summer vacations.
- August/September is the planning period for fall vacations.

# The Media Plan

## *Media Selection*

A combination of television, newspaper, transit are recommended during the Spring/Summer/Fall 1988 period.

### *Rationale:*

1. Television has been recommended for the following reasons:
   a) The use of sight, sound and motion will convince Montreal residents that Ontario is a vibrant, exciting and entertaining place to vacation.
   b) In media terms, television provides an excellent reach of all target groups. The weekly reach of adults 18 + is 99%.
2. Newspapers have been recommended for the following reasons:
   a) Newspapers provide an excellent market penetration.
   b) Newspapers provide Montrealers with a more detailed description (vs broadcast/outdoor) of the many vacation benefits available in Ontario.
   c) Newspapers provide the flexibility to buy regionally and to select the day and the section of the newspaper with the suitable environment for the product/service advertised. The Saturday Travel section is recommended as it provides the proper environment for travel advertising, also the additional circulation offered in the Saturday edition of the newspapers.

## Weight/Duration

| Media | Type/Unit | Schedule | Duration | Levels |
|---|---|---|---|---|
| | | *Montreal (Fr.)* | | |
| Television | 30″ | March 28–April 10 | 2 weeks | 200 GRP's/wk |
| | | April 11–May 8 | 4 weeks | 150 GRP's/wk |
| | | May 30–June 26 | 4 weeks | 150 GRP's/wk |
| | | *Montreal (E.)* | | |
| | | March 28–April 10 | 2 weeks | 150 GRP's/wk |
| | | April 11–May 8 | 4 weeks | 125 GRP's/wk |
| | | May 30–June 26 | 4 weeks | 125 GRP's/wk |
| Newspapers | Full Page | May | 1 insertion | |
| | B/1 color | June | 1 insertion | |
| | | Mid-August to Mid-October | 5 insertions | |
| Transit | Exterior Bus | April/May | 8 weeks | 291 Panels |
| | Boards | Sept./Oct. | 8 weeks | 291 Panels |

## *Unit: Full Page B/1 color*

| PUBLICATION | CIRCULATION (Saturday) | UNIT |
|---|---|---|
| Montreal – *La Presse* | 321 468 | 1860 MAL |
| *Journal de Montreal* | 368 639 | 1400 A. Li. |
| *Gazette* | 274 072 | 1860 MAL |

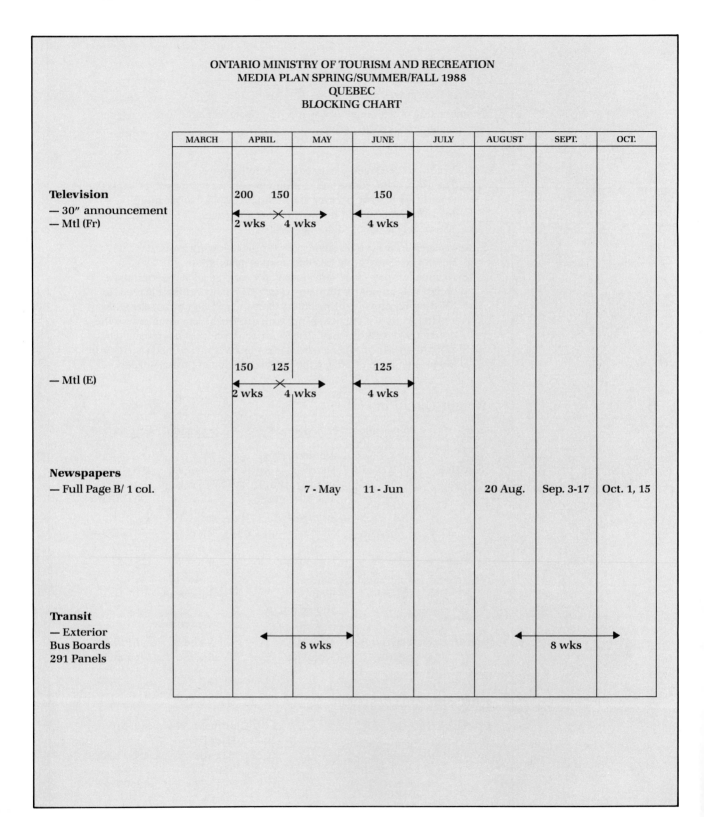

ONTARIO MINISTRY OF TOURISM AND RECREATION
MEDIA PLAN SPRING/SUMMER/FALL 1988
QUEBEC
BLOCKING CHART

| | MARCH | APRIL | MAY | JUNE | JULY | AUGUST | SEPT. | OCT. |
|---|---|---|---|---|---|---|---|---|
| **Television**<br>— 30″ announcement<br>— Mtl (Fr) | | 200    150<br>◄——✕——►<br>2 wks   4 wks | | 150<br>◄——►<br>4 wks | | | | |
| — Mtl (E) | | 150    125<br>◄——✕——►<br>2 wks   4 wks | | 125<br>◄——►<br>4 wks | | | | |
| **Newspapers**<br>— Full Page B/ 1 col. | | | 7 - May | 11 - Jun | | 20 Aug. | Sep. 3-17 | Oct. 1, 15 |
| **Transit**<br>— Exterior<br>Bus Boards<br>291 Panels | | | ◄——►<br>8 wks | | | | ◄——►<br>8 wks | |

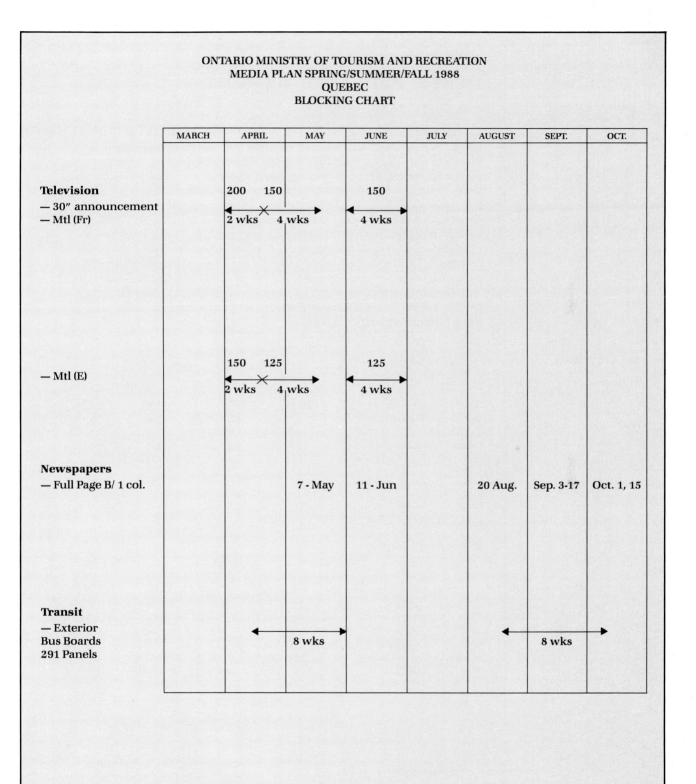

ONTARIO MINISTRY OF TOURISM AND RECREATION
MEDIA PLAN SPRING/SUMMER/FALL 1988
QUEBEC
BLOCKING CHART

| | MARCH | APRIL | MAY | JUNE | JULY | AUGUST | SEPT. | OCT. |
|---|---|---|---|---|---|---|---|---|
| **Television** — 30″ announcement — Mtl (Fr) | | 200  150 2 wks  4 wks | | 150 4 wks | | | | |
| — Mtl (E) | | 150  125 2 wks  4 wks | | 125 4 wks | | | | |
| **Newspapers** — Full Page B/ 1 col. | | | 7 - May | 11 - Jun | | 20 Aug. | Sep. 3-17 | Oct. 1, 15 |
| **Transit** — Exterior Bus Boards 291 Panels | | | 8 wks | | | | 8 wks | |

# APPENDIX —
# OTHER PROVINCE MARKET

## 1. SOCIO-ECONOMIC OUTLOOK

Quebec has posted a strong 5% real economic growth in 1987. However, the downturn in housing starts which commenced late this year may suppress the province's growth in 1988 and 1989. While the unemployment rate remains somewhat above the national average, employment growth should remain strong along with gains in personal disposable income. Canadian tax reform scheduled for 1988 should stimulate consumer demand. Slightly rising interest rates will also tend to dampen demand. It is likely that consumer spending will weaken somewhat in 1988, however this will probably pertain to durable purchases, as expenditures on semi-durable and service should remain positive.

Manitoba's real economic growth, while much lower than Quebec's, should be steady. However, personal disposable income gains will be relatively lower along with employment growth. The unemployment rate will still remain relatively high. The affects of tax reform are discussed above. Consumer spending on services will be probably much slower.

ECONOMIC INDICATORS

% Change

| | 1987 | | 1988 | |
|---|---|---|---|---|
| | Quebec | Manitoba | Quebec | Manitoba |
| Real Domestic Product | 5.0 | 2.2 | 2.6 | 2.5 |
| Employment | 3.3 | 1.0 | 2.4 | 0.8 |
| Unemployment Rate | 10.7 | 7.4 | 10.7 | 7.3 |
| Personal Disposable Income | 6.2 | 5.3 | 8.6 | 7.3 |

Source: The Conference Board of Canada

## 2. OTHER PROVINCE TRAVEL IN ONTARIO

a) Number of Travellers

| | Quebec | % Change From Previous Year | Manitoba | % Change From Previous Year | Other Province | % Change From Previous Year |
|---|---|---|---|---|---|---|
| 1982 | 1,895,000 | − 9.3% | 425,000 | − 3.0% | 805,000 | 12.9% |
| 1983 | 1,900,000 | 0.3 | 427,000 | 0.5 | 809,000 | 0.5 |
| 1984 | 1,564,000 | − 17.7 | 392,000 | − 8.2 | 741,000 | − 8.4 |
| 1985 | 1,580,000 | 1.0 | 395,000 | 0.8 | 749,000 | 1.1 |
| 1986 | 2,882,000 | 82.4 | 532,000 | 34.7 | 843,000 | 12.6 |
| 1987P | 2,971,000 | 3.1 | 549,000 | 3.1 | 869,000 | 3.1 |

P – Preliminary

Source: Tourism Canada, *Canadian Travel Survey for 1982, 1984, 1986* – other years estimated by Tourism Canada and MTR.

All of the markets had declined significantly since the recession, however the recovery in 1986 was most dramatic, and is probably attributable to pent-up demand and strong economic growth.

b) Expenditure in Ontario

| | Expenditure, 1986 (In millions of current $) | |
|---|---|---|
| | $ | % |
| Quebec | 264 | 44.1 |
| Manitoba | 77 | 12.9 |
| Other Provinces | 257 | 43.0 |
| TOTAL | 598 | 100.0 |

Source: Tourism Canada, *Canadian Travel Survey*

Of the total $598 million spent in the province, about 96% was generated by overnight travel only. In 1986, the average expenditure per trip per visitor from Quebec was $92, and per day it was $57. The averages for Manitoba were $145 and $29, respectively.

c) Expenditure by Destination Region, any length of Stay

| | Per Cent of Expenditures, 1985 | |
|---|---|---|
| Destination Region | Quebec | Manitoba |
| Southwestern Ontario | 3.3% | 4.1% |
| Niagara & Mid-Western Ontario | 7.6 | 15.9 |
| Georgian Lakelands | 3.0 | 1.7 |
| Metro Toronto | 39.3 | 39.5 |
| Central Ontario | 5.2 | 2.5 |
| Eastern Ontario | 36.7 | 9.5 |
| Ontario North | 4.9 | 26.7 |
| | | |
| TOTAL | 100.0 | 100.0 |

Source: MTR, *Ontario Exit Survey, 1985.*

• Both Metro Toronto and Eastern Ontario captured over one third of the total expenditure in the province by Quebec residents.

• The highest incidence of spending by Manitobans accrued to Metro Toronto (about 40%), followed by Ontario North at 27%.

d) Region of Destination, by Length of Stay, 1985

| | Per Cent Of Quebec Travellers | |
|---|---|---|
| Destination Region | Same Day | Overnight |
| | % | % |
| Eastern Ontario | 96 | 39 |
| Metropolitan Toronto | 3 | 32 |
| Niagara & Midwestern Ontario | * | 8 |
| Southwestern Ontario | * | 4 |
| Georgian Lakelands | — | 5 |
| Central Ontario | * | 8 |
| Ontario North | — | 5 |
| TOTAL | 100 | 100 |

*Less than 0.5 per cent

Source: MTR, *Ontario Exit Survey, 1985.*

Quebec same day visitors tend to visit Eastern Ontario, while overnight visitors travel to Eastern Ontario as well as Metropolitan Toronto.

e) Region of Destination, by Length of Stay, 1985

| Destination Region | Per Cent Of Manitoba Travellers | |
| --- | --- | --- |
| | Same Day | Overnight |
| Ontario North | 87 | 62 |
| Metropolitan Toronto | 10 | 18 |
| Eastern Ontario | 2 | 6 |
| Niagara & Midwestern Ontario | 1 | 6 |
| Southwestern Ontario | — | 3 |
| Central Ontario | — | 3 |
| Georgian Lakelands | — | 2 |
| TOTAL | 100 | 100 |

Source: MTR, *Ontario Exit Survey, 1985.*

Almost 9 in 10 same-day travellers visit Ontario North. Overnight travellers tend to visit Ontario North and Metropolitan Toronto.

f) Activities Participated in at Ontario Main Destination, 1985

| Activities | In Per Cent Of Travellers From | |
| --- | --- | --- |
| | Quebec | Manitoba |
| Shopping | 45 | 46 |
| Visiting Friends/Relatives | 35 | 46 |
| Restaurant Dining | 31 | 47 |
| Sightseeing/Touring | 21 | 46 |
| Outdoor/Sporting | 20 | 39 |
| Personal | 17 | 9 |
| Historical Sites | 10 | 11 |
| Attractions/Zoos/Amusement Parks | 10 | 8 |
| Business/Convention | 8 | 12 |
| Exhibitions/Fairs/Special Events | * | 9 |

*Less than 8 per cent

Source: MTR, *Ontario Exit Survey, 1985.*

For Quebec travellers, the most popular activities participated in focused on general activities such as shopping, visiting friends/relatives, restaurant dining, etc.

The same activity pattern holds for Manitoba visitors.

g) Type of Accommodation Used, 1985

| Accommodation Used | In Per Cent Of Person-Nights | |
|---|---|---|
| | Quebec | Manitoba |
| Friends/relatives | 49 | 38 |
| Hotel/motor hotel | 7 | 24 |
| Motel | 7 | 5 |
| Resort lodge | * | 1 |
| Commercial cottage/cabin | 4 | 2 |
| Private cottage | 11 | 17 |
| Camping/trailer | 21 | 8 |
| Outfitter/outpost | — | — |
| Marina/unorganized anchorage | * | * |
| All other types | 2 | 4 |
| TOTAL | 101 | 99 |
| | | |
| Average length of stay (nights) in accommodation: | 4.04 | 5.94 |

Source: MTR, *Ontario Exit Survey, 1985.*

*\*Less than 0.5%*

About 50 per cent of Quebeckers person-nights were spent with friends/relatives, followed by 21 per cent camping. Manitobans also spent 38 per cent with friends/relatives, followed by hotels/motor hotels at 24 per cent.


3. TRAVEL TRENDS

*Leading Indicators*
The Canadian Conference Boards' survey of travel intentions indicates that 24% of Quebec residents plan to take a vacation in the next six months (as of the third quarter survey, 1987), which is up noticeably from the 14% recorded at the same time in 1986. There was no comparable change for the Prairies in the incidence planning to travel.

a) Main Purpose of Trip, By Province of Origin.

| | In Per Cent of Overnight Travellers | | | | | |
|---|---|---|---|---|---|---|
| | Quebec | | | Manitoba | | |
| | 1980 | 1984 | 1986 | 1980 | 1984 | 1986 |
| Visiting Friends/Relatives | 39.3 | 44.4 | 40.5 | 16.2 | 27.3 | 24.3 |
| Recreation/Pleasure | 26.5 | 29.7 | 24.4 | 58.6 | 51.9 | 51.1 |
| Personal Business | 4.6 | 4.9 | 4.4 | 4.2 | 3.3 | 4.0 |
| Business/Convention | 29.0 | 21.0 | 30.7 | 20.6 | 17.4 | 20.6 |
| TOTAL | 100.0 | 100.0 | 100.0 | 100.0 | 100.0 | 100.0 |

Source: Tourism Canada, *Canadian Travel Survey, 1980, 1984, 1986.*

It does not appear as if significant changes have occurred in the main purpose of overnight trips taken by both Quebec and Manitoba residents in Ontario during the 1980 to 1986 period.

b) <u>Benefits and Products Sought by Travel Orientation Typologies</u>

### Benefits

| | | |
|---|---|---|
| • Safe and secure.<br>• See as much as possible. | • Rest/relaxation.<br>• Many points of interest in short distance.<br>• Physically active.<br>• Meeting people with similar interests.<br>• Pampered/all needs attended to. | • Feel at home away from home.<br>• Being a family.<br>• VFR.<br>• Meet people with similar interests. |

### Products

| | | |
|---|---|---|
| • Place to stroll.<br>• Historic sites/parks.<br>• Live theatre/musicals/ festivals.<br>• Museums/art galleries.<br>• Big cities.<br>• Shopping.<br>• Elegant restaurants. | • Beautiful scenery/ undisturbed nature/ wilderness.<br>• Mountains.<br>• Natural/provincial parks.<br>• Reduced fares.<br>• Big cities.<br>• Smaller towns/villages.<br>• Inexpensive meals.<br>• Camping/hiking/ canoeing.<br>• Budget accommodation.<br>• Skiing/snowmobiling/ winter sports.<br>• Attend professional sporting events.<br>• Outdoor sports. | • Place to stroll.<br>• Wilderness/undisturbed nature.<br>• Smaller towns/villages. |

Denotes high future potential to Ontario. These types plan to travel to Ontario.

Source: MTR, *Ontario Tourism Attitude & Motivation Study, Montreal, 1987*.

c) <u>Potential Visitor Profile by Travel Orientation Typologies</u>*

| Total Traveller | Urban | Active/Passive | Middle-of-the-road |
|---|---|---|---|
| • Under 35 years | 34–54 years | | |
| • Post secondary/university education | | Post secondary | |
| • Professional/owners/managers & skilled labour | | Skilled labour | Skilled labour |
| • $30 000 or more | | Male | |

Source: MTR, *Ontario Tourism Attitude & Motivation Study, Montreal, 1987*

## 4. SITUATION ANALYSIS

*Quebec*

- Quebec has realized strong economic growth.

- Strong gain expected in 1988 in personal disposable income, along with positive outlook for consumer spending on services/travel.

- Growth rate in visitation to Ontario in 1988 should be moderate, but will lead other provinces' performance.

- Most of the tourism spending in Ontario accrues to overnight travellers. Metro Toronto and Eastern Ontario are destinations accounting for the highest share of expenditures.

- Shopping is the major activity participated in along with Visiting Friends and Relatives, and Restaurant Dining.

- The two major accommodation types are Staying with Friends/Relatives and Campgrounds.

- No significant changes have occurred from previous years in the main purpose of overnight trips.

# The Financial Implications of Marketing Practice

The objective of this appendix is to illustrate the financial implications of marketing decisions. Readers must recognize that marketing actions and results are measured quantitatively. It can be said that marketing actions directly affect the financial well-being of an organization.

This appendix presents some of the key financial areas for marketing managers: namely, the operating statement and the balance sheet (plus the various ratios obtained from these), and markups and markdowns.

## ⟩⟩⟩⟩ Operating Statement

One of the major financial statements of an organization is the operating statement, often referred to as an income statement or a profit-and-loss statement. It shows whether a business achieved its primary objective — earning a profit. A profit or net income is earned when revenues exceed expenses (losses occur when expenses exceed revenues).

Revenues are inflows of cash or other properties received in exchange for goods or services provided to customers. Expenses are goods and services consumed in operating a business. From the various figures included in an operating statement ratios are calculated and reviewed so that the financial performance of the firm can be assessed. For the purposes of analysis and control, the marketer can relate each component of an operating statement to sales. Operating statements are used for comparative purposes. For example, the ratios on the latest statement can be compared to past ratios or to planned ratios for a given period. The analysis of ratios indicates problems that management may try to correct through marketing and financial decisions.

# Important Components of the Operating Statement

*Sales*   The top line of any operating statement is sales; in the sample statement for KJT Enterprises, the top lines are gross sales and net sales. The level of sales is influenced by numerous marketing decisions, such as pricing strategy and the budget allocated to generate sales. Returns and allowances must be deducted from gross revenues, as net sales are the actual revenues received by the firm. Returns and allowances include returned merchandise (i.e., faulty or damaged products) and partial refunds or rebates to the customer. Since customer service is an important element of the marketing process, an organization should not view returns and allowances negatively. How product returns are handled has a direct impact on the level of customer satisfaction.

*Cost of Goods Sold*   Cost of goods sold in a manufacturing organization includes the costs of work in process and the inventory costs of raw materials and finished goods. In a retailing environment, cost of goods sold refers to the value of inventory offered for sale. Firms attempt to minimize the cost of goods sold wherever possible. The lower the cost of goods sold, the higher the gross profit.

*Operating Expenses*   These expenses are costs other than the merchandise costs and inventory costs cited in the cost-of-goods-sold explanation. Typically, operating expenses include marketing or selling expenses (advertising, sales expenses, and other related expenses), general expenses (rent, salaries, utilities, telephone, etc.) and interest expense. The objective of the firm is to control such expenses as much as possible, thereby improving profitability.

Let's assume that the operating statement KJT Enterprises, Inc. is as follows:

**OPERATING STATEMENT**
as at December 31, 19x1

|  | $ Value | % of Net Sales |
|---|---|---|
| Gross Sales | 820 000 | 102.5 |
| *Less:* Returns & Allowances | 20 000 | 2.5 |
| Net Sales | 800 000 | 100.0 |
| *Less:* Cost of Goods Sold | 480 000 | 60.0 |
| Gross Profit | 320 000 | 40.0 |
| *Less:* Operating Expenses | 200 000 | 25.0 |
| Net Profit before tax | 120 000 | 15.0 |
| Income Tax | 40 000 | 5.0 |
| Net Profit after tax | 80 000 | 10.0 |

# The Operating Statement and Ratio Analysis

These ratios are worthy of explanation:

1. *Gross Profit Percentage*   This percentage indicates the average profit margin on all merchandise sold during a period. Such information can be compared to past results, to a plan for the year, or to industry averages, if such information is known. If margins are too far above or below industry averages, it may indicate a cost problem or a pricing problem in the firm.

2. *Operating Expense Ratio* This ratio is needed to control individual expense categories and to evaluate performance. Ratios in this area have a direct relation to marketing activity, since marketing budgets are included in operating expenses. The challenge for managers is to minimize operating expenses (lower the ratio) while maximizing sales.

3. *Net Profit Percentage* This is a ratio that takes into account prices, costs, and all other expenses, and is, therefore, a reflection of the firm's bottom-line profit. Since the bottom-line profit is often used to determine the objectives of the firm, it is a figure scrutinized very closely by managers, shareholders, and potential investors. The net profit percentage clearly relates the quality of a firm's decisions to the revenue it generates. Decisions that reduce costs and expenses while maintaining or increasing sales revenue have a positive effect on the net profit percentage.

The ratios for the sample operating statement for KJT Enterprises are calculated by means of the following formula.

$$\text{Operating ratio} = \frac{\$ \text{ Value of Component}}{\text{Net Sales}} \times 100\%$$

Each ratio compares a particular component to net sales, the actual amount of revenue received by KJT Enterprises.

Therefore,

$$\text{Cost of Goods Sold} = \frac{\text{Cost of Goods Sold}}{\text{Net Sales}} \times 100\%$$

$$= \frac{480\ 000}{800\ 000} \times 100\%$$

$$= 60.0\%$$

$$\text{and, Gross Profit} = \frac{\text{Gross Profit}}{\text{Net Sales}} \times 100\%$$

$$= \frac{320\ 000}{800\ 000} \times 100\%$$

$$= 40\%$$

$$\text{and, Operating Expenses} = \frac{\text{Operating Expenses}}{\text{Net Sales}} \times 100\%$$

$$= \frac{200\ 000}{800\ 000} \times 100\%$$

$$= 25.0\%$$

$$\text{and, Net Profit before tax} = \frac{\text{Net Profit Before Tax}}{\text{Net Sales}} \times 100\%$$

$$= \frac{120\ 000}{800\ 000} \times 100\%$$

$$= 15.0\%$$

and, Net Profit

$$\text{after tax} = \frac{\text{Net Profit After Tax}}{\text{Net Sales}} \times 100\%$$

$$= \frac{80\ 000}{800\ 000} \times 100\%$$

$$= 10.0\%$$

KJT Enterprises would compare the above ratios to those of a plan or those of past years to determine if the financial results are satisfactory.

## ⟩⟩⟩⟩ *The Balance Sheet*

The purpose of a balance sheet is to show the financial position of a business on a specific date. The financial position is shown by listing the assets of the business, its liabilities or debts, and the equity of the owners. The balance sheet of an organization allows an organization to evaluate its earnings in a given period against the amount of money invested in the organization. Managers, therefore, assess ratios from both the profit-and-loss statement and the balance sheet.

Assume that the balance sheet for KJT Enterprises is as follows:

BALANCE SHEET
as at December 31, 19x1

| | |
|---|---:|
| **Assets** | |
| Cash | $200 000 |
| Accounts Receivable | 100 000 |
| Inventory | 100 000 |
| Facilities | 200 000 |
| Equipment | 50 000 |
| Total Assets | 650 000 |
| | |
| **Liabilities** | |
| Accounts Payable | 120 000 |
| Long-term liabilities | 100 000 |
| Total Liabilities | 220 000 |
| | |
| **Owner's Equity** | |
| Capital | 330 000 |
| Retained Earnings | 100 000 |
| Total Owner's Equity | 430 000 |
| | |
| Total Liabilities and Owner's Equity | 650 000 |

## The Balance Sheet and Ratio Analysis

*Return on Investment (ROI)*   This ratio compares earnings directly against investment in a particular year. Return on investment is calculated using the formula:

$$\text{ROI} = \frac{\text{Net Profit (Net Income)}}{\text{Average Assets}} \times 100\%$$

Therefore, following the sample statements of KJT Enterprises, Inc., the calculation would be:

$$ROI \quad = \quad \frac{120\ 000}{650\ 000}$$

$$= \quad 18.5\%$$

For the purposes of this calculation, the net profit before taxes was compared to the value of the firm's assets at the end of the period. Another way to look at the 18.5% ROI percentage is to say that for every dollar of assets held by the firm there was a return of 18.5 cents. These figures, like those derived from the operating statement, can be compared to past years, plans, or industry averages.

*Return on Equity (ROE)*   This ratio compares the firm's earnings directly with the amount of money an owner has invested in the business, an amount called *owner's equity*. Return on equity is calculated using the formula:

$$ROE \quad = \quad \frac{Net\ Profit}{Owner's\ Equity} \quad \times \quad 100\%$$

Therefore, using the sample statements of KJT Enterprises, Inc., the calculation would be:

$$ROE \quad = \quad \frac{120\ 000}{430\ 000} \quad \times \quad 100$$

$$= \quad 27.9\%$$

This figure can be used by the organization to assess the worth of the investment. If the return on equity is below that of potential returns on bank deposits and certificates, the firm would question the value of being in business. On the other hand, if the ratio is very high, effort could be put into growth and expansion plans for the business.

# ⟩⟩⟩⟩ *Markups and Markdowns*

Markups and markdowns are a form of financial analysis commonly used by members of a channel of distribution (wholesalers and retailers).

## Markups

A markup involves adding a predetermined amount to the cost of a product to determine a selling price. If a product costs $10.00 and sells for $14.00 the difference between the two prices is the markup. Markup is the difference between selling price and the cost. Markups can be expressed as:

$$Markup \quad = \quad Retail\ Price \quad - \quad Cost$$
$$or$$
$$Cost \quad + \quad Markup \quad = \quad Retail\ Price$$

Markups should be high enough to cover operating expenses and desired profit. The percentage markup can be computed in two ways (i.e., by markup on cost or by markup on sales).

The formula for calculating markups are as follows:

$$\text{Markup (MU) on Cost} = \frac{\text{Dollar Markup}}{\text{Purchase Cost}} \times 100\%$$

$$\text{Markup (MU) on Sales} = \frac{\text{Dollar Markup}}{\text{Selling Price}} \times 100\%$$

To illustrate these formulae, let's assume the following figures. The product has a cost of $200.00 and the desired profit is $80.00. Therefore,

$$\text{Markup (MU) on Cost} = \frac{80}{200} \times 100\%$$

$$= 40\%$$

$$\text{and, Markup (MU) on Sales} = \frac{80}{280} \times 100\%$$

$$= 28.6\%$$

Both of these figures are used in many ways by wholesalers and retailers. Markup on cost is a method of setting prices. In the example above, the cost was $200.00 and the desired markup was $80.00, resulting in a selling price of $280.00.

## Markdowns

A markdown refers to a downward adjustment in selling price. For example, if a $30.00 jacket is marked down $5.00, the new selling price is $25.00. Retailers express the markdown as a percent of the new selling price. To compute the markdown percent, the following formula is used:

$$\frac{\text{Markdown}}{\text{New Selling Price}} = \text{Markdown Percentage}$$

$$\frac{\$ \ 5.00}{25.00} = 20\%$$

When a retailer offers a price reduction (e.g., for an item on sale), the markdown is expressed as a percentage of the original selling price for the consumer's benefit. The markdown formula in this case would be:

$$\frac{\text{Markdown}}{\text{Old Selling Price}} = \text{Markdown Percentage}$$

$$\frac{\$ \ 5.00}{30.00} = 16.66\%$$

Internally, the markdown is usually based on a net sales figure rather than the original sales figure. To illustrate the offset of markdowns on a larger scale, consider an example where the total value of the markdowns is $60 000. The calculation for markdown would be as follows:

$$\text{Markdown percentage} = \frac{\text{Markdown on \$}}{\text{Net Sales}} \times 100\%$$

Therefore, if net sales are $240 000 and the markdown in dollars is $60 000, the calculation would be:

$$\text{Markdown percentage} = \frac{60\ 000}{240\ 000} \times 100\%$$

$$= 25\%$$

In the example, the markdown represents 25 percent of net sales. Markdowns are frequently used by wholesalers and retailers to promote sales items, to reduce inventories of certain goods, or to balance out sales volume over a period. The results of such marketing decisions can be viewed in light of previous years' activities.

# Cases

# ❱ ❱ ❱ ❱ *1. Dow Chemical Canada Inc.*

In the marketplace of today, business organizations are very conscious of the impact their activities have on the environment. As consumers and businesses move towards the next century, being environmentally concerned is an "in" trait. However, the managing of environmental issues is not a simple task because the solutions for one environmental issue can cause problems in other environmental areas. This is a situation Dow Chemical faces in the marketing of Styrofoam brand insulation.

As a company, Dow is fully committed to protecting the environment. This commitment is a key element of its corporate values, and the reason for its position as a responsible member of the Canadian Chemical Association. The company recognizes the importance of the environmental lobby in Canada, but expresses deep concern for its focus on solutions that, while practical and necessary, may not consider the impact on other environmental issues. Similar to many other large organizations and consumers, Dow feels there is a strong need to address the issue of fossil-fuel consumption as well as greenhouse gas (i.e., global warming). One way to increase energy conservation is to improve insulation in homes and other buildings. Styrofoam, a trademark of Dow, is one of the polystyrene foam insulation products that have proven to be effective insulators. Blue in colour, the product is commonly seen during the construction stage of new homes or commercial buildings across the country. However, the manufacture of Styrofoam includes CFCs (chlorofluorocarbons), which, an internationally funded study has concluded, contribute to the depletion of the ozone layer, a cause of global warming. It would seem that while CFCs help resolve one environmental problem by conserving energy, they create another problem by increasing the possibility of a greenhouse effect.

At a meeting of major free world countries in Montreal in 1987, a draft agreement was struck that would reduce and ultimately eliminate the use of CFCs by the year 2000. Known as the Montreal Protocol on Substances that Deplete the Ozone Layer, the agreement was signed by 33 countries in 1989. Dow is a major user of CFCs in the manufacture of Styrofoam brand insulation products. CFCs are part of the foaming system that improves the plastic's natural thermal insulation characteristics. Ironically, CFCs were the chosen material in the sixties, as they helped solve some environmental issues of that era, namely flammability and toxicity. Styrofoam is non-flammable and non-toxic.

As early as the 1970s, when the ozone depletion issue surfaced, Dow began investigating alternative foaming systems. Its research goal was to find a commercially available substitute material that would be as effective in providing insulation properties as its current Styrofoam product is. After much research and development, a substitute product was ready for testing in 1987.

Prior to taking action, Dow had to answer two questions. First, did Styrofoam have a long-term value in the marketplace, and, second, did the company have the capability to change? The company concluded that Styrofoam was a viable product since it encouraged fuel conservation. Also, the company could move immediately on the change, but it recognized that this solution was only an interim one. Further research and development was required to find a long-term solution.

In June 1988, Dow announced that CFCs would be eliminated from Styrofoam by the end of 1989. Three of its chemical plants would be converted to accommodate the manufacture of Styrofoam with new replacement materials. The change was received positively by Environment Canada, but Dow had some reservation about its competitiveness. If competitors delayed in converting to a similar process, or, even worse, did not convert, then Dow would suffer a cost disadvantage. Insulation is a competitive market, and since substitute products used in the new Styrofoam product are significantly more expensive than CFCs, Dow would penalize itself financially and lose market share for being a good corporate citizen. To further complicate the situation, consumers have indicated that they will only pay more for environmentally friendly products where there are no choices.

To avoid this situation, Dow presented Environment Canada with a "retirement option." Under this plan, any CFCs not used by Dow due to its conversion would be taken off the market (i.e., made unavailable to other firms). This would keep supply and demand in balance and keep up the price of competitive insulation products for which CFCs were still used. Dow feels that such action is in line with the federal government's objective of reducing CFC consumption, but, as of yet, the plan has not been included in any regulations brought forth by the government.

To further ensure that the other firms convert, Dow, as of 1988, has offered its patented process and alternate foaming agent technology to other polystyrene insulation manufacturers through a licensing agreement. These organizations have not taken advantage of this option yet.

## 〉〉〉〉 QUESTIONS

1. What is the major problem that Dow faces?
2. Should the government intercede and force other companies to follow Dow's leadership? If so, what action might the government take?
3. If Dow's perception of the competitive situation is correct, should it proceed with the conversion? Defend your position.
4. Should Dow advertise the fact that it markets a product free of CFCs?
5. What is your opinion of Dow's "retirement option"?

Adapted from Daniel Carruthers, "Dow's environmental high-wire act", *Marketing*, September 18, 1989, pp.B4,B12.

# ❯❯❯❯ *2. Spinning Wheels: The Big Three*

In the mid-1980s, the Canadian automobile industry successfully used a variety of price incentives to reduce inventories in the month of August, a period when car manufacturers and dealers prepare for the launch of new models for the next year. These incentive programs included cash rebates, low-interest financing, and free option packages.

By 1989, price incentives had lost their impact. All manufacturers were offering incentives in what appeared to be a useless scramble to build market share in a stagnant market. According to Bill Pochiluk, president of Autofacts Inc., an industry research firm, "incentives are so entrenched they produce 40 percent less business in the U.S. and 20 percent less in Canada than they did in the mid-1980s." Despite this, the market is simply too competitive for one company to give up price incentives on its own, and a follow-the-leader approach has been adopted by the big three domestic auto makers. None of the Big Three — General Motors, Ford, or Chrysler — dares to pull out of the discounting battle for fear of losing market share.

In 1989, incentives were offered in a bewildering variety that probably confused consumers that were comparative shopping. Among the more popular incentives were rebates in the range of $500 to $2 000 depending on the make, model, and base price of the car. Another incentive was discount financing as low as 6.9% and as high as 9.9%, a rate still well below financing rates offered by banks and trust companies. Finally, all manufacturers offered a variety of option packages, including free air conditioning and automatic transmissions, with certain models. Although these incentive programs were common in the industry in 1989, their effect was in question. At the end of the first five months, total car sales in the industry were down 3.9 percent from sales during the same period a year earlier. Truck sales, a much smaller segment, were only up 3.6 percent. The truck segment was also subjected to the price incentive strategy. With sales results like these, the value and impact of incentive programs has to be questioned.

According to Paul Sullivan, director of Business Strategy at General Motors of Canada Ltd., "incentives on their own will not increase the size of the total market, but they certainly could have the potential for moving it from one car company to another." Patrick Smorra, Chrysler Canada's vice-president of Marketing also adds that "our products are not priced adequately to recover the costs of incentives . . . so in fact it's cutting into our profitability." Industry analysts, however, doubt this claim. They estimate that the cost of incentives is US $600 per vehicle in the U.S. and that these costs are built into the base price of the automobiles. According to Smorra, the incentives add to short-term variable costs, so profits are reduced, but this money will be gained back in the longer term. In effect, consumers who save today will pay tomorrow if the automobile companies are to stay afloat financially.

The outlook for the industry is gloomy. It was estimated that in 1990 the North American-produced car supply would exceed demand by 2.2 million vehicles. Consequently, price incentives will probably remain the preferred marketing tactic of the industry in its bid to stimulate car purchases by consumers.

>>>> QUESTIONS

1. What is the real problem facing the Canadian automobile industry?
2. Are price incentives such as those mentioned in this case the best way to remedy the problem?
3. What environmental factors are probably affecting the demand for automobiles?
4. What effect have price incentives had on consumer behaviour?
5. Should other elements of the marketing mix be given priority over pricing incentives? If so, what do you recommend?

Adapted from Mark Hallman, "Automakers spin wheels in endless incentives race", *Financial Post*, June 19, 1989, pp.1,4.

# ❯ ❯ ❯ ❯ *3. Imperial Tobacco*

When Bill C-51, the Tobacco Products Control Act, came into effect on January 1, 1989, all brand name sponsorships by tobacco products stopped. Advertising for cigarette brands in magazines and newspapers also stopped, and tougher new health warnings on packaging and any remaining form of advertising began. Advertising on outdoor billboards and on point-of-purchase material was to be phased out gradually over a three-year period, from 1989 to 1991. There is controvery surrounding the new laws governing the advertising of tobacco and the prospect of banning the advertising of tobacco products. On one side are organizations such as the Canadian Cancer Society and the Non-Smokers Rights Association, which applaud Bill C-51. On the other side are the tobacco growers and manufacturers such as Imperial Tobacco and Rothmans Benson & Hedges, which find the new laws an infringement of their rights. These companies are good corporate citizens and pay large sums in taxes to governments. As such, they feel that they should not lose the right to advertise a product legally sold in Canada. Nonetheless, the law is the law, and all companies must conform to the law.

In terms of sponsorships, Bill C-51 stated that all brand sponsorships would be frozen at 1987 spending levels and that the use of brand names could only continue until the existing contracts expired with the event organizers. New or renewed sponsorship agreements cannot use brand names. Instead, corporate names could be used. In other words, a well-known event such as the Player's Tennis challenge would become the Imperial Tobacco Challenge.

The reaction of Don Brown, the vice-president of marketing for Imperial Tobacco was, "we're going to look into every avenue to provide support for events and to continue to sponsor things. One way to find out what opportunities exist is to sponsor under corporate names like the du Maurier Company or the Player's Company."[1] Such a strategy by Imperial Tobacco has been perceived by critics of the tobacco industry as being in violation of the spirit of the law.

Soon after the new law came into effect, Imperial Tobacco did proceed with the structuring of new corporate entities to take advantage of gaps that existed in the government's Tobacco Products Control Act. To run sponsorships no longer allowed under brand names, Imperial established du Maurier Limited, Player's Limited, and Matinée Limited. Officials of the Tobacco Products Unit of Health and Welfare Canada were very quick to say that they thought this move violated the spirit of the law, and probably the letter of the law. According to Don Sweanor, the legal counsel for the Non-Smokers Rights Association, this action demonstrated that the cigarette industry will "use every loophole it can" to get around the law.[2]

The industry interpretation of the law was quite different. Their position was that the intent of the law was not to stop sponsorships. In effect, the law allowed sponsorships if they were promoted under corporate names. Thus all its new sponsorships would be under new corporate names. The 1989 tennis championships held in Toronto were promoted as the 1989 Player's Ltd. Challenge Tennis Championships. In accordance with the law, Imperial Tobacco also continued with two brand sponsorships contracted prior to the 1989 deadline. These were the du Maurier Classic, a ladies professional golf tour event, and the du Maurier International, an equestrian event. Imperial Tobacco remains very active in the sponsorship field and supports many cultural and sporting events. Its investment in sponsorships on an annual basis is estimated to be $10 million.[3]

## ⟩⟩⟩⟩ QUESTIONS

1. Is it right to ban advertising for products that are produced and marketed legally in Canada? What are your views on this issue?
2. Are the actions taken by Imperial Tobacco ethical in view of the intent of Bill C-51? What is your opinion of Imperial's new marketing strategies?

## ⟩⟩⟩⟩ REFERENCES

1. "Imperial Looks to Skirt Tobacco Advertising Ban", *Marketing*, April 29, 1989, p.3.
2. "Imperial Exploits Gap in Ad Ban", *Marketing*, April 13, 1989, pp.1,4.
3. "Tobacco Sponsorship Still Alive", *Marketing*, April 3, 1989, p.2.

# 〉 〉 〉 〉 *4. Foster Grant Sunglasses*

Foster Grant is one of the best-known names in the global market for sunglasses. Despite the high level of awareness and acceptance of the product by the mass market of sunglass wearers, the Foster Grant Corporation has fallen upon hard times. As of 1988, Foster Grant's market share of the mass market in North America had fallen as low as 15 percent, down considerably from a high of 30 percent in 1983.

Other manufacturers, including Bausch & Lomb of the United States, Vuarnet of France, and Optyl of Austria, have enjoyed booming business throughout the 1980s, taking market share away from Foster Grant. These companies have specialized in the expensive and more stylish segment of the sunglasses market. Certain occurrences contributed to the growth of these specialized brands. The appearance in 1980 of the *Blues Brothers* with John Belushi and Dan Aykroyd, and then of *Risky Business* with Tom Cruise, created a high demand for Bausch & Lomb's Wayfarer sunglasses. Prior to 1980 the company sold less than 10 000 pairs of Wayfarer glasses a year, but in the early eighties the volume sold had increased to millions of pairs per year.

Practical concerns also helped spur growth in the market. Consumers' concerns about exposure to ultraviolet light and blue light, which cause eye damage, had to be addressed by the manufacturers of sunglasses. It is now common for manufacturers to indicate the level of protection their sunglasses provide. Concerns for health have led a segment of the market to spend more on sunglasses with sophisticated lenses. Foster Grant, however, does not concentrate on this segment. Lens manufacturers such as Pilkington of Britain and Corning of the United States are investing much more than Foster Grant in research and development to meet the demand for better lenses.

The market for sunglasses is divided into two price segments: those selling for less than $30.00 and those selling for more than $30.00. Sales growth is quite different in each segment, as indicated by the following figures:

|  | U.S. Dollar Sales (in millions) | | |
|---|---|---|---|
|  | *1983* | *1988* | *Growth* |
| Less than $30.00 | $570 | $742 | + 30% |
| More than $30.00 | 231 | 696 | +200 |

According to Imperial Optical, one of Canada's largest makers of sunglasses, these sales trends hold true in Canada, where the strongest growth area by far is in the making or the importing of "designer" sunglasses that range in price from $100.00 to $500.00.

To meet demand for this segment, Imperial Optical imports and distributes designer sunglasses from France, Italy, and the United States. Among domestic manufacturers, the most successful have, in the mid to late 1980s, also concentrated on more expensive product lines. While Foster Grant has been sliding, manufacturers such as Bausch & Lomb, Tropi-Cal, and Riva have increased market share. As well, European manufacturers anxious to have a piece of the North American pie have expanded rapidly by establishing new distribution networks. Vuarnet from France and Luxottica and Safilo from Italy have followed this path.

While the designer segment is the fastest growing and most profitable segment, mass market manufacturers such as Foster Grant have struggled in the face of slower growth and intense competition from companies in Hong Kong, Taiwan, and the Philippines. Products from these countries sell for as low as $3.00 to $5.00 in drug stores, compared to Foster Grant's, which are priced in the $12.00 to $18.00 range.

### ⟩⟩⟩ QUESTIONS

1. What are the problems that the Foster Grant Corporation faces?
2. What factors have contributed to the growth in the designer segment of the sunglasses market? Do you think this trend will continue?
3. What marketing strategies would you recommend that Foster Grant adopt in order to reestablish its position in the sunglasses market?

Adapted from Alice Rawsthorn, "Cheap sunglasses left in the shade", *Financial Post*, August 14, 1989, pp.1,4.

# ⟩ ⟩ ⟩ ⟩ *5. The Canadian Distilling Industry*

Four companies control approximately 75 percent of the total Canadian hard liquor production, a market estimated to be worth $3.1 billion in consumer dollar sales. In the early 1980s it was common to see these companies — Seagram's, Gilbey's, Hiram-Walker, and Corby's — advertising their respective brands of liquor by associating them with lifestyles. The imagery suited the market at the time. These strategies had changed by the end of the decade, when liquor advertising became more focused on the product than on the customer. The emphasis shifted to the quality or smoothness of the brand. This development shows that attitudes are changing among drinkers.

The biggest change is that people are drinking less. According to Tim Woods of the Association of Canadian Distillers, "people just aren't drinking as much as they used to." Industry officials contend that the decrease in consumption is due to the higher taxes imposed by governments and to changing taste preferences among Canadian drinkers. While overall consumption is down, with spirits showing the greatest decline, followed by beer, Canadians have developed a taste for wine and spirit-based coolers. The movement is towards lighter products with less alcohol content.

Statistics Canada figures for the year ending March 31, 1989 illustrate the changing habits of Canadian drinkers:

|  | 1980 | 1988 |
|---|---|---|
| Amount Spent on Alcohol per Capita | $225 | $450 |
| Consumption per Capita: |  |  |
| Beer | 112.6 ℓ | 104.1 ℓ |
| Wine | 9.5 ℓ | 12.8 ℓ |
| Spirits | 10.8 ℓ | 7.9 ℓ |

While the amount of alcohol consumed per capita shows a decline, for the first time since 1982, 1988 did show sales increases in all three types of alcohol beverages: spirits, wine, and beer. It seems that while Canadians who do drink are drinking less, more people are drinking than ever before. The growth also came from a new type of product. The volume of spirits sold in Canada increased by 1 percent in 1988. The increase was due to a booming demand for spirit-based coolers, rather than a growth in the sales of straight spirits. Coolers represent a real growth segment in an otherwise dwindling market. In 1988, sales of coolers reached 6.8 million litres compared to only 2.2 million litres in 1987. In the traditional spirits segment, on the other hand, sales continue to fall as indicated by the following:

| | Sales Volume in Litres (in millions) | |
| --- | --- | --- |
| | 1980 | 1988 |
| Rye | 76.0 | 51.0 |
| Rum | 28.0 | 25.0 |
| Vodka | 21.0 | 21.5 |

These trends in consumption are expected to continue; hard liquor sales will decline modestly each year, and any growth that does occur will be marginal at best. All Canadian liquor companies face the same situation and must identify new opportunities and marketing strategies to keep their bottom lines healthy.

❭❭❭❭ QUESTIONS

1. What factors are contributing to the growth trends in the liquor industry?
2. Given the trends in the marketplace, what strategies would you recommend to a company like Seagram's or Gilbey's?
3. Will free trade have a positive or negative influence on the marketing activities of Canadian liquor producers? Explain your viewpoint.

Adapted from Philip Demont, "It's enough to drive you to . . .", *Financial Times of Canada*, April 10, 1989, pp.12–13, and "Canadians are drinking less", *Whig-Standard*, September 5, 1989, p.18.

# ❯ ❯ ❯ ❯ *6. Rogers Communications Inc. and Videotron Ltée*

Two of the key players in Canada's cable television industry are concerned about growth prospects. Rogers Communications Inc. of Toronto and Videotron Ltée of Montreal are evaluating different strategies in hopes of producing financial growth for their companies. Industry analysts estimate that competing companies will invest as much as $1 billion by 1995 in new technology to serve new market segments and thus offset the slower growth predicted for existing business.

The existing business of cable companies is comprised of basic cable service, which includes commercial channels, cable channels, and specialty channels. Specialty channels include networks such as MuchMusic, The Sports Network (TSN), and the Youth channel (YTV). A look back at the growth of cable television reveals that consumers first subscribed to the service to receive a clearer signal from the large U.S. networks (NBC, CBS, and ABC). In the seventies and early eighties, cable companies added stations to their service at an alarming rate. In Toronto, for example, as many as 50 stations are available, and there is demand for even more. Most often, consumers subscribe to the basic service and then purchase a package of specialty channels in accordance with their interests. Among these options are First Choice (movies), MuchMusic (rock videos), and The Nashville Network (country music).

The market leader in Canada is Rogers Cablesystems, which controls 24 percent of the market. Rogers is followed by Videotron Ltée., Maclean Hunter, and Shaw Cablesystems. The number of subscribers to each company is as follows:

| Company | Subscribers (in thousands) | Markets |
|---------|---------------------------|---------|
| Rogers Cablesystems | 1 500 | Toronto, Vancouver |
| Videotron Ltée | 927 | Quebec |
| Maclean Hunter | 440 | Southern Ontario |
| Shaw Cablesystems | 367 | Alberta, Nova Scotia and British Columbia |
| Cablecasting | 298 | Calgary, Toronto |

The penetration rate of cable television is of concern to cable companies, since penetration is now so high that pursuing further opportunities has become increasingly difficult. As of 1988, the national penetration rate was 67 percent, and in major urban markets it was even higher: Vancouver (91 percent), Toronto (85 percent), Montreal (74 percent), Calgary and Edmonton (72 percent) and Winnipeg (70 percent)[1]. A further indication of how the Canadian cable television market is developing is the fact that Canada is the second most cabled country in the world. Only Belgium exceeds Canada in terms of penetration. In a market where relatively few companies maintain control and the rate of penetration is so high, it is difficult for companies to grow through existing business.

To grow in this situation, Rogers has adopted a strategy whereby it uses its network to transmit data for business and to enter the long distance market as a competitor to

Bell Canada. That the company might follow this course was suggested when Rogers Communications Inc. purchased a 40 percent interest in CNCP Telecommunications in April of 1988. Rogers is also investing heavily in the development of fibre-optic technology. Fibre optics is a hair-thin glass strand along which pulses of laser light are capable of carrying extraordinary amounts of information. The corporation will concentrate on using fibre optics in Toronto initially and then use it in Vancouver. This new technology will replace the present system of transmitting television signals by copper cable and by microwave. The company estimates that by the year 2000 fibre-optic cables will reach Canadian households directly, a circumstance that will turn Rogers into a long distance telephone company. To achieve this goal, Rogers is now recruiting smaller cable companies to form Cablecom Canada, a consortium that would use non-regulated portions of its cable service to transmit data.

In contrast, Videotron Ltée. is investing in the development of interactive television, a technology that allows viewers to actively participate in the programs. Called "Videoway", the system consists of a small box connected to the television set. It offers access to a variety of data banks, electronic mail, video games, and educational programs. For the sports fan, different camera angles are possible on command, as are instant replays. Videotron estimates that 50 percent of its revenue will be generated by Videoway within ten years.

## 〉〉〉 QUESTIONS

1. Identify the type of marketing strategies that Rogers and Videotron are considering? What risks can you identify in these strategies?
2. In view of the information in the case, would you say there are any other marketing strategies worth pursuing? If so, which?
3. If Rogers does enter the long distance market, what strategies and actions will be necessary to motivate personal and business customers to use their service? Can you anticipate any reaction from Bell Canada?

Adapted from Jaimie Hubbard, "Cable-TV firms seeking to conquer rich new worlds", *Financial Post*, September 16, 1989, pp.1,4.

## 〉〉〉 REFERENCES

1. *The Canadian Media Distributors' Council Media Digest*, 1988–89, pp.21–22.

# ❱❱❱❱ *7. Canadian Produce Corporation: The Lichee Fruit Decision*

Sharon Nelson let out a big sigh, placed the letter she had just read on the corner of her desk, and wondered what she could do about the writer's problems. Sharon's position as national sales manager of Canadian Produce Corporation gave her a say in product decisions, but she was only one in a team of three people who made the final choices of what would be offered. Fruits and vegetables were among the products sold by the company to retail food stores across Canada. The letter from Mr. Wang was only one of a number of similar letters Canadian Produce had received during the past year from various people of diverse ethnic backgrounds.

Mr. Wang, an engineering student from Guang Tong province in the People's Republic of China, was voicing frustration with his inability to buy lichee fruit in the Kingston, Ontario area. Lichee fruit is a sweet Chinese delicacy sold in large quantities during the summer months in China. A typical lichee fruit looks like a small, yellow chestnut and is eaten after the scaly outer skin is peeled off, much as if it were an orange. In China, India, and the Philippines, hundreds of millions of dollars worth of the fruit is sold, and some villages even hold festivals celebrating it, much like the wine festivals of Europe. In some Chinese provinces, private farms permit customers to pick their own lichee fruit, a custom similar to the Canadian custom of strawberry picking.

Sharon appreciated that language and culture have a great influence on the Canadian marketplace. She realized that more than one quarter of Canada's total population comes from a French ethnic background and has its own distinct culture and lifstyle.

Another quarter of the population consists of people with neither an English nor a French ethnic background. These people have a diverse cultural heritage, many coming from such countries as Italy, Germany, Japan, the Ukraine, Africa, the West Indies, and China. Sharon understood that some of Canada's most successful marketers were those who were taking steps to recognize the truly unique character of the nation's diverse cultural mosaic. Whereas the practice in the United States is to assimilate cultural minorities as rapidly as possible, in Canada the practice has been to encourage cultural diversity and to view it as a positive force for national development. However, the wide range of ethnic backgrounds in Canada puts tremendous pressure on marketers to satisfy diverse needs.

Canadian Produce had largely ignored the various ethnic markets because business in its traditional markets had been strong during its first ten years in business. Sharon reflected on Wang Shang Yu's letter and wondered if Canadian Produce should consider supplementing its product mix of traditional fruits and vegetables such as oranges, apples, bananas, corn, carrots, and so on. The firm had been under a fair bit of pressure from competition recently, so Sharon had severe reservations about whether the management committee would change the product mix.

〉〉〉 QUESTIONS

1. Do you feel Canadian Produce should seriously consider Wang Shang Yu's request and offer lichee fruit in the Canadian market? Why or why not?

2. What type of research would have to be undertaken to prove that a viable market opportunity exists?

3. Identify some of the significant difficulties Canadian Produce might encounter in attempting to add lichee fruit to its product mix.

Case prepared by Gerald B. McCready, Professor of Marketing, St. Lawrence College.

# 〉 〉 〉 〉 *8. Jaftek Ventures Inc.*

Jaftek Ventures Inc. is a small Calgary-based company that claims it will revolutionize the dental floss market, worth $150 million worldwide. Through its research subsidiary, Princeton Pharmaceuticals Inc. of Patterson, New Jersey, Jaftek is developing a medicated, flavoured floss that contains stannous fluoride. This compound kills microbes that cause gum diseases such as gingivitis. Other flosses on the market, a market dominated by Johnson & Johnson, only cleanse the teeth to prevent plaque build up and to fight tooth decay.

Stannous fluoride is not new in the market for dental products. It was popularized by numerous toothpaste brands in the 1970s, but in 1980 was removed from these products because the compound broke down quickly and lost its effectiveness. Jaftek and Princeton Pharmaceuticals now claim, however, that they can stabilize stannous fluoride so that such products as dental flosses, mouth sprays and rinses can be impregnated with it. The company is aiming to achieve over-the-counter sales in drug stores and supermarkets within the next three years.

Unfortunately, Jaftek is not alone on this project. Much larger companies, already established in similar product categories, are clamouring for a technological breakthrough as well. For this reason, Jaftek is not keeping its product a secret. It would consider participating in some kind of joint venture or licensing agreement; it would even consider selling its technology to companies such as Procter & Gamble, Colgate-Palmolive, or Warner-Lambert, all market leaders in many personal-hygiene product categories. The company is busy contemplating its options for the next few years and is not certain which direction to pursue.

〉〉〉 QUESTIONS

1. Is a dental floss containing stannous fluoride unique enough to be successful on the market?

2. What obstacles will Jaftek face if it decides to market the product on its own?
3. What marketing strategies and actions would you recommend to Jaftek Inc. as it enters this market? Consider the fact that it is a small company when developing your strategies.
4. Should Jaftek pursue agreements and partnerships with the much larger and established companies in the market?

# 》 》 》 》 *9. Porsche*

Porsche, Jaguar, Audi, BMW, Saab, Mercedes — are these the cars of the future or the cars of the past? Conflicting information on the direction the luxury car segment is taking is causing a stir in the automobile industry. The car market is segmented on the basis of price, and up until 1986 the fastest-growing segment of the market was the luxury segment. Generally speaking, the minimum sticker price for a true luxury car is $40 000. In Canada, this luxury segment accounts for 40 000 units in sales, spread across major names such as Porsche, BMW, and Jaguar, and the market is expected to remain strong through the early 1990s.

Who buys these expensive cars? Industry research shows luxury car buyers to be classic movers and shakers. Jaguar, for example, which sells about 2 000 cars a year in Canada, affirms that 80 percent of its buyers are male, 45 to 50 years of age, and earning $250 000 a year. That's affluence!

British and European automakers hold high expectations for the North American market but are disturbed by recent sales trends in the United States. Canada, a much smaller market, is generally healthier in terms of sales. Sir John Egan, the Chairman of Jaguar PLC of Great Britain, is very optimistic about Canada, stating that "the number of people getting into their prime Jaguar-buying years is growing by 10 to 15 percent per annum." It would appear that demographic shifts are on the side of Jaguar and other luxury automobiles.

Actual volume sales in the market suggest something different. Apparently, this affluent group of consumers who have been known to purchase Audis, BMWs, Jaguars and Mercedes are now spending their money elsewhere. These automakers and others in the same market segment are on the latest list of losers in the North American car market. Each of these automakers has experienced a serious decline in sales between 1986 and 1989. Commenting on the reasons for the decline, a Volvo executive stated, "Being showy with your car is no longer in." Perhaps this comment is indicative of recent consumer behaviour.

Porsche is very concerned about its North American operations, since its market has all but disappeared. Porsche has embarked on numerous cost-cutting programs in its German factories, and layed off 46 people from its sales and distribution network in the United States. The sales of Porsche, once considered the "king of sports car hill", have slipped at a staggering rate in the United States. Volume in 1986 was 30 000 units and in 1988, 15 000 units. Projections for 1989, another bad year, were as low as 7 500 units. With a revised marketing strategy, Porsche's goal is to level off at 10 000 to 11 000 units a year in the U.S. market. This decline in volume has forced Porsche to re-evaluate its role in the North American market. It could enter the fray of North American marketing hype and start using cash rebates, discount financing, and free accessories as a means of attracting customers, or it could remain as a small, "exclusive" car producer — exclusive in price and quality.

Industry analysts link the decline to the inroads made by Japanese automakers. The successes of the Honda Accura and Toyota Lexus have had a negative impact on the sale of European-made cars in North America. The Japanese cars are less expensive, but offer the quality and image that is attractive to the affluent car buyer. With the introduction in 1991 of the top-of-the-line Infiniti by Nissan of Japan, the luxury car market becomes even more crowded. From Europe, Volvo is introducing a $50 000 coupe and Audi a $60 000 sedan.

The effect of these introductions is unpredictable, given the changing demographics and recent buyer behaviour. Some industry executives think these new cars will attract additional buyers and expand the luxury market segment. Others see the pie being resliced at the expense of existing European cars. Regardless, the greater the force from Japan, the greater the need for European automakers to be more cost-efficient in production and marketing.

## >>>> QUESTIONS

1. Could the luxury car segment rebound under these circumstances or are the trends toward disaster likely to persist? Why?

2. Apart from Japanese competition, what other environmental or behavioural factors are, in your view, affecting volume trends in the luxury car segment?

3. Develop a consumer profile for what you perceive to be the typical Porsche buyer. Your profile should include demographic, psychographic, and geographic variables.

4. What recommendations do you have for Porsche in terms of product, price and promotion strategy? Should they change their positioning strategy in the North American market?

5. Do you think that the luxury car segment will expand or that the existing market will be divided among more competitors if new models enter the market? Defend your position.

Adapted from James Risen, "Sagging sales make European luxury car losers in the U.S.", *Toronto Star*, September 16, 1989, p.G14., and John Schreiner, "Luxury cars picking up speed", *Financial Post*, July 10, 1989, p.8.

# ❯ ❯ ❯ ❯ *10. Lepage's Canada Limited*

In the glue industry, Lepage's is a firmly established leader. Recognition of Lepage's as a glue producer is extremely high. In fact, a research survey conducted in January of 1989 revealed that recognition of Lepage's glue was at 100 percent. Among their competitive rivals, Krazy Glue was second with 97 percent recognition, and Elmer's third with 64 percent recognition.

Given such recognition for a line of highly specialized products, one would expect Lepage's sales to be booming, and that the manufacturer, the retailers carrying the product, and the consumers would be content with the state of affairs in the marketplace. Quite the contrary, however, is the situation, according to Laird Robertson, the product manager responsible for Lepage's consumer glue lines. Robertson feels there are numerous problems associated with the marketing and displaying of glue products. Among his concerns are the following:

1. *Consumer Confusion and Loyalty*  It seems that consumers examine the glues available in stores but walk away, frustrated, from the section or displays. There are too many alternatives within a product line to choose from, and consumers can't easily determine the best product for the job. It is common for a consumer to postpone purchase or simply to decide not to repair the item.

2. *Disappointment and Consumer Dollars Wasted*  The consumer buys the wrong glue for the job. Lepage's uses a system of picture applications on the packages. Those pictures that do appear are confusing, and many applications are not communicated due to lack of space. This creates confusion in the customer's mind.

3. *Higher Manufacturing and Marketing Costs*  Lepage's has a total of 30 items in its product line. A source of confusion for consumers, this number also means smaller production runs and inefficient distribution, which add to the cost structure of each item.

4. *Poor Merchandising*  Shelf space in retail stores is limited in the first place, and because glue is a low-interest item, it is not a focus of display activity. It is, however, the type of product people will search for when needed. Glue is generally a regular stock item, space permitting, in the general supplies section of a retail store. Drug stores, book and stationery goods stores, discount department stores, and department stores are the types of stores that carry the Lepage's line of products.

Lepage's has helped create its own problems. Product manager Robertson states that "the industry puts out products faster than anybody can [understand], and all we've managed to do is cover the shelves with stuff that's become confusing and overwhelming."

Since there is a general lack of understanding about what each product will do, consumers must go to the trouble of educating themselves each time they contemplate a glue purchase.

>>>> QUESTIONS

1. Lepage's is facing two key problems. Can you identify what these problems are?
2. What potential actions do you recommend to Lepage's to overcome these problems? Justify your recommendations.

Adapted from Ken Riddell, "Less stock, more loyalty", *Marketing*, September 18, 1989, pp.B1,B5.

# 〉 〉 〉 〉 *11. Steel Desk Corporation*

Founded in the early 1900s, the Steel Desk Corporation (SDC) long enjoyed an enviable reputation as one of Canada's leading producers and marketers of high quality office furnishings. The company held a 24 percent share of the Canadian market and prided itself on outstanding relations with its broad network of dealers, agents, and distributors. Business organizations that purchase their furnishings have expressed a high level of satisfaction with the quality of the company's products.

As part of the company's plans for the 1990s, work had progressed on the development of a new "state of the art" line of furniture specifically designed to accommodate computer equipment and electronic devices. The company was particularly proud of having reduced the weight of desks by as much as 30 percent through an alternative materials program. Selective desk parts were redesigned using a material called ABS plastic, which was an industry "first." Management felt the new line was as good in quality as the traditional all-steel desks, and had many advantages. Besides being lighter than steel, ABS plastic does not rust, helps reduce office noise, and can be colour matched to any standard.

However, Rob Woodward, SDC's marketing manager, had some reservations about the new desks. Already, a number of the sales representatives had voiced concern about the new product line. They wondered how they were going to deal with customers' questions. Rumour had it that the company was making the move to plastic components to save money, and several of the salespeople had asked if product prices would be coming down. Recently, an article had appeared in the leading furniture trade magazine which criticized producers for using "inferior" materials. One of their big retail clients had called SDC saying he had heard rumours the company was having financial difficulties. Compounding Rob's problems was the fact that the supplier of the new ABS parts was a subsidiary of SDC's parent firm and had been assured that they would get the business when the changeover in product design took place. Rob pondered his problem and decided to get some additional advice from Donna Burt, SDC's sales manager, and Bill Elliott, the production chief. In three days time, Woodward had to face the company's board of directors and review the marketing plans for the coming year. This would include his recommendation on whether or not to proceed with the revised product lines.

⟩⟩⟩⟩ Q U E S T I O N S

1. What kind of difficulties do marketing people have when changes must be made in the composition or construction of their firm's products?
2. What type of advice should Rob Woodward seek from the sales and production managers to help in his decision?
3. If you were an SDC sales representative, what would your major concerns be in this situation?

Case prepared by Gerald B. McCready, Professor of Marketing, St. Lawrence College.

# ⟩ ⟩ ⟩ ⟩ *12. Video Wars: NEC vs Nintendo*

The undisputed leader of the North American home video game market in 1989 was Nintendo Company Limited. Between 1985 and 1988, Nintendo vaulted from virtual obscurity to become a household name with seven- to fourteen-year-old boys, the primary users of the games. Nintendo is the dominant leader in the second wave of game sales in the industry's short history. It controls 80 percent of the market. The remaining 20 percent is shared by Atari Corporation, the original leader, and Tonka Corporation, which is predominantly a manufacturer of children's toys.

Nintendo takes full credit for the renewed interest in home video games. In contrast, Atari faced a big crash in 1985 when it watched sales drop from $3 billion in 1983 to $100 million in 1989. Atari attributes the crash to its having games that were poorer in quality than the games Nintendo was offering.

The video game market is one in which technology is the lifeline to consumer fun and company profits. It seems that users want increasingly sophisticated, life-like games. Nintendo's present game system has an eight-megabyte memory, though most of the games it sells in North America use only one megabyte. Since the system has been endowed with a great memory capability, Nintendo is ready to produce more sophisticated games. The addition of more megabytes improves the colour and the graphics, and makes play action more complicated. In Japan, Nintendo has successfully marketed games using two and four megabytes of memory. Japan has proven to be a good testing ground for games that are eventually introduced to the North American market. Twenty million consumers have already purchased the eight-megabyte system in North America, so they will be ready to purchase the more powerful games without having to spend a lot of extra money. Nintendo's basic system starts at $160, and games generally cost between $45 and $60 each. Being the leader, Nintendo has a huge catalogue of games, and its plan is to launch as many as 150 new games by the end of 1991.

In 1989, the NEC Corporation, a multi-billion-dollar computer maker and the world's 47th largest company, issued a challenge to Nintendo. Feeling that Nintendo was slow in exploiting the potential of the eight-megabyte system, NEC jumped a step and launched a sixteen-megabyte system in North America. Offering twice as much power, the system, known as Turbo Grafx-16 (or TG-16), had been marketed in Japan in the previous two years. Characters in the games are much larger, and simulated eye-movements, grimaces, and bleeding are all part of new game action. NEC claims that the new games, in conjunction with the system's more powerful memory, provide better colour, graphics, and sound than Nintendo. Being the first to market such powerful games to the home video market, NEC further claims that Nintendo's eight-byte system is obsolete and dares players to compare the two systems.

NEC's North American product is equipped with a stereo soundtrack; a compact disc player is optional. With such technological capabilities, NEC thinks its system has the potential to become the family home-entertainment center of the future. The TG-16 product launch was supported by $20 million in advertising, an indication of how serious NEC is about establishing its presence in this market. By the end of 1989, NEC was marketing twenty games in the North American market.

## 〉〉〉 QUESTIONS

1. Should Nintendo be seriously concerned over the acitivities of the NEC Corporation? If so, what specific strategies might Nintendo consider adopting?
2. To remain successful in the home video market, what factors must manufacturers of games address?
3. The core users of home video games are boys seven to fourteen years old. Is this market sufficient to sustain growth or should the market be expanded? If so, what expansion would you recommend and what products would you market?
4. What type of pricing strategy should NEC use to launch its new TG-16 system?

Adapted from *Karen Benzing*, "NEC fires phasers in video battle of the bits," *Financial Post*, September 16, 1989, pp.1,4.

# 〉〉〉〉 *13. HiTech Security Systems Limited*

You are the product manager at HiTech Security Systems Limited, responsible for the development of a new line of home door-locks. Knowing the market and the competition, you are in a quandary over the potential demand for the lock. Your company already has a few home locks on the market that are doing reasonably well. The sale of this lock could affect the sale of others, and vice versa. On the low side you estimate demand to be 2 000 units annually and on the high side 10 000 units. As part of your initial proposal to the senior executives of the firm, you have been asked to prepare a breakeven analysis. This analysis will have a bearing on whether senior management will approve the project for further development.

Your strategy for the proposal is to calculate the breakeven point in units and dollars, using the current estimates of costs and the price you think you can charge distributors. Due to the uncertainty of demand, you will illustrate the cost and revenue situation in intervals of 2 000 units of volume (from 2 000 to 10 000 units).

To assist you in this task, the production department has advised you that *total fixed costs* are $60 000 annually and that *average variable costs* are $20.00 per unit. Because of competitive factors, you decide that $30.00 per unit is the maximum price you can charge distributors. This is the price you will use in your analysis.

Senior executives have indicated to you informally that the introduction of the new line must generate $40 000 in its first year of production; otherwise, the project is in doubt. This goal might have some impact on your analysis.

## ⟩⟩⟩⟩ Q U E S T I O N S

1. Prepare the breakeven analysis for this case and indicate what action should be taken by the firm.

# ⟩ ⟩ ⟩ ⟩ *14. Sears Canada Inc.*

In February 1989, Sears Roebuck, the leading department store retailer in the United States, startled the retailing world by announcing that it was eliminating "special sales" from its promotion mix strategies. In a rather bold change of direction, Sears stated that an "everyday-low-price" strategy would be instituted. Following the announcement, Sears closed all of its stores for two days to mark down prices on as many as 50 000 items. Sears Canada, the subsidiary company of Sears Roebuck, did not follow the lead of its parent company.

## The United States Market

The U.S. market is very competitive, because a wide range of stores serves each segment of the department store market: there are high-end retailers, middle-of-the-road retailers, and discount retailers. Sears Roebuck is a successful retailing operation that has appealed primarily to the middle-of-the-road segment. Company profits have been lower than anticipated in recent years. Part of Sears Roebuck's strength is the popularity of its well-known and firmly established house brand names such as DieHard, Kenmore, and Craftsman. Sears Roebuck has been affected by the activities of competitors such as Wal-Mart and K Mart, both of which are growing much more rapidly than Sears. Sears Roebuck's financial results over the five-year period spanning 1984 to 1989 show sales growth of only 12 percent while Wal-Mart has grown by 242 percent. In the past ten years, 1980 to 1989, Sears' share of the market for general merchandise retailers dropped from 18 percent to 13 percent. Faced with these figures, a shift in marketing strategy, such as the one Sears Roebuck announced, seemed appropriate. Sears Roebuck finally realized that it had been relying too heavily on a "sale" strategy to drive the business.

Today's consumer is very conscious of price and is willing to shop around for good buys, particularly on hard goods, durable goods, and fashion apparel, all items carried by Sears Roebuck. The toy market also reveals a high interest in continuous low prices. The Toys 'R Us chain changed the face of toy retailing with its everyday-low-price strategy. The strategy helped vault Toys 'R Us into a leadership position in toy retailing, where it now controls a quarter of total sales. Its growth took business away from traditional retailers, including Sears Roebuck and J.C. Penny.

Whether or not Sears Roebuck made the right decision is open to debate. According to *USA Today*, sales revenue for March 1989, the first month following the announcement, was up 8.9 percent over March 1988. Sales in July and August, however, were down 2.4 percent and 1.1 percent respectively compared to the same months a year before.

## The Canadian Situation

Sears Canada continued with the sales approach that has made it Canada's leading individual department store retailer (see exhibit 1). This indicates that the management of Canadian operations is autonomous from the United States parent company. Because a different strategy is used in Canada, there is no opportunity for Sears to capitalize on any advertising overflowing from the U.S., a factor that needs to be considered in future marketing strategy. The content of advertising messages would vary from one country to the other.

EXHIBIT 1

**CANADIAN DEPARTMENT STORE**

**Market Shares, 1989**

| 1988 Sales (in millions) | $13 277 |
|---|---|
| | **Market Share** |
| Sears | 21.0% |
| Zellers | 15.2 |
| Eaton's | 14.6 |
| The Bay | 13.0 |
| Woolco | 12.7 |
| K Mart Canada | 9.2 |
| Woodward's | 5.3 |
| Simpsons | 4.7 |
| Towers/Bonimart | 3.6 |
| M-Stores | 0.4 |
| Others | 0.3 |

Perhaps the Canadian retailing market is not quite the same as the U.S. market. In Canada, Sears has a conservative and positive image; it offers "value" for consumers in a family department store." Sears sells the same brand names as the U.S. company, and it is particularly strong in men's and women's clothing. The combination of its catalogue and retail sales makes it the largest retailer of women's clothing in Canada, but it is not recognized as a fashion leader. The Arnold Palmer line of men's leisure clothing is extremely popular. Good, basic, everyday value is what Sears provides its customers with. Sears Canada is in a situation unusual among Canadian subsidiaries of U.S. companies: it operates more profitably than the parent company. This is another reason it resisted change, and did not follow the lead of the U.S. company.

In Canada, the market is not as competitive. Fewer chain stores control the market and there is less distinction between the various price segments than in the U.S. A chain such as Zellers has been very successful in recent years with its Club Z promotion (a system whereby the customer accumulates, with each purchase, points that are redeemable on catalogue merchandise at a later date) and its "low price law" strategy (it will match any of its competitor's prices). Woolco has succeeded by promoting sales heavily, using advertising slogans such as the "Big Sales Event" and "Full Scale Sales" to attract customers. The Bay also promotes sales, offering discounts in the 10–50 percent range in one-day sales events such as "Scratch and Save Saturdays." Sears' strength in Canada is largely due to its stores being located in regional malls where they literally "own" the market area in many cases.

Sears' financial performance in Canada for the first six months of 1989 was average. Sales slightly exceeded $2 billion, an increase of 7.7 percent over the previous year. Net profits rose from $20.7 million to $29.7 million in the same period. In such a dynamic market, projecting similar growth for the future is difficult. According to Paul Page, the corporate communications manager at Sears, "Sears finds itself competing for the same customers as other major retailers, and almost all of us are aimed at the middle-of-the-road consumer." Woolco, K Mart, Sears, Eaton's and The Bay carry similar merchandise. In effect, a "look-alike" merchandising strategy is developing where stores, and even shopping malls, are becoming similar in appearance and in the merchandise they offer. It seems that not much attention has been focused on developing and marketing true competitive differentiation.

## ⟩⟩⟩ QUESTIONS

1. Should Sears Canada adopt the pricing policy of the U.S. parent company? Why or why not?
2. Given the current situation, are Sears' marketing strategies appropriate for the next five years? If changes are necessary, what changes would you recommend?
3. Should Sears be respositioning itself in the department store segment of Canada's retailing market?
4. Are there other competitive influences that Sears should be evaluating?
5. How important is price strategy in department store retailing?

Adapted from Martin Mehr, "Sears: debating pricing policies", *Marketing*, September 25, 1989, pp.24–25, and Morris Saffer, "EDLP: the end of the sale era," *Marketing*, September 25, 1989, pp.24–25.

# ⟩ ⟩ ⟩ ⟩ *15. Kellmar Canada*

Kellmar Canada Inc. (Kellmar) was a multinational manufacturer and marketer of a number of heavily advertised lines of canned fruits and vegetables, hot and cold cereals, and pet foods, with 1982 Canadian sales of $100 000 000 and profits of $5 000 000. In November 1983, Kellmar's national sales manager, Frank Rivers, was preparing for a meeting with Bill Hawke, regional manager – Atlantic,[1] to discuss Hawke's proposal to terminate their brokerage arrangement in Newfoundland and move to using salaried salespeople. The notion of moving to a direct sales operation in Newfoundland, similar to that utilized in the remainder of Canada, was not new. However, in the past the costs involved could not be justified by acceptable revenue-increase projections.

O'Neil Brokerage Ltd. (O'Neil) had represented Kellmar in Newfoundland for over 30 years. Their principals were well-known and well-liked by the grocery trade in Newfoundland as a result of their continuing service and their historic coverage of the remote 'outports'.

Bill Hawke, (32), the regional manager, had been appointed in January 1982 after a seven-year successful track record in sales and sales supervision in Nova Scotia and New Brunswick. Prior to January 1982, Atlantic was an area reporting to the Quebec Region. It was now the smallest region, with 7 sales representatives and a regional manager while other regions had 15 to 30 sales representatives and 1 to 3 area managers reporting to a regional manager. Hawke was viewed by management as an upwardly mobile individual who clearly hoped to achieve success in his current assignment with a view to moving on to a bigger region or to a position at Head Office.

Newfoundland, with a population of 585 000 (see exhibit 1), represented 2.4 percent of Canada's population and had historically been viewed as a 'have not' province. The economy was changing, however, and according to Statistics Canada was showing growth for 1980 on a number of dimensions as compared to some other provinces: disposable income was up 13.5 percent in Newfoundland compared to 10.1 percent for the Maritimes; jobs were up 7.5 percent versus 3.5 percent; retail trade was up 13.2 percent versus 11.1 percent; and food sales were up 20.1 percent versus 15.3 percent.

In the report Bill Hawke had submitted, he pointed out that Kellmar's dollar volume in Newfoundland accounted for 17 percent of the combined volume for the Maritime provinces, while the ratio for three other major food manufacturers who used their own salesforce rather than brokers ranged from 19.5 percent to 51.3 percent (see exhibit 2). Unfortunately market share data by brands or product lines were not currently available from the major reporting services although they would be including Newfoundland in their reports starting in 1983. In Hawke's view there were opportunities for growth by Kellmar in Newfoundland, as a number of Kellmar brands and sizes were not sold; and merchandising, shelf space, and shelf position for many Kellmar products were limited at the retail level. The major problem in Hawke's opinion was that while the broker maintained a salesforce of seven people, Kellmar only received about 10 percent of their sales time and effort. The broker, who represented six major national manufacturers including Kellmar, as well as a few regional manufacturers, not surprisingly claimed that Kellmar received more effort than that. According to Hawke, however, O'Neil's sales people had too many

**EXHIBIT 1**

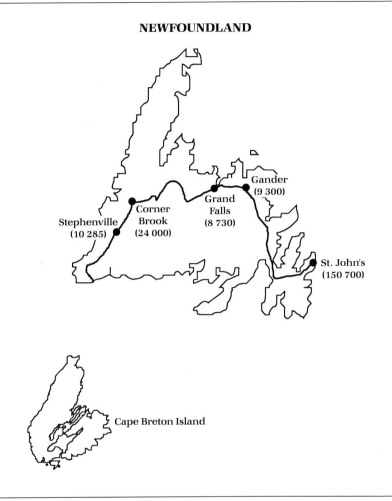

**NEWFOUNDLAND**

Gander
(9 300)

Grand
Falls
(8 730)

Corner
Brook
(24 000)

Stephenville
(10 285)

St. John's
(150 700)

Cape Breton Island

products to handle and were inclined to think of Kellmar as fourth or fifth on their list of priorities.

Bill Hawke had originally believed that Kellmar should have a sales supervisor based in St. John's and account representatives in St. John's and Grand Falls. Corner Brook would be covered from Cape Breton as was done by a few other manufacturers which unfortunately involved considerable travel time and expense. In his formal proposal, he recommended that the company install a supervisory level representative in St. John's and account representatives in St. John's and Grand Falls, with no support from Cape Breton. After applying Kellmar's sales-call-frequency decision model[2], which considered individual store volume and decision-making power at the store level, Hawke had calculated that 3.4 salespeople would be required to cover Newfoundland. He felt that a complement of three would still give sufficient coverage as in his view there were a number of smaller volume direct accounts which should be buying from wholesalers and could receive less sales time. The total cost of the sales group of three would amount to about $100 000 (see exhibit 3) and

---

**EXHIBIT 2**  Analysis of Competitive Salaried Sales Force Deployment

---

*Company A — 22.5% ratio Newfoundland to Maritimes Sales*

1 District Manager, St. John's

2 Representatives, St. John's

1 Representative, Grand Falls

1 Representative, Corner Brook

*Company B — 19.5% ratio Newfoundland to Maritimes Sales*

1 District Manager, St. John's

2 Representatives, St. John's

1 Representative, Corner Brook

*Company C — 51.3% ratio Newfoundland to Maritimes Sales*

1 Division Supervisor, St. John's

1 Representative, St. John's

1 Representative, Grand Falls

1 Representative, Corner Brook

*Company D — 26% ratio Newfoundland to Maritimes Sales*

1 District Manager, St. John's

1 Representative, St. John's

1 Representative, Grand Falls

Corner Brook covered from Cape Breton

*Common Elements*

A.  Supervisory personnel in St. John's

B.  Coverage in three district geographical areas — St. John's, Grand Falls and Corner Brook.

C.  All sales forces composed of at least four individuals.

---

compared favourably with the previous year's brokerage commissions of about $150 000.[3] With the added sales effort and greater control over the sales force, Hawke expected to increase sales from $2 100 000 to $2 500 000 in the next fiscal year, at an average contribution margin of 25 percent. Hawke proposed that, after formal termination of O'Neil's contract with six month's notice, a letter be mailed out to all accounts (exhibit 4). In the six month's period preceding the actual termination, Hawke proposed to recruit, train, and organize a sales team that would cover the territory for a number of months in conjunction with the broker's efforts. Sales for that period would be credited to the broker's commission. Hawke stated that he did not expect O'Neil to be pleased with the decision, but that they would be co-operative until the end of the contract time in order to maximize commission income.

Although Frank Rivers shared Bill Hawke's interest in growth, he was concerned that Hawke had not calculated all the costs involved in the proposal. He anticipated that a number of headquarters costs could increase immediately such as travel,

---

**EXHIBIT 3**   Newfoundland Sales Force Feasibility Study as Submitted by Bill Hawke

In confirming the cost of establishing a sales group on the island, the following figures substantiate approximately $100 000.00.

The $100 000.00 is the actual outlay of expenses needed to sustain a three-person sales force for a year. This does not include the cost of office or stenographic help, which at this point will not be required, nor does it include communications. There is also another factor of interest, the investment of three cars. In round figures, if we say each car is worth $10 000.00, we will have $30 000.00 invested at 17 percent, which is $5 100.00. I am not sure where this figures into the hard figures; however, it is certainly something one should keep in mind.

*Salary*

| | | | | | |
|---|---|---|---|---|---|
| 1 Supervisor Level | | | | | |
| Representative  $486.00[1] per week  ×  52 | | | | = | $ 25 272.00 |
| 2 Account Reps  $375.00[1] per week  ×  52 | | | | = | 39 000.00 |
| 3 Car Expenses  ×  $350.00[2] per month  ×  12 | | | | = | 12 600.00 |
| 3 Car Depreciation  ×  $150.00[2] per month  ×  12 | | | | = | 5 400.00 |
| 3 Travel and Subsistence  ×  $450.00[2] per month  ×  12 | | | | = | 16 200.00 |
| Total | | | | | $98 472.00 |

[1]Includes benefit costs such as pension, insurance etc. per the personnel department, but this does not include any expenses included in the sales department expenses categories (sales meetings, awards etc.)
[2]Same as used for budgeting purposes for Maritime Provinces salespeople.

---

**EXHIBIT 4**   Proposed Letter to All Newfoundland Accounts

The Kellmar Company of Canada Inc. is pleased to announce the establishment of its own sales force for Newfoundland, effective January 1, 1983.

O'Neil Brokerage Limited has represented Kellmar very well over the years, and their efforts and accomplishments are appreciated. However, we believe that we can service our Newfoundland customers even more effectively with our own sales force selling Kellmar products exclusively.

It is our intention to hire only within Newfoundland to ensure that the Kellmar sales force is well experienced in your marketplace and that solid relationships continue with our valued customers.

Our sole intention in this move is to improve service to our customers and thereby fully realize the potential of the Newfoundland market. We look forward to servicing you in this new capacity; your Kellmar sales representative will call to meet you in the very near future.

Sincerely,

National Sales Manager

---

national sales meetings, sales contests etc. and that in the future there would be pressures for regional administrative and supervisory support. Nor was he convinced that the transition would flow that easily. The broker had shown steady sales increases for Kellmar over the years, and had dealt quickly and well with any and all issues that had arisen with retailers and wholesalers in the province. Frank still had in his files letters received from three major accounts some years ago when there were rumours that Kellmar would be replacing O'Neill with a direct salesforce. The strongest one stated that "We are making plans to delete fifty percent of your goods from our inventory but hope you will change your mind". The other two were most supportive of O'Neil and clearly stated that they would be most unhappy with such a decision and would take some action. Six accounts out of fifty accounted for 65 percent of Kellmar's total dollar sales (ranging from a high of 15 percent to 6 percent) in Newfoundland. The support of those six accounts, only two of which were national accounts, was critical. If any of those key accounts chose to resist the changeover, it would create a host of problems and Kellmar's sales could be seriously affected.

## >>>> QUESTIONS

1. In Mr. River's place, would you approve the proposal? Consider the financial implications when making your decision.
2. From Mr. Hawke's point of view, how important is the decision? Keep in mind the relevant financial considerations.
3. If you were a principal of O'Neil Brokerage, what would you do?

## >>>> NOTES

1. "Atlantic" includes the four provinces of New Brunswick, Nova Scotia, Prince Edward Island and Newfoundland. "Maritimes" includes New Brunswick, Nova Scotia and Prince Edward Island.

2. For each store weekly estimated sales volume, store control over shelving and space allocations, store control over displays and deal support and store control over distribution were considered to determine maximum quarterly sales call frequency which ranged from 0 to 6. Stores where sales people could accomplish little because of low volume or because key decisions were made at the store headquarters received few calls.

3. The $150 000 was composed of contracted sales commissions of $115 000 on Kellmar products shipped by Kellmar's Newfoundland warehouse and a supplement of $35 000 instituted in 1980 when Kellmar had increased its salesforce size in Canada by 25 percent to improve effort and coverage at the retail level. They had increased the broker's commissions at that time to attain comparable coverage and effort increases. The broker had increased his sales complement from six to seven as a result.

Prepared by Adjunct Professor David G. Burgoyne, supported by funding from the Commercial Travellers Association of Canada. Copyright © 1983, The University of Western Ontario. This case was prepared as a basis for classroom discussion only. All names of companies, products and people have been disguised. Corporate financial data have been adjusted but relationships of data have been maintained.

# ❱ ❱ ❱ ❱ *16. Canada's Franchised Fast Food Industry*

Fast food franchises have long been considered a safe bet for making a quick buck. Growth in the industry throughout the seventies, when franchising started to boom, and in the early eighties was always in double digits. Consumers' love affair with hamburgers and chicken fuelled rapid franchise expansion among operations such as McDonald's, Kentucky Fried Chicken, Harvey's, Burger King, and Wendy's. The latest sales and market share statistics for the leaders in the industry are contained in Exhibit 1.

EXHIBIT 1

|  | 1987 | | 1988 | |
|---|---|---|---|---|
|  | Sales (in millions) | Share | Sales (in millions) | Share |
| McDonald's | $1 500 | 34.2% | $1 800 | 40.0% |
| Kentucky Fried Chicken | 500 | 11.4 | 500 | 11.1 |
| Burger King | 232 | 5.3 | 250 | 5.3 |
| Harvey's | 183 | 4.2 | 200 | 4.4 |
| A&W | 140 | 3.2 | 140 | 3.1 |
| Wendy's | 119 | 2.7 | 140 | 3.1 |

*Source:* "Who's on First", *Financial Post*, December 4, 1989, p.A4.

Franchising is a concept that has been very successful in encouraging rapid growth in the industry, but now sales growth is sluggish, creeping along in the 5–6 percent range annually. As the fast food industry moves further into the nineties, the situation it confronts will be quite different from that in the past. The market is now saturated, and in such an environment, franchisees are facing competition at every street corner. The days of the quick buck are disappearing fast. With prospects of slower growth overall, the opportunity to attract new customers has dwindled. Now the marketing battle among competitors has intensified as companies try to take business from each other, seeing this strategy as the best means of securing growth. Franchises find themselves forced to offer discounts in an attempt to lure customers away from the competition.

Another change from the past, and one that is compounding the woes of franchisees, is the difficulty of finding reliable help, while paying entry level wages in a tight labour market. Many franchises now use younger (fourteen years old) part-time employees (15 hours a week and less) who have uncertain loyalties to their employer. Such a practice threatens to undermine the stringent quality standards that have been a trademark of successful fast food franchises in the past (the concept of product uniformity, quality, and service standards).

Many franchisees now complain that fast food chains overbuilt in the eighties because of their desire to dominate and that this excessive expansion has led to the troubled times of the present. In good times such a strategy appears sound, but when leaner times prevail there is less business available for greater numbers of outlets. Even the biggest franchised chain, McDonald's, is not immune to the cycles in the business or to the finicky eating habits of the public. Like the others, it must be in tune with the consumers' needs if growth is to continue in the nineties. A bone of contention among Harvey's outlets, and not uncommon among some other franchise operations, is that each franchisee's company-defined territory is shrinking. New locations are popping up very close to existing franchised locations. In some cases, and especially in downtown areas, franchisees are competing against franchisees of the same chain. Current franchisees have the right of first refusal on such new locations (i.e., they must be given the first chance to buy the new franchise proposed by the franchisor); however, present franchisees cannot afford to take advantage of the opportunity when facing tight times with their existing franchise. Such action by franchisors can damage the franchisor-franchisee relationship, and indicates that entrepreneurs have little muscle in dealing with franchisors.

## Current Marketing Strategies

Given the current environment of the fast food industry, the weapon of choice in the battle for market share is the $0.99 hamburger special or the 2-for-1 offer. Many franchisees complain to the franchisor that such specials erode profit margins considerably. In virtually all cases, the specials are mandatory directives from the franchisor. The franchisors may not like this particular practice either, but they acknowledge that such tactics are necessary if they are to stay in the game. Further, discounts do serve a purpose. In the short-term, discounts can increase consumer traffic during the slower winter months or boost sales of a sagging menu item. But too much price slashing can cheapen the product in the eyes of consumers. For an image-conscious company such as McDonald's, price-slashing is not a desirable strategy, particularly if viewed as a long-term solution to sluggish sales. Perhaps it is new products that offer greater potential. After all, it was McDonald's who virtually created the breakfast-sandwich market with the Egg McMuffin in the 1970s.

Another development in the industry has seen the franchisor buying back franchises from the franchisee. Burger King, for example, bought back twelve existing franchises in the Toronto market in 1989. The company moved to a greater concentration of corporate ownership because it felt that franchises in the Toronto market were too complex an undertaking for most owner operators and that growth opportunities were better if greater control of operations were in their hands. According to William Bullis, president of Burger King Canada Inc., "we're prepared to make an investment in a store and wait longer for a return on it than most franchisees would." Future expansion by Burger King will be at the corporate ownership level. Harvey's is the only national operation to resist this trend, as indicated by exhibit 2.

It appears certain that the fast food industry has entered a mature state, and that

EXHIBIT 2    Canadian Outlets, 1989

|  | *Total Outlets* | *Franchised Outlets* |
|---|---|---|
| Kentucky Fried Chicken | 783 | 753 |
| McDonald's | 602 | 334 |
| A&W | 375 | 248 |
| Harvey's | 244 | 244 |
| Burger King | 206 | 140 |
| Wendy's | 130 | 46 |

uncertain and lean times lie ahead. The companies currently operating in the industry will have to look at new strategies if they are to survive the nineties. Any new strategies must consider that consumers are increasingly finicky about what they will eat and how much they will pay. In what direction companies need to go to establish a lasting relationship with such a consumer remain uncertain.

#### ⟩⟩⟩⟩ QUESTIONS

1. What environmental or behavioural factors besides those mentioned in this account are contributing to sluggish growth in the fast food industry? (Hint: Are there other forms of competition?)
2. Since the current strategies appear to be short-term in their solution, what marketing strategies can you recommend for the long-term? (Hint: Consider the stage in the product life cycle and the competition you identified in the first question).
3. What new market opportunities do you see for the fast food chains in Canada?
4. Are there any lessons to be learned about franchising from this case? What are the prospects for franchising in the fast food industry in the nineties? In other service-related industries?

Adapted from Colin Languedoc, "Pickings get slim for fast food franchises", *Financial Post*, December 2, 1989, p.1,4., and Brian Bremner, "McDonald's stoops to conquer", Business Week, October 30, 1989, p.120,124.

## ⟩⟩⟩⟩ *17. Cambridge Meat Packers*

Barbara Norris enthusiastically accepted her appointment to the position of product manager at Cambridge Meat Packers. A business administration graduate with a specialty in marketing, Barbara had spent four years in a junior position with a competitive company before joining Cambridge.

Cambridge Meat Packers has been in the meat processing field since 1909. It started as a public slaughterhouse, killing cattle, sheep and pigs for local farmers. In time, the company grew, supplying independent meat stores across southern Ontario with sides of beef, lamb, and pork. The company's forcemeat products — wieners, bologna and farmer's sausage — were very well respected in the trade.

In 1980 Cambridge expanded its product mix through the acquisition of a small poultry plant. The plant processed dressed chickens and turkeys, together with a premium-priced product line of turkey cold cuts, which acquired a significant and very profitable share of the sliced meat market.

The company decided in 1986 to build on the success of the turkey cold cuts with the addition of a new line of specialty cold cuts, including sliced ham, pastrami, and variety meat packs. The marketing department reasoned that the potential was there for Cambridge Premier slices to become the third best selling cold cuts line on the market by the end of 1989.

The Premier Slices line was launched with great expectations. The 1980s had seen the arrival of yuppies and the departure of wine and cheese parties. Fondue sets gathered dust on shelves. Consumers sought variety in their fast foods. Muffin stands and submarine shops sprang up everywhere. Consumers wanted different tastes and greater convenience in their foods. Sliced meats offered both difference and convenience. It seemed to Cambridge Meat Packers that the day of the deli had arrived.

But the product line failed to meet sales expectations. In fact, sales in 1989 declined. Barbara Norris concluded that consumer tastes had changed since the introduction of Premier Slices. There had been a much publicized swing away from red meat, as consumers had become increasingly health-conscious. Barbara felt that sliced ham shouldn't be classified as red meat, but, nevertheless, consumers had turned away from pork products because of a perceived fat content.

In fact, a consumer perception study had shown that consumers did not know the calorie and fat content of the Cambridge sliced meat products. Focus-group participants estimated that a single ham slice had between 150 and 250 calories when it in fact had fewer than 30 calories.

Barbara's predecessor, marketing director Walter Keta, attributed the sales decline to packaging problems. Early in 1989 he had introduced improved vacuum packs to end a discoloration problem; however, a number of retailers, especially a small supermarket chain of independent food outlets, was hesitant to shelve the repackaged line. Keta insisted that the market for cold cuts, particularly for the sliced ham, was assured. He said his forecasts were realistic, his revised sales targets were easily attainable, and he felt comfortable passing the responsibilities of product manager over to Barbara.

At a recent executive meeting where the ailing product line was discussed, it appeared that other company executives did not share Keta's unbounded confidence in the product. Vince Patterson, plant manager for twenty years at Cambridge, believed that the cold cuts line was unsuccessful and should be dropped, at least for the present. He felt it might be possible to revive it in a few years when market tastes changed. Comptroller Jim Andrews, while acknowledging that the line had failed to show a profit, noted that revenue was meeting most costs; thus he favoured retaining the line because of the considerable investment that the company had made in the product.

Barbara consulted Rick Yeates, account executive with the company's advertising agency Barker Donaldson Limited. The agency argued that a heavy print-advertising campaign would reach the target market most efficiently and would bring retailers on side, supporting the Cambridge sales force in its efforts to gain greater distribution for the Premier Slices line.

The target market for Premier Slices is almost exclusively adult and primarily women, with dual-income households constituting a substantial segment of the market. The agency therefore developed a creative package that marketed Premier Slices as "adult food." Magazine advertisements in the proposed package, Yeates pointed out, were aimed at the "active women who may or may not be working outside the home." Yeates explained that the agency's proposal also called for coupons to be included with some of the magazine advertising as well as a direct-mail coupon program.

Yeates assured Barbara that the campaign would be favoured by the executive board at Cambridge. He knew them well, having handled the account since 1982. Barbara stalled Yeates. She wanted to consider her options in this situation.

1. What problem does Barbara Norris face with the Premier Slices line?
2. What changes have occurred among consumers since the product was launched to affect their acceptance of it?
3. Is the positioning strategy for Premier Slices correct? Should alternative positioning strategies be considered?
4. What recommendations would you make to Barbara Norris?

Case prepared by Ron Kelly, Professor of Marketing, St. Lawrence College.

# ›››› *18. The Canadian Football League*

The 1980s were not kind to the Canadian Football League. It was a decade in which the league experienced sharp declines in attendance, even in traditionally strong cities such as Toronto, Edmonton, and Vancouver. The B.C. Lions were a dominant force at the box office in the early years of the decade, but experienced severe financial difficulty in the latter years. Calgary and Ottawa also faced financial pressure, and their very existence was threatened as a result of it. Even Harold Ballard, owner of Maple Leaf Gardens (a building often referred to as the Carlton Street cash box) and the Toronto Maple Leafs, a man known for making money, could not turn a profit in Hamilton during the years he owned the Tiger Cats.

Perhaps the league hit its lowest point in June 1989 when officials quietly announced that the annual player awards, sponsored by Schenley since 1953, would no longer be called the Schenleys. The 1989 outstanding player awards would not have a corporate sponsor. These annual awards showcase the best talent in the league and pit the best players in the East against the best in the West. The categories include "most outstanding player", "best defensive player", "best offensive player", and "outstanding Canadian player". Over the years the Schenleys grew to become a gala event, and at one time they were televised live, a true testimonial to their popularity and the league's popularity. The Schenleys added prestige to a league that otherwise was fading fast in the eyes of the Canadian sports fan. In 1989 some interest was renewed as television audiences grew modestly from recent years, and there was a lot of hype and excitement surrounding the 77th Grey Cup game that was played in Toronto's SkyDome. Traditionally, the Grey Cup game is successful, but one game does not a season make, and critics still feel the league has long since passed its glory days.

Schenleys absence from the player awards symbolizes the CFL's predicament as it struggles to prove to fans and marketers alike that it is "big-league" enough to warrant attention in the super-saturated sports and entertainment environment. There is a perception among Canadians that the CFL is inferior to the NFL, and this is why attendance is declining and interest in the league is generally low. The league has acknowledged that it needs a more contemporary positioning. Consider the following viewpoints regarding the league's current state of affairs:

"Reveen the Impossiblist couldn't save the CFL."
(Jamie Wayne, *Financial Post*)

"Everybody's looking over their shoulders at the States. You've got a more exciting, interesting brand of televised sport in football just south of the border. That screws up everything. Then you've got a sheer marketing problem . . . which appears to lie with the franchises themselves. They aren't good marketers of their own product in their own communities."
(Dick Moore, vice-president, International Management Group)

"You'd better have a pretty solid marketing plan. Football competes not only with other sports, but for the general entertainment dollar. They've got to figure out what their competition is in each market."
(Chris Lang, Chairman, Christopher Lang and Associates)

Could it be that a common marketing strategy is what the league needs to turn it around? Bill Baker, the newly apppointed president for the 1989 season, spent the year promoting the "new CFL." His own assessment of the situation was that the sports marketplace had changed dramatically since the heydays of the sixties and early seventies. Baker contended that the CFL is not the NFL. The NFL lives for television and is structured and paced to appeal to TV audiences and advertisers. The 28-team NFL generates 60 percent of its revenues from television, with this percentage very likely to increase when the next round of negotiations with the U.S. networks are completed. In contrast, the CFL only generates 20 percent of its revenues from television. Says Baker, "We are in the live entertainment business, not as a lot of other sports are, the television presentation business."

Going into 1989 the league had high expectations because of the appointments of Roy McMurtry as chair and Bill Baker as president, which were seen as moves to stabilize the league administration. Despite this optimism, both of the new executives faced numerous setbacks that had to be overcome before they could start to move ahead. For example, there was some serious talk of a new NFL franchise for Toronto, where the SkyDome awaits another big league tenant. One of the backers of the Toronto franchise idea was Carling O'Keefe (now Molson because of the 1989 takeover), which was one of the CFL's own sponsors. Such talk created one giant headache for the CFL. Critics feel that if Toronto folds, the league will follow suit, and there is no way a CFL team would survive in Toronto if the NFL came to town.

On the field, some franchises were having problems. Toronto, playing in the beautiful, expansive SkyDome, was attracting 34 000 fans per game, up 47 percent from a year ago when the team played at Exhibition Stadium. But hardly anyone noticed; Toronto's true love, the Blue Jays, had sellouts game after game. In Ottawa, Baker had to lobby local governments to provide funds to keep the Rough Riders afloat, and a new owner had to be found for the B.C. Lions, a team that was $8 million in debt at the time. With problems like these apparently under control, the league faced another embarrassing setback in October, when Bill Baker announced his resignation from the presidency, citing personal reasons.

Recognizing that marketing was an issue, the league did hire a marketing director,

Morrey Rae Hutnick, for the 1989 season. Her view is that the league is a mature product that needs an overhaul. The challenge for Hutnick was to create a new and greater visibility for the league nationally. Going into the 1990s, the league had a core group of corporate sponsors that included Molson, the Royal Bank, Canada Post, Pepsi's 7Up brand, Gatorade, and Culinar's Vachon division. If attendance and television audiences were to continue declining, the commitment of these sponsors over the longer term could weaken. The second challenge for Hutnick was to attract additional corporate sponsors that would bring financial support to the league in the longer term.

What the league had to do was to encourage the teams to market themselves with some sophistication. Some critics said that more of what's happening in Hamilton should be done elsewhere. Some said Hamilton's advertising was the best they had seen for the CFL in a long time. "The Cat's Back" campaign developed for the 1989 season for new owner David Braley (he purchased the club from Harold Ballard in March 1989) featured in one of the commercials a slab of raw beef tossed in the direction of the television viewer. It resulted in instances of fans throwing meat onto the playing field during games. Print ads also featured the raw beef and the slogan "It's feeding time." It was an image the Hamilton fans liked and one that symbolized the type of football that Hamilton was once noted for. Hamilton also got back into the promotion business. Each game had a festive atmosphere, with bands playing before the game and during half-time. For one game, Tim Horton Donuts sponsored a three-ring circus at half-time that proved a good drawing card for the family target market. As part of the promotion, Tim Horton gave away 10 000 dashboard coffee holders. As a result of such activities, attendance for Hamilton's first seven games increased 25 percent over what it had been a year earlier. Average attendance was 18 511 a game, a figure that might seem small to larger cities, but is very reasonable for Hamilton. It indicated that a coordinated marketing effort in the community could help rekindle fan interest.

## ⟩⟩⟩⟩ QUESTIONS

1. What are the problems the CFL faces?
2. What is the marketing problem in this case?
3. What external factors have contributed to the demise of the CFL? Why is fan interest so low?
4. If you were in Hutnick's shoes (director of marketing) what would you do? What marketing strategy would you recommend, particularly in the long term?
5. For the CFL team closest to your school, make some specific marketing recommendations that would help promote the product in the local community.
6. Identify some potential corporate sponsors that the CFL could pursue.

Adapted from Stan Sutter, "The CFL runs for its life", *Marketing*, November 6, 1989, pp.14–15.

# ❭ ❭ ❭ ❭ *19. Commonwealth Hospitality Limited (A)*

Commonwealth Hospitality Limited currently operates 34 Holiday Inns in Canada and is aggressively pursuing expansion and growth through renovation, upgrading, and the addition of new properties. In Canada's lodging industry, Holiday Inn ranks third in dollar sales behind the market leaders: Four Seasons Hotels Inc., and Canadian Pacific Hotels and Resorts. Sales revenue figures for the leading hotel chains in Canada are provided in exhibit 1.

**EXHIBIT 1**

| | Sales (in millions) | | |
| | 1987 | 1988 | Units |
|---|---|---|---|
| 1. Four Seasons Hotels Inc. | $297.1 | $312.6 | 22 |
| 2. Canadian Pacific Hotels | 202.2 | 243.6 | 25 |
| 3. Commonwealth Hospitality | 207.3 | 155.0 | 34 |
| 4. Westin Hotels | 131.9 | 132.0 | 6 |
| 5. Delta Hotels & Resorts | 105.5 | 113.6 | 15 |
| 6. The Sheraton Corp. | 117.0 | 106.0 | 18 |
| 7. Journey's End Hotels | 66.0 | 100.0 | 125 |
| 8. Hilton Canada Inc. | 93.0 | 96.0 | 9 |
| 9. Ramada Canada | 78.0 | 91.0 | 30 |
| 10. York-Hanover Hotels | 81.0 | 83.0 | 9 |

Source: "Marketing With a Difference", *Foodservice and Hospitality*, September 1989, p54.

Holiday Inns has grown from rather modest beginnings to become a leading name in the Canadian lodging market. The first Holiday Inn was opened by company founder, Kemmons Wilson, in Memphis, Tennessee, in 1952. He saw freshly paved highways crossing the United States and the consumers' love affair with the automobile as a business opportunity. Wilson promised his customers "no surprises", a tag that still remains with the hotel chain to this day. The hotel offered air conditioning, private baths, and in-room telephone service, all amenities that are common today, but were very new in the early fifties. A booming economy and a good product made Holiday Inn an overnight success.

Holiday Inns opened in Canada in 1962. The first location was in London, Ontario. By 1968 the company had expanded to 30 hotels and the corporate name changed to Commonwealth Holiday Inns of Canada Limited. In keeping with the American style, the Canadian operation used the "no surprises" formula, and the value-for-your-money image strongly appealed to the consumers of the sixties and seventies. Throughout the 1970s growth continued, and the well-known roadside chain underwent physical evolution. Holiday Inns went downtown and built highrise style complexes to compete with the likes of Westin, Sheraton, Canadian Pacific, and others. Despite this change, Holiday Inns still appealed primarily to the same target market — the value-conscious leisure traveller (e.g., the vacationing couple or family).

So successful were the 1970s that the need for marketing strategy at Holiday Inn was virtually nonexistent. Activity that did occur relied heavily on the spillover of advertising from the United States. All of the leading chains were building new properties, and more and more rooms were added to the market.

In the 1980s, Holiday Inn operations came unhinged. The industry was changing and the market was now highly segmented on the basis of price. During this decade the Canadian hotel industry matured, and major chains concentrated on segmentation strategies that clearly divided the market according to price. At the low end were chains such as Journey's End, Comfort Inn, and Relax Inn; in the mid-price range were Holiday Inn and Ramada; and in the luxury segment were Four Seasons, Westin, and Canadian Pacific. Everybody seemed to be expanding and room supply mushroomed. Holiday Inn estimated that in 1986 alone, 20 000 rooms were added to the mid-price market segment. With demand being stable and room supply abundant, the competition for customers was fierce.

The fight was on for Holiday Inn and others to maintain occupancy rates at reasonable levels. The new low-end, basic-service hotel emerged as a popular alternative for the value-minded traveller. The Journey's End chain came from nowhere in the early eighties to rank seventh in the industry by 1988. Even luxury hotels weren't immune to the activities of budget hotels, for they, too, had to offer discounted rates to hold onto market share. According to Michael Beckley, president of Commonwealth Hospitality, Holiday Inn found itself, "in the middle of the market with a somewhat aging physical product — just being squeezed."[1]

For Holiday Inn, a change in management philosophy was needed. Michael Beckley's mandate as head of the operation was to change the image of Holiday Inn. Consumer research clearly indicated that Holiday Inn was perceived as "clean, comfortable, and boring."[2]

## ❭❭❭❭ QUESTIONS

1. What is the major problem facing Holiday Inn? What factors are contributing to this problem?
2. Holiday Inn is attractive to the leisure traveller. Are alternate targets necessary if Holiday Inn is to grow in the future?
3. Given the information provided in the case and your own perception of Holiday Inn, what marketing mix strategies would you recommend for the chain? Your answer should consider the needs of any new target markets.
4. How can Holiday Inn go about changing its image, an image that is firmly entrenched in the minds of consumers?

## ❭❭❭❭ REFERENCES

1. "Commonwealth Hospitality Ltd.", *Foodservice and Hospitality*, September 1989, p.4.
2. "Marketing with a Difference", *Foodservice and Hospitality*, September 1989, p.20.

# 〉 〉 〉 〉 *20. Commonwealth Hospitality Limited (B)*

As part of Commonwealth Hospitality's growth plans for the 1990s, company executives made the decision to enter the high-end, luxury segment of the hotel industry. Commonwealth Hospitality, through its chain of Holiday Inns which extend from coast to coast in Canada, is an established brand leader in the mid-priced segment of the market. Its desire to expand into the luxury segment coincided with the expansion plans of Radisson Hotels of the United States, which wanted to enter the Canadian market. An agreement was struck between the two parties whereby Commonwealth would have a financial interest in Radisson properties in Canada, and would operate and manage facilities under the Radisson brand name.

Radisson was not a household name in Canada. When a Canadian thinks of luxury hotels, he or she is likely to think of the Royal York in Toronto, the Chateau Laurier in Ottawa, Hotel Vancouver or the Banff Springs in Banff (all of which are Canadian Pacific Hotels), or the Westin or Four Seasons Hotel chains. Yet David MacMillan, vice-president of Operations at Commonwealth, explains the lack of awareness of Radisson as a potential advantage, "It's reputation was virgin — it had made no mistakes in Canada."[1]

By 1989, Commonwealth had opened five Radisson Hotels in Canada. Three Holiday Inns, in London, Ottawa, and Toronto, were refurbished and converted to Radissons, and new hotels were opened in St. John's and Winnipeg. The Winnipeg hotel is an all-suite hotel, a new trend in the hotel industry. To create an awareness for the Radisson name, a theme using a "What's a Radisson?" headline was developed, an interesting strategy given the name's relative obscurity in Canada. Planning for the future, Commonwealth has its sights set on opening as many as fifteen more Radissons by the middle of the 1990s.

According to Warren Adamson, vice-president of Development, four types of Radissons will appear in Canada:

1. *Radisson Plaza Hotels*   Located in city centres, these are full-service, top quality hotels that appeal to upscale leisure travellers and business travellers unconcerned with accommodation costs.

2. *Radisson Hotels*   These are full-service hotels, located in busy commercial and shopping districts, that include restaurants, entertainment, and banquet and meeting rooms. The Toronto, Ottawa and London hotels are in this category.

3. *Radisson Suite Hotels*   Appealing to leisure and business travellers, these hotels offer the comfort of two rooms — a bedroom and sitting room — and they feature full-service restaurants and cocktail lounges. They are located in downtown and preferred suburban locations.

4. *Radisson Resorts*   Aimed at leisure travellers and conference planners, these hotels will have recreational destinations and feature full service restaurants, entertainment, meeting and recreational facilities.

Commonwealth executives are relying heavily on being helped by the strength of the Radisson name outside of Canada. It is the tenth largest and fastest growing chain of hotels in continental United States. A new Radisson opens every ten days somewhere in the world. However, the situation in Canada is quite different. A research study conducted in November 1987 revealed that among many segments of business travellers awareness of the name Radisson as a hotel chain was virtually "zero."[2] Does this represent a problem or an opportunity for Commonwealth?

#### ⟩⟩⟩⟩ QUESTIONS

1. To create awareness for the Radisson name, what strategies would you recommend? Your answer should consider the physical product itself as well as other relevant elements of the marketing mix.

2. What are the risks associated with Commonwealth's venture into the luxury segment of the hotel market?

3. Will the variety of hotel offerings planned by Commonwealth confuse or complement its marketing strategy?

4. What target markets must Commonwealth pursue if the Radisson division is to be successful? What amenities must it stress to differentiate its product?

#### ⟩⟩⟩⟩ REFERENCES

1. "Development and Diversification", *Foodservice and Hospitality*, September 1989, p.8.

2. "Marketing with a Difference", *Foodservice and Hospitality*, September 1989, p.23.

# ⟩ ⟩ ⟩ ⟩ *21. Biathlon Canada: A Sport Marketing Case*

Rick Nickelchok settled into his new office and wondered when he would get time to clear the backlog of paperwork on his desk. As the new executive director of Biathlon Canada, Nickelchok was responsible for the overall operation of the national office of this small sport-governing body. The organization's offices are located in the new Canadian Sport and Fitness Administration Centre on James Naismith Drive in the Gloucester area of Ottawa. About 80 percent of all Canada's recognized sport-and-recreation organizations have their national headquarters at this national center so that they can be close to the body responsible for making most of the funding and major policy decisions that affect them — Fitness and Sport Canada.

Large sport and recreation organizations such as the Canadian Amateur Hockey Association, the Coaching Association of Canada, and the Canadian Soccer Association have substantial budgets and staffs. Small organizations such as Softball Canada, the Canadian Archery Association, and Biathlon Canada operate on a financial shoestring and are staffed accordingly. Biathlon Canada employs five people. There are over 50 000 non-profit organizations like Biathlon Canada operating throughout the country in health, sport, recreation, social services, and the arts. Biathlon Canada incorporated itself in 1985.

## History of the Sport

Biathlon Canada was founded in 1972 to help prepare a Canadian entrant for the 1976 Olympics in Montreal. The sport was not popular in Canada at the time, and consequently Biathlon Canada focused primarily on building the skills of a dedicated group of enthusiastic athletes, whose goals were to compete internationally. The sport combines cross-country skiing and rifle marksmanship in a gruelling test of skill, speed, finesse, and endurance. Europeans, in particular, enjoy the biathlon, and an athlete's success in the sport is very much a source of national pride for his or her country.

The word "biathlon" stems from the early Greek term meaning "two tests." The roots of the biathlon have been traced to Scandinavian natives of old, who hunted game on skis as their principal means of survival. The Norwegians call it *Skiskyting* (sky-shooting) and the Finns call it *Ampumchinto* (shoot-skiing). Canadians have chosen the word *biathlon* to convey that two activities are combined in the sport.

Like the sport of dog sledding in northern Canadian communities, the biathlon has become an important part of life in many European countries. Perhaps inevitably, competitions commenced between the best biathloners of various communities. Over time, the broad acceptance of biathlon led to its inclusion as a winter Olympic event. Canada ranks among the top twenty nations of the world in biathlon, but needs more and better athletes, qualified coaches, major competitions and facilities to move ahead in this demanding sport. And this all takes money! One major breakthrough for the biathlon is the introduction of female competitors in the Albertville Winter Olympics in 1992. This innovation was a result of Canadian sport administrators lobbying international officials for a female event at the 1988 Calgary Olympics.

## Sport Marketing

Since the early 1980s, considerable financial pressure has been placed on the sport and recreational community in Canada. The sport industry has a history of being a pawn of the political winds prevailing at any given point in time. Thus, in Canada, if a particular sport achieves significant prominence, the political winds become favourable, and increased funding from the government is allotted to that sport. For example, Canada's win in the famous hockey series of 1972 against the Soviets led to increased funding for hockey. Performances by Canadian athletes in recent Olympic and World Figure Skating championships similarly produced additional funding for figure skating. However, the trauma of the Ben Johnson steroid affair, the negative publicity it generated, and the Dubin enquiry, which investigated the use of steroids by track and field athletes, put a blanket of gloom over Canadian sport as the industry entered the 1990s. Such unfortunate occurrences could have a negative influence on public funding of sport.

**EXHIBIT 1**

Professor Jim Roberts
St. Lawrence College
Kingston, Ontario
K7L 5A6

Dear Jim:

It was great talking to you recently and I really appreciated your telephone call. Things are relatively in control here at Biathlon and soon we hope to be able to move "full steam ahead." We have a good staff and working environment but still need some outside guidance to help us in specialty areas.

As I mentioned to you on the telephone, we would like to offer you the Marketing Chair position for Biathlon Canada on an interim basis, to help assure our strategies are sound.

The Marketing Goal:
To develop a realistic and professional marketing plan.

Objectives:
1. To increase the percentage of non-government funding.
2. To attract new sponsors for programs, events, and equipment.
3. To evaluate current event promotions.
4. To develop a new biathlon image program through media and public relations.
5. To increase participation in the biathlon.

Time Commitment:
Intermittent involvement for about six months.

Benefits:
No compensation for Chair work but potential to work as our paid consultant in the future.

Jim, I do not see this position as being too demanding on your time as Biathlon Canada has already done some work in the area and we plan to use several college and university work-placement and internship students to help us. However, please base your decision on your interests, needs, etc. Looking forward to hearing from you in the near future.

With kind regards,

Rick Nickelchok
Executive Director

Biathlon Canada, along with numerous other sport bodies, has a growing need to find the right formula for marketing success. Chief among the arguments put forward to make the biathlon appear attractive is the claim that the sport is a healthy outdoor activity that demands stamina and a high level of skill. The national association is always seeking financial support for various competitive events, special promotions, newsletter advertising, equipment subsidies, and athlete sponsorships.

The board of directors gave the responsibility of developing a suitable marketing plan and attracting funding support to the executive director, Rick Nickelchok, who felt that this was his biggest challenge and one that could make or break the sport in Canada. In order to get something happening, Nickelchok decided to call for the assistance of one of his former college marketing professors whom he knew had an interest and background in sport. His letter outlined the nature of the organization's goals and issues that could be looked at (see exhibit 1).

## Governance and Administration

Canadian sport and recreation is governed by some 80 national governing bodies and their provincial counterparts. Each of these organizations has a board of directors made up primarily of concerned volunteers, often the parents of present or past participants in the particular sport or recreational activity.

Boards of directors normally meet between three and six times a year, and committees of the board meet in the interim to conduct research and shape policy recommendations. Ongoing topics of concern for most sport and recreation organizations typically include dates and venues for competitions, rules and regulations, athlete and team rankings, policies on travel expenses, coaches fees, training programs, equipment purchases, the association's annual budget, and so on. In the 1980s, new topics of concern came to the forefront: drugs, ethics, women in sport, competitive pressures on athletes, and funding development.

Each sport or recreation organization is led by an executive director, who manages the administrative affairs of the national or provincial office. The director's activities involve managing the budget, handling all personnel issues, communicating with the board and committees, organizing innumerable meetings, and completing all necessary reports and correspondence. They are also held responsible for developing fund-raising programs, stimulating media attention for their sport, and maintaining sound government relations. Some executive directors find their work a thankless task, while others revel in the challenges presented by the need to occupy diverse roles. Most executive directors come to sport with a college or university degree in business or sport administration and several years of experience in a preparatory position (e.g., as a program coordinator).

Besides the obvious time-pressures of the job, several other factors contribute to making the executive director's role complex. In many sport and recreational associations, the nature of the job is such that a considerable focus on technical matters is required. For example, the director may be responsible for ensuring that correct training procedures are followed by coaches so that the performance or well-being of developing athletes is enhanced. However, most sport and recreation organizations now employ a full-time technical director who takes on matters that directly concern athlete preparation, performance standards, rules and regulations, coaching, and major competitions. While this division of administrative and technical work in sport is for the most part good, it can also lead to disagreement over policy decisions and the allocation of money. One solution that has been tried successfully is the addition of a full-time (rather than volunteer) president, but the costs of such a change are immense and would not generally be feasible for fledgling sports.

>>>> QUESTIONS

1. What problems do you see in the implementation of a marketing concept for an amateur sport organization such as Biathlon Canada?

2. What relative strengths and weaknesses does Biathlon Canada possess as it seeks to achieve the goals stated in Nickelchok's letter?

3. If you were Roberts, what marketing steps would you take, if you decided to accept the position of marketing chair?

4. Aside from fund raising, how can marketing help a non-profit organization? Discuss at least three areas of benefit.

5. There are over 50 000 non-profit organizations in Canada in the health, social service, sport, recreation and arts communities. Name five non-profit organizations operating in your community. Contact one such organization and report on how it performs its marketing function.

6. Suggest a realistic timetable for the accomplishment of the Biathlon Canada goals. How will these goals be achieved. Who will do the work?

Case prepared by Gerald B. McCready, Professor of Marketing, St. Lawrence College.

# 〉 〉 〉 〉 *22. Marks and Spencer*

Marks & Spencer PLC is Britain's largest and most profitable retailing chain. Despite its success at home, it has never really found a winning formula in Canada. The company burst onto the Canadian retailing scene in 1972 in a joint venture with People's Department Stores Limited. People's is a junior department store chain located primarily in Quebec. In 1972, Marks & Spencer also purchased D'Allairds, a rather conservative chain of ladies clothing stores. A few years later, Marks & Spencer purchased a 55 percent interest in People's Department Stores Limited. Included in this deal were 43 Walker & Smith stores that were quickly converted to Marks & Spencer stores.

Marks & Spencer's retailing concept is quite different from those of most Canadian-based chains or United States-based chains operating in Canada. In an era where specialization and store image dominate retailing, it is quite common to see, in the typical Marks & Spencer store, products such as meat pies, frozen fish, and cookies displayed a few feet from sweaters, blouses, and lingerie. The company has tried to market under one roof a combination of high quality clothing and prepared food, both of which are marketed under the St. Michael brand name.

Since its inception in Canada, the company has tinkered with its merchandising mix and the store's appearance in an attempt to match the success of British operations. Initially, the stores had a generic, "no frills" appearance and did not include dressing rooms, both features that were inconsistent with the quality image the company was striving to present. In the 1980s, attempts were made to improve the stores' appearance, shopping environment, and image. New lighting and new carpeting enhanced the appearance, and dressing rooms were added for shoppers' convenience.

Despite these changes, the flow of red ink that started in the seventies continued in the eighties, and the British management showed more concern for the health of the Canadian operations. Financial trouble in Canada had gone unnoticed by British management for a long time, since operations here were just a tiny part of the Marks & Spencer PLC empire. This situation changed in 1988 when Marks & Spencer PLC bought Brooks Brothers, a trendy men's clothier, from the Campeau Corporation. All of a sudden Canada was part of a North American operations group. On financial statements for North American operations, the losses in Canada looked much larger than they had in previous financial reporting. In 1988, the Canadian operations lost close to $16 million based on revenues and profits from 74 Marks & Spencer stores, 78 Peoples stores, and 117 D'Allairds stores. In contrast, Marks & Spencer PLC showed a net profit of $910 million in the same period.

To get the company back on track, the parent company ordered an in-depth study of its Canadian operations. Among some of the initial suggestions to improve the situation were:

1. The closure of Marks & Spencer stores in western Canada (ten stores). Many of these stores were built in Alberta during the oil-boom years of the early eighties.
2. The closure of rural market stores so that the company could concentrate on mall locations. In the 1970s, 32 small store-front locations were closed in the Maritimes, so this tactic was not new to the company.

3. To sell People's and D'Allairds so that cash could be generated for the beleaguered Marks & Spencer stores.

It should be noted that Peoples lost $5.7 million in 1988 while D'Allairds generated $5.4 million in net income in the same period. D'Allairds was the only part of the Canadian operations making money.

It is possible that Marks & Spencer PLC fell into a classic trap when it entered the Canadian market. Its strategy was to transplant a U.K. formula to the Canadian marketplace. Perhaps its century-old formula, which combines high quality clothing and prepared food, is difficult for Canadian consumers to accept.

## ⟩⟩⟩⟩ QUESTIONS

1. What is the major problem that Marks & Spencer faces? Are there any related problems that must be addressed?
2. What is your opinion of Marks & Spencer's marketing strategy for the Canadian market? What factors has it neglected that might have had impact on its strategy?
3. What recommendations for improving its position in Canada do you have for Marks & Spencer? Support your recommendations with appropriate rationale.

Adapted from Mark Evans, "Marks & Spencer battles on", *Financial Post*, December 11, 1989, p.32.

# *Glossary*

›››

**Absolute advantage**   A situation in global marketing where only one country provides a good or service, or where one country produces a product at significantly lower cost than do other countries.

**Accumulation**   The purchase by wholesalers of quantities of goods from many producers for redistribution in smaller quantities to retailers they serve.

**Adoption**   A series of stages a consumer passes through on the way to purchasing a product on a regular basis.

**Advertising**   Any paid form of nonpersonal sales presentation and promotion of goods and services by an identified sponsor.

**Advertising agency**   Service organizations responsible for creating, planning, producing and placing advertising messages for clients.

**Advocacy advertising**   Advertising designed to communicate a company's position on a particular issue, usually an issue that affects it directly.

**Allocation**   The division of available goods by a producer or wholesaler among its various customers.

**Applied research**   Research undertaken to resolve a specific problem.

**Approach**   In selling, the initial contact with the prospect, usually a face-to-face encounter.

**Assorting**   Having an adequate variety of merchandise available in terms of brand name, price range, and features.

**Atmosphere**   The physical characteristics of a retail store or group of stores that are used to develop an image and attract customers.

**Attitude**   An individual's feelings, favourable or unfavourable, towards an idea or object.

**Auction company**   A commission merchant that brings together sellers and buyers at a central location to complete a transaction.

**Back end testing**   In direct marketing, the measurement of a campaign's degree of success or failure when the campaign is over.

**Bait and switch**   A situation where a company advertises a bargain price for a product that is not available in reasonable quantity; when customers arrive at the store they are directed to another product, often more highly priced than the product advertised.

**Basic research**   Research undertaken to develop new knowledge and discover new information.

**Behaviour response segmentation**   The division of buyers into groups according to the occasions they have for using a product, the benefits they require from a product, the frequency of use, and the degree of their brand loyalty.

**Belief**   The strongly held convictions on which an individual's actions are based.

**Bid**   A written tender submitted in a sealed envelope by a specified deadline.

**Bounce back**   An offer that rides along with a product shipment or with an invoice from a previous order.

**Boycott**   An organized refusal to buy a specific product.

**629**

**Branch office**   A regional office of a national firm that performs both sales and distribution functions within a designated area.

**Brand**   A name, term, symbol or design, or some combination of them that identifies the goods and services of an organization.

**Brand loyalty**   The degree of consumer attachment to a particular brand, product or service.

**Brand name**   That part of a brand that can be vocalized.

**Brandmark**   That part of a brand identified by a symbol or design.

**Breadth (of selection)**   The number of goods classifications a retail store carries.

**Breaking bulk**   The delivery of small quantities to customers (quantities that are usually below the weight requirement established by transportation companies)

**Break-even point**   That volume, either in units or dollars, where total revenue equals total costs.

**Broker**   A sales agent who represents suppliers, usually small suppliers, to the wholesale and retail trade in a particular industry.

**Business goods**   Products purchased by business, governments and institutions that facilitate the operations of the buying organization.

**Business-to-business advertising**   A business advertising its products, services, or itself to other businesses.

**Business-to-business market**   Individuals in an organization responsible for purchasing goods and services that the organization needs to produce a product or service, promote an idea, or produce an income.

**Buying center**   An informal purchasing process where individuals in an organization perform particular roles but may not have direct responsibility for the actual decision.

**Buying committee**   A formal purchasing process involving members from across a business organization who share responsibility for making a purchase decision.

**Capital goods**   Expensive goods with a long life span that are used directly in the production of another good or service.

**Cartel**   A group of firms or countries which band together and conduct trade in a manner similar to a monopoly.

**Cash cows**   Usually an established product characterized by high market share in a low growth market.

**Cash discount**   A discount granted for prompt payment within a stated period.

**Cash-and-carry outlet**   A limited-service merchant wholesaler who provides stock in small quantities to independent retail customers. Customers come to the outlet to pick up the goods they require.

**Catalogue showroom**   A form of discount retailer that lists its merchandise in catalogues, and displays selected lines of merchandise in a showroom where customers come to place their orders.

**Category manager**   An individual assigned responsibility for developing and implementing marketing activity for a group of related products or product lines.

**Causal research**   Research conducted to determine cause-and-effect relationships.

**Central business district**   Normally it is the hub of retailing activity in the heart of the downtown core, that is, the main street and busy cross-streets in a centralized area.

**Chain store (retail chain store)**   An organization operating four or more retail stores in the same kind of business under the same legal ownership.

**Channel captain**   A leader that integrates and coordinates the objectives and policies of all other members of a channel of distribution.

**Channel length**   The number of intermediaries or levels in the channel of distribution.

**Channel width**   The number of intermediaries at any one level of the channel of distribution.

**Circulation lists**   Magazine subscription lists that target potential customers by an interest or activity.

**Closed bid**   A written, sealed bid submitted by a supplier for review and evaluation by a purchaser on a particular date.

**Closing**   That point in the sales presentation where the seller asks for the order.

**Cognitive dissonance**   An individual's unsettled state of mind due to an action he or she has taken.

**Commercialization**   The full-scale production and marketing of a product on a regional or national basis.

**Commission merchant**   A wholesaling merchant who receives and sells goods for suppliers in centralized markets on consignment.

**Common market**   A regional or geographical group of countries that agree to limit trade barriers among its members and apply a common tariff on goods from non-member countries.

**Comparative advantage**   A situation in global marketing in which one country produces and markets an item more efficiently or abundantly, as well as more cheaply, than other countries.

**Comparative testing**   Used in direct marketing, it is the altering of one component of the proposed campaign to judge the effect of the change on the acceptability of the offer.

**Competitive bidding**  A situation where two or more firms submit written price quotations to a purchaser based on specifications by the purchaser.

**Compiled lists**  Lists prepared from government, telephone, warranty and other public information.

**Concept test**  The presentation of a product idea in some visual form, with a description of the product characteristics and benefits, in order to get customer reaction to it.

**Consumer analysis**  The monitoring of consumer behaviour changes (tastes, preferences, lifestyles, etc.) so that marketing strategies can be adjusted accordingly.

**Consumer and Corporate Affairs**  A government department that serves as the focal point of the legal environment of marketing practice and is responsible for laws that help consumers and businesses to function in Canada.

**Consumer behaviour**  The acts of individuals in obtaining goods and services, including the decision processes that precede and determine these acts.

**Consumer goods**  Goods and services purchased by consumers for personal use.

**Consumer promotion**  Activity promoting extra brand sales by offering the consumer an incentive over and above the product's inherent benefits.

**Consumerism**  A social force within the environment designed to aid and protect the consumer by exerting legal, moral and economic pressure on business.

**Containerization**  The grouping of individual items into an economical shipping quantity that is sealed in a protective container for intermodal transportation to a final customer.

**Contingency plan**  The identification of alternate courses of action that can be used to modify an original plan if and when circumstances change.

**Continuity**  The length of time required to create an impact on the target through a particular medium.

**Contract manufacturing**  A situation where a manufacturer stops producing a good domestically, preferring to find a foreign country that can produce the good to its specifications.

**Convenience goods**  Those goods that consumers purchase frequently, with a minimum of effort and evaluation.

**Convenience store**  A food-oriented store, situated in a busy area of a community, that sells limited numbers of lines over long hours.

**Conversion rate**  Used in direct marketing, it is the ratio of orders delivered as a percentage of the enquiries received.

**Cooperative advertising**  Funds allocated by a manufacturer to pay for a portion of a retailer's advertising.

**Copyright**  The exclusive right to reproduce, sell, or publish the matter and form of a dramatic, literary, musical, or artistic work.

**Corporate advertising**  Advertising designed to convey a favourable image of a company among its various publics.

**Corporate culture** The values, norms, and practices shared by all employees of an organization.

**Corporate planning**  Planning that includes three variables: a mission statement for the organization; corporate objectives; and corporate strategies.

**Cost reductions**  Cost-cutting measures taken by a firm as a means of protecting profit margins.

**Cost-based pricing**  A type of pricing whereby a company calculates its total costs and then adds a desired profit margin to arrive at a list price for a product.

**Cost-benefit analysis**  Used in the evaluation of price by a customer in a purchase situation, it is a procedure whereby all associated costs of the product are measured against the benefits of the product.

**Countertrading**  A system of exchange in which something other than currency or credit is used as a form of payment.

**Country-centered strategy**  The development of unique marketing strategies for each country a product is marketed in.

**Coupons**  Price-saving incentives, offered to consumers by manufacturers or retailers, that stimulate purchase of a specified product.

**Coverage**  A term used in media planning. The number of geographic markets where advertising is to occur for the duration of the media plan.

**Creative boutique**  A specialist advertising agency that concentrates on the design and development of the advertising message only.

**Creative execution**  The formation of precisely defined strategies for presenting a message to a target market.

**Creative objectives**  Statements of what information is to be communicated to a target market.

**Creative strategy**  Statements outlining how a message is to be communicated to a target market.

**Cross-elasticity of demand**  The degree to which the demand for one product will increase or decrease in response to changes in price of another product.

**Culture**   Behaviour, learned from external influences such as family and education, that feeds into the value systems held strongly by individuals.

**Customary pricing**   A price that matches the buyers' expectations: the price reflects tradition or is a price that people are accustomed to paying.

**Data analysis**   The evaluation, in marketing research, of responses on a question-by-question basis whereby meaning is given to the data.

**Data interpretation**   Relating accumulated data to the problem under review, and the objectives and hypotheses of the research study.

**Database marketing**   The process of analyzing customer and prospect data contained in a data base to identify new markets and selling opportunities, and to prepare marketing programs targeted to customers most likely to buy.

**Dealer premium**   An incentive offered a distributor by a manufacturer to encourage a special purchase (e.g., a specified volume of merchandise) or to secure additional merchandising support.

**Demand-based pricing**   A pricing strategy whereby the firm calculates the markup needed to cover selling expenses and profits and determines the maximum it can spend to produce the product; the calculations work backwards since they initially consider the price the ultimate consumer will pay.

**Demographic segmentation**   The division of a large market into smaller segments based on combinations of age, sex, income, occupation, education, marital status, household formation, and ethnic background.

**Department store**   A large general-product line retailer that sells a variety of merchandise in a variety of price ranges.

**Depth (of selection)**   The number of brands and styles carried by a retail store in each product classification.

**Derived demand**   Demand for a product in the business market that is based on consumer demand, that is, on demand created by the final user.

**Descriptive research**   Research undertaken to identify the characteristics of consumer groups.

**Diffusion**   The manner in which different market segments accept and purchase a product between product introduction and market saturation.

**Direct advertising**   Advertising delivered directly to prospects by mail, telephone, or in person by salespeople.

**Direct channel**   A short channel of distribution.

**Direct exporting**   A form of international distribution whereby the exporting company itself strikes agreements with local market companies that would be responsible for distribution in the foreign country.

**Direct home retailing**   The selling of merchandise by personal contact in the home of the customer.

**Direct home shopping**   A shopping service provided by cable television stations whereby products are offered for sale by broadcast message (e.g., Canadian Home Shopping Network).

**Direct mail**   A form of direct advertising whereby the advertising message is communicated to prospects through the postal service.

**Direct marketing**   An interactive marketing system fully controlled by the marketer, who develops products, promotes them directly to customers through a variety of media, accepts orders directly from customers, and distributes products directly to consumers.

**Direct-response advertising**   Messages that prompt immediate action, such as advertisements containing clipout coupons, response cards, and order forms; such advertising goes directly to customers.

**Discount department store**   A store that carries a full line of merchandise at low prices while offering consumers limited customer service.

**Discount supermarket (warehouse store)**   A supermarket offering limited lines, limited assortment of brands, few services, low margins, and low prices.

**Distribution planning**   A systematic decision-making process regarding the physical movement and transfer of ownership of goods and services from producers to consumers.

**Distribution strategy**   The selection and management of marketing channels, and the physical distribution of products.

**Diversification**   A firm's movement into a totally new area, such as a new industry, market, or product category.

**Dogs**   Products characterized by low market share in a low growth market.

**Double ticketing**   A situation in which more than one price tag appears on an item.

**Drop shipper**   A merchant wholesaler who contacts customers and puts together carload quantities of goods that can be delivered to those customers.

**Dumping**   The practice of selling goods in a foreign market at a price lower than the price at which they are sold in the domestic market.

**Durable goods**   Tangible goods that survive many uses.

**Early adopters**   A large group of opinion leaders who like to try new products when they are new.

**Early majority**   A group of consumers that represents the initial phase of mass market acceptance of a product.

**Economic order quantity (EOQ)**   The actual amount of goods ordered that will strike a balance between the cost of ordering goods and the cost of carrying goods in inventory.

**Elastic demand**   A situation in which a small change in price results in a large change in volume.

**Embargo**   A trade restriction that disallows goods from entering a foreign country.

**Emergency goods**   Goods purchased immediately when crisis or urgency arises.

**End-product advertising**   Advertising by a firm that makes part of a finished product.

**Event**   A theme activity created by a special interest group.

**Event marketing**   The process, planned by a sponsoring organization, of integrating a variety of communication elements behind an event theme.

**Event sponsorship**   A situation in which a sponsor agrees to support an event financially in return for advertising privileges associated with the event.

**Exclusive distribution**   The availability of a product in only one outlet in a geographic area.

**Execution (tactics)**   Action plans that outline in specific detail how strategies are to be implemented.

**Experimental research**   Research where one or more factors are manipulated under controlled conditions, while other elements remain constant, so that respondents' reactions can be evaluated.

**Exploratory research**   A preliminary form of research that clarifies the nature of a problem.

**F.O.B. (free on board) origin pricing**   A geographic pricing strategy whereby the price quoted by a seller does not include freight charges (the buyer assumes title when the goods are loaded onto a common carrier).

**F.O.B. destination (freight absorption) pricing**   A geographic pricing strategy whereby the seller agrees to pay freight charges between point of origin and point of destination (title does not transfer to the buyer until the goods arrive at their destination).

**Fact gathering**   The compilation of already discovered data which is published for reasons that have nothing to do with the specific problem under investigation.

**Fad**   A product that has a reasonably short selling season, perhaps one or a few financially successful seasons.

**Family brand**   The use of the same brand name for a group of related products.

**Family life cycle**   A series of stages a person undergoes starting with the stage of bachelorhood, progressing to the stages of marriage and parenthood, and ending with the stage of solitary survivor.

**Fashion**   A cycle for a product that is recurring through many selling seasons (a style or type of product that stays popular for a considerable period).

**Fixed costs**   Costs that do not vary with different quantities of output.

**Flexible pricing**   Charging different customers different prices.

**Flight (flighting)**   The purchase of media time and space in planned intervals, separated by periods of inactivity.

**Focus group**   A small group of eight to ten people with common characteristics brought together to discuss issues related to the marketing of a product or service.

**Follow-up**   An activity that keeps salespeople in touch with customers after the sale has been made to ensure that the customer is satisfied.

**Franchise**   A contractual agreement according to which a franchisee (retailer) conducts business using the franchiser's name and operating methods in exchange for a fee.

**Free ride**   An extra offer that rides free or piggybacks with a primary offer.

**Free-standing store**   An isolated store usually located on a busy street or highway.

**Freight forwarder**   A firm that consolidates small shipments — shipments that form less than a carload or truckload — from small companies.

**Frequency**   The average number of times an audience is exposed to an advertising message over a given period, usually a week.

**Front end testing**   Used in direct marketing. Involves measuring the effectiveness of activity on a sample of the market to determine the feasibility of extending the activity to the rest of the market.

**Fulfillment**   The processing, in direct marketing, of an order, information request, premium, or refund.

**Full-service agency**   An advertising agency that offers a complete range of services to its clients.

**Full-service merchant wholesaler**   A wholesaler that assembles an assortment of products in a central warehouse and offers its customers a full range of services, including delivery, storage, merchandising support, credit and planning support.

**Funnelling**   The narrowing down of a subject to manageable variables so that specifically directed research can be conducted.

**General merchandise wholesaler**   A wholesaler that carries a full line or wide assortment of merchandise that serves virtually all of its customers' needs.

**Generic brand**   A product without a brand name.

**Geodemographics**   The isolation of dwelling areas through a combination of geographic and demographic information. Based on the assumption that people seek out residential neighbourhoods in which to cluster with their lifestyle peers.

**Geographic segmentation**   The division of a large geographic market into smaller geographic or regional units.

**Global strategy**   A marketing strategy whereby a product is marketed in essentially the same way whatever the country, though some modification to particular elements of the marketing mix is often necessary.

**Grey market**   A market segment based on age and lifestyles of people who are over the age of fifty-five.

**Harvest**   A strategy whereby a company divorces itself from a product category or market through sale or liquidation of the product or through withdrawing the product from the marketplace.

**Horizontal conflict**   Competition between similar organizations at the same level in the channel of distribution.

**Horizontal marketing system (horizontal integration)**   A situation where channel members at one level in the channel have the same owner.

**Idea marketing**   Encouraging the public to accept and agree with certain issues and causes.

**Impulse goods**   Goods bought on a sudden whim, without forethought.

**Inbound telemarketing**   The reception of calls by an order desk, customer service enquiry, and direct response calls, often through toll-free telephone numbers.

**Independent retailer**   A retailer who operates one to three stores, even if the stores are affiliated with a large organization.

**Indirect channel**   A long channel of distribution.

**Indirect exporting**   A form of international distribution where a company employs a middleman or trading company to establish a distribution network in a foreign country.

**Individual brand**   The identification of a product in a company's product mix with its own name.

**Industrial advertising**   Advertising by source supplier such as a manufacturer that directs messages at members of a channel of distribution.

**Industrial advertising**   Advertising by industrial suppliers directed at industrial buyers.

**Industrial goods**   Those products and services purchased by business, industry, institutions, and governments that are used directly or indirectly in the production of another good or service for resale to another user.

**Inelastic demand**   A situation in which a change in price does not have a significant impact on the quantity purchased.

**Inflation**   A rising price level for goods and services, resulting in reduced purchasing power.

**Innovators**   The first group of consumers to accept a product.

**Instant bust**   A product that a firm had high expectations for, but that, for whatever reasons, was rejected by consumers very quickly.

**Instant wins**   A type of contest where a package contains winning certificates which consumers redeem for prizes.

**Intensive distribution**   The availability of a product in the widest possible channel of distribution.

**Intermediary**   A distributing agent that offers the producers of goods and services the advantage of making goods and services available to target markets efficiently.

**Intertype conflict**   Competition between different types of middlemen at the same level in the channel of distribution.

**Inventory management**   A system that ensures continuous flow of needed goods so that the quantity in inventory matches sales demand so that neither too little nor too much stock is carried.

**In-home selling**   A form of personal selling whereby an individual uses a network of local people to sell products in their communities, often at home parties.

**In-pack or on-pack premium**   A free item placed inside the package or attached to a package and overwrapped for protection and security.

**Joint demand**   A situation in which products can only be used in conjunction with each other, so the production and marketing of one product is dependent upon another.

**Joint venture**   In a global marketing situation, a partnership between a domestic and a foreign company.

**Just-in-time inventory (JIT Inventory)**   An inventory system based on frequent ordering of small quantities of needed goods.

**Laggards**   The last group of people to purchase a product.

**Late majority**   A group of consumers who represent the latter phase of mass market acceptance of a product.

**Licensing**   A temporary agreement allowing a company (the licensee) to use a trademark, patent, copyright, or manufacturing process of another company (the licensor).

**Licensing**   One firm legally allowing another firm to use its brand name or trademark for a certain period (the brand name or trademark used in such a way is called a licensed brand).

**Lifestyle**   A person's pattern of living as expressed in his or her activities, interests, and opinions.

**Limited-service merchant wholesaler**   A wholesaler that is selective in the functions it performs.

**List broker**   A specialist who makes all of the arrangements for one company to use the lists of another company.

**List price**   The rate normally (initially) quoted to potential buyers.

**Loss leaders**   Products offered for sale at or slightly below cost.

**Macro-segmentation**   The process, in business-to-business marketing, of identifying a market according to characteristics of the buying firm and of the buying situation.

**Mail-in premium**   An item offered free or at a bargain price to consumers who buy another item.

**Manufacturer wholesaling**   When a producer undertakes the wholesaling function, feeling that it can reach customers effectively and efficiently through direct contact.

**Manufacturers' agent**   A sales agent who carries and sells similar products for non-competing manufacturers in an exclusive territory.

**Market**   A group of people who have a similar need for a product or service, the resources to purchase the product or service, and the willingness and ability to buy it.

**Market analysis**   The collection of appropriate information (e.g., information regarding demand, sales volume potential, production capabilities and resources necessary to produce and market a given product) to determine if a market is worth pursuing.

**Market development**   A strategy whereby a company attempts to market existing products to new target markets.

**Market differentiation**   Targeting several market segments with several different products and marketing plans.

**Market Integration**   A strategy whereby a company or product expands from a single segment into other similar segments.

**Market leader**   The firm that is the largest in the industry and is a leader in strategic action.

**Market nicher**   A firm that concentrates resources on one or more distinguishable market segments.

**Market penetration**   A strategy whereby a company attempts to improve the market positions of existing products in existing markets.

**Market segmentation**   The division of a large market into smaller homogeneous markets (targets) based on common needs and/or similar lifestyles.

**Market share**   The sales volume of one competing product or company expressed as a percentage of total market sales volume.

**Marketing**   The process of anticipating, stimulating, developing, managing and satisfying customer needs based on exchanges between the organization and the customer.

**Marketing audit**   A systematic, critical, and unbiased review and appraisal of the basic objectives and policies of the marketing function, and of the organization, methods, procedures and people employed to implement the policies.

**Marketing channel**   A series of firms or individuals that participate in the flow of goods and services from producer to final users or customers.

**Marketing communication**   The process of sending an understood message between a marketing organization and another business organization or consumer.

**Marketing concept**   The process of determining the needs and wants of a target market and delivering a set of desired satisfactions to that target market more effectively than does the competition.

**Marketing control**   The process of measuring and evaluating the results of marketing strategies and plans, and taking corrective action to ensure that marketing objectives are attained.

**Marketing culture**   The philosophy or attitude of an organization regarding how it should deal with customers.

**Marketing information system (MIS)**   People and equipment organized to provide the continuous, orderly collection and exchange of information (internal and external) needed for a firm's decision-making process.

**Marketing mix**   The four strategic elements of product, price, place, and promotion.

**Marketing objectives**   Statements outlining what a product or service will accomplish in one-year, usually expressed in terms of sales volume, market share, or profit.

**Marketing planning**   The analysis, planning, implementation, evaluation, and control of carefully formulated and coordinated initiatives to satisfy target market needs while achieving organization objectives.

**Marketing research**   A function that links the consumer, customer, and public to the marketer through information — information used to define marketing opportunities and problems; generate, refine and evaluate marketing actions; and monitor marketing performance.

**Marketing strategies**   The process of identifying target markets and satisfying those targets with a combination of marketing mix elements within budget constraints.

**Mass marketing**   The use of one basic marketing strategy for a broad range of consumers without addressing any distinct characteristics among them.

**Media billings**   The total dollar volume of advertising time and space handled by an agency in a one-year period.

**Media-buying service**   A specialist advertising agency that concentrates on planning and purchasing the most cost-efficient time and space in the media for their clients.

**Media objectives**   Media planning statements that consider the target market, the presentation of the message, geographic market priorities, the best time to reach the target, and the budget available to accomplish stated goals.

**Media planning**   A precise outline of media objectives, media strategies and media execution, culminating in a media plan that recommends how funds should be spent to achieve advertising objectives.

**Media strategy**   Statements that outline how media objectives will be accomplished; typically, they outline what media will be used and why certain media were selected and others rejected.

**Merchandise assortment**   The total assortment of products a retailer carries.

**Micro-segmentation**   Used in business-to-business marketing, it is the process of analyzing a buying situation based on qualitative factors such as buying motives, purchasing strategy, and the importance of the purchase to the customer.

**Mission statement**   A statement of purpose for an organization reflecting the operating philosophy and direction the organization is to take.

**Modified rebuy**   The purchase by an organization of a medium-priced product on an infrequent basis.

**Monopolistic competition**   A market where there are many competitors selling products that are similar but perceived to be different by consumers.

**Monopoly**   A market where there is a single seller of a particular good or service for which there are no close substitutes.

**Motive**   A condition which prompts action to satisfy a need.

**Multinational corporation**   A firm that operates in several countries and usually has a substantial share of its total assets, sales and labour force in foreign subsidiaries.

**Multiple channel**   A type of channel of distribution in which different kinds of intermediaries are used at the same level.

**Multiple-unit pricing**   Offering items for sale in combinations, usually at a price below the combined regular price of each item.

**National advertising**   Advertising of a trademarked product or service wherever the product or service is available.

**Nationalization**   A form of expropriation whereby a government of a country takes control of operations of a foreign company operating in that country.

**Needs**   A state of deprivation; the absence of something useful.

**Negative action**   A situation in direct marketing where the customer agrees that the product will be sent unless a reply, refusing to accept a shipment, is made to a notice.

**New product** A product that is truly unique and meets needs that have been previously unsatisfied.

**New task purchase** The purchase of an expensive product by a business for the first time.

**Niche marketing** Targeting a product line to one particular segment and allocating all marketing resources to the satisfaction of that segment.

**Nondurable goods** Tangible goods normally consumed after one or a few uses.

**Nonprofit marketing** The marketing effort and activity in not-for-profit organizations.

**Objection** An obstacle that the salesperson must confront and resolve if the sales transaction is to be completed.

**Objectives** Statements that outline what is to be accomplished in a corporate plan or marketing plan.

**Observation research** A form of research where the behaviour of the respondent is observed and recorded.

**Odd-even pricing** A psychological pricing strategy that capitalizes on the effectiveness of odd numbers in prices as opposed to rounded-off numbers.

**Off-invoice allowance** A temporary allowance that is deducted from the invoice at the time of customer billing.

**Oligopoly** A market situation in which a few large firms control the market.

**Open bid** An informal submission by a supplier of a price quotation in written or verbal form.

**Orderly market agreement** An agreement by which nations share a market by eliminating trade barriers between one another.

**Organization marketing** Marketing that seeks to gain or maintain acceptance of an organization's objectives and services.

**Organizational buying** A decision-making process firms follow to establish what products they need to purchase, and to identify, evaluate and select a brand and supplier for those products.

**Outbound telemarketing** The calls a company makes to a customer in order to develop new accounts, generate sales leads, qualify prospects, and conduct marketing research.

**Packaging** Those activities related to the design and production of the container or wrapper of a product.

**Patent** A provision that gives a manufacturer the sole right to develop and market a new product, process, or material.

**People marketing** The marketing of an individual or group of people to create a favourable impression of that individual or group.

**Perception** How individuals receive and interpret messages.

**Performance allowance** Discounts offered by manufacturers to distributors for performing a promotional function on the manufacturer's behalf.

**Personal selling** Face-to-face communication involving a presentation of features and benefits of a product or service by a seller to a buyer for the purpose of making a sale.

**Personality** Those distinguishing psychological characteristics of a person which produce relatively consistent and enduring responses to the environment in which that person lives.

**Physical distribution** The range of activities involved in the delivery of goods to designated places, at designated times, and in proper condition.

**Piggybacking** A system whereby the entire load of a truck trailer is transferred to a rail flatcar for movement from one place to another.

**Place marketing** Drawing attention to and creating a favourable attitude toward a particular place, be it a country, province, region, or city.

**Planning** The process of anticipating the future business environment and determining the courses of action a firm will take in that environment.

**Point-of-purchase material (POP)** Self-contained, specifically designed merchandising units that either temporarily or permanently display a manufacturer's product.

**Portfolio analysis** A process of reviewing the business categories or market segments that a firm operates in based on the fact that the total company can be divided into strategic units.

**Positioning** Creating appropriate marketing appeals that will produce a desirable image of a product, service or company in the minds of customers.

**Positive action** A situation in direct marketing in which the customer must take action to receive the offer (e.g., sign a return-response card).

**Post-testing** The evaluation of an advertisement, commercial or campaign, during or after its implementation.

**Predatory pricing** A situation in which a large firm sets an extremely low price in an attempt to undercut all other competitors, thus placing those competitors in a difficult financial position.

**Premium**  An item offered free or at a bargain price to consumers who buy a specific item.

**Presentation (sales presentation)**  The persuasive presentation and demonstration of a product's benefits.

**Prestige pricing**  A situation in the sale of luxury goods where a high price contributes to the image of a product and to the status of the buyer.

**Pretesting**  The evaluation of an advertisement, commercial or campaign to determine the strengths and weaknesses of the message prior to final creative production.

**Price**  The exchange value of a good or service in the marketplace.

**Price lining**  The adoption of price points for the various lines of merchandise a retailer carries.

**Price penetration**  Establishing a low entry price in order to gain wide market acceptance quickly.

**Price skimming**  Establishing a high entry price so a firm can maximize its revenue early.

**Price strategy**  The development of a pricing structure that is fair and equitable to consumers and profitable for the organization.

**Primary package**  The package containing the actual product (e.g., the jar that contains the jam).

**Primary research**  Data collected and recorded for the first time to resolve a specific problem.

**Private label brand**  A brand designated by a wholesaler or retailer, usually carrying its company name or a brand name it has developed.

**Problem children (question marks)**  Products characterized by low market share in a high growth market.

**Product**  A bundle of tangible and intangible benefits that a buyer receives in exchange for money and other considerations.

**Product development**  A strategy whereby the company markets new products to existing customers, or markets modified existing products to current users.

**Product differentiation**  A strategy that focuses on the unique attributes or benefits of a product that distinguish it from another product.

**Product item**  A unique product offered for sale by an organization.

**Product life cycle**  The stages a product goes through from its introduction to the market to its eventual withdrawal.

**Product line**  A grouping of product items that have characteristics in common (e.g., type of product, market it is directed at, or channel of distribution)

**Product manager**  An individual assigned responsibility for developing and implementing marketing programs for a specific product or group of products.

**Product mix**  The total range of products offered for sale by a company.

**Product strategy**  Making decisions on variables such as product quality, product features, brand names and packaging, customer service guarantees, and warranties.

**Product stretching**  The sequential addition of products to a product line to increase its depth or width.

**Product testing**  In direct marketing, the testing of the viability of a product to see how acceptable it is to the target market.

**Profile matching**  A media strategy whereby the advertising message is placed in media where the profile of the readers, listeners or viewers is reasonably close to the profile of the product's target market.

**Promotion mix**  The combination of five promotional elements: advertising, sales promotion, personal selling, public relations, and event marketing and sponsorships.

**Promotion planning**  A systematic decision-making process regarding the use of various elements of the promotion mix in marketing communications, whereby objectives and strategies are outlined.

**Promotion strategy**  The blending of advertising, sales promotion, personal selling and public relations activity to present a consistent and persuasive message about a product or service to a target market.

**Promotional pricing**  The temporary lowering of prices to attract customers.

**Prospecting**  A systematic procedure for developing sales leads.

**Protectionism**  A belief that foreign trade should be restricted so that domestic industry can be preserved.

**Prototype**  A physical version of a potential product, that is, of a product designed and developed to meet the needs of potential customers; it is developmental in nature and refined according to feedback from consumer research.

**Psychographic segmentation**  Market segmentation based on the activities, interests, and opinions of consumers.

**Psychological pricing**  Pricing strategies that appeal to tendencies in consumer behaviour other than rational tendencies.

**Public image**   The reputation that a product, service or company has among its various publics.

**Public relations.**   A variety of activities and communications that organizations undertake to monitor, evaluate, and influence the attitudes, opinions, and behaviours of their publics.

**Publicity**   The communication of newsworthy information about a product, service, company, or idea, usually in the form of a press release.

**Pull strategy**   Creating demand by directing promotional efforts at the consumers or final users of a product, who in turn put pressure on the retailers to carry it.

**Pure competition**   A market in which many sellers market the same basic product to many buyers.

**Push strategy**   Creating demand for a product by directing promotional efforts at middlemen who in turn promote the product to consumers.

**Qualifying**   The procedure for determining if a prospect needs the product, has the authority to buy it, and has the ability to pay for it.

**Quantity discount**   A discount offered on the basis of volume purchased in units or dollars for a specified period.

**Question marks (problem children)**   Products characterized by low market share in a high growth market.

**Quota**   A specific limit imposed on the amount of goods that may be imported into a country.

**Rack jobber**   A specialty merchandise wholesaler who stocks display racks it owns in a retail outlet, in which products it carries are displayed.

**Rain-cheque**   A guarantee by a retailer to provide an original product or one of comparable quality to a consumer within a reasonable time.

**Reach**   The total, unduplicated audience potentially exposed to a message, one or more times, in a given period, usually a week.

**Rebate**   A temporary price discount in the form of a cash return made directly to the consumer, usually by a manufacturer.

**Recall test**   A message-effectiveness test that measures consumers' comprehension of key selling points following exposure to a message.

**Recognition test**   A message-effectiveness test that determines the level of consumer awareness of an advertisement.

**Redemption rate**   The number of coupons returned to an organization expressed as a percentage of the total number of coupons in distribution for a particular coupon offer.

**Reference group**   A group of people with a common interest that influences the participants' attitudes and behaviour.

**Refund (rebate)**   A predetermined amount of money returned to consumers by the manufacturer after the purchase has been made.

**Reorder point**   An inventory level at which new orders must be placed in order to maintain normal production operations or satisfy demand for finished products.

**Repositioning**   Changing the place a product occupies in the consumer's mind, relative to competitive products.

**Response list**   A purchasable list that identifies people as mail-order buyers.

**Response rate**   A measurement used in direct marketing, it is the number of responses received and expressed as a percentage of the total distribution.

**Retail advertising**   Advertising used by a retail operation to communicate name, image, store sales and variety of merchandise carried.

**Retail cooperative**   A group of retailers who join together to establish a distribution center that performs the role of the wholesaler in the channel.

**Retail in-ad coupon**   A coupon distributed in a retailer's advertising, either in the newspaper or in supplements inserted in the newspaper.

**Retailing**   Activities involved in the sale of goods and services to final users for personal, family, or household use.

**Rifle strategy**   The selection of media that appeal specifically to an interest common to a particular target market.

**Rollout**   A strategy used in direct marketing, it is the distribution of an offer to the remaining names on a mailing list after a portion of that list has been successfully tested.

**Sales forecast**   A prediction of sales volume over a period of time.

**Sales office**   A regional office of a national company that performs a sales function, but does not distribute products from that location.

**Sales promotion**   Activity that provides special incentives to bring about immediate action from consumers, distributors, and an organization's sales force.

**Sample**   A representative portion of an entire population used to obtain information about that population.

**Sample (free sample)**   A free product distributed to potential users either in a small trial size or in its regular size.

**Sampling frame**   A listing that can be used to access a population for research purposes.

**Scrambled merchandising**   The addition, in retailing, of unrelated products and product lines to an original business.

**Seasonal discounts**   Discounts that apply to off-season or pre-season purchases.

**Secondary data**   Data that has been compiled and published for purposes other than that of solving the specific problem under investigation.

**Secondary package**   An outer wrapper that protects the product; that part of the package that is discarded once the product is used the first time.

**Selective distribution**   The availability of a product in only a few outlets in a particular market.

**Service**   The activity and benefits provided by an organization whose principal benefits satisfy the buyers' needs without conferring ownership of tangible goods.

**Service mix**   The complete listing of all services that a supplier offers.

**Services**   Intangible goods; activities and benefits of which a consumer takes advantage, but not possession.

**Shopping goods**   Goods that the consumer compares on such bases as suitability, quality, price, and style, before making a selection.

**Shopping mall**   A centrally owned, managed, planned and operated shopping facility comprised of a balanced mix of retail tenants and adequate parking for customers.

**Shotgun strategy**   The selection of general interest media to reach a broad cross-section of a market population.

**Slippage**   A situation in which a consumer starts collecting proofs of purchase for a refund offer, but neglects to follow through and submit a request for the refund.

**Social class**   The division of people into orderly groups based on similar values, lifestyles, and social history.

**Social marketing**   Marketing activity that increases the acceptability of social ideas.

**Social responsibility**   The possession of a corporate conscience; anticipating and responding to social problems due to a sense of moral obligation.

**Societal marketing concept**   Determining and delivering needs more efficiently and effectively than competitors, and in such a way that consumers' and society's well-being is preserved or enhanced.

**Sorting**   The classification of merchandise into grades, colours, and sizes.

**Sorting process**   The accumulation, allocation, classifying, and assorting of merchandise.

**Source list**   A list maintained by the Ministry of Supply and Services that includes the names, products, and services of all companies that have expressed an interest in dealing with the federal government.

**Specialty goods**   Goods that consumers will make an effort to find and purchase because the goods offer some unique or important characteristics.

**Specialty merchandise wholesaler**   A wholesaler that carries a limited number or narrow line of products but offers an extensive assortment within these lines.

**Specialty store**   A store selling a single line or limited line of merchandise.

**Standard industrial classification (SIC)**   A numbering system that allows a supplier to track down customers who can use their goods and services within an industry category.

**Staple goods**   Products that are needed or used on a regular basis.

**Stars**   Products characterized by high market share and high profit in a high growth market.

**Stock balance**   The practice of maintaining an adequate assortment of goods that will attract customers while keeping inventories of those goods at reasonable levels.

**Stockturn**   The number of times during a specific period that the average inventory of a store is sold.

**Straight (full) rebuy**   The purchase of inexpensive items on a regular basis by an organization.

**Strategic business unit (SBU)**   A unit of a company that has a separate mission, and that can be planned independently from other company businesses.

**Strategic planning**   The process of determining objectives and identifying those strategies and tactics within the framework of the business environment that will contribute to the achievement of objectives.

**Strategies**   Statements that outline how objectives will be achieved.

**Strip cluster**   The grouping of food, lodging and entertainment establishments on main routes in and out of cities and towns.

**Subculture**   A subgroup of a culture that has a distinctive lifestyle based on racial, religious, or geographic factors, while retaining important features of the dominant culture.

**Supermarket** A departmentalized food store selling packaged grocery products, produce, dairy, meat, frozen food and general merchandise.

**Superstore** A diversified supermarket that sells a broad range of food and non-food items.

**Supplies** Those goods purchased by business and industry which do not enter the production process but facilitate other operations of the organization.

**Survey research** Data that is collected systematically through some form of communication with a representative sample.

**Sweepstakes** A type of contest in which large prizes such as cash, cars, homes and vacations are given away.

**Target market** A group of customers that can be defined based on similar characteristics (e.g., similar needs, habits, and lifestyles).

**Target pricing** A pricing strategy that is designed to generate a desirable rate of return on investment and is based on the full costs of producing a product.

**Tariff** A tax or duty imposed on imported goods.

**Telefocus marketing** In direct marketing, the combining of telemarketing, direct mail, and video brochures into one integrated campaign.

**Telemarketing** The use of telecommunications to promote the products and services of a business.

**Test marketing** Placing a product for sale in one or more representative markets to observe performance under a proposed marketing plan.

**Trade advertising** Advertising directed at channel members by a source supplier such as a manufacturer.

**Trade promotion** Promotional activity directed at distributors that is designed to increase the volume they purchase and to encourage merchandising support for a manufacturer's product.

**Trademark** That part of a brand granted legal protection, so that only the owner can use it.

**Trial close** An attempt to close that failed.

**Truck jobber** A specialty wholesaler that sells and delivers goods to retail customers during the same sales call.

**Uniform delivered pricing** A geographic pricing strategy that includes average freight charges for all customers regardless of their location.

**Unit pricing** The expression of price in terms of unit of measurement (e.g., cost per gram or cost per millilitre).

**Unsought goods** Goods of which consumers are unaware that they have a need or about which they lack knowledge.

**USP (unique selling point)** The one variable that distinguishes a product from competing products.

**Utility** The want-satisfying power of a product or service.

**Variable costs** Costs that change according to the level of output.

**Variety store** A store selling a wide range of staple merchandise at low or popular prices.

**Vendor analysis** An evaluation of a potential supplier based on factors such as technological ability, consistency in meeting product specifications, quality, delivery, and the ability to provide needed quantity.

**Venture team** A group of individuals brought together by an organization to devote all of their time to the development of a product concept of high market potential.

**Vertical conflict** Conflict that occurs when a channel member feels that another member at a different level is engaging in inappropriate conduct.

**Vertical marketing system (VMS)** The linking of channel members at different levels to form a centrally controlled marketing system dominated by one member; also called vertical integration.

**Voluntary chain** A wholesaler-sponsored buying organization composed of a group of independent retailers who agree to buy from a designated wholesaler.

**Warehouse club (discount supermarket)** A supermarket offering limited lines, limited assortment of brands, fewer services, lower margins, and lower prices.

**Wholesaling** The buying and handling of merchandise and its subsequent resale to organizational users, other wholesalers, and retailers.

**Zone pricing** The division of a market into geographic zones and the establishment of a uniform delivered price for each zone.

# >>>> *Index*

# ›››› *Photo Credits*

**647**